CW01095663

About this book

The Traveller's *Yellow Pages and Handbook for St. Petersburg* 1993/94, (2nd, ed.) is designed especially to fill the need for an up-to-date accurate "Yellow Pages" telephone book for St. Petersburg, Russia for travelers and foreigners living, visiting and working there. This second edition has 88 more pages, about 950 more numbers, new and updated essays, and more descriptive lines for each firm than the first edition, yet it still remains compact, practical and reader-friendly.

The concept of a "Yellow Pages" designed especially for travelers and foreign residents evolved from our 1991 proposal to the Leningrad Telephone Company to do a full size Yellow Pages in Russian. In October 1991 InfoServices International, Inc. was founded to publish a series of *Traveller's Yellow Pages* for major cities in Russia, CIS and Eastern Europe. In March, 1992, we opened Telinfo A/O in St. Petersburg, Russia to do research and to bring the concept of advertising in the Yellow Pages to the business community of St. Petersburg. The first edition was published in September, 1992 and was an instant success. The 1994 Goodwill Games Organizing Committee in Saint Petersburg selected The *Traveller's* Yellow Pages for Saint Petersburg and its companion *Traveller's* Yellow Pages City Map to be the "Official Visitor's Directory" and the "Official Visitor's Map" for the 1994 Goodwill Games. In March 1993 we began work on the Moscow edition of a Traveller's Yellow Pages, which will appear in November 1993. Work is now in progress on the Baltics and Northwest Russia editions.

This practical telephone book and handbook for St. Petersburg has more than 4300 telephone numbers and addresses of shops, restaurants, hotels, services, institutions and everything else useful for visitors and residents of St. Petersburg. These were selected from more than 8,000 addresses of firms and establishments. Hundreds of small informational ads were written by the Russian and American staff together with the advertisers. All this information is classified under 412 categories of goods and services, like the well-known "Yellow Pages" used throughout the world. Our book, written in English, is designed for the world traveler and has indexes in English, Russian, German, French, Swedish and now Finnish.

The *Traveller's* Yellow Page for St. Petersburg is designed to be a convenient up-to-date and accurate reference book and directory for travelers and residents which compliments a full-sized Yellow Pages Telephone Book. Our goal was to include all or some of the best listings for each category, or at least five or six good verified listings.

The information is up to date as of July 1, 1993, but St. Petersburg is changing rapidly. Even as the book goes to press, we are discovering new shops, little cafes, more good doctors, and special craftsmen. Old shops and institutions are closing for "remont" and repair. Some are simply disappearing forever.

We need your help to make the next edition even better. Tell us about your special findings: a good clothing shop, a great restaurant, a fascinating tour guide, a little cafe, a new stationery shop, or a talented artist. Tell us what new information you want. And above all, tell us about incorrect numbers, bad experiences with any listings in our book and any wrong information. Write us, fax us or even call us. We want to hear from you.

Acknowledgments

The staff:

The second edition of *The* Traveller's *Yellow Pages and Handbook for Saint Petersburg 1993/94* was researched and produced by American and Russian staffs in St. Petersburg, Russia. Their long hours, dedication to the concept of the book and enthusiasm were essential to the success of this project.

Special acknowledgment must be given to the following: To Michael B. Lisyuk, Ph.D. the Manager of Telinfo, St. Petersburg, Russia, who coordinated the collection and reverification of over 8,000 telephone numbers and addresses, and supervised the editing of the final copy.

To Paul Tush, Associate Editor, who applied his expertise in journalism and photography to coordinating and writing the ads. Copy for our ads was written by Paul Tush and our very able translator, Svetlana V. Tkachenko, who also proof read the final copy.

To Aleksandr G. Zakirov for his excellent designs and creative graphics, and for managing our computer resources, and to Dmitriy A. Gudramovich for designing ads.

To Marina Golli, MD. for managing a successful advertising campaign. To Olga A. Kholodova, Elena M. Botvinnik, and Vera G. Zhgun for managing records and keeping the office running. To Kirill A. Smirnov for managing our book sales. To Igor A. Gudramovich for keeping the data base healthy. To Lyudmila P. Ershova who kept us well fed and our spirits high.

The rest of the staff included: Valentin V. Romanov; Anna V. Anisimova, Marina V. Bochenina, Vitaliy V. Gorenoy, Yuliya S. Korshun, Natalia I. Zimina, Arina I. Romanyuk, Marina M. Zabruskova; Karl Pezzold, Andrey A. Belykh, Ph.D., Ph.D., Maria N. Zubacheva, Valeriy Yu. Starostin, Marina G. Nemanova, Irina G. Logancheva; Olga L. Boykova, Lyudmila S. Chesnokova, Lidia I. Demicheva, Stanislav P. Demichev, Galina M. Dmitrieva, Solomon L. Erpert, Daredzhan M. Fedorova, Olga E. Gazina, Galina I. Kuznechenkova, Ekaterina F. Lipina, Elena S. Lisyuk, Maria G. Markova; Lyudmila N. Samoylova; Anatoliy M. Sysoev, Elena N. Yanchenkova; Aleksandr V. Anisimov, Irina V. Yakovleva, Eric Abbruzzese, Susan Smith, Alla V. Belykh. Computer support was provided by Evgeniy E. Vasilev, Aleksey M. Yazev, Ph.D., Victor V. Botvinnik, Irina I. Popova, Svetlana A. Padubotskaya, Michael I. Chusovitin, and Tatyana A. Tikhomirova .

A special thanks is given to our 353 advertisers which include the leading Russian and Western firms in St. Petersburg. Their support and confidence are making a major contribution to the economic prosperity of their city.

The text and informational commentary were written by the editor with the help of the Russian and American staff. Rita Stasiak and the technical staff of Accurate Web, a major printer of directories in New York, provided technical advice, enthusiastic encouragement, fast press times and infinite patience. Eric Barnes and Robert Geiger at Scanachrome provided assistance in the production of our color ads. Special thanks goes to Christopher Jannuzzi, manager of the US office and international sales whose enthusiasm, hard work and creativity kept us going in the US and made it possible for us to come to Russia.

Special appreciation goes to Blanche B. Dohan, Associate Editor and Vice President of InfoServices, for her management skills and for her constant support which kept me going throughout the project.

> Michael R. Dohan, Ph.D.
> Editor and Publisher
> Cold Spring Harbor, New York, USA and St. Petersburg, Russia

About the editor:
The editor, Michael R. Dohan, received his Ph.D. in Economics from the Massachusetts Institute of Technology. He is a specialist in Soviet (now Russian) economics and is currently an Associate Professor of Economics at Queens College of the City University of New York and Director of the Social Science Laboratory for Research and Teaching.

About the typography and printing
The book was written using Word for Windows 2 on Dell 386 20 MHz laptops , 486 50 MHz desktop systems and a Zeos 486 66 MHz system. The essays are set in 7 pt Univers (W1) and the listings in 6 and 7 pt Switzerland. The Russian Glasnost fonts were designed by Cassidy and Greene of California. The manuscript was prepared for printing on a Hewlett Packard Laserjet 4. The cover was printed by Levon Graphics Corp. NY, USA on 10 pt coated 2 sides, and the book was printed by Accurate Web Press, Long Island, NY, USA on 40 lb. offset paper especially selected to keep the book compact. Color separation was done by Scanachrome, Farmingdale, NY, USA.

THE *TRAVELLER'S* YELLOW PAGES

and HANDBOOK for

SAINT PETERSBURG

Vyborg and Suburbs of Lomonosov, Pavlovsk, Peterhof and Pushkin

1994

Жёлтые Страницы
с алфавитным указателем
для иностранных гостей
Санкт-Петербурга

Gelbe Seiten
für Reisende mit
deutschem Suchwortregister

Pages Jaunes
pour le voyageur
avec index en français

Gula Sidorna
för resande
med anvisning på svenska

Keltaiset Sivut
suomenkielinen
aakkosellinen hakemisto

Michael R. Dohan, Ph.D.
Editor
with the assistance of
Michael Lisyuk, Paul Tush and
Blanche B. Dohan
Associate Editors
Alexander Zakirov, Designer

Selected as
Official
Visitor's
Directory
by the St. Petersburg
Organizing
Committee

When calling from outside
of St. Petersburg
The City Code For
Saint Petersburg

812

The Country Code For
Russia

7

INFOSERVICES INTERNATIONAL, INC.,
New York, USA

The *Traveller's* Yellow Pages and Handbook
for Saint Petersburg
1993-1994

Michael R. Dohan, Ph.D., Editor

Published by InfoServices International, Inc., NY, USA
Distributed in Russia by Telinfo, Saint Petersburg, Russia

Copyright © 1993 by InfoServices International, Inc., NY, USA
*Telinfo, Saint Petersburg, Russia, is a wholly-owned subsidiary of
InfoServices International, Inc., NY, USA*

All rights reserved. No part of this book may be reproduced or transmitted in any form or by any means, electronic or mechanical including photocopying, recording or by any informational storage or retrieval system – except by a reviewer, who may quote brief passages in a review to be printed in a magazine or newspaper – without permission in writing from the publisher.

For information, contact:
InfoServices International, Inc., 1 Saint Marks Place, Cold Spring Harbor, New York, 11724, USA (516) 549-0064, Fax: (516) 549-2032.
In Russia, contact Telinfo, Saint Petersburg, Russia, 190000, Nab. reki Moyki, 64, Tel: (812) 315-64-12, Fax: (812) 312-73-41.

Large volume purchases with your imprint for promotional purposes or premiums are available at a special discount.

The name "The *Traveller's* Yellow Pages" and "Information for the World Traveller" are registered trademarks.

ISBN 1-881-832-01-5
First Printing: September 15, 1993

Although the editors, staff and publishers have made every effort to insure the accuracy and completeness of the information contained in this book, we assume no responsibility for errors, inaccuracies, omissions or any inconsistency herein or for any harm or any inconvenience from using this book or from being included in or omitted from this book. Readers should be aware of the rapid changes in telephone numbers and business conditions in Saint Petersburg, Russia and should take appropriate measures to verify the information. We are grateful for corrections and suggestions for improvement.

PRINTED IN THE UNITED STATES OF AMERICA

TABLE OF CONTENTS
Содержание, Inhaltsverzeichnis, Sommaire
Innehållsförteckning, Sisällysuettelo

СОДЕРЖАНИЕ
Содержание, Inhaltsverzeichnis, Sommaire
Innehållsförteckning, Sisällysuettelo

❖INHALTSVERZEICHNIS❖

☎•••••✉•••••✉•••••☎

Die Gelben Seiten St. Petersburg
Telefonnummern und Adressen

•••••••••••••

❖SOMMAIRE❖

☎•••••✉•••••✉•••••☎

Page Jaunes pour Saint Peterbourg
Numéros des téléphones et adresses

•••••••••••••

❖INNEHÅLLSFÖRTECKNING❖

❖SISÄLLYSLUETTELO❖

Introduction

The Traveller's *Yellow Pages and Handbook for Saint Petersburg, 1993/94*, (2nd ed.) contains over 4300 up-to-date addresses and telephone numbers most frequently needed by travelers to (and residents of) Saint Petersburg, and nearby suburbs. You will find everything from art galleries and airlines to veterinarians and video rentals, all organized in over 412 categories of goods and services like the well-known "Yellow Pages" telephone books. All page headings are in English, with indexes and category headings in English, Russian, German, French, Swedish and Finnish. The book has more than 140 essays and tables of information on telephone services, personal safety, driving, train travel, radio stations, postal rates, sizes and measures, customs regulations, medical care, Cyrillic alphabet, climate, etiquette, safety, visas, seating charts for major concert halls, a checklist of what-to-bring and more. It has a walking map of Nevskiy Prospect, a bilingual metro map (subway or underground) and a new large fold-out street map of Saint Petersburg with transport routes, and new street names.

How to live and shop: *The* Traveller's *Yellow Pages* is especially designed to help you enjoy this beautiful city by showing you how to live, work, dine and shop in St. Petersburg, to make international phone calls, buy good theater tickets, hail a taxi, find flowers, listen to jazz, mail a package home, picnic in the park, get a replacement contact lens, and do your laundry as well as visit museums, dine at great restaurants, browse in old book stores and take an architectural tour with an art historian. It is the perfect companion to a good guidebook such as Baedeker's *Guide to Leningrad (St. Petersburg)*, or Fodor's *Guide to Russia and the Baltics*. See "TRAVEL BOOKS" under "T". A good way to start is by reading the white pages and the essays on SHOPPING, MARKETS, VISAS, CURRENCY EXCHANGE, ETIQUETTE, CUSTOMS, TELEPHONES and SAFETY.

On business: When coming here on business, you will find everything you need for working, living and running a business: banks, auditing firms and business consultants, shipping, trucking, and customs clearance, fax and E-mail, computers, cellular phones, office space, furniture and apartments, car rentals and repairs, presentation banquets, temporary help and translators, advertising agencies, business service centers, accountants and lawyers, and more.

Learn the Cyrillic Alphabet: Visitors, who do not know Russian, will find many aids to help them get about the city. The Cyrillic alphabet is on the back cover, the transliteration and pronunciation guides are on page 13. It is well worth the few hours needed to learn the 33 letter Russian Cyrillic alphabet. You will soon be able to recognize street signs, shops, and Metro stations. In the book, the names of many signs and shops are not only translated, but are also given in Cyrillic and transliterated into Latin letters. The foreign languages spoken in shops, restaurants, etc. are indicated in most listings.

Suburbs and nearby cities: Our section with telephone numbers and addresses for the suburbs of Lomonosov, Pavlovsk, Peterhof and Pushkin and for the nearby city of Vyborg is one of the few sources of this information in Russia as well as abroad.

New Names: Names are still changing in St. Petersburg. In general *old* Soviet-era names in Russia have been dropped in favor of the *new* tsarist names. In this second edition, we use the *new* tsarist names for streets, Metro, bridges, theaters, concert halls and shops. Many but not all street signs, stationery, business cards, etc. have been changed to the new names. Consult the list of the *old* Soviet-era and *new* tsarist street names on pages 14-15.

Transliteration: There is no agreed upon system for writing (transliterating) Russian words in regular "Latin" letters. We chose the simplest system possible as discussed on page 13 "The Russian Cyrillic Alphabet".

What and who is included: This is not a complete Yellow Pages for all the shops and firms in St. Petersburg. We have *selected only those shops, restaurants, firms and agencies of the greatest interest to the foreign resident and traveler* and these we included *free of charge*. These are usually better known, better quality and located in the central part of Saint Petersburg. More than 353 of these establishments have chosen to describe their specialties, services, products, qualifications, hours, currencies, credit cards, location and languages spoken in informative ads. Please patronize our advertisers!

A complex changing economy: In St. Petersburg the visitor will find a very complex economy using two currencies with different price levels, rapid inflation of ruble prices and absurd distortion in relative prices. This book will help both visitors and residents to shop for lower prices and a wider variety of goods and services. In some areas there remains the old fashioned "official" price discrimination against foreigners and foreign firms, but this is slowly disappearing under the pressure of increased competition among firms.

Keeping up-to-date and the Contributing Reader: Saint Petersburg is changing rapidly. New shops, restaurants and businesses open every day, and many firms close for "renovation" and maybe "forever". About 20% of the firms disappeared or changed names or addresses in the past year. All numbers were verified as of July 1993. We know, however, that numbers change rapidly, business conditions change, and errors can be made. Our research staff verifies numbers all year round to keep our book up-to-date. A supplement will be published and delivered to all readers who return their mailing list card. We also ask your help in keeping our *Traveller's* Yellow Pages up-to-date by becom-ing a *Contributing Reader* (see pages 345-351). Send us your evaluations about your favorite (or least favorite) restaurant or shop. Tell about errors and correc-tions, and suggestions for improvements. You can call us while you are in St. Petersburg at 812-315-64-12, fax us at 812-312-73-41, or send a note to Telinfo, 64 Moyka Embankment, St. Petersburg, Russia 190000. Outside of Russia, contact us at: InfoServices International Inc., 1 Saint Marks Place, Cold Spring Harbor, New York 11724, USA. Fax 516-549-2032 and Tel. 516-549-0064.

Michael R. Dohan, Ph.D.
Editor and Publisher

HOW TO USE THE *TRAVELLER'S* YELLOW PAGES

Categories of goods and services are arranged in English alphabetical order: The stores, restaurants, services, institutions and information are classified into more than 412 different categories of goods, services and topics, which are *organized in the* Yellow Pages *in alphabetical order according to their English headings.* These headings are also given in Russian, German, French, Swedish and Finnish.

Within each category, the listings are also arranged alphabetically, usually by the English name, unless the "transliterated" Russian name is simpler and more useful to the reader; then, both are often given.

Essays organized together with categories. The short essays about topics such as restaurants, train travel, shopping, flowers are included under the related categories e.g., types of restaurants under RESTAURANTS.

Where and what to expect at each firm: Most firms listed here are located in the center of the city. Unless otherwise stated, they accept rubles, do not speak much English and are open normal working hours. (See HOURS.)

What we have not included: We have not included factories, most wholesale suppliers, detailed listings of government agencies, local schools, etc. Similarly, the many hundreds of food stores, cafeterias and clinics, especially if located in the outlying regions of St. Petersburg, have been omitted. Listings of these stores and institutions are available in other telephone books. We refer you to *Ves Sankt-Peterburg - 1993 (Ves St. Pb 93)* and *Saint Petersburg Yellow Pages 1993 (St. Pb. Yellow Pages 93)* for more information on the old state sector. See TELEPHONE BOOKS.

Similarly, this is not a traditional travel guide book and thus it has little information about history, culture and arts. See TRAVEL BOOKS.

Use the indexes: Look directly in the Yellow Pages for the categories most closely related to the product, service or information you are seeking. Or use the indexes in English, Russian, German, French, Swedish, and Finnish. For example, to extend your visa, look under "VISA"; to buy a cake, look under "BAKERIES"; to reschedule your flight, look under "AIRLINES"; to find out the average temperature in November, look under "CLIMATE"; for official holidays and vacations, look under "HOLIDAYS". Before you pack, see WHAT-TO-BRING.

If you don't find the category for a specific good, service or information, look under *related* categories. For "paper", look under "STATIONERY" and for a winter coat, look under "CLOTHING".

Use the many cross references to related categories. Related firms are contained in the *cross references,* which are given in CAPITAL LETTERS. For example, under the category of RESTAURANTS, you are given the following "cross reference" to other related categories:

See also CAFES, PIZZA, FAST FOOD, FOOD DELIVERY, DELICATESSENS *and* ICE CREAM.

Translation and transliteration of Russian words: In the text, we often give the English *translation* (bakery) so you can understand it, the English *transliteration* of the Russian word so that you can pronounce it (bulochnaya), and the Russian word in *Cyrillic* (булочная) so that you can recognize it in Russian. Thus, for example, you will see "bakeries" (bulochnaya, булочная).

We use a simple English system of transliteration, described in *The Russian Cyrillic Alphabet* on page 13 and printed also on the back cover. Our system is compared with other systems on page 13 and differs from other systems in that we substitute "y" for the Russian й regardless of where it occurs in the word. Thus, "Nevsky" becomes "Nevskiy" and "Bolshoi" becomes "Bolshoy".

What is in each listing: Each listing includes the name, address and telephone. Additional information is often listed (especially in the ads), including fax, telex, hours of operation, currencies and credit cards accepted, languages spoken and nearest metro station and map coordinates. Here are some conventions used in our listings.

City Code for Saint Petersburg   All telephone numbers are local telephones in St. Petersburg. To call into Saint Petersburg from outside the city, use the **Saint Petersburg City Code 812**

Hours of operation are given on the 24 hour clock, so that 8:00 is 8 a.m. and 20:00 is 8 p.m.. The notation "0-24" means "24 hours per day".

English shown as *Eng* means that some English is spoken by some personnel. Similarly with German (*Ger*), French (*Fr*), Swedish (*Swed*) and Finnish (*Finn*).

**The symbol $** alone means that the establishment accepts only "hard currency". This always includes US dollars and depending on the establishment may also include German and Finnish marks. French and Swiss francs, Scandinavian currencies, English pounds and other currencies are more difficult to use. The symbol *$ & Rbls* means that both dollars and rubles are accepted *or* that part of the cost is in hard currency and part is in rubles. *Rbls* alone means that only rubles are accepted.

For public transportation routes, *Tram* refers to trams (called "streetcars" or "trolleys" in the US), ***T-bus*** refers to trolleybus, ***Bus*** refers to what is called an "avtobus" in Russian and "bus" in English. ***Metro*** refers to the Metro station (called "Underground" in England, "Subway" in the US). The map coordinates refer to the location on The *Traveller's* Yellow Pages City Map. On The *Traveller's* Yellow Pages City Map, tram routes and route numbers are black, bus lines are blue , T-bus routes are red, and Metro lines are heavy blue.

How street names are listed: The names of all streets, prospects, lanes, boulevards, avenues, etc. are listed with the **principal name first** *followed* by *ul.* (street), *pl.* (square), etc. regardless of their actual order in Russian. Thus we write *Sadovaya ul.* rather than *Ul. Sadovaya*. This simplifies finding streets on maps, etc. Our map follows the same system.

Abbreviations of Russian words for street, etc.: The Russian words are used for street (*ulitsa*), square (*ploshchad*), etc. rather than their English translations (e.g. street, square, etc.), because this helps you (and Russians) find the right street or square more quickly. The abbreviation **V.O.** after a street name refers to its location on Vasilevskiy Ostrov (Island) on the northwest side of the Neva River and **P.S.** refers to Petrogradskaya Storona (side) on the north side of the Neva across from the Hermitage.

ul.	=	ulitsa	⇒	улица	=	street
pr.	=	prospekt	⇒	проспект	=	prospect or avenue
kan.	=	kanal	⇒	канал	=	canal
pl.	=	ploshchad	⇒	площадь	=	square
per.	=	pereulok	⇒	переулок	=	lane
Nab.	=	naberezhnaya	⇒	набережная	=	embankment
V.O.	=	Vasilevskiy Ostrov	⇒	Васильевский Остров	=	Vasilevskiy Island
P.S.	=	Petrogradskaya Storona	⇒	Петрогадская Сторона	=	Petrogradsky Side

A full list of abbreviations is given on page 48.

The Russian Cyrillic Alphabet
Its Transliteration and Pronounciation

TRANSLITERATION of Cyrillic letters into our Latin letters is difficult because there is no international agreement among experts on a single unified system of converting from Cyrillic into Latin letters. Indeed, each language has one or more methods of converting Russian into English or German or French, based on their own pronunciation of letters. In addition there is an official Russian of transliteration from Cyrillic. In the text of the Traveller's Yellow Pages, (TYP) we usually use a simplified system of transliteration based on the English system of transliteration.

The principal differences between the simplified English transliteration used in the text of the Traveller's Yellow Pages and the German and official Russian transliterations are for the letters Й, Я, Ч, Ш, and Щ.

RUSSIAN Cyrillic Alphabet		Traveller's Yellow Pages	English System in Use	German System In Use	Russian Official Method	GUIDE TO PRONUNCIATION Like the letter	in the word
А	а	a	a	a	a	a	father
Б	б	b	b	b	b	b	bank
В	в	v	v	w	v	v	victor
Г	г	g	g	g	g	g	good
Д	d	d	d	d	d	d	dog
Е	е	e	e, ye	je	e, je	ye	yes
Ё	ё	e	yo	jo	o, jo	yo	yogurt
Ж	ж	zh	zh	sh	ž	g	massage
З	з	z	z	s, z	z	z	zebra
И	и	i	i	i	ji, i	ee	see
Й	й	y	j	j	i, y	*In the following combinations*	
						oy	toy
						y	goodbye
						ay	hay
Ê	ê	k	k	k	k	k	kangaroo
Л	л	l	l	l	l	ll	fill
М	м	m	m	m	m	m	mouse
Н	н	n	n	n	n	n	north
О	о	o	o	o	o	o	port
						Like "ah" if not stressed	
П	п	p	p	p	p	p	pepper
Р	р	r	r	r	r	r	red
						Rolled at the tip of the tongue	
С	с	s	s	s	s	s	soon, yes
Т	т	t	t	t	t	t	tea
У	у	u	u	u	u	oo	fool
Ф	ф	f	f	v, f	f	f	fire
Х	х	kh	kh	ch	ch	ch	*Scottish* loch
Ц	ц	ts	ts	z	c	ts	sits
Ч	ч	ch	ch	tsch	č	ch	chair
Ш	ш	sh	sh	sch	š	sh	short
Щ	щ	shch	shch	stsch	sč	shch	fresh cheese
Ъ	ъ	*Hard sign not pronounced*				*Hard sign not pronounced*	
Ы	ы	y	y	y	y	i	ill
Ь	ь	*Soft sign not pronounced (j)*				*Soft sign not pronounced*	
Э	э	e	e	e	e	e	let
Ю	ю	yu	yu, iu	ju	u, ju	you	youth
Я	я	ya	ya, ia	ja	ja	ya	yacht

NEW NAMES IN SAINT PETERSBURG

Names are being changed quickly in Saint Petersburg. The name of Leningrad was formally changed to SANKT-PETERBURG (САНКТ-ПЕТЕРБУРГ) after a vote by the citizens in June 1991. Even before that vote, street names were being changed. Soviet-era name plates were being removed from street signs, and statues of Lenin and other Soviet heroes were disappearing. After the vote, the process accelerated and now more than 60 street names have been changed back to their original pre-1917 names. Some of these have been listed below.

New Street, Metro and Bridge Names: In the second edition of *The* Traveller's *Yellow Pages for Saint Petersburg*, we have used only the "new" post-Soviet names (often pre-1917 names) for streets, Metros and bridges. Remember, however, that some people, some signs and most pre-1993 guide books still use the old Soviet-era names. Streets names now in (legal) transition are denoted by an asterisk (*).

Other New Names: Many other Soviet-era and Communist names for hospitals, universities and institutes have also changed. For example, the "Opera and Ballet Theater named after Kirov" has been changed back to "Mariinskiy Theater." Often, pre-1917 institutions took back their pre-1917 names. Many names with "Leningrad" have been changed to "Saint Petersburg". For example, the "Leningrad State University" is now the "St. Petersburg State University" and the hotel "Leningrad" is now the hotel "Saint Petersburg". Some venerable institutions, have been broken up into several small parts. For example Intourist lost most of its hotels when they became independent organizations, its transportation branch is now the independent "Intourist Transport", and its travel agency functions now survive in the much smaller "Travel Agency of Saint Petersburg". We have used the newest names available for theaters, universities, enterprises, and so forth. In sum, life and names are changing quickly in Saint Petersburg. Very confusing, but very exciting as the new system emerges from the old.

Street, Metro and Bridge Names- Old and New

НАЗВАНИЯ УЛИЦ, МЕТРО И МОСТОВ -СТАРЫЕ И НОВЫЕ

STRASSENNAMEN - ALTE und NEUE	NOMS DES RUES - VIEUX & NOUVEAUX
GATUNAMN - GAMLA och NYA	KATUEN NIMILUETTELO - VANHA ja UUDET

Old Soviet-era names	New names	Старое название	Восстановленное название
STREET NAMES			
Anny Ulyanovoy ul.	Polozova ul.	ул. Анны Ульяновой	ул. Полозова
Bratstva ul.	Malyy Sampsonievskiy pr.	ул. Братства	пр. Малый Сампсониевский
Brodskogo ul.	Mikhaylovskaya ul.	ул. Бродского	ул. Михайловская
Voynova ul.	Shpalernaya ul.	ул. Войнова	ул. Шпалерная
Voytika ul.	Vitebskaya ul.	ул. Войтика	ул. Витебская
Gaza pr.	Staro-Petergofskiy pr.	пр. Газа	пр. Старо-Петергофский
*Gertsena ul.	*Bolshaya Morskaya ul.	ул. Герцена	ул. Большая Морская
*Gogolya ul.	*Malaya Morskaya ul.	ул. Гоголя	ул. Малая Морская
Dzerzhinskogo ul.	Gorokhovaya ul.	ул. Дзержинского	ул. Гороховая
Zhelyabova ul.	Bolshaya Konyushennaya ul.	ул. Желябова	ул. Большая Конюшенная
Kalyaeva ul.	Zakharevskaya ul.	ул. Каляева	ул. Захарьевская
Karla Marksa pr.	Bolshoy Sampsonievskiy pr.	пр. Карла Маркса	пр. Большой Сампсониевский
Kirovskiy pr.	Kamennoostrovskiy pr.	Кировский пр.	Каменноостровский пр.
Kommunarov pl.	Nikolskaya pl.	пл. Коммунаров	Никольская пл.
Krasnoy Konnitsy ul.	Kavalergardskaya ul.	ул. Красной Конницы	Кавалергардская ул.
Mayorova pr.	Voznesenskiy pr.	пр. Майорова	Вознесенский пр.
Maksima Gorkogo pr.	Kronverkskiy pr.	пр. Максима Горького	Кронверкский пр.
Marii Ulyanovoy ul.	Grafskiy per.	ул. Марии Ульяновой	Графский пер.

Old Soviet-era names	New names	Старое название	Восстановленное название
Ploshchad Mira	Sennaya pl.	Площадь Мира	Сенная пл.
Smirnova pr.	Lanskoe shosse	пр. Смирнова	Ланское шоссе
Ogorodnikova pr.	Rizhskiy pr.	пр. Огородникова	Рижский пр.
Olega Koshevogo ul.	Vvedenskaya ul.	ул. Олега Кошевого	Введенская ул.
Petra Lavrova ul.	Furshtatskaya ul.	ул. Петра Лаврова	Фурштатская ул.
Podbelskogo per.	Pochtamtskiy per.	пер. Подбельского	Почтамтский пер.
Profsoyuzov blvd.	Konnogvardeyskiy blvd.	бульвар Профсоюзов	Конногвардейский бульвар
Rakova ul.	Italyanskaya ul.	ул. Ракова	Итальянская ул.
Skorokhodova ul.	Bolshaya Monetnaya ul.	ул. Скороходова	Большая Монетная ул.
Sofi Perovskoy ul.	Malaya Konyushennaya ul	ул. Софьи Перовской	Малая Конюшенная ул.
Tolmacheva ul.	Karavannaya ul.	ул. Толмачева	Караванная ул.
Fotievoy ul.	Eletskaya ul.	ул. Фотиевой	Елецкая ул.
Fofanovoy ul.	Enotaevskaya ul.	ул. Фофановой	Енотаевская ул.
Khalturina ul.	Millionnaya ul.	ул. Халтурина	Миллионная ул.
Shchorsa pr.	Malyy pr. P.S.	пр. Щорса	Малый пр. П.С.
Skver na Ostrovskogo pl.	Ekaterininskiy skver	сквер на пл. Островского	Екатерининский сквер
Vosstaniya pl.	Znamenskaya pl.	пл. Восстания	Знаменская пл.
Dekabristov pl.	Senatskaya pl.	пл. Декабристов	Сенатская пл.
Ostrovskogo pl.	Aleksandriyskaya pl.	пл. Островского	пл. Александрийская
Pestelya ul.	Panteleymonovskaya ul.	ул. Пестеля	Пантелеймоновская ул.
Revolyutsii pl.	Troitskaya pl.	пл. Революции	Троицкая пл.
Stachek pl.	Narvskaya pl.	пл. Стачек	Нарвская пл.
Truda ul. & pl.	Blagoveshchenskaya ul. & pl.	ул. и пл. Труда	Благовещенская ул и пл.
Metro Stations			
Ploshchad Mira	Sennaya pl.	Площадь Мира	Сенная пл.
Komsomolskaya	Devyatkino	Комсомольская	Девяткино
Krasnogvardeyskaya	Novocherkasskaya	Красногвардейская	Новочеркасская
Bridges			
Kirovskiy most	Troitskiy most	Кировский мост	Троицкий мост
Komsomolskiy most	Kharlamov most	Комсомольский мост	Харламов мост
Leytenanta Shmidta most	Nikolaevskiy most	Лейтенанта Шмидта мост	Николаевский мост
Liteynyy most	Aleksandrovskiy most	Литейный мост	Александровский мост
Pestelya most	Panteleymonovskiy most	мост Пестеля	Пантелеймоновский мост
Pionerskiy most	Silin most	Пионерский мост	Силин мост
Narodnyy most	Politseyskiy most	Народный мост	Полицейский мост
Stroiteley most	Birzhevoy most	Строителей мост	Биржевой мост
Svobody most	Sampsonievskiy most	мост Свободы	Сампсониевский мост
Canals			
Krushteyna kan.	Admiralteyskiy kan.	кан. Круштейна	Адмиралтейский кан.
Griboedova kan.	Ekaterininskiy kan.	кан. Грибоедова	Екатерининский кан.
Parks			
Detskiy park Oktyabrskogo rayona	Yusupovskiy sad	Детский парк Октябрьского района	Юсуповский сад
Sad imeni F.E.Dzerzhinskogo	Lopukhinskiy sad	Сад им. Ф.Э. Дзержинского	Лопухинский сад
Park Chelyuskintsev	Udelnyy park	Парк Челюскинцев	Удельный парк

Outside of Russia, Order extra copies of
The *Traveller's* Yellow Pages of St. Petersburg from

InfoServices International, Inc.

1 Saint Marks Place, Cold Spring Harbor,
NY 11724 USA
☎ (516) 544-0064.   ☎ (516) 544-2032

Как разместить рекламу в
**The *Traveller's* Yellow Pages and
Handbook for Saint Petersburg 1994-95**
*Жёлтые Страницы с алфавитным
указателем для иностранных гостей
Санкт-Петербурга*
Лучшее в Санкт-Петербурге 1994
*Новый справочник на русском языке
из серии The Traveller's Yellow Pages.*

**Worldwide (except Russia)
InfoServices International, Inc.**
✉ 1 Saint Marks Place
Cold Spring Harbor, NY 11724, USA

Tel........................... USA (516) 549-0064
Fax .... (516) 549-2032
Telex............................ 221213 TTC UR

In Russia, TELINFO
✉190000, St. Petersburg, Russia
Nab. Reki Moyki, 64
Tel..315-64-12
Fax 312-73-41

Geschäft in Russland und Osteuropa?

Inserieren Sie Ihre Reklame in

THE *TRAVELLER'S* YELLOW PAGES

MOSCOW 1994
Closing October 15, Pub: Nov. 15 1993
NORTHWEST RUSSIA, 1994/95
from Murmansk to Novgorod, Pub: July 1994
ESTONIA 1994-95
Including Tallinn and major towns, Pub. July 1994
SAINT PETERSBURG 1994-95
Sonderaufgabe für die 1994 Goodwill Games in Sankt Petersburg in Juli-August 1994. Pub: June 1994

☙ Лучшее в ❧ *Das Beste in*

Unseren Gelben Seiten auf russisch besonders für die Einwohner

Лучшее в Санкт-Петербурге 94-95
Das Beste in Sankt-Petersburg 1994-95
Лучшее в Москве 1994/95
Das Beste in Moskow 1994-95

AUCH *KIEV-1995, LATVIA-1994, LITHUAINIA-1994 RUSSIAN FAR EAST-1995, BUCHAREST-1996, BUDAPEST-1995/96, WARSAW-1995 / 96, PRAGUE-1995/96*

SEHEN SEE, BITTE, SEITE 327 & 330

Business in Russia?

**Marketing to the English
speaking foreign residents,
businessmen and visitors**

*Advertise in
the coming editions of*

**THE *TRAVELLER'S*
YELLOW PAGES**

SEE PAGE 327

Annonsera i nästa nummer av

THE *TRAVELLER'S* YELLOW PAGES

MOSCOW 1994
Closing October 15, Pub: Nov. 15 1993
NORTHWEST RUSSIA, 1994/95
from Murmansk to Novgorod, Pub: July 1994
ESTONIA 1994-95
Including Tallinn and major towns, Pub: July 1994
SAINT PETERSBURG 1994-95
Special Edition for the 1994 Goodwill Games in Saint
Petersburg in July-August 1994. Pub: June 1994

Лучшее в ꙮ
Det Bästa i

*Nya Gula Sidor på ryska
för ryska invånare*
ЛУЧШЕЕ В САНКТ-ПЕТЕРБУРГЕ **94-9**
Det Bästa i St. Petersburg 1994-95
ЛУЧШЕЕ В МОСКВЕ 1994/95
Det Bästa i Moskva 1994-95

*KIEV-1995, LATVIA-1994, LITHUAINIA-1994,
RUSSIAN FAR EAST-1995, BUCHAREST-1996, BUDAPEST-
1995/96, WARSAW-1995 / 96, PRAGUE-1995/96*

SE SIDORNA 327 - 330

Business in Russia

Marketing to the English speaking foreign residents, visitors and businessmen in Russia

Advertise in

THE *TRAVELLER'S* YELLOW PAGES

MOSCOW 1994
Closing November 27, 1993

NORTHWEST RUSSIA 1994/95
from Murmansk to Novgorod.
Closing May 1994, Pub: July 1994

ESTONIA 1994-95
Including Tallinn and major cities and town
Closing June 1994, Pub. July 1994

SAINT PETERSBURG 1994-95

Special Edition for the 1994 Goodwill games in Saint Petersburg in July-August 1994. 6000 copies distributed free: Closing: May 15, Pub: June 1994
See page 327 for details on advertising.

The *Traveller's* Yellow Pages and Handbook Series
Written for the world traveller, foreign resident, businessman and visitor
Michael R. Dohan, Ph.D., Editor

❖ ❖ ❖ *Forthcoming editions in 1994* ❖ ❖ ❖
Northwest Russia (June 1994) and Estonia (June 1994),
Latvia (August 1994), and Lithuania (October 1994),
Kiev (late 1094), Moscow, *2d ed.* (late 1994),
Saint Petersburg *3d ed.* (late June, 1994)

For your Russian friends, look also for similar editions in Russian for Moscow and Saint Petersburg in mid-1994 (see page 329). In 1995, look for new English editions for Warsaw, Prague, Budapest, Bucharest and selected islands in the Caribbean.

Each edition of **The *Traveller's* Yellow Pages and Handbook** features:

• **Written in English**, with headings and indexes in major foreign and local languages. Easy to use.

• **Contains 1000's of addresses,** including the most extensive lists of restaurants, hotels, fine shops and quality service firms of special interest to foreign residents and visitors on business and pleasure.

• **Organized like the Yellow Pages** with **more than 400 categories** of goods, services and topics of interest from accounting, airlines and auto rentals to universities, video rentals, water, yacht clubs and zoos

• **Is a useful and easy-to-use directory** because many listings include not only the name, address, telephones, but also **fax numbers, hours, currencies, languages spoken, public transport and a short description.** Each contains hundreds of informative ads for local firms. Most shop names are given in both English and the local language, e.g., Russian, Estonian, etc.

• **Contains more than 100 short practical essays and informative tables** on taxis, safety, shopping, currency exchange, climate, time, distances, radio stations, weights, sizes, water quality, what to bring, local etiquette and holidays, etc.

• **Is accurate and up-to-date** because each number is verified twice by our resident staff before printing.

• **Includes a full size fold-out city and/or country map** along with detailed maps of main shopping areas and other useful illustrations.

• **Priced between $7.00 and $12.00** depending on edition, includes free supplements when published. Sold by mail and in bookstores and hotels throughout the world.

For advertising information, see pages 327-331.

TO ORDER FORTHCOMING EDITIONS, CALL, FAX OR WRITE:

TRAVELLER'S YELLOW PAGES

EDITORIAL OFFICES
THE *TRAVELLER'S* YELLOW PAGES™

InfoServices International, Inc.
✉ 1 Saint Marks Place
Cold Spring Harbor, NY 11724, USA

Tel	USA (516) 549-0064
Fax...................	(516) 549-2032
Telex	221213 TTC UR

Editorial offices also in Saint Petersburg and Moscow.

Information for the World Traveller™

2500 WORLD-CLASS ATHLETES WILL BE WALKING, RUNNING, LEAPING AND FLYING TO GET TO ST. PETERSBURG, RUSSIA IN JULY 1994

*W*hen the historic and beautiful city of St. Petersburg presents the 1994 Goodwill Games, it will be the first major international athletic competition in the new Russia. World-class athletes from over 50 nations will compete in 24 sports, bringing together a diversity of athletic events with centuries of history, art and culture.

Please join us in uniting the world's best athletes in an atmosphere of international goodwill.

GOODWILL GAMES '94
St. Petersburg, Russia

© 1993 Turner Broadcasting System Inc. All Rights Reserved.

МЕДИ

DENTAL CENTER
DENTAL SUPPLY

OPEN 24 HOURS
7 DAYS A WEEK
EVERYTHING FOR DENTISTS

Dentistry materials, equipment and instrument sales. Our sales representatives are experienced dental consultants. All materials and instruments have been tested at the MEDI Dental Center.

DENTAL CENTER St. Petersburg, 10ya Sovetskaya, 13
Tel: (812) 274-64-80

DENTAL SUPPLY St. Petersburg, Zanevskiy pr., 43
Tel: (812) 528-88-88, tel./fax: (812) 528-42-63

THE MAJOR B·A·N·K IN ST. PETERSBURG

Ruble & currency accounts • All foreign exchange operations • Direct currency transfer • SWIFT member • Documentary operation • Cash letters of credit • FX operations • Moscow Interbank Currency Exchange

CORRESPONDENT WITH:

Norwest Bank • Deutsche Bank • Barclays Bank • Midland Bank • Credit Lyonnais • Kansallis-Osake-Pankki • ABN Bank • Credit Suisse • The Bank of Tokyo • & major Western banks

BANK "SAINT-PETERSBURG"

Admiralteyskaya Emb., 8
Ostrovskogo Sq., 7
Tel.: 315-8327, 310-3357
Fax: 315-8327
Telex: 121226 LBANK SU
SWIFT JSBSRU2P
Office 8:30 - 17:00
Banking Operation 9:30 - 13:00
English spoken

BANK "SAINT-PETERSBURG"

Daily Flights
to HELSINKI & to

- **North America**

- **Europe**

- **Scandinavia**

- **Far East**

In Moscow
Kamergerskiy per., 6
Tel.: 292-87-88, 292-33-37,
292-17-58, Fax: 292-49-48

In Saint Petersburg
Office at Gogolya ul., 19
Tel.: 315-97-36, Fax: 312-04-59
Airport Pulkovo-2: Tel. 104-34-39

CENTER OF MANAGEMENT AND MARKETING PROGRESS

MANAGEMENT TRAINING AND PROFESSIONAL ADVICE FOR YOUR PERFOMANCE IN RUSSIA

In cooperation with:
European Bank for Reconstruction and Development
Manchester Business School
Bildungswerk
der Baden-Württembergischen Wirtschaft

Member of ERIDO

Phone:
(812) 552-1338
(812) 552-6962
(812) 552-2817

Fax:
(812) 552-7728
(812) 552-2398

E-mail:
cmm@sovam.com

Joint-Stock Company

UNiREM

Russia, St.Petersburg,190000, Konnogvardeyskiy blvd., 1
Tel: 311-78-93; Fax:312-79-58; Telex: 121054 UREM SU

See our ads under
BEER • COMPUTER STORES • FOOD STORES • GAS STATIONS
BUILDING SUPPLIES • TRAVEL AGENCY • TRUCKING
SHIPPING • THEATER/BALLET

FINNAIR CARGO

Daily flights to Helsinki
from Moscow and St. Petersburg.
Trucking service AY 9029
Moscow - Helsinki, St. Petersburg - Helsinki.
Short transit time in Helsinki and
good connections to all
Finnair onward destinations.

Finnair Cargo in St. Petersburg:
Pulkovo Airport, Terminal 2
Tel: 104-34-39
Telex: 121533

Finnair Cargo in Moscow:
Sheremetievo-2 Airport 6th floor,
Tel.: 578-2718
Telex: 413902
Mobile tel.: 941-6080

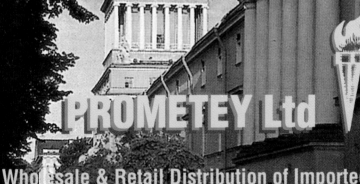

PROMETEY Ltd

Wholesale & Retail Distribution of Imported Food Products & Tobacco in St.Petersburg

Ochakovskaya ul., 7, St.Petersburg, 193015, Russia
Tel.: (812) 274-76-54, (812) 274-78-84; Fax. (812) 274-77-62

RUSSIAN ABBREVIATIONS AND WORDS USED IN ADDRESSES

Blvd.	Boulevard	Бульв.	Бульвар
Der.	Village	Дер.	Деревня
D.	House/Apt.	Д.	Дом
Entr.	Entrance	Под.	Подъезд
G.	City/Town	Г.	Город
Gos.	State (adj)	Гос.	Государственный
Im.	Named after	Им.	Имени
In-t	Institute	Ин-т.	Институт
K	Room	К.	Комната
Kan.	Canal	Кан.	Канал
Kv.	Apartment	Кв.	Квартира
Kladb	Cemetery	Кладб.	Кладбище
Km.	Kilometer	Км.	Километр
Korp.	Building Number	Корп.	Корпус
Mag	Shop/ Store	Маг.	Магазин
Min	Ministry	Мин.	Министерство
Nab	Embankment	Наб.	Набережная
O.	Island	О.	Остров
Per.	Lane	Пер.	Переулок
P.S.	Petrogradsky Side	П.С.	Петроградская Сторона
Pl.	Square	Пл.	Площадь
Pos	Planned Settlement	Пос.	Поселок
Pr	Prospect	Пр.	Проспект
St.	Station	Ст.	Станция
Tel.	Phone	Тел.	Телефон
Ul	Street	Ул.	Улица
V.O.	Vasilevskiy Ostrov	В.О.	Васильевский Остров
Z-d	Plant	З-д.	Завод

ENGLISH ABBREVIATIONS and TERMS USED IN ADS AND LISTINGS

Mon	Monday	понедельник
Tue	Tuesday	вторник
Wed	Wednesday	среда
Thu	Thursday	четверг
Fri	Friday	пятница
Sat	Saturday	суббота
Sun	Sunday	воскресенье
apt	apartment	квартира
bldg	building	корпус
floor	floor	этаж
rm	room	комната
Clsd	Closed	закрыто
Hrs	Time on the 24 hour clock	время работы
Rbls	Accepts only rubles	рубли
CC	Accepts Credit Cards	кредитные карточки
$	Accepts only hard currency	валюта
$/rbls	Accepts hard currency & rubles	валюта и рубли
Eng	English spoken to some extent	английский
Ger	German spoken to some extent	немецкий
Fren	French spoken to some extent	французкий
Finn	Finnish spoken to some extent	Финский
N.A.	Named after	имени
St. Pb.	Saint Petersburg	Санкт-Петербург
TYP	*Traveller's* Yellow Pages	*Traveller's* Yellow Pages
Ves St Pb 93	Ves Sankt-Peterburg 1993	Весь Санкт Петербург 1993Ц
Yellow Pages St Pb 93		Желтые Страницы
	Yellow Pages Saint Petersburg 1993	Санкт Петербург 1993

☎ ACCOUNTING AND AUDITING FIRMS
АУДИТОРСКИЕ ФИРМЫ
FINANZBERATUNG-UND
ABWICKLUNGSFIRMEN
COMPTABILITE, SOCIETES DE
REVISORER,
OCH HANDELSKONSULTER
KIRJANPITO -
TILINTARKASTUSTOIMISTOT

Russian and Western accounting methods and tax systems differ considerably. Get an expert to manage your books and tax accounts.

ARTHUR ANDERSEN
Saint Petersburg Office, Russia
Audit and Business Advisory
Tax and Legal Services
Systems Consulting

V.O., Bolshoy pr., 10 350-49-84
....350-48-13
Fax....................................213-78-74

Auditor Cooperative
&ω Independent Auditors ଔ
&ω Complete Accounting Services ଔ

Dumskaya ul., 1/3.........................110-59-77
Fax 314-15-73

Audit & Management International
Griboedova kan. nab., 34, rm. 210..... 110-57-20
Bosi
1-ya Krasnoarmeyskaya ul., 11, rm. 85 292-56-58

Coopers &Lybrand | Solutions for Business
Moscow & St. Petersburg
Accountants, Management Consultants
Tax Advisers

In Saint Petersburg
At the Astoria Hotel, Room 528
Gertsena ul., 39 .... (812) 210-55-28
Fax .... (812) 210-55-28
In Moscow
Shchepkina ul., 6 .... (095) 288-98-01
Fax .... (095) 284-52-73

Deloitte & Touche
DRT - Inaudit
St. Petersburg Office
Accounting and Auditing
Management Consulting
and Tax Services

Petropavlovskaya krepost, 11
(812) 850-15-09

Diskont, *Mon-Fri 9-21; Rbls, $*
Bolshoy Smolenskiy pr., 6.............. 567-49-18
Fax..567-53-18

⧗ ERNST & YOUNG
St. Petersburg

Auditing, Management Consulting, Tax & Accounting
Gogolya ul., 11, St. Petersburg
Tel. .... (812) 312-99-11
.... (812) 312-81-29
Int. Tel. .... (7-812) 850-85-00
Fax .... (812) 312-53-20
Telex ....612135 STPETE SU

Express-Pravo-Information
Malaya Konyushennaya ul., 7 315-96-30
    Mon-Fri 9-18; Rbls, $; Eng
Inaudit AKG, *Mon-Fri 9:30-18; Rbls, $*
Italyanskaya ul., 33 311-61-53
Fax..310-53-33

INFRAUDIT Ltd.
Malaya Posadskaya ul., 22 259-58-54
....246-50-90
    Auditing & Tax Consulting

Intekhcenter, *Auditing, Bookkeeping & Accounting*
Chkalovskiy pr., 52........................ 234-92-23
Fax..230-13-07
 Mon-Fri 9-18; Rbls, $; Eng, Ger; Metro Petrogradskaya

Institute of Independent Social &
Economic Investigations   IISEI

*Auditing - Consulting -
Tax Services - Management Training*
Kanal Griboedova, 34   Tel. 110-5720
office 210   Fax: 110-5751

iCPA inter corp.
Russian-American Stock Company

Member of St. Petersburg Chamber of Chartered Accountants

- **Accounting**
- **Consulting**
- **Auditing**

(812) 312-23-39, 311-61-30

Invest
Gertsena ul., 18 319-39-54
Fax 311-95-84
Mon-Fri 9:30-17:30; Rbls, $; Eng

A/O Investkon
Financial Consulting, Auditing & Licenses
III-go Internatsionala ul., 3, apt. 2
Tel 246-50-90
.... 158-59-08

KPMG
St. Petersburg

- *Auditors*
- *Accountants*
- *Advisors and Consultants*

Canal Griboyedova 7, 3rd floor
☎ 314-52-09; Fax 312-71-32

Lenaudit
Nevskiy pr., 7/9 315-89-85
Kazanskaya ul., 36 312-56-73
Accounting, preparation of taxes & financial records
Mon-Fri 9-18; Rbls; Ger

Max
Akademika Konstantinova ul., 8/2, 6th floor
.... 550-87-02
Fax 550-70-16
Mon-Fri 10-18; Rbls; Eng
Marketing Consulting Design - *See ad below*
Piterkonto
Sredniy pr., 28 310-47-18
Mon-Fri 9-17; Rbls, $; Eng, Ger

Country code for Russia - 7
City code for St. Petersburg - 812

Marketing Consulting Design

- One of the First Auditing Companies in St. Petersburg
- Domestic & Foreign Auditing
- Tax and Legal Consulting
- Assistance in Company Registration
- Construction & Renovation Consulting
- Financial Analysis

Shpalernaya ul., 52, apt. 13 275-54-55
Tel./Fax 275-56-23

We Think About Tomorrow

St. Petersburg Audit Service
Obvodnogo kan. nab., 53 164-25-84
Mon-Fri 9:30-18; Rbls; Eng
Yurie
Aptekarskiy pr., 6 234-43-84
Fax 234-15-33
Mon-Fri 8:30-17; Rbls, $; Eng

☎ ACUPUNCTURE
АКУПУНКТУРА
AKUPUNKTUR
ACCUPUNCTURE
AKUPUNKTUR
AKUPUNKTIO

Acupuncture & Reflexology Office
Perekupnoy per., 7/9 274-92-73
Mon-Sat 16-19; Rbls
Acupuncture & Reflexology Office
Sezdovskaya Liniya, 15 213-22-18
Mon-Fri 9-17; Rbls; Eng, Ger
Gippokrat Pediatrician
Please call 107-37-92
Daily 9-21; Rbls
Kalashnikov Center
Blagodatnaya ul., 7 292-51-12
Fax 292-50-12
Karlson, *Home and hotel visits*
Oleko Dundicha ul., 26, bldg. 2, floor 1, rm. 1
☎ 177-74-36
Mon-Sat 9-20; Rbls
Mokhov Dmitriy E., *Manual therapy & massage*
Please call 225-87-78

☎ ADDRESSES
АДРЕСА
ADRESSENBÜROS
ADRESSES, BUREAU D'
ADRESSBYRÅER
OSOITETOIMISTOT

How To Get An Address
Use the "Address Bureau" for help in finding new telephone numbers and addresses. This bureau was traditionally run by the Ministry of Internal Affairs (MVD). There are two offices, one that you must visit in person and another that you may phone. Unfortunately, many new numbers and firms are not listed.

Address Bureau - in Person
Liteynyy pr., 6 278-31-19
*The only information given by phone is the bureau's
location and working hours. Mon-Fri 9-17*
Address Bureau - by Phone
Dial 061 + your own phone number.

*If you tell them a person's full name, date
and place of birth, they will give you a
St. Petersburg address within one hour. If
the address is outside of St. Petersburg,
you will get the information in 2-2.5 hrs.
Information is available only in Russian.*

How To Find An Address Location
*It is recommended that you call the
organization or host to get detailed
directions (literally) on <u>how to find their
door</u>. House numbers are few and far
between, difficult to see and refer to the
entire building, not the number of the
entrance. Ask the firm if they have a sign
or some other way of finding the front
door. Even better, get written (faxed)
instructions in English and Russian.*

*"Metro stations" are often used as a
"point of reference". So use the Metro
stations or map coordinates on the back of
The Traveller's Yellow Pages City Map to
help find the street.*

Finding the actual door
*The street number given in the text is the
number for the whole building, called a
"house" (dom, дом). A "house" can cover
a whole city block and may include several
different separate buildings called "korpus"
and may have several entrances (podezd,
подъезд). These entrances may be located
not only on the street but also in
courtyards.*

Thus an address in Russian might read:
дом 2, корпус 3, подъезд 3, квартира 22
which means:
house 2, bldg. 3, entrance 3, apt. 22
*The street number of the house can also
have a letter, for example дом 51г. In such
cases we give a transliteration - house 51g.*

*Offices are referred to in different ways
depending on where they are located. In
office buildings an office is referred to as an
apartment, (kvartira, квартира) or office
(ofis, офис). In hotels and business
centers, they are referred to as "room"
(komnata, комната).*

Getting In and Permits
*Ask if you or any Russian colleagues will
need a permit (propusk, пропуск) to get into
the building. At some banks, however,
both Westerners and Russians need to
show passports to get in.*

☞ **Shop for food in FOOD STORES,
DELICATESSENS, BAKERIES, MARKETS
and even SUPERMARKETS**

☎ **ADVERTISING AGENCIES**
РЕКЛАМНЫЕ АГЕНСТВА
WERBEAGENTUREN
PUBLICITE, AGENCES DE
REKLAMBYRÅER
MAINOSTOIMISTOT

See also BUSINESS PUBLICATIONS, MAGAZINES
AND NEWSPAPERS, RADIO STATIONS,
TELEVISION STATIONS, CABLE TV, &
VIDEO /FILM PRODUCTION

Aktsioner
Full Service Advertising Agency
Shpalernaya ul., 52, apt. 19 272-90-94
Fax 275-76-11

Alenmaks
Liteynyy pr., 20, rm. 14 278-86-81
Fax 394-02-10
Mon-Fri 10-18; Rbls, $; Eng, Finn

a d v e r t i s i n g
Alexander
a g e n c y
design, direct mail, billboards
Konnogvardeyskiy blvd., 4, apt. 11
☎ 312-94-76
☎ 311-78-22
Fax 312-36-94

ARIADNA
Advertising, Design & Agent Training
Kostyushko ul., 1/1 123-19-33

ART GRAPHIC™
DESIGN & PRINTING   311 59 23

Association of Ballroom Dance
Display advertising at international dance competitions
Reki Moyki nab., 94, rm. 96 314-89-95
Fax 310-47-76
Daily 11-19; Rbls, $; Eng
Aviaprocess
Advertising in Pulkovo 1 domestic airport
Pulkovo I 104-37-82
Avir
Mokhovaya ul., 31 275-62-57
Mon-Fri 10-18; Rbls; Eng, Ger
BMP Reklama *Mass media ads in St. Pb.*
Mezhevoy kan., 5 114-95-41
Fax 186-83-44
Mon-Fri 8:35-17:35; Rbls, $; Eng, Ger, Fr

Blaze Productions *TV commercials and corporate video. See our ad under* VIDEO/FILM PRODUCTION

Bolton
Gertsena ul., 28, rm. 525 315-47-81
Fax 315-30-00
Daily 8-20; Rbls, $

The Bronze Lion Ltd.
We/Мы   Advertising/Distribution
Tel/Fax 314-72-92

Commersant *Publishing House*
St.Petersburg Representation
Nevskiy pr., 3, office 25.............315-04-29
Fax.......................................315-79-67
Hrs: 10-20, English, German, French

DAB'S
Aleksandrovskiy park, 4 233-49-56

Decor
Apraksin Dvor, rm. 333 310-22-94
Public transportation advertising
Mon-Fri 10-18; Rbls

DELOVIE LYUDI

provides valuable and unique information on the CIS market enabling decision makers and entrepreneurs to follow the market economy transition in the former USSR.

DELOVIE LYUDI
also offers foreign business people an exceptional medium for communicating details concerning their companies, products and services.

DELOVIE LYUDI
is published in both English and Russian by a Moscow editorial team.

DELOVIE LYUDI
is independent, objective and thorough.

Profsoyuznaya ul., 73...........(095) 333-33-40
Fax.......................................(095) 330-15-68

US Offices
1560 Broadway, 5th floor, N.Y., N.Y. 10036
2865 East Coast Hwy. Suite 308
Corona del Mar, CA. 92625

Electronic Display Newspaper
Nevskiy pr., 52.................................. 310-17-68

Emets
Rubinshteyna ul., 13 112-43-95

Florman Information Russia
Kamennoostrovskiy pr., 14b........... 232-02-51
Fax... 232-80-17
Media relations, press and TV advertising

Foyender, *Daily 0-24; Rbls, $; Eng*
Povarskoy per., 8 311-06-82
Fax... 112-53-59

Igrek Agency
Konnogvardeyskiy blvd., 19, floor 5, rm. 112 .
☎... 311-95-95
Fax... 311-92-19

IMA-Press, *Newspaper and radio advertising*
Zodchego Rossi ul., 1/3 110-46-51
Fax... 314-48-23

IMPEX *Service*

Advertising in Pulkovo-1 & Pulkovo-2 Airports

Neon signs & Billboards

Advertising on vehicles

Advertising through mass media

Some References: Gillette, DHL, SMIRNOFF, SCANSPED, Industry and Construction Bank, Delta Telecom, PETERSTAR, etc.

Advertising agency

ul. Belinskogo, 13, St. Petersburg, 191104, box 39
Phone: (812) 2757968, 2758559   Fax: (812) 2724654

Impex, *Mon-Fri 9-18; $; Eng, Ger, Fr*
Gertsena ul., 35.............................. 310-94-41
Fax... 319-97-09

INFOSERVICES INTERNATIONAL
Information for the World Traveller
PUBLISHER OF

TRAVELLER'S YELLOW PAGES

THE *TRAVELLER'S* YELLOW PAGES FOR **SAINT PETERSBURG**

THE CITY MAP OF SAINT PETERSBURG

Official Visitor's Directory and Map for the 1994 Goodwill Games in Saint Petersburg.
Upcoming Editions for Moscow (Nov. '93), Northwest Russia, and Estonia, Latvia, and Lithuania

1 Saint Marks Place
Cold Spring Harbor, NY 11724, USA
Tel .... USA (516) 549-0064
Fax .... (516) 549-2032
Telex .... 221213 TTC UR
Represented in Russia by
TELINFO, St. Petersburg
✉190000, St. Petersburg, Russia:
Nab. reki Moyki, 64 315-64-12
Fax 312-73-41
Mon-Fri 9-18; Metro Sadovaya

INI-Press, *Radio, television ads, brochures*
Shpalernaya ul., 52, rm. 19, ... 272-90-94
Fax 275-76-11
Mon-Fri 10-17; Rbls; Metro Chernyshevskaya

*i*НОСТРАНЕЦ

Advertising, Classifieds & Public Relations
Inostranets provides you with specialists
and business contacts throughout Russia
and the former USSR
Circulation: 100,000 throughout
the former USSR. 32 pages.

125080, Russia, Moscow, P.O. Box 21
Khoroshovskoe shosse, 17
Moscow .... (095) 941-09-00
.... (095) 137-58-88
Fax .... (095) 940-04-68

Internad Medica
*Medical equipment and pharmaceutical advertising
in "Internad Media", "Peterburg-Europe" and other
mass media*
Novolitovskaya ul., 15 245-53-92
Fax 245-51-28
Mon-Fri 10-18; Rbls, $
Izdatel-Kommersant
Nauki pr., 12, bldg. 7, rm. 24 555-08-39
Klin,   *Mon-Fri 9-18; Rbls, $; Eng, Ger*
Olgina ul., 2 b 235-30-80
Kommet, *Advertising on St. Petersburg metro*
Moskovskiy pr., 28, rm. 450 259-74-15
Fax 251-65-53
Mon-Fri 9-15; Rbls
LenEXPO Exhibition
20 years experience in publicizing exhibitions
Bolshoy pr., V.O., 103 217-11-12
Fax 355-19-85
Daily 10-18; Rbls, $; All European Languages
Lengorspravka
Ligovskiy pr., 29 272-08-34
*Advertising notices on glass covered billboards
throughout the city. Mon-Fri 9-18; Rbls*

*LIC Information
& Publishing
Agency Ltd.*

**Gertsena ul., 20
191065, St. Petersburg, Russia
Tel.: 314-59-82
Fax: 315-35-92**

Likran
Please call 232-55-12
Fax 232-25-88
Mon-Fri 10-19
Media
Yuriya Gagarina pr., 28, bldg. 1 264-03-54
Fax 299-39-82
Mon-Fri 11-17; Rbls; Bus 13; Metro Park Pobedy
Mika
Kamennoostrovskiy pr., 34 232-08-23
Fax 312-41-28
Mon-Fri 10-20; Rbls, $; Eng
Monte Ltd.
Yuriya Gagarina pr., 28, bldg. 1 264-03-54
Fax 299-39-82
Mon-Fri 11-17; Rbls; Eng

WHAT'S HAPPENING IN ST. PETERSBURG

NEVA NEWS

*An English language newspaper
for foreign readers
in Russia & abroad*

**Our prices for advertisements &
classifieds are very competitive**

Postal address: Pravdy ul., 10,
St. Petersburg, 191126, Russia

Tel/Fax: 164-47-65

Novocom-Studio, *Television advertising*
Kamennoostrovskiy pr., 60 234-65-69
Fax 234-36-63
Daily 10-22; Rbls, $; Eng, Ger
Peleng
Gospitalnaya ul., 4 274-03-05
Fax 274-32-34
Mon-Fri 10-18; Rbls, $
Petersburg Advertising Agency
Gorokhovaya ul., 38 310-81-23
Mon-Fri 10-19; Rbls
PolyPlan St. Petersburg, *Cartographers*
*Cartographer for the Traveller's Yellow Pages
Advertising on Maps and Guides*
Shaumyana pr., 18 528-96-80
Fax 528-97-02
Mon-Fri 10-18
Potentsial, *Advertising spots on TV-1 in Russia*
Pavlovskaya ul., 42, Kolpino 481-95-24
Fax 463-90-00
Mon-Fri 8:15-17:15; Rbls, $; Hun
Prime
Pirogova per., 15, 191025, P.O. Box 226
.... 315-76-80
Fax 314-53-63
Mon-Fri 10-18; Rbls; Bus 22; Metro Sennaya Ploshchad
Pulkovo Advertising Agency,
Advertising stands at Pulkovo - 1, 2 airports
Pilotov ul., 18/4, Aviagorodok 122-98-51
Daily; $; Eng, Ger, Finn, Swed, Ital
Ralan Agency
Reki Moyki nab., 61 312-15-78

REKLAMA SHANS

Publishers of the Reklama-Shans newspaper,
weekly circulation: 120,000.

Complete advertising campaign services
in St. Petersburg, Moscow and NW Russia.

Western quality at Russian prices.

Reki Fontanki nab., 59, apt. 116, St. Petersburg

Tel. 210-84-57
Fax 315-62-83

Rial
Proletarskoy Diktatury pl., 6, rm. 424
☎ 271-14-81
Fax 271-02-86
Bus 22; Metro Chernyshevskaya; Rbls
Rossi Advertising Agency
Advertising on computerized screens
Reki Fontanki nab., 51/53, apt. 17...... 310-10-68
Mon-Fri 9:30-19; Rbls, $; Eng, Ger
Rostorgreklama
TV, films and radio advertisements
Sedova ul., 13................................ 567-47-15

RTE Press
PUBLISHING HOUSE

Full Service Advertising Agency

- Mass Media Advertising
- Design & Printing
- Consulting & Marketing Research
- Public Relations

Russia, 191014,
St.Petersburg, P.O. Box 151
Tel.: 164-41-78
Fax: 164-21-93

Rumb
Zaytseva ul., 41 183-46-39
Fax 185-08-69
8:30-12, 13-18:30; Rbls
Russian Business Review
Pochtamtskaya ul., 5, apt 30 315-52-25
Fax 315-47-74
Russian Press Service
Advertising agency & printing service
Pochtamtskaya ul., 5, apt 30 314-23-67
Fax 315-47-74
Russian Trade Express, *See RTE ad above*
Pavlogradskiy per., 6 164-41-78
Fax 164-40-78
*Advertising to the business community in English
Mon-Sat 10-19; $*
Russkoe Video, *Advertising Center*
Obukhovskoy Oborony pr., 163...... 262-05-98
Fax 262-14-05

Santa Ltd. Advertising Agency
Makarova nab., 30 218-39-47
Fax 218-06-15
*Publisher of St. Petersburg Today & Tonight
Daily 9-18; Rbls, $; Eng, Ger*

SEVERO-ZAPAD
BUSINESS
NEWS
INFORMATION

On your desk every morning, daily reports
on business related news in St. Petersburg
and throughout Russia.
Thorough reporting on issues
in business and economics.
Transmitted by fax or E-mail
in Russian and English.
The most available and useful source
of information in St. Petersburg.

Reki Fontanki nab.,75/1 310-11-01
Fax 310-11-74

SignArt, *Posters, signs, Mon-Fri 10-21*
Leninskiy pr., 168 290-20-02

SLAVIC BAZAAR
published by
Litera-Nord

Associated Advertising Agency
*We Publish Commercial &
Classified Advertisements
Distributed in CIS & Europe
Circulation 70,000 copies*
Tel 296-33-75
Fax 298-99-25

Smart
Admiralteyskiy pr., 8/1 110-66-55
Fax 110-65-70
Mon-Fri 10-18; Rbls, $; Eng, Ger, Fr, Finn, Swed, Ital
Sonex, *Newspapers, radio & TV*
Professora Popova ul., 7/8, apt. 6 234-58-00
Fax 234-55-04
Mon-Fri 11-18; Rbls, $; Eng; Bus 10; Metro Petrogradskaya
Sovmarket, *Newspapers, TV-1 in Russia*
1-ya Sovetskaya ul., 10 277-53-71
Mon-Fri 10-17; Rbls; Tram 10; Metro Ploshchad Vosstaniya
Spar-Galaktika, *Television and radio advertising*
Bolshoy pr., V.O. 83, 4th floor, off. 84
.... 217-53-26
Mon-Fri 10-18; Rbls, $; Eng
Spark, *Advertising billboards and city transport ads*
Reki Moyki nab., 28, 1st floor........ 314-14-47
Fax.. 315-46-17

Sports and Concert Complex (SKK)
Advertising stands in the complex
Yuriya Gagarina pr., 8 298-21-64
Fax 298-01-07
Mon-Fri 9:30-17; Rbls, $; Eng, Ger; Bus 12; Metro Elektrosila

St. Petersburg Chamber of Commerce & Industry Advertising Agency
Chaykovskogo ul., 46-48 272-71-36

St. Petersburg Press
Professora Popova ul., 47 234-52-27
Fax 234-98-18

Start Plus
Ulyany Gromovoy per., 8 277-53-18
Mon-Fri 9:30-17; Rbls, Eng, Ger, Finn, Swed

Stiba
Malaya Posadskaya ul., 8 233-32-74
Fax 235-22-88
Mon-Fri 10-18; Rbls; Eng

Svega, *Light panels with running lines on buildings*
Nevskiy pr., 52/14 310-17-68
Mon-Fri 8:30-17:30; Rbls; Bus 22; Metro Gostinyy Dvor

Transport, *On the side of cargo vehicles*
Energetikov pr., 50 222-43-61
Mon-Fri 9:30-17:15; Rbls

TVID, *A full service ad agency*
Kamennoostrovskiy pr., 42, rm. 430
P.O. Box 97 230-80-22
Fax 230-85-55
Daily 12-20; Rbls, $; Eng, Bus 46; Metro Petrogradskaya

Ves Peterburg Association
Sadovaya ul., 2, rm. 46 210-48-79
.... 272-36-89
Mon-Fri 9-17; Rbls; Eng; Tram 2; Metro Gostinyy Dvor

Vil-Mobil
Please call 550-16-16
Fax 550-09-28
Mon-Fri 10-18; Rbls, $; Eng, Finn

[I] Wennergren Williams AB

When It's Important To Be Seen
150 Free Standing Billboards in Saint Petersburg

Intersot - Wennergren - Williams

Admiralteyskiy pr., 10 275-45-69
Fax 275-04-39
Telex .... 121614 CENTR SU

Outside of Russia, To order extra copies of the TYP of St. Petersburg write/call/fax

InfoServices International, Inc.
1 Saint Marks Place, Cold Spring Harbor, NY 11724 USA
☎ (516) 549-0064, Fax (516) 549-2032

☎ AIR CARGO
АВИАПЕРЕВОЗКИ
FLUGTRANSPORT
AIR CARGAISON
FLYGTRANSPORT
LENTORAHTI

See also EXPRESS MAIL & PARCEL SERVICE, FREIGHT FORWARDING AGENTS, SHIPPING, TRUCKING

Air Cargo Offices at Pulkovo-2
Located on the 2nd floor
of the Central Building at Pulkovo-2 Airport
Air France Cargo 104-34-33
Austrian Airlines Cargo 104-34-31
Delta Airlines Cargo 104-34-38
Finnair Cargo 104-34-39
KLM Cargo (FTE) 104-34-49
SAS 104-34-30

Aero-Balt Service Company
Shturmanskaya ul., 12 104-18-12
Fax 104-36-84
Mon-Fri 9-17:30; Rbls, $

Aeroflot
Aviagorodok, Pilotov ul., 18, bldg. 4
Domestic air cargo 104-34-11
.... 104-34-48
Pulkovo-2
International air cargo 104-34-95

AEROCOURIER
АЭРОКУРЬЕР

Air express parcel & cargo shipping
Domestic & international
courier service
Charter cargo & passenger flights
European & other foreign
destinations handled by
Hamann International GmbH

In St. Petersburg:
Pilotov ul., 18 104-34-96
Telex .... 121172 AISCU SU
In Germany:
D-6000 Frankfurt am Main
FZF Gebäude 453, Flughafen
Tel 069/69 19 19
Fax 069/69 22 34
Telex 4032348

ATRUVERA *Air Cargo*
Lensoveta ul., 29 293-50-40

EuroDonat   *FREIGHT FORWARDERS AND TRANSPORT*

TRUCK, SHIP, AIR, RAIL
Specializing in transport to/from
Russia, the Baltic States, CIS,
USA, Canada & Europe
Customs Document Service
Modern Truck Fleet
St. Pb. Warehouse

Yakornaya ul., 17

Tel ....(812) 224-11-44
Fax..........................(812) 224-06-20
Telex .... 121118 DFS SU
Hrs: 9-18, $ & Rubles, English

FINNAIR
CARGO

2 Day Delivery from
New York
London
Western Europe
From 1 kg to 1 ton
Customs Clearance
Trucking

Pulkovo-2 Airport
Tel...............................104-34-39
Telex 121533
Daily 0-24; English, Finnish, German
Metro Moskovskaya; Bus 13

Official KLM agent
AIR CARGO AGENCY
FTE CORPORATION

Prof. Popova ul., 47, apt. 607...... 104-34-49
Fax: 234-51-92

Petersburg Vneshtrans,   *Mon-Fri 8:30-17:15*
Mezhevoy kan., 5......................... 251-18-77
See our ad on page 167
Sofi
Volkhonskoe shosse, 111 138-98-50
Air cargo, customs clearance, storage & delivery;
Mon-Fri 9-18; Rbls, $; Eng

T|N|T **Express Worldwide**
St. Petersburg
Liteynyy pr., 50

Express Parcels & Documents
Express Freight
Over 200 Countries Worldwide
Door to Door in 2-3 Days
Direct through Helsinki
Customs Clearance in St. Pb.

Immediate free pick-up.... 273-60-07
.... 272-58-86
Fax 104-36-84
Telex .... 121741 ABS SU
Moscow Office: (095) 156-57-71

VneshTransAvia Co. Ltd
Pilotov ul., 18, Pulkovo 2 104-34-97
See our ad on page 167

☎ **AIR CHARTER, RENTALS**
АВИАЦИЯ,
АРЕНДА АВИАСРЕДСТВ
FLUGZEUGVERMIETUNG
AVIONS, BAIL
FLYGPLAN, ATT HYRA
LENTOKONEVUOKRAUS

 AiR LeN

See St. Petersburg, Peterhof, Pushkin, Pavlovsk
from a Bird's-Eye View. Comfortable 9 & 20-Seat
Business-Class Helicopters

Please call: 104-16-76   Fax: 251-20-49
Hrs: 9-17, Rbls., $, German

 A L A K
A I R T A X I
ALAK-AT

Domestic & International
Business Flights
• *Leasing* • *Chartering*
• *Ground Services*
• *Insurance Customs*

Pilotov ul., 8 178-27-25
Tel/Fax..................................178-27-71
Rbls & $, Eng., Ger., Finn.

Prof. Popova ul., 47, apt. 607
FTE CORPORATION   Tel./Fax: 234-51-92
AIRPLANE CHARTER

Kustanay Air,   *Daily 9-18*
Please call.......................................465-88-10

VneshTransAvia Co. Ltd
Pilotov ul., 18 Pulkovo 2 104-37-25
See our ad on page 167

☎ **AIR TRAVEL**
АВИАПУТЕШЕСТВИЯ
FLUGZEUGREISE
VOYAGE PAR AVION
FLYGRESA
MATKA JUNALLA

*Approximate times and distances for
selected cities are listed below.*

City	Distance (km)	Time
Alma-Ata	3500	7 hrs
Amsterdam	1700	4 hrs 40 min
Berlin	1300	2 hrs 20 min
Budapest	1500	4 hrs
Frankfurt	1700	3 hrs
Helsinki	320	0 hrs 55 min
Kiev	1000	2 hrs
London	2200	3 hrs 30 min
Moscow	650	1 hr
New York	8200	10 hrs
Omsk	2100	4 hrs
Paris	2000	3 hrs 25 min
Prague	1500	3 hrs
Riga	530	1 hr
Rome	2300	4 hrs
Simferopol	1600	2 hrs 55 min
Sochi	1700	3 hrs 10 min
Stockholm	710	1 hr 20 min
Tallinn	300	0 hrs 40 min
Tokyo	8100	10 hrs
Vladivostok	7000	11 hrs
Warsaw	1000	2 hrs

☎ **AIRLINES**
АВИАЛИНИИ
FLUGGESELLSCHAFTEN
AVION (LIGNES AERIENNES)
FLYGBOLAG
LEHTOYHTIÖT

*On Aeroflot, bring along your own food
and beverages for long trips.*
Aeroflot
Nevskiy pr., 7/9 104-38-22

AIR FRANCE ////

Daily flights
to and from Paris

Pulkovo-2, Airport office
104-34-33

Austrian Airlines - *See SAS ad on next page.*
Balkan, Bulgarian Airline, *See ad on this page.*
British Airways
Gertsena ul., 36 311-58-20
Mon-Fri 9-13, 14-17; $; Eng

BALKAN
BULGARIAN AIRLINES

Direct flights to Sofia
Convenient connections to
Europe, Asia, Africa & USA

Bolshaya Morskaya (Gertsena) ul., 36
Information 315-50-30
Fax 315-50-19

CSA *CZECHOSLOVAK AIRLINES*

*Flights to Prague,
Europe & USA*

Bolshaya Morskaya ul., 36 315-52-59
.... 315-52-64
Pulkovo-2, Airport 104-34-30

Delta Airlines
Gertsena ul., 36 311-58-20
.... 311-58-19
*Convenient connections to the USA
Mon-Fri 9-13, 14-17; $; Eng*

FTE
CORPORATION

Official KLM agent
TRAVEL AGENCY

Prof. Popova ul., 47, apt. 607 234-47-25
Tel./Fax: 234-51-92

Finnair - *See ad on next page*
BEST TO THE WEST
*Daily Flights to Helsinki & to New York, London,
Moscow, St. Petersburg, Vladivostok, Tallinn, Vilnius*
Gogolya ul., 19 104-34-39
*Mon-Sat 9-17; $, CC; English, Finnish, German
Metro Nevskiy Prospekt;
Bus 22; Trolleybus 1, 5, 14, 22*

USA TRAVEL AGENCY IN RUSSIA

**GRIPHON
TRAVEL**

• **Any Destination • Any Airline**
• **Lowest Airfares on the Market**
Moskva Hotel, Service Bureau 274-00-22
*Hrs: 10-18, $, English
Subsidiary of Griphon Travel, USA
Representation in St. Petersburg*

**FINNAIR**

Daily Flights to Helsinki & Other Convenient Connections to:

- **North America**
- **Europe**
- **Scandinavia**
- **Far East**

Gogolya ul., 19 315-97-36
Fax 312-04-59
Airport Tel/Fax 104-34-39
Telex .... 121533 FNAIR SU

*English, Finnish, German; $, CC
Metro Nevskiy Prospekt;
Bus 22; Trolleybus 1, 5, 14, 22*

 Lufthansa

**Now 6 times a week nonstop
St. Petersburg - Frankfurt**

Voznesenskiy pr., 7 314-4979
.... 314-5917
Fax 312-3129
Pulkovo 2, Airport 104-3432
We serve your destination - Call us.

MALEV Hungarian Airlines

From St. Petersburg via Budapest
to 43 destinations in Europe,
Middle East & North America

Voznesenskiy pr., 7 314-63-80
.... 315-54-55
Pulkovo-2, Airport 104-34-35

KLM

The Reliable Airline

Pulkovo-2, Airport office
Tel. 104-34-40
Tel. 104-34-41
Amsterdam - Gateway to Europe

KLM Representation -
See FTE ad on previous page

POLISH AIRLINES

**LOT**

Karavannaya ul., 1
(entrance from Manezhnaya pl.)............ 273-57-21
.... 272-29-82
Fax 279-53-52
Pulkovo-2, Airport........................ 104-34-37

**Direct flights to Warsaw
Convenient connections via Warsaw
to Southeast Asia, North America & Europe**

SHOULD YOUR AD BE HERE?

The most effective use of your
advertising dollar in St. Petersburg

Call InfoServices International
USA + 516 549-0064

*AUSTRIAN* **swissair**

SAS

Nevskiy pr., 57
314-50-86

☎ **AIRPORT TRANSPORTATION**
АЭРОПОРТЫ,
ТРАНСПОРТ К НИМ
TRANSPORT ZU FLUGHÄFEN
AEROPORTS, TRANSPORT
FLYGTAXI
LENTOKENTTÄKULJETUS

*The two Pulkovo airports are 17 km
south of St. Petersburg, 30 minutes by taxi
from the center of St. Pb. Taxi prices vary,
from hotels it can cost $15, in rubles $3-5.*

*There is good, frequent, comfortable
Airport Express Bus service to and from
Pulkovo I, the Domestic Airport. Catch the bus
at the corner of Gertsena ul., 13. To return
from the airport, take the express bus right
outside the terminal. Buy tickets on the
bus. The trip takes 45 minutes. Buses
leave about every 20 minutes during the
day, 30-40 minutes in the morning and
evening, and every one and a half hours at
night.*

*Getting public buses to Pulkovo - 2
International Airport is more difficult. Bus
No. 13 from Hotel Pulkovskaya is*

infrequent and not recommended. Instead call AIRPORT TRANSPORTATION SERVICES *or* TAXI *or* LIMOUSINE *listed below.*

Ask to be met at Pulkovo -2 by a driver or order a taxi ahead. Getting to the center of St. Petersburg from the airport by bus with heavy bags is burdensome and taxi drivers at the airport ask for $25 from foreigners; part is shared with their "dispatcher"

Matralen, *Featuring Fords*
Lyubotinskiy proezd, 5 298-12-94
(See our ad in TAXI*) Mon-Sat 8-20; Rbls, $; Eng, Ger*

Svit, *Taxi and limousine services 24 hours/day*
Korablestroiteley ul., 14 356-10-74
Fax 356-00-94
Daily 0-24; Rbls, $; Eng, Ger, Finn

Taxi (on call)
Konyushennaya pl., 2 312-00-22
Daily 0-24; Rbls; Eng, Ger

☎ **AIRPORTS**
АЭРОПОРТЫ
FLUGHÄFEN
AEROPORTS
FLYGPLATSER
LENTOKENTÄT

See also AIRPORT TRANSPORTATION

There are two major airports in St. Petersburg, Pulkovo - 1 for domestic flights and Pulkovo - 2 for international flights. The airports share the same runway, but have separate terminals about five kilometers apart. There are two smaller airports, Rzhevka Airport providing service to Northwest Russia and Levashovo used by many flying clubs.

Facilities: At Pulkovo -2 *Arrivals, there is an* Airport Duty Free *shop for last minute gifts. At* Departures*, after you pass through customs and passport control there is a larger* duty-free *shop, and a* bar *with draft beer and light snacks.*

Pulkovo-1
Pilotov ul., 18, bldg. 4
Domestic Flights 104-38-22
Information 293-90-21, 293-90-31
Air Cargo 104-34-11, 104-34-48
Bus 39 from Metro Moskovskaya, Daily 0-24; Rbls

Pulkovo-2
International Arrival/Departure 104-34-44
Tickets 310-45-81
International Air Cargo 104-34-95
Customs 104-34-08
.... 104-34-09
Customs- Cargo 104-34-16
Daily 0-24; Rbls, $; Eng, Ger, Fr

Rzhevka
Poselok Kovalevo, Vsevolozhsk...... 527-52-08
Fax 527-39-82

Levashovo Sports Airport
Call St. Petersburg City Air Club 210-46-62
For info call 594-95-19

The Airport Shops
At St. Petersburg Airport

A LENRIANTA AEROFLOT Joint Venture

Largest selection of international brand goods, liquors, electronics and the best Russian souvenirs at real duty free prices.

The cafe bars at both terminals serve hot and cold drinks and snacks.

See our ad under INTERNATIONAL SHOPS

☎ **ALARM SYSTEMS & DEVICES**
СИГНАЛИЗАЦИЯ
ALARMANLAGEN
SYSTEME D'ALARME
ALARM, UTRUSTNING
HÄLYTYSLAITTEET

See also SECURITY

Most apartments have heavy duty double locks on the doors and if they are on the first floor, iron grates (reshetka, решетка) over the windows. Businesses, especially with expensive equipment, have monitored alarm systems tied into the militia.

Alarm
Furmanova ul., 28 352-21-86
Daily 10-18; Rbls, $; Eng

Alex Security Ltd.

Fully Licensed Security Service
Offices, Industries, Banks & Hotels
Transport & Technical Systems Security
Licensed Training School
Branches & Subsidiaries Throughout
Russia

Security Doesn't Cost...It Pays

St. Petersburg .... (812) 352-59-42
Moscow .... (095) 318-03-11
Fax .... (095) 318-50-01

Armus
Pionerskaya ul., 65 230-88-62
Mon-Fri 10-18

Bikar Alarm Systems

Installation, Repair & Technical Service

3-ya Sovetskaya ul., 19 271-13-02

Fax 274-42-91

Break Point
Mirgorodskaya ul., 16 277-78-11
Dispatcher 597-67-70
Automobile alarm systems, Russian and imported
Daily 9-21; Rbls, $

Business Security
Shkapina ul., 4 252-45-22

Contact
Moskovskiy pr., 182, P.O. Box 752
☎ 294-04-75
Fax 298-86-35
Mon-Fri 9-17; Rbls; Eng; Tram 15; Metro Elektrosila

Home □ Center

Authorized Abloy Lock dealer

For Home Security

We install what we sell.

Located in S.E. St. Pb., minutes from city center
Slavy pr., 30 261-15-50
Fax 260-15-81
Daily 10-20; $, FIM, DM, Rbls; Eng, Finn, Ger
Metro Moskovskaya, then Bus 31, 114, T-bus 29

Jonathan Club
Lermontova ul., 4/41 132-37-22
Fax 145-14-50
Mon-Fri 8-18

K-Keskus
Sound Surveillance System
Surface Reed Contacts

232-07-23, 233-48-33

Kredo
196070, P.O. Box 231 293-68-80

Quazar - Center
Zhdanovskaya ul., 8 230-83-58
Mon-Fri 9-17

RDW
Kuybysheva ul., 21 232-04-02
Mon-Fri 10-18; Rbls, $

SBS-Neva
Svechnoy per., 9 112-30-19
Fax 164-94-94
Mon-Fri 10-17; Rbls, $; Eng

Shchit *Metal doors, window bars* **Shield**
2-ya Liniya, 49 350-03-53
Daily 9-21; Rbls, $; Eng, Ger

Sokol
Chkalovskiy pr., 12 235-27-85
Mon-Fri 10-18; Rbls, $

Sredstva Bezopasnosti
                        Security Items Store
Rubinshteyna ul., 9 315-47-74
Metro Vladimirskaya

Zashchita   **Defense**
Dobrolyubova pr., 13 233-82-62
Mon-Fri 9-18; Rbls, $

Zim
Boytsova per., 4 567-11-97
Mon-Fri 9-17; Rbls

☎ **ALCOHOL/OFF-LICENSE/LIQUOR**
СПИРТНЫЕ НАПИТКИ,
ПРОДАЖА
SPIRITUOSEN, VERKAUF
ALCOOL, VENTE
SYSTEMBOLAG
ALKOHOLIJUOMAT

Liquor, wine and beer are available on almost every street corner kiosk, especially around Metros and train stations, in most commercial shops and now in many "state shops". Many kiosks and a few commercial shops stay open 24 hours a day. See section in FOOD STORES called OPEN 24 HOURS.

Buyer beware! Refilling old bottles or "changing labels" is not unknown. Do not buy bottles with damaged labels. Look for tamper- resistant tops on bottles such as "Stolichnaya" or "Absolut". You will find many unrecognizable brands of scotch, creams, innumerable imported vodkas, Amaretto, liquors of Kiwi, Bananas, etc. and throat-numbing "spirits" (which may actually do harm).

The most reliable and best selection of imported name brands of liquor and beer at reasonable prices is in the INTERNATIONAL SHOPS and a few of the better state stores. A "best buy" is "Stolichnaya Vodka" (check the cap and label before buying). Russian beer is an acquired taste (See BEER), but Russian champagne is quite good and very reasonable.

Dagestan "Cognac & Wine"
Excellent wines from Dagestan
Nevskiy pr., 172 277-43-12
Fax 315-05-22
Mon-Sat 9-14, 15-21; Rbls

EmBI

Authorized Distributors
of the Pierre Smirnoff Company

SMIRNOFF

Bolshaya Konyushennaya 27

314-76-62

Gera, *Open 24 Hours*
Bolshaya Konyushennaya ul., 1 315-74-90
Daily 0-9; 10-15, 16-24; Rbls, $

Konyak, Shampanskoe
                        Cognac, Champagne
Nevskiy pr., 130 277-18-26
Good selection of wines, cognacs and champagnes from
Russia and CIS; Daily 9-20; Rbls

Krepkie Napitki   **Liquor**
Gogolya ul., 4 315-89-78
Mon-Sat 11-21; Rbls

Livag
Sinopskaya nab., 56-58 274-59-82
Mon-Fri 9-17; Rbls, $; Eng
Markit (*wholesale*)
Reki Moyki nab., 48 311-88-66
Fax 312-42-16
Nektar, *Testing hall and store*
Malodetskoselskiy pr., 25/12 292-52-44
Fax 292-76-67
Daily 11-21; Rbls

Vino, Vodka	Wine, Vodka
Вино, Водка	

- Gorokhovaya ul., 34 310-82-70
  Mon-Sat 11-20; Rbls
- Griboedova kan. nab., 152 114-08-36
  Mon-Sat 11-19; Rbls
- Karavannaya ul., 2 210-47-37
  Mon-Sat 11-22; Rbls
- Moskovskiy pr., 38 292-33-83
  Daily 10-22; Rbls
- Moskovskiy pr., 74 292-34-83
  Open 24 Hours; Rbls
- Nevskiy pr., 130 277-18-26
  Daily 9-20; Rbls
- Nevskiy pr., 156 277-10-63
  Daily 9-19; Rbls

☎ **AMBULANCE**
СКОРАЯ ПОМОЩЬ
AMBULANZEN/KRANKENWAGEN
AMBULANCE
AMBULANSTJÄNST
AMBULANSSI

FOR MEDICAL EMERGENCIES
See EMERGENCY MEDICAL CARE
AMBULANCE 03

☎ **AMERICAN EXPRESS OFFICE**
АМЕРИКАН-ЭКСПРЕСС
AMERICAN-EXPRESS-BÜROS
AMERICAN EXPRESS BUREAU
AMERICAN EXPRESS
AMERICAN EXPRESS

See also TRAVELER'S CHEQUES

American Express *now has a full-service office in the Grand Hotel Europe (right off Nevskiy pr.) at Mikhaylovskaya ul., 1/7, where they sell* TRAVELER'S CHEQUES, *arrange travel and provide all the services expected by card holders. They are most helpful.*

To purchase Traveler's Cheques: *You will need your* American Express Card, *passport and personal check. Your check is used to purchase the* TRAVELER'S CHEQUES, *your card guarantees the check. With a green card you can purchase $1,000, with a gold $5,000 every 21 days.*

Mail Service: *Of special interest is their quick mail service for cardholders only. To receive mail from the US or Western Europe, send letters, (no packages) to:*

Name of Card Holder
C/O American Express, P.O. Box 87
SF-53501 Lappeenranta, Finland
You must present your American Express Card to pick up your mail.

AMERICAN EXPRESS TRAVEL SERVICE
In the Grand Hotel Europe

Air Tickets • Business Travel
Card member Services • Foreign Exchange
Mikhaylovskaya ul., 1/7 119-60-09
Fax 119-60-11
Telex .... 621198 AMEX SU

☎ **ANTIQUARIAN SHOPS**
(Old Books)
АНТИКВАРНЫЕ КНИГИ
ANTIQUARIATE
ANTIQUAIRES LIBRAIRIES
ANTIKVITETS AFFÄRER
ANTIKVAARISET KIRJAKAUPAT

These shops carry used books, old books, and sometimes engravings, stamps & coins.

Bukinist na Liteynom, *Books from Tsarist times*
Old Books on Liteynyy
Liteynyy pr., 59 273-25-04
Mon-Fri, 10-20; Rbls
Kniga *Used Soviet and Western books* **Book**
Nevskiy pr., 18 312-66-76
Mon-Sat 10-19; Rbls; Eng, Fr; Bus 22; Metro Gostinyy Dvor
Natasha
Rizhskiy pr., 19 251-48-36
Mon-Sat 10-15, 16-19; Rbls
Petersburg
Nevskiy pr., 54 311-40-20
.... 311-20-57
Mon-Sat 10-14, 15-19; Rbls; Metro Nevskiy Prospekt

Staraya Kniga	Old Books
Старая Книга	

- Bolshoy pr., P.S., 19 272-97-14
  232-17-65
  Mon-Sat 10-19; Rbls
- Bolshoy pr., V.O., 29 218-42-86
  Mon-Sat 10-18; Rbls, Tram 1; Metro Vasileostrovskaya
- Marata ul., 43 164-94-15
  Mon-Sat 10-19; Rbls

Staraya Tekhnicheskaya Kniga
Used Technical Bookstore
Zhukovskogo ul., 2 273-33-84
Mon-Sat 10-14, 15-19; Rbls

☎ **ANTIQUES**
АНТИКВАРИАТ
ANTIQUITÄTEN (GESCHÄFTE)
ANTIQUITES
ANTIKVARIAT
ANTIIKKILIIKKEET

See also ART GALLERIES *and* ART APPRAISERS,
ARTS & HANDICRAFTS, COMMISSION SHOPS

Antiques are not only sold in antique shops, but also in ART GALLERIES, *in* COMMISSION SHOPS *or in street markets. On the street buy for "beauty", not value, and beware of pre-aged "authentic" icons and samovars.*

Customs regulations for exporting authentic antiques are strict and you must have a certificate proving that your "antique" is not old or its export will not diminish the cultural heritage of Russia. Good shops will assist you in export formalities. See CUSTOMS REGULATIONS *for the formalities of export.*

AKAHT AKANT

Restoration of Antique Furniture
Manufacturing of Exact Replicas
Koroleva ul., 47, bldg. 2 306-49-03
Fax 306-00-07
Hrs: 9-17, Rubles

Alfa, *Appraisers*
Saltykova-Shchedrina ul., 43 279-39-13
Mon-Fri 10-18; $; Eng
Antiques
Pochtamtskaya ul., 5 311-26-43
Mon-Sat 11-19; Rbls, $
Commission Store No. 76
Kazanskaya ul., 39 312-72-53
Mon-Sat 10-19; Rbls

'HERITAGE'

Representative work from the finest weavers, painters, silversmiths, woodcarvers, & potters

Paintings, tapestry, embroidery, jewelry, Palekh boxes, samovars china, silver, ceramics

Nevskiy pr., 116 279-50-67
Daily 10-14, 15-19, Rbls, Eng & Ger

Izmaylovskiy
7-ya Krasnoarmeyskaya ul., 23 112-74-28
Mon-Fri 11-19; Rbls
Lavka Antikvara   **Antique Store**
Coins, Icons, Stamps
Moskovskoe shosse 16, bldg. 1 293-73-00

NA LITEINOM
Books, engravings, antiques
Liteynyy pr., 61 (entrance in courtyard)
☎ 275-38-73
Hrs 10:30-19, Closed Sunday, English

Na Mokhovoy
Mokhovaya ul., 31 272-40-46
Mon-Sat 11-15, 16-20
Salon Petersburg
Nevskiy pr., 54 311-20-57
Daily 11-19; Rbls; Eng
Shop Petersburg
Furshtadtskaya ul., 42 273-03-41
Mon-Sat 11-14, 15-17; Rbls; Eng

Russkaya Bronza   **Russian Bronze**
Zhukovskogo ul., 36/1 279-72-39
.... 279-72-38
Mon-Sat 11-14, 15-19; Rbls

☎ **APARTMENT CLEANING**
КВАРТИРЫ, УБОРКА
GEBÄUDEREINIGUNG,
WOHNRÄUME
APPARTEMENTS NETTOYAGE
STÄDNING
ASUNTOJEN SIIVOUS

Best hire a trusted "Babushka" who needs extra money, she might even cook for you.

Agenstvo po Uborke Kvartir
           Apartment Cleaning Service
Zakharevskaya ul., 14 273-38-51
Daily 10-17:30; Rbls
Apartment Cleaning Service No. 8
Staro-Petergofskiy pr., 52 252-04-63
Daily 9-17:30; Rbls; Tram 31; Metro Narvskaya
Apartment Cleaning Service No. 7
Rizhskaya ul., 12 221-25-49
Mon-Fri 8:30-17:15; Rbls
Cleaning Services "Losk" *(for offices only)*
Shpalernaya ul., 30 272-91-41
Daily 9-17:30; Rbls, T-bus 49; Metro Chernyshevskaya
Gefest
Marshala Govorova ul., 31 252-25-26
Mon-Sat 10-17; Rbls, Bus 66; Metro Prospekt Veteranov
Peterburgskie Zori
Nevskiy pr., 95, floor 5 277-45-47
.... 277-17-17
Mon-Fri 9-18; Rbls

☎ **APARTMENT RENTALS**
КВАРТИРЫ, АРЕНДА
WOHNUNGEN, VERMIETUNG
APPARTEMENTS, LOCATION
LÄGENHETER, ATT HYRA
ASUNTOJEN VUOKRAUS

See also HOTELS, MOTELS, BED & BREAKFASTS, DACHA RENTALS *and* REAL ESTATE AGENTS

Apartments *can be rented in St. Pb. for longer stays. Prices for foreigners range from a very cheap $50 per month to an outrageous $1000 per month for a 3 room apartment. It all depends on connections, currency, location and negotiating ability.*

Staying in a private apartment legally is still tricky from the viewpoint of old regulations and should be clarified. For example, prolongation of a visa often requires that your passport be registered with the "Registration Office" OVIR (ОВИР) *and this in turn requires permission to stay in other than an official hotel or as an invited guest in someone's home. See* VISA. *If you want to rent an apartment and observe legal regulations, then you need to have a contract with the proprietor. Many apartments, however, are rented informally on the basis of a handshake, even those which are offered to you by apartment rental services.*

Rooms can be found with many families who will free up their living room for a very reasonable rate. There are a growing number of real BED & BREAKFASTS that can offer you a room of your own and meals.

Hint: Look for apartments with a gas or electric hot water heater (see WATER). Find out about trash disposal, cable TV, where to pay your phone bill, and how to get communal repairs done, especially lights in stairwell. Ask if there is a "babushka" or someone who will clean, do your laundry, cook and shop for you. This can save hours.

Astoria-Service
Borovaya ul., 11/13, apt. 65 164-96-22
Mon-Fri 9-17; Rbls, $; Eng

Avokar
Kuznetsovskaya ul., 22 296-31-01
Mon-Fri 11-17:30; Rbls

Burgo, *Opening September 1993*
Myasnikova ul., 4, apt. 11 113-41-11
Mon-Sat 9-18:30; Rbls, T-bus 1; Metro Nevskiy Prospekt

А Г Е Н Т С Т В О
DOM PLUS Agency
Dvortsovaya nab., 16 312-88-73
Real estate agency

HOME SWEET HOME
Apartment Rentals
Please call .... 535-92-29 (24 Hrs.)

Inpredservice
Kutuzova nab., 34 272-15-00
Fax 279-50-24
Service to foreign representatives and their staff.
Mon-Fri 9-13, 14-18; Rbls, $, CC;
Bus 26; Metro Chernyshevskaya

K·Keskus
*Wide Selection of Apartments
in the Best Districts of the City*
232-07-23, 233-48-33

Peterburgskie Zori
Nevskiy pr., 95, floor 5................... 277-45-47
Mon-Fri 9-18; Rbls

| **Petersburg Properties** |
Nevskiy pr. 275-41-67

Pomoshchnik
Reki Moyki nab., 72 310-00-52
Fax 164-37-26
Daily 9-18; Rbls; Bus 22; Metro Gostinyy Dvor

RENTAL
We Sell & Rent Apartments & Office Space
Babushkina ul., 3 592-96-45
.... 567-49-21

Yuniks Inc.
Gorokhovaya ul., 38 310-81-23
Mon-Fri 10-18; Metro Sadovaya

☎ APARTMENT REPAIRS
КВАРТИРЫ, РЕМОНТ
WOHNUNGEN, RENOVIERUNG
APPARTEMENTS,
PETITEREPARATION
LÄGENHETER, REPARATION
ASUNTOJEN KORJAUS

See also CARPENTERS, ELECTRICAL INSTALLATION, LOCKSMITHS, RENOVATION and PLUMBERS

Apartment repairs are carried out by three groups.

Most large apartment repairs, such as painting, are supposed to be done by local "municipal repair offices" listed below under "District Apartment Repair". Repairs and small installations of electrical outlets and wiring, locksmiths, heating, plumbing systems, and water, in theory, can be solved with the help of "PREO" (ПРЭО) and "REU" (РЭУ) offices. These operate on a very specific district basis, almost street by street, so you'll have to find the right office to solve your problem. Your best bet is to look in the Short Leningrad Telephone Book 1991, Ves St. Pb 93, or St. Pb. Yellow Pages 93. The emergency numbers for PREO and REU as well as other emergency services are listed under our category EMERGENCY ASSISTANCE.

The second major provider of repair services are the **Nevskie Zori** (Невские Зори) *and* **Peterburgskie Zori** (Петербургские Зори) *who provide all sorts of services on an individual craftsman basis from locksmiths to electricians to carpenters and painters. These services can be done on a pay-as-you-go basis.*

Third, many people look for good individual craftsmen to get work done more quickly. Ask a friend and/or look under CONSTRUCTION AND RENOVATION, CARPENTERS, LOCKSMITHS, PLUMBERS, PAINTERS, *and* ELECTRICIANS.

PREO DISTRICT
MAIN APARTMENT REPAIR OFFICES

Dzerzhinskiy District
Chaykovskogo ul., 15 273-23-52
Mon-Sat 11-21; Rbls, Bus 47; Metro Chernyshevskaya
Frunzenskiy District
Budapeshtskaya ul., 37, apt. 120.... 260-74-88
.... 177-71-66
Mon-Fri 9:30-20; Rbls, Bus 31; Metro Elektrosila
Kirovskiy District
Veteranov pr., 21 156-07-24
Mon-Fri 10-19; Rbls, Bus 68; Metro Prospekt Veteranov
Leninskiy District
Moskovskiy pr., 61.......................... 292-21-02
Mon-Fri 10-19; Rbls, Tram 2; Metro Frunzenskaya
Moskovskiy District
Kosmonavtov pr., 42...................... 299-80-07
Mon-Fri 9-18; Rbls, Bus 11; Metro Moskovskaya

Nevskiy District
Babushkina ul., 42, bldg. 1 560-55-96
Mon-Fri 10-19; Rbls, T-bus 44; Metro Lomonosovskaya

Oktyabrskiy District
Gorokhovaya ul., 49 310-85-56
Mon-Fri 10-20; Rbls, Tram 2; Metro Sennaya Ploshchad

Petrogradskiy District
Bolshaya Monetnaya ul., 23 233-25-22
Mon-Fri 10-18:30; Rbls, Bus 1; Metro Gorkovskaya

Primorskiy District
Reki Chernoy nab., 51 242-04-64
Mon-Sat 10-21; Rbls, Bus 101; Metro Pionerskaya

Smolninskiy District
Suvorovskiy pr., 47 275-64-36
*Mon-Sat 9:30-17:30; Rbls,
Bus 30; Metro Ploshchad Aleksandra Nevskogo*

Vasileostrovskiy District
11-ya Liniya, 40 213-13-78
Mon-Fri 8-17; Rbls, Tram 1; Metro Vasileostrovskaya

OTHER REPAIR COMPANIES

Arian
Revolyutsii shosse, 15 227-16-96
Mon-Fri 10-19; Rbls;Bus 22; Metro Novocherkasskaya

Ecopolis
Zanevskiy pr., 32, bldg. 2 528-26-66
Mon-Fri 9:30-18; Rbls, $; Eng

Grif
Ruzovskaya ul., 16 292-57-57
Mon-Fri 8-17; Rbls

K-Keskus
Ordinarnaya ul., 7 232-07-23
Mon-Sat 10-17:30; Rbls; Bus 10; Metro Petrogradskaya

Max Shatornyy
Dimitrova ul., 6, bldg. 1 101-67-22
Mon-Fri 10-19; Rbls

Otis, *Elevator installation & service*
(*See our ad under* CONSTRUCTION)
Khimicheskiy per., 12 252-37-58
.... 252-36-94
Fax 252-53-15

Peterburgskie Zori
Nevskiy pr., 95, floor 5................ 277-45-47
Mon-Fri 9-18; Rbls

Vika
Mytninskaya ul., 19 274-48-04
Daily 9-18; Rbls

☎ **ARBITRAGE COURT**
АРБИТРАЖНЫЙ СУД
SCHIEDSGERICHT
ARBITRAGE
ARBITRAGE
VÄLITYSTOIMISTO

See also LAW FIRMS & LAWYERS

Commercial disputes are usually resolved by the Arbitrage Court. Foreign companies can only utilize arbitrage procedures if they are legally registered on the territory of Russia. For legal consultation or assistance, contact one of the many LAW FIRMS *in St. Petersburg.*

Arbitrage Court
Gertsena ul., 30 312-70-94

☎ **ARCHITECTS**
АРХИТЕКТОРЫ
ARCHITEKTEN
ARCHITECTES
ARKITEKTER
ARKKITEHDIT

Arcon
Pestelya ul., 11, apt. 63 ....No ☎
Mon-Fri 10-18; Rbls

Bureau-2
Povarskoy per., 9, apt. 10 591-49-42
Mon-Fri 10-17; Rbls, $; Eng

ARCHITECTS
Staff of 60 Architects Engineers & Designers
European Architectural Standards
International Fashion Center, Moscow, 1992
Commissioned by Steilman & Kronen, Germany
Buildings in St. Pb, Black Sea, & Vyborg
From a single apartment to an entire building
Zanevskiy pr., 32, Bldg. 2, No. 3
☎ **528-26-66**
Mon-Fri 9:30-18; Rbls, $; Eng

Palachev Nikolay
Personal Creative Architectural Studio
Pushkinskaya ul., 10, rm. 102 310-69-24
Daily 9-20

St. Petersburg Union of Architects of Russia
Gertsena ul., 52.......................... 312-04-00
Mon-Sat 12-22; Rbls, $

☎ **ARCHIVES**
АРХИВЫ
ARCHIVE
ARCHIVES
ARKIV
ARKISTOT

Many state archives are now more accessible for research, but services suffer from underfunding. You may be charged a hefty fee for using the research material.

**Central Historical Archives
of St. Petersburg**
Pskovskaya ul., 18 219-79-61
Mon-Fri 8:30-17:30

**Central State Archives
of Film & Photo Documentary**
Myasnoy per., 2 310-52-48
Mon-Tue, Thu 9-17; Rbls

**Central State Archives
of Literature & Art of St. Petersburg**
Shpalernaya ul., 34 272-53-97
Mon-Fri 9:30-17:30; Rbls; Tram 1; Metro Chernyshevskaya

Central State Archives of St. Petersburg
Varfolomeevskaya ul., 15 560-68-62
Mon-Fri 9-17; Bus 114; Metro Elizarovskaya

Central State Historical Archives
Krasnogo Flota nab., 4 311-09-26
Mon-Fri 9-18; Rbls

Department of Archives, Mayor's Office
Krasnogo Flota nab., 4 311-14-89
Mon-Tue, Thu-Fri 10-13, 15-17; T-bus 5

Military Medical Archives
Furshtadtskaya ul., 52 272-26-41
Mon-Sat 11-21; Rbls, $; Eng

St. Petersburg Branch Archive
of the Russian Academy of Sciences
Universitetskaya nab., 1 218-05-12
Mon-Fri 9-17; Bus 47; Metro Nevskiy Prospekt

ZAGS Archives (Vital Statistics of St. Pb.)
Births, marriages, divorces & deaths
Furshtadtskaya ul., 52 272-26-41
Mon-Fri 9-14, 15-18

☎ ART APPRAISERS
ХУДОЖЕСТВЕННАЯ
ЭКСПЕРТИЗА
GUTACHTEN,
KUNSTGEGENSTÄNDE
ART, EXPERTISE D'
KONST.VÄRDERINGSEXPERT
TAIDEARVIOITSIJAT

Alfa, *Appraisers*
Saltykova-Shchedrina ul., 43 279-39-13
Mon-Fri 10-18; $; Eng

Palitra, *Art appraisers and restorers*
Sredniy pr., 55 350-94-95
Fax 274-09-11
Mon-Fri 11-18

Peyzazh   **Landscape**
6-ya Liniya, 11 213-52-96
Fax 213-42-78
Mon-Fri 10-17; Rbls; Eng, Ger

Sovetskaya Zhivopis   **Soviet Painting**
Izmaylovskiy pr., 2, apt. 104 259-11-11
Daily 10-18; Rbls, $; Eng, Fr

☎ ART GALLERIES
ХУДОЖЕСТВЕННЫЕ ГАЛЕРЕИ
KUNSTGALERIEN
ART, GALLERIES D' /
GALLERIES D'ART
KONSTGALLERIER
TAIDEGALLERIAT

*The art galleries listed here specialize in
paintings & graphics and often have
permanent exhibitions of contemporary
Russian painters. For sculpture, tapestry,
embroidery, and Russian handicrafts, see*
ARTS & HANDICRAFTS. *See* CUSTOMS
REGULATIONS *for formalities of export.*

Aida Art Salon   *Daily 10-20; Rbls*
Yakubovicha ul., 5 311-06-46

Anna (in the Iskusstvo Store)
Nevskiy pr., 16 312-85-35
Mon-Sat 10-14, 15-19; Rbls

Ariadna
Best of the modern artists in St. Petersburg
Konnogvardeyskiy blvd., 11, rm. 17 ... 311-69-97
Mon-Fri 9:30-18; T-bus 5; Metro Nevskiy Prospekt

Art Gallery of the Academy of Arts
Nalichnaya ul., 21 355-12-74
.... 217-10-10
11-14, 15-19; Rbls, $; Eng, Fr

Atus Gallery
Ispolkomskaya ul., 9/11 275-32-15
Mon-Sat 11-19; Rbls; Eng; Metro Ploshchad Vosstaniya

Baltica   **Baltic Gallery**
Pravdy ul., 10 315-01-53
Fax 164-10-18
Tue-Sun 13-19

Blok Library Art Gallery   *Mon-Fri 12-19*
Nevskiy pr., 20 311-77-77
Fax 311-22-49

BOREYARTGALLERY
Liteynyy pr., 58 273-36-93
Fax 273-53-76

Delta
Pochtamtskaya ul., 4 314-79-14
Tue-Sun 12-19

FORUM ART GALLERY
V.O., 6-ya Liniya, 17 213-67-87
Fax 511-72-23

Gallery 102
Nevskiy pr., 102 275-57-66
Mon-Sat 11-20; Rbls; Eng, Finn, Ital

Garmoniya
Kamennoostrovskiy pr., 26/28 .... No ☎
Bus 46; Metro Gorkovskaya

Golubaya Gostinaya   **Blue Drawing Room**
Gertsena ul., 38 315-74-14
Featuring well known artists of the Realism movement
Tue-Sun 13-20

Graphic Arts Center
St. Petersburg Artist Union
Sverdlovskaya nab., 64 224-06-15

GRIFFON
Paintings & Folk Art with Export Documents
Gertsena ul., 33

Guild of Masters
*Oils, graphics, tapestries, ceramics, batik, jewelry,
glassware by well-known artists*
Nevskiy pr., 82 279-09-79

Helen   *Mon-Sat 10-19*
Morskaya nab., 15 356-03-13

'HERITAGE'
*Representative work from the finest
weavers, painters, silversmiths,
woodcarvers, & potters*

*Paintings, tapestry, embroidery,
jewelry , Palekh boxes, samovars
china, silver, ceramics*

Nevskiy pr., 116 279-50-67
Hrs: 10-19, Rbls, Eng & Ger

HIRON ART GALLERY

Modern Figurative Art

3-ya Sovetskaya ul., 8 113-32-07

Initsiativa
Nevskiy pr., 104 272-09-06
Mon-Fri 10-18

Klenovaya Alleya
Klenovaya ul. 219-21-29
A large outdoor market of Russian art and handicraft
Daily 9-18

KOLOMNA Art Gallery
Professional Artists of St. Petersburg
School of Art
Rimskogo-Korsakova pr., 24
.... 114-31-50

Lavka Khudozhnikov   Artist's Shop
Nevskiy pr., 8 312-61-93
Mon-Sat 10-14, 15-19; Rbls, $; Eng, Ger, Fr
T-bus 1; Metro Nevskiy Prospekt

LenArt
Reki Fontanki nab., 34 275-75-10
Fax 275-50-96
Mon-Fri 9-18; Rbls, $; Eng, Finn; Metro Mayakovskaya

Lipetsk Art International
Partizana Germana ul., 3, apt. 428 .... No ☎
Bus 68; Metro Prospekt Veteranov

Milena, *Private collection*
Exhibition of St. Petersburg's best painters
Muchnoy per., 2 110-59-70
Fax 311-46-33
Mon-Fri 9:30-18:30; Rbls, $

Modern Art
Reki Moyki nab., 83 314-47-34
Classic, realist and avant garde graphics and paintings
Mon-Fri, Sun 13-18

Musaget
Bolshaya Konyushennaya ul., 27 .... No ☎
Daily 12-20; Rbls; Eng, Ger, Fr

Navicula
Truda pl., 4 219-81-00
Fax 312-19-13
Mon-Sat 12-18; Rbls

New Passage Art Gallery

Liteynyy pr., 57 273-16-23
Fax 273-57-92
Hrs 11-19, Eng., Ger.

PALITRA ART GALLERY
An Exquisite Art Gallery

Oils, watercolors, graphics, sculptures, & ceramics
by F. Volosenkov, A. Gerasimov, I. Cholariya,
A. Ivanov and other recognized & new young stars
Sit with a cup of coffee and chat with
artists about displayed works.
Visit our shops in London & Szczecin
Nevskiy pr., 166 277-12-16
Fax 274-09-11
Mon-Sat 11-19; Rbls; Eng, Fr, Ital
Metro Ploshchad Aleksandra Nevskogo, T-Bus 1

ART CLUB
A / O   P e t r o a r t

View the art & relax in our cafe.
Theater parties & meetings of artists
& critics arranged.
Nab. kan. Griboedova, 3 210-75-49
Near the Church of our Savior on the Blood

PETROPOL
G A L L E R Y

MAMMOTH-IVORY
and
Peter the Great's Turnery

27 Millionnaya St. 315-34-14
Hrs: 10-18, Rbls, English

Russian Art Ltd.

In the Senate-Synod Building

Near the Bronze Horseman
Exhibition & Sale of Traditional Russian
Arts & Handicrafts
Wide Selection of Jewelry & Antiques
Cossack Theater
Dekabristov pl., 1 210-98-08
Hrs: 10-19, Rubles, English, German

Sankt-Peterburgskiy Khudozhnik
                    Saint Petersburg Artist
Nevskiy pr., 31 110-50-05
Mon-Sat 10-19; Rbls; Eng, Ger, Fr

Sidlin School Art Gallery
Grafskiy per., 7 113-22-45
Mon-Sat 11-18; Rbls; Eng; Metro Mayakovskaya, Dostoevskaya

St. Petersburg Art Union of Russia
                    Exhibition Center
Gertsena ul., 38 314-30-60
Fax 314-64-12
Exhibition and sale of paintings graphics & sculptures
Tue-Sun 13-19; Rbls, $; Eng

STARAYA DEREVNYA
Savushkina ul., 72
239-00-00
Cafe and Modern Art
Daily 12 noon to evening

The Art of Russia
Nevskiy pr., 147 277-18-93
Mon-Sat 10-14, 15-19; Rbls, $; Eng

The Russian Arts
Saltykova-Shchedrina ul., 53 275-69-60
Master craftsmen of glass and decorative arts
Tue-Sun 11-17

The Trojan Horse
Voznesenskiy pr., 41, off. 32 .... No ☎
Mon-Fri 11-20; Rbls, $; Eng, Finn

Modern Art Museum
Tsarskoe Selo Collection
Pushkin, Karla Marksa pr., 40
Director 466-55-81
Exhibition 466-04-60
Open Saturday, Sunday 11-17

Vasilevskiy Ostrov
Sredniy pr., 37 213-28-35
Mon-Fri 11-14, 15-19; Metro Vasileostrovskaya

VZGLYAD Art Center
Paintings, graphics, applied art at Museum of Urban Sculpture
Al. Nevskogo pl., 1 277-17-16

Zerkalo Gallery   **Mirror**
Nekrasova ul., 11 272-40-58
Fax 273-37-04
Mon-Sat 11-19; Rbls; Eng; Metro Chernyshevskaya

☎ **ART MUSEUMS**
See MUSEUMS

☎ **ART SUPPLIES**
ХУДОЖЕСТВЕННЫЕ
ПРИНАДЛЕЖНОСТИ
KÜNSTLERBEDARF
ARTISTES, MAGASINS POUR
KONSTMATERIAL
TAITEILIJANTARVIKKEET

Lavka Khudozhnikov   **Artist's Shop**
Nevskiy pr., 8 312-61-93
Paints, brushes, canvases
Mon-Sat 10-14, 15-19; Rbls, $; Eng, Ger, Fr
T-bus 1, Metro Nevskiy Prospekt

Peyzazh   *Oil Paints*   **Landscape**
6-ya Liniya, 11 213-52-96
Fax 213-42-78
Mon-Fri 10-17; Rbls; Eng, Ger

Roma
Serdobolskaya ul., 68 242-28-96
Fax 245-15-40
Mon-Fri 9-17; Rbls, $; Eng

The Factory of Artistic Beauty
Serdobolskaya ul., 68 245-36-68
Fax 245-15-40
Mon-Fri 8:30-17; Rbls, $; Eng

U Fontanki   **Near Fontanka**
Pestelya ul., 8 273-54-04
Everything for artists; Mon-Sat 10-19; Rbls

Look in
Traveller's Yellow Pages
before calling!

☎ **ARTISTS**
ХУДОЖНИКИ
KÜNSTLER
ARTISTES
KONSTNÄRER
TAITEILIJAT

To find artists, try also ART GALLERIES and ARTIST ASSOCIATIONS

The streets of St. Petersburg are not only decorated with the work of contemporary artists but by the artists themselves.

Art and Artists on the street. The following are known for the sale of art: near the Circus on Klenovaya Alleya, on the embankment opposite the Aurora cruiser, Petrogradskaya nab., on Nevsky pr. near the Grand Hotel Europe, the Literary Cafe and near Dom Knigi (House of Books) and by the Peter and Paul Fortress.

Abramov Leonid
Lensoveta ul., 91, rm. 52 127-09-37
Burtas Viktor
Zvezdnaya ul., 8, apt. 217 126-91-30
Grigorev Vadim
Kolomenskaya ul., 15, bldg. 17, rm. 71
☎ 312-80-80

Guild of Masters
Oils, graphics, tapestries, ceramics, batik, jewelry, glassware by well-known artists
Nevskiy pr., 82 279-09-79

 Igor KUPRIN
Graphics, oils, book illustrations
Please call 314-30-67

Slava Rozhkov
Russian Orthodox themes in oils, graphics, watercolors
Please call 311-72-14

Snail Lover's Club   **Artist Workshop**
Pushkinskaya ul., 10/50 164-48-73
Troitskiy Konstantin
Reki Fontanki nab., 26, rm. 23 272-98-91
Vlasova Irina, *Ceramic toys, theatrical costumes*
Pushkinskaya ul., 106, apt. 130 164-53-71
Volosov Vladimir - *Lyrical Landscape*
Korablestroiteley ul., 44, bldg. 2, apt. 188
.... 351-41-30
Yakhnin Oleg
Please call 350-34-30
Oils, watercolors, lithographs, wood block prints
Yakovlev Aleksey
Antonenko per., 2, apt. 19 315-63-53
.... 306-97-11

Zhilkin Vladimir
Kultury pr., 19, apt. 84 166-03-78
.... 557-50-38
Tram 22; Metro Prospekt Prosveshcheniya

📞 **ARTISTS' ASSOCIATIONS**
ХУДОЖНИКИ, АССОЦИАЦИИ
KÜNSTLERVERBÄNDE
ARTISTES, ASSOCIATIONS DES
ARTISTFÖRMEDLING
TAIDESEURAT

Association of Free Artists
of St. Petersburg
Nevskiy pr., 20.......................... 311-01-06
Daily 12-20

┌─────────────────────────────────────┐
│ ΣΓ-ΣΣ-ϤΙΣ............................Fax. │
│ 9Ζ-ΣΣ-ϤΙΣ....'ΖΣ 'ɐʎɐuuɐɥsnʎuoʞ ɐʎɐɥsʅo8 │
│ ǝɔıɟɟO ǝɥʇ ɹoɟ sƃuıʇuıɐԀ │
│ **ИƆIᗺ∃D** • sɔıɥdɐɹ⅁ • **∀ Ɔᗺ∀** │
│ uƃısǝ⅁ ɹoıɹǝʇuI │
│ This ad was designed by ABC & Design │
└─────────────────────────────────────┘

Free Culture Humanities Foundation
Pushkinskaya ul., 10, apt. 1 164-53-71
Fax 164-52-07
Eng, Ger; Metro Ploshchad Vosstaniya

House of Artists
Gertsena ul., 38 314-64-32
Tue-Sun 13-19; T-bus 17; Metro Nevskiy Prospekt

Snail Lover's Club   *Art-Cafe*
Pushkinskaya ul., 9..................... 164-52-07
Fax 164-52-07
Daily 19-24; Metro Ploshchad Vosstaniya
Performances by well-known & undiscovered artists, &
musicians. Try us.

St. Petersburg Artists Union of Russia
Gertsena ul., 38 314-77-36
Mon-Fri 14-20; Eng; T-bus 5; Metro Nevskiy Prospekt

📞 **ARTS & HANDICRAFTS**
(National Crafts)
ХУДОЖЕСТВЕННЫЕ
ПРОМЫСЛЫ
VOLKSHANDWERK
KUNSTHANDWERK
ARTS et ART MANUEL
BOUTIQUES D'
KONST OCH HANTVERKSAFFÄRER
TAIDE-JA KÄSITYÖLIIKKEET

The shops and galleries listed here carry a
variety of handicrafts from traditional
Palekh painted boxes, Pavlov-Posadskiy &
Orenburgskiy scarves, Khokhloma painted
wooden ware, and matreshkas to beautiful
silver, glassware, tapestry, jewelry and
sculptures by contemporary Russian
artisans and artists.

A Q U I L O N
Traditional Handmade Russian Clothes
Konnogvardeyskiy blvd., 4 (office).....311-68-51
Kamennoostrovskiy pr., 6 (salon) 232-67-83

Art Boutique
Nevskiy pr., 51 113-14-95
Mon-Sat 10-14, 15-19; Rbls, $; Eng

The Borey Art Gallery
Liteynyy pr., 58 273-53-76
Mon-Sat 11-20; Rbls; Metro Mayakovskaya

Heritage
Nevskiy pr., 116 279-50-67
Daily 10-14, 15-19; Rbls, $; Eng, Ger

Izoproduktsiya
Pestelya ul., 8 273-54-04
Mon-Sat 10-19

┌─────────────────────────────────────┐
│ ⛪ 🏛 **MARBLE**   │
│   **PALACE**   │
│ Fine collection of Russian gifts   │
│   by individual artists   │
│ Millionnaya ul., 5/1 ....312-18-59 │
└─────────────────────────────────────┘

Nekrasova 6
Nekrasova ul., 6 273-26-03
Mon-Sat 10-19; Rbls; T-bus 15; Metro Vladimirskaya

┌─────────────────────────────────────┐
│ **NEW SAINT PETERSBURG TRADE HOUSE** │
│ Reki Fontanki nab., 76..........315-77-65 │
│ Fax..............................315-34-00 │
│ *Selling Graphic Prints & Art Works* │
└─────────────────────────────────────┘

Plakat   **Poster**
Lermontovskiy pr., 38 251-94-97
Mon-Fri 10-14, 15-19; Rbls; Eng; T-bus 3;
Metro Baltiyskaya

Polyarnaya Zvezda   **Pole Star**
Nevskiy pr., 158 277-09-80
Mon-Fri 10-14, 15-19; Rbls

RosVuzdizain
Solyanoy per., 13 279-41-97
Fax.. 279-41-96
Mon-Fri 11-18; Rbls, $; Eng

Russia
Bolshaya Konyushennaya ul., 5 315-29-70
Mon-Sat 10-19; Rbls

Russian Style
Birzhevoy proezd, 6....................... 218-54-02
Daily 9-19

Russkiy Dom   **The Russian House**
Chaykovskogo ul., 65.................... 275-15-65
Mon-Fri 9-18; Rbls, $; Eng, Ger, Fr

┌─────────────────────────────────────┐
│ ⛪ 🏛 **STROGANOV**   │
│   **PALACE**   │
│ Wide Selection of Traditional   │
│ Russian Arts & Handicrafts   │
│ Nevskiy pr., 17 ....312-18-59 │
└─────────────────────────────────────┘

The Art of Russia
Nevskiy pr., 147 277-18-93
Mon-Sat 10-14, 15-19; Rbls, $; Eng

The Trojan Horse
Voznesenskiy pr., 41, off. 32 ....No 📞
Mon-Fri 11-20; Rbls, $; Eng, Finn

Vesta-M
Bolsheokhtinskiy pr., 25/5.............. 227-16-43
Mon-Fri 11-14, 15-19; Rbls
Bus 22; Metro Novocherkasskaya

VITYAZ

Paintings, Ceramics, Lacquer boxes,
Pavlovo Posad Shawls, Matreshkas,
and other Russian Crafts

Tsarskoe Selo, Moskovskaya ul., 20

466-43-18

☎ **ASSOCIATIONS &
PROFESSIONAL
ORGANIZATIONS**
АССОЦИАЦИИ И
ПРОФЕССИОНАЛЬНЫЕ
ОРГАНИЗАЦИИ
VEREINE UND VERBÄNDE,
BERUFSGESELLSCHAFTEN
ASSOCIATIONS, CLUBS et
SOCIETES PROFESSIONNELLES
FÖRENINGAR, KLUBBAR
PROFESSIONELLES
KERHOT, YHDISTYKSET

See also BUSINESS ASSOCIATIONS, CLUBS,
CHESS CLUBS, INTERNATIONAL ASSOCIATIONS,
ORGANIZATIONS *and* SPORTS CLUBS

*There are many clubs, societies and
charitable associations in St. Pb. from the
Amateur Hand Weaving Association to the
War Veterans. Get a copy of the Leningrad
Business Guide 1993 or the Ves St. Pb. 93,
or St. Pb. Yellow Pages 93 (See* BUSINESS
DIRECTORIES). *For a list of local clubs, see*
CLUBS. *Here we list associations.*

**Association of the Victims of
Stalin's Repression**
Reki Moyki nab., 59 .... No ☎
Mon, Wed-Thu 14-16

Center of Citizens' Initiatives
Kvarengi per., 4, rm. 418 113-58-96
Fax 271-04-67
Mon-Fri 10-17; Eng

Cinematographers Union
Karavannaya ul., 12 314-71-43
Mon-Sat 18-22; Bus 22; Metro Gostinyy Dvor

Dental Cooperation with Foreign Countries
Tverskaya ul., 12/15........................ 110-06-54
Fax 245-67-00
*Training in latest Western techniques; Mon-Fri 9-19; Eng,
Ger, Finn; T-bus 15; Metro Chernyshevskaya*

Designer's Union
Reki Moyki nab., 8 311-72-63
Daily 10-18; Rbls

Justice Free Trade Union   **Spravedlivost**
Belinskogo ul., 13 272-15-51
Daily 10-21

Jewish Association of St. Petersburg
Ryleeva ul., 29-31 275-61-03

**Leningrad Children
of the Blockade 900 Society**
Saltykova-Shchedrina ul., 34.......... 275-76-73
Mon-Fri 11-13, 14-17

Petersburg Informational Channel
Rubinshteyna ul., 8 312-95-72
Fax 314-43-48

Russian Geographic Society
Grivtsova per., 10 315-85-35
Mon-Sat 15-19; Rbls

St. Petersburg Diabetic Association
Rubinshteina ul., 3 112-41-36
Metro Vladimirskaya

St. Petersburg Dyagilev Club
Please call....................................... 310-82-72
Fax... 310-71-96

St. Petersburg Union of Architects
Gertsena ul., 52............................. 312-04-00
Mon-Fri 11-14:30, 15-19:30; Rbls, $; Eng, Ger, Fr, Ital, Sp

Theater Union
Nevskiy pr., 86.............................. 272-94-82
Mon-Fri 11-18

Union of Composers
Gertsena ul., 45............................. 311-18-33

Union of Journalists
Nevskiy pr., 70.............................. 272-85-13

Znanie   **Knowledge**
Kazanskaya ul., 36, rm. 321, 322
Fax... 314-78-90
Mon-Fri 9-17:30

☎ **AUCTIONS**
АУКЦИОНЫ
AUKTIONEN
VENTE AUX ENCHERES
AUKTIONER
HUUTOKAUPAT

See also FURS, REAL ESTATE AGENTS *and*
CURRENCY EXCHANGE

Alfa *(appraisers)*
Saltykova-Shchedrina ul., 43 279-39-13
Mon-Fri 10-18; $; Eng

Pushnoy Auktsion   **Fur Auction**
Moskovskiy pr., 98....................... 298-45-43
Fax... 293-34-59
*Fur auctions are held three times per year: October,
January, May or June. Mon-Fri 8:30-18:30; Rbls, $; Eng*

☎ **AUDIO EQUIPMENT**
АУДИО-ВИДЕО СЕРВИС
HIFI-/VIDEOGERÄTE/ ANLAGEN
AUDIO-VISUEL, SERVICES D'
AUDIO/VIDEO UTRUSTNING
HIFI-JA VIDEOLAITTEET

*Imported audio equipment from a simple
Walkman to a surround-sound system with
a CD player can be purchased in a wide
variety of shops in St. Petersburg. Look at*
COMMERCIAL STORES *and* COMMISSION STORES,
ELECTRONIC GOODS, INTERNATIONAL SHOPS *and*
TELEVISION SALES.

The Electronic Store at the Airport Shop
Airport Pulkovo-1 123-87-78
.... 104-34-87
*Top selection of consumer electronics at reasonable
prices. A Lenrianta shop $, CC; Eng, Ger*

Baltica
Toreza pr., 2/40............................. 247-82-03
Fax... 247-23-79
Mon-Fri 10:30-20; Rbls

Bang and Olufsen, *See* **Electrolux** *on next page.*

Electrolux, *Distributor of Bang & Olufsen*
Robespera nab., 16........................ 275-55-12
.... 275-00-52

Kovcheg
Chernyshevskogo pr., 9 294-34-59
Mon-Sat 11-14, 15-19; Rbls

Kvark
Leni Golikova ul., 60, apt. 216........ 156-70-97
Fax 157-67-41
Mon-Fri 10-18; Rbls, $

Mitsar
Bolshoy pr., P.S., 15...................... 232-04-82
Fax 233-87-41
Mon-Sat 10-14, 15-19; Rbls, $; Eng

 MS·AUDIOTRON

Professional audio, video and lighting
equipment for concert halls, theaters and studios.
Complete Installation • Musical Instrument Sales
P.O. Box 28, 00421 Helsinki, Finland
St. Petersburg:
Tel 310-55-13
Fax 310-48-01

Nakamichi
Full range of Nakamichi audio
Marata ul., 22 314-42-27

National / Panasonic / Technics
Matsushita Electric Industrial Co., Ltd

National

Nakhimova ul., 7, office 39
Tel.: 356-36-35, 355-63-05; Fax: 356-83-33
Telex: 121309 ledka su

Nautilus
Gorokhovaya ul., 61 310-23-02
Fax 310-19-15
Mon-Sat 11-20

Panasonic, *see* National Panasonic Technics

Penguin
Zagorodnyy pr., 10 314-32-30
Mon-Sat 11-19; Rbls; Eng

Peterhouse
Chekhova ul., 14 272-30-07
Fax 272-63-57
Mon-Fri 10-19; Rbls, $; Eng, Ger, Metro Chernyshevskaya

Philips Electronics
A full line of Philips Audio Video
Suvorovskiy pr., 2.......................... 277-43-19
.... 277-22-25
Daily 10-14, 15-20; Rbls, $; Eng

Pioneer Electronics
Zagorodnyy pr., 11 314-23-14
Mon-Sat 11-19; Rbls; Eng, Ger, Fr
T-bus 3, 5, 8, 15, 17; Metro Pushkinskaya

Quazar, *Pioneer audio equipment*
Kamennoostrovskiy pr., 5 233-40-33
Fax 232-49-44
Mon-Sat 10-19; Rbls, $; Eng

Sadko, *Authorized Panasonic audio/video dealer*
Petra Alekseeva ul., 11 315-63-09
Mon-Sat 11-14, 15-19

SAMSUNG, *see* UMA Electronics *ad below.*

 LTD

Authorized **SAMSUNG ELECTRONICS** Distributor
Dealer for **Supra**
Malookhtinskiy pr., 68 528-95-66
.... 528-00-51
Fax... 528-84-00

☎ **AUTO PARKS**

See PARKING LOTS

☎ **AUTOMOBILE ACCIDENTS**
ДОРОЖНО-ТРАНСПОРТНЫЕ
ПРОИСШЕСТВИЯ
VERKEHRSUNFÄLLE
AUTOMOBILE, ACCIDENTS D'
BILOLYCKORVAD GÖRA INSTR.
AUTO-ONNETTOMUUDET

See also DRIVING *for traffic rules.*

*In case of an automobile accident, call the
traffic police, called "GAI", (ГАИ) (State Auto
Inspectorate) at 02 or 234-26-46. Don't
touch, move or even mark the car's position
with chalk, even though it may take several
hours for the GAI to come and write a report. Be prepared to present all your papers
to the GAI. Beware that for minor fender-
benders in private vehicles, Russians like to
reach an agreement and drive on. If there
is any question about fault, get the names
of witnesses and a lawyer experienced in
such matters. Especially if charged with
drunk driving, a very serious charge. See*
LAW FIRMS. *To tow or transport your car,
see listings under* AUTOMOBILE EMERGENCY
ASSISTANCE.

State Auto Inspectorate (GAI), *Hrs 0-24*
Professora Popova ul., 42 234-26-52
.... 234-26-46

☎ **AUTOMOBILE EMERGENCY
ASSISTANCE**
АВТОМОБИЛИ,
СРОЧНАЯ ПОМОЩЬ
RETTUNGSDIENST
AUTOMOBILE,
ASSISTANCE D'URGENCE
BIL BÄRGNING
AUTOJEN HÄTÄAPU

See also DRIVING

*Getting emergency assistance in the case
of a breakdown is difficult. Try calling the
GAI (State Auto Inspectorate) or the com-
panies listed below. See also* MILITIA
(Police). Try some of the shops listed under
AUTOMOBILE SERVICE.

Avto Technica Towing Service A/O
Service 24 hours per day
Call us for assistance
Office at Nekrasova ul., 14a............ 273-24-26
.... 273-32-68
Daily 0-24, Rubles

Sovinteravtoservice (towing service)
5-y Predportovyy proezd................ 290-15-10
Daily 9-17

Tekhnotransservice
Tambasova ul., 5 130-33-23
Fax 130-08-07
Daily 9-16; Rbls, $; Eng; Bus 130; Metro Prospekt Veteranov

Avtopark Towing Service
    Avtopark Avtotekhobsluzhivaniya
Towing of automobiles and trucks
Udelnyy pr., 28 554-08-64
Service Daily from 8-21; Rbls

☎ **AUTOMOBILE PARTS**
    АВТОМОБИЛИ, ЗАПЧАСТИ
    AUTOERSATZTEILE
    AUTOMOBILE,
      PIECES DE RECHANGE D'
    BILDELAR
    AUTONVARAOSAT

See also AUTOMOBILE SALES, AUTOMOBILE
SERVICE & REPAIRS *and*
ALARM SYSTEMS & DEVICES

Parts for Russian cars are usually supplied by the specific service stations for that model or in auto parts shops (Zapchasti, Запчасти). Parts for most foreign cars are increasingly available as the number of authorized dealers of imported cars continues to grow. For a price, most other parts can be ordered for quick delivery from Western Europe.

On weekend mornings, hundreds of car owners gather at the corner of Prazhskaya and Fuchika ul. in the Kupchino District to buy and sell auto parts, mostly for Russian models.

Aleks-Avto
Ispytateley pr., 1 a 393-18-19
Fax 393-29-39
Daily 10-20; Rbls

Aniko Automarket
Sytninskaya ul., 9 230-70-56
Mon-Sat 10-18

Auto Parts
• Mira ul., 5, In the Dry Cleaners....... 232-79-80
Mon-Sat 10-19; Rbls; Ital
• Vosstaniya ul., 22
Fax 272-67-95
Mon-Sat 11-19; Rbls
• Kurchatova ul., 6 ☎ *changing*...... 552-54-53
Mon-Sat 10-14, 15-19; Rbls
T-bus 3; Metro Chernyshevskaya
• Shkolnaya ul., 9 239-71-36
.... 239-60-30
Mon-Sat 10-19; Rbls
• Zagorodnyy pr., 3 271-26-35
Mon-Sat 11-13, 14-20; Rbls; Eng

Automobile Parts and Registration
Zamshina ul., 31 543-98-72
Mon-Sat 11-19; Rbls

Avtohaus Saint Petersburg
Mercedes Benz Orders
Rubinshteyna ul., 6-8 312-69-72
Mon-Sat 10-18; Rbls

Avtopribor
Khudozhnikov pr., 9, bldg. 1......... 594-07-84
Mon-Sat 10-17; Rbls; Eng

Automobile Glass   **Avtosteklo**
Marata ul., 76................................ 164-87-45
Mon-Sat 10-18; Rbls, $

AVTOTUR   **BOSCH** (B)

    Automotive
    Sales Center
    Auto services

Energetikov pr., 65 226-95-39
Fax.................................... 226-26-78

Borskoe Steklo
Nalichnaya ul., 9........................... 311-71-01
Mon-Fri 9-18; Rbls, $

Bosch Shop
Apraksin Dvor, bldg. 1, section 50.........No ☎
Mon-Sat 10-14, 15-18; Rbls, $

Digest-1
Kazanskaya ul., 9 312-47-03
Mon-Fri 10-13, 14-19; Rbls

Elena
Kolomenskaya ul., 29.................... 312-70-72
Mon-Sat 10-19; Rbls; Eng

Go Star
Kremenchugskaya ul., 19.............. 277-29-37
Mon-Sat 9:30-18; Rbls; Metro Ploshchad Vosstaniya

Home □ Center
Auto Parts Center

Auto Body Repair Tools & Supplies
Air compressors and spray paint, auto body repair
materials, wet sand paper, paints & finishes,
Turtle Wax and polishes

Car Repair and maintenance
If we don't have it, we can order it for you
from our parts catalog.

Special automotive tools, jacks, engine parts and
repair manuals for Lada and Volvo in English.

Michelin & Nokia Tires
Seat covers, batteries, lubricants,
Bosch windshield wipers, and head lamps

Located in S.E. St. Pb., minutes from city center

Slavy pr., 30.................................. 261-15-50
.... 261-04-02
Fax.. 260-15-81
Daily 10-20; $, FIM, DM, Rbls; Eng, Finn, Ger
Metro Moskovskaya, then Bus 31, 114, T-bus 29

Inavtoservice, *Windshields for European cars*
Vitebskiy pr., 17/2 298-39-10
Mon-Fri 10-18; Rbls, $

Kulttovary
Robespera nab., 8 279-20-66
Mon-Sat 10-14, 15-19

LondLen
Gertsena ul., 42 314-77-15
Fax 311-88-78
Mon-Fri 9-18; Rbls; Eng, Ital

Masla, Smazki　　　　　　**Oil & Lube**
Komissara Smirnova ul., 5/2 542-23-51
Mon-Fri 10-19; Rbls

Motor
Engelsa pr., 66............................. 553-87-23
Mon-Sat 10-14, 15-19; Rbls

Nord Camp, *Windshields for all cars*
Martynova nab., 6.......................... 230-97-81
.... 230-97-82

PLT
Authorized Toyota Dealer, parts & service
Malaya Balkanskaya ul., 57 101-52-13
Fax 101-64-26

Pyatoe Koleso　　　　　　**Fifth Wheel**
Tire and wheel specialists
Sinopskaya nab., 30...................... 274-00-51
Mon-Sat 10-14, 15-19; Rbls

Sirius-3
Novatorov blvd., 32 255-76-38
Mon-Sat 11-19; Rbls

AUTO PARTS

*Parts, accessories & supplies
for foreign cars, trucks & buses
Visit Our Shop on Gogolya ul. 19,
near the Astoria Hotel*

Gogolya ul., 19 315-97-58
Malodetskoselskiy pr., 26 ...292-77-18
Telex .... 121412 LTOS SU
Fax.................................... 292-00-28
M-F, 10 a.m. -6 p.m.; Eng; Rbls & $

Sport
Shaumyana pr., 2.......................... 224-28-74
Mon-Sat 10-14, 15-19; Rbls

Universal
Lebedeva ul., 31 541-81-87
Mon, Fri-Sun 10-19; Rbls

☎ **AUTOMOBILE RENTAL**
АВТОМОБИЛИ, ПРОКАТ
AUTOVERMIETUNG
AUTOMOBILE, LOCATION
BILUTHYRNING
AUTONVUOKRAUS

See also DRIVING

*Automobiles, mini-vans and buses can be
rented in St. Petersburg with driver. Car
rentals without drivers are also available.
Renting a car with a driver, however, can
be less expensive, safer and more
comfortable than without.*

Eight good reasons for hiring a car with

"driver": *language, driving rules, vigilant
GAI (traffic police), one-way streets, roads
in disrepair, road hazards, poor night
visibility, and bad street signs. Need we
say more!*

Astoria Rent-A-Car
Gertsena ul., 39............................ 210-58-58
Fax.. 542-87-98
Rbls, $

Autotur, *Chauffeur driven cars*
Energetikov pr., 65....................... 226-95-39
Fax.. 226-26-78
Mon-Fri 9-18; Rbls, $

AVIS RENT A CAR

Konnogvardeiskiy blvd., 4, apt. 34, entr. 6
.... 312-63-18
Fax.. 312-72-92
Remeslennaya ul., 13 235-64-44

Avtodom, *Serving groups by appointment only*
Reki Moyki nab., 56 315-90-43
Mini-buses with drivers; Daily 10-18

Interavto
Hertz Representative, choice of cars & minibuses
Ispolkomskaya ul., 9/11 277-40-32
Fax.. 274-25-62
Daily 0-24; Rbls, $; Eng, Ger

Intourist Transport, *Cars, minivans, buses, drivers*
Sedova ul., 5................................. 567-82-46
Fax.. 567-88-97
Mon-Fri 8-16:30; Rbls, $; Eng, Ger

Itmaz, *Cars with drivers for enterprises & firms*
Bogatyrskiy pr., 7/5, rm. 4-14 395-35-04
Mon-Fri 10-18; $

Kareliya, *Cars with drivers for enterprises and firms*
Petrovskaya nab., 29..................... 238-41-49
Mon-Fri 9-17; Rbls

TAXI & LIMOUSINE

At the Hotel Pulkovskaya
Featuring FORD automobiles & mini-vans
Lyubotinskiy proezd., 5 298-36-48
.... 298-12-94
Fax 298-00-73
Telex .... 121028 MATRA SU
24 Hours Daily, $, English, German

Mobil-Service, *Cars with drivers*
Borovaya ul., 11/13, apt. 65, rm. 2..... 164-60-66
Fax.. 108-51-05
*Mon-Fri 9-17; Rbls, $; Eng, Finn
Tram 11; Metro Pushkinskaya*

STV
Konnogvardeyskiy blvd., 4 315-29-55
Mon-Fri 9-17; Rbls

Soppol, *Secure transport of passengers & cargoes*
2-ya Krasnoarmeyskaya ul., 7......... 110-14-32
Fax.. 110-12-09
*Mon-Fri 10-18; Rbls, $; Eng, Ger
Bus 10; Metro Tekhnologicheskiy Institut*

AUTOMOBILE RENTAL

At Pribaltiyskaya Hotel

Taxi and Limousine Service
24 Hours/Day,
Featuring Fords
With Our Skilled Drivers

Korablestroiteley ul., 14

Dispatcher	356-93-29
Director	356-10-74
Fax	356-00-94
Fax	356-38-45

$, English, German, Finnish

RENT A CAR
TRANSWELL
TROIKKA LTD.

Passenger Cars, Minivans and Trucks
Drivers Available

Lermontovskiy pr., 37 113-72-53
Fax 114-38-03
Monday-Friday 9-21, Sat. 9-18, Sun. 9-12
English, Finnish, $, rubles

☎ **AUTOMOBILE SALES**
АВТОМОБИЛИ, ПРОДАЖА
AUTOVERKAUF
AUTOMOBILES, VENTE
BILFÖRSÄLJNING
AUTOLIIKKEET

New Russian cars are ruggedly built for Russian roads and gasoline. Some prices as of July 1993: Moskvich $3,500 - 4,000, NIVA $5,300, Zhiguli 4,800 - 6,600 depending on the model, Volga $10,000 - 12,000. These prices are beyond the means of most Russians. Try the NIVA for a four wheel drive vehicle. Imported cars should be modified for the Russian market, especially stronger shock absorbers and carburetor adjustment for Russian gasoline. Lead-free gasoline is difficult to find, so it is best not to have a catalytic converter.

Alpia
Baykonurskaya ul., 19, bldg. 3 393-11-77
Fax 552-36-52
Mon-Fri 12-18; Rbls, $; Eng

Ancher Auto Sales
Prosveshcheniya pr., 80 530-84-90
Fax 530-97-85
Mon-Sat 9-18; Rbls, $; Eng

Aniko Automarket
Sytninskaya ul., 9 232-79-98
Mon-Sat 10-14, 15-18

ARS Auto Showroom
Audi, BMW, Mercedes-Benz, Volvo
Leninskiy pr., 121 255-14-67
Fax 254-76-11
Mon-Sat 11-20; Rbls, $; Eng, Finn

Audi - *See* ARS, Ow Quast
Auto Saint Petersburg,   *10-20; Rbls, $*
Chekistov ul., 13 130-02-30
Fax 130-45-09
Autotechnical Service, *All models, all makes*
Apraksin Dvor, bldg. 1, rm 34 314-89-77
Fax 110-60-99
Mon-Sat 10-19; Rbls, $; Eng
Avtohaus Saint Petersburg
Rubinshteyna ul., 6-8 113-18-95
Fax 314-05-97
Mercedes Benz Orders, Mon-Fri 10-18; $

OPEL   **GM**

Avto Motors Oy
Novoizmaylovskiy pr., 4   296-55-87
Kubinskaya ul., 81   122-54-18

Avtostar
Energetikov pr., 65 226-99-80
Fax 226-10-34
Mon-Fri 10-18; Sat 10-16; Rbls, $; Eng

Axel
• Savushkina ul., 15; ☎/Fax 239-98-19
Daily 10-19; Rbls
• Rustaveli ul., 31 a 538-67-81
Daily 10-14, 15-19; Rbls, $

BMW- *See* ARS
Chrysler - *See Below*
Chrysler-Novek-Motors
Slavy pr., 5 260-41-06
Fax 273-97-77
Mon-Fri 10-20, Sat 10-17; Rbls, $; Eng
T-bus 27, 35; Metro Moskovskaya

Citroën - *See* Tiitus
Consultant
Bolshaya Podyacheskaya ul., 24 312-79-44
Fax 312-81-84
Mon-Fri 10-18; Rbls, $; Eng, Fr; Metro Sennaya Ploshchad

Continent-7, *RAF Mini-buses*
Zhukovskogo ul., 49, apt. 18 275-61-83
Fax 275-40-91
Mon-Fri 10-18; Rbls, $; CC; Eng, Ger

Crosstown Motorcity, *Auto Showroom*
Krasnoputilovskaya ul., 38 184-98-43
Fax 183-51-49
Mon-Sat 10-14, 15-19; Rbls, $; Ger

Dejur
Sofiyskaya ul., 8 269-54-47
Fax 269-55-47
Mon-Fri 8-16; Rbls, $; Ger

East Trade Polmot Holding
Nakhimova ul., 7, apt. 102 356-33-64
Mon-Fri 8-14; Rbls, $; Eng, Ger, Pol

EASTMARKET Motors
Bolshaya Konyushennaya ul., 27 312-27-29
Fax 314-22-73
Mon-Fri 10-18; Rbls, $; Eng, Ger, Finn

Euro-Ros-Company,   *Mon-Fri 10-18; Rbls, $*
Ispolkomskaya ul., 4/6, off. 14 277-04-45
Fax 277-24-42

Ford - *See* TDV Auto & Sovavto
Galant-1 Auto Showroom
Zhdanovskaya ul., 2, at the Sport Palace "SKA"
☎ 230-78-10
Fax 230-78-21
Mon-Sat 10-20; Rbls, $; Eng

General Motors GM - *See* Avto Motors OY
Global USA - *See our color ad*
  Moscow, Usacheva ul., 35
  .... (095) 245-56-57
Honda - *See* PetroHonda - AutoBaltService
Hyundai - *See* San Shop
Iantovski, *Volvo cars*
  Nevskiy pr., 48, in Passage, 1st floor
  ☎ 219-17-92
  Rbls; Metro Nevskiy Prospekt
ICD Avto, *Used foreign cars, parts, service*
  Kalinina ul., 59 a 252-29-21
  Fax 186-36-79
  Mon-Sat 10-19; Rbls, $; Eng
Inavtoservice, *Volvo cars, Metro Park Pobedy*
  Vitebskiy pr., 17/2......................... 294-05-33

INSTANT
Automobile Import-Export
Zheleznodorozhnyy pr., 40 560-66-85
Fax 560-43-85

 Korona-LogoVaz

Mercedes Benz Automobile Sales
Kamennoostrovskiy pr., 5 238-19-15
Hrs: 9-19; English, German, French

Automobile Showroom in St. Petersburg
LogoVAZ
Models from Leading
Automobile Manufacturers
Oktyabrskaya nab., 6..................... 223-52-33
Fax 221-93-22
Hrs: 9-19; English, German, French

LogoVAZ
Representative in St. Petersburg
Rubinshteyna ul., 25 314-17-18
Fax 315-79-81
Hrs: 9-19; English, German, French

Laktio Star, *Foreign cars* *Mon-Fri 10-18*
  Trefoleva ul., 2.............................. 186-34-13
Leader, *VAZ* *Mon-Fri 10-18; Rbls, $*
  Bronnitskaya ul., 17 110-10-93

RENAULT TRUCKS

Sales & Leasing
Lyubotinskiy proezd., 5 298-36-48
.... 298-12-94
Fax 298-00-73
Telex .... 121028 MATRA SU
24 Hours Daily, $, English, German

Mercedes Benz - *See* ARS, Avtohaus Saint
  Petersburg & Korona LogoVaz
Neva-Leasing
  Galernaya ul., 58 312-72-60
  Fax... 312-07-00
  Mon-Fri 9-13, 14-18; Rbls
Opel - *See* Avto Motors OY & Sovavto
Ortex
  Ordzhonikidze ul., 42..................... 264-60-12
  Fax... 293-08-85
  Mon-Fri 9-14, 15-18; Rbls, $, CC

ST. PETERSBURG
• Sales / Service
• Parts
• Accessories
• Warranty Service
The Best Cars & Service
in St. Petersburg
Morisa Toreza ul., 40
Tel/Fax: 247-89-25
Hrs: 9-18, Rubles & $

DELOVIE LYUDI
INDEPENDENT • OBJECTIVE • THOROUGH
Profsoyuznaya ul., 73; Tel.: (095) 333-33-40; Fax: (095) 330-15-68

Peter-Lada
Kingiseppskoe shosse 50, Krasnoe Selo
☎ 132-17-15
Fax 132-83-47
Daily 10-14, 15-19; Rbls, $

Petex
Sverdlovskaya nab., 64 224-78-75
Fax 310-14-26
Mon-Sat 11-14, 15-19; Rbls, $

Petroff Motors, *Good selection of foreign cars*
Sverdlovskaya nab., 62 227-09-12
Daily 10-20; $, CC; Eng, Finn
Bus 22, 174; Metro Novocherkasskaya

PetroHonda - AutoBaltService

Authorized St. Petersburg Distributor

 HONDA

Sales, Warranty & Service
Nakhimova ul., 5, blg.1
Tel.: 356-45-25   Fax: 355-04-40

PLT, *Authorized Toyota Dealer*
Malaya Balkanskaya ul., 57 101-52-13
.... 172-21-03
Fax 101-64-26
Modified for Russian conditions, parts & service

RAF, *Mini-vans from Estonia*
Bratyev Radchenko ul., 3 482-77-90
Mon-Fri 8-17; Rbls, $

Renault - *See* Teknesis
Renault Trucks - *See* Matralen
Saab - *See* Avto Motors OY
San Shop, *Hyundai*
Torzhkovskaya ul., 2, bldg. 1 246-53-95
Tues-Sat 11-19; Rbls, $

Sovtransavto

SOVAVTO ST. PETERSBURG
with Klein Trucks, Netherlands

Imported Automobiles

Wide selection of used foreign cars
Volvo, Opel, Ford Scorpio or by order
Excellent prices

Vitebskiy pr., 3 298-46-50
Fax.. 298-77-60
Telex .... 121535 AVTO
Hrs. 8:30-17:30, English, German

Teknesis, *Renault automobile by order*
Reki Fontanki nab., 76, 4th floor 112-58-32
Fax 112-58-26
Mon-Fri 9-16; $; Eng, Fr, Ger

Tiitus, *Citroën*
Leninskiy pr., 168 290-46-02
Mon-Fri 10-18; $; Eng

VOLVO

swed car
SANKT-PETERSBURG

Official Import-Dealer

Prospect Bolshevikov 33, korpus 1,
St. Petersburg, 193232, Russia
Tel.: 812/586 77 18
Fax: 812/586 74 77

 TDV-AUTO ТДВ-АВТО

NEW CAR SALES & WARRANTY SERVICE

Authorized Dealer of Ford Europe

in St. Petersburg & NW Russia

FORD-EUROPE CARS & MICROBUSES
Adapted To Russian Road Conditions

Showroom, Service & Parts
Kommuny ul., 16 521-46-14
.... 521-77-19
Fax.. 521-85-47
Telex .... 121263 TDV SU
Hrs: 9-18, Closed Sunday, $ & Rubles, CC, English

Transco N.V. & DTI Holdings (Belgium)
& LRC Avto-Vaz.

Tekhnotransservice
Tambasova ul., 5........................... 130-33-23
Fax.. 130-08-07
Daily 9-16; Rbls, $; Eng
Bus 130; Metro Prospekt Veteranov

Toyota - *See* PLT
Triada
Zhukovskogo ul., 22...................... 275-79-22
Fax.. 272-59-17
Mon-Fri 9:30-18; Rbls, $

Volkswagen - *See* Ow Quast
Volvo - *See* ARS, Iantovski, Inavtoservice,
Sovavto, Swed Car

 The *Traveller's*
Yellow Pages

To Direct Dial The USA
DIAL 8, wait for Dial Tone
DIAL 101 + Area Code + #

☎ AUTOMOBILE SERVICE AND REPAIRS
АВТОСЕРВИС
AUTOWERKSTÄTTEN
AUTOMOBILE, REPARATION D'/ (GARAGE)
BIL SERVICE, BILVERKSTÄDER
AUTOHUOLTO JA-KORJAUS

See also AUTOMOBILE SALES

Autobaltservice, *Honda sales & service*
Nakhimova ul., 5, bldg. 1 356-77-01
Fax 355-04-40
Daily 8-12, 13-20; Rbls, $; Eng, Ger

Autoservice
Leninskiy pr., 142 a 254-79-49

Avto Dvor
Rustaveli ul., 7 249-13-70
Daily 10-18; Rbls

Avtomobilist
Lodeynopolskaya ul., 7 235-70-78

Chrysler-Novek-Motors
Primorskiy pr., 202, Motel-Camping Retur
☎ 237-75-33

Dejur
Sofiyskaya ul., 8 269-54-47
Fax 269-55-47
Mon-Fri 8-16; Rbls, $; Ger

Forward
Luzhskaya ul., 3 530-47-82
Fax 531-66-93
Daily 8-20; Rbls

Inavtoservice, *Volvo cars & service*
Vitebskiy pr., 17/2 298-39-10

InNis, *Nissan Service*
Primorskoe shosse, 18 238-37-09
Fax 542-87-98
Daily 9-17; Rbls, $; Eng

Kameya, *Window tinting*
Zhukovskogo ul., 5 273-44-69
Mon-Fri 9-18

Kareliya VAZ
Petrovskiy Ostrov, 2 g 238-40-47
Mon-Fri 10-18; Rbls

Moskvich Warranty Service
Malaya Balkanskaya ul., 59 101-54-01
Daily 8-20:30; Rbls

Peter-Lada
Kingiseppskoe shosse, 50 132-44-50
Daily 0-24; Rbls, $; Eng

Petroservice
Leninskiy pr., 160 295-54-49
Mon-Fri 9-17; Rbls, $, CC; Eng

PLT, *Authorized Toyota dealer*
Malaya Balkanskaya ul., 57 101-52-13
Fax 101-64-26

Pyatoe Koleso *Tires & wheels* **Fifth Wheel**
Sinopskaya nab., 30 274-00-51
Mon-Sat 10-14, 15-19; Rbls

Repair and Service Station
Bogatyrskiy pr., 12 395-31-34
Fax 395-36-96
Mon-Fri 9-12, 13-17

Service Station No. 1 (VAZ)
Salova ul., 70 166-47-06
Daily 8-12, 13-20; Rbls; Tram 15; Metro Elektrosila

Service Station No. 3 (GAZ & VAZ)
Staroderevenskaya ul., 5 239-22-31
Daily 7-20; $

Service Station No. 4 (ZAZ)
Kosmonavtov pr., 69 126-02-20
Daily 8-13, 14-21; Rbls

Shuvalovo
Prokofeva ul., 10 515-14-08
Daily 9:30-20; Rbls

Foreign Car Service

Predportovyy proezd, 5 290-15-10
(Next to Hotel Pulkovskaya)
Daily, 9 a.m. - 8 p.m., Eng, $ & Rbls.

For other services, call
Malodetskoselskiy pr., 24... 292-77-18
Fax 292-00-28
Telex .... 121412 LTOS SU

STTM
AUTOSERVICE

Auto Repair, Bodywork and Painting

Sofiyskaya ul., 8 269-87-28

Swed Car, *Volvo*
Energetikov pr., 59/3 225-40-51
Mon-Fri 10-19, Sat 10-15; Rbls, $

 TDV-AUTO ТДВ-АВТО

WARRANTY SERVICE & REPAIRS
PARTS, TIRES & ACCESSORIES
Authorized Dealer of Ford Europe
in St. Petersburg & NW Russia

Kommuny ul., 16 521-46-13
Fax 521-85-47
Telex ....121263 TDV SU
Hrs: 9-18, Closed Sunday, $ & rubles, CC, English

Transco N.V. & DTI Holdings (Belgium)
& LRC Avto-Vaz

Tiitus, *Citroën*
Leninskiy pr., 168 290-46-02
Mon-Fri 10-18; Rbls, $

VAZ Warranty Service (Peter-Lada)
4-y Verkhniy per., 1 a, Promzona Parnas
☎ 557-39-07
Fax 558-81-83
Daily 8-21:30; Rbls

VAZ Warranty Service Rzhevka
Kommuny ul., 16 521-46-13
Fax 521-85-47
Mon-Sat 9-18; Rbls, $; Eng

ZAZ Warranty Service
Simonova ul., 13..........................515-38-03
Mon-Sat 9-20; Rbls, $; Eng, Ger

☎ AUTOMOBILE WASH

See CAR WASHES

☎ BABY FOOD
ДЕТСКОЕ ПИТАНИЕ
BABYNAHRUNG
BEBES, NOURRITURE POUR
BARNMAT
VAUVANRUOKA

Special shops, called Baby food (Malysh, Малыш) *sell prepared baby food and they often have a good selection of regular food products. With a prescription, baby food is available at subsidized prices. Many Russians and most Westerners, however, prefer imported baby food, formula and disposable diapers which are available in* COMMERCIAL SHOPS, INTERNATIONAL SHOPS, *and* PHARMACIES, *and even some street kiosks.*

Dieta No. 18   **Diet**
Sadovaya ul., 38 315-94-53
Mon-Fri, Sun 9-14, 15-21; Rbls

Dobrota No. 12
Moskovskiy pr., 23 292-31-57
Mon-Fri, Sun 8-14, 15-20; Rbls

Malysh   **Baby Food**
• Bolshoy pr., P.S., 5......................233-56-14
Mon-Sat 9-21; Rbls
• Bolshoy pr., P.S., 51 232-67-21
Mon-Fri 8-20; Rbls
• Malyy pr., V.O., 13 213-08-42
Mon-Fri 10-19; Rbls; Ger
• Nevskiy pr., 30............................312-16-33
Mon-Fri, Sun 9-21; Rbls

Zdorove   **Health**
Moskovskiy pr., 172 296-17-20
Mon-Fri, Sun 8-14, 15-21; Rbls

☎ BAKERIES
БУЛОЧНЫЕ, КОНДИТЕРСКИЕ
BÄCKEREIEN, KONDITOREI
BOULANGERIES , CONFISERIES
BAGERIER, KONFEKTAFFÄRER
LEIPOMOT

See also FOOD STORES, SUPERMARKETS, *and* SHOPPING

Russian bread is excellent and inexpensive. Baked without preservatives, it is often delivered fresh to the bakery several times a day. You can get fresh and sometimes even hot bread (goryachiy khleb) everyday. Bread and rolls are not packaged, so take along plastic bags. Russians often ask if the bread is "Svezhiy" (Свежий) fresh and/or myagkiy (Мягкий) soft. Sometimes a fork is provided to test the bread or the clerk might even advise you as to the best bread that day.

There are two types of bakeries: Bulochnaya (Булочная), *of which there are about 300, almost one on every block, and more than 30* Konditerskaya (Кондитерская).

A bulochnaya *generally has fresh bread, rolls, and occasionally cakes and pastries, while a* Konditerskaya *has pastries, cakes, cookies, candy and often coffee, cognac and in some even ice cream, but no bread. A few of the better* "Bulochnaya" *and* "Konditerskaya" *are listed below.*

Types of Bread (khleb, хлеб)*:*

Baton (Батон) = *oval white loaf,* Belyy Kirpich (Белый кирпич) = *"white brick" loaf,* Chernyy Kirpich (Черный кирпич) = *"dark brick" loaf,* Belyy Kruglyy (Белый Круглый) = *round white loaf,* Chernyy Kruglyy (Черный Круглый) = *round dark loaf,* Bulochki (Булочки) = *tasty rolls, may be with a bit of conserve inside,* Tort (Торт)=*Very fancy, sweet cake.*

Le Café Bahlsen
Fresh Bread and Pastries, Bakery on Premises, German Bahlsen Cakes, Cookies, Pastries
Nevskiy pr., 142 271-28-11
Daily 8-12, 15-20, (15-19 Sun); Metro Ploshchad Vosstaniya

Belochka   **Squirrel**
Sredniy pr., 28 213-17-63
Mon-Sat 9-21; Rbls

Bulochnaya   **Bakery**
• Bolshaya Konyushennaya ul., 7 314-15-58
Chorek Georgian bread, rolls, hamburgers Baking on premises; Daily 11-20
• Bolshoy pr., P.S., 4 232-02-91
Daily 9-21; Rbls
• Bolshoy pr., P.S., 61 232-87-84
Daily 8-14, 15-22; Rbls
• Nevskiy pr., 66 314-85-59
Daily 9-21; Rbls
• Nevskiy pr., 74 273-50-23
Daily 9-21; Rbls
• Nevskiy pr., 93 277-08-81
Daily 9-13, 14-21; Rbls
• Nevskiy pr., 139 277-15-97
Daily 8-20; Rbls

Cakes, *Daily 9-21; Rbls*   **Torty**
Nevskiy pr., 10 312-60-86

Cakes   **Torty, Pirozhnye**
Nevskiy pr., 154 277-29-16
Daily 11-21; Rbls

Cakes, to Order   **Tort na Zakaz**
Makarova nab., 32 213-42-74
....213-66-24
Mon-Fri 8:30-16; Metro Vasileostrovskaya

Dr. Oetker Nevskiy, 27
Freshest bread and pastries in St. Pb.
Nevskiy pr., 27 312-10-80
Daily 8-20; Rbls

Dr. Oetker Nevskiy, 40, *Konditorei*
Nevskiy pr., 40 312-24-57
....311-90-66
Daily 12-24; $

Hot Bread   **Горячий Хлеб**   **Goryachiy Khleb**
Bread factory "window shops" selling hot bread
Chernyshevskogo pr., 16................272-68-97
Ligovskiy pr., 74 164-97-88

Karavay   Round Loaf Bakery
The Scottish Baker with Great Pastries and Black Bread
Tavricheskaya ul., 33 275-69-18
Daily 9-14, 15-20; Rbls

Kylon, *Fresh salted roulettes*
Bolshekov pr., 3............................. 588-63-28
Russkiy Khleb   Russian Bread
Saltykova-Shchedrina ul., 19.......... 273-55-84
Fresh Russian Bagels (Bubliki)
Sever, *Famous for their cakes*   **North**
Nevskiy pr., 44................................ 311-25-89
Mon-Fri, Sun 10-19; Rbls
Vostochnye Sladosti
Eastern Sweets Pastry Shops
Candies, cakes and cookies
• Moskovskiy pr., 27 292-75-56
Mon-Fri, Sun 9-21; Rbls
• Nevskiy pr., 104........................... 273-74-36
Mon-Sat 8-20
Yubileynyy Bakeries   Jubilee
• Chernyshevskogo pl., 3................. 298-15-47
Daily 9-20; Rbls
• 7-ya Liniya, 40............................. 213-11-62
Daily 9-21; Rbls
Zolotoy Uley   Golden Hive
Nevskiy pr., 22............................... 312-23-94
Mon-Sat 9-14, 15-21; Rbls

☎ **BALLET**

See THEATERS/BALLET

☎ **BANKS**
БАНКИ
BANKEN
BANQUES
BANKER
PANKIT

See also CURRENCY EXCHANGE, and TRAVELER'S CHEQUES

BANKING: St. Petersburg is rapidly becoming a banking center with more than 60 commercial banks, some new, some from the old state banking structure. These banks perform most of the usual banking operations including deposits, transfers, lending, and often currency exchange.

PERSONAL ACCOUNTS: Foreigners can open hard currency accounts at major banks. Withdrawals and deposits are usually done in person, in cash, and without restriction, but banking and currency laws change.

For example, in late July the Central Bank called in all pre-1993 bank notes (1,2,5,10 rubles notes were later excluded from this rule because of the lack of change). People could exchange 35,000 rubles in cash (later changed to 100,000); the rest had to be deposited in the Savings Bank and frozen for six months. The status at press time was in flux.

COMMERCIAL ACCOUNTS: Transactions are more cumbersome and restricted, because cash withdrawals are restricted to certain operations (wages, primarily) while all other transactions among firms are supposed to be made by "inter-bank transfers". This system of "transfer requests" is cumbersome because the transfer request must be taken in person to the payer's bank which then transfers funds to the payee's bank rather than the payer simply sending a check to the payee for deposit.

The commercial banking industry is growing rapidly in a very uncertain economic climate and changing regulations. Foreign firms should look for banks with good foreign departments and the right to buy and sell foreign currency. The stability of banks should also be investigated carefully before making significant deposits since many banks have folded. We list some of the larger and better known banks.

GETTING CASH IN ST. PETERSBURG

It is much easier now to get cash in St. Petersburg.

Western Union. Money can be wired to you overnight by Western Union via Moscow in your name to the account of the Bank Saint-Petersburg. It cost from 15% for small sums to 4.5% for large sums.

VISA card cash advances. Take your passport and VISA card to Bank Saint Petersburg (Ostroskogo pl., 7) or to the St. Petersburg Savings Bank branches (see ad), or go to Credo Bank branches at the Astoria Hotel, the Hotel Moskva, and the Morskoy Vokzal Ship Terminal. The bank commission is usually 5% of the total advance, plus any charge from your credit card company.

Getting American Express Traveler's Cheques. Take your personal check, passport and American Express Card to the office in the Grand Hotel Europe on Mikhaylovskaya ul., 1/7 (& Nevskiy) and buy American Express Traveler's Cheques at a 1% commission. You can cash them right there (if there are enough dollars available), at branches of Credo Bank, or at other banks listed in TRAVELER'S CHEQUES. Commissions range from 3-4%.

✳ **BABYLON**
SUPER
Mon-Sat 10-21 Sun 12-20
Exchange office

Breakfast from Super Babylon with sliced cheeses & smoked meats, bacon, fresh fruit on Kellogg cereals or Museli, Dutch butter, jams & jellies on hot French bread or rolls, fruit juices, skim milk, 1.5% and whole milk, or cream and coffees and teas.
P.S., Maly pr., 54 & 56 230-80-96
In the former Okean store off Bolshoy Prospekt

Changing money or Traveler's Cheques. See CURRENCY EXCHANGE and TRAVELER'S CHEQUES.

Money Wire Transfers: Banks that do wire transfers are usually members of the "SWIFT currency transfer" system. If you are really organized and plan ahead, it is best to ask about wire transfers before you leave home. Ask your bank if they have a "correspondent bank" in St. Petersburg. Otherwise you can transfer money by wire at the following banks listed below. Some require that you open an account with a deposit varying from $10 - $1000 and some do not. They usually charge a fee of 1 - 4% of the amount transferred, and it takes from 2 to 10 days.

Banks Which Transfer Funds
Acct = Account required,
No acct = Account not required
% ? = Fee not known or varies

AvtoVaz Bank	acct., %?
Bank of New York	
Inter-Maritime Bank	no acct.,3.5%
Bank Saint Petersburg	no acct., 1%
Credo Bank	no acct., %?
Kuban-Bank St. Petersburg	acct., 4 %
Russian Commercial	
Industrial Bank	acct., 3.2%
St. Petersburg Commercial	
Agricultural Industrial Bank	acct., %?
Severnyy Torgovyy Bank	acct., 4%
Vneshtorg Bank	no acct., 2%

Be sure to get a receipt called a razreshenie (разрешение) to permit you to take the money out of Russia with you. Keep it with your "declaration". See CUSTOMS.

Western Banks: As of July 1, 1993 several Western banks, including Bank of New York, Deutsche Bank, and Bank Nationale de Paris have representatives in St. Petersburg, but still do not directly carry out banking operations. Dresdner Bank and Credit Lyonnais plan to start operations in September, 1993. Many Western banks have offices in Moscow. See The Traveller's Yellow Pages and Handbook for Moscow 1993-1994.

Aeroflotbank

Gertsena ul., 28	315-51-57
	312-96-34
Fax	314-93-88
Mon-Fri 9-17	

Association of Commercial Banks of Saint Petersburg - Banks Only

Kazanskaya ul., 36, rm. 707	319-95-47
Fax	319-92-49
Mon-Fri 9-18; Metro Sadovaya	

Astrobank

Nevskiy pr., 58	311-36-00
Fax	311-08-25
Mon-Fri 9:30-13; Metro Nevskiy Prospekt	

AVTOVAZBANK
St. Petersburg Branch

Full Service Bank:
➥ Ruble & Currency Accounts
➥ Currency Exchange
➥ Direct Correspondent Account
   with Union Bank of Finland Ltd.
➥ Over 100 correspondent
   banks world-wide
2-ya Sovetskaya ul., 3/7

Tel	274-49-48
Fax	277-41-80
Telex	121288 SPAVB SU

Mon.-Fri.: 8:30-13, 14-17:15, Clsd. Sat., Sun. English

Baltiyskiy Bank, Daily 10-13; Fr, Ger, Finn

Sadovaya ul., 34	310-05-80
Fax	310-92-74

Bank Nationale de Paris Representative

Mikhaylovskaya ul., 1/7, rm. 110	119-60-00
Fax	119-60-01

Bank of New York Inter-Maritime Bank, Geneva, Mon-Fri 9-18

Dumskaya ul., 1/3	110-49-86

Bank Saint-Petersburg, See ad on next page
Professional banking services
for the foreign resident and guest
Bank Saint-Petersburg, opens personal accounts for foreigners, cashes all traveler's cheques for dollars, provides VISA cash advances and Western Union wire transfers. Correspondent banks in the USA include Bankers Trust and Chase Manhattan.

Central Bank of Russia
Tsentralnyy Bank Rossii

Reki Fontanki nab., 70/72	312-39-40
Fax	311-70-60
Working only with St. Petersburg banks	
Mon-Fri 9:30-13; Eng, Fr	

Central Bank of Russia, Main Office
Tsentralnyy Bank Rossii

Griboedova kan. nab., 13	311-00-34
Fax	311-08-75
Working only with banks in the Leningrad Region	
Daily 9:30-13	

DELOVIE LYUDI

INDEPENDENT • OBJECTIVE • THOROUGH
Profsoyuznaya ul., 73; Tel.: (095) 333-33-40; Fax: (095) 330-15-68

BANK SAINT PETERSBURG

- Ruble & Currency Accounts
- All Foreign Exchange
  Operations
- Direct Currency Transfer
- SWIFT Member
- Documentary Operations
- Letters of Credit
- Moscow Interbank
  Currency Exchange

Admiralteyskaya emb., 8
Ostrovskogo sq., 7
Tel.: 310-33-57
Tel./Fax: 315-46-01
Telex: 121226 LBANK SU
SWIFT: JSBSRU2P
Office Hours: 8:30-17,
Banking Hours: 9:30-13
English

Industry & Construction Bank
Saint Petersburg, A/O

Est. Volzhsko-Kamskiy Bank 1863

The widest network of branches
in St. Petersburg
Correspondent with 12
Major Foreign Banks
Worldwide Service with Payments,
Letters of Credit
Documentary Collection, Secured Loans
Traveler's Cheque Cashing,
Currency Exchange
Points at over 8 Locations
(See our color ad for addresses)

Nevskiy pr., 38
Tel.: 110-49-58, Fax: 310-61-73
Telex: 121612 ICB SU
Mon-Sat 10-20; Metro Nevskiy Prospekt

Industry & Construction Bank
is also called **Promstroy Bank**

Credit Lyonnais Russie
Planned opening September 1993, Mon-Fri 9-18
Nevskiy pr., 12 210-31-00
Fax 210-33-90

Credobank, *Mon-Fri 9:30-13, 14-18*
Mokhovaya ul., 26 275-06-06
Fax 275-03-31

Deutsche Bank Representative
Griboedova kan. nab., 101 315-02-16
Fax 315-06-55

Dresdner Bank
Isaakievskaya pl., 11 312-16-20
Fax 312-26-11

Ekaterinenskiy Bank
Vyborgskaya nab., 61 245-34-71
Fax 245-17-70
Mon-Fri 9:30-14, 15-15:30

Elektrobank, *Mon-Fri 9:30-13*
Mitrofanevskoe shosse, 5 v 186-46-14
Fax 168-22-93

Energomashbank, *Mon-Fri 10-13; Eng*
Karavannaya ul., 1 315-73-52
Fax 315-99-27

Industrial & Construction Bank -
See ad above

INKOMBANK

St. Petersburg Branch
Ruble & Hard Currency Services
Official SWIFT member

Banking & Office Hours: 9 - 17
Komsomola ul., 41
Tel.: 542-36-11
Fax: 542-38-07
$ TR, English, French, German

Innovation Bank
Chaykovskogo ul., 24, apt. 8 279-00-04
Fax 279-02-81
Mon-Fri 9:30-17:30; Eng, Ger

Investorbank, *Mon-Fri 9:30-13*
Rimskogo-Korsakova pr., 47 113-70-99
Fax 113-70-99

Konversbank, *Mon-Fri 9:30-18*
Reki Chernoy nab., 24 239-80-53
Fax 239-75-01

Kuban Bank - St. Petersburg
A Full Service Bank
Hard Currency & Ruble Accounts
Correspondent with:
Dresdner Bank AG
Turkiye Garanti Bankasi AS
Manhattan Bank

In St. Petersburg:
Nalichnaya ul., 20 352-37-55
Fax..352-37-48
In Krasnodar:
Ordzhonikidze ul., 29
Tel................................. (8612) 52-29-77

Ladabank, *Mon-Fri 9:30-12:30*
Zanevskiy pr., 6 528-59-01
Lesopromyshlennyy Bank
Krapivnyy per., 5............................ 541-82-17
Fax 541-83-93
Mon-Fri 9:30-12:30; Eng
Ligobank, *Mon-Fri 9-18*
Ligovskiy pr., 56 164-03-03

Full Service Banking Operations in
Rubles & Hard Currency

Correspondent with:

Banka Agricola Mantovana
Mantova, Italy

Moskov Narodny Bank
London, England

Commerz Bank
Frankfurt Am Main, Germany

Moscow Office ....(095) 239-16-97
  (095) 239-15-76
  (095) 350-42-47
Fax...........................(095) 238-56-77
When travelling, call our branches in:
Izhevsk ....(3412) 75-65-55
Kiev.............................(044) 245-79-98
Lubertsy....................(095) 554-73-23
Orenburg..................(35300) 3-67-26
Sovetsk ....(011161) 7-20-15
Surgut ....(35461) 2-42-13
Tomsk ....(3822) 21-43-93
Ukhta ....(82147) 6-30-56
In St. Petersburg call
Tel. ....(812) 252-38-46
Fax...........................(812) 252-11-03
Hrs: 9:30-17:30, Clsd. Sat, Sun;
All currencies; Eng, Ger, Fin

Otechestvo Bank
Mytninskaya nab., 13 238-97-91
Fax..238-97-50
Mon-Fri 9-16; Eng, Ger, Fr
Peterburgskiy Aktsionernyy
                Narodnyy Bank (PAN Bank)
Chernoy Rechki nab., 41/15
Tel/Fax 246-91-08
Daily 9-18; Eng
Petroagroprombank, *Mon-Fri 9:30-13*
Griboedova kan. nab., 13............315-44-92
Petrovskiy Bank, *Daily 9:30-13; Eng*
Ruzovskaya ul., 8, ☎/Fax 292-53-22
Zakharevskaya ul., 14....................275-76-36
Fax..275-76-35
Promstroy Bank
See ad for **Industry & Construction Bank**
Rossiya, *Mon-Fri 9:30-13; Eng, Ger, Fr*
Kvarengi per., 4.............................278-10-48
Tel/Fax 278-10-78

 Russian Commercial Industrial Bank

Hard Currency and Ruble Accounts
Safe deposit • Certificates of Deposit
International Transfers

Gertsena ul., 15 314-69-32
Fax 311-21-35
Hours for International Payments:
9-12:30, English

Russkiy Torgovopromyshlennyy Bank
Gertsena ul., 15..............................314-69-32
Fax..311-21-35

**ST. PETERSBURG COMMERCIAL
AGRICULTURAL INDUSTRIAL BANK**

Complete Range of Banking Services
Operations in Rubles & Hard Currency
23 branches in St. Petersburg & Region
Correspondent with: Dresdner Bank,
Kansallis-Osaka-Pankki, Svenska-Handelsk

Nab. Kan. Griboedova, 13
Tel.................................... 110-49-33
Fax 314-37-15
Telex ....121205 LK APB
Hrs: 9:30-13

St. Petersburg Saving Bank - *See next page*
Severnyy Torgovyy Bank
Nekrasova ul., 14 275-87-98
Fax..275-45-59
Mon-Thu 10-17, Fri 10-13; Eng

SAINT - PETERSBURG
BANK

St. Petersburg Savings Bank

Largest Bank in Saint Petersburg
Five million accounts • 23 Full Service
Branches • 254 Savings Bank Offices
18 Currency Exchange Offices

A LEADER IN BANKING INNOVATION
Sberbank Cash Card & Visa Cash Advance

A FULL SERVICE BANK
Foreign Currency & Ruble Accounts
All Lending & Credit Operations
International Currency Transfer

VISA $ CASH ADVANCE

At Hotel Pulkovskaya
Pobedy pl., 2 264-57-22
At Branch No. 1991
Nevskiy pr., 38.......................... 110-47-91
Nevskiy pr., 82 272-90-89
Business Center
Vladimirskiy pr., 9 113-16-71
International Airport
Pulkovo-2................................. 104-34-27
In The House of Books
Nevskiy pr., 28 219-94-17

CURRENCY EXCHANGE OFFICES
18 Currency Exchange Offices in St. Pb.
Head Office: Voznesenskiy pr., 16
Tel 314-60-95
Fax 110-49-69
Telex.................................121353 LSB SU
Hrs: 9-18

Stankinbank
Baskov per., 12.............................. 273-16-71
Fax 275-55-23
Mon-Fri 10-13; Eng, Ger

TECHNOCHIMBANK

Nab. Krasnogo Flota, 10................. 311-68-36
Tel/Fax 311-69-94

Tekobank, *Mon-Fri 9:30-13*
Ispolkomskaya ul., 7/9 271-18-75
Fax 271-48-10
Tokobank, *Mon-Fri 9:30-12:30*
Zagorodnyy pr., 5 112-43-80
Vikingbank, *Mon-Fri 9:30-15:30*
Reki Moyki nab., 72 314-73-88
Fax 314-61-31
Vladimirskiy pr., 17......................... 310-31-71

Vitabank, *Mon-Fri 9:30-13; Eng, Fr*
Gertsena ul., 59.............................. 311-51-93
Fax.. 311-83-61
Vneshtorgbank, *Mon-Fri 9:30-13; Eng, Ger, Fr*
Gertsena ul., 29.............................. 314-60-59
Fax.. 312-78-18

☎ BARBER SHOPS

See HAIRCUTTING

☎ BARS
БАРЫ
BARS
BARS
BARER
BAARIT

There are many types of "bars" in St. Pb.
from the 61 simple bars (bary, бары) and
beer joints (pivnoy bar, пивной бар) and
smoky grill bars to authentic German
"Bierstubes" and English pubs with beer on
tap, sophisticated hotel bars and swinging
"Night Bars" and "Night Clubs" with live
music and dancing.

Westerners tend to gather at "hard
currency only". Western-style bars located
in hotels and restaurants. There are many
good "ruble" bars and restaurants with a
more limited selection accepting rubles
which serve wine, champagne, cognac, and
vodka. Sometimes, imported liquor is sold
for hard currency and meals for rubles.

Imported Draught Beer. While most bars
have imported beer in bottles and cans,
some bars and restaurants have imported
draught beer on tap. These are noted after
the name, e.g., Carlsberg

HOTEL BARS

Angleterre at the Hotel Astoria *Carlsberg*
Gertsena ul., 39.............................. 210-59-06
Mon-Fri 12-1, 8-2; $, CC; Eng
The Astoria Night Bar, *Block B*
Gertsena ul., 39.............................. 311-42-06
Live Music & Dancing; 22-5; $, CC; Eng, Ger
Bavaria at the Hotel Sovetskaya *Warsteiner*
Lermontovskiy pr., 43 259-22-25
Daily 12-3
Carlsberg at the Hotel Saint Petersburg
Vyborgskaya nab., 5/2.................... 542-90-55
Fax.. 248-80-02
Mon-Fri 8-14, 15-2; $; Eng
The Bar at the Grand Hotel Europe
One of the most elegant places to meet in St. Pb.
Mikhaylovskaya ul, 1/7 119-60-00
Hotel Kareliya, 2nd floor
Marshala Tukhachevskogo ul., 27/2 226-57-31
Mon-Fri 12-2; $; Eng, Ger, Finn
Hotel Kareliya, 8th floor
Marshala Tukhachevskogo ul., 27/2 226-30-78
Mon-Fri 24-6, 9-21; $; Eng
Hotel Kareliya, 11th floor
Marshala Tukhachevskogo ul., 27/2 226-30-79
Mon-Fri 12-24; Rbls
Hotel Moskva, *Stella*
Aleksandra Nevskogo pl., 2 274-00-26
Mon-Fri 9-4; $; Eng, Ger, Finn

Hotel Pribaltiyskaya Bars
Night Club, Mon-Sat 20-4; $; Eng
Night Bar, 15 floor, *Heineken*
   Daily 18-8; Rbls, $, CC; Eng, Ger; A-6
Panorama Bar, 15th floor
   Great view of Gulf. Mon-Fri 8-4; $; Eng;
Stella Beer Bar, Daily 8-4; Rbls, $
Korablestroiteley ul., 14 356-30-01

Hotel Sovetskaya, *Mon-Fri, Sun 14-17; Rbls*
Lermontovskiy pr., 43/1, 6th floor 259-39-15

Summertime rendezvous
under the midnight sun.
Open daily, 15.00 to 03.00,
mid-May until mid-Sept.

Hotel Olympia, Sea Glory
Square, 199106 St.Petersburg,
Russia. Phone: 119 68 00.

OTHER BARS

The Beer Garden, *Carlsberg & Lapin Kulta*
   With outdoor bar, live music in restaurant
Nevskiy pr., 86 275-76-20
   Daily 14-2; Metro Mayakovskaya; $
The Beer Stube
   Carlsberg, Pripps & non-alcoholic beer
Nevskiy pr. 57, 1 st floor Nevskij Palace
☎ ....Ext. 115, 275-20-01
   Tues-Thurs 12-1, Fri-Sat 12-3; $; Eng, Ger
Chayka, *Jever, Astra*
Griboedova kan. nab., 14 312-46-31
Daily 11-5, Winter 11-3; $; Eng, Ger;Metro Nevskiy Prospekt
Dr. Oetker Nevskiy, 40, *DAB*
Nevskiy pr., 40 312-24-57
   Daily 12-24; Rbls; Eng, Ger
Fortetsiya, *DeKoninck*
Kuybysheva ul., 7 233-94-68
   Daily 12-17, 19-24; Rbls, $
Galspe at Palanga, *Pripps, Daily 17-6*
Leninskiy pr., 127 254-55-82

JohnBull

The English Pub

Nevskiy pr., 79 164-98-77
   Hrs: 12-5, Rbls & $; English
   Metro: Ploshchad Vosstaniya

John Bull serves both John Bull & Skoll on draught.

Joy, *Three Western Bars, discotheque, casino*
Lomonosova ul., 1/28 311-35-40
   Daily 22-5; Metro Gostinyy Dvor
Kurazh, *Mon-Fri 10-22; Rbls*
Mokhovaya ul., 41 273-53-79
Leda Grill Bar, *Daily 11-23; Rbls*
Beloostrovskaya ul., 27 245-51-11
Petro Star, *Holsten, Daily 13-24; Rbls*
Bolshaya Pushkarskaya ul., 30 232-40-47
Fax... 232-10-80
Petrograd
Bolshoy pr., P.S., 17 232-34-93
Daily 9-14, 15-22; Rbls; T-bus 1; Metro Petrogradskaya
Petrovskiy
Mytninskaya nab., 3, on the ship Petrovskiy
☎ 238-47-93
   Daily 12-24; Rbls, $; Eng
Prestol Beer Hall, *Daily 10-21; Rbls*
Mayakovskogo ul., 2/94 272-27-90

Sadko's, *Falcon on draught*
   at the Grand Hotel Europe
Mikhaylovskaya ul., 1/7 119-60-00
   Daily 12-24; $; CC; Eng, Ger, Fr, Swed

Schwabski Domik, *Alpersbacher*
Krasnogvardeyskaya pl., 28/19 528-22-11
   Daily 11-2; Rbls, $; Eng, Ger
Sirin Bar, *Daily 11-23; Rbls*
1-ya Liniya, 16 213-72-82
Skif, *Zhigulevskoe on draught*
Babushkina ul., 105 262-11-48
   Daily 12-16, 17-23; Rbls; Eng
Viktoriya   **Victoria**
Bolshaya Monetnaya ul., 10 232-42-34
   Mon-Fri 10-20; Rbls
Visla Beer Restaurant
Gorokhovaya ul., 17 210-68-07
   Mon-Fri 13-23; Rbls
Warsteiner Forum, *Warsteiner*
Nevskiy pr., 120 277-29-14
   Daily 12-2; $; Eng, Ger
White Nights   **Belye Nochi**
Voznesenskiy pr., 41 314-84-32
   Daily 12-17, 18-23; Rbls
Zhiguli Beer Bar
Vladimirskiy pr., 8 113-16-68
   Mon-Fri 10-15, 16-21; Rbls; Metro Dostoevskaya

☎ BATHS, RUSSIAN
    БАНИ
    BÄDER
    BAINS
    BAD, RYSKT
    SAUNAT, VENÄLÄINEN

See also SAUNAS

*There are more than 30 "Russian baths"
in St. Petersburg. Baths of the highest
class often have a sauna room, showers*

✳ BABYLON SUPER

IMPORTED WINES & BEERS AT SUPER BABYLON
Wide selection of European wines, aperitifs by Martini and Rossi,
Heineken and many other fine beers, and tonics and mixers, sodas and
juices to make any cocktail. Get some cheese, crackers
and pretzels, too.

Mon-Sat 10-21 Sun 12-20   P.S., Malyy pr., 54 & 56 230-80-96
Exchange office   *In the former Okean store off Bolshoy Prospekt*

and a small swimming pool. Men and women always attend separately designated facilities and therefore bathing suits are not customary in the saunas or pools. Private reservations for groups are available in rubles.

Russian baths are "steam baths", while Finnish "Saunas" have hot dry air from heated rocks, onto which you can ladle water, sometimes scented with pine pitch.

Banya, *Highest class*
Olgi Forsh ul., 6 592-76-22
Wed-Sun 8-22; Rbls; Metro Prospekt Prosveshcheniya

Banya Lux No. 57,   *Wed-Sun 8-22; Rbls*
Gavanskaya ul., 5 356-63-00

Banya No. 13, *Large outdoor heated pool*
Karbysheva ul., 29 a 550-09-85

Banya No. 26
Tallinnskaya ul., 11 221-34-53

Banya No. 43,   *Daily 8-22; Rbls*
Fonarnyy per., 1 312-31-51

Banya No. 50,   *Wed-Sun 8-22; Rbls*
Malaya Posadskaya ul., 28 233-50-92

Imbir,   *Mon-Tue, Fri-Sun 8-21; Rbls*
5-ya Liniya, 42 213-42-75

Kruglye Bani   **Round Baths**
Karbysheva ul., 29 a 550-09-85
Mon-Tue, Fri-Sun 8-20; Rbls; Metro Ploshchad Muzhestva

Nevskie Bani, *First Class, Wed-Sun 8-22; Rbls*
Marata ul., 5/7 ....No ☎

Pravoberezhnye Bani
Novoselov ul., 51 266-20-87
Wed-Sun 8-22; Rbls; Metro Ulitsa Dybenko

Superlux,   *0-24; Rbls*
Chaykovskogo ul., 1 272-09-11

Termy, *Luxury class facility*
Degtyarnaya ul., 1 a 274-56-21
Daily 9-21; Rbls

☎ BATTERIES
БАТАРЕЙКИ
BATTERIEN
PILES
BATTERIER
PARISTOT

See AUTOMOBILE PARTS, ELECTRONIC GOODS, AND WATCH BATTERIES

Virtually any regular battery from standard D-cells to tiny watch batteries can be found in St. Petersburg (except for obscure hearing aid and special purpose batteries). Imported alkaline batteries tend to be expensive. A small inexpensive ($3-4) 220 volt transformer with voltage selector can be found in some kiosks.

☎ BEACHES
ПЛЯЖИ
STRÄNDE
PLAGES
STRÄNDER
UIMARANNAT

See SWIMMING

For swimming, the nearest good sand beaches are on the Gulf of Finland in nearby

Sestroretsk, Repino and Solnechnoe, about 40 minutes by train from Finlyandskiy Vokzal (Finland Station, see our map). Take a picnic or buy some snacks. For sunbathing, try a park. See PARKS. *Many people sunbathe on the small beach in front of the Peter & Paul Fortress, but don't swim there.*

☎ BEAUTY SALONS
САЛОНЫ КРАСОТЫ
SCHÖNHEITSSALONS
SALONS DE BEAUTE
SKÖNHETSSALONGER
KAUNEUSHOITOLAT

See MEDICAL CONSULTATIONS

For women's hairdressers and beauty salons, see HAIR SALONS. *The so-called "cosmetic salons" (Kosmeticheskie salony, Косметические салоны) have nothing to do with cosmetics, but instead involve plastic surgery and dermatology.*

☎ BED & BREAKFAST
ПАНСИОН С ЗАВТРАКОМ
ÜBERNACHTUNG MIT FRÜHSTÜCK
CHAMBRE AVEC PETIT DEJEUNER
PENSIONAT/RUM MED FRUKOST
YÖPYMINEN AAMIAISINEEN

See also DACHA RENTALS, HOTELS *and* MOTELS

Many families are now opening up their homes to foreign visitors as "bed and breakfasts". Some services will arrange the invitation necessary for obtaining a VISA, provide you with a private room in an apartment, or sometimes an entire fully furnished apartment, and provide as many meals as you want. Often they will guide you around the city, arrange for tickets, get translators, and arrange meetings with people in business and government. Be clear about what is included in the cost of an overnight's stay.

There are organizations in many foreign countries who can arrange such home stays. There is at least one you can call directly in St. Petersburg. You can often find people offering a room to stay in at the Moskovskiy Vokzal or advertised in the newspapers. The prices can be very reasonable.

Host Families Association
Stay with English or French speaking, college educated host families in St. Petersburg, Pskov, Moscow, Vladimir, Irkutsk, Kiev, Minsk, Vilnius, Riga, Tallinn, Alma-Ata, Bishkek, Tashkent, Samarkand and Bukhara. Home Meals, Family Car, Cultural Program, Family & Professional Guide, Russian Tutor Apartments Arranged, Visa Invitations

Tel/Fax .... (812) 275-19-92

ST. PETERSBURG'S
MODERN BUDGET
"WESTERN STYLE" **ЯUSSIAN**
YOUTH HOSTEL
An American-Russian Joint Project

Tourist visas available!

3rd Sovetskaya Ulitsa, 28	277-05-69
Fax	277-51-02
International Reservation in USA..+1 (310) 379-4316	
Fax	+1 (310) 379-8420

☎ BEEPERS
БИПЕРЫ
BEEPER
BEEPER
PERSONSÖKARE
HAKULAITTEET

Pocket pagers or beepers have arrived in St. Petersburg although service has not yet begun. For equipment try the following:

Absolyut St. Petersburg
Kosmonavtov pr., 54 264-65-15
Beepers are sold on the third floor of the Children's Clinic and are available only with answering machines. Beepers are imported from Taiwan; the answering machines from Japan. Mon-Fri 10-19; Rbls; T-bus 45

MKS St. Petersburg, *Beepers from Hong Kong*
16-ya Liniya, 11 213-64-47
Mon-Fri 10-17: Rbls; Eng

Seldom
Kutuzova nab., 10 275-31-67
Fax 275-09-73
Mon-Fri 10-18; Rbls, $; Eng; Metro Chernyshevskaya

Venta, *Chinese beepers and Japanese phones*
Kosygina pr., 28 bldg., 1 521-09-16
Fax 521-77-62
Mon-Fri 10-17; Rbls, Metro Ladozhskaya

☎ BEER

ПИВО
BIER
BIERE
ÖL
OLUT

See BARS, ALCOHOL, BEVERAGES

Dozens of imported beers from Bud and Beck's to Tuborg and Stella Artois are sold in kiosks and shops. Even more unknown brands are bottled especially for the Russian market.

Draught Beer. A dozen or more different imported draught beers are now available in St. Petersburg. Draught beers are given for each bar where available. See BARS.

Russian Beer. Most Russian beer (pivo, пиво) is unpasteurized and should be enjoyed fresh and cold. It's inexpensive and declared "excellent" by some cognoscenti and an "acquired taste" by others. According to our staff the best Russian beers in St. Petersburg are: Baltika Originalnoe (pasteurized), Tverskoe, Nevskoe, Martovskoe, Petrovskoe, Admiralteyskoe, Novgorodskoe and Rizhskoe. Western brewing techniques are being introduced (Baltika). Russian beverage bottles are recycled.

UniRem Beer

Wholesale Distributors of the Famous European Beer "Kronenbourg"

Nab. kan. Griboedova, 27
Tel: 314-72-68; Fax: 312-79-58

☎ BERIOZKA SHOPS
ВАЛЮТНЫЕ МАГАЗИНЫ
БЕРЕЗКА
BERIOZKA- GESCHÄFTE (DEVISEN)
BERIOZKA, BOUTIQUE
AFFÄRER HÅRDVALUTA
BERIOZKA SHOP

See INTERNATIONAL SHOPS

Beriozka shops were a monopoly of hard currency shops run by a former state trade organization to sell Russian art, handicraft, jewelry, vodka, cigarettes and a selection of other imported goods for hard currency. At present, the system is being "reorganized" and privatized. For a complete listing, see INTERNATIONAL SHOPS.

☎ BEVERAGES / SOFT DRINKS
НАПИТКИ
GETRÄNKE
BOISSONS
DRYCKER
VIRVOITUSJUOMAT

See also ALCOHOL

Beer, Mineral Water, Juice (sok, сок), Coca-Cola & Pepsi, fruit punch (Limonad, Лимонад) are sold everywhere including shops called Mineral Water (Mineralnye Vody, Минеральные Воды), Fruit Juice & Water (Soki-Vody, Соки-Воды), and Fruit Juice (Soki-Frukty, Соки-Фрукты). Some have been taken over by a chain of stores called "Germes" which sells drinks and snacks.

Pepsi, Coca Cola, and imitations, however, are battling for the Russian market, and imported soft drinks have flooded the kiosks and state shops. This has driven many domestic beverages out of the shops including juices (soki, соки), salty mineral water and kvas (квас) (lightly fermented drink made from rye bread and raisins).

Tea (chay, чай) and coffee (kofe, кофе) are very popular in Russia with tea being the national drink. The Russians prepare very strong tea in a small tea pot, kept warm on top of an electric samovar. This is diluted with hot water and lots of sugar. Lemon is considered a treat.

Coca-Cola Saint Petersburg Bottlers
Shpalernaya ul., 55, 2nd floor 278-18-99
Fax 274-26-78
Mon-Fri 9-18; Rbls; Eng

East-Rest Beverage Distributor
Podolskaya ul., 23 292-63-22
Daily 10-18; $
Markit (wholesale)
Reki Moyki nab., 48 312-46-16
Melpomeny Tradehouse
Vladimirskiy pr., 12........................ 164-65-85
Mon-Sat 10-14, 15-20; Rbls
Mineralnye Vody   Mineral Water
Kamennoostrovskiy pr., 20 232-60-13
Daily 10-14, 15-19; Rbls
Pepsi Bottlers, *Mon-Fri 13-15; Rbls*
Marshala Tukhachevskogo ul., 4 226-57-44
Saint Petersburg-Pure Water
Tavricheskaya ul., 10 275-40-55
Mon-Fri 9-18
Soki-Frukty   Fruit and Fruit Juice Shop
Bolshaya Konyushennaya ul., 6...... 311-54-39
Mon-Sat 8:20-14, 15-20; Rbls

☎ **BICYCLING (Rentals, Clubs)**
ВЕЛОСИПЕДЫ, ПРОКАТ,
КЛУБЫ
FAHRRADVERLEIH, CLUB
BICYCLETTE, LOCATION DE
CYKELAFFÄRER
PYÖRÄILY (VUOKRAUS, KERHOT)

See also RENTALS

Regular bicycles can be bought in SPORTS
EQUIPMENT SHOPS *and* DEPARTMENT STORES.

*Touring, racing, and "mountain" bikes
and bicycling clothes can be bought in a
"market" held on Thursdays from 4 p.m. to
8 p.m. (best time around 6) at a little park
on the left hand side of Korolenko ul. off
Nekrasova ul. and Liteynyy pr.*

*You can rent bicycles from the following
organizations for a modest sum. The 1st
and 2nd are sport schools for children, the
3rd is the Sports Club "Burevestnik" which
also organizes bicycling tours.*

Admiralteets, *Rental,   Daily 16-18; Rbls*
Truda pl., 6 311-25-90
Bicycling at the Sport-School for Girls
Vyborgskoe shosse, 34 553-69-94
Rental; Daily 15-22; Rbls
Burevestnik Cycling Club
Cycling school for children, cycling tours
Engelsa pr., 81 554-17-41
Daily 10-18; Rbls
Motolyubitel   Auto Enthusiast
Apraksin Dvor, bldg. 1, sect. 50-63.... 310-06-31
Mon-Sat 10-14, 15-19; Rbls
Profi-Tandem, *Cycling tours,   Daily 9-21*
Lensoveta ul., 10 293-72-95
Sport, *Mon-Sat 10-14, 15-19; Rbls*
Shaumyana pr., 2........................... 224-28-74

☎ **BOAT EXCURSIONS**
ЭКСКУРСИИ ВОДНЫЕ
BOOTSAUSFLÜGE
EXCURSIONS EN BATEAU
BÅTTURER
VESIREITIT

See RIVER TERMINALS

*St. Petersburg is the Venice of the North
and many firms now offer boat trips on the
canals and rivers as well as hydrofoils out
on the Gulf of Finland to Petrodvorets. The
large sightseeing tours leave from piers
opposite the Hermitage & the Square of the
Decembrists* (Ploshchad Dekabristov E-6)
*which has the famous Bronze Horseman
statue of Peter the Great.*

Trips on the canals. *Many canal boat
trips in small motor boats leave from the
corner of Nevskiy & Fontanka at the
Anichkov Bridge* H-5. *See ads for boat trips.*

To Petrodvorets *(May to October). The
hydrofoil to Petrodvorets leaves from the
Neva Embankment* F-6 *opposite the Hermitage every 30 minutes beginning at 9:20
in the morning. As of June 1993 it cost
1,000 rubles. You cannot buy tickets in
advance. Admission to the park is an
additional charge.*

To Kronshtadt *(May to October). With
the proper passes, you can take the hydrofoil "Meteor" to the* **restricted city of** *Kronshtadt. It leaves from the Tuchkov Most
dock on Vasilevskiy Ostrov, next to the
Hotelship Peterhof, from 6:30 to 21:05.
Boats leave every 30-40 minutes.*

Boating Excursions on the Neva. *Boat
excursions on the Neva leave either from
the Dvortsovaya Embankment opposite the
Hermitage Museum or a bit further west
near the Admiralty. The schedule in the
summer is about every two hours.*

A Night Trip on the Neva. *During the
summer and especially during the White
Nights, there are boats tours at night on the
Neva and canals. One trip leaves from the
Dvortsovaya Embankment (near the
Hermitage) at 10:00 p.m. and lasts about 1
hour. Another leaves from Anichkov Bridge
at 12 midnight, returning at 5 a.m..*

ae aqua·excurs

Explore the rivers and canals
of St. Petersburg any time of the day.
Excursions begin from
Nevskiy Prospect near Kazan Cathedral.
Tours in English
Reki Moyki nab., 8 314-56-45
.... 292-30-54
Reservations: 9-22, May - October, $

Passazhirskiy Port
Kutuzova nab., 14 311-87-71

REGATA
Nab. Maloy Nevki
at Kamennoostrovskiy Bridge
271-75-65

Saint Petersburg
Isaakievskaya pl., 1 312-36-66

☎ BOAT RENTALS
ЛОДКИ, ПРОКАТ
BOOTSVERLEIH
BATEAUX, LOCATION
BÅTUTHYRNING
VENEEN VUOKRAUS

See PARKS, BOAT EXCURSIONS, *and*
YACHT CLUBS

*Row boats can be rented in Moskovskiy
Park Pobedy, Primorskiy Park Pobedy, and
Park TsPKO. For sail boats see,* YACHT
CLUBS.

---

aqua·excurs

Explore the rivers and canals
of St. Petersburg any time of the day.
Excursions begin from
Nevskiy Prospect near Kazan Cathedral.
Tours in English

Reki Moyki nab., 8 314-56-45
.... 292-30-54

Reservations: 9-22, May - October, $

☎ BOOK BINDERS
КНИГИ, ПЕРЕПЛЕТ
BUCHBINDEREIEN
RELIURE, ATELIER DE
BOKBINDARE
KIRJANSITOMOT

*Book binders abound in St. Petersburg.
Book binding is called* Pereplet, (Переплет).

Book Binding   **Pereplet**
• Detskaya ul., 28 217-05-24
Mon-Fri 8:30-16; Rbls; Tram 40; Metro Vasileostrovskaya
• Lanskoe shosse, 20 246-20-18
Mon-Tue 9-18; Rbls; T-bus 6, 31; Metro Chernaya Rechka
• Nekrasova ul., 41 279-54-53
• Sedova ul., 37 560-33-03
Mon, Wed-Fri 11-14, 15-19; Rbls
• Zaozernaya ul., 4 292-56-74
Mon-Fri 10-16; Rbls, $
Knigolyub Book Binding
Rybatskaya ul., 4 230-71-24
Mon-Fri 10-18; Rbls; T-bus 7; Metro Petrogradskaya
Vial Book Binding, *Mon-Sat 11-14, 15-19; Rbls*
Belinskogo ul., 11 272-35-92

☎ BOOKS
КНИГИ
BUCHHANDLUNGEN
LIVRES
BÖCKER
KIRJAKAUPAT

*Book sellers line the street around Dom
Knigi selling books of interest to residents
and tourists alike. For old books and
second hand books, see* ANTIQUARIAN SHOPS.

*Note, most Western books can not be
found in St. Petersburg. See* TRAVEL BOOKS
*for recommendations on what to bring.
There is a chain of general bookstores
called "books" (kniga, книга).*

Akademkniga   **Academic Books**
• Liteynyy pr., 57 272-36-65
Scientific and Technical Literature
• Tamozhennyy per., 2 218-32-11
*Books on the humanities
Mon-Sat 10-14, 15-19; Rbls*
Bukinist, *Second Hand Books*   **Old Book Shop**
Liteynyy pr., 59 273-25-04
Mon-Sat 11-14, 15-20; Rbls
Burevestnik   **The Stormy Petrel**
Nevskiy pr., 141 277-15-22
General Book Store. Mon-Sat 10-14, 15-19; Rbls
City Antiques Book Store
Reki Moyki nab., 32 312-77-25
Mon-Sat 10-14, 15-19; Rbls; Eng
Detskiy Knizhnyy Mir
       Children's Book World
Ligovskiy pr., 105 164-23-94
Daily 10-14, 15-19; Rbls

Dom Knigi (House of Books)
Largest Selection of Books in St. Petersburg
Nevskiy pr., 28 219-94-43
Hrs: 9-20 Clsd: Sun. & first Fri. of the month; Rbls

Dom Stroitelnoy Knigi
       Construction Books
Bolsheokhtinskiy pr., 1 224-08-73
*Specializing in construction books
Daily 10-14, 15-19; Rbls*
Dom Voennoy Knigi, *Fiction*   **Military Books**
Nevskiy pr., 20 311-07-51
Mon-Sat 10-19; Rbls
Ekonomicheskaya Literatura "Business Press"
       Economics Books
Razyeszhaya ul., 16/18 312-95-00
Fax 312-41-28
Mon-Sat 11-14, 15-19; Metro Vladimirskaya
Ekstern, *Fiction*
Lomonosova ul., 11 .... No ☎
Mon-Fri 10-19; Metro Dostoevskaya
Energia   **Energy**
Moskovskiy pr., 189 293-01-47
Technical, art, politics & more; Mon-Sat 10-14, 15-19;
Gelios   **Helios**
Bolshevikov pr., 19 588-57-07
Literature of all kinds; Mon-Sat 10-14, 15-19;
Gippokrat, *Medical Books*   **Hippokrat**
Lenina ul., 20 232-54-69
Mon-Sat 10-14, 15-19; Rbls
Grenada Politics, *poetry and literature for all ages*
Soyuza Pechatnikov ul., 6 114-51-14
Mon-Sat 10-14, 15-19
Iskatel   **Seeker**
Reki Moyki nab., 51 312-71-14
*Subscription sales of famous author sets, stamps & coins
Mon - Sat 10-14, 15-19*
Iskusstvo   **Art Books**
Nevskiy pr., 52 311-16-51
Mon-Sat 10-14, 15-19; Rbls
Knizhnaya Lavka Pisatelya, *Modern Fiction*
       Writer's Book Corner
Nevskiy pr., 66 314-54-58
Mon-Sat 10-14, 15-19

Kniga Pochtoy   **Books by Mail**
Petrozavodskaya ul., 7 235-40-64
Books from Nauka publishers; Tues-Sat 10-14, 14-18

Knigi   **Books**
• Bolshoy pr., P.S., 34 233-41-33
• Bolshoy pr., P.S., 70-72................. 232-96-41
    Mon-Fri 10-14, 15-19
• Bolshoy Sampsonievskiy pr., 92 245-46-47
• Bolshoy Sampsonievskiy pr., 44 542-50-79
    Daily 10-19
• Liteynyy pr., 63 272-80-85
    Mon-Sat 10-14, 15-19
• Ploshchad Truda, 4 312-51-17
    Trade Union books; Mon-Fri 930-16
• Suvorovskiy pr., 17....................... 271-44-88
    Preparation books for entrance exams, and more
    Mon-Fri, 10-14, 15-19

Knigi dlya Uchiteley   **Books for Teachers**
Zagorodnyy pr., 24 112-50-32
Text books and teaching materials; Mon-Sat 10-14, 15-18

Maska, *Theater and Drama Books*   **Mask**
Nevskiy pr., 13............................. 311-03-12
    Mon-Sat 10-14, 15-19; Rbls

Mir, *Books from Eastern Europe*   **World**
Nevskiy pr., 13............................. 311-51-46
    Mon-Sat 10-14, 15-19; Rbls

Na Liteynom   **On Liteynyy**
Liteynyy pr., 61 275-38-73
    Mon-Sat 10:30-14, 15-19; Rbls; Eng

Nauka   **Science**
Liteynyy pr., 64............................ 273-50-12
    Mon-Sat 10-14, 15-19; Rbls

Otkrytka   **Post Cards**
Liteynyy pr., 63............................ 273-48-97
    Mon-Sat 10-14, 15-19; Rbls; Eng
    T-bus 22; Metro Ploshchad Vosstaniya

Planeta

Liteynyy pr., 30 273-88-15
....273-88-10
A Large Variety of Imported Books.
Mon-Sat 10-14, 15-19; Rbls; Eng, Ger, Fr

Plakat, *Posters*   **Poster**
Lermontovskiy pr., 38................... 251-94-97
    Mon-Fri 10-14, 15-19; Rbls; Eng; T-bus 3;
Podpisnye Izdaniya, *Book subscriptions*
Liteynyy pr., 57 273-50-53
    Subscriptions to all types of book sets
    Mon-Sat 10-14, 15-19

RAPSODIYA

Sheet Music and Music Books.

Bolshaya Konyushennaya, 13......... 314-48-01

Staraya Kniga, *Second hand books*   **Old Books**
Nevskiy pr., 18............................. 312-66-76
    Daily 10-14, 15-19; Rbls

Sudostroitel   **Shipbuilder**
Sadovaya ul., 40 315-31-17
    Books on Shipbuilding & Fiction
    Mon-Sat 9-20; Rbls

Tekhnicheskaya Kniga   **Technical Books**
Pushkinskaya ul., 2....................... 164-65-65
    Books on electronics, computers
    Mon-Sat 10-14, 15-19; Rbls

Transportnaya Kniga
         Transportation Books
Pushkinskaya ul., 20 164-98-07
    Books on transport; Mon-Sat 10-14, 15-19; Rbls

Variant   **Variant**
Komsomola ul., 15.......................... 542-49-71
    Medical and other text books, literature
    Mon-Sat 10-14, 15-19

☎ BOOKS, OLD

See ANTIQUARIAN SHOPS

☎ BOWLING
КЕГЕЛЬБАН
KEGEL UND BOWLINGBAHNEN
BOWLING
BOWLING
KEILAILU

Bowling at Kirov Stadium
Morskoy pr., 1 235-68-04
    Tue-Sun 14-22; Rbls, $
Bowling in Hotel Pribaltiyskaya
Korablestroiteley ul., 14.................356-16-63
Fax..356-03-72
    Daily 12-22; $; Eng, Ger, Fr

☎ BRIDGES
МОСТЫ
BRÜCKEN
PONTS
BROAR
SILLAT

There are about 332 bridges (Bridge, Most, Мост) in St. Petersburg; 21 are draw bridges.

The main bridges over the Neva and Nev-ka Rivers in the city are raised between April and November (depending on ice and weather) to allow ships to sail up the rivers from the Baltic Sea. This causes major problems in getting home across the rivers late at night. On the 1st & 2nd of May, 7th & 8th of November holidays, the bridges are not raised. Call 063 + your number for (pay) information on bridge openings. The main bridges are listed below. The first group of bridges are opened according to schedules. The other bridges are opened at night only as needed.

DAILY DRAW BRIDGE OPENINGS:
(APRIL - NOVEMBER)

Aleksandra Nevskogo Most, J-5 ....2:35-4:50
Birzhevoy (Stroiteley) Most,
        F-7 2:25-3:20 & 3:40-4:40
Bolsheokhtinskiy 2:45-4:55
Dvortsovyy (Palace) Most
        F-6 1:35-3:05 & 3:15-4:45
Finlyandskiy Most (Railway Bridge)
        K-3,4 2:35-4:45
Ladozhskiy Most   *(30 km from St. Petersburg*
on Murmanskoe shosse)   8:00-9:00, 14:00-15:00
Leytenanta Shmidta Most E-6 1:55-4:50
Liteynyy (Foundry) Most H-7 2:10-4:40
Troitskiy (Kirovskiy) Most F-10 2:00-4:40
Tuchkov Most.............E-7 2:00-3:10 & 3:40-4:40
Volodarskiy Most.............Out of map 2:00-5:50

DRAW BRIDGE OPENINGS BY REQUEST
(APRIL - NOVEMBER)

Bolshoy Petrovskiy C-9	**Grenaderskiy Most** G-9
Elagin 1 C-11	**Kamennoostrovskiy Most** E-10
Elagin 2 D-10	**Kantemirovskiy Most** F-10
Elagin 3 C-9	**Krestovskiy Most** D-9

FAMOUS BRIDGES OVER RIVERS & CANALS

Anichkov Most *(1849/50) - Four bronze horses and riders on Nevskiy Prospect over Fontanka. A meeting place for Russians and tourists.* H-5

Lomonosovskiy Most *(1785-87) - Stone bridge over Fontanka.* G-5

Siniy Most *(1842-44) - This is the widest bridge in St. Petersburg & forms part of St. Isaac's Square. It crosses Moyka River* F-5

Kazanskiy Most *(1765/66) - Over Griboedova Canal on Nevskiy Prospekt in the heart of St. Petersburg.* G-6

Bankovskiy Most *(1825/26) - Foot bridge over Griboedova Canal with four gilded Griffins.* G-5

Lion Most *(1825/26) - Foot bridge with four lion figures over Griboedova Canal.* E-5

☎ BROKERS
БРОКЕРСКИЕ КОНТОРЫ
MAKLER
AGENTS DE CHANGE
MÄKLARE
MEKLARIPALVELU

Alexander
Konnogvardeyskiy blvd., 4, apt. 13
.... 311-61-50
.... 312-26-70
Fax 311-78-22

Alfa
Reki Fontanki nab., 7 314-02-01
Fax 312-39-12
Mon-Thu, Sat-Sun 9:30-17:30; Rbls, $; Eng, Ger, Ital, Bul

Avesta, *Mon-Fri 10-17; Rbls*
Vladimirskiy pr., 18/2, apt. 28 312-15-49

BST, *Mon-Fri 10-19; Rbls, $, CC; Eng*
Shkolnaya ul., 6 246-15-32

Besik, *Mon-Fri 10-17; Rbls*
Kolokolnaya ul., 2, apt. 28 164-12-52

Bosi
1-ya Krasnoarmeyskaya ul., 11 292-56-58
.... 292-15-95
Mon-Fri 10-13, 14-18; Rbls, $

Brok Master in the Hotel Moskva
Aleksandra Nevskogo pl., 2 274-21-45
Fax 274-21-39
Mon-Fri 9:30-18; Rbls

Brok-Pozitron
Kurchatova ul., 10 552-36-05
Fax 552-88-38
Mon-Fri 9-18; Rbls, $, CC; Eng, Ger, Pol

Broker-Signal, *Mon-Fri 9-17; Rbls*
Shpalernaya ul., 52, rm. 23 273-21-24

Conbi, *Mon-Fri 9-18; Rbls; Eng, Ger*
Lesnoy pr., 64 542-88-94

Disla
5-ya Krasnoarmeyskaya ul., 20, rm. 6
☎ 292-14-52
Member: Moscow International Stock Exchange
Mon-Fri 9-17; Rbls

Inros-Broker
Kazachiy per., 9, apt. 129 272-88-15
Mon-Fri 10-18; Rbls, $, CC; Eng, Fr, Ital

Itek, *Mon-Fri 9-18; Rbls*
Manezhnyy per., 19 275-87-20

Keen Inc., *Mon-Fri 9-18; Rbls, $*
Chernyakhovskogo ul., 73 164-64-24

Kronverk St. Petersburg
Major Stock Exchanges
Gertsena ul., 56 311-70-27
Mon-Fri 10-19; Rbls, $; Eng, Ger, Fr, Finn, Swed, Ital

Kuban
Morskaya nab., 15, entr. 10 356-53-60
Mon-Fri 10:30-17:30; Rbls, $, CC; Eng, Ger

L.O.V.E. Enterprises
192281 St. Pb. P.O. Box 83 172-54-51
Business Consulting, Brokerage, Promotion &
Presentation Group

Miko
Nevskiy pr., 41, entr. 2, rm. 1 315-57-55
Mon-Fri 9-18; Rbls, $; Metro Mayakovskaya

Montazhsnab, *Mon-Fri 8:30-19:30; Rbls*
Apraksin per., 4 310-73-00

On Liteynyy-57
Liteynyy pr., 57 273-06-94
Mon-Fri 9-12, 13-17; Rbls, $; Eng, Ger, Fr
T-bus 3; Metro Vladimirskaya

Orimi-Broker
Kostyushko ul., 3, bldg. 2 290-78-55
Mon-Sat 10-18; Rbls, $; Eng, Ger

Orion
Ligovskiy pr., 87 164-12-85

Peter-West Brok, *Mon-Fri 9-18; Rbls; Eng, Fr*
26-ya Liniya, 9 a 217-17-54

Roster, *Mon-Fri 9-19; Rbls*
Griboedova kan. nab., 15 314-52-96

Sampo, *Mon-Fri 9:30-17; Rbls, $, CC; Eng*
Bolshoy pr., V.O., 83, off. 336 217-58-20

Spektr
Blagodatnaya ul., 40 528-84-54
Brokerage Services for St. Petersburg and
Kaliningrad Stock Exchanges
Mon-Fri 9-17; Rbls, $

St. Petersburg Brokerage Company
8-ya Liniya, 61 213-06-13
Mon-Sat 9:30-18; Rbls

Trust-Center, *Mon-Fri 9:30-12:30; Rbls*
Babushkina ul., 3 567-21-34

Trilogika, *Mon-Fri 10-18; Rbls*
Millionnaya ul., 27, apt. 46 184-06-88

Vostok
Tavricheskaya ul., 39, rm. 347 271-41-04

Zarto, *Mon-Fri 9:30-17:30; Rbls*
Lermontovskiy pr., 54 259-94-97

☎ BUILDING SUPPLIES
СТРОИТЕЛЬНЫЕ МАТЕРИАЛЫ
BAUSTOFFE
CONSTRUCTION, MATERIAUX DE
BYGGNADSMATERIAL
RAKENNUSTARVIKKEET

See also HARDWARE STORES *and* PAINT STORES

Building supplies and lumber are bought in shops called "building materials" (Stroymaterialy, Стройматериалы) *and in the increasing number of private shops. The supply and quality of domestic lumber, bricks, and hardware is variable, an increasing supply of imported materials is available.*

Adamant, *Bosch electrical supplies, tools*
8-ya Sovetskaya ul., 9 279-27-82
Mon-Fri 10-19; $

Alisa - Petersburg

Home Building Supplies
Wholesale Distributors

• *Rugs*

• *Decorating Materials*

• *Lacquer Paint Products*

ПЕТЕРБУРГ • *Appliances*

Zanevskiy pr., 6 221-47-01
.... 528-77-38
Fax 528-62-11

Avesta, *Metal Structures,   Mon-Fri 10-17; Rbls*
Vladimirskiy pr., 18/2, apt. 28 312-15-49

Ca Gi Ve
Nevskiy pr., 49/2........................... 113-15-79
Bathroom fixtures, drywall, insulation from Italy
Mon-Sat 10:30-13, 14:30-19:30; Rbls, $; Ital

A/O ELEMENT
Precast Element Manufacturing
Tsentralnaya ul., 6, Promzona Parnas
Tel./Fax... 598-86-13

Elias
Lermontovskiy pr., 9 113-80-06
Fax 113-80-05
Electrical appliances, tiles, windowsills, door frames
Daily 10-14, 15-19; Rbls; Eng

Hilti, *Electric construction tools*
Dekabristov per., 20........................ 350-58-86
Mon-Fri 9-13, 14-19; Rbls, $; Eng, Ger

Home ☐ Center- *See ad below*

Iskra-Soft, *Linoleum, wallpaper, rugs*
Lesnoy pr., 65, bldg. 6 f 245-36-82
Daily 10-20; Rbls

Komfort
Pestelya ul., 10/23 272-89-02
Electrical goods, housewares, door locks, glass and mirrors cut to size; Mon-Fri 10-14, 15-19

LEN-BERG
Manufacturer of Premium Building Supplies
Kalinina ul., 22 186-74-49

Lenfinstroy, *Lumber*
8-ya Krasnoarmeyskaya ul., 23 113-01-55
Mon-Fri 9-18:Rbls, $; Eng

LES Company
Custom Wood Floors Using Laser Technology
Engelsa pr., 154a............515-24-33

Marshal, *Marble, granite, travertine*
Furshtadskaya ul., 43 275-35-30
Mon-Fri 9-21; Rbls

Home ☐ Center

The Complete Hardware Source

Wide selection of tools including
Ryobi electric hand tools, Stanley and
Ironside tools including chisels, levels,
pliers, cutters, planes, screwdrivers,
hammers, axes, hex wrenches, socket
wrenches, and more

Items For The Dacha,
McCulloch chain saws, pruning shears,
rakes, shovels, and portable gas stoves and
wood stoves, a bocci set and English darts.

Hardware For The Home
from door sets and heavy duty locks to
nails, screws, nuts and bolts.

Large Electrical Supply and Parts Dept

Plumbing Supplies and Fixtures
PVC pipe and fittings

Complete Paint Department
Custom-Mixed Paints

Located in S.E. St. Pb., minutes from city center
Slavy pr., 30...................... 261-15-50
.... 261-04-02
Fax 260-15-81
Daily 10-20; $, FIM, DM, Rbls; Eng, Finn, Ger
Metro Moskovskaya, then Bus 31, 114, T-bus 29

METRA Engineering
• Mechanical engineering
• Building material technology
• Porcelain bathroom fixtures
Bolshoy Sampsonievskiy pr., 31
Tel... 542-06-59
Tel/Fax.. 542-68-42

Mipros, *Metal structures*
Lenina pr., 101, Kolpino 484-91-04
Fax.. 484-18-88
Mon-Fri 9-18; Rbls, $; Eng, Ger, Fr

Okhta
Bolshaya Pushkarskaya ul., 20 232-01-47
Fax... 277-23-12
Italian bathroom fixtures, Mon-Fri 10-19; Rbls, $

Plumbing Center
Tukhachevskogo ul., 22 225-15-15
American bathroom fixtures; Mon-Sat 11-20; Rbls

Renlund
Bolshaya Zelenina ul., 14................ 232-36-07
Finnish fixtures and building materials to meet all your needs; Mon-Fri 10-14, 15-19; Rbls, $; Finn

Rossa Trade,   *Moving in September 1993*
Khlopina ul., 11.............................. 534-10-86
Lumber; Mon-Fri 9-19; Rbls, $

Salon Store,   *Mon-Sat 10-14, 15-19; Rbls*
Krasnykh Zor blvd., 8/10 267-39-56

Spicc, *Glass*
Makarenko per., 9 114-44-55

Stroitelnye Materialy   Building Supplies
Here you can find a variable supply of goods from paint to electrical appliances.
• Babushkina ul., 71 262-16-22
Mon-Sat 10-19; Rbls

- Baskov per., 36 279-18-56
  Paint, lacquer; Mon-Sat 10-18; Rbls
- Grecheskiy pr., 27 271-21-74
  Mon-Sat 10-19; Rbls
- Kultury pr., 29, bldg. 1 559-93-88
  Tile, lumber, paint; Mon-Sat 10-19
- Mokhovaya ul., 28 273-40-26
  Bathroom fixtures, doors; Mon-Sat 10-14, 15-19
- Moskovskiy pr., 4 310-17-29
  Paint, tiles, bathroom fixtures
  Mon-Sat 10-14, 15-19; Rbls
- Moskovskiy pr., 134 298-21-15
  Electrical appliances; Mon-Sat 10-19; Rbls
- Stachek pr., 54 184-82-69
  Tiles, paint; Mon-Fri 10-19; Rbls

Supplies for Apartment Renovation
Reki Chernoy nab., 6 239-84-90
  Mon-Sat 11-19; Rbls

Vesta Tradehouse
Lanskoe shosse, 16 246-32-48
Fax 242-17-63
  Wallpaper, rugs, tile, bathroom fixtures
  Mon-Fri 10-14, 15-19; Rbls, $; Eng

ZODCHIY

BUILDING SUPPLY STORE

- Hanging Grid Ceilings
- Partitions for Banks & Offices
- Floor & Wall Coverings for Greater
  Warmth & Sound Insulation
- High Quality Building
  & Decorating Supplies

Zagorodnyy pr., 1
Tel.: 311-60-98   Tel/Fax: 314-41-33
Hrs: 9-24, Rbls & $

Joint-Stock Company UniRem

☎ **BUS & MINIVAN CHARTER**
АВТОБУСЫ, ПРОКАТ
BUSVERLEIH, KLEINBUSVERLEIH
BUS ET MICROBUS, BAIL
BUSS OCH SKÅPBILAR ATT HYRA
LINJA-AUTOJEN JA MINIBUSSIEN
VUOKRAUS

See also AUTOMOBILE RENTAL

FINNORD
BUS & MINIVAN CHARTERS

**TO FINLAND & FOR EXCURSIONS
ST. PETERSBURG & SUBURBS**
Beautiful Comfortable Coaches

Italyanskaya ul., 37 314-89-51
Fax 314-70-58
Telex .... 121496 FIRD, SU
  Hrs. 9 - 18, English, Finnish

Intourist Transport
Sedova ul., 5 567-82-46
  567-82-26
Fax 567-88-97
  Mon-Fri 8-16:30; Rbls, $; Eng, Ger

MATRALEN *(See our ad under TAXI)*
Lyubotinskiy proezd, 5 298-12-94
  298-36-48
  Mon-Sat 8-20; Rbls, $; Eng, Ger

☎ **BUSES (City & Municipal)**
АВТОБУСЫ, ГОРОДСКИЕ
BUSVERBINDUNGEN, STADT
BUS (MUNICIPAL)
BUSSAR LOKALTRAFIK
LINJA-AUTOT, LÄHILIIKENNE

People rely largely on public transportation in St. Petersburg and the city and nearby suburbs are covered with bus, tram and trolley bus routes. In addition to the regular buses, there are red express busses (Экспресс) that charge higher prices, are uncrowded and stop upon request. "Marshrutnoe" taxi mini-buses follow a fixed route, e.g. to the airport

Paying for the bus. You need one coupon (talon, талон) for each ride, or use a monthly transportation card. Coupons and cards can be bought in some kiosks, in the metro or from bus drivers. See TRAM and METRO for further information on how to use public transportation.

Bus Stops are denoted by "A" on the side of the street and its routes are usually listed on signs. Note that due to budget cutbacks, some lines have been discontinued. Bus lines operating as of June 1993 are noted on our Traveller's Yellow Pages City Map. See MAPS for the best public transport map.

TRANSPORT SIGNS

| BUS | TRAM | TROLLEYBUS |
| Автобус | Трамвай | Троллейбус |

☎ **BUSES INTERCITY &
INTERNATIONAL**
АВТОБУСЫ, МЕЖДУГОРОДНЫЕ
И МЕЖДУНАРОДНЫЕ
BUSVERBINDUNGEN, ÜBER LAND
BUS, LONGUE DISTANCE
BUSSAR, INRIKES
LINJA-AUTOT, KAUKOLIIKENNE

Buses serve many of the nearby areas, such as Novgorod, Vologda, Narva and the Baltic States. They leave from the two terminals listed below. There is also daily express bus service to Finland (FINNORD or Sovinteravtoservice).

BUS TERMINALS - INTERCITY

Bus Terminal No 1   Avtovokzal No. 1
Buses to Vyborg, Priozersk on Lake Ladoga, Volosovo, Kingissepp and other cities in Leningrad Oblast (region)
Nab. kan. Obvodnogo, 118 292-16-83
Daily 0-24; Rbls; Metro Baltiyskaya

Bus Terminal No 2   Avtovokzal No. 2
Buses to the Northern Region, Vologda, Petrozavodsk, Estonia, Novgorod, Pskov and Pushkinskie Gory.
Nab. kan. Obvodnogo, 36 166-57-77
Daily 0-24; Rbls; Metro Ligovskaya

BUSES INTERNATIONAL

FINNORD
DAILY EXPRESS BUS

SAINT PETERSBURG
VYBORG, HELSINKI
LAKHTI (FINLAND) &
SAINT PETERSBURG

Quick, Convenient, Comfortable

Italyanskaya ul., 37 314-89-51
Fax 314-70-58
Telex ....121496 FIRD, SU
Hrs. 9 - 18, English, Finnish

Sovtransavto
SOVAVTO ST. PETERSBURG

Express Bus to Finland
St. Petersburg - Helsinki
St. Petersburg - Lappeenranta
Vyborg - Lappeenranta
The quick, comfortable way to Finland in modern new coaches at a reasonable cost.

Daily Departures to/from Helsinki
Astoria, Helen, Grand Hotel Europe and Pulkovskaya Hotel

For Reservations
Inquire at the hotel desks
or call Sovavto at.......... 298-13-52
Fax..............................298-77-60

Ticket Offices
Ploshchad Pobedy, 1,
Hotel Pulkovskaya 264-51-25
Kamennoostrovskiy pr., 39
☎ 234-1057

☎ BUSINESS ASSOCIATIONS AND CLUBS
БИЗНЕС-АССОЦИАЦИИ
WIRTSCHAFTSVERBÄNDE
BUSINESS ASSOCIATIONS DE AFFÄRSKLUBBAR
KAUPALLISET KERHOT JA YHTEISÖT

There are many "Business Associations" in St. Pb. See the business directories listed under BUSINESS PUBLICATIONS. *See also* BUSINESS CONSULTANTS, ASSOCIATIONS, CLUBS, CHAMBER OF COMMERCE, *and* INTERNATIONAL ASSOCIATIONS. *See* CONSULATES *for trade delegations and commercial attaches. A few of the larger and more active associations are listed below.*

Aveks
3-ya Krasnoarmeyskaya ul., 12.......292-48-37
Fax.....................................292-14-53
Mon-Fri 10-18; Rbls, $

Baltica
Please call....................................164-53-38
Fax.....................................311-48-64
Mon-Fri 9-17; Rbls, $; Eng

Business Association of Medium Sized Firms
Kazanskaya ul., 36, rm. 602-607 315-79-54
Fax.....................................312-07-08
Mon-Fri 9-18; Rbls, $; Eng, Ger

∬ Financial Group
JEM Holding
• Real Estate Investments
• Financial & Real Estate Brokers
• Business Consultants
10-ya Krasnoarmeyskaya ul., 11
Tel......................................113-00-33
Fax.....................................251-60-56
Hrs: 10.30-18, Rbls & $, English, German

Progress Management and Marketing Center - *See our color ad*
Institutskiy pr., 22.......................552-13-38
Mon-Fri 10-18; Rbls

Provisional Rotary Club St. Petersburg Downtown
Dvorets Truda 172-54-51
Meetings: Thurday 6:30; Eng; President: Vadim Panov

St. Petersburg American Association
Meets the 2nd Tuesday of each month at various locations.
Executive secretary 273-01-08
Fax.....................................272-80-31

St. Pb. Association of Joint Ventures
Kazanskaya ul., 36, rm. 602-605 312-79-54
Mon-Fri 9-19, Eng

St. Pb. Foreign Economic Association of Small and Medium Sized Enterprises
Zagorodnyy pr., 68.......................292-14-55
Fax.....................................113-01-14
Mon-Fri 10-18; Rbls, $; Eng, Ger, Fr

Tekhnoimpeks, Foreign Economic Association
6-ya Liniya, 27 213-06-05
Fax.....................................218-42-75
Mon-Fri 9-18; Rbls, $; Eng, Ger, Fr

☎ BUSINESS CARDS
ВИЗИТНЫЕ КАРТОЧКИ
VISITENKARTEN
CARTES DE VISITE
VISITKORT
KÄYNTIKORTIT

Business cards (vizitnye kartochki, визитные карточки) *are handed out freely in Russia. It is best to have them printed here with English on one side and Russia on the other. We print our colored logo on 80# stock in the US and then bring it to Russia for printing.*

Ayu
Voronezhskaya ul., 33 166-03-20
Mon-Fri 9-17; Rbls, $, Metro Ligovskiy Prospekt

EXPRESS-PRINT

Pushkinskaya ul., 20 113-18-08
Express Printing of Business Cards
Hrs: Mon.-Fri. 10 - 19
Metro Mayakovskaya

Institute of Printing, *Mon-Fri 10-16; Rbls*
Galernaya ul., 3 315-24-36

DESIGN & PRINTING

Printers to the banks, businesses & government of Saint Petersburg

Stationery and Business Cards
Logos & Trademarks
Kronverkskaya ul., 10 251-88-90
Fax 232-18-90
Mon-Sat 9-21; Rbls, $, CC; Eng, Ger, Fr

POLYGON®   *Design & Print Bureau*

Stationery, Business Cards, Logos, etc.
Tel 525-16-95
.... 298-57-35

Rikki-Tikki-Tavi, *Mon-Fri 9-18; Rbls, $; Eng*
Dekabristov ul., 62 219-76-92
Fax 114-19-20
Skif, *Mon-Fri 9-18; Rbls, $; Eng, Ger, Fr*
Vosstaniya ul., 32 275-53-45
Fax 275-58-71
Tram 5; Metro Chernyshevskaya
Trud, *Mon-Fri 10-17; Rbls*
Saltykova-Shchedrina ul., 30 275-77-07
Fax 275-74-34

Vial Stationers
Holographic Business Cards
Belinskogo ul., 11 278-86-80

☎ BUSINESS CENTERS
БИЗНЕС-ЦЕНТРЫ
BUSINESS CENTERS
BUSINESS CENTERS
AFFÄRSCENTER
LIIKEALAN PALVELUT

See also EXPRESS MAIL/PARCEL SERVICE, FAX SERVICES, COMPUTERS, PHOTOCOPYING, TELEPHONES, TELEX, TELEGRAM, BUSINESS CARDS, BUSINESS CONSULTANTS, OFFICES, and OFFICE EQUIPMENT.

BUSINESS CENTERS *provide temporary office space, conference rooms, communication facilities, computers, etc. to visiting businessmen. The best offer the following: all types of communications (usually by satellite), fax, secretarial support, conference rooms, translators and interpreters, computers and laser printers, photocopying, audio visual equipment and reference materials.*

 Ltd.

Project Rental Space &
Investment Assistance
On Site Business Accommodations
❖❖❖
Nevskiy pr., 176, P.O. Box 140
Tel 585-21-12
Tel/Fax 585-90-57

Alliance Business Center
at the Sovetskaya Hotel

Fax, Copies, Telex, International
Telephone, Meeting Rooms,
Rental Cars, Tourist Services
Lermontovskiy pr., 43/1 259-34-42
Fax 251-88-90
Telex .... 121705 HOTS SU

AsLANTIS

Fax Translation & Transmission
Photocopies (RISOGRAPH) & E-mail
Desk: House of Books, Ground Floor
    Nevskiy pr., 28; *Hrs: 16-20*
Dibunovskaya ul., 24, office 7
Tel./Fax 239-36-45
English, French, Metro: Chernaya Rechka

Cities of Russia - St. Petersburg Branch
Voznesenskiy pr., 41 310-74-83
Fax 272-34-76
Mon-Fri 9:30-18; Rbls

Crossroads
Poltavskaya ul., 10.........................277-41-97
Fax...273-43-04
Mon-Fri 10-18; Rbls; Eng

DHL
Griboedova kan. nab., 5, rm. 325 ... 311-26-49
....210-76-54
Fax...314-64-73
Mon-Fri 9-18; Rbls, $, CC

BUSINESS CENTER **GRAND HOTEL EUROPE**

★★★★★
ST. PETERSBURG RUSSIA

Fax, telex, photocopies, telephones, computers,
Audio-visual support and projectors
Secretaries and interpreters
Six meeting rooms

Mikhaylovskaya Street 1/7
Saint Petersburg, 191011

Info/Switchboard .... 119-60-00, Ext. 6234
Fax: 119-60-01

Hotel Helen
Lermontovskiy pr., 43/1 259-20-48
Fax...113-08-60
Mon-Fri 9-18; $; Eng

Innovations of Leningrad Institutes
Professora Popova ul., 47, rm. 1-7, floor 11
☎...234-04-96
Fax...234-98-18
Mon-Fri 9-18; Rbls, $; Eng

The LDM Complex

The LDM offers a variety of
services for businessmen & visitors
Hotel, Restaurant, Bars, Casino,
Business Center, Concert Hall,
Movie Theater, Winter Garden &
Indoor Swimming Pool

Professora Popova ul., 47 ...234-44-94
....234-97-93
Fax....................................234-98-18
Telex ....614002 LDM SU
Metro Petrogradskaya

Len-Uton
Nevskiy pr., 30..............................312-14-90
Fax...315-59-48
Daily; Eng

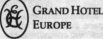 **MMIR Business Center**

A Full Range of Services for
Foreign Businessmen
Imported Product Display
Marketing & Advertising Assistance
Leninskiy pr., 161, bldg. 2.............108-54-11
....108-44-23
Fax...293-56-03
Telex...............................121665 PCSUS SU

 business centre **NEPTUN**

Hotel & Office for Business
Assistance with Business Meetings, Conferences, Presentations & Hotel Accommodations. Technical, Social & Business Consulting

Obvodnogo kan. nab., 93a.............210-17-07
Fax...311-22-70
Metro Pushkinskaya

Hotelship Peterhof ★★★★
The Business Center
Nab. Makarova, near the Tuchkov Bridge
....213-63-21

Pribaltiyskaya Hotel Business Center
Korablestroiteley ul., 14.................356-45-63
Fax...356-00-94
Rainbow International
Moskovskiy pr., 79 a.....................198-03-58
Mon-Fri 10-17:30; Rbls; Eng
Retur Business Center at the Hotel Astoria
Gertsena ul., 39, 2nd floor.............311-73-62
Fax...311-42-12
Daily 9-23; $, CC; Eng, Fr
St. Petersburg Telephone Station
Gertsena ul., 3/5............................274-93-83
Fax...315-17-01
Daily 0-24; Rbls, $; Eng
St. Petersburg Center of International Commerce
Proletarskoy Diktatury ul., 6, rm. 417-419
☎...274-19-70
Mon-Fri 9-18; Rbls, $; Eng
Smart
Admiralteyskiy pr., 8/1 110-66-55
Fax...110-65-70
Mon-Fri 10-18; Rbls, $; Eng, Ger, Fr, Finn, Swed, Ital
World Trade Center
Tambovskaya ul., 12 112-92-72
Mon-Fri 9-18; Eng

☎ BUSINESS CONSULTANTS
БИЗНЕС-КОНСУЛЬТАЦИИ
WIRTSCHAFTSBERATER
BUSINESS, CONSULTATIONS DE
AFFÄRSKONSULTER
LIIKEKONSULTAATIO

See also ACCOUNTING and LAW FIRMS.

Business consultants specialize in helping with the start up of firms, finding contacts in government and at the universities, getting information, and market surveys.

A. J. EST S.U.

Representative for

French & Spanish firms in Russia

Konnogvardeyskiy blvd., 4, Entry 6

Tel 110-64-96
Telex .... 121732 CGTT SU

ABC
Sadovaya ul., 55/57, rm. 505 310-84-36
Fax 315-77-14
Mon-Fri 9-17; Eng

Alfa-ABM
Zakharevskaya ul., 25, rm. 6 355-10-91
Mon-Fri 10-18; Rbls

Alkor
Apraksin Dvor, 33, 2nd floor 310-44-70
Fax 255-76-56
Mon-Fri 10-18; Rbls, $; Eng, Fr

Alkor - Consulting
Varshavskaya ul., 37, bldg. 1 295-83-90
Mon-Fri 10-19; Rbls, $; Eng

Alliance at the Hotel Sovetskaya
Lermontovskiy pr., 43/1 259-34-42
Fax 251-88-90
Mon-Fri 9:30-17:30; Rbls, $; Eng

Arktis
Promyshlennaya ul., 14 a 252-95-87
Fax 186-28-30
Mon-Fri 10-18; Rbls; Eng, Ger, Fr

AsLANTIS

License & Patent Law

Dibunovskaya ul., 24, office 7

Tel./Fax 239-36-45

English, French; Metro: Chernaya Rechka

Audit & Management International
Griboedova kan. nab., 34, rm. 210 110-57-20
Fax 110-57-51
Mon-Fri 9-18; Eng, Fr

BALFORT, Inc. Law Firm

Bolshoy Smolenskiy, 36

....568-04-91
Fax...568-04-93

Noted lawyers from St. Petersburg University
LL.D. A.Ivanov, LL.D. Medvedev, I.Yeliseyev

English speaking staff; weekdays: 10-18; $, Rbl

Baltic International Technopark
1-ya Krasnoarmeyskaya ul., 13 251-11-62
Fax... 315-17-01
Mon-Sat 8:30-18; Rbls, $

Bazis, *Mon-Fri 9:30-18; Rbls*
Bolshoy pr., V.O., 4 213-48-89

Bosi
1-ya Krasnoarmeyskaya ul., 11 292-56-58
Mon-Fri 10-13, 14-18; Rbls, $

Business Link Company
13-ya Liniya, 14 218-69-00
Fax... 218-79-40
Mon-Sat 9-18; Rbls, $; Eng, Ger

Business Management International
Bolshaya Konyushennaya ul., 9, rm. 50
☎ 311-40-72
Mon-Fri 8:30-18:30; Rbls, $; Eng

Businessinvest Group, *Mon-Fri 10-19*
Reki Fontanki nab., 92 164-89-56
Fax... 164-27-07

Central Europe Trust
Mayakovskogo ul., 46 275-58-20
Fax... 279-28-69
Mon-Fri 10-18:30; Rbls, $; Eng; Metro Chernyshevskaya

Concord Agency
Rubinshteyna ul., 3 315-18-32
Fax... 315-06-59
Mon-Fri 10-18; Rbls, $; Eng

Consofin T.V. Fin (Technical)
Rizhskiy pr., 58 259-91-06
Fax... 251-76-11
Mon-Fri 8:30-17; Rbls, $; Eng

Coopers & Lybrand | Solutions for Business

Moscow & St. Petersburg

Accountants, Management Consultants
Tax Advisers

In Saint Petersburg

At the Astoria Hotel, Room 528
Gertsena ul., 39 .... (812) 210-55-28
Fax.................................. (812) 210-55-28

In Moscow

Shchepkina ul., 6 .... (095) 288-98-01
Fax............................... (095) 284-52-73

Delegation der Deutschen Wirtshaft
Delegation of German Economics
Bolshoy pr., V.O., 10 213-79-93
Fax... 350-56-22
Mon-Fri 9-18; Eng, Ger

Ernst and Young
(See our ad under Accounting and Auditing Firms)
Gogolya ul., 11 312-99-11
Fax... 312-53-20
Daily 9-18; $; Eng; Bus 22, 27; Metro Nevskiy Prospekt

⬭ HS Petersburg AG

Consulting, Engineering & Development

V.O., Bolshoy pr., 9/6 218-55-37

**INTERNATIONAL
BUSINESS SERVICES**
Russian-American JV

Rubinshteyna ul., 8, 2nd floor, office 4

(812) 311-58-38, (812) 311-31-93

Fax: (812) 311-31-93

Inaudit AKG
Italyanskaya ul., 33 311-61-53
Fax 310-53-33
Mon-Fri 10-18; Rbls, $

Inkomstroy, *Mon-Fri 9-18*
Kazanskaya ul., 36, rm. 301 315-45-34

Institute of Independent Social &
Economic Investigations   **IISEI**

*Auditing - Consulting -
Tax Services - Management Training*
Kanal Griboedova, 34   Tel. 110-5720
office 210   Fax: 110-5751

Inter-Consult
Kazanskaya ul., 36, rm. 404 312-85-48
Fax 355-19-85
Mon-Fri 9-17

**International Fund For Support of
Economic Reforms in Russia**
Galernaya ul., 22, off. 52 312-33-06

Intourist-Nauka-Service
Egorova ul., 18 292-50-13
Fax 292-77-29
Mon-Fri 9-18; Rbls, $; Eng

**Lecturers Association of Innovative
Consulting Center of St. Petersburg**
Universitetskaya nab., 7/9 218-97-17

L.O.V.E. Enterprises
192281, St. Pb., P.O. Box 83 172-54-51
Fax 113-58-96
*Business Consulting, Brokerage, Promotion &
Presentation Group*

Maynor-Neva
Serpukhovskaya ul., 4 292-44-66
Fax 112-73-36
Daily 19-21; Rbls, $; Eng, Fr

MBCo Methodological & Business Consulting
We Understand the Russian Business World
Management Consulting, Evaluation of Company
Projects, Business Plans, Personnel Employment
Assistance in Negotiations
Labutina ul., 20 114-37-70
Fax 114-37-63
Hrs: 10-18, $ & Rbls, English, Norwegian

Method
Antonenko per., 6 b 312-93-12
Fax 314-74-19
Mon-Fri 10-18; Rbls, $; Eng, Ger, Fr

Natari
Antonenko per., 6 319-92-59
Fax 315-74-20
Mon-Fri 9-18; Rbls, $; Eng

Neva-Commerce
Gertsena ul., 41/11 314-93-66
Fax 312-26-11
Mon-Fri 10-17

New Saint Petersburg
Reki Fontanki nab., 76 315-77-65
Fax 315-34-00
Mon-Fri 10-18; Rbls, $; Ger

Pari
Nekrasova ul., 40 273-67-46
Mon-Fri 10-18; Rbls

Pearl Oyster on Neva
191025, P.O., Box 203 312-22-46
Mon-Fri 10-18

Permafrost Consultants - *See our ad under*
ENGINEERING CONSULTANTS

Personnel Corps
Nevskiy pr., 104 275-83-23
.... 275-45-86
Fax 275-83-23

Pinta Stock Co.
Professora Popova ul., 47 234-51-78
Mon-Fri 10-19

**Center of Management &
Marketing**

"PROGRESS"
—CMM—

Management
Training
&
Professional
Advice

Institutskiy pr., 22
Telephone:
552-13-38
552-69-62
552-28-17
Fax:
552-77-28
552-23-98

Prolog
Kamennoostrovskiy pr., 21 230-10-47
Fax 232-23-04
Mon-Fri 9:30-18; Rbls, $; Eng, Ger

Rainbow International
Moskovskiy pr., 79 a 198-03-58
Mon-Fri 10-17:30; Rbls; Eng

Reforma
Griboedova kan. nab., 32, rm. 323
☎ 110-55-90
Mon-Fri 9-18

RusTex International (USA)
Investment, Securities, & Privatization
Victor Konovalenko & Cheryl Ann Sigsbee
Tel/Fax 109-69-14

**SKL Motoren und System Technik
AG vorm Buckau-Wolf**
Stavropolskaya ul., 10 271-09-04
Fax 271-12-95
Mon-Fri 9-17; $; Ger

Selena
Liteynyy pr., 20 278-86-94
Mon-Fri 10-18; Rbls

Sigmatek
Krasnogo Flota nab., 8 312-28-73
Fax 315-27-98
Mon-Fri 10-20; Rbls, $

Smena, *Mon-Fri 9-18; Rbls, $; Eng, Nor*
Labutina ul., 20............................ 114-37-70
Soppol, *Mon-Fri 10-18; Rbls, $; Eng, Ger*
2-ya Krasnoarmeyskaya ul., 7 110-14-32
SOU, *Mon-Fri 9-18; Rbls, $*
Nevskiy pr., 177, rm. 6 277-44-94

Stern & Co
Nevskiy pr., 104............................. 275-58-64
Fax.. 275-45-87

St. Petersburg Chamber of Commerce & Industry Business Consultants
Chaykovskogo ul., 46-48................ 273-99-14

Tellus, *Daily 9-18; Rbls, $; Eng, Ger, Finn*
Egorova ul., 18 292-50-13

VANA Information A/O
VANA Public Relations
VANA Press Clipping
Millionnaya ul., 11
☎ 311-17-17, 315-95-85
Fax 311-33-91

Vneshvuz Center
Morskaya nab., 9 355-60-56
Fax 355-69-87
Mon-Fri 10-18; Rbls, $; Eng, Ger, Finn
Vostochnyy Predprinimatelskiy Express
Gogolya ul., 14 110-66-58
Mon-Fri 9-18; Rbls, $; Eng

☎ **BUSINESS INSTITUTES**
БИЗНЕС-ИНСТИТУТЫ
WIRTSCHAFTSSCHULEN
BUSINESS, INSTITUTS DE
AFFÄRSINSTITUT
KAUPALLISET OPISTOT

There are more than a dozen new private
BUSINESS INSTITUTES, *some even offering the*
equivalent of MBA's. Several are operated
jointly with Western universities. Others
teach basic secretarial, computer, and
business skills.

THE FUQUA SCHOOL OF BUSINESS
Associated with Duke University, USA
Please call 314-64-93
MBA programs in Russia

Institute of Independent Social & Economic Investigations   IISEI
Auditing - Consulting - Tax Services - Management Training
Kanal Griboedova, 34   Tel. 110-5720
office 210   Fax: 110-5751

International Banking Institute
Nevskiy pr., 58, rm. 103.................. 311-12-19

International Management Institute of
St. Petersburg (IMISP)
Smolnyy, entr. 9............................ 271-34-33
Fax.. 271-07-17
Mon-Fri 9-18; Rbls, $; Eng
MMT International
Shvetsova ul., 22 252-34-08
Mon-Fri 9-14, 15-18; Rbls, $; Eng, Ger, Fr
Polyus, *Mon-Fri 10-17; Rbls, $; Eng*
Shpalernaya ul., 24 279-36-84
PROGRESS MANAGEMENT AND
MARKETING CENTER - *See our color ad*
Institutskiy pr., 22 552-13-38
Fax.. 552-77-28
School of Managers, *Mon-Fri 10-18; Rbls, $*
Sadovaya ul., 21, rm. 336 110-55-81

![Sozidanie logo] Sozidanie
CENTER OF BUSINESS TRAINING & EDUCATION
Management School
Sadovaya ul., 21, rm. 336 110-55-81
Fax.. 110-57-33

St. Petersburg University of Finance &
Economics-Post Graduate Studies
Griboedova kan. nab., 34................ 310-52-31
Metro Nevskiy Prospekt
Vneshvuz Center
Morskaya nab. 9 355-60-56
Mon-Fri 10-18; Rbls, $; Eng, Ger, Finn
Znanie Society
                    International Business School
Bolshoy Sampsonievskiy pr., 88............No ☎

☎ **BUSINESS PUBLICATIONS**
ДЕЛОВЫЕ ИЗДАНИЯ
WIRTSCHAFTSPUBLIKATIONEN
PUBLICATIONS D'AFFAIRE
AFFÄRSFÖRLAG
KAUPALLISET JULKAISUT

See also NEWSPAPERS, MAGAZINES,
DIRECTORIES, *and* TELEPHONE BOOKS

SELECTED BUSINESS BOOKS AND
DIRECTORIES IN ENGLISH

BUSINESS CONTACT - *See ad below*
13461, Moscow, Kakhovka ul., 31
☎.. 331-89-00
Fax.. 310-70-05
Information Moscow, *One of the most useful guides*
for Moscow. pp. 304, semi-annual.
Moscow............................(095) 135-11-64
The Economist Guide, USSR. *Outdated, but useful.*
Published by The Economist, 1990, UK

Russia Survival Guide, 4th Edition, 1993.
Essential reading for anybody doing business in Russia.
Many reference sources. Russian Information Services,
Montpelier, VT, USA
Severo-Zapad, *daily news by fax*
See ad on next page

St. Petersburg Business Guide (in English)
Very useful for foreign businessmen
Gertsena ul., 20............................ 314-59-82
Fax.. 315-35-92
Published by LIC

SEVERO-ZAPAD ®

BUSINESS
NEWS
INFORMATION

On your desk every morning, daily reports
on business related news in St. Petersburg
and throughout Russia.

Thorough reporting on issues
in business and economics.

Transmitted by fax or E-mail
in Russian and English.

The most current and useful source
of information in St. Petersburg.

Reki Fontanki nab.,75/1 310-11-01
Fax 310-11-74

TRAVELLER'S
YELLOW
PAGES

THE *TRAVELLER'S*
YELLOW PAGES
FOR
SAINT PETERSBURG
AND
THE CITY MAP OF
SAINT PETERSBURG

*The essential reference guide for living
and doing business in St. Petersburg,
352 p.p., $8.95 plus S&H.
Updated annually*

*Buy or order a copy from our distributors
listed on page 349 or order directly from*

InfoServices International, Inc.
1 Saint Marks Place, Cold Spring Harbor,
New York 11724, USA

Tel .... USA (516) 549-0064
Fax .... (516) 549-2032
Telex .... 221213 TTC UR

In Russia, get sales information at
Telinfo ✉190000, St. Petersburg, Russia:
Nab. reki Moyki, 64 315-64-12
Fax 312-73-41

*Telinfo is a wholly-owned subsidiary of
InfoServices International, Inc. NY, USA*

St. Petersburg Yellow Pages-93
See TELEPHONE DIRECTORIES
Yellow Pages Moscow, pp. 421, 45$
Moscow .... (095) 202-95-05

SELECTED BUSINESS BOOKS AND DIRECTORIES IN RUSSIAN

Buznes v Sankt-Peterburge 1993
Business in Saint Petersburg
Gertsena ul., 20 314-59-82
Fax 315-35-92
Published by LIC in Russian

Delovaya Kniga RAU Rossiya - 93
*Published by Obozrevatel, Moscow 1993,
Vol. I, II, III. Excellent collection in Russian on
business regulations and information*

Spravochnik Delovogo Peterburzhtsa
*Directory of Petersburg Businessman
Published annually by Agency Igrek*
Konnogvardeyskiy blvd., 19, floor 5, rm. 112
.... 311-95-95
Fax 311-92-19

St. Petersburg Representative
Nevskiy pr., 3, apt. 25 315-04-29
Fax 315-79-67
Mon-Fri 10-18; Rbls
Ves Peterburg-93, *A Yellow Pages*
*The Whole Saint Petersburg-93
Business Directory*
See TELEPHONE DIRECTORIES

SELECTED MAGAZINES AND NEWSPAPERS IN ENGLISH

BUSINESS
CONTACT
ДЕЛОВЫЕ СВЯЗИ

• The business magazine bringing you
news on the cutting edge of banking,
privatization, industry trends and up-
coming meetings in Russia.
• The most influential guide for industry
leaders throughout the CIS and abroad
• Bi-monthly, published in English &
Russian.
• Advertise today and reach a readership
of 35,000!
• Subscribe for a yearly price of $54!

113461, Moscow, Kakhovka ul., 31
☎ 331-89-00; Fax 310-70-05

City Life
GUIDE

A Monthly Bulletin of
Coming Events in
Russian & English

• Public Life
• Business
• Culture
• Religion
• Entertainment
• Sport

Gertsena ul., 20
191065, St.Petersburg, Russia
Tel.: 314-59-82 Fax.: 315-35-92
LIC Information & Publishing Agency Ltd.

*Commersant, *Weekly, English*
Summary of daily Commersant (in Russian), the most respected business newspaper in Russia.

*Delovie Lyudi, *Monthly, English*
Outstanding business journal. A "must " read.
, Profsoyuznaya ul., 73 .... (095) 333-33-40
Mon-Fri 10-18; $ for Eng, Rbls for Rus

Russian Guide
Mainly information on Moscow companies some information on St. Petersburg companies
Moscow, Bolshoy Cherkasskiy per., 15

Russian Business Review, *Monthly, English*
Interesting collection of articles on business
Postchentskaya, ul., 5 office 30...... 315-52-25

Russian Trade Express, *English, monthly*
Pavlogradskiy per., 6 164-41-78
Fax 164-40-78
Mon-Sat 10-19; $

Saint Petersburg Premier, *English, quarterly*
Professora Popova ul., 47, off. 709...... 234-53-34
Fax 110-73-93

NEWSPAPERS IN RUSSIAN

There are at least a dozen newspapers about business, banking and privatization.
See NEWSPAPERS

☎ BUSINESS SERVICE CENTERS

See BUSINESS CENTERS

☎ CABLE TELEVISION

See TELEVISION, CABLE

☎ CAFES
КАФЕ
CAFES
CAFES
KAFÉR
KAHVIOT

See also RESTAURANTS

There are more than 100 establishments in St. Petersburg calling themselves "CAFES". They are usually smaller than restaurants and serve a lighter menu and a variety of drinks (but not always coffee). Some only offer "stand-up" tables. The better ones are under RESTAURANTS. For fast service, look for "Cafe Express" or "Bistro".

Actor, *Open 24 Hours*   **Akter**
Voznesenskiy pr., 4 315-06-75
Daily 0-24; Rbls; F-6

Alina, *Pelmeni (Siberian Meat Dumplings)*
Suvorovskiy pr., 1 277-15-49
Daily 9-15, 16-20; Rbls; I-5

Aliviya, *Grill*
Bolshoy pr., P.S., 13/4 235-48-69
Daily 9-15:30, 16:30-21; Rbls; F-9

Bagdad *Uzbek Cuisine (Central Asian)*
Furshtadtskaya ul., 35 272-35-33
Fax 272-46-39
Daily 12-23; Rbls; Eng; H-7

Bahlsen***, *see Le Café*
Nevskiy pr., 142 271-28-11
Fax 271-30-60
Daily 12-21; I-5

Bristol, *Pizza, Khachapuri*
Nevskiy pr., 22 311-74-90
Daily 10-22; Eng, Bus 22; Metro Nevskiy Prospect; G-6

Cafe at the Saint Petersburg Restaurant
Griboedova kan. nab., 5 210-76-73
Daily 16-21; G-6

Cafe-Bar
Suvorovskiy pr., 42 274-99-11
Daily; Rbls; $; Eng; I-6

Canon
Stachek pr., 67.............................. 184-68-19
Daily 11-14, 16-19; Rbls

Charodeyka   **Nymph**
Nevskiy pr., 88.............................. 273-15-94
Daily 11-23; Rbls; Eng, Fr; H-5

Chas Pik, *Hamburgers*
Bolshaya Konyushennaya ul., 29 314-08-37
Daily 10-16, 17-20; Rbls; G-6

Diez Grill*, *Whole Grilled Chickens - Take-out*
Kamennoostrovskiy pr., 16............ 232-42-55
Daily 10-21; Rbls; F-8

Donuts   **Pyshki**
Nevskiy pr., 119...................................No ☎
Metro Ploshchad Vosstaniya; I-5

Dr. Oetker Nevskiy 40
BAKERY-KONDITOREI-CAFE
Fine pastry, sweets and great bread
Enjoy coffee, fresh-baked cakes and pastries
Nevskiy pr., 40 312-24-57
Daily 12-24; Rbls, G-8

Frox Pool Ice-Cream
Nevskiy pr., 24 311-00-71
Daily 11-20; G-6

Gloria
Dekabristov ul., 32/2 312-38-07
Daily 10-20; Rbls; E-7

***Grand Hotel Europe Mezzanine Cafe
Mikhaylovskaya ul., 1/7 119-60-00
An elegant cafe in the beautiful atrium of the Grand Hotel Europe. See our ad under RESTAURANTS
Daily 11-23, Sunday 15-23; $, Eng

DELOVIE LYUDI

INDEPENDENT • OBJECTIVE • THOROUGH
Profsoyuznaya ul., 73; Tel.: (095) 333-33-40; Fax: (095) 330-15-68

Kafe　　　　　　　　　　　**Cafe**
• Bolshoy pr., P.S., 7 232-69-04
　　　Mon-Sat 9-20; Rbls; F-9
• Suvorovskiy pr., 65 271-92-47
　　　Mon-Sat 12-16, 17-22; Rbls; J-6
• Zagorodnyy pr., 2 315-84-21
　　　Daily 8-23; Rbls; H-5

Kameya　　　　　　　　　　**Cameo**
Furmanova ul., 32 272-60-66
　　　Daily 12-16, 17-23; Rbls; H-7

Kurazh　　　　　　　　　　**Courage**
Mokhovaya ul., 41 273-53-79
　　　Mon-Fri 10-22; Rbls; H-6

Le Café

Nevskiy Prospect 142,
Tel. 271-2811, 271-3037
Fax. 271-3060

Literary Cafe　　　　　**Literaturnoe Kafe**
Nevskiy pr., 18............................... 312-60-57
.... 312-85-43
　　　Daily 12-16:30, 19-23; Rbls; $; F-6

Metekhi
Belinskogo ul., 3 .... No ☎
　　　Daily 11-20; Rbls; H-6

Na Sadovoy　　　　　　　**On Sadovaya**
Sadovaya ul., 59 312-35-16
　　　Daily 11-24; Rbls; F-5

Nevsky Melody
Sverdlovskaya nab., 62 227-26-76
.... 222-51-80
Fax 227-15-96
　　　Daily 9-4; Rbls; $; CC; Eng, Ger, Fr, Swed; K-7

Nik Bistro
Pestelya ul., 23 .... No ☎
　　　Daily 12-16, 17-1; Rbls, H-6

Hotelship Peterhof ★★★★
Nab. Makarova, near the Tuchkov Bridge; D-7
.... 213-63-21

Petersburgers on Neva
Leninskiy pr., 115 153-80-22
　　　Mon-Sat 12-19; Rbls
The first of a chain of 150 planned cafes to be opened
throughout St. Petersburg

Petroart
Griboedova kan. nab., 3 210-75-49
Fax 275-10-86
　　　Mon, Wed-Sun 11-19; Rbls, $; Eng, Bus 6;
　　　Metro Gostinyy Dvor; G-6

Pingvinchik　　　　　　**Little Penguin**
Nevskiy pr., 54............................... 312-24-60
　　　Daily 10-15, 16-22; Rbls; G-6

Polar
Moskovskiy pr., 222....................... 293-18-09
Fax.. 293-04-08
　　　Daily 9-17; Rbls, $; Eng, Finn

Retro
Malyy pr., P.S., 24 230-83-91
　　　Daily 12-23; F-9

Rioni
Nevskiy pr., 136............................. 277-58-93
　　　Daily 11-20; I-5

Rosa Vetrov　　　　　　　**Wind Rose**
Moskovskiy pr., 204....................... 293-08-66
　　　Metro Park Pobedy

Russkie Bliny
Furmanova ul., 13 279-05-59
　　　Mon-Fri 11-18

Saigon-Neva, *Vietnamese*
Kazanskaya ul., 33 315-87-72
　　　Mon, Wed-Sun 12:30-23; Rbls, $; Eng; F-5

Snail Lover's Club, *Art-Cafe*
Pushkinskaya ul., 9 164-52-07
Fax.. 164-52-07
　　　Daily 19-24; Metro Ploshchad Vosstaniya
Evening performances of well-known and undiscovered
performers, artists, and musicians

Sonety　　　　　　　　　**Sonnets**
Karavannaya ul., 8......................... 314-74-45
　　　Metro Nevskiy Prospekt; G-6

Store No. 42 Cafe
Potemkinskaya ul., 7 272-91-57
　　　Mon-Fri 10-14, 15-19; Rbls; I-7

Sudarynya
Rubinshteyna ul., 28 312-63-80
Daily 12-23; Rbls; Eng, Ger, Fr; Metro Dostoevskaya; H-5

Syurpriz　　*More than a cafe*　　**Surprise**
Nevskiy pr., 113............................. 277-24-31
　　　Daily 12-22; I-5

U Vasiliya　　　　　　　**At Vassily's**
8-ya Liniya, 71 218-34-10
　　　Daily 12-23; Rbls; D-7

Vecher　　　　　　　　　**Evening**
Tallinnskaya ul., 20 221-16-76
　　　Daily 12-24; Rbls; K-5

Vechernee Kafe　　　　　**Evening Cafe**
Chaykovskogo ul., 75 272-95-16
　　　Daily 12-23; Rbls; I-7

Zakarpate　　　　　　　　*T-bus 5,22; F-6*
Gertsena ul., 14............................. 110-69-97

Zerkalnoe　　　　　　　　**Mirror**
Zagorodnyy pr., 8........................... 315-89-48
Fax.. 542-86-38
　　　Daily 10-15, 16-21; Rbls; Metro Dostoevskaya; H-5

Zhemchuzhina　　　　　　**Pearl**
Suvorovskiy pr., 57 275-77-68
　　　Mon-Fri 10-20; Rbls; I-6

CHILDREN'S CAFES

Konek-Gorbunok
Industrialnyy pr., 10....................... 520-20-33
　　　Daily 12-21

BABYLON SUPER
Mon-Sat 10-21 Sun 12-20
Exchange office

COME TO SUPER BABYLON ON A COLD WINTER NIGHT
For hot chocolate with whipped cream and cookies. Heat up
some soup, hot rolls and French bread with a plate of cheese, a
crisp apple and a glass of wine. Can of imported beer and a bag
of chips by the fire. All at the Super Babylon Supermarket.
P.S., Maly pr., 54 & 56 230-80-96
In the former Okean store off Bolshoy Prospect

Shokoladnitsa   **Chocolatier**
Pestelya ul., 19 272-98-46
Daily 9:30-21:30; H-6

RUSSIAN CUISINE

Cafe 01 (Nol Odin)
Karavannaya ul., 5 .... No ☎
Daily 12-16, 16:45-23; Metro Gostinyy Dvor; G-6
Cafe-Automat
Nevskiy pr., 45............................. 311-45-60
Daily 10-15, 16-21; Rbls; H-5
Cafe-Ice Cream, *Daily 11-22;* H-6
Belinskogo ul., 6 273-64-98
Evropa, *Near Mariinskiy Theater*
Soyuza Pechatnikov ul., 19 113-60-72
Daily 12-23; E-4
Fregat, *18th Century Russian Cuisine*   **Frigate**
Bolshoy pr., V.O., 39....................... 213-49-23
Daily 11-22; H-5
Kot   **Cat**
Stremyannaya ul., 22 311-33-77
Daily 13-16, 17-24; Metro Mayakovskaya; H-5
Petrogradskoe   *Daily 12-24;* E-8
Bolshoy pr., P.S., 88 232-34-55
Sirin-Bar, *Daily 11-24;* E-6
1-ya Liniya, 16............................. 213-72-82
U Samovara   *Great bliny*   **At the Samovar**
Piskarevskiy pr., 52 538-30-95
Mon-Sat 10-20; Rbls; K-9

CAUCASIAN CUISINE

Iveriya
Marata ul., 35 164-74-78
Daily 11-22; Rbls, Metro Vladimirskaya; H-4
Klassik   **Classic**
Ligovskiy pr., 202 166-01-59
Daily 11-20; Rbls, $; Eng, Finn; H-3
Pirosmani
Bolshoy pr., P.S. 14 235-64-56
Daily 12-23; Metro Petrogradskaya; F-9
Pitsunda
Kamennoostrovskiy pr., 12 233-16-86
Metro Gorkovskaya; E-8
Rioni *(under repair)*
Shpalernaya ul., 24 273-32-61
Mon-Sat 11-23; Rbls; H-7

☎ CALLING HOME

See TELEPHONE INTERNATIONAL CALLS

☎ CAMERAS

See PHOTOGRAPHY FILM & DEVELOPING,
PHOTOGRAPHY-CAMERAS *and* SUPPLIES

☎ CAMPING
КЕМПИНГ
LEIRENTÄALUEET

There are only one or two public camping
sites near St. Petersburg. Going to some
one's dacha is a close substitute sometimes
and great fun. Many organizations operate
campsites especially around the lakes.

Olgino Motel Camping
Primorskoe shosse, 18 km
Sestroretsk 238-35-52
Fax 238-39-54
Daily 0-24; Rbls, $

RETUR - Camping

CAMPING
On the beautiful Gulf of Finland

Comfortable 2-rm Cottages with Bath,
Breakfast, Bar & Restaurant
Sauna, Russian Baths
Heated Swimming Pool & Tennis

Car Rental & Caravan Camping
with Hot Showers
Secure Parking Guaranteed

29 km from Saint Petersburg
on St. Pb.- Helsinki highway

Primorskoe shosse, 29 km
Tel 237-75-33
Fax 273-97-83
Open 24 hrs, $, English, German, Finnish

☎ CAMPING SUPPLIES
ТОВАРЫ В ДОРОГУ
CAMPINGZUBEHÖR
CAMPING, FOURNITURES
CAMPINGUTRUSTNING
RETKEILYVÄLINEET

See also DEPARTMENT STORES, SPORTS
EQUIPMENT *and* HUNTING & FISHING EQUIPMENT

Camping supplies can be bought in
special travel stores called "Tourist" (Turist,
Турист), *in* DEPARTMENT STORES *and in*
SPORTING GOODS *stores.*

Gostinyy Dvor, Department Store:
Perinnaya, Sadovaya Linii
Nevskiy pr., 35, floor. 1 312-41-74
Mon-Sat 10-21; Rbls
Kompas   **Compass**
Malaya Posadskaya ul., 30 238-78-57
Mon-Fri 9-17; Rbls, $; Eng, Ger
ORT Ltd.
Bolshaya Pushkarskaya ul., 41 234-03-22
Fax.. 234-36-20
Tents, auto covers, beach umbrellas
Mon-Fri 9-19
Ring
Apraksin Dvor, bldg 1, rm. 85-95....... 310-18-93
Fax.. 310-41-38
Daily 10-19; Rbls
Rybolov, *Rods, lures, reels, etc.*   **Fishing**
Kamennoostrovskiy pr., 4............... 232-08-52
Snaryazhenie, *Tents & backpacks*   **Equipment**
Akademika Pavlova ul., 16B............ 232-02-58
Mon-Sat 10:30-13:30, 15-19; Rbls
Tourist   **Turist**
Nevskiy pr., 122.............................. 277-02-79
Mon-Sat 10-14, 15-19; Rbls

☎ CANDY STORES
КОНФЕТЫ
SÜßWAREN
BONBONS
KONFEKTYR
KARKKIKAUPAT

Try a box of Russian chocolates
(Shokolad, Шоколад) *which tends toward
dark bittersweet or hard candy. Candy is
sold by the pound in "confectionery" shops*
(Konditerskaya, Кондитерская) (*see*
BAKERIES). INTERNATIONAL SHOPS *usually have
a good selection of imported candy. Many
kiosks have imported candy bars and gum,
Snickers, Mars, Wrigley's and others.
Gostinyy Dvor has a whole department
selling candy.*

Bakery
Nevskiy pr., 134.............................. 277-19-12
Mon-Sat 11-14, 15-19; Rbls

Belochka
Sredniy pr., 28................................. 213-17-63
Mon-Fri 9-14, 15-21; Rbls

Estafeta   **Relay Race**
Moskovskiy pr., 189 293-50-54
Mon-Sat 9-13, 14-21; Rbls

Mars
Nevskiy pr., 40............................... 311-90-66
Daily 12-24; Rbls, $

Mechta Confectionery Shop
Nevskiy pr., 72............................... 272-98-56
Mon-Sat 8.30-14, 15-20
T-bus 1; Metro Mayakovskaya

Vostochnye Sladosti   **Eastern Sweets**
• Moskovskiy pr., 27 292-75-56
Mon-Fri, Sun 9-21; Rbls
• Nevskiy pr., 104............................ 273-74-36
Mon-Sat 8-20

Zolotoy Uley   **Golden Bee Hive**
Nevskiy pr., 22............................... 312-23-94
Mon-Sat 9-14, 15-21; Rbls

☎ CAR ACCIDENTS

See AUTOMOBILE ACCIDENTS *and* DRIVING

☎ CAR PHONE

See CELLULAR PHONES

☎ CAR RENTAL

See AUTOMOBILE RENTAL

☎ CAR REPAIR

See AUTOMOBILE SERVICE & REPAIR

☎ CAR SALES

See AUTOMOBILE SALES

☎ CAR WASHES
АВТОМОБИЛИ, МОЙКА
AUTOWASCHANLAGEN
VOITURES, LAVAGE
BILTVÄTT
AUTOPESUT

Auto Service No. 6
Bolshaya Zelenina ul., 34............... 235-49-23
Daily 8-20; Rbls

Autobaltservice, *One of the best*
Nakhimova ul., 5, bldg. 1 356-77-01
Fax... 355-04-40
Daily 8-12, 13-20; Rbls, $; Eng, Ger

Car Wash No. 1
Salova ul., 70................................. 166-47-06
Daily 8-21; Rbls; Tram 15; Metro Elektrosila

Car Wash No. 3, *One of the best*
Staroderevenskaya ul., 5 239-22-31
Daily 7-20; Rbls, $

Forward Car Wash
Luzhskaya ul., 3 530-47-82
Fax... 531-66-93
Daily 8-20; Rbls

Inautoservice, *One of the best*
Vitebskiy pr., 17, bldg. 2 298-46-08
Fax... 294-16-60
Daily 9-22; Rbls, $; Eng

Kupchino Auto Service
Malaya Balkanskaya ul., 57........... 178-16-29
Daily 7-19; Rbls; Eng

Lada-EN 65 Car Wash
Energetikov pr., 65........................ 226-56-78
Daily 8-21; Rbls

Service Station No. 4 (ZAZ)
Kosmonavtov pr., 69...................... 126-02-20
Daily 8-13, 14-21; Rbls

Vasilevskiy Ostrov Auto Service
Uralskaya ul., 33 351-58-85
Daily 10-19; Rbls

☎ CARPENTERS
ПЛОТНИКИ, СТОЛЯРЫ
SCHREINEREIEN TISCHLEREIEN
CHARPENTIERS
SNICKARE OCH HANTVERKARE
KIRVESMIEHET

Grif
Ruzovskaya ul., 16........................ 292-57-57
Mon-Fri 8-17; Rbls

Lassa, *Windows, doors*
Obvodnogo kan. nab., 4 567-10-85
Mon-Fri 10-17; Rbls

Max Shatornyy
Dimitrova ul., 6, bldg. 1................. 101-67-22
Mon-Fri 10-19; Rbls

S & Co., Ltd., Carpenters
*Russian-style wood houses
Custom carpentry, Russian Saunas
We ship throughout Russia and Europe.*

✉ *The Kirov Stadium, Bldg. 1
Krestovskiy Ostrov, Morskoy Pr.*

Tel 235-57-87
Fax... 235-54-35
Mon-Sat 9-18; Rbls, $

Sosna   **Pine**
  Yuzhnoe shosse, 61 269-30-94
     Mon-Fri 9-18; Rbls, $; Eng
Stroitel   **Builder**
  Tsiolkovskogo ul., 10 251-26-16
Uyut, *Curtain Rods*
  Reki Fontanki nab., 73 310-88-62
     Mon-Fri 9-18; Rbls

☎ CARPETS & RUGS

See RUGS & CARPETS

☎ CASINOS
КАЗИНО
CASINO
CASINOS
CASINO
KASINOT

There are a growing number of casinos and "lanes of one-armed bandits". These are some of the better casinos.

CASINO

Admiral®

In the Hotel Astoria

Gogola ul., 20

Hrs: 6 p.m. - 6 a.m.; $; English

CASINO

Admiral®

In the Leningrad Youth Palace

Pr. Popova ul., 47

Hrs: 6 p.m. - 6 a.m.; Rbls; English

Casino 777, *Daily 11-24; Rbls*
  Malaya Konyushennaya ul., 7 311-31-41
  Fax 274-37-12
Casino at the Hotel Pribaltiyskaya
  Korablestroiteley ul., 14 356-41-53
     Daily 22-4; $

CONTI Casino

European style casino for rubles
Kondratievsky av., 44

540-15-65

Galspe at Palanga, *Bingo*
  Leninskiy pr., 127 254-55-82
  Fax 255-51-60
     Daily 17-6; Rbls, $, CC
Joy
  Lomonosova ul., 1/28 311-35-40
     Daily 22-5; Metro Nevskiy Prospekt

Nevsky Melody
  Sverdlovskaya nab., 62 227-26-76
  Fax 227-15-96
     Daily 9-4; Rbls, $, CC; Eng, Ger, Fr, Swed

New Palanga,   *Daily 18-5; Rbls, $*
  Leninskiy pr., 127 254-21-92
Nord-West WBA
  Kima pr., 4 350-12-91
     Mon-Fri 11-19; Rbls, $; Eng, Ger

ST. PETERSBURG PALACE CASINO
Professional Croupier from England
Bar with Free Coffee & Soft Drinks
Beautiful Decor
Aleksandrovskiy Park, 4
(inside Music Hall) 233-05-42
Hrs: 16-4 a.m., Rbls & $

☎ CATERED BUSINESS FUNCTIONS
ПРЕЗЕНТАЦИИ
PRÄSENTATION
PRESENTATIONS
MATCATERING
PRESENTAATIO

Many RESTAURANTS *and* CONFERENCE HALLS *will also "cater" your party.*

Ivan & Co., *Finland,*   *Mon-Fri 9-17*
  294-02-52
  Fax 298-13-06
Pavlosk Palace
  Revolyutsii ul., 20 (Pavlovsk) 470-21-55

Potel & Chabot

Premier French Caterer and Organizer of Prestige Events

In the tradition of fine French cuisine and presentation, Potel & Chabot organize exceptional receptions in superb sites in Saint Petersburg as well as Moscow.

For lunch, dinner, buffet á la fourchette, gala evening, cocktail or traditional Russian menu, let us create the ideal service for any occasion.

In Saint Petersburg, please contact us at:
  Dvortsovaya nab, 10 314-60-00
  Tel ....(812) 315-63-05
  Tel./Fax ....(812) 315-06-69
  Telex .... 12646 BU3RC SU
In Moscow:
  Bolshaya Kommunisticheskaya, 2a
  (inside Moscow Commercial Club)
  Tel ....(095) 271-07-07
  ....(095) 274-00-81
  Fax ....(095) 274-00-80

CELLULAR PHONES
РАДИОТЕЛЕФОНЫ
MOBILTELEFONE
RADIOTELEPHONE
MOBILTELEFONER
MATKAPUHELIMET

See also COMMUNICATIONS *and*
TELEPHONE SERVICE

Cellular Radio Telephone
In Saint Petersburg
Gateway to the World

Instant Access • Direct Dial
Local and international phone & fax
From your home, office or car
Single calls & short-term rentals
Long-term subscriptions
Bolshaya Morskaya ul., 22 314-61-26
Fax 314-88-37
.... 275-08-86
Fax. 275-01-30

☎ **CEMETERIES**
КЛАДБИЩА
FRIEDHÖFE
CIMETIERES
KYRKOGÅRDAR
HAUTAUSMAAT

*Some cemeteries are split into two parts
for Orthodox Russians and non-orthodox
Russians and some include a necropolis
reserved for the graves of famous people.
There are churches at all cemeteries.*

Armenian Smolenskoe Cemetery
Reki Smolenki nab., 29 350-06-42
Daily 9-18, Metro Primorskaya, C-7

Bogoslovskoe Cemetery
Laboratornaya ul., 4 a 544-75-24
Daily 10-16, Metro Ploshchad Muzhestva

Bolsheokhtinskoe Cemetery
Metallistov pr., 5 224-27-29
Daily 9-16; Bus 22; Metro Novocherkasskaya

Evreyskoe (Jewish) Cemetery
Aleksandrovskoy fermy pr., 66 a 262-03-97
Daily 10-18; Metro Obukhovo

GVF & Co.
9-go Yanvarya ul. 262-10-88
*Cemetery services for Jewish people
Daily 9-16; Rbls; Metro Obukhovo*

Kazanskoe Cemetery
Yunnatov ul., 34 107-55-44
9-18; Metro Rybatskoe

Levashovskoe Memorial Cemetery
Contains graves of recently found victims of Stalinism.
Gorskoe shosse, 135, Poselok Levashovo
☎ 594-95-14

**Literary Necropolis
of the Volkovskoe Cemetery**
Famous poets, artists, composers, scientists, writers
Rasstannaya ul., 30 166-23-83
Mon-Wed, Fri-Sun 11-19; Rbls, H-2

Necropolis at *1765*
 Aleksandro-Nevskaya Lavra
Consists of three separate cemeteries
Nikolskoe Cemetery, *1862*
Reki Monastyrki nab., 1 274-29-52
Mon-Fri 10-15
Lazarus Cemetery *1716*,
*Graves of famous officials and noble families and some
famous writers, artists, and actors,
Daily 11-19, Closed Thur*
Tikhvin Cemetery *1823*
*Graves of famous sculptors, scientists, architects
Daily 11-19, Closed Thur*

Novo-Volkovskoe Cemetery, *Daily 10-16*
Salova ul., 80 298-09-29

Piskarevskoe Memorial Cemetery
*Final resting place of more than 420,000 Leningraders
who perished during the 1941-44 Siege*
Nepokorennykh pr., ... 247-57-16
Daily 10-18, Metro Ploshchad Muzhestva, then Bus 123, 131

Serafimovskoe Cemetery
Serebryakov per., 1 a 239-31-51
Tue-Sun 9-17; Metro Chernaya Rechka; C-11

Severnoe Cemetery, *Modern cemetery*
Pargolovo 594-86-26
Daily 10-16, Electric train from Finland Station

Shuvalovskoe Cemetery
Vyborgskoe shosse, 106 a 554-16-59
Daily 10-16, Electric train from Finland Station

Smolenskoe Cemetery
Graves of famous people from early 1700's.
Kamskaya ul., 24 355-99-93
Daily 10-15, Metro Primorskaya; C-7

Volkovskoe (Lutheran) Cemetery
Part of Volkovskoe Cemetery for the Non-Orthodox
Reki Volkovki nab., 1 166-33-34
Mon-Fri 11-19, Metro Ligovskaya; H-2

Volkovskoe (Orthodox) Cemetery *1756*
Rasstannyy proezd, 7 a 166-04-00
Mon-Sat 10-16, Metro Ligovskaya; H-2

Yuzhnoe Cemetery, *Modern cemetery*
Volkhonskoe shosse, 1 183-15-34
Daily 10-19, Metro Moskovskaya

Zelenogorskoe Cemetery
Lenina pr., Zelenogorsk 231-32-19
Mon-Fri 9-18, Electric train from Finland Station

☎ **CERAMICS**

See CRYSTAL & PORCELAIN

☎ **CHAMBERS OF COMMERCE**
ТОРГОВЫЕ ПАЛАТЫ
HANDELSKAMMERN
CHAMBRES DE COMMERCE
HANDELSKAMMARE
KAUPPAKAMARIT

See also CONSULATES *for commercial attaches
and commercial trade delegations.*

Finnish-Russian Chamber of Commerce
4-ya Krasnoarmeyskaya ul., 4 a 292-16-41
Fax 112-72-52
Mon-Fri 9-17; Finn

St. Petersburg Chamber of Commerce & Industry
Chaikovskogo ul., 46-48
....273-48-96
Fax ....272-64-06 .
Telex ....121324 LTPP SU
See also ADVERTISING AGENCIES, BUSINESS CONSULTANTS, PUBLISHERS, QUALITY CONTROL, TRANSLATION SERVICES, LANGUAGE COURSES

Vneshposyltorg
Moskovskiy pr., 98 298-67-25
Mon-Fri 10-17; Rbls, $

☎ CHARITIES
БЛАГОТВОРИТЕЛЬНЫЕ ОБЩЕСТВА
SPENDENGESELLSCHAFTEN
SOCIETE DE BIENFAISANCE
VÄLGÖRENHETSORGANISATIONER
HYVÄNTEKEVÄISYYS

Evfimiya Christian Girls Pension
Malookhtinskiy pr., 51 528-62-02
International Charitable Foundation for the Renaissance
Please call 278-18-02

·NEVSKIY ANGEL·
CHARITABLE   SPb   SOCIETY

We invite you to take part in any of our 17 charitable programs aiding invalids, orphans, the chronically ill & the elderly
Gorokhovaya ul., 5 315-54-45
Fax 315-14-63
Hrs: 11-18, clsd. Sat., Sun., English, German

Red Cross Society of Russia
Italyanskaya ul., 25 311-36-96
Mon-Fri 9-17; T-bus 1; Metro Gostinyy Dvor

Salvation Army
Nevskiy pr. 60..................Ask for new phone.
Metro Nevskiy Prospekt

Sochuvstvie   Compassion Charity Society
9-ya Sovetskaya ul., 23 271-11-80

☎ CHESS CLUBS
ШАХМАТНЫЕ КЛУБЫ
SCHACHVEREINE
ECHECS CLUBS
SCHACK KLUBBAR
SHAKKI

Chess Club of St. Petersburg University
Morskaya nab., 15 351-71-78
Daily 15-19

City Chess Club,
Major chess club; organizes tournaments
Bolshaya Konyushennaya ul., 25 314-75-61
Mon-Sat 16-22:30; Rbls
Intellekt, *Mon-Sat 16-19:30*
Dunayskiy pr., 48/1 172-16-16
Ladya, *Mon, Wed-Fri 15-18*
Vladimirskiy pr., 3 311-71-60

☎ CHILD CARE
НЯНИ
KINDERMÄDCHEN
BONNES D'ENFANTS
DAGHEM, BARNPASSNING
LASTENHOITO

See also CHILDREN in ST. PETERSBURG

Most baby-sitting is done by grand-mothers or by well-known, highly recommended older women. The American system of baby-sitting is still developing. Children are usually sent to nursery schools and kindergartens.
Kompleks   Complex
Voznesenskiy pr., 16 298-85-76
Daily 20-22; Rbls

MORIS
Child Care, Maids, Interpreters w/refs.
Fonarnyy per., 3 552-62-97

Peterburgskie Zori, *Mon-Fri 9-18; Rbls*
Nevsky pr., 95, 5th floor 277-45-47

RIKKI-TIKKI-TAVI
TRAINED NANNIES & TUTORS
FOR CHILDREN 3 to 8
Nursery care, kindergarten,
play groups for languages & arts
References on request
Inquire about our private school for children
Dmitrovskiy per., 16 311-80-19
Mon-Fri 10-21; English, French and German

☎ CHILDREN IN ST. PETERSBURG
ДЕТИ В САНКТ-ПЕТЕРБУРГЕ
KINDER
LES ENFANTS
BARN I ST. PETERSBURG
LAPSET MITÄ TEHDÄ LASTEN KANSSA PIETARISSA

St. Petersburg is full of things to do with children and teenagers. Try the ZOO, the CIRCUS, take a BOAT EXCURSION on the Neva, a hydrofoil to Peterhof, tour the Aurora Cruiser or visit the PLANETARIUM.
Museums. *Try the following MUSEUMS. The Artillery Museum is a favorite of children fond of climbing over tanks and real military equipment and looking at the rich collection of arms and armor. The Railroad Museum has large operating displays of model trains. The House of Nature is a natural history museum with*

many native animals. The small Space Museum *illustrates the Soviet space program.* The Central Naval Museum *has models of ships.* The Kunstkammer *has fascinating curious relics collected by Peter the Great. Try also the* Botanical Museum, Peter the Great's Cottage, *the* Mining Museum, *and even* The Hermitage *and* Russian Museum.

Sports. *Watch a world-class football, basketball, volleyball practice or visit sports events at local* STADIUMS. *Go* BICYCLING, SKATING, SAILING, SWIMMING, TENNIS, *and* HORSEBACK RIDING *or take a carriage ride around the Winter Palace and down Nevskiy Prospect.*

Concerts. *Schedules for* THEATERS, CONCERTS, JAZZ PROGRAMS, *and* ROCK CONCERTS *(held in stadiums) are in the local newspapers.*

Parks and Amusements. *The Parks of Culture and Recreation at TsPKO* (C-10) *and Park Pobedy have mini-amusement parks* (Attraktziony, Аттракционы) *with rides for children; some have row boats, pony rides, playgrounds, band shells with music, and plenty of room to walk, run, and play. Tavricheskiy Park* (I-7) *has been a children's park for years.*

Almost every apartment complex or small park has a playground, many quite imaginative, but in recent years the equipment may have been neglected and less attention paid to safety standards. So check the equipment first and then, let your children loose.

Children's Railway. *(Wed-Sat 10-17) is at Railway Station Shuvalovo ten minutes from the Finlyandskiy Railway Station.*

Libraries and Books. *Children's* LIBRARIES *are found in each district where books in English can sometimes be found. Also look in a children's bookstore, or in the children's and foreign language sections of a large bookstore for English books. Books in Russian are plentiful and inexpensive.*

Toys and Clothing. *The shop* DLT (ДЛТ) *Leningrad Trading House, traditionally a shop for children, still has a large selection of children's clothing, furnitures, toys. The Russian metal scale-models of trucks and cars, Playmobils, Barbie dolls and Lego, and stuffed animals are favorites for children. See* TOYS. *Metal soldiers are often found on tables along the street. Part of the fun is hunting for the particular soldier, book, etc. that you want.*

Joining a SPORTS CLUB *might be good for long term foreign residents or participating in a chess, rowing or other clubs.*

Indoors During Winter. *Try swimming, tennis and bowling or outdoor skating, cross-country skiing, or even watch ski-jumping.*

Country Dacha and Forest. *The country is enjoyed by all ages and there are kindergartens and programs similar to our summer camps for Russian children. If you*

have an adventuresome child, inquire about joining. At the dacha you would probably go fishing, garden, and pick mushrooms, all favorite pastimes.

Infants: *Baby food, disposable diapers, cribs, strollers, and good medical care are widely available. Look in* DEPARTMENT STORES, FURNITURE STORES *or even rent equipment if needed. There are special shops called* Malysh (Малыш) *or* Magazin Dieta (Магазин Диета) *where you can buy baby food, formula, milk and pure foods . Western baby products are easy to find, but be sure to bring along any special medicines. See also* BABY FOOD, CLOTHING, CHILDREN, MEDICAL CARE, TOYS, *and* SCHOOLS.

☎ CHILDREN'S CLOTHES

See CLOTHING, CHILDREN

☎ CHINA & CRYSTAL STORES

See CRYSTAL & PORCELAIN

☎ CHURCHES, OTHER
ЦЕРКВИ РАЗЛИЧНЫЕ
KIRCHEN, VERSCHIEDENE
EGLISES: AUTRES
KYRKOR: ALLMÄN
KIRKOT MUUT

See also SYNAGOGUES

ARMENIAN APOSTOLIC CHURCHES

Armenian Church of St. Catherine, *1771*
Nevskiy pr., 40/42 311-57-95
Metro Nevskiy Prospect; G-6
Armenian Church of the
Holy Resurrection, *1791*
Smolenskaya ul., 29 350-53-01
Daily 9-21; C-7

BAPTIST CHURCH

Baptist Church, *1900*
Bolshaya Ozernaya ul., 29 a 553-45-78
Daily 10-20

EVANGELICAL CHRISTIAN CHURCHES

Dom Evangeliya
Borovaya ul., 52 166-28-31
Daily 12-18
Evangelical Christian Church (Pentecostal)
Slavyanskaya ul., 13...................... 100-40-92
Daily 10-21
Evangelical Christian Church
Polevaya ul., 21, Pargolovo 594-89-97
Grace Missionary Center
Obukhovskoy Oborony pr., 223, rm. 12
☎ 262-01-20
Daily 11-18
Salvation Army
Nevskiy pr. 60 .... Ask for new phone.
Metro Nevskiy Prospekt
Seventh Day Adventists
Internatsionalnaya ul., 7 138-98-11
Daily 9-20

LUTHERAN CHURCHES

Dutch Church, *1830-33*
Gollandskaya Tserkov
Nevskiy pr., 20.....................................Inactive
Metro Nevskiy Prospect; G-6
Evangelical Lutheran Church of St. Maria (Finnish)
Bolshaya Konyushennaya ul., 8...... 314-08-48
German and Evangelical Lutheran Church
Saltykova-Shchedrina ul., 8..............No Phone
Lutheran Church
Pushkin, Proletkulta ul., 4 470-99-63
Lutheran Church of Saint Peter *1832-8*
Nevskiy pr., 22.....................................Inactive
Currently used as a swimming pool
Metro Nevskiy Prospekt; G-6

ROMAN CATHOLIC CHURCHES

Roman Catholic Church
Nevskiy pr., 34...................................Inactive
Metro Nevskiy Prospect; G-6
**Roman Catholic Church
of Our Lady of Lourdes**
Kovenskiy per., 7 272-50-02
Daily 11-18; F-8

CHURCHES CHRISTIAN - OTHER

CHRIST CHURCH - Spirit-filled Church
Sergei Timokhin, pastor
*English Translation Available
for All Services*
Prof. Popova ul., 47 (concert hall)
....110-18-70
......................................234-45-71
Fax 234-97-81
Worship service: Wed. 18:00, Sun. 12:00,

Temple of the Gospel
Borovaya ul., 52............................. 166-44-19
Metro Ligovskiy Prospect; H-3

OLD-BELIEVERS CHURCH

Znamenskaya Church of the Pomorskiy Persuasion, *at Kazanskoe Cemetery*
Yunnatov ul., 32 262-07-42
**Pokrovskaya Church
of the Belokrinitskiy Persuasion**
Aleksandrovskoy Fermy pr., 20 ....No ☎

HOUSES OF WORSHIP - NON-CHRISTIAN

Buddhist Temple, *1905-1915,* C-11
Primorskiy pr., 91.......................... 239-13-41
**Choral Synagogue
& Jewish Religious Center,** *1891*
Sinagoga-Evreyskaya Obshchina
Lermontovskiy pr., 2..................... 114-11-53
Daily 10-17; E-5
Synagogue
Aleksandrovskoy Fermy proezd, 2.. 264-39-81
Bus 51
Mosque of the Congregation of Moslems
Kronverkskiy pr., 7........................ 233-98-19
Daily 10-19; Rbls; Metro Gorkovskaya; F-8

☎ **CHURCHES RUSSIAN ORTHODOX**
ЦЕРКВИ ПРАВОСЛАВНЫЕ
KIRCHEN,ORTHODOXE
EGLISES: ORTHODOXES
KYRKOR: ORTODOX
KIRKOT ORTODOKSISET

There are 100's of church buildings in St. Petersburg. Some hold services, some are museums, others warehouses and swimming pools. Many are being restored and reopened as churches. Included here are both open and closed churches of historical significance.

One church can have several names, for example, the Church on the Blood, Church of the Redeemer, and Church of the Resurrection are the same. And the same name has been given to different churches in different areas. Take note of this when trying to find a church. To help identify a church, we give the traditional English name first, then the Russian name and map location.

Alexander Nevskiy Church, *1890*
Tserkov Aleksandra Nevskogo
Krasnoe Selo, Shuppa per., 10, ... 136-46-16
Daily 6:30-12, 15-19

Alexander Nevskiy Church, *1886*
Tserkov Aleksandra Nevskogo, Shuvalovskiy District
Vyborgskoe shosse, 106 a 595-06-66
Daily 9-11; Bus 262; Metro Ozerki

Alexander Nevskiy Monastery, *1713*
*Complex of religious buildings including Cathedral
of the Holy Trinity, Nunnery, and Necropolis*
Reki Monastyrki nab., 1.................. 274-04-09
Daily 8-14; Metro Ploshchad Aleksandra Nevskovo; I-4

Cathedral of the Holy Trinity *1776-90 by Starov*
At Alexander Nevskiy Monastery
Svyato-Troitskiy Sobor
Aleksandro-Nevskoy Lavry
Reki Monastyrki nab., 1.................. 274-04-09
Daily 8:14; Metro Ploshchad Aleksandra Nevskovo; I-4

Cathedral of Prince Vladimir, *1741-47*
Knyaz-Vladimirskiy Sobor
Blokhina ul., 16 232-76-25
Daily 7-12, 15-19; E-7

Cathedral of the Transfiguration, *1827-29*
Spaso-Preobrazhenskiy Sobor
Preobrazhenskaya pl., 1 272-36-62
Daily 6:30-13, 17-20; Metro Chernyshevskaya; H-6

*Cathedral of the Icon of the Lady of Kazan
Kazan Cathedral   **Kazanskiy Sobor**
*Built in 1801-11, is a Museum of Religion, but services
are held on holidays. Icon of the Virgin of Kazan and
grave of the famous Russian General Kutuzov.*
Kazanskaya pl., 2 311-04-95
Hrs 11-18, Closed Wednesdays, Metro Nevskiy Prospect; G-6

Chesmen Church, *1777-80*
Chesmenskaya Tserkov
*Commemorates the 1770 naval victory at Chesma.
Branch of the Central Naval Museum*
Lensoveta ul., 14-16 ....No ☎

Church of Nativity of John the Baptist, *1776*
Tserkov Rozhdestva Ioana Krestitelya
Kamennoostrovskiy pr., 7
Daily 7-12, 15-19; Bus 46; Metro Petrogradskaya; E-10

Church of the Valaam Monastery, St. Pb.
1905-10 Tserkov Valaamskogo Monastyrya
Narvskiy pr., 1/29 252-20-66
Daily 10-18; D-3

Church of the Holy Trinity, *1785-90*
Svyato-Troitskaya Tserkov
Obukhovskoy Oborony pr., 235 262-13-87
Daily 10-12, 17-19; Bus 11; Metro Elizarovskaya

Church of the Icon of the Lady of Kazan
Tserkov Ikony Kazanskoy Bogomateri
In Zelenogorsk
Primorskoe shosse, 547 231-80-06
Sat-Sun 10-18

Church of the Icon of the Lady of Smolensk, *1785*
Tserkov Ikony Smolenskoy Bogomateri
Kamskaya ul., 24 213-54-24
Sat-Sun 7-16; Bus 41; Metro Vasileostrovskaya; C-7

Church of the Icon of the Lady of Vladimir
1760   Tserkov Vladimirskoy Bozhey Matery
Vladimirskaya pl., 20 113-16-14
Daily 9-20; Metro Vladimirskaya; H-5

Church of the Resurrection, *1904-08*
Voskresenskaya Tserkov
Obvodnogo kan. nab., 116 292-00-93
Metro Baltiyskaya; F-3

---

*Church on the Blood, *1883-1907, also known as*
Church of the Resurrection, *and*
Church of the Redeemer
Tserkov Spasa-na-Krovi
Built by Alexander III on the spot where his father Tsar Alexander II was assassinated in 1881. Modeled on St. Basil's Church in Moscow. Mosaic decoration
Griboedova kan. nab., 2 a 314-40-53
Metro Nevskiy Prospect; G-6

Church of the Serafim, *1906*
Serafimovskaya Tserkov
Serebryakov per., 1 239-15-50
Sat-Sun 7-16

Spasskaya Church, *1876-80*
Spasskaya Tserkov
Vyborgskoe shosse 106 a 554-16-58
Mon-Fri 9-16; Bus 262; Metro Prospect Prosveshcheniya

Spasskiy Cathedral, *1817-23   Spasskiy Sobor*
Konyushennaya pl., 1 ....No ☎
Metro Nevskiy Prospect; G-6

St. Andrew Cathedral, *1764-80*
Sobor Svyatogo Andreya
6-ya Liniya, 11 213-17-32
Sat-Sun 9-12, 18-20; Metro Vasileostrovskaya; D-6

St. Dmitriy Church, *1906*
Tserkov Svyatogo Dmitriya
1-ya Nikitinskaya ul., 1 a 395-34-10
Daily 10-18

St. Ilya Church in Porokhovye, *1781-85*
Tserkov Svyatogo Ili
Revolyutsii shosse, 75 227-88-15
Daily 7-12, 15-19; Bus 27; Metro Ladozhskaya

St. Iov's Church
Tserkov Svyatogo Iova
Kamchatskaya ul., 6 166-27-49
Sat-Sun 7-16; H-2

***St. Isaac's Cathedral, *1828-58*
Isaakievskiy Sobor
Built by Montferrand of multi-colored granite from Finland. Go up to the terrace of the dome (101 meters) for the best view of St. Petersburg.
Isaakievskaya pl. 315-97-32
.... 210-92-06
Mon-Tue, Thu-Sun 11-19; Trolleybus 5; F-6

St. Nicholas Cathedral, *1753-63*
Nikolskiy Sobor
Nikolskaya pl., 1 114-08-62
Daily 7-12, 15-19; Tram 14; F-4

St. Nicholas Church, *1812-18*
Tserkov Svyatogo Nikolaya
Metallistov pr., 5 224-27-08
Sat-Sun 10-19

**St. Peter & Paul Cathedral, *1712-33*
Petropavlovskiy Sobor
Oldest church in St. Petersburg with tall gold spire & beautiful bells . Graves of Peter the Great & Tsars
Petropavlovskaya Krepost 238-45-11
Metro Gorkovskaya; F-7

St. Peter's Church, *1893-99*
Tserkov Svyatogo Petra
Lakhtinskiy pr., 94 ....No ☎
Sat-Sun 7-16

RUSSIAN ORTHODOX CHURCH IN EXILE

Church of the Transfiguration of the Virgin Mary
Tserkov Bozhiey Materi Preobrazhayushcheysya
Moskovskiy pr., 188 294-03-74

Kazan Church   *Kazanskaya Tserkov*
Former Novodevichiy Monastery
Moskovskiy pr., 100 ....No ☎

☎ CINEMAS, MOVIES
КИНОТЕАТРЫ
FILMTHEATER
CINEMAS
BIOGRAFER
ELOKUVATEATTERIT

Tickets can be bought only for the day of the show at the ticket office (Kassa, касса); shows start about every two hours. The schedule is printed in Kinonedelya (кинонеделя), Film Weekly for the following week. Most films are dubbed Western films. The first showing (at 10 or 12) is often for children. Some theaters also have "theme weeks" that feature American, German, French, and other films.

Avrora, *Daily 11-21*   **Aurora**
Nevskiy pr., 60 315-52-54
Barrikada, *Daily 12-21:30*   **Barricade**
Nevskiy pr., 15 315-40-28
DK Lensoveta
Lensoviet House of Culture
Kamennoostrovskiy pr., 42 230-80-14
Daily 9:40-22:10
Gigant, *Daily 11-21*   **Giant**
Kondratevskiy pr., 44 540-13-55
Dom Kino, *Mon-Fri, Sun*   **House of Films**
Karavannaya ul., 12 314-81-18

Khudozhestvennyy, *Daily 10-22* **Artist**
Nevskiy pr., 67 314-00-53
Kolizey, *Daily 10-22* **Coliseum**
Nevskiy pr., 100 272-87-75
Ladoga, *Daily 15-21*
Revolyutsii shosse, 31 227-24-18
Leningrad, *Daily 11-22*
Potemkinskaya ul., 4 273-31-16
Meridian, *Daily 14-22*
Novo-Izmaylovskiy pr., 48 295-76-70
Molniya, *Daily 12-22* **Lightning**
Bolshoy pr., P.S., 35 233-11-36
Molodezhnyy, *Daily 12-21* **Youth**
Sadovaya ul., 12 311-00-45
Moskva, *Daily 13-21* **Moscow**
Staro-Petergofskiy pr., 6 251-29-18
Neva, *Daily 12-22*
Nevskiy pr., 108 273-75-52
Parisiana, *Daily 12-22* **Paris**
Nevskiy pr., 80 273-48-13
Prometey, *Daily 12-21* **Prometheus**
Prosveshcheniya pr., 80 531-77-82
Rodina, *Daily 13-21* **Motherland**
Karavannaya ul., 12 312-15-23
Rubezh, *Daily 12-21:30* **Border**
Veteranov pr., 121 135-17-44
Slava, *Daily 14-21* **Glory**
Bukharestskaya ul., 47 260-87-26
Smena, *Daily 12-21:30* **New Generating**
Sadovaya ul., 42 310-13-01
Spartak *Old films, foreign and Russian* **Spartak**
Saltykova-Shchedrina ul., 8 272-78-97
Daily 12-21
Stereokino **Stereocinema**
3-D films with paper glasses, *Daily 11-21*
Nevskiy pr., 88 272-27-29
Titan, *Daily 10-22; Rbls* **Titan**
Nevskiy pr., 47 319-97-26
Zenit, *Daily 12-22* **Zenith**
Gastello ul., 7 293-13-20
Znanie, *Documentary and art films* **Knowledge**
Nevskiy pr., 72 273-51-83
Daily 10:30-21; Rbls

☎ CIRCUS
ЦИРКИ
ZIRKUS
CIRQUES
CIRKUS
SIRKUKSET

On the Scene, *Daily; Rbls*
Sergeya Tyulenina per., 4 312-01-10
Shapito (Big Top) Summer Circus
Avtovskaya ul., 1 a 183-15-01
Daily; Rbls

The State Circus

Nab. reki Fontanki, 3
Administrator 314-84-78

Tutti
Nevskiy pr., 134, apt. 7 274-21-73
Fax 274-09-11
Daily 10-18; Rbls

☎ CITY GOVERNMENT

See ST. PETERSBURG CITY GOVERNMENT;
MAYOR'S OFFICE

☎ CLEANING SERVICES

See APARTMENT CLEANING

☎ CLIMATE
КЛИМАТ
KLIMA
CLIMAT
KLIMAT
ILMASTO

Weather systems *in St. Petersburg
usually come from the Baltic Sea and the
Gulf of Finland. The weather is highly
changeable with crystal clear sunshine
followed by heavy showers and again by
sunshine, especially in summer.*

What to Bring. *A collapsible umbrella that
opens automatically is essential. A good
raincoat (with liner) will be useful from
March to October. It can get chilly in summer, so a sweater and/or wind breaker is
useful, especially for evenings. Something
warmer is needed from November to February. A good warm top coat, fur coat, or
ski parka with scarf, gloves, a ski or fur hat
and warm zip-up boots (in dark brown or
black) will be necessary. Note that the interiors of most buildings are usually well
heated. Dress in "layers".*

*In summer, temperatures range from a
cool, wet 45°F to an occasional hot, humid
90°F.*

	Average Temperature			
	Fahr	Celsius	Days with	
	Low/High	Low/High	Rain	mm
January	8/19	-13/-7	21	35
February	11/22	-12/-5	17	30
March	18/32	-8/0	14	31
April	33/46	0/8	12	36
May	42/59	6/15	13	45
June	51/68	11/20	12	50
July	55/70	13/21	13	72
August	55/69	13/20	14	78
September	47/60	9/15	17	64
October	39/48	4/9	14	76
November	28/35	-2/2	18	46
December	18/26	-8/-3	22	40

☎ CLINICS

See MEDICAL CARE AND CONSULTATIONS

☎ CLOCKS/WATCHES

See WATCHES

☎ CLOTHING
ОДЕЖДА
BEKLEIDUNG
VETEMENTS
KLÄDER
VAATETUS

See also CLOTHING-CHILDREN'S, CLOTHING-MEN'S, CLOTHING-WOMEN'S, FASHION SALONS, DEPARTMENT STORES, COMMERCIAL SHOPS, INTERNATIONAL SHOPS *and* COMMISSION SHOPS, FURS *and* SHOES, HATS, TAILORS *and* HABERDASHERY

These clothing stores carry both men's and women's clothing and often shoes. You can also find both domestic and imported clothing at the better DEPARTMENT STORES *Gostinyy Dvor, Passage, DLT, Tsentr Firmennoy Torgovli and other Univermags. Imported clothing can also be bought throughout St. Petersburg in* FASHION SALONS, COMMERCIAL SHOPS, COMMISSION SHOPS, *and* INTERNATIONAL SHOPS, *raincoats and coats at the large* DEPARTMENT STORES. *Sports clothing and swim suits are available at* SPORTS SHOPS.

Many Russian women sew their own clothing (FABRICS) *or have them tailored* (TAILORS). *Used clothing can be bought in* COMMISSION SHOPS. *See* TABLES OF SIZES, *p. 343 for international size comparisons*

Alexander
italian style
Apparel, Footwear, Costume Jewelry & Accessories
V.O., Bolshoy pr., 99.............355-40-20
Hrs: 10-14, 15-19; Clsd Sun, Mon; $, Rbls; English, Italian

Alina
Moskovskiy pr., 138 298-20-11
Mon-Sat 10-14, 15-19; $; Metro Elektrosila
Alivekt, *Shops specializing in clothing*
• Kuybysheva ul., 11 233-82-97
Mon-Sat 11-14, 15-19; $; Eng
• Nevskiy pr., 23 311-46-45
Mon-Sat 10-19; $; Metro Nevskiy Prospekt
• Nevskiy pr., 112 295-01-04
Mon-Sat 11-14, 15-19; $; Eng

ARTICA
Tyushina ul., 11 164-92-08
Tel./Fax.. 164-47-13

Babylon - *See ad below*
Benetton, *Informal stylish fashions*
Nevskiy pr., 147 277-17-32
Mon-Sat 10-14, 15-19; $, CC

BABYLON
shops
No. 1 The Clothing Store
Clothes for the Entire Family
Men's and Women's Suits, Shirts, Skirts & Blouses, Casual Clothes, Warm-up Suits & Bathing Suits, Jackets & Raincoats, Scarves, Shoes & Socks,
Imported from the Netherlands.
Liteynyy pr., 61 273-42-12
Daily 10-14, 15-20; Rbls Metro Mayakovskaya

Beriozka Shops
• Morskaya nab., 9 356-55-98
Mon-Sat 10-19; $
• Morskaya nab., 15 355-18-75
• Nevskiy pr., 7/9 315-51-62
Daily 10-21; $
Bogatyr, *Big sizes for men and women*
Nalichnaya ul., 33 352-76-46
Mon-Sat 10-14, 15-19; Rbls
Bosco
• Ligovskiy pr., 130 166-00-11
• Nevskiy pr., 8 219-18-56
• Ulyany Gromovoy per., 3...............275-57-11
Daily 11-15, 16-20; Rbls, $; Eng
• Zhukovskogo ul., 8........................273-70-92
Mon-Sat 11-20; Rbls, $; Eng
Boutique Couture, *Mon-Sat 11-19; Rbls, $*
Chaykovskogo ul., 18 275-82-59
Boutique-Joy, *High fashion*
Zagorodnyy pr., 9...........................315-53-13
Mon-Sat 11-14, 15-20; Rbls, $; Eng, Ital; Metro Dostoevskaya

---

capricorn
EXPORT IMPORT

IMPORTED
MEN'S & WOMEN'S CLOTHES
WHOLESALE & RETAIL
Varshavskaya ul., 51 296-27-09
Fax...296-43-51
Telex....................121194 RUB SU

Chao-Chao, *Clothing, shoes and perfume*
Reki Fontanki nab., 5......................314-00-80
Mon-Sat 10-19; Rbls, $; Eng; Tram 5
City, *Clothing, shoes, audio/video, food*
Malaya Konyushennaya ul., 7 311-80-20
Cristian, *Italian fashions for men and women*
Voznesenskiy pr., 46 310-39-22
Mon-Sat 10:30-19; $
Diesel International, *Clothing, shoes*
Kamennoostrovskiy pr., 37.............233-47-20
Mon-Sat 11-18; $; Eng, Ger
DLT (Leningrad Trading House)
Mainly for children, it also has clothing, footwear, housewares, toys, and a shoe boutique, too.
Bolshaya Konyushennaya ul., 21/23
☎ 312-26-27
Mon-Sat 10-20; Rbls, $; Eng

Dom Mody, *Branch store*   **Fashion House**
Marshala Tukhachevskogo ul., 22
☎ 225-19-19
Mon-Sat 11-20

Dom Mody, *Main store*   **Fashion House**
Kamennoostrovskiy pr., 37 234-90-55
Mon-Fri 10-15, 16-19; Rbls; Eng

Ezhen, *Panty hose and stockings*
Nevskiy pr., 105 275-39-56
Daily 10-20; Rbls

Furshtadt, *Mon-Sat 11-14, 15-19; Rbls*
Furshtadtskaya ul., 42 272-66-33

Future Vision, *Daily 10:30-19; $; Eng*
Belinskogo ul., 13 272-79-43

Gloria, *Women's dresses and shoes, cosmetics
men's jackets and trousers*
Nevskiy pr., 168 277-41-09
Mon-Sat 8-20; Rbls

Godiva
Imported coats, skirts, trousers, leather jackets
Moskovskiy pr., 179 .... No ☎
Daily 10-20; $; Metro Park Pobedy

Gorokhovaya-38, *Mon-Sat 10-14, 15-19; Rbls*
Gorokhovaya ul., 38 310-79-25

Iantovski, *Imported Swedish clothing*
Nevskiy pr., 48, Passage, 1st floor.... 219-17-92
Mon-Sat 10-21; Rbls

Kosmos, *Expensive clothing*
Mokhovaya ul., 39 273-34-05
Mon-Sat 11-15, 16-20, Sun 11-17; Rbls

Luhta
Nevskiy pr., 48, Passage, 2nd floor.... 219-17-58
Imported clothing; Mon-Sat 10-21; Rbls, $

Melpomeny Tradehouse, *Russian & imported*
Vladimirskiy pr., 12 164-65-85
Mon-Sat 10-14, 15-20; Rbls

Merkuriy, *Small, but good*   **Mercury**
Moskovskiy pr., 41 .... No ☎
Mon-Sat 10-15, 16-21; Rbls

Monolith-8, *Imported clothing*
Kamennoostrovskiy pr., 42 .... No ☎
Mon-Sat 11-15, 16-19; Rbls; Eng

Nautilus, *Imported sports and day wear*
Gorokhovaya ul., 61 310-23-02
Fax 310-19-15
Mon-Sat 11-20

Nika, *Imported men's & women's clothing*
Vladimirskiy pr., 2 314-00-48
Mon-Sat 11-14, 15-19; Rbls

Novyy Rim   **New Rome**
Nevskiy pr., 48, at the Passage, 2nd floor
☎ 219-17-83
Wonderful Russian styles; Mon-Sat 10-21; Rbls

Oksana
Lomonosova ul., 11 314-25-17
Mon-Sat 10-14, 15-19; Rbls; Metro Dostoevskaya

Okhta, *Mon-Fri 10-19; Rbls, $*
Bolshaya Pushkarskaya ul., 20 232-01-47
Fax 277-23-12

Real Music
Nevskiy pr., 54 310-59-22
Fax 310-40-80
Mon-Sat 10-14, 15-19; Rbls, $; Eng, Ger

Rifle-Petrograd, *Jeans, clothing, Daily 10-20; $; Eng*
Kamennoostrovskiy pr., 54 234-43-77

Rospol
Sofiyskaya ul., 30, bldg. 2 269-24-20
*Mon-Fri 10-14, 15-18; Rbls, $; Eng, Fr
Bus 114; Metro Moskovskaya, Elizarovskaya*

Salon No. 1
Suvorovskiy pr., 30 271-20-92
Mon-Sat 10-14, 15-19; $; Eng

Skif
Griboedova kan. nab., 28 312-16-14
Daily 10-20; Rbls, $, CC

Sonya
Nevskiy pr., 78 272-95-98
Mon-Sat 11-14, 15-20; Rbls, $

Stollen
Sadovaya ul., 32 310-06-65
Mon-Sat 11-14, 15-19; $

Teatralnyy
Saltykova-Shchedrina ul., 24 272-19-77
Mon-Sat 11-13, 14-20; Rbls

Tradehouse of Holland
Malookhtinskiy pr., 68 528-82-25
*Large selection of clothing, shoes and food from Holland
Mon-Sat 11-19; Rbls, $*

Tradehouse on Moyka
Reki Moyki nab., 59 315-60-38
Mon-Sat 10-14, 15-19; Rbls, $

Troika, *Imported clothing for men & women*
Bolshaya Konyushennaya ul., 17 314-13-21
*Mon-Sat 11-14, 15-20; Rbls; Eng, Ger, Fr
Bus 47; Metro Nevskiy Prospekt*

☙ **TROЇKA RO** ℞
A. O. TROIKA
Fashionable Men's & Women's Clothing
Zagorodnyy pr., 28 112-47-46

Tsentr Firmennoy Torgovli
    Center of Fashion Trade
Stylish Russian clothing for men and women
Novo-Smolenskaya nab., 1 352-11-34
Mon-Sat 10-20

VIB Style
Sadovaya ul., 55/57 113-76-75
*Women's dresses, men's suits, men's and women's shoes
Daily 10-14, 15-19; Rbls*

VISHNU
Priya International Co Ltd.
V.O. 19 Liniya, 12, 199026, St. Petersburg
*Importers of Fine Fashion Clothing
for Men & Women from England,
Europe, Hong Kong & USA.
Pure Wool, Genuine Leather Garments,
Shoes & Accessories from India*
V.O., 19 Liniya, 12 213-99-99
Fax 218-14-49
S t . P e t e r s b u r g

Voski
Chaykovskogo ul., 36 275-71-47
Mon-Sat 10-14, 15-19; Rbls

Yubiley
Sverdlovskaya nab., 60 224-25-98
Mon-Sat 10-20; Rbls, $

☎ CLOTHING, CHILDREN'S
ОДЕЖДА ДЕТСКАЯ
KINDERBEKLEIDUNG
VETEMENTS POUR, ENFANTS
KLÄDER, BARN
VAATETUS, LASTEN

Children's clothing can be bought in the DEPARTMENT STORE DLT (ДЛТ) *and its branches as well as special children's shops called "Children's World" (Detskiy Mir, Детский Мир). Many* DEPARTMENT STORES *have special departments for children.*

Aist
Sredniy pr., 16 213-26-37
Clothing for infants
Mon-Sat 10-19; Rbls

Alenka
Stachek pr., 80 183-01-60
For young girls
Mon-Fri 10-14, 15-19; Rbls; Tram 36; Metro Avtovo

Andreyka
Stachek pr., 55 183-04-88
For young boys
Mon-Sat 11-14, 15-19; Rbls

Bele Dlya Detey
Clothing for Infants & Young Children
• Bolshoy pr., P.S., 25 233-56-36
Mon-Sat 10-14, 15-19; Rbls
• Nevskiy pr., 63.............................. 311-45-33
Mon-Sat 10-19; Rbls

Detskiy Mir   Children's World
Детский Мир
Children's clothing & toys.
• Bolshoy pr., P.S., 25 233-56-36
Mon-Sat 10-14, 15-19; Rbls
Bus 10; Metro Petrogradskaya
• Moskovskiy pr., 191 293-50-75
Mon-Sat 10-19; Rbls
Bus 3; Metro Moskovskaya
• Prosveshcheniya pr., 46, bldg. 1 597-63-38
Mon-Sat 10-14, 15-19; Rbls
• Sedova ul., 69.............................. 560-61-92
Mon-Sat 10-14, 15-19; Rbls
• Shkolnaya ul., 6 239-85-50
Mon-Sat 11-14, 15-19; Rbls

DLT   Leningrad Trading House
Store for children with clothing, children's furniture,
cribs, strollers, and toys
Bolshaya Konyushennaya ul., 21/23
☎ 312-26-27
Fax 315-21-92
Mon-Sat 10-20; Rbls, $; Eng

Lyudmila
Prosveshcheniya pr., 46-1 597-33-16
Fashion for girls & women
Mon-Sat 10-19; Rbls

Moda Detyam   Fashion for Children
Kuznechnyy per., 19 113-17-96
Mon-Sat 10-20, Sun 11-16

Odezhda   Clothing
Stakhanovtsev ul., 10..................... 528-17-63
Mon-Sat 10-14, 15-19; Rbls

Peggy
Liteynyy pr., 8/21 272-49-40
English Children's Clothing
Mon-Sat 10-20; Sun 12-17; Rbls, $

☎ CLOTHING, MEN'S
ОДЕЖДА МУЖСКАЯ
HERRENBEKLEIDUNG
VETEMENTS POUR, HOMMES
KLÄDER, HERR
VAATETUS, MIESTEN

See comments under CLOTHING.
See DEPARTMENT STORES, COMMERCIAL STORES, INTERNATIONAL SHOPS, COMMISSION STORES, SHOES *and* HABERDASHERY.

The best places to buy men's clothing are the DEPARTMENT STORES *Gostinyy Dvor, Apraksin Dvor, Univermags and the Babylon shops. Belts and neckties can be bought at* HABERDASHERY *shops. Neckties can also be found at shops, called "Neckties" (Galstuki, Галстуки).*

Andy's Fashion Hong Kong, *Custom tailoring*
By appointment............................. 556-08-09
(See our ad under TAILOR/SEAMSTRESS)

✳ BABYLON
shops

No. 4 Clothing for Men

Exclusive Men's Shop
Featuring Hugo Boss Clothing
Choose from a wide selection of
Imported Suits, Shirts, Ties,
Sports Clothes, & Underwear
Belts, Cuff Links, Briefcases
Top it all off with our fine Dutch Cigars.

Sadovaya ul., 26 310-18-15
Daily 10-14, 15-20; Rbls
Currency exchange in store
Metro Gostinyy Dvor

Elegant, *Men's Department*
Bolshoy pr., P.S., 55 232-86-01
Mon-Sat 10-14, 15-19; Rbls

Heinemann *at the Grand Hotel Europe*
Elegant imported men's clothing,
Scottish sweaters, leather accessories
1st floor, right side....................... 312-00-72
Daily 8-21; Metro Nevskiy Prospekt

Littlewoods, *Imported clothing for men*
Nevskiy pr., 35, Gostinyy Dvor, Sadovaya Liniya
.... 110-59-67
.... 110-54-47
Mon-Fri 9-18; Rbls, $; Eng

Lux-L, *Imported clothing*
Nevskiy pr., 63 113-15-60

Muzhskaya Odezhda   Men's Apparel
Stachek pl., 21 186-78-49
Mon-Fri 10-14, 15-19; Rbls; Bus 2; Metro Narvskaya

Odezhda   Clothing
Stakhanovtsev ul., 10..................... 528-17-63
Mon-Sat 10-14, 15-19; Rbls

Rassvet, *Only men's shirts*
Ligovskiy pr., 38 314-42-20
Mon-Sat 10-14, 15-19; Rbls

Sokol   **Falcon**
Metallistov pr., 77 540-21-01
Mon-Sat 10-14, 15-19; Rbls

❦ TROĬKA RO ℞
A. O. TROIKA
Fashionable Men's & Women's Clothing
Zagorodnyy pr., 28 112-47-46

☎ CLOTHING, SPORT
ОДЕЖДА СПОРТИВНАЯ
SPORTBEKLEIDUNG
VETEMENTS DE SPORT
SPORT KLÄDER
VAATETUS URHEILU

Danskin, *First Danskin shop in St. Pb.*
Complete line of Danskin for women and girls;
Givenchy, Round the Clock and Anne Klein
pantyhose; Leotards.
Kazanskaya ul., 60 315-15-65
Mon-Sat 11-20; Rbls, $

New Balance, *Shoes & sports attire*
Bolshoy pr., P.S., 65 230-80-43
Daily 11-19; Rbls

Trust, *Adidas*
Nevskiy pr., 86 275-12-23
Mon-Sat 12-20; Rbls, $

☎ CLOTHING, WOMEN'S
ОДЕЖДА ЖЕНСКАЯ
DAMENBEKLEIDUNG
VETEMENTS POUR, FEMMES
KLÄDER, DAM
VAATETUS, NAISTEN

See comments under CLOTHING.
See also FASHION SALONS, DEPARTMENT
STORES, COMMERCIAL STORES, INTERNATIONAL
SHOPS, COMMISSION STORES, FURS, SHOES *and*
HABERDASHERY

The best places to buy women's clothes
are the stylish Dom Mod, Passage, Gos-
tinyy Dvor, better Univermags and the Bab-
ylon shops. **FASHION SALONS, COMMERCIAL**
SHOPS *and* **INTERNATIONAL SHOPS** *often carry*
imported clothing.

Andy's Fashion Hong Kong, *Custom tailoring*
By appointment 556-08-09

(See our ad under TAILOR/SEAMSTRESS*)*

Aquilon
Kamennoostrovskiy pr., 6 232-67-83
Fabrics, shoes, furs
Mon-Sat 10-18; Rbls

Ariadna
Kazanskaya ul., 40 315-62-48
Knitted clothing, skirts
Mon-Fri 9-13, 14-18; Rbls

Avrora
Prosveshcheniya pr., 5 599-69-51
Mon-Sat 11-14, 15-19; Rbls

BABYLON
shops

No. 6 Clothing for Women
Elegant Imported Fashions
Evening Dresses, Suits, Handbags, Shoes,
Coats, Lingerie, Panties, Panty Hose
& Bras from *Dim* of France.
Toiletries from Procter & Gamble.

P.S., Bolshoy pr., 94 234-90-68
Daily 10-14, 15-20; Rbls
Metro Petrogradskaya

BOLSHEVICHKA
Ligovskiy pr., 107 164-94-33
"Bolshevichka" collection designed by the
Leningrad House of Fashion, known for
elegance and style
Mon-Sat 11-14, 15-19; Rbls

Boutique-Joy, *An elegant shop with imported*
clothing and cosmetics, lingerie, shoes
Zagorodnyy pr., 9 315-53-13
Mon-Sat 11-14, 15-20; Rbls; Eng, Ital; Metro Dostoevskaya

Elegant Women's Department
Bolshoy pr., P.S., 55 232-86-01
Mon-Sat 10-14, 15-19; Rbls

Elsy
Zagorodnyy pr., 12 ....No ☎
Mon-Sat 13-18; Rbls; Eng, Ger

Escada *High fashion imported for women*
Dresses, skirts, blouses, lingerie.
Nevskiy pr., 48, at the Passage, 2nd floor
Mon-Fri 10-21, Sat 10-18

Dom Mody *Best selection* **House of Fashion**
See description under FASHION SALON
Marshala Tukhachevskogo ul., 22 225-18-18
Mon-Sat 10-14, 15-20; Rbls

Dom Mody *Main store* **House of Fashion**
Kamennoostrovskiy pr., 37 234-90-55
Mon-Fri 10-15, 16-19; Rbls; Eng

Gostinyy Dvor Department Store
Good selection of Russian-made coats, suits, dresses,
blouses, lingerie, furs, & shoes. Littlewoods Fashion
Salon of imported women's clothing.
Nevskiy pr., 35 110-54-08
Daily 9-21; Rbls

Littlewoods, *Fashionable imported clothing*
Nevskiy pr., 35, Gostinyy Dvor, Sadovaya Liniya
.... 110-59-67
.... 110-54-47
Mon-Fri 9-18; Rbls, $; Eng

Lux-L, *Lingerie, shoes*
Nevskiy pr., 63 113-15-60

Natali
Moskovskiy pr., 10/12 ....No ☎
Mon-Fri 9-13, 14-18; Rbls

Passage *Collection of Boutiques*   **Passazh**
Nevskiy pr., 48 311-70-84

Prestige, *Blouses, jabot*
Reki Moyki nab., 3 312-77-18
Mon-Fri 9-18; Rbls

RUNO clothing for women
Hand-tailored blouses, dresses, skirts
P.S., Bolshoy pr., 22/24 233-67-18
Mon-Sat 11-14, 15-19; Rbls; Eng; Metro: Petrogradskaya

Stefanel
Nevskiy pr., 70.............................. 164-64-03

TROÏKA RO
A. O. TROIKA
Fashionable Men's & Women's Clothing
Zagorodnyy pr., 28 112-47-46

Voski, *Women's dresses*
Chaykovskogo ul., 36..................... 275-71-47
Mon-Sat 10-14, 15-19; Rbls
Yaroslavna, *Shoes, dresses, blouses, lingerie*
Narodnaya ul., 5 263-81-90
Mon-Sat 10-14, 15-19; Rbls
Yubiley, *Wedding and evening gowns*
Sverdlovskaya nab., 60................... 224-25-98
Mon-Sat 10-14, 15-20; Rbls, $

☎ CLUBS & SOCIETIES
КЛУБЫ И ОБЩЕСТВА
VEREINE UND VERBÄNDE
CLUBS ET SOCIETES
KLUBBAR OCH FÖRENINGAR
KERHOT JA SEURAT

See also AIRPORTS, ASSOCIATIONS, BICYCLING, BUSINESS ASSOCIATIONS, CHESS CLUBS, HUNTING & FISHING, ROWING CLUBS, SKATING, SKIING, VOLLEYBALL CLUBS, SPORTS CLUBS, YACHT CLUBS.

St. Petersburg is full of sports clubs, chess clubs, music clubs, and many other "voluntary associations". Here are a few. For a full list of clubs, see Ves St. Pb. 93 *and* Yellow Pages St. Pb 93.

Airplane Model Club, *Mon-Fri 15-20; Rbls*
Novo-Izmaylovskiy pr., 101............ 295-15-50
Atlantis School of Photomodels
Amateur Photographers
Obvodnogo kan. nab., 114 554-29-83
Mon-Fri 15-19; Rbls
Automotive Society
Zhukovskogo ul., 55 272-11-21
Mon-Fri 9-17:40; Rbls; Bus 174; Metro Ploshchad Vosstaniya
Aviation and Parachute Club
Kosmonavtov pr., 28/8................... 299-08-26
Mon-Fri 11-17; Rbls
Book Lovers Club-Stables of Biron
Bironovy Konyushni
Reki Moyki nab., 12 311-06-19
Fax 311-38-01
Bridge Club, *Tue-Wed, Sun 18:15-22*
Tambovskaya ul., 63, rm. 3............ 166-46-96

Cat Lovers Club   Kis
Chkalovskiy pr., 56........................ 230-26-27
Mon-Sat 15-19; Rbls
Fireplace Vegetarian Club   Ochag
Kutuzova nab., 8 106-59-76
Daily 19-21; Rbls
House of Nature   Dom Prirody
Bolshaya Konyushennaya ul., 8 314-08-48
Mon-Sat 11-19; Rbls
Hunting and Fishing Club   Sreda
Reki Pryazhki nab., 32................... 219-70-74
Mon-Sat 15-19; Rbls
Musical Society
Muzikalnoe Obshchestvo
Reki Moyki nab., 20 315-43-49
Mon-Fri 11-15, 16-19
Petersburg Rock-Club
Peterburgskiy Rok-Klub
Rubinshteyna ul., 13, Tel/fax 314-96-29
Philatelist Union   Soyuz Filatelistov
Griboedova kan. nab., 27................ 314-72-78
Mon-Fri 15-19; Rbls
Society of Collectors
Obshchestvo Kollektsionerov
Rimskogo-Korsakova pr., 53 114-33-41
Mon-Fri 11-19
Women's Club   Zhenskiy Klub
Rubinshteyna ul., 28 312-63-80
Mon-Fri 16-20; Rbls; T-bus 3; Metro Vladimirskaya
World of Hobbies   Mir Uvlecheniy
Srednyaya Podyacheskaya ul., 1.....311-85-36
Mon-Fri 9-18; Rbls, $; Eng, Ger
Youth for the Renaissance of St. Petersburg
Nevskiy pr., 39.............................. 314-57-52

☎ COMMERCIAL STORES
КОММЕРЧЕСКИЕ МАГАЗИНЫ
KOMMERZIELLE LÄDEN
MAGASIN COMMERCIAL
AFFÄRER, PRIVATÄGDA,
KOMMERSIELLA
KAUPALLISET KAUPAT

See also SHOPPING

The term "COMMERCIAL SHOP" was originally used by the Russians to indicate shops that were free to set their own (higher) prices in contrast to "state shops" which had fixed prices. As of June 1993 most prices are "free" (to rise, usually) and the distinction became less meaningful. Even state food stores with controlled prices have "commercial" sections. Now only a few products such as food staples, gas, electricity, telephone, and official rentals still have low subsidized prices.

Small variety stores: There are literally hundreds of "commercial shops" now in St. Petersburg from tiny hole-in-the-walls to elegant fashion salons. Here we list only these smaller shops that have no clear specialty and sell a variety of imported and Russian goods, including liquor, shoes, TV/radios/videos, soft drinks, cigarettes, jeans, clothing, etc. They usually sell for rubles (occasionally for dollars). The selection is remarkably similar from shop to shop. Many more such little shops are stashed away in courtyards and corners of stores.

Shops with a clear specialty have been placed in the appropriate category e.g., CLOTHING, ELECTRONICS.

Adamant, *Cold soda, snacks, water heaters*
Reki Moyki nab., 72 ....No ☎
Daily 10-14, 15-21; $, Rbls

ADS-Luma, *Mon-Sat 10-15, 16-19; Rbls, $; Eng*
Nevskiy pr., 164 277-45-62

Akka
Bolshaya Konyushennaya ul., 3 311-92-75
Women's clothing, men's clothing, leather jackets, refrigerators, microwave ovens. Daily 11-19; Rbls

Alivekt, *Mon-Sat 10-19; Metro Nevskiy Prospekt*
Nevskiy pr., 22/24 315-59-78
Fax 234-90-96

Ameros Business Company
Ligovskiy pr., 87 164-21-28
Fax 112-18-44
Mon-Sat 10-18; Rbls, $

Babylon Shops
A leading retailer with 10 stores. See ads under CLOTHING, CLOTHING-MEN, CLOTHING-WOMEN, ELECTRONICS, FABRICS, HOUSEWARES, *and* SUPERMARKETS.

Baltica Shop, *Mon-Sat 9-14, 15-19; Rbls; Eng*
Timurovskaya ul., 8 592-78-82

Boston, *Mon-Sat 10-19; Rbls*
Shvernika pr., 37 552-22-18

Butterfly
Moskovskiy pr., 63 292-48-93

Capricorn, *See our ad under* CLOTHING
• Varshavskaya ul., 51 218-11-23
  Fax 296-43-51
• Moskovskiy pr., 39 292-68-01
  Fax 292-79-05
Mon-Sat 11-14, 15-20; Rbls

Commission Store No. 64
Clothing, Costume Jewelry
Apraksin Dvor , Section 25-27 310-36-29
Mon-Sat 10-14, 15-19; Rbls

Christmas   **Rozhdestvo**
Toreza pr., 43 247-09-45
Daily 10-14, 15-19; Rbls; Metro Politekhnicheskaya

Gallery 102, *Clothing, lingerie, purses, leather jackets, shoes, audio-video equip., telephones*
Nevskiy pr., 102 275-57-66
Mon-Sat 11-20; Rbls; Eng, Finn, Ital

Gera, *Glassware, alcoholic drinks*
Bolshaya Konyushennaya ul., 5 311-02-53
Mon-Sat 10-14, 15-19; Rbls; Eng

Griffon, *Audio-video equipment, women's bathing suits, shoes, lighting fixtures*
Zagorodnyy pr., 28 113-27-95
Fax 113-16-60
Daily 10-14, 15-19; Rbls; Metro Dostoevskaya

Iris, *Daily 11-20; Rbls*
Liteynyy pr., 23 273-21-53

Kantemirovskaya 17, *Mon-Sat 10-19; Rbls*
Kantemirovskaya ul., 17 542-88-89

Kometa, *Mon-Fri 9-17; Rbls*
Yuriya Gagarina pr., 42 127-97-40

Kosmos, *Food, clothing*
Mokhovaya ul., 39 273-34-05
Mon-Sat 11-15, 16-20, Sun 11-17

Kraun, *Audio, clothing, dishes*
Bolshoy pr., P.S., 72 232-25-10
Mon-Fri 10-19; Rbls

Leo, *Mon-Sat 11-20; Rbls, $; Eng*
Zhukovskogo ul., 8 273-70-92

Ligovskiy 142, *Daily 9-19; Rbls*
Ligovskiy pr., 142 166-42-74

Meridian Tradehouse, *Mon-Sat 10-14, 15-19*
Varshavskaya ul., 58 293-33-44

Metro, *Mon-Sat 10-20; Rbls*
Griboedova kan. nab., 16 ....No ☎

Micas AG, *Mon-Sat 10-14, 15-19; Rbls, $*
7-ya Krasnoarmeyskaya ul., 6/8 112-75-04

Milena, *Mon-Fri 10-14, 15-19; Rbls*
Razezzhaya ul., 8 315-98-81

Nevskiy Prospect   **Dom Modeley**
Souvenirs, costume & fine jewelry, custom-made dresses. See our ad under CLOTHING.
Nevskiy pr., 21 311-44-48
Mon-Fri 8-17; Rbls; Eng, Fr

Nina
Audio-video equipment, clocks, women's clothing
Sadovaya ul., 89 114-43-52
Mon-Sat 10-19; Rbls

Novinka
Costume jewelry, car audio, women's dresses
Vladimirskiy pr., 17 112-52-22
Fax 164-02-82
Mon-Fri 11-19; Rbls, $; Eng

Oggo, *Mon-Sat 10-14, 15-19; Rbls; Eng*
Suvorovskiy pr., 26 271-77-94

Oksana
Lomonosova ul., 11 314-25-17
Mon-Sat 10-14, 15-19; Rbls; Metro Dostoevskaya

Onega
Suvorovskiy pr., 54 274-38-12
Fax 110-71-18
Daily 10-14, 15-20; Rbls

Orion
Volynskiy per., 8 314-15-59
Imported and Russian watches, cosmetics, men's and women's clothing; Daily 10-20; Rbls; Eng, Finn

Peter's Island   **Petrovskiy Ostrov**
Kronverkskiy pr., 65 232-45-96
Fax 233-75-41
Daily 9-14, 15-20; Rbls; Eng

Real Music
Nevskiy pr., 54 310-59-22
Mon-Sat 10-14, 15-19; Rbls, $; Eng, Ger

Rozhdestvenskaya
Nevskiy pr., 120 277-59-05
Fax 277-31-03
Video equipment, dresses, blouses, shirts, suits, jeans, trousers and shoes. Mon-Sat 9-19; Rbls

Sadko
Petra Alekseeva ul., 11 315-63-09
Two entrances, one sells audio/video equipment, telephones, faxes, the other liquor and soft drinks. Daily 11-19; Rbls, $

Skif
Crystal, audio/video equipment, clocks, clothing
• Leninskiy pr., 124 254-21-84
  Daily 10-14, 15-19; Rbls
• Lomonosova ul., 1/28 312-16-14
  Daily 10-14, 15-20; Rbls

Soto
Novocherkasskiy pr., 21 528-89-55
*Daily 11-14:30, 15-19; Rbls; Eng
Tram 7; Metro Novocherkasskaya*

Sovex, *Mon-Sat 11-14, 15-20; Rbls, $*
Sredneokhtinskiy pr., 41 224-29-93

Store No. 114, *Mon-Sat 10-14, 15-19; Rbls*
Novo-Izmaylovskiy pr., 40, bldg. 1 295-90-28

Store-Salon
Women's and men's clothing, cosmetics, glassware
Furshtadtskaya ul., 42.................... 272-66-33
Mon-Fri 11-14, 15-19; Rbls

Surf, *Daily 11-14, 15-20; Rbls; Eng, Ger*
Mashkov per., 5............................. 312-04-29
Fax 311-82-82

Temp, *Daily 10-14, 15-21; Rbls; Eng*
Sredneokhtinskiy pr., 47 227-48-20

Top, *Mon-Sat 10-19; Rbls*
Apraksin dvor , rm. 35-36 310-30-58

Torbi, *Tue-Sun 10-19; Rbls*
Sadovaya ul., 51 315-98-34

Tradehouse of Holland
See CLOTHING and FOOD

Troika
Bolshaya Konyushennaya ul., 17 314-13-21
Mon-Sat 11-14, 15-20; Rbls; Eng, Ger, Fr
Bus 47; Metro Nevskiy Prospekt

Union, *Cosmetics, clothing, shoes, liquor*
Gorokhovaya ul., 13 314-84-44

Universal, *Mon-Sat 11-14, 15-20; Rbls*
Moskovskiy pr., 4 310-14-76

Vesta Tradehouse
Lanskoe shosse, 16 246-32-48
Fax 242-17-63
Mon-Fri 10-14, 15-19; Rbls, $; Eng

Vika
Bolshaya Konyushennaya ul., 6-8 312-96-72
Audio-video equipment, televisions, men's and women's clothing; Mon-Sat 10-14, 15-19; Rbls; Eng

☎ COMMISSION STORES
КОМИССИОННЫЕ МАГАЗИНЫ
KOMMISIONSLÄDEN
SECOND-HAND-LÄDEN
MAGASINS D'OCCASION
PROVISIONS AFFÄRER
OSTO- JA MYYNTILIIKKEET

See also PAWN SHOPS, ANTIQUES

There is a long established tradition in Russia of selling goods bought abroad for resale here, and selling Babushka's heirlooms to stay afloat. Thus there are many Commission Shops (Second-hand stores), called Komissionnyy magazin (Комиссионный магазин) *which specialize in consignment buying and selling of second-hand clothes, footwear, furniture, refrigerators, carpets, electronics, automobiles, etc. These shops are worth a visit because you may find old silver, jewelry, or antiques. In contrast to* Commercial Stores, *where things are not necessarily new and charge the seller up to 25% commission. Some commission shops now have commercial departments as well.*

Specialized commission shops may also be found under ART GALLERIES, FURS, ANTIQUES, JEWELRY, *and* PAWN SHOPS.

15-Elit, *Audio and radio*
Moskovskiy pr., 50 292-54-52
Mon-Sat 10-19; Rbls

Bolshoy 44, *Shoes*
Bolshoy pr., P.S., 44...................... 232-01-29
Mon-Sat 10-19; Rbls

Commission Store No. 10 (Under Repair)
Apraksin dvor , Section 35-36........ 310-30-58
Mon-Sat 10-14, 15-19; Rbls

Commission Store No. 16
Apraksin dvor, Section 32-34 110-45-59
Clothing, shoes, rugs, building supplies
Mon-Sat 10-14, 15-19; Rbls

Commission Store No. 35, *Fabrics, shoes, furs*
Nevskiy pr., 124 277-23-01
Mon-Sat 10-14, 15-19; Rbls
T-bus 1; Metro Ploshchad Vosstaniya

Commission Store No. 42
Marata ul., 53................................. 164-75-33
Furniture, TV's, refrigerators
Mon-Sat 10-14, 15-19; Rbls

Commission Store No. 76, *Art*
Kazanskaya ul., 39 312-72-53
Mon-Sat 10-14, 15-19; Rbls

Farfor, Khrustal, Bronza
                    China, Crystal, Bronze
Kamennoostrovskiy pr., 4............... 232-85-80
Mon-Sat 10-14, 15-19; Rbls; Eng

Na Gorkovskoy, *Furs*
Kamennoostrovskiy pr., 2............... 233-51-53
Mon-Sat 11-14, 15-20

Petersburg, *Antiques*
Nevskiy pr., 54............................... 311-40-20
Mon-Sat 10-14, 15-19

Svetla, *Lighting fixtures, housewares*
Stachek pr., 82............................... 183-42-74
Mon-Sat 10-14, 15-19; Rbls; Bus 66; Metro Avtovo

Vizit, *Shoes, dresses, lingerie*
Ligovskiy pr., 96 164-98-65
Mon-Sat 10-14, 15-19; Rbls

☎ COMMODITY EXCHANGE

See STOCK & COMMODITY EXCHANGE

☎ COMMUNICATIONS
СВЯЗЬ, УСЛУГИ
NACHRICHTENWESEN/POST-
UND FERNMELDEWESEN
COMMUNICATION
TELEKOMMUNIKATION
TIETOLIIKENNE

See also TELEPHONE-INTERNATIONAL, TELEPHONE, TELEGRAM, EXPRESS MAIL/PARCEL SERVICE, ELECTRONIC MAIL, TELEX, FAX, *and* CELLULAR PHONE.

BUSINESS CENTERS *often specialize in international communications via satellite.*

Alcatel
Gertsena ul., 16.............................. 315-89-38
Fax... 315-94-74
Mon-Fri 9-18; Rbls, $; Eng, Fr, Finn, Ital

┌───┐
BCL (*See our ad under* TELEPHONE SERVICE)
Konnogvardeyskiy blvd., 4 311-14-88
Fax... 314-86-60
Mon-Fri 8-17; $; Eng
└───┘

┌───┐
Bikar Communications
Communication Systems Installation
& Technical Service
3-ya Sovetskaya ul., 19 274-42-91
Fax 110-49-69
└───┘

Dauer
  Ispolkomskaya ul., 4/6 277-54-85
Delta Telecom *See our ad in* CELLULAR PHONES
  Gertsena ul., 22 314-61-26
  Fax 314-88-37
        Mon-Fri 9-18; Rbls, $
Express-Post, *Mon-Fri 10-18*
  Konnogvardeyskiy blvd., 4, off. 22 311-23-46
Informcomset
  Yuriya Gagarina pr., 1, rm. 312, 313
  ☎ 294-86-97
  Fax 294-88-91
        Mon-Fri 9-18; Rbls; Eng
Inros-Broker, *Mon-Fri 10-17; Rbls, $*
  Kazachiy per., 9, apt. 129 310-49-38
Kaiya, *Mon-Fri 11-19; Rbls, $*
  Myasnikova ul., 6 235-30-76
LDM (Leningradskiy Dvorets Molodezhi)
  Professora Popova ul., 47 234-06-96
        Mon-Fri 11-18; Rbls
Lenbell, *Telephone systems*
  Malookhtinskiy pr., 68 528-02-35
  Fax 528-74-14
        Mon-Fri 10-18
Lenceltel, *Mon-Fri 9:30-17; Rbls; Eng*
  Kostromskaya ul., 7 274-46-41
Lenfincom
  Gertsena ul., 3/5 110-69-17
  Fax 312-32-73
Mon-Fri 8:30-17; $; Eng; T-bus 5; Metro Nevskiy Prospekt
Masshtab
  Kantemirovskaya ul., 6 245-51-65
  Mon-Fri 8-17; Rbls, $; Eng; T-bus 46; Metro Petrogradskaya
Novintech-Infopro, *Mon-Fri 10-19*
  Gdanskaya ul., 17 553-94-05

PETERSTAR, *See* - TELEPHONE SERVICE
  Bldg. 31, Line 16, V.O., 199178, St. Petersburg
  Tel 119-60-60
  Fax 119-90-02

St. Petersburg City Telephone Company
    Sankt-Peterburgskaya Gorodskaya
        Telefonnaya Stantsiya
  Gertsena ul., 3/5 274-93-83
  Fax 315-17-01
        Daily 0-24; Rbls, $; Eng
Silex, *Mon-Fri 9-19; Rbls, $*
  Volodi Ermaka ul., 9 219-75-87
  Fax 219-70-00
Sprint Network, *Daily 0-24; Rbls; Eng*
  Sinopskaya nab., 14 265-05-71
  Fax 274-26-21
Transelectro OY, *Mon-Fri 9-18; Rbls, $*
  Moskovskiy pr., 171 294-06-35
  Fax 294-04-43

☎ **COMPACT DISKS**
   КОМПАКТ-ДИСКИ
   COMPACT DISCS
   COMPACTES-DISQUES
   SKIVOR, CD
   CD-LEVYT

See also RECORDS, MUSIC STORES

Compact disks are available throughout St. Pb. in electronic stores, kiosks, and music stores. The selection is highly variable. Buy it when you see it. Prices are

about the same as in the USA. For compact disk players, see AUDIO-VIDEO *and* ELECTRONICS.

DLT (Leningrad Trading House)
  Bolshaya Konyushennaya ul., 21/23 312-26-27
  Fax 315-21-92
        Mon-Sat 10-20; Rbls, $; Eng
Diez Record Store, *Mon-Sat 11-19; Rbls*
  Transportnyy per., 6 164-95-79
Electronica Gallery and Shop
  Yuriya Gagarina pr., 12 299-38-49
     Mon-Sat 10-14, 15-19; Rbls, $
Gostinyy Dvor, *Perinnaya Liniya*
  Nevskiy pr., 35 310-53-66
        Mon-Sat 10-21; Rbls
Gramplastinki   **Records**
 • Nevskiy pr., 32-34 311-74-55
     Mon-Sat 11-14, 15-19; Rbls
 • Moskovskiy pr., 34/36 292-35-05
     Tue-Sun 10-14, 15-19; Rbls
 • 7-ya Liniya, 40 213-35-88
       Mon-Sat 10-19; Rbls
Severnaya Lira   **Northern Lira**
    Musical literature, compact disks
  Nevskiy pr., 26 312-07-96
  Mon-Sat 10-14, 15-19; Rbls; Metro Nevskiy Prospekt
Tradehouse on Moyka
  Reki Moyki nab., 59 315-60-38
     Daily 10-14, 15-19; Rbls, $

☎ **COMPUTER COURSES**
   КОМПЬЮТЕРНЫЕ КУРСЫ
   COMPUTERKURSE
   ORDINATEUR, COURS
   DATAKURSER
   ATK-KURSSIT

Many institutes offer computer courses.

Center for Computer Technology at the Technical University
  Politekhnicheskaya ul., 29 552-76-62
      Mon-Sat 9:30-17:30; Rbls
Humanities Center
  Griboedova kan. nab., 92/1 310-20-90
       Mon-Fri 9-17:30; Rbls
Independent College of Humanities
  Voznesenskiy pr., 34 b 314-35-21
       Mon-Fri 10-22; Rbls
Obuchenie *Computer programming* **Education**
 • Leninskiy pr., 149 259-60-65
      Mon-Fri 10-16; Rbls, $
 • Zagorodnyy pr., 58 292-40-05
   Daily 10-19; Rbls, $; Eng, Ger, Fr, Finn, Ital

Progress Management and Marketing Center, *See our color ad*
  Institutskiy pr., 22 552-13-38
  552-69-62
  Fax 552-77-28
        Mon-Fri 10-18; Rbls

Scientific-Training Center
  Energetikov pr., 60, bldg. 2 226-07-48
  Mon-Fri 10-17; Rbls; Bus 102; Metro Ploshchad Lenina
Spektr NPO, *Mon-Fri 10-17*
  Moiseenko ul., 15/17 271-68-05
St. Petersburg Educational Center
  Aerodromnaya ul., 4 394-50-04
      Mon-Fri 9:30-18:30; Rbls, $

☎ COMPUTER PROGRAMMING
КОМПЬЮТЕРЫ,
ПРОГРАММИРОВАНИЕ
COMPUTER, PROGRAMMIERUNG
ORDINATEUR,
PROGRAMME INFORMATIQUE
DATAPROGRAMMERING
ATK-OHJELMOINTI

St. Petersburg abounds with excellent programmers to write specialized software and do designs.

Ajax Ltd., *Mon-Fri 10-17:30; Rbls, $; Eng, Ger*
Galernaya ul., 55 314-39-45
Fax 312-24-79
Ascon, *Mon-Fri 10-20; Rbls; Eng*
Obvodnogo kan. nab., 132 259-18-00
Askod, *Mon-Fri 10-19; Rbls, $; Eng*
Reki Fontanki nab., 6 275-58-14
Fax 275-58-16
Association of Artificial Intelligence
Gastello per., 12 293-05-40
Mon-Sat 9-16
Center for Computer Technology at the Technical University
Politekhnicheskaya ul., 29 552-76-62
Mon-Sat 9:30-17:30; Rbls
Defis, *Mon-Fri 10-17; Rbls, $; Eng*
Reki Fontanki nab., 117 278-50-88
Dialogue-Invest, *Mon-Fri 9-18; Rbls, $; Eng*
Dostoevskogo ul., 19/21 164-89-56
Elinor, *Mon-Fri 10-16*
Millionnaya ul., 27 311-78-46
Etlas (Official Borland Dealer)
14-ya Liniya, 39 218-08-87
Mon-Fri 11-19; Rbls, $
Infotran, *Mon-Fri 10-18; Rbls, $; Eng, Ger*
Ligovskiy pr., 275, apt. 42 112-87-60
Fax 166-36-14
Intellekt Bank, *Mon-Fri 9-20; Rbls, $; Eng*
197046 P.O. Box 401 272-30-38
Intercompex, *Mon-Fri 9-18; Rbls; Eng*
Kalinina ul., 13 221-76-31
Fax 186-33-90
LIPK, *Mon-Fri 11-16; Rbls*
Metallistov pr., 115 540-93-69
Obuchenie, *Computer courses*   **Education**
See listing in computer courses
Service-Informatika, *Mon-Fri 10-16; Rbls, $*
Nevskiy pr., 81 277-04-80

☎ COMPUTER REPAIR
КОМПЬЮТЕРЫ, РЕМОНТ
COMPUTER, REPARATUR
ORDINATEURS, REPARATION
DATAREPARATIONER
ATK-KORJAUKSET

See also COMPUTER STORES*, especially for authorized service.*

Arnica Prima
Aptekarskiy pr., 10, apt. 2
Tel 234-20-18
Fax 234-21-18
*Computers, copiers, software
service, repair, Cyrillic fonts*

Bereg, *Mon-Fri 10-19; Rbls*
Bolshaya Raznochinnaya ul., 4, apt. 36
☎ 230-00-32
Fax 230-11-93

Bikar Computer Repair
Office Electronics Repair & Technical Service
3-ya Sovetskaya ul., 19
Tel/Fax 274-42-91

Business Project, *Mon-Fri 10-18; Rbls, $*
Aptekarskiy pr., 10, apt. 8 234-32-70
Fax 234-52-45
Computer Wave, *Mon-Fri 10-17; Rbls, $; Eng*
Dostoevskogo ul., 6 224-04-55
Fax 164-83-08
Dialogue-Invest, *Mon-Fri 9-18; Rbls, $; Eng*
Dostoevskogo ul., 19/21 164-89-56
Elinor, *Mon-Fri 10-16*
Millionnaya ul., 27 311-78-46

JV **MacTech**
St. Petersburg

Authorized Dealer 🍎 Apple Computer
Russia, 191025
Povarskoy per., 8 112-38-44
Fax 112-53-59
Telex 121222

Mak, *Mon-Fri 9-13, 14-18; Rbls, $; Eng*
Novocherkasskiy pr., 12, bldg. 2 528-48-50
Mister PC, *Mon-Fri 10-14, 15-18; Rbls, $*
Shvernika pr., 49 110-77-64
Nienschanz, *Mon-Fri 10-18; Rbls, $*
Orenburgskaya ul., 4 542-91-67
Fax 542-55-47
Procom, *Mon-Fri 10-19; Rbls; Eng*
Stachek pr., 47 183-61-14
Fax 184-98-46
St. Petersburg Business Center
Marata ul., 78 164-40-37
Mon-Fri 10-19; $
Stalker, *Mon-Fri 9-13:30, 14:30-18; Rbls*
25-ya Liniya, 8 217-90-01
UMA, *See our ad under COMPUTER STORES*
Malookhtinskiy pr., 68 528-95-66

☎ COMPUTER SOFTWARE
КОМПЬЮТЕРНО-
ПРОГРАММНЫЕ ПРОДУКТЫ
COMPUTER, SOFTWARE
ORDINATEUR,
COMPUTER SOFTWARE
DATATILLBEHÖR, MJUKVARA
ATK-OHJELMAT

There are now many authorized dealers of Western software, some in Russified versions. Russian and American programmers have produced a large number of joint Latin-Russian fonts according to a standard protocol that allows for simple switch between the Cyrillic and Latin

Keyboards. These fonts sort properly in both languages. Such fonts are used to produce The Traveller's *Yellow Pages.*

Arnica Prima, *Software, Cyrillic fonts*
Aptekarskiy pr., 10, apt. 2 234-20-18
Fax 234-21-18

Amira, *Mon-Fri 9-18; Rbls; Eng, Arab*
Kalinina ul., 22 186-57-57
Amos
Pavlogradskiy per., 6/10 164-40-78

Tyushina ul., 11 164-92-08
Tel./Fax... 164-47-13

ComputerLand ®

Saint Petersburg
SALES, SERVICE, TRAINING
SUPPORT
Personal computer systems
Office electronics
Complete solutions
Authorized Dealer
IBM, Compaq, Minolta
and other leading brands
Nab. Sverdlovskaya, 64 224-04-55
Fax....................................224-09-32

EVM-Frederiksson, *Mon-Fri 10-18; Rbls, $*
Tyushina ul., 3 164-61-85
Fax 166-72-85
East Concept, *Mon-Fri 9:30-18; Rbls; Eng*
Baltiyskaya ul., 26 185-07-81
ELCO - Technology - *See ad below*
Etlas (Official Borland Dealer)
14 Liniya, 39 218-08-87
         Mon-Fri 11-19; Rbls, $
Intellekt Bank, *Mon-Fri 9-20; Rbls, $; Eng*
197046, P.O. Box 401 272-30-38
Intersoft, *Mon-Fri 10-18*
Leninskiy pr., 160 290-91-67
Iteks, *Mon-Fri 9:30-18; Rbls, $; Eng*
Lesnoy pr., 61, bldg. 1, entr. 8 245-55-12
Institute of Simulation Technology
   Computer Center
Liteynyy pr., 57 113-55-35
         Mon-Fri 10-19
Leningradintekh
Chkalovskiy pr., 52 235-58-74
Fax 230-13-07
   Mon-Fri 9-13, 13:45-17:45; Rbls, $; Eng, Ger, Fr
Link, *Mon-Fri 9-18; Rbls, $; Eng*
Ropshinskaya ul., 1 230-67-95
Fax 235-48-31
Mac-Tech St. Petersburg, *See ad on page 121.*
Microfort, *Mon-Fri 9-18; Rbls*
Zelenkov per., 7 a 542-29-07
Fax 542-12-67

ELCO
TECHNOLOGY
Electronic & Computer Technology, Ltd.

Authorized Distributor
NOVELL Inc. & DELL Computer Corp.
NetWare systems.

Moscow, 9/10 Vernadskogo pr.,
Russia, 117311
Tel : (+7-095) 131-5555
Fax: (+7-095) 131-1684
St. Petersburg, 26 Goncharnaya st.,
Russia, 193036
Tel : (+7-812) 277-7175
Fax: (+7-812) 277-5807

NOVELL D&LL

JV MacTech
St. Petersburg

Authorized dealer Apple Computer
Russia, 191025
Povarskoy per., 8 112-38-44
Fax.. 112-53-59
Telex 121222

Monolit-Info, *Mon-Fri 10-20; Rbls, $; Eng*
Ryleeva ul., 29 273-53-33
Neyvo, *Mon-Fri 10-20; Rbls; Eng*
Izmaylovskiy pr., 2 259-50-14
Novell Netware *See ELCO and Soft-Tronik ads*
Novintech-Infopro, *Mon-Fri 10-19*
Gdanskaya ul., 17........................... 553-94-05

OLLY Ltd. SCO Authorized Reseller
V.O., 14-ya Liniya, 39 218-04-50
Fax 213-33-88
       Hrs: 9-18; Eng

РУБИКОН
Rubicon
Lesnoy pr., 19
542-00-65, 248-83-06
Fax.............542-09-89
Telex 121194 Rub SU

Official Business Partner
IBM
MINOLTA
Gold Star
Hewlett Packard

soft-tronik ™
creative computer technology

Authorized distributors in Russia
Novell Netware & SCO Unix
Networks and Multi-User Systems

Nab. reki Fontanki, 88	*........315-92-76*
Fax	*...................311-01-08*
Telex	*...................121-184 SOFT SU*

Hrs: 9-18, $ & rbl

☎ **COMPUTER STORES**
КОМПЬЮТЕРЫ, ПРОДАЖА
COMPUTER, FACHGESCHÄFTE
ORDINATEURS, MAGASINS D'
DATAAFFÄRER
ATK-LIIKKEET

See also COMPUTER REPAIR *and* COMPUTER
SOFTWARE

Aerotelekom ATS
Tukhachevskogo ul., 27, rm. 1507, Hotel Kareliya
Fax 226-57-11
Daily 0-24; Rbls, $; Eng, Ger

Ailend
Nevskiy pr., 102........................ 272-22-67
Mon-Fri 10-19; Rbls

Ajax Ltd.
Galernaya ul., 55...................... 314-39-45
Fax 312-24-79
Mon-Fri 10-17:30; Rbls, $; Eng, Ger

Algonik
Bolshaya Konyushennaya ul., 2....... 312-20-21
Mon-Sat 10-19; Rbls; Eng

Amos
Pavlogradskiy per., 6/10 164-40-78

Argo
Kuybysheva ul., 38/40................... 232-72-56
Mon-Sat 10-14, 15-19; Rbls; Ger
Tram 30; Metro Gorkovskaya

Arnika-Prima
Aptekarskiy pr., 10, rm. 2.............. 234-20-18
Fax 234-21-18
Mon-Fri 10-18; Rbls, $; Metro Petrogradskaya

ASKoD
Reki Fontanki nab., 6 275-58-14
Fax 275-58-16
Mon-Fri 10-19; Rbls, $; Eng

Baltex
Blagodatnaya ul., 55 294-10-23
Mon-Fri 10-19; Rbls; Eng, Ger, Fr

Bereg
Bolshaya Raznochinnaya ul., 4, apt. 36
☎ 230-00-32
Fax 230-11-93
Mon-Fri 10-19; Rbls

Biem
Oktyabrskaya nab., 6.................... 532-06-13
Mon-Sat 10-13, 14-19; Rbls

Bive
Konnogvardeyskiy blvd., 4, entr. 4, apt. 20
☎ 312-78-35
Fax 315-39-51
Mon-Fri 10-17; Rbls; Eng, Ger

Business Project
Aptekarskiy pr., 10, apt. 8 234-32-70
Fax................................. 234-52-45
Mon-Fri 10-18; Rbls, $

Compan MK
Marshala Govorova ul., 52.............. 252-02-68
Fax....................................... 252-17-73
Mon-Fri 9-18; Rbls, $; Eng, Ger

Computer Gallery
Nab. Kutuzova, 10
Tel. 275-09-73
Fax: 272-79-68
Address to be changed

Computer Systems
1-ya Krasnoarmeyskaya ul., 18....... 292-40-20
Fax....................................... 292-21-67
Mon-Fri 10-19; Rbls, $; Eng

Computer Wave
Dostoevskogo ul., 6 224-04-55
Fax....................................... 164-83-08
Mon-Fri 10-17; Rbls, $; Eng, Ger

ComputerLand ®

Saint Petersburg
**SALES, SERVICE, TRAINING
SUPPORT**
**Personal computer systems
Office electronics
Complete solutions**
Authorized Dealer
IBM, Compaq, Minolta
and other leading brands

Nab. Sverdlovskaya, 64 224-04-55
Fax 224-09-32

Computer, video, graphics
CREAT

**The Solution to All Your Business
Computer Needs**
• Computers & Local Area Networks
• Complete Line of Computer
  Accessories
• SCSI Systems
• Video Studios -
  BETACAM SP, S - VHS
• Professional Videocassettes
• Computer Design
• Video Advertisements

Kazanskaya ul., 49
Tel. 311-13-01   Fax: 312-43-12

 HEWLETT PACKARD | SONY | IBM

Dell Computers
See ELCO ad in COMPUTER SOFTWARE

Dialogue-Invest
Dostoevskogo ul., 19/21 164-89-56
Mon-Fri 9-18; Rbls, $; Eng

Diskom, *Authorized Citizen dealer*
Volkovskiy pr., 146, bldg. 3............ 268-45-86
Fax 268-05-04
Mon-Fri 9-14:30

Doovesta Sau
10-ya Krasnoarmeyskaya ul., 19, rm. 239
☎ 259-23-78
Fax 542-86-38
Mon-Fri 9-17:30; Rbls, $; Eng

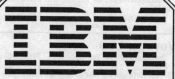

EASTMARKET
Bolshaya Konyushennaya ul., 27
Tel 312-88-39; 315-87-38
Fax 314-22-73

EVM-Frederiksson, *Equipment, software*
Tyushina ul., 3 164-61-85
Fax 166-72-85
Mon-Fri 10-18; Rbls, $

Elinor, *Mon-Fri 10-16*
Millionnaya ul., 27 311-78-46

Evrika
Reki Fontanki nab., 6 275-58-15
Fax 275-58-16
Mon-Fri 10-19; Rbls, $; Eng, Ger, Fr

Fanni, *Mon-Sat 12-20; Rbls; Eng*
Bolshaya Konyushennaya ul., 27 315-13-36

Fotrelle, *Mon-Fri 10-18; Rbls, $; Eng*
Nevskiy pr., 58........................... 312-32-01

Global USA - *See our color ad*
Moscow, Usacheva ul., 35
☎ .... (095) 245-56-57

IBM
ST.PETERSBURG OFFICE
Computers
Information Systems
Marketing & Services

Admiralteyskiy pr., 6	Адмиралтейский пр., 6
191065, St.Petersburg	191065, С.-Петербург
Tel. (812) 312-60-17	Тел. (812)312-60-17
Fax (812) 312-38-87	Факс.(812)312-38-87

ТОО *ИНГРЕСС СП* ※ *INGRESS SP* Ltd.
‖‖‖‖‖‖‖‖‖‖‖‖‖‖‖‖‖‖‖ **SALES** ‖‖‖‖‖‖‖‖‖‖‖‖‖‖‖‖‖
COMPUTERS, PRINTERS, COMPUTER SYSTEMS
Dekabristov ul., 35, Saint Petersburg, 190121
Tel. (812) 114-11-35, Tel./Fax (812) 114-37-44

Ingress
Shpalernaya ul., 40 275-64-88
Mon-Fri 10-15, 15:30-20; Rbls, $

Intercompex
Kalinina ul., 13 221-76-31
Fax.. 186-33-90
Mon-Fri 9-18; Rbls; Eng

Irik
Reki Monastyrki nab., 3 274-38-88
Mon-Fri 10-13, 14-17; Rbls, $; Eng

Ivanov A. P. Tradehouse
Please call.............................. 310-57-86
Mon-Sat 10-20; Rbls, $

Konkom
Reki Fontanki nab., 102, apt 13 167-04-56
Daily 11-20; Rbls, $; Eng

Kontur
Sredneokhtinskiy pr., 6, apt. 40...... 222-54-90
Fax.. 222-26-91
Mon-Fri 10-18; Rbls, $

Kopiya   Copy
Partizana Germana ul., 37, apt. 4 130-78-00
Fax.. 130-80-98
Mon-Fri 9-18; Rbls, $; Eng, Ger

Kvant-Neva, *Authorized Hayes Dealer & Intermed distributor, sales, service, computer networks*
Shvedskiy per., 2 311-97-85
Fax.. 314-18-59
Mon-Fri 9:30-18, Rbls; Eng

Lance
Reki Fontanki nab., 48.................. 113-26-59
Fax.. 314-12-73
Mon-Fri 10-14, 15-18; Rbls, $; Eng, Ger; Metro Dostoevskaya

Linkomp
Kuybysheva ul., 28 232-53-45
Fax.. 232-60-96
Mon-Fri 10-18; Rbls, $; Eng

Lyumena, *Will open in October 1993.*
5-ya Sovetskaya ul., 18 528-96-06
Fax.. 528-96-12
Mon-Fri 8:30-18; Rbls, $; Eng, Ger

 JV MacTech
St. Petersburg

Authorized Dealer 🍎 Apple Computer
Russia, 191025
Povarskoy per., 8................ 112-38-44
Fax 112-53-59
Telex................................ 121222

Mak
Novocherkasskiy pr., 12, bldg. 2 528-48-50
Mon-Fri 9-13, 14-18; Rbls, $; Eng

Mega
Komsomola ul., 41 248-42-32
Fax.. 542-55-45
Mon-Fri 10-17; Rbls, $; Eng

MKS St. Petersburg
16-ya Liniya, 11 213-64-47
Mon-Fri 10-17; Rbls; Eng

Neko
Kutuzova nab., 10 275-09-73
Fax 278-88-56
Mon-Fri 10-18; Rbls, $; Eng; Metro Chernyshevskaya
Nienschanz, *Mon-Fri 10-18; Rbls, $*
Orenburgskaya ul., 4 542-91-67
Fax 542-55-47
Novoindeks, *Mon-Sat 10-18; Rbls*
Mozhayskaya ul., 6 292-27-85

OLLY
SCO Authorized Reseller
SCO UNIX Multi-Processor Computers &
Workstations for Banks, Factories,
Hospitals, Exchanges, etc.
V.O., 14-ya Liniya, 39 218-04-50
Fax 213-33-88
Hrs: 9-18; Eng

Online, *Mon-Fri 10-18; Rbls, $; Eng*
Izmaylovskiy pr., 14 .... No ☎
Peterburzhets, *Mon-Fri 9-12, 12:45-18:30; Rbls*
Zagorodnyy pr., 40 164-29-00

 POLRADIS
computer systems

STAR MICRONICS - printers
authorized distributor

IBM - computer systems
business partner,
local service organization

sales, installation & support

NETWORK DESIGN & INSTALLATION

Gagarina pr., 1
tel.294-85-41, 294-85-85, fax.294-87-83
Telex: 121 025 LIPVM SU
Metro: Elektrosila, hrs 10AM-8PM

$ & Rbl, English

Procom
Stachek pr., 47 183-61-14
Fax 184-98-46
Mon-Fri 10-19; Rbls; Eng
R+P Superwave Electronic GmbH
Yakubovicha ul., 6
Fax 110-63-69
Mon-Fri 10-19; Rbls, $

 **RAMEC**

Personal computers from our in-store stock
Custom configurations from
brand name components
2 Year Warranty and Service
Local Networks & Peripherals
Obruchevykh ul., 1
Tel/Fax 277-69-60

Renaissance
Malaya Posadskaya ul., 17 233-44-17
Fax 232-12-90
Mon-Sat 11-20; Rbls, $; Eng

 РУБИКОН   *Official*
Business
Partner
Rubicon   **IBM**
Lesnoy pr., 19   **MINOLTA**
542-00-65, 248-83-06   **Gold Star**
Fax.............542-09-89   **Hewlett Packard**
Telex 121194 Rub SU

Sinus
Morskoy Pekhoty ul., 8, bldg. 1, apt. 4
☎ 157-57-94
Mon-Fri 10-17; Rbls, $; Eng, Fr, Finn
Soft-tronik, *See ad on next page*
Reki Fontanki nab., 88 315-92-76
Fax 311-01-08
Unirem, *See ad on next page*
Dobrolyubova pr., 6/2 232-61-55
Vesta
Vyborgskaya nab., 27 542-88-09
Mon-Fri 9-19

Voyager LTD
Vosstaniya ul., 18, apt. 40 275-49-43
Fax 275-49-45
Hrs: 10-19, rbl & $, Metro Ploshchad Vosstaniya

DELOVIE LYUDI
INDEPENDENT • OBJECTIVE • THOROUGH
Profsoyuznaya ul., 73; Tel.: (095) 333-33-40; Fax: (095) 330-15-68

soft-tronik™
creative computer technology

Branch office St. Petersburg
soft-tronik GmbH, *Germany*
Specializing in
Networks and Multi-User Systems
Authorized distributors in Russia
Novell Netware & SCO Unix,
3Com, U.S. Robotics, APC ups, Wyse
Complete systems, sales and service
from small shops and offices
to large banks and factories
Nab. reki Fontanki, 88.......315-92-76
Fax 311-01-08
Telex .... 121-184 SOFT SU
Hrs: 9-18, $ & Rbls

UNIREM COMPUTERS

Authorized Hewlett Packard Dealer
Laser Printers, Scanners, Plotters
& Computer Systems
Sales & Service
Up to a 2 Year Guarantee
Authorized Farbax Dealer
Inkjet, Laserjet & Photocopier
Refill & Refurbishing
Select from Black,
Blue & Brown Toner
Dobrolyubova pr., 6/2
Tel.: 232-61-55; 235-22-98;
Fax: 232-21-11
Hrs: 10-18, Friday 10-17

UMA LTD

Authorized **SAMSUNG ELECTRONICS** Distributor
Dealer for **Hewlett Packard, Compaq, 3M**
Malookhtinskiy pr., 68 528-95-66
.... 528-00-51
Fax 528-84-00

☎ COMPUTER SUPPLIES
КОМПЬЮТЕРНОЕ
ОБОРУДОВАНИЕ
COMPUTER, ZUBEHÖR
ORDINATEURS, FORNITURES
DATAMATERIAL
ATK-TARVIKKEET

Alternativa Sinitsy, *Mon-Fri 10-18; Rbls*
Dostoevskogo ul., 6 184-75-33
Fax..164-77-42
ASKoD, See Computer Stores
Bive, See Computer Stores
Compan MK, See Computer Stores
Creat
Savushkina ul., 28.........................239-99-60
Mon-Fri 10-18
Bakunina pr., 1/7............................274-54-39
EVM-Frederiksson, See Computer Stores
Eltek
Rozenshteyna ul., 19, rm. 306........252-75-76
Mon-Fri 10-17; Rbls; Eng
IBM Representation *(computer systems)*
Admiralteyskiy pr., 6 312-60-17
Fax..312-38-87
InfTel
Moldagulovoy ul., 7/6, 5th floor, rm. 51-52
☎ 224-39-61
InformPap, *Mon-Fri 9-17:30; Rbls*
Babushkina ul., 3 567-20-95
Fax..567-20-05
Ingress, See Computer Stores
Lek Tradehouse
Mytninskaya ul., 19/48, apt. 20 271-14-29
Mon-Fri 10-17; Rbls. $; Eng, Fr
Linkomp, See Computer Stores

JV **MacTech**
St. Petersburg

Authorized Dealer ⌘ Apple Computer
Russia, 191025
Povarskoy per., 8..................112-38-44
Fax......................................112-53-59
Telex 121222

Marine Computer Systems
Babushkina ul., 80 568-38-44
Mon-Fri 9-17:30; Rbls, $; Eng
Polradis
Yuriya Gagarina pr., 1 297-89-66
Mon-Fri 10-20; Rbls, $; Eng, Ger
Bus 12; Metro Elektrosila

РУБИКОН

Rubicon
Lesnoy pr., 19
542-00-65, 248-83-06
Fax.............542-09-89
Telex 121194 Rub SU

Official
Business
Partner
IBM
MINOLTA
Gold Star
Hewlett Packard

Spektr NPO
Moiseenko ul., 15/17 271-68-05
Mon-Fri 10-17
Vesta, *See* COMPUTER STORES

☎ **CONCERT HALLS**
КОНЦЕРТНЫЕ ЗАЛЫ
KONZERTSÄLE
CONCERT, SALLES DE
KONSERTHUS
KONSERTIT

See also THEATERS/BALLET, JAZZ and ROCK
CONCERTS.

*Concerts are held in the following halls.
We have* SEATING PLANS *on pages 336 for
the Bolshoy Philharmonic Hall, Glinka
Cappella (Choral Hall), Mariinskiy Opera and
Ballet (Kirov), Malyy Opera and Ballet, and
Oktyabrskiy Concert Hall.*

*For advanced ticket sales in rubles, go to
any* THEATRICAL TICKET OFFICE, *which sells
tickets for all concerts, theaters, circus and
other public events. You can also go to the
Box Office of the Concert Hall.*

Teatralnaya Kassa
        Theatrical Tickets - Main Office
Nevskiy pr., 190............................ 277-59-24
*Mon-Sat 11-18; Rbls, Near the Hotel Moskva,
Metro Ploshchad Aleksandra Nevskogo*
Central Box Office No. 1
Nevskiy pr., 42 311-31-83
Daily 11-19; Rbls
T-bus 1, 10, 14, 22, 7; Metro Nevskiy Prospekt

Anichkov Palace Concert Hall
      Kontsertnyy Zal Anichkova Dvortsa
Nevskiy pr., 39............................... 310-48-22
Bolshoy Philharmonic Hall (Large Hall)
      Bolshoy Zal Filarmonii
Mikhaylovskaya ul., 2..................... 110-42-90
Bosse Mansion, *Chamber Music Concert Hall*
      Osobnyak Bosse, Kamernyy Zal Kapelly
4-ya Liniya, 15............................... 213-34-88
Composers House   *Dom Kompozitorov*
Gertsena ul., 45 311-02-62
Daily 10-18; Rbls; Eng, Ger
Hotel St. Petersburg Concert Hall
Vyborgskaya nab., 5/2 542-90-56
Fax 315-96-63
Daily 10-20; Rbls
Glinka Kappella, *Choral Hall*
Reki Moyki nab., 20 314-11-59
15 mins from Metro Nevskiy Prospect
Jubilee Sports Palace, *Rock concerts*
      Dvorets Sporta Yubileynyy
Dobrolyubova, pr., 18 238-40-49
Metro Gorkovskaya
LDM Youth Palace Concert Hall
      Kontsertnyy Zal Dvortsa Molodezhi
Professora Popova ul., 47 .... 234-42-15`
Lensovet Palace of Culture
      Dvorets Kultury im. Lensoveta
Kamennoostrovskiy pr., 42 233-85-54
Metro Petrogradskaya
Malyy Theater of Opera and Ballet
Malyy Teatr Opery i Baleta (im. Musorgskogo)
Iskusstv pl., 1 212-20-40
5 mins from Metro Nevskiy Prospect

**Malyy Zal (Glinka Chamber Hall) of the
Philharmonia of St. Petersburg**
Beautiful old chamber music hall with great acoustics
Nevskiy pr., 30 312-45-85
Daily 11-20; Rbls, $
Mariinskiy Theater *(former Kirov Theater)*
      Mariinskiy Teatr Opery i Baleta
Teatralnaya pl., 1.......................... 114-43-44
**Mirror Palace Hall of
Princes Beloselskiy-Belozerskiy**
      *Zerkalnaya Gostinaya Dvortsa
      Beloselskikh-Belozerskikh*
Nevskiy pr., 41 315-38-21
Neva-Concert
Lenina pl., 1 542-09-44
Daily 9-21; Rbls
Neva-Concert, State Concert Association
Reki Fontanki nab., 41 310-49-52
.... 110-40-00
Daily 10-19; Rbls
Oktyabrskiy Concert Hall   *Seats 4000*
      Kontsertnyy Zal Oktyabrskiy
Ligovskiy pr., 6 277-69-60
Metro Ploshchad Vosstaniya
**Smolnyy Cathedral Concert &
Exhibition Complex**   **Smolnyy Sobor**
Concerts of Russian sacred music.
Rastrelli pl., 3/1............................. 311-35-60
Mon-Wed, Fri-Sun 11-16:30; Rbls, Bus 14; Metro Chernyshevskaya
Sports and Concert Complex (SKK)
      Sportivno-Kontsertnyy Kompleks
Hosts popular foreign stars and rock groups
Yuriya Gagarina pr., 8 298-21-64
Fax.. 298-01-07
Mon-Fri 9:30-17; Rbls, $; Eng, Ger; Bus 12; Metro Park Pobedy
**St. Petersburg State Conservatory Theater
of Opera and Ballet**
      Munitsipalnyy Teatr pri St.Pb. Konservatorii
Teatralnaya pl., 3............................ 312-25-07
Fax.. 311-50-34
Mon, Wed-Sun 12-18; Rbls
Tram 1, 5, 11, 31, 33; Metro Sennaya Ploshchad; E-5
**Tovstonogov Russian Academic Bolshoy
Dramatic Theater**
      *Russkiy Bolshoy Dramaticheskiy Teatr
      im. Tovstonogova*
Reki Fontanki nab., 65 310-92-42
Fax.. 110-47-10
Tues-Sun, 11-17, Rbls; Metro Gostinyy Dvor
Vremya Concert Hall
      Kontsertnyy Zal Vremya
Stachek pr., 105 158-12-04

☎ **CONFECTIONARY SHOPS**

See BAKERIES *and* CANDY STORES

☎ **CONFERENCE ROOMS**
КОНФЕРЕНЦ-ЗАЛЫ
KONFERENZRÄUME
CONFERENCES, SALLES DE
KONFERENSLOKALER
KOKOUSTILAT

See also BUSINESS CENTERS

Commodore Hotel, *See* HOTELS
Dom Arkhitektora   **Architect's House**
Gertsena ul., 52.............................. 312-04-00
Mon-Fri 11-20; Rbls, $

Dom Ofitserov   **Officer's House**
Liteynyy pr., 20.............................. 278-86-40
Tue-Sun 8-20; Rbls, $; T-bus 3; Metro Chernyshevskaya

BANQUET &
CONFERENCE FACILITIES
GRAND HOTEL EUROPE
★★★★★
ST. PETERSBURG RUSSIA

Kryscha Ballroom, Conference & Meeting Rooms
Simultaneous interpretation, overhead projector
TV & VHS-videos, PA-system, large screen

Mikhaylovskaya Street 1/7
Saint Petersburg, 191011

Info/Switchboard ....119-60-00, Ext. 6230
Fax 119-60-01

Hotelship Peterhof ★★★★

Nab. Makarova, near the Tuchkov Bridge
.... 213-63-21

House of Scientists   **Dom Uchenykh**
Dvortsovaya nab., 26 312-82-58
Mon-Fri 10-18; Rbls

LDM Complex
(former Leningradskiy Dvorets Molodezhi)
Professora Popova ul., 47 234-97-93
Daily; Rbls; Bus 25; Metro Petrogradskaya

Pribaltiyskaya Hotel
Korablestroiteley ul., 14 356-60-75
Fax 356-00-94
Daily; Rbls

Pulkovskaya Hotel
Pobedy pl., 1 264-51-79
Fax 264-63-96
Daily 10-22; Rbls

Tavricheskiy Palace
Shpalernaya ul., 47 278-95-85
Daily 9-19; Rbls, $

Zarya
Primorskoe shosse, 423, Repino.... 231-65-39
Fax 231-65-10
Daily 8-23; Rbls

☎ **CONSTRUCTION &**
RENOVATION
СТРОИТЕЛЬСТВО
И РЕКОНСТРУКЦИЯ
BAU UND RENOVIERUNG
CONSTRUCTION ET RENOVATION
BYGGNATION
RAKENTAMINEN
JA REMONTTEERAUS

Adzhi Corporation
Severnyy pr., 8/3, rm. 84 510-24-12
Mon-Fri 10-19; Rbls

AKOC   • *Construction work*
AKOS   • *Reinforced Concrete*
         Structures Manufacturing
Tyulenina ul., 3 311-74-95
Fax 311-34-48

Alyuma System Monolitstroy
Ryleeva ul., 29 273-26-46
Fax.. 272-79-30
Mon-Fri 9-18; Rbls; $; Eng

AMO *Private Construction Company*
Kolpino, Sapernyy per., 17
Tel................................... 482-12-46

Anata
Izmaylovskiy pr., 14 112-66-78
Mon-Fri 10-17; Rbls

Angar-Metall
Galernaya ul., 22, rm. 8.................. 210-94-06
Fax.. 210-97-96
Mon-Fri 9-17; Rbls, $

Avielein
Pilotov ul., 18, bldg. 4 104-37-02
Mon-Fri 8:30-13, 14-17:30; Rbls, $; Eng

B & T
1-ya Krasnoarmeyskaya ul., 16....... 110-18-92
Mon-Fri 9-17

 A/O Bumar Warinski

Construction Equipment, Sales & Repairs
Moscow office: Mira pr., 74, apt. 190
Tel./Fax.............................(095) 284-45-55
In St. Petersburg: Yakornaya ul., 9
Tel./Fax.............................(812) 528-84-90

Comfort   **Komfort**
Bolshaya Porokhovskaya ul., 24 224-27-52
Mon-Sat 11-18; Rbls

Cottage
Ligovskiy pr., 35 274-49-08
Mon-Sat 10-21; Rbls, $; Eng, Ger

 Ecopolis GENERAL CONTRACTORS

CONSTRUCTION MANAGEMENT
DESIGN & BUILDING RENOVATION
Large Staff of Architects, & Engineers
Best craftsmen & sub-contractors in St. Pb.
Designer and General Contractor
Swimming Facility & Circus Arena
St. Petersburg 1994 Goodwill Games

Zanevskiy pr., 32, Bldg 2, No. 3
☎...............................528-26-66
Mon-Fri 9:30-18; Rbls, $; Eng

Evista, *Mon-Fri 10-18*
Radishcheva ul., 42...................... 273-31-06
Fax.. 272-88-85

Gera
Svetlanovskiy pr., 93...................... 538-70-08
Mon-Fri 10-17; Rbls

Germes
Nevskiy pr., 57 112-55-16
Mon-Fri 10-17; Rbls, $; Eng, Ger, Fr

A/O FILCO General Construction
Nab. reki Moyki, 11
Tel.....................................+7-812-311-05-30
Fax.....................................+7-812-110-68-43

Grif
Ruzovskaya ul., 16.......................... 292-57-57
Mon-Fri 8-17; Rbls

AN INTERNATIONAL CONSTRUCTION SERVICES COMPANY

Haka has over 20 years of construction experience in the CIS. We combine quality thinking and project management skills with a thorough knowledge of local markets.

▆▆HAKA

HAKA-STROI CORPORATION:
P.O. Box 309, SF 00531 Helsinki, Finland
Tel. 358-0-77-05-1
Fax 358-0-77-05-24-89

Haka in St. Petersburg:

A/O **PETER-HAKA** Real Estate Development Services
Admiralteyskiy pr., 6, 191065, St. Petersburg
Tel .... +7-812-312-31-18
Fax .... +7-812-315-93-58

A/O **FILCO** General Construction
Nab. reki Moyki 11, 191065, St. Petersburg
Tel .... +7-812-311-05-30
Fax .... +7-812-110-68-43

A/O **ELEMENT** Precast Element Manufacturing
Tsentralnaya ul., 6, Promzona Parnas
Tel./Fax .... +7-812-598-86-13

Ibar
Energetikov pr., 24.......................... 227-47-98
Fax 227-47-14
Mon-Fri 9-18; $; Eng

Inform-Future
Tambovskaya ul., 12...................... 315-17-01
Fax 312-30-78
Mon-Fri 9-18; Rbls, $; Eng, Ger

Jupiter-Service
Grazhdanskiy pr., 105, bldg. 1, P.O. Box 25
☎ 249-44-91
Daily 10-13, 14-19; Rbls; Eng

Karella
Zodchego Rossi ul., 1, rm. 313 110-45-40
Mon-Fri 10-17; Rbls, $

Lenstroyinter
Ryleeva ul., 1 312-60-42
Mon-Fri 10-19; Rbls

MDN
Kantemirovskaya ul., 5................... 550-26-37
Fax 245-51-86
Mon-Fri 9-16:30; Rbls, $; Ger, Hun

Malakhit
Novo-Aleksandrovskaya ul., 22
☎ 227-29-20
Mon-Fri 9-17; Rbls, $; Eng, Ger

Mauntex
Nevskiy pr., 102, apt. 31 272-13-68
.... 275-57-29
Mon-Fri 9-18; Rbls; Metro Ploshchad Vosstaniya

Megapolis
Smolnyy pr., 11 278-52-69
Fax................................... 110-02-66
Mon-Fri 9:30-18:30; Rbls

Montazh
Vereyskaya ul., 31 292-25-32
Mon-Fri 9-17; Rbls

Neva
Svetlanovskiy pr., 42
Tel./Fax 555-04-06
Mon-Fri 8:30-17

Oreol
Liflyandskaya ul., 3 186-48-93
Mon-Fri 9-18; Rbls

OTIS

OTIS St. Petersburg

◆◆◆

Featuring the "EUROPA-2000" model passenger elevators manufactured in our new factory in St. Petersburg.

We also offer the complete line of elevators from our other OTIS factories worldwide.

All OTIS products include installation, adjusting and handover by OTIS' own mechanics.

We service and/or modernize all types of elevators

◆◆◆

Khimicheskiy per., 12 252-36-94
Fax................................... 252-53-15

◆◆◆

OTIS St. Petersburg Today Services 10,000 Elevators in St. Petersburg and Northwest Russia

Parquet Floors	**Nastilka Parketa**
Please call................................... 186-35-16	

Daily 20-23; Rbls

Pegas International Ltd.
Tambasova ul., 27, bldg. 2 130-14-79
Mon-Fri 9:30-18, Rbls, $; Metro Prospekt Veteranov

Permafrost Consultants Soil Mechanics & Engineering Cryology

Put Your Enterprise on Solid Ground

Frost Heaving & Soil Mechanics,
Experts on Soil Conditions in Russia
Specifications for Road Surfaces, & Paving,
Construction, Dams, Large Structures &
Refrigerated Storage.
Contact: O.R. Golli.
Laboratory of Engineering Geology,
Geocryology and Soil Mechanics, Research
Instititute of Hydraulic Engineering
**Gzhatskaya ul., 21
(812) 535-88-68**

Quality, *Mon-Fri 9-18; Rbls*   **Kachestvo**
Rimskogo-Korsakova pr., 5............ 311-84-95

S & Co., Ltd

*Russian-style wood houses
Custom carpentry, Russian Saunas
We ship throughout Russia and Europe.*

✉ *The Kirov Stadium, Bldg. 1
Krestovskiy Ostrov, Morskoy Pr.*

Tel 235-57-87
Fax 235-54-35
*English, translators available
Mon-Sat 9-18; Rbls, $*

Skanlen
Kazanskaya ul., 36, rm. 701 312-84-34
Fax 312-78-91
Mon-Fri 9:30-18

Sodruzhestvo
Sverdlovskaya nab., 14/2 524-89-26
Fax 524-57-12
Mon-Sat 8-19; Rbls; Eng

Sport-Stroy, *Daily 10-15; Eng*
Karpinskogo ul., 73, rm. 14............. 232-56-63

St. Petersburg Construction & Renovation Enterprise
Griboedova kan. nab., 174 a........... 114-27-80
Fax 114-19-49
Mon-Sat 10-19; Rbls; Eng

St. Petersburg Revival Fund Perspective Technologies Center

Project design & construction
Nab. Sinopskaya, 24, apt. 12.......... 110-77-64

STTM
Renovation, Plumbing, Electrical
Sofiyskaya ul., 8 269-40-51

 Unique Cottage Construction

Please call 213-65-87

Vneshstroyservice
Galernaya ul., 6............................... 315-26-10
Mon-Fri, Sun 9-18; Rbls, $; Eng; T-bus 5

Vysotnik
Bolshoy Smolenskiy pr., 2.............. 567-98-34
.... 567-95-50

☎ CONSULATES
КОНСУЛЬСТВА
KONSULATE
CONSULATS
KONSULAT
KONSULAATIT

See also EMBASSIES

Consulates offer a variety of services and assistance to foreign nationals. For example, the American, German, and French consulates in St. Petersburg do the following: passport replacements, notary services, birth certificates, absentee voting, federal income tax forms and emergency help.

In Case of an Emergency Only. *The consulate "duty officer" of many consulates can be reached 24 hours a day. Call immediately in case of arrest or other legal difficulties, they can contact an attorney or act on your behalf. They will also provide medical evacuation and assistance in the event of a death. In an emergency only they can perform money transfers.*

Travel Advisories. *If you plan to travel anywhere else, especially to one of the former republics, they issue timely travel advisories and information about obtaining visas, etc.*

Registration. *For your safety you are advised to register with your consulate so that you may be easily contacted in case of emergency.*

Schools Here. *The American consulate also houses the American School for children in pre-school & grades 1-6, which is the St. Petersburg branch of the Anglo-American School of Moscow. The school is planning to move in the near future.*

Business Assistance. *The US., Hungarian, Chinese People's Republic, Finnish, and German consulates have commercial or trade delegations in St. Pb. The US Commercial Department is on the Hotelship Peterhof. See below.*

Bulgaria
Ryleeva ul., 27 273-73-47
Fax.. 272-57-18
Mon-Fri 14-16

China, (People's Republic of)
3-ya Liniya, 12 218-17-21
Commercial Department................. 213-79-63
*Visa applications Mon, Wed 9:30-11:30
Operating hours Tues, Thur 9-12*

Cuba
Ryleeva ul., 37 272-53-03
Mon-Fri 9-13

Czech and Slovak Federal Republics
Tverskaya ul., 5............................. 271-04-59
Fax.. 271-46-15
Opening September 1993; Mon-Fri 9:30-12:30

Denmark
Bolshaya Alleya 13, Kamennyy Ostrov
.... 234-37-55
Mon-Fri 9-13

Estonia
Bolshaya Monetnaya ul., 14
Tel/Fax.. 333-55-48

Finland
Chaykovskogo ul., 71...................... 273-73-21
Emergencies.................................... 116-06-52
Visa applications *Mon-Fri 9-12* 272-42-56
Visa applications *Mon-Fri 14-16*...... 272-42-43
Commercial Department
4-ya Krasnoarmeyskaya ul., 4 a...... 292-16-41
Mon-Fri 9-17

France
Reki Moyki nab., 15 314-14-43
Visa applications Mon-Fri 9:30-11

Germany
Furshtadtskaya ul., 39.................... 273-55-98
.... 279-32-07
Fax 279-32-42
Mon-Fri 9-16

Great Britain
Proletarskoy Diktatury pl., 5 119-60-36
Fax 119-60-37
Mon-Fri 9:30-17:30

Hungary
Marata ul., 15 312-67-53
Commercial Department 312-64-58
Fax 312-64-32
Tues, Wed, Fri 10-12

India
Ryleeva ul., 35................................ 272-19-88
.... 272-17-31
Mon-Fri 10:30-12:30, 14:30-16:30

Italy
Teatralnaya pl., 10 312-32-17
.... 312-31-06
Fax 312-28-96
Visa Applications: Mon, Wed, Fri 10-12
Visa Pick-up: Tues, Thur 10-12

Japan
Reki Moyki nab., 29 314-14-18
.... 314-14-34
Mon-Fri 9:30-18

Latvia
Galernaya ul., 69 (In courtyard)...... 315-17-74
Fax 311-31-82
Mon-Fri 10-12 (Visa applications), 15-16 (Visa pick-up)

Netherlands
Engelsa pr., 101.............................. 554-49-00
.... 554-48-90
Fax 554-36-19
Mon-Fri 10-12

Poland
5-ya Sovetskaya ul., 12/14 274-41-70
Fax 274-43-18
Mon-Fri 8:30-12:30

South Africa
Toreza pr., 118 554-17-49
.... 553-17-42
Fax 553-57-18
Moving Fall 1993 to Reki Moyki nab., 11.
Telephones will be changed; Mon-Fri 9:30-12

Sweden
10-ya Liniya, 11 213-41-91
Visa applications............................. 218-35-27
.... 218-35-26
Mon-Fri 9-13, 14:30-17

United States
Furshtadtskaya ul., 15 274-86-89
.... 274-85-68
Visa Wed, Fri 9-12; Operations Mon-Fri 9-17:30
Commercial Department
In the Hotelship "Peterhof" 213-65-37
Fax.. 213-69-62
Mon-Fri 9-17:30

☎ CONSULTING FIRMS

See BUSINESS CONSULTANTS

☎ CONTACT LENSES
ЛИНЗЫ КОНТАКТНЫЕ
KONTAKTLINSEN
VERRES DE CONTACT
KONTAKT LINSER
PIILOLINSSIT

Concor
Voznesenskiy pr., 9 311-50-93
Mon-Fri 11-19; Rbls, $; Eng

Contacor
Liteynyy pr., 25 272-05-03
.... 272-32-13
Mon-Fri 9-20; Rbls, $; Eng, Ger, Fr

Contact-Inter
Izmaylovskiy pr., 23 315-41-78
Mon-Fri 9:30-19; Rbls, $

Exclusive
Nevskiy pr., 20............................... 311-45-88
Daily 10-14, 15-20

Lincon
• 14-ya Liniya, 97 355-83-88
Mon-Fri 10-20; Rbls; Eng
• Furshtadtskaya ul., 36.................. 272-28-52
In Polyclinic No. 39; Mon-Fri 10-20; Rbls; Eng
• Liteynyy pr., 39 275-45-24
Mon-Fri 10-20; Rbls; Eng
• Lensoveta ul., 80.......................... 127-09-74
In Medsanchast No. 6; Mon-Fri 10-20; Rbls; Eng
• Nevskiy pr., 86............................. 275-69-98
In Polyclinic No. 40; Mon-Fri 10-20; Rbls; Eng

Linkor-Contact
Galernaya ul., 46 312-10-92
Mon-Fri 9-19; Rbls

VISION EXPRESS
THE LENS MASTERS
®

of St. Petersburg

Eyeglasses • Contact lenses
Imported from Europe & USA
Eye examination • 1 hour Service

Lomonosova ul., 5 310-15-95
Hrs: 10-20, English
A Russian-British firm

Vizus
Kosygina pr., 11, in Ochki Store 520-45-51
Mon-Sat 10-18; Rbls

☎ COPYING (PHOTOCOPYING)

See PHOTOCOPYING, *and* BUSINESS CENTERS

☎ COSMETICS
КОСМЕТИКА
KOSMETIKA
PRODUITS DE BEAUTE
KOSMETIKA
KOSMETIIKKA

See also HABERDASHERY, DEPARTMENT STORES
and INTERNATIONAL SHOPS

*A wide selection of Western and Russian
cosmetics and perfumes are now sold in
"Parfyumeriya" (Парфюмерия), in
haberdashery shops "Galantereya"
(Галантерея), in some specialty shops and
INTERNATIONAL SHOPS. There are several
shops along Nevskiy Prospect selling well
known French and American cosmetics.*

Adonis
Dumskaya ul., 3 312-51-48
Mon-Fri 10-19, Sat 11-18; Eng, Fr
**Baltic Star International Shopping at
Pribaltiyskaya Hotel**
Korablestroiteley ul., 14 356-41-85
Fax 356-01-14
Daily 8-23; $, CC; Eng, Ger
Bolgarskaya Roza   Bulgarian Rose
Nevskiy pr., 55 112-14-75
Mon-Fri 10-19; Rbls
Debyut   Debut
Nevskiy pr., 54 312-30-26
Mon-Sat 9-21; $, CC; Eng, Ger
Henkel
Nevskiy pr., 48, at Passage, 2nd floor.... 219-17-77
Kosmos   Cosmos
Mokhovaya ul., 39 273-34-05
Mon-Sat 11-15, 16-20, Sun 11-17
Krasota   Beauty
Nevskiy pr., 90 272-93-25
Mon-Sat 10-19; Rbls
Lancome
Nevskiy pr., 64 312-34-95
Mon-Sat 10-19; Rbls, $

Neva Star International Shopping
at the Moskva Hotel
Aleksandra Nevskogo pl., 2 274-00-24
Daily 8-23; $
T-bus 1; Metro Ploshchad Aleksandra Nevskogo

Rifle-Petrograd
Kamennoostrovskiy pr., 54 234-43-77
Fax 234-98-69
Daily 10-20; Rbls, $; Eng, Ital
Rosgalantereya
Salova ul., 48/50 166-25-40
Fax 166-48-22
Mon-Fri 9-17:30; Rbls
Saturn
Moskovskiy pr., 34 292-35-88
Mon-Sat 10-14, 15-19; Rbls

Sharm
Nevskiy pr., 27 314-27-58
Mon-Sat 10-14, 15-19; Rbls
Siren
Nevskiy pr., 76 272-10-03
Mon-Sat 10-14, 15-19; Rbls; Metro Mayakovskaya
Troika
Bolshaya Konyushennaya ul., 17
☎ 314-13-21
*Mon-Sat 11-14, 15-20; Rbls; Eng, Ger, Fr
Bus 47; Metro Nevskiy Prospekt*
Wanda, *Mon-Fri 8-19; Rbls*
Nevskiy pr., 111 277-00-44

ЯR   Yves Rocher

Sadovaya ul., 42

Tel./Fax 310-92-15
Metro: Sadovaya, French, German

Yves Rocher
Nevskiy pr., 61 113-14-96
*Mon-Sat 10-14, 15-19; Rbls, $; Eng, Fr
Metro Mayakovskaya*

☎ COURIER SERVICES

See EXPRESS MAIL/PARCEL SERVICE

☎ COURSES
КУРСЫ
KURSE
COURS
KURSER
KURSSIT

See also BUSINESS INSTITUTES, EDUCATIONAL
PROGRAMS, LANGUAGE COURSES,
UNIVERSITIES, *and* COMPUTER COURSES.

Advanced Humanities Courses
Vysshye Gumanitarnye Kursy
Voznesenskiy pr., 34 b 314-35-21
Fax 315-39-17
Mon-Fri 10-22; Rbls
Garantiya (Warranty) Center
Bolshoy pr., V.O., 88, rm. 110 217-26-70
Closed in July, August; Mon-Fri 9-19
Humanities Center, *Mon-Fri 9-17:30; Rbls*
Griboedova kan. nab., 92/1 310-20-90
Nevskiy Angel Charity Society
See our ad under CHARITIES
Obuchenie   Education
• Leninskiy pr., 149 259-60-65
Mon-Fri 10-16; Rbls, $
• Zagorodnyy pr., 58 292-40-05
*Daily 10-19; Rbls, $; Eng, Ger, Fr, Finn, Ital
Metro Tekhnologicheskiy Institut*

**✳ BABYLON
SUPER**
Mon-Sat 10-21 Sun 12-20
Exchange office

GET YOUR PERSONAL PRODUCTS AT SUPER BABYLON

A full range of Procter and Gamble toiletries and personal care
products. Tissues, mirrors, combs and hairbrushes. Band-aids and
personal health care products, too. Come to Super Babylon.

P.S., Maly pr., 54 & 56 230-80-96
In the former Okean store off Bolshoy Prospekt

**Progress Management and
Marketing Center**
Institutskiy pr., 22.......................... 552-13-38
Fax 552-77-28
Mon-Fri 10-18; Rbls

☎ CREDIT CARDS
КРЕДИТНЫЕ КАРТОЧКИ,
KREDITKARTEN
CARTES DE CREDIT
KREDITKORT
LUOTTOKORTIT

*Use: Many establishments accept foreign
currency, especially hotels, airlines, restaurants and shops, such as international
shops, accept VISA, Master Card, and
American Express. In many other shops,
however, credit cards are still not accepted.*

*Cash advances: For cash advances from
your VISA card, try Bank Saint Petersburg,
St. Petersburg Savings Bank (see ad in
BANKS and CURRENCY EXCHANGE) and Credo
Bank at three locations including the Astoria
Hotel. See also BANKS.*

*Stolen credit cards: Call the American
Express Office in St. Petersburg (812) 119-
60-09, fax 119-60-11 or Moscow (095)
230-68-87 to report a lost or stolen American Express Card. For other cards, try
calling (095) 284-41-51 or the numbers in
your home country.*

*Keep a photocopy of your credit card
number, passport, visa, and "stolen or lost
credit card" telephone numbers in a secure
place.*

*Credit card fraud is increasing and you
will often be asked to show your passport
when using one.*

☎ CRYSTAL & PORCELAIN
ХРУСТАЛЬ, ФАРФОР
KRISTALL UND PORZELLAN
CRISTAL ET PORCELAINE
KRISTALL OCH PORSLIN
KRISTALLI JA POSLIINI

Farfor, Khrustal, Bronza
                    China, Crystal, Bronze
Kamennoostrovskiy pr., 4 232-85-80
Mon-Sat 10-14, 15-19; Rbls; Eng
Farfor, Khrustal   China and Crystal
• Bolshoy pr., P.S., 92 234-93-65
*Mon-Sat 10-14, 15-19; Rbls
T-bus 1; Metro Petrogradskaya*
• Nevskiy pr., 64 314-42-63
Mon-Sat 10-19; Rbls, $; Eng
Farfor, Steklo, Khrustal
                    China, Glass and Crystal
Sadovaya ul., 38 310-07-34
Mon-Sat 10-14, 15-19; Rbls

Gera Stores
• Bolshaya Konyushennaya ul., 1 315-74-90
Daily 0-15, 16-24; Rbls, $
• Iskusstv pl., 4 352-18-18
Wed-Sun 10-22; Rbls; Eng; Tram 14; Metro Gostinyy Dvor
• Zheleznovodskaya ul., 9 350-74-98
Mon-Fri 11-19; Rbls, $

Glazur
Furshtadtskaya ul., 42 279-33-55
Mon-Sat 11-14, 15:30-19; Rbls
Iskusstvo Rossii   Arts of Russia
Nevskiy pr., 147 277-18-93
Daily 10-14, 15-19; Rbls
Markus, *Daily 10-14, 15-19; Rbls*
Nevskiy pr., 147 277-18-93
Mikhaylovskaya Ploshchad
Isskusstv pl., 3 ....No ☎
Sovex, *Mon-Sat 11-14, 15-20; Rbls, $*
Sredneokhtinskiy pr., 41 224-29-93
Wanda, *Porcelain*
Nevskiy pr., 111 279-43-41
Mon-Sat 10-14, 15-19; Rbls; Eng, Finn

☎ CURRENCY EXCHANGE
ВАЛЮТА, ОБМЕН
GELDWECHSEL
DEVISES, CHANGE DE
VALUTAVÄXLING
VALUUTANVAIHTO

See also BANKS and TRAVELER'S CHEQUES

*Rubles: You will need rubles as most
goods and services are sold for rubles, even
to foreigners. In reality, US dollars circulate
as a second currency only in a few sectors
of the economy. Some elements of the
tourist industry, however, try to demand
payment in dollars, and few refuse dollars
when offered. Deutsch marks and Finn
marks, are more difficult to use, Swiss &
French francs, English pounds, etc. are
almost impossible to use.*

*What dollar bills to bring. Bring along all
denominations ($1's, 5's, 10's, & 20's for
purchases and $100's for changing money.
The bills should be in good condition without writing or marks on them as soiled bills
are not accepted.*

*Traveler's Cheques and Credit Cards. For
information on cashing traveler's cheques,
see TRAVELER'S CHEQUES, on receiving cash
advances on credit cards, see CREDIT CARDS,
for wire transfer of money, see BANKS.*

*Official Currency Exchange Offices, called
"Obmen valyuty" (Обмен валюты or Пункт
обмена валюты) are scattered throughout
the city, in hotels, stores, and banks. At
these official offices, often branches of
banks, you can "officially" change money
and receive the proper receipts, which may
be required to take some types of purchases out of the country.*

GUIDELINES ON EXCHANGING
DOLLARS FOR RUBLES

*The Exchange rate is stated as **rubles per
dollar** and is called the "kurs" (курс). In
banks the "kurs" can vary as much as 10%
between the lower buying rate and the
higher selling rate of dollars. On the street it
is about 3-5%. In addition, some places
assess a service charge from zero to 5%.*

*When exchanging dollars officially, **shop
around for the best bank buy rate.***

The current "kurs" is quoted on TV every morning. The Moscow Currency Exchange "kurs" as well as an average "kurs" is given.

*While changing money with private persons is technically illegal, the actual legal risks of unofficial money changing are low. The principal problem is not having the receipts. You will find many "unofficial" places to change money, on the street (dangerous), in hotels (better), etc. **This can be risky, especially if changing large sums of money.** If you insist on changing money "on the street", go with two friends to watch the transaction. Watch for the "slight of hand" trick of wrapping small denomination bills in larger ones. **Avoid money changers in Gostinyy Dvor!***

*To get the best rate. First, ask to sell dollars to you and to get a selling rate. Now, you know the maximum they can give you when they buy your dollars. **You should get a buying rate of about 2-5% lower than their selling rate.** For example, if the sell rate is 1000 rubles for $1, then the buy rate should be around 950 rubles for $1.*

Note, that the rates on the street vary according to supply and demand and whether or not banks are open. Thus, at night, on holidays and weekends, the ruble/dollar rate is lower. Also, greater fluctuations in the kurs increase the gap between buy and sell rates.

Counterfeit Bills. Counterfeit US dollar bills have flooded Russia, so don't be offended when your dollars are carefully examined. Also, torn or soiled bills with writing or ink stamps will not be accepted. Be careful yourself when accepting dollars. One test for genuine dollars is that the ink rubs off on white paper.

"Old Soviet" Pre-1993 Rubles. As of July 25, all ruble bills issued before 1993 are no longer valid and have been replaced with new "Russian" rubles. Do not accept pre-1993 ruble notes when exchanging money unless you want them for souvenirs. New notes in circulation include 100, 200, 500, 1,000, 5,000, 10,000, and 50,000. The new coins include 1, 5, 10, 20, 50 and 100 rubles.

Interbank Information Service
Nevskiy pr., 16...............................315-39-42
Currency Exchange Info 311-69-84
Information and Financial Services, Financial Management Consulting, Mon-Fri 10-18

BANKS AND EXCHANGE OFFICES

AVTOVAZBANK
Currency exchange
- 2-ya Sovetskaya ul., 3/7 277-51-58
Mon-Fri: 9-13, 14-20
- Sapernyy per., 11................................No ☎
Mon-Fri: 9:30-13, 14-16
- Vyborg, Progonnaya ul., 1, office 2
Tel ....(278) 2-57-06, (278) 3-38-80
Daily 9-21

Bank Saint Petersburg Exchange offices
- Gostinnyy Dvor,
Sadovaya Linya, 2nd floor ....No ☎
- Nevskiy pr., 13, in Maska store ....No ☎
- Nevskiy pr., 21, in Modnyy Dom.........No ☎
- Nevskiy pr., 31, in Lavka Khudozhnika...No ☎
- Nevskiy pr., 47/1, in Germes Store ....No ☎
- Ostrovskogo pl., 7..........................310-35-75
Mon-Sat 10-19

Industry & Construction Bank
Mikhaylovskaya ul., 4.................110-49-09
Daily 9:30-17:30

Ladabank, Exchange Offices
- Moskovskiy pr., 189
in Izumrud Store ....No ☎
Mon-Fri 10-14, 15-19
- Slavy pr., 5, in Zhemchug Store ....No ☎
Mon-Fri 10-14, 15-19
- Kuznechnyy per., 4 311-49-89
Daily 0-24
- Zanevskiy pr., 6...........................528-59-01
Fax...528-03-03
Mon-Fri 9-13

Lesopromyshlennyy Bank, Exchange offices
- Krapivnyy per., 5
Answering Machine......................541-86-09
Fax...542-83-93
Mon-Fri 10-13, 13:30-15:30
- Gertsena ul., 24, in Yakhont Store ....No ☎
Tue-Sat 11-14, 15-18
- Millionnaya ul., 10...............................No ☎
Mon-Fri 9:30-13, 13:30-16:30
- Nevskiy pr., 69, In Biryuza Store............No ☎
Mon-Fri 9:30-13, 13:30-16:30

 Russian Commercial Industrial Bank

- Bolshaya Morskaya ul., 15 210-07-56
- Kamennoostrovskiy pr., 39 234-10-57
- Nevskiy pr., 111......................279-43-41
- Chernyshevskogo pl., 11
(Russia Hotel, 1st floor) 296-72-01
Leninskiy pr., 120
(Narvskiy Department Store)..........158-18-33

SKV Bank, Exchange office
Bolshoy Smolenskiy pr., 12............567-88-27
Fax...567-95-91
Mon-Fri 9:30-12:30, 13:30-16

Vitabank at the Hotel Pribaltiyskaya
Korablestroiteley ul., 14................356-38-79
Daily 9-14, 15-19

Vneshtorgbank, Exchange offices
- Gertsena ul., 29..............................312-79-09
Fax...312-78-18
Mon-Fri 9:30-13; Eng, Ger, Fr
- Gertsena ul., 35..............................312-22-59
Mon-Fri 9:30-13, 14-16; Eng, Ger, Fr
- Gorokhovaya ul., 4 110-68-53
Mon-Fri 9:30-13, 14-16; Eng, Ger, Fr
- Mikhaylovskaya ul., 1/7 American Express Office
at the Grand Hotel Europe ....No ☎
Daily 8-20; Eng, Ger, Fr

SAINT - PETERSBURG
BANK

St. Petersburg Savings Bank
CURRENCY EXCHANGE

CURRENCY EXCHANGE OFFICES
with VISA $ CASH ADVANCE

◆ **At Hotel Pulkovskaya, 1st floor**
  Pobedy pl.,2 299-92-17
  Hrs: 9 - 21 Every Day
◆ **Department store "Moskovskiy"**
  Moskovskiy pr., 205 291-28-20
◆ **At Branch No. 1991, Nevskiy pr., 38**
  Tel 110-40-17
  Fax 110-47-91
  Hrs: 10-18, Closed Sun, English
◆ **Nevskiy pr., 82** 272-90-89
  In the House of Books
  Nevskiy pr., 28 219-94-17
◆ **Business Center**
  Vladimirskiy pr., 9 113-16-71
◆ **International Airport**
  Pulkovo-2 104-34-27

CURRENCY EXCHANGE OFFICES
  Hrs: 10-18, Closed Sat & Sun, English
◆ **Branch No. 1877 (Moskovskiy)**
  Basseynaya ul., 7 290-14-15
◆ **Branch No. 2006 (Frunzenskiy)**
  Bukharestskaya ul., 23 109-85-51
◆ **Branch No. 2002 (Vasileostrovskiy)**
  V.O., Bolshoy pr., 57/15 213-09-02
◆ **Branch No. 1879 (Petrogradskiy)**
  Lva Tolstogo pl., 2 232-35-20
◆ **In the Palace of Youth**
  Prof. Popova ul., 47
◆ **Branch No. 2005 (Leninskiy)**
  Moskvinoy pr., 7 251-53-65
  Moskovskiy pr., 39 292-64-03
◆ **Branch No. 2004 (Kalininskiy)**
  Nepokorennykh pr., 2 247-17-98
◆ **Operations Office (Dzerzhinskiy)**
  Nab. Robespera, 6 275-39-78
◆ **Branch No. 1874 (Oktyabrskiy)**
  Voznesenskiy pr., 37 314-32-87
◆ **Branch No. 1880 (Vyborgskiy)**
  Lesnoy pr., 75 245-03-78
◆ **Branch No. 2003 (Primorskiy)**
  P.S., Bolshoy pr., 18 230-92-60
◆ **Branch No. 7884 (Peterhof)**
  Mezhdunarodnaya ul., 10 427-94-47
◆ **Branch No. 8074 (Krasnogvardeyskiy)**
  Krasnogvardeyskiy pr., 12/1
  Tel 528-94-82

HOTEL EXCHANGE BUREAUS

Grand Hotel Europe, *by Vneshtorgbank*
  in the American Express Office
  Mikhaylovskaya 1/7 .... No ☎
Hotel Astoria, *by Credobank*
  Gertsena ul., 39 210-58-78
  Daily 9-13:30, 14:30-21
Hotel Moskva, *by Vitabank*
  Aleksandra Nevskogo pl., 2 274-21-27
  Daily 8:30-12, 13-19
Hotel Pribaltiyskaya, *by Vitabank*
  Korablestroiteley ul., 14 356-38-79
  Daily 0-24
Hotel St. Petersburg, *by Petroagroprombank*
  Vyborgskaya nab., 5/2 542-80-45
  Daily 8:30-13, 14-18, 18:30-20
Hotel Sovetskaya, *by Promstroybank*
  Lermontovskiy pr., 43/1
  Main hotel number 259-25-52
  Daily 10-13, 15-18; Eng
  Metro Tekhnologicheskiy Institut
Nevskij Palace, *by Inkombank, 1st floor*
  Nevskiy pr., 57 .... Phone to be installed

OTHER EXCHANGE BUREAUS

Exchange Bureau at Maska Store
  Nevskiy pr., 13 .... No ☎
  Mon-Sat 11-18
Exchange Bureau at Mir Store
  Nevskiy pr., 13 .... No ☎
  Mon-Sat 10-17
Exchange Bureau in Mebel (Furniture) Store
  Novocherkasskiy pr., 22 .... No ☎
  Mon-Sat 10-18:30
OGGO Exchange Bureau in Shop-Salon
  Suvorovskiy pr., 26 168-48-04
  Mon-Sat 10-14, 15-18
Parisiana Box Office Currency Exchange
  Nevskiy pr., 80 .... No ☎
  Mon-Sat 10-16:30

☎ **CUSTOMS**
  ТАМОЖНЯ
  ZOLL
  DOUANE
  TULL
  TULLI

---

*See also CUSTOMS CLEARANCE and CUSTOMS
REGULATIONS*
  *Customs officials are generally reasonable
people and most guests pass through
entrance customs without difficulty. Exit
customs can occasionally be a problem. Be
sure to read CUSTOMS REGULATIONS. The
customs official's job is difficult because
rules are vague, contradictory, absurd, and
changing, so that each official has
considerable latitude to interpret the code.
Politeness, patience and understanding go a
long way. Arrogance and rudeness get you
nowhere. Enlist their help and sympathy in
solving any problems.*

Customs, Airport Pulkovo-2
  Customs 104-34-08, 104-34-09
  104-34-01
  Customs- Cargo 104-34-16
  Daily 0-24; Rbls, $; Eng, Ger, Fr

Customs, Sea Cargo Department
Mezhevoy kan., 5 114-97-76
Fax 113-97-40
9-21; Rbls, $; Eng, Ger, Fr, Finn

Northwestern Customs Administration
Furmanova ul., 1, apt. 28 275-76-95
.... 273-16-19
Fax 275-31-54
Daily 9-17:45; Eng, Fr

St. Petersburg Customs Administration
9-ya Liniya, 10 350-63-74
.... 213-75-63
Fax 213-80-17
Mon-Fri 9-13, 14-18; Rbls, $

St. Petersburg Customs Trucking Department
Yakornaya ul., 17 227-67-15
Mon-Fri 9-18; Rbls

☎ CUSTOMS CLEARANCE
ТАМОЖЕННЫЕ ПОШЛИНЫ, ОСВОБОЖДЕНИЕ
ZOLLDEKLARATION
DEDOUANEMENT
TULLDEKLARATIONER
TULLISELVITYKSET

Custom clearance firms stay up-to-date on current changes in regulations and can greatly expedite getting through customs.

Acto-VneshTrans Co. Ltd
Zaozernaya ul., 4 294-86-75
See our ad on page 167

A E S
Transportation & Distribution

International and CIS Freight Forwarding
&
Customs clearance for air and surface cargo
Contact Moscow Office at: .... (095) 256-45-02
Fax .... (095) 254-28-76

Kirovspek
Stachek pr., 47 183-67-38
Fax 252-17-30
Mon-Fri 8:30-17

PetersburgVneshTrans
Mezhevoy kan., 5 251-95-48
See our ad on page 167

Rosvneshterminal
Belinskogo ul., 11 279-75-86
.... 275-89-89
Fax 279-75-62
Mon-Fri 9:30-13, 14-18:30; Rbls, $; Eng

Runo
Bolshoy pr., P.S., 22/24 233-67-18
Rbls; Tram 6; Metro Gorkovskaya
Sovavto - *See ad below*

VneshTransAvia Co. Ltd
Pilotov ul., 18 Pulkovo 2 104-34-97
See our ad on page 167

SOVAVTO ST. PETERSBURG

CUSTOMS CLEARANCE

Experienced and knowledgeable staff of the largest freight carrier in Northwest Russia is ready to assist you in clearing your cargo through Russian customs

All documents and operations

Conveniently located next to the Customs Office in St. Petersburg

Vitebskiy pr., 3 298-46-50
Fax 298-77-60
Telex .... 121535 AVTO
Hrs. Same as Customs, English, German

☎ CUSTOMS REGULATIONS
ТАМОЖЕННЫЕ ПРАВИЛА
ZOLLVORSCHRIFTEN
DOUANE, REGLEMENT DE
TULLFÖRESKRIFTER
TULLIMÄÄRÄYKSET

See also CUSTOMS CLEARANCE, and CUSTOMS

Customs regulations change frequently, and to our knowledge no complete up-to-date printed copy of the regulations existed as of June, 1993. Try the following for summaries and updates of customs regulations:

COMMERCIAL CUSTOMS REGULATIONS.

For exact information on imports and exports, consult a CUSTOMS CLEARANCE *broker, or call or visit the* CUSTOMS OFFICE.

Rules and Regulations of Russia, *published by the RTE (Russian Trade Express), often contains information on customs. See* PUBLISHERS.

St. Petersburg Customs Administration
V.O., 9-ya Liniya, 10
Information 213-75-63
Secretary 213-07-91

TOURIST REGULATIONS, ARRIVING

Items Allowed: *All items for personal use in reasonable quantities except those expressly limited (prohibited). Hint: You may bring as "personal luggage" a reasonable amount of (legal) items for personal use plus gifts up to $5,000 . If you think that you will be having items sent over later, fill out the section called "Baggage to Follow"* with "X" number of pieces. This will reduce the chance of being charged import duty when your items arrive latter. The total value of "accompanied" and "to follow" baggage is limited to $5,000.

Limited: Spirits 1½ liters, Wine 2 liters.

Forbidden Items: Illegal drugs, weapons, pornography, some fruits, vegetables and meats, and also rubles.

Currency: Any amount of almost any currency _except rubles_ is allowed to be brought in if declared in your declaration (Deklaratsiya, Декларация). If you want to take it out again, "declare" it when you bring it in.

How to fill out a "Deklaratsia": The purpose of the declaration is to prevent the flight (export) of capital from Russia. Thus, fill out your "declaration" listing all currency and traveler's cheques you have with you. You are supposed to include any other valuables, desktop computers, expensive cameras, precious stones, art works, icons, antiques, and especially gold jewelry of Russian or CIS origin, or any other items that you want to take out again.

Keep the stamped "declaration" with your passport and VISA. Make a photocopy, if you can.

TOURIST REGULATIONS, LEAVING

Items allowed: You can take out the items and money you stated on your declaration.

Items purchased in International Shops for hard currency with a proper receipt (this includes caviar) or from any art shop or other shop from which you have a receipt and appropriate papers.

Restricted Items: Art works, manuscripts, musical instruments, coins, clothing, jewelry, antiques, old books or similar items you received as gifts or bought on the "street" that could have value as a "national cultural treasure". Get a permit for export from:

The Department of the Representative of the Ministry of Culture
Griboedova kan. nab., 107 314-82-34

Even new paintings need permission from the authorities to be exported.

300 Ruble Rule. According to Customs Regulations on June 1, 1993, all items purchased for rubles above the value of 300 rubles (less than 30 cents) are subject to a 600% export tax payable in rubles at the airport. We have known of some zealous customs officials who try to enforce this regulation. These rules, however, were not available in print, so check before getting overly concerned.

For some paid advice on this subject, contact:

Tirex
Ligovskiy pr., 230 166-13-52

Experts on Control of Import-Export of Cultural Items
Griboedova kan. nab., 107 314-82-34
Mon-Tue, Thu-Fri ; Rbls
Rosvneshterminal
Belinskogo ul., 11 279-75-86
Fax.. 279-75-62
Mon-Fri 9:30-13, 14-18:30; Rbls, $; Eng: Metro Gostinyy Dvor

☎ DACHA RENTALS
ДАЧИ, АРЕНДА
WOCHENDHAUS, VERMIETUNG
DATCHAS, LOUAGE
FRITIOSHUS, UTHYRES
LOMA-ASUNTOJEN VUOKRAUS

On a summer Friday afternoon, the trains and roads are packed with people off to the "dacha" (дача) for the weekend to tend the garden, take walks, and just relax. Backpacks will be stuffed with food and plants, and cars will be piled high with wood and supplies to take to the country.

Dachas are privately owned country houses or cottages located anywhere from the near suburbs to over 200 kilometers away. It is possible to rent a dacha (or a room in a dacha) for a whole season or for a shorter time. Look for rentals in newspapers or see also APARTMENT RENTAL and REAL ESTATE AGENTS.

Dachas are built of wood or brick and can be quite large. The bath facilities vary; luxurious occasionally, simple frequently. Running water in a dacha is a luxury, the toilet is often in a separate building in the yard, showers are a rarity, separate Russian-style bath houses, located near a lake or river, are more frequent. Most dachas have electricity, telephones are few and the stove provides heating. In general, they are a special place to be in the summer.

Gardening is a major activity and almost every respectable dacha has a large garden with flowers, berries, fruits and vegetables.

The most fashionable areas are on the Finland Gulf Coast. Dachas there have better facilities, more stores nearby, hotels with restaurants and better roads.

Dacha Rental No. 2 in Zelenogorsk
Primorskoe shosse, 521 231-39-57
Mon-Sat 10-19; Rbls

Inpredservice
Kutuzova nab., 34 272-15-00
Fax.. 279-50-24
Mon-Fri 9-13, 14-18; Rbls, $, CC; Bus 26

☎ DANCE INSTRUCTION
ТАНЦЫ, ШКОЛА
TANZSTUDIOS, TANZSCHULEN
DANSE, STUDIOS DE
DANSSTUDIER/DANSLEKTIONER
TANSSIKOULUT JA-STUDIOT

Ballroom dancing is popular in Russia and many "Houses of Culture" (Dom Kultury, Дом Культуры) offer specialized courses for 1, 3, 6 months or even a year. It's a great *way to meet people, and learn Russian and dancing at the same time. There are also discotheques in many of the Houses of Culture listed below.*

Association of Ballroom Dance
Reki Moyki nab., 94, rm. 96 314-89-95
Fax 310-47-76
Daily 11-19; Rbls, $; Eng

Gaz House of Culture
Stachek pr., 72 184-35-83
Mon-Wed, Sun 15-17; Rbls

Kirov House of Culture
Bolshoy pr., V.O., 83 217-58-64
Daily; Rbls

Lensovet House of Culture
Kamennoostrovskiy pr., 42 230-82-24
Daily; Rbls

Santa (in Hotel Kareliya)
Marshala Tukhachevskogo ul., 27, bldg. 2
☎ 226-35-58
Rbls; Metro Ploshchad Muzhestva

☎ DANCING
ДИСКОТЕКА
DISKOTHEKEN
DANSE
DANS
TANSSIMINEN

See RESTAURANTS, NIGHTTIME
ENTERTAINMENT, DISCOTHEQUES,
DANCE INSTRUCTION

Many restaurants and bars in hotels have live music and a dance floor. Look for dancing in the display ads of RESTAURANTS, CAFES, BARS, *and* NIGHTTIME ENTERTAINMENT.

☎ DATABASES
See INFORMATION SERVICES

☎ DECORATING
See INTERIOR DESIGNERS

☎ DELICATESSENS
КУЛИНАРИИ
FEINKOSTGESCHÄFTE
DELICATESSES
DELIKATESSAFFÄRER
HERRKUKAUPAT

The closest Russian equivalent to a delicatessen is the Kulinariya, (Кулинария). *Look at the one on Nevskiy. Many* INTERNATIONAL SHOPS *and the larger* FOOD STORES, *selling for hard currency or rubles such as Spar Market, Super Babylon and Stockmann, carry a selection of imported*

cheese, sausages, smoked salmon, beverages, crackers, etc.

Kulinariya
Malaya Sadovaya ul., 8 319-99-52
Daily 9-13, 14-21; Rbls

Metropol
Sadovaya ul., 22 310-18-45
Daily 12-24; Rbls, $; Eng, Ger

Kulinarnyy Magazin Nevskiy
Nevskiy Delicatessen

At Entrance of Metro Mayakovskaya

Prepared Foods To Go • Microwave ready
Meats, Fish, Pizza, Baked Goods, Cakes
Pastries, Vegetables, Fruit & Cereals
Corner of Marata ul., 1 and Nevskiy pr., 71
☎ 164-85-81
Daily 9-15, 16-20, Rbls, Eng, Finn

☎ DENTISTS
СТОМАТОЛОГИ
ZAHNÄRZTE
DENTISTES
TANDLÄKARE
HAMMASLÄÄKÄRIT

Russian dentistry has improved greatly in the past few years as Russian dentists have finally gained access to Western materials, techniques, and equipment. (Some of our staff have had good experiences with Nordmed.)

Aura
Sedova ul., 12 567-86-64
Daily 12-19; Rbls

Avicenna
Professora Popova ul., 15/17 234-50-28
Mon-Fri 9-17; Rbls; Eng

Central Dental Clinic No. 1

Fillings, Extractions, Anesthesia
Dental Implants & Dentures

Nevskiy pr., 46 311-83-28
Tel 110-50-54
Telex .... 621470 DENTA
Also Call St. George Hospital Dental Clinic
Severnyy pr., 1 511-97-94

✳ BABYLON SUPER
Mon-Sat 10-21 Sun 12-20
Exchange office

GOING ON A PICNIC? COME VISIT THE DELI SECTION
For fresh hot bread, sliced meats and cheese, a jar of pickles, bags of chips, some fresh fruit, potato salad, a few cans of beer or soda and a great bottle of wine. Need cups, plates, paper napkins, plastic knives & forks? We even have charcoal for the barbecue.

P.S., Maly pr., 54 & 56 230-80-96
In the former Okean store off Bolshoy Prospekt

Delta-Albion
Akademika Baykova ul., 9, bldg. 2.. 555-79-24
Daily 9-15, 16-20; Rbls, $
T-bus 13; Metro Politekhnicheskaya

Denta
Kazanskaya ul., 3 311-09-50
Daily 9-21; Rbls; Eng

Dental Clinic for Children
Voznesenskiy pr., 34 314-25-65
Daily 9-20; Rbls

DENTAL POLICLINIC No. 3

Highly qualified experienced dentists
Extractions, fillings, root canals
Peridontal, checkups & dentures
Imported equipment & materials
24 hours emergency service available
Reasonable fees

21-ya Liniya, 12 213-75-51
Night emergency care.........213-55-50
Mon-Sat: 8-21, Rbls

Diksi
Liteynyy pr., 31 272-13-08
Mon-Sat 9-20; Rbls

DENTAL CENTER

OPEN 24 HOURS 7 DAYS A WEEK

Western Style Dental Care
St.Petersburg, 10ya Sovetskaya, 13
Tel: (812) 274-64-80

Dental Surgery
Mayakovskogo ul., 5 275-35-86
Mon-Fri 10-16; Rbls, $; Eng

Dentists
Bolshoy pr., P.S., 8, rm. 13............ 238-40-68
Mon-Fri 9-19; Rbls

Medikon
Borovaya ul., 55............................ 168-32-06
Mon-Fri 9-19; Rbls; Metro Ligovskiy Prospekt

TRAVELLER'S YELLOW PAGES

Please say that
you found them in
The *Traveller's*
Yellow Pages

NORDMED

A Private Dental Clinic

Specializing in
Bridges, Crowns & Root Canals,
Fillings, Extractions & Implants

Our staff graduated from leading dental
schools, trained in Europe & now teach
in leading institutes in St. Pb.

German & Finnish Equipment
Latest Western Materials

✉193124, Saint Petersburg, Russia
Tverskaya ul., 12/15

Tel... 110-06-54
Duty Doctor Weekends & Evenings ... 110-04-01
Fax 110-02-06
Hrs: 9-17:30, Thursday 9-20, English & German

St. Petersburg Policlinic No. 2

An Independent Medical Group
Dental clinic *with highly trained*
dentists and Finnish equipment
Over 25 years serving diplomats and visitors

Clinic hours: M-F, 9:00 to 21:00
Sat. 9:00 to 15:00

Moskovskiy pr., 22 292-62-72

Polimed
Nastavnikov pr., 22 521-46-33
Ulybka, *Mon-Fri 9-20; Rbls*   **Smile**
Salova ul., 37 166-76-50
Veronika, *Mon-Sat 9-14, 16-20; Rbls; Eng*
Serebryakov per., 11 239-98-34

☎ **DEPARTMENT STORES**
УНИВЕРМАГИ
KAUFHÄUSER
GRANDS MAGASINS
VARUHUS
TAVARATALOT

*The Russian equivalent of a department
store is called an "Univermag" (Универмаг).
These resemble Western department stores
and have departments for clothing, coats,
shoes, kitchen supplies, housewares, art
supplies, sporting goods, musical instruments,
stationery, souvenirs, gifts, electronics, etc.*

✳ **BABYLON**
SUPER
Mon-Sat 10-21 Sun 12-20
Exchange office

SHOP AT SUPER BABYLON SUPERMARKET
THE LARGEST SUPERMARKET IN RUSSIA
SELLING FOR RUBLES

ONE-STOP SHOPPING AT SUPER BABYLON

P.S., Maly pr., 54 & 56 230-80-96
In the former Okean store off Bolshoy Prospekt

The best known ones are Gostinyy Dvor, Passage, DLT, Apraksin Dvor, Tsentr Firmennoy Torgovli and the Moskovskiy Univermag.

Gostinyy Dvor has departments spread out over 2 floors and is divided into four "lines" named according to the streets they face: Sadovaya, Perinnaya, Nevskaya & Lomonosovskaya. It includes a few foreign shops. Stop in at Littlewoods for fashionable clothing.

The Passage (Passazh) is a 3-floored department store and has more foreign shops and is now the most upscale department store. Try Escada for women's clothing (including underwear) and accessories, lantovski for leather goods, Henkel for cosmetics, and Sylvi for personal hygiene products. The Passage even houses a small Volvo showroom.

The Apraksin Dvor department store has really become a row of COMMISSION *and* COMMERCIAL SHOPS *competing with street vendors under an arcade on Sadovaya. The courtyard inside is an open-air bazaar and auto show room. Interesting, but be careful of pick pockets.*

The DLT is a children's department store with lots for adults, including an Italian shoe boutique. Toy selection is one of the biggest in St. Pb.

Best Department Store
Kupchinskaya ul., 15 261-64-53
Daily 9-20; Rbls

DLT (Leningrad Trading House)
A department store for children, and adults, too
Bolshaya Konyushennaya ul., 21/23
.... 312-26-27
Fax 315-21-92
Mon-Sat 10-20; Rbls, $; Eng

Frunzenskiy Univermag
Kuznetsovskaya ul., 10 296-10-52
Mon-Sat 10-14, 15-19; Rbls

BOLSHOY GOSTINY DVOR

The largest Department Store in St. Pb.
❖ ❖ ❖
Two Floors of Stores including
Imported Foods, Footwear, Clothes,
Electronics, Jewelry etc.
❖ ❖ ❖
Currency Exchange &
Littlewoods International Shop
located in Sadovaya Line

Nevskiy pr., 35 312-41-65
Fax 314-98-81
Mon-Sat 10-21

Kalininskiy Univermag
Kondratevskiy pr., 40 540-29-35
Fax 310-25-18
Mon-Sat 10-20; Rbls

Kirovskiy Univermag, *Mon-Sat 10-21; Rbls*
Stachek pr., 9 186-59-80

A/O KUPCHINSKIY UNIVERMAG
A Variety of Items for Men, Women & Children
Housewares, Appliances
Reasonable Prices

Slavy pr., 4, 12, 16 261-99-81
Fax 260-23-67
Hrs: 10-20, Closed Sunday

Fairn & swanson

Lama Trading
N e v s k y   p r . ,   9 6
275•53•85

**Housewares,
Large Appliances
Electronics, Toys**

Corporate Offices
in Moscow:
Olimpiyskiy pr., 18
Tel. (095) 288-15-12
Fax (095) 288-46-53
Wholesale Division:
Tel. (095) 288-60-66

Rbls & $

—Littlewoods—

Wide Selection of Imported & Domestic
Goods at Competitive Prices

Gostinyy Dvor,
Sadovaya Line 110-54-21
Daily 10-20, Clsd. Sun.; Rubles, $

Moskovskiy Univermag
One of the best in the city
Moskovskiy pr., 205, 220 293-44-55
Mon-Sat 10-21; Rbls

Narvskiy Univermag
Leninskiy pr., 120-138 255-84-29
Mon-Sat 10-21; Rbls

PASSAZH (PASSAGE)
Latest fashions, clothing, shoes, fabrics,
sport clothing, lingerie, hats & handbags,
electronics, cosmetics, watches, jewelry
Imported & domestic
Nevskiy pr., 48. 311-70-84
Mon-Fri 10-21, Sat 10-18

Severomurinskiy Univermag
Prosvshcheniya pr., 87................ 531-04-44
Mon-Sat 10-19; Rbls

"SHOPPING CENTER"
Tsentr Firmennoy Torgovli
The best domestic and imported goods
Specializing in apparel, footwear &
electronics, furs, and cosmetics.
Novosmolenskaya nab., 1. . .352-06-32
Mon-Sat 10-20

Voennyy Univermag
                      Military Supply Store
• Nepokorennykh pr., 6.................... 247-19-14
• Nevskiy pr., 67.......................... 311-77-33
Mon-Sat 11-14, 15-19; Rbls

Yubiley, *A great store for newlyweds*
Sverdlovskaya nab., 60 224-25-98
Mon-Sat 10-20; Rbls

Yunost, *Youth fashions*
Novo-Izmaylovskiy pr., 4................ 296-62-64
Mon-Sat 10-19; Rbls

☎ **DESKTOP PUBLISHING**
   НАСТОЛЬНЫЕ ИЗДАТЕЛЬСКИЕ
   СИСТЕМЫ
   DESKTOP PUBLISHING
   DESKTOP PUBLISHING
   DESKTOP PUBLISHING
   DESKTOP PUBLISHING

See also BUSINESS CARDS, PRINTING,
PHOTOCOPYING *and* PUBLISHERS

Desktop publishing thrives in St.
Petersburg. Some firms listed under
PUBLISHING *and* PRINTING *are really desktop*
publishers.

Amos, *Specialists in desktop publishing*
Pavlogradskiy per., 6/10 164-40-78

☎ **DIESEL FUEL**
   ДИЗЕЛЬНОЕ ТОПЛИВО
   DIESELKRAFTSTOFF
   DIESEL FUEL
   DIESEL BRÄNSLE
   DIESELPOLTTOAINE

Diesel Station in Sestroretsk
Primorskoe shosse, 18 km............. 238-30-49
Daily 0-24; Rbls
Diesel Station No. 45
Avangardnaya ul., 36 135-58-67
Daily 0-24; Rbls, $

☎ **DIRECTORIES**
   СПРАВОЧНИКИ
   ADRESSBÜCHER
   ANNUAIRES
   ADRESS KATALOG
   OSOITE LUETTELO

See also BUSINESS PUBLICATIONS *and*
TELEPHONE DIRECTORIES.

DIRECTORIES IN RUSSIAN

Everyday Services of Leningrad, Sluzhby
Byta Leningrada, Службы быта
Ленинграда, 1990

St. Petersburg for Motorists, Sankt
Peterburg avtomobilistu, Санкт-Петербург
автомобилисту, 1993

Thousands of Services for St.
Petersburgers, Tysyacha uslug Sankt-
Peterburzhtsam, Тысяча услуг Санкт-
Петербуржцам, 1992
   Volume 1. Services for the Family
   Volume 2. Medical Services
   Volume 3. Employment Services

St. Petersburg for Children, Teenagers &
Parents, Sankt Peterburg dlya detey,
podrostkov i roditeley, Санкт-Петербург
для детей, подростков и родителей, 1992.
An excellent directory.

☎ **DISCOTHEQUES**
   ДИСКОТЕКИ
   DISKOTHEKEN
   DISCOTEQUES
   DISKOTEK
   DISKOT

See also DANCE INSTRUCTION *and* RESTAURANTS

NIGHT CLUB
ELDORADO
HOTEL KARELIA - ST. PETERSBURG
Tukhachevskogo ul., 27/2
226-3110
BAR, DISCO, DANCE SHOW, CASINO
OPEN DAILY 8 p.m. - 5 a.m., $

Europa Plus, Dance Hall
Kamennoostrovskiy pr., 68...................No ☎
Fri, Sat 23-6; Rbls, $
Galspe at Palanga
Leninskiy pr., 127 254-55-82
Fax... 255-51-60
Variety Show; Daily 17-6; Rbls, $, CC
Joy, *Western style discotheque*
Lomonosova ul., 1/28 311-35-40
Daily 22-5; Metro Nevskiy Prospekt
Kuryer, *Sat 24-6*
Gertsena ul., 58............................. 311-46-78

🕊 *NEVSKY*
MELODY

European & Russian Cuisine,
Disco, Bars, Roulette, Blackjack.
Nab. Sverdlovskaya, 62 227-15-96
Tel/Fax 222-51-80
Hrs: 12-18 for Rubles, 18-1 $ & Rbls, $ for drinks.,
discotheque 21-1; CC; English, German, French

Relax, *Discotheque*
Prosvshcheniya pr., 80, bldg. 2 514-75-22
Fri, Sat 22-6

U Lissa, at the Sports and Concert Complex (SKK)
Yuriya Gagarina pr., 8 298-21-64
Sat & Sun; Metro Park Pobedy

Star Dust Night Discotheque
Alexandrovskiy Park, 4 233-27-12
Tue-Sun 10-16:30; Rbls; Metro Moskovskaya

☎ DOCTORS
ВРАЧИ
ÄRZTE
DOCTEURS
LÄKARE
LÄÄKÄRIT

See MEDICAL CARE & CONSULTATIONS,
HOSPITALS *and* EMERGENCY MEDICAL
ASSISTANCE

☎ DOGS AND KENNELS
СОБАКИ, ПРОДАЖА
HUNDE UND HUNDEHÜTTEN
CHIENS, VENTE
HUNDAR OCH KENNLAR
KOIRAT JA KENNELIT

See also PETS
*Russians love dogs, especially pedigree.
Don't be surprised if you see a dog walking
down the street with a parcel in its mouth,
or on trams. Most dogs are well trained &
cared for. Kennels listed here are
"breeding" kennels and do not board dogs.*

DOSAAF Dog Kennel, *Breeding*
• Rasstannaya ul., 10 166-36-41
Mon, Wed-Thu 14-20; Rbls
• 6-ya Sovetskaya ul., 30 271-45-78
Mon, Wed-Thu 14-20; Rbls
• Bolshaya Podyacheskaya ul., 16..... 311-58-57
Mon, Wed-Thu 14-20; Rbls

St. Petersburg Dog Breeding Club
17-ya Liniya, 38 213-75-60
Mon-Fri 11-18; Rbls, $

☎ DRIVING
ПРАВИЛА ВОЖДЕНИЯ
AUTOFAHREN
CONDUITE
TRAFIK REGLER
AJAMINEN

See also MILITIA, AUTOMOBILES,
and ACCIDENTS

License: *To drive in Russia, an international drivers license is required with a
Russian translation along with your national
driver's license.*

Rules: *Most international rules apply.
The official speed limits are 60 kph/37 mph
in the city, 90 kph/56 mph in unpopulated
areas and 120 kph/72 mph on open
highways.*

*At intersections, the vehicle on the right
has the right of way. At traffic lights you
can not turn right on red. Do not block intersections. The blue and white traffic
arrows over the lanes of major thorough-
fares and solid and dotted lines indicate
turns and no-turns; observe carefully. To
turn left, you must often turn right first,*

*make a U-turn and go back across the
intersection. Parking lights are required
from dusk to dawn, but full headlights are
not usually used at night. Lights are
flashed to warn other cars and pedestrians,
horns are not permitted except in emergencies. Wear your seat belt; it is the law!*

Driving Conditions: *City roads contain
many unmarked hazards: pot holes, missing
manhole covers, excavations and more.
Trolley tracks are especially treacherous.
Night driving in the city in winter with poor
street lighting and dirty windshields is only
for the experienced.*

*Russian city drivers are amazingly skillful
and have become more courteous in recent
years. Many, however, drive very fast and
take incredible risks, especially when pass-
ing on the open highways. If you have a
driver, don't let him take these risks.
Always drive defensively.*

Traffic Police: *Most traffic officers (GAI,
ГАИ) usually wear either gray or dark blue
uniforms and carry black and white batons
which they wave at you to signify that you
should pull over. If a traffic officer signals
to you, best obey. For minor violations
such as a missing tail light or an illegal
turn, they can collect a small fine immediately. It is easiest to pay on the spot; ask
for a receipt. With serious violations, they
take your license on the spot forcing you to
retrieve it at the GAI. Driving after the use
of any alcohol is severely punished. If such
a violation is alleged, get a good lawyer
immediately.*

Accidents and Insurance *Be sure to
have auto insurance coverage in Russia.
Look under* INSURANCE.
*In case of an accident, do not move the
involved cars until the traffic police arrive
and measure everything. It can take several
hours for them to arrive, so Russians often
work things out between themselves. Sign
nothing without consulting a lawyer. For
towing, see* AUTOMOBILE EMERGENCY ASSIS-
TANCE; *for repairs see* AUTOMOBILE PARTS,
and AUTOMOBILE SERVICE & REPAIRS.

Parking Precautions. *Theft of windshield
wipers, radios, wheels and entire cars is
frequent. Try to park in watched* AUTO PARKS
*around hotels or on well-traveled streets.
Many Russians have installed* AUTOMOBILE
ALARMS *and regularly remove their
windshield wipers.*

Gas, Petrol, Lubricants, Tires, Auto Parts
*A reasonable supply is available even for
imported cars. See* GAS STATIONS *and*
AUTOMOBILE PARTS *and* TIRES.

Street names and signs. *Street names
are written in Russian on the walls of buildings at intersections. Building numbers are
posted once or twice on white signs each
street block. Because of the recent
changes in street names, many signs do not
correspond to the new street names. See*
NEW NAMES, *pp. 14-15. Major highways are
marked by blue and white route numbers.
For example the highway to Moscow*

is M10. Try to learn the Cyrillic alphabet if you plan to drive. Our Traveller's Yellow Pages City Map for St. Petersburg *has both English and Russian street indices to help you find your way and shows all streets in the central part of the city. See also* FINDING YOUR WAY.

For auto route maps of the surrounding regions, see MAPS.

☎ **DRUG STORES**
   АПТЕКИ
   APOTHEKEN
   PHARMACIES
   APOTEK
   APTEEKIT

See PHARMACIES

There is no equivalent to the "American Drug Store" that fills prescriptions _and_ sells sundries in Russia. For medicine and drugs, try PHARMACIES *and for sundries look in Western style* DEPARTMENT STORES *or* SUPERMARKETS. *You can also find toothpaste, personal hygiene products, etc. now and again in* KIOSKS, *and* COMMERCIAL SHOPS.

☎ **DRY CLEANING**
   ХИМЧИСТКА
   CHEMISCHE REINIGUNGEN
   NETTOYAGE A SEC
   KEMTVÄTT
   KUIVAPESULAT

Dry cleaning *service* (Khimchistka, Химчистка) *is provided in most major hotels, usually payable in hard currency and in these stores.*

Khimchistka	Dry Cleaners
Химчистка	

* Barmaleeva ul., 6 232-44-56
   Mon-Sat 9-14, 15-19; Rbls
* Izmaylovskiy pr., 12 292-33-47
   Mon-Sat 9-19; Rbls
* Lermontovskiy pr., 1/44 114-19-04
   Mon-Sat 9-14, 15-19:30; Rbls
* Metallistov pr., 73 540-19-36
   Mon-Fri 8-14, 15-19; Rbls
* Razezzhaya ul., 12 164-77-01
   Mon-Sat 9-14, 15-20; Rbls
* Salova ul., 57 166-13-28
   Mon-Sat 8-21; Rbls, $
* Zanevskiy pr., 37 528-84-65
   Mon-Sat 8-21; Rbls

☎ **DUTY-FREE SHOPS**
   МАГАЗИНЫ БЕСПОШЛИННОЙ
   ТОРГОВЛИ
   DUTY-FREE-LÄDEN
   DUTY FREE SHOPS
   TAX FREE
   TAX FREE

See INTERNATIONAL SHOPS

The only real duty free shops are the Lenrianta Airport Shops in Arrivals & Departures at the Airport Pulkovo-2. The rest are really shops featuring imported goods and are usually called "hard currency

shops" ("Valyutnye magaziny", Валютные магазины). *If shops specialize in a product such as clothing or electronics, we list them under that category. Shops with a small selection of a wide variety of goods such as alcohol, candy, perfume, electronics, some jeans, and a few food items are listed under* INTERNATIONAL SHOPS.

Many other shops, called "COMMERCIAL STORES", *however, now sell a large variety of imported goods, too, but for rubles.*

☎ **EDUCATIONAL PROGRAMS**
   ОБРАЗОВАНИЕ, УЧРЕЖДЕНИЯ
   WEITERBILDUNG
   INSTITUTS EDUCATIFS
   UTBILDNINGSINSTITUT
   KOULUTUS

See also UNIVERSITIES *and* INSTITUTES

These private organizations offer educational programs to Russian and foreign students.

Advanced Humanities Courses
   Voznesenskiy pr., 34 b 314-35-21
   Fax.. 315-39-17
   Mon-Fri 10-22; Rbls
Alliance Francaise
   Reki Moyki nab., 20 311-09-95
   Mon-Sat 10-19; Rbls; Fr
Baltic International Institute of Tourism
   Morskoy pr., 29 230-21-16
   Mon-Fri 10-17; Rbls
Center for International Education - CIE
   Smolnogo ul., 1/3, entr. 9, rm. 304 143-85-21
   Mon-Fri 10-18; Rbls; Eng
Humanities Center
   Griboedova kan. nab., 92/1 310-20-90
   Mon-Fri 9-17:30; Rbls
International Management Institute of St. Petersburg-IMISP
   Smolnyy , entr., 9 271-34-33
   Fax.. 271-07-17
   Mon-Fri 9-18; Rbls, $; Eng
LETI-Lovanium
   Professora Popova ul., 5 234-02-12
   Mon-Fri 9-19; Rbls; Eng
Progress Management and Marketing Center
   Institutskiy pr., 22 552-13-38
   Fax.. 552-77-28
   Mon-Fri 10-18; Rbls

THE FUQUA SCHOOL OF BUSINESS
Associated with Duke University, USA
Please call 314-64-93

☎ **ELECTRICAL INSTALLATION**
   ЭЛЕКТРООБОРУДОВАНИЕ,
   УСТАНОВКА
   ELEKTROINSTALLATIONEN
   ELECTRICITE(ELECTRIQUE,
   INSTALLATION)
   EL INSTALLATION
   SÄHKÖASENNUKSET

See also ELECTRICITY, EMERGENCY SERVICES *and* APARTMENT REPAIR

These firms install wiring and circuits. Electrical outlets are few and far between.

So when setting up an office or apartment, you need to know how many outlets (Rozetki, Розетки) you have. Remember, circuits are not usually grounded and ground-fault interrupters are unknown. Outlets take a plug with two round pins. Troynik (тройник) are the adapters that convert one outlet to three. Extension cords are called udlinitel (удлинитель).

Khronotron
Dostoevskogo ul., 44 315-19-21
Fax 315-68-79
Mon-Fri 8-13, 14-17; Rbls; Ger

LEMK
Ligovskiy pr., 82 164-12-59
Mon-Fri 9:30-13, 14-18; Rbls, $

Tyazhpromelektroproekt
Bukharestskaya ul., 6 166-38-56
Mon-Fri 8:30-13:30, 14:30-17:30; Rbls
Bus 74; Metro Ligovskiy Prospekt

☎ **ELECTRICAL APPLIANCE REPAIR**
ЭЛЕКТРОПРИБОРЫ, РЕМОНТ
ELEKTROGERÄTE, REPARATUR
ELECTRICITE(ELECTRIQUES, REPARATIONS)
ELEKTRIKER (ELEKTRISKA REP.)
SÄHKÖKORJAUKSET

See also EMERGENCY SERVICES *and* REPAIR

These shops repair a variety of small appliances, radios, lamps, etc.

Electrical Repair Shop
• Bogatyrskiy pr., 10......................... 394-71-29
Mon-Fri 10-14, 15-19; Rbls; Bus 93; Metro Pionerskaya
• Lenina ul., 16................................. 232-06-48
Mon-Sat 10-14, 15-19; Rbls; Bus 10; Metro Gorkovskaya
• Tipanova ul., 29 299-87-51
Mon-Sat 11-19; Rbls; Bus 11; Metro Moskovskaya

Reved
Bryantseva ul., 7 531-76-95
Mon-Sat 10-14, 15-19; Rbls

St. Petersburg Corporation
Reki Fontanki nab., 116 g, apt. 45 259-50-11
Mon-Fri 10-14, 15-19; Rbls; Eng

☎ **ELECTRICAL SUPPLIES AND GOODS**
ЭЛЕКТРОТОВАРЫ
ELEKTROZUBEHÖR
ELECTRICITE(ELECTRIQUES, FOURNITURES)
ELTILLBEHÖR
SÄHKÖTARVIKKEET

See also LIGHTING FIXTURES, BUILDING SUPPLIES, COMPUTERS, OFFICE EQUIPMENT, TELEVISION SALES, VIDEO EQUIPMENT, PHOTOCOPIERS, INTERNATIONAL SHOPS, *and* ELECTRONICS

Shops called Electrical Goods, (Electrotovary, Электротовары) sell lamps, lighting fixtures, bulbs, heaters, coffee mills, etc. Buy light bulbs when you see them. They are often in "deficit".

ABO
Bolshevikov pr., 38, bldg. 2............. 595-90-57
Mon-Fri 9-18; Rbls, $

Adamant, *Bosch electrical supplies, tools*
8-ya Sovetskaya ul., 9 279-27-82
Mon-Fri 10-19; $

Babylon No. 2
See ad under HOUSEWARES

Elektrolux *All Electrolux appliances*
Robespera nab., 16........................ 275-55-12
Daily 10-20; Rbls, $; Eng, Fr

Elektrotovary   **Electrical Goods**
• Grecheskiy pr., 27 271-21-74
Mon-Sat 10-14, 15-19; Rbls
• Kamennoostrovskiy pr., 18............. 232-78-22
Mon-Sat 10-14, 15-19; Rbls; Metro Gorkovskaya
• Lanskoe shosse, 69 246-48-44
Mon-Sat 10-14, 15-19; Rbls
• Liteynyy pr., 27 272-45-98
Mon-Sat 10-14, 15-19; Rbls
• Moskovskiy pr., 134....................... 298-21-15
Mon-Sat 10-14, 15-19; Bus 3; Metro Moskovskie Vorota
• Pestelya ul., 10/23 272-89-02
Mon-Sat 10-13, 14-19
• Zagorodnyy pr., 9.......................... 314-18-15
Mon-Sat 10-14, 15-19; Rbls

Elma
Lesnoy pr., 73............................... 245-45-88
Mon-Fri 10-19; Rbls; Eng, Ger

Home ☐ Center
Electrical Center
Professional or do-it-yourself
Supplies for electrical repair or installation
A large selection of plugs, outlets, switches, light fixtures, bulbs, cable and cord, circuit breakers, fasteners, crimping tools and testers.

Located in S.E. St. Pb., minutes from city center
Slavy pr., 30................................... 261-15-50
.... 261-04-02
Fax 260-15-81
Daily 10-20; $, FIM, DM, Rbls; Eng, Finn, Ger
Metro Moskovskaya then Bus 31, 114, T-bus 29

Lek Tradehouse
Mytninskaya ul., 19/48, apt. 20 271-14-29
Mon-Fri 10-17; Rbls, $; Eng, Fr

Line
1-ya Liniya, 44 213-26-19
Mon-Sat 10-14, 15-19

Neva Star International Shopping
(at the Moskva Hotel)
Aleksandra Nevskogo pl., 2 274-00-24
Daily 8-23; $; T-bus 1; Metro Pl. Aleksandra Nevskogo

Philips Electronics
Full range of Philips home appliances
Suvorovskiy pr., 2........................ 277-43-19
Daily 10-14, 15-20; Rbls, $; Eng

Svet
Moskovskiy pr., 163...................... 298-37-57
Mon-Sat 10-13, 14-19; Rbls

Svetlyachok, Electrical Goods No. 164
Nevskiy pr., 65.............................. 311-04-45
Mon-Sat 11-14, 15-19; Rbls

Vega Shop-Salon
Lermontovskiy pr., 27 114-45-91
Mon-Fri 10-14, 15-19; Rbls

☎ ELECTRICITY
ЭЛЕКТРИЧЕСТВО
ELEKTRIZITÄT
ELECTRICITE
ELEKTRICITET
SÄHKÖ

The electricity in St. Petersburg is 220 volt, 50 Hz.

Some newer appliances, such as laptop computers, battery chargers and travel appliances, automatically adapt to this voltage & cycles/herz. Check your appliances and look for a label stating "110-220 volt, 50-60 hertz". Sometimes you must change a switch manually.

You need a round two-pin plug adapter, also a surge protector is recommended. Buy some plugs and adapters before you arrive and check that the pins are the right size and not too thick. Note that some Russians routinely unplug electronic equipment when not in use to protect against power surges.

A transformer can convert from 220 volt to 110-130 volt without problems. It is not possible, however, to easily convert 50 Hz to 60 Hz, so be sure that your appliances or equipment can work with 110 volt, 50 Hz power. (US market photocopiers will not work here without modification).

The small travel transformers are effective for small appliances & hair dryers, but not large motors, appliances and photocopiers. A 300 watt transformer for computers weighs about 10 pounds and a 1,000 watt transformer for laser printers and photocopiers weighs about 30 pounds. Transformers can be purchased in St. Petersburg at Computerland. Most power sources are ungrounded, but running a wire to a water pipe usually does the job.

Computerland
Sverdlovskaya nab., 64 224-04-55

☎ ELECTRONIC GOODS
(Stereos, Radio-TV's, VCR's, CD players)
ЭЛЕКТРОНИКА
ELEKTRONIK
ELECTRONIQUE, MATERIEL
ELEKTRONISKA APPARATER
ELEKTRONIIKKA

Many shops sell a wide variety of Western electronic goods from TVs & VCRs to computers & photocopiers. Many are now authorized dealers and can provide warranty services. For specific products see also AUDIO EQUIPMENT, COMPUTERS, OFFICE EQUIPMENT, PHOTOCOPIERS, TELEPHONE EQUIPMENT, TELEVISION, and VIDEO EQUIPMENT.

7 Ogney
Novocherkasskiy pr., 22 528-55-12
Fax 114-84-33
Mon-Sat 11-14, 15-19; Rbls, $; Eng

Adzhi Shop
Prosveshcheniya pr., 80, bldg. 2 530-97-75
Daily 9-20; Rbls, $
Afina Shop No. 4
8-ya Sovetskaya ul., 6/8 271-20-73
Mon-Sat 10-14, 15-19; Rbls
Afina Shop No. 5
Komsomola ul., 51 542-04-66
Mon-Fri 9-13, 14-18; Rbls
Ajax Ltd.
Galernaya ul., 55 314-39-45
Fax 312-24-79
Mon-Fri 10-17:30; Rbls, $; Eng, Ger
Alivekt
Nevskiy pr., 23 311-46-45
Mon-Sat 10-19; $; Metro Nevskiy Prospekt
Argus
Olminskogo ul., 6 567-26-10
Mon-Fri 10-18; Rbls, $
Baltex
Blagodatnaya ul., 55 294-10-23
Mon-Fri 10-19; Rbls; Eng, Ger, Fr
Baltic Star International Shopping
(at Pribaltiyskaya Hotel)
Korablestroiteley ul., 14 356-41-85
Fax 356-01-14
Daily 8-23; $, CC; Eng, Ger

BALTICA

AUTHORIZED **BOSE** DISTRIBUTOR

Better Sound Through Research
A wide range of professional hi-fi audio systems and equipment for any purpose you can imagine

M. Toreza pr., 2/40 247-82-03
Fax 247-23-79

Beriozka
Morskaya nab., 9 356-55-98
Mon-Sat 10-19; $
Calculators
Kamennoostrovskiy pr., 2 233-50-53
Mon-Sat 10-14, 15-19; Rbls
Creat
Kazanskaya ul., 49 311-13-01
Fax 312-43-12
Mon-Fri 10-14, 15-18; Rbls, $; Eng, Ger; Metro Sadovaya
Electronica Gallery and Shop
Yuriya Gagarina pr., 12 299-38-49
Mon-Sat 10-14, 15-19; Rbls, $
Elektronika
Italyanskaya ul., 14 .... No ☎
Mon-Sat 11-14, 15-19; $; Eng, Ger
Elektronika-Video
Lesnoy pr., 22 542-62-17
Mon-Fri 10-19; Rbls
Eridan
Zagorodnyy pr., 11 314-23-18
Mon-Sat 10-14, 15-19; Rbls
T-bus 3, 8; Metro Dostoevskaya, Vladimirskaya

FAIRN & SWANSON
Electronics, Housewares, Toys
See our ad under DEPARTMENT STORES
Nevskiy pr., 96 275-53-85
Fax 275-53-86
Daily 9-14, 15-21; Rubles; English

Global USA - *See our color ad*
Moscow, Usacheva ul., 35
☎ ....(095) 245-56-57
Goldstar
Lesnoy pr., 20 542-19-59
Fax 542-09-89
Mon-Sat 10-19; Rbls, $; Eng
Gorizont, *Daily 10-14, 15-19; Rbls*
Shvernika pr., 14 550-44-84
Fax 552-35-21

*Number 1 in Electronics
and Electrical Appliances*

HI·LIFE ELECTRONICS

*Номер 1 в электронике и
электрической бытовой технике*

Visit our shop
on Karavannaya ul., 16
Tel/Fax: 314-98-61

Home ▢ Center
TV video/audio center

Coming soon at the Home Center

Located in S.E. St. Pb., minutes from city center
Slavy pr., 30 261-15-50
.... 261-04-02
Fax 260-15-81
*Daily 10-20; $, FIM, DM, Rbls; Eng, Finn, Ger
Metro Moskovskaya, then Bus 31, 114, T-bus 29*

Intep, *Daily 10-19; Rbls, $; Eng*
Ryleeva ul., 10 275-53-27
Fax 275-53-60
Kris Agro, *Audio/video*
Bakunina pr., 29 274-78-89
Fax 271-31-61
Mon-Sat 11-14, 15-19; Rbls, $
LEMI'S, *Mon-Sat 10-14, 15-19; Rbls, $*
Moskovskiy pr., 20 110-12-95
Lance
Reki Fontanki nab., 48 113-26-59
Fax 314-12-73
*Mon-Fri 10-14, 15-18; Rbls, $; Eng, Ger
Metro Dostoevskaya*
Leninets, *Mon-Fri 9:30-17:30; Rbls*
Moskovskiy pr., 212 293-71-78
Fax 291-81-38

MS-Audiotron
4-ya Krasnoarmeyskaya ul., 4 a 310-55-13
Fax... 310-48-01
Daily; Rbls
Micas AG
7-ya Krasnoarmeyskaya ul., 6/8...... 112-75-04
Fax... 315-70-56
Mon-Sat 10-14, 15-19; Rbls, $
Mipros
Lenina pr., 101, Kolpino 484-91-04
Fax... 484-18-88
Mon-Fri 9-18; Rbls, $; Eng, Ger, Fr

National Panasonic Technics
See our ad under AUDIO EQUIPMENT
Nakhimova ul., 7, off. 39 356-36-35
Fax..356-83-33

Ortex
7-ya Krasnoarmeyskaya ul., 30....... 264-60-08
.... 251-90-69
Panasonic-*See National Panasonic Technics*
Philips Electronics
Suvorovskiy pr., 2........................277-43-19
Daily 10-14, 15-20; Rbls, $; Eng
Penguin
Zagorodnyy pr., 10........................314-32-30
Mon-Sat 11-19; Rbls; Eng
Pioneer Electronics
Zagorodnyy pr., 11........................314-23-14
*Mon-Sat 11-19; Rbls; Eng, Ger, Fr
T-bus 3, 5, 8, 15, 17; Metro Pushkinskaya*
Progress Service
Reki Moyki nab., 59, floor 2 315-86-63
Fax..213-53-56
Mon-Fri 11-14, 15-19; Rbls; Tram 2, 28, 3; Metro Sadovaya
Quazar
Kamennoostrovskiy pr., 5...............233-40-33
Fax..232-49-44
Mon-Sat 10-19; Rbls, $; Eng
Radiotekhnika
Sverdlovskaya nab., 64 224-04-57
Fax..224-29-28
Daily 11-19; Rbls, $
Record-Service
Rubinshteyna ul., 20 310-59-71
Mon-Sat 10-14, 15-19; Rbls; Metro Dostoevskaya
Records, Radio, Watches, Photo
Obukhovskoy Oborony pr., 81 265-13-01
Mon-Sat 10-19; Rbls
Rigonda
• Makarova nab., 28 213-27-80
Fax..213-78-42
Mon-Fri 10-19; Rbls
• Moskovskiy pr., 171....................298-08-40
Daily 11-20; Rbls

DELOVIE LYUDI
INDEPENDENT • OBJECTIVE • THOROUGH
Profsoyuznaya ul., 73; Tel.: (095) 333-33-40; Fax: (095) 330-15-68

Official Business Partner

IBM
MINOLTA
Gold Star
Hewlett Packard

РУБИКОН

Rubicon
Lesnoy pr., 19
542-00-65, 248-83-06
Fax.............542-09-89
Telex   121194 Rub SU

Samsung, *See UMA Electronics ad below.*
Sansui, *Daily 11-15, 16-19; Rbls; Eng*
  Chekhova ul., 14 312-73-58
  Fax 310-82-11
Selena, *Mon-Fri 9-14, 15-18; Rbls*
  Reki Moyki nab., 74 314-94-88
Sever, *Mon-Sat 9:30-18; Rbls*   **North**
  Gertsena ul., 18 311-81-66
Shop No. 28, *Mon-Fri 10-19; Rbls*
  Bolshoy pr., P.S., 72 232-25-10
Siemens AG
  Gogolya ul., 18/20 315-31-97
  Fax 315-36-21
            Mon-Fri 9-17; Rbls, $; Eng, Ger
Sinus
  Morskoy Pekhoty ul., 8, bldg. 1, apt. 4
  ☎ 157-57-94
            Mon-Fri 10-17; Rbls, $; Eng, Fr, Finn
So-Eks
  Professora Popova ul., 7/8, apt. 8 234-58-00
  Fax... 234-02-52
            Mon-Fri 11-18; Rbls, $; Eng
Soniko, *Mon-Sat 9-18*
  Moskovskoe shosse, 16................. 127-58-30
Sovlyuks
  Orlovskiy per., 7/3 277-40-83
            Mon-Fri 10-18; Rbls, $; Eng, Ger, Fr, Bul
Tankur, *Panasonic electronics*
  Energetikov pr., 60, bldg. 2 225-00-19
  Fax 535-35-34
                     Mon-Sat 10-18
Tekhkompakt, *Mon-Fri 10-17; Rbls, $; Eng*
  Moskovskiy pr., 181 291-00-48
  Fax 108-48-65

★★ The Electronic Store at the Airport Shop
  Airport Pulkovo-1............................ 123-87-78
  104-34-87
  Top selection of consumer electronics at reasonable prices. A Lenrianta shop $, CC; Eng, Ger

LTD

Authorized SAMSUNG ELECTRONICS Distributor

Dealer for Supra

Malookhtinskiy pr., 68 528-95-66
.... 528-00-51
Fax 528-84-00

Vega Shop-Salon, *Mon-Fri 10-14, 15-19; Rbls*
  Lermontovskiy pr., 27 114-45-91
Vesta-Tauras, *Mon-Sat 10-19; Rbls*
  Primorskiy pr., 27 239-97-61
Vilma, *Mon-Fri 9-17; Rbls*
  Ligovskiy pr., 65 310-30-29
Vychislitelnaya Tekhnika *Calculators*
  Vladimirskiy pr., 2.......................... 113-14-45
            Mon-Sat 10-14, 15-19; Rbls
Zolotoy Klyuchik   **Golden Key**
  Marshala Govorova ul., 10............. 184-83-18
            Mon-Sat 10-14, 15-19; Rbls

☎ **ELECTRONIC GOODS REPAIR**

See ELECTRONICS GOODS, TELEVISION REPAIRS,
COMPUTER REPAIRS, *and* REPAIR SERVICES

☎ **ELECTRONIC MAIL, E-MAIL**
     ЭЛЕКТРОННАЯ ПОЧТА
     E-MAIL, ELEKTRONISCHE
     NACHRICHTENÜBERMITTLUNG
     ELECTRONIQUE, COURRIER
     ELEKTRONISK POST
     TELEPOSTI

Electronic mail (E-mail) is a cheaper and quick way to send information between cities and countries. Because of poor phone lines, it is necessary to have a good **2400 Baud modem that supports MNP5 Error Correction or telecommunications software** *such as METZ, that does error correction. For a good discussion of E-mail resources in Russia and US, see* "Business Survival Guide" *under* BUSINESS PUBLICATIONS.

Many Western services go through VNIIPAS computer in Moscow.

Glasnet
  Los Angeles, CA...................(415) 948-57-53
  Fax...(415) 948-14-74
  Moscow Fax............................(095) 216-60-33
Infocom *Extensive world network, Infonet especially in Europe*
  USA.......................................(800) 766-87-37
  Moscow..................................(095) 925-12-35
Masshtab
  Kantemirovskaya ul., 6 245-51-65
  Mon-Fri 8-17; Rbls, $; Eng; T-bus 46; Metro Petrogradskaya
Relcom *Largest Russian/CIS network with access to Western E-mail services*
  14-ya Liniya, 39 218-18-35
  Fax... 237-45-14
            Mon-Fri 10-18; Rbls, $; Eng

Sovam Teleport
*All International Electronic Mail Services (Bitnet, Internet, MCI, Mercury, Transpak, etc.)
Local Access to International Databases, Express Fax and Telex Links.*

Short-term E-Mail Accounts for Visitors
Nevskiy pr., 30................................. 311-84-12
Fax.. 311-71-29
Telex .... 158-230564 PETERS
In USA call .... (800) 257-51-07

Int'l E-Mail: spbsovam@sovamsu.uucp
Mon-Fri 9-18

Sprint Net
Sinopskaya nab., 14......................265-05-71
Fax 274-26-21
Mon-Fri 9-18; Rbls; Eng

☎ EMBASSIES
ПОСОЛЬСТВА
BOTSCHAFTEN
AMBASSADES
AMBASSADER
SUURLÄHETYSTÖT

All embassies are located in Moscow.
See CONSULATES *for the numbers &*
addresses of consulates in St. Petersburg.
Our Moscow book has a complete list of
the more than 100 embassies in Moscow.
Embassies will usually answer 24 hrs a day
for emergencies on a call back basis.

IN MOSCOW

Australia, *Daily 0-24*
Kropotkinskiy per., 13...........(095) 956-60-70
Belgium, *Mon-Fri 9-17:30*
Malaya Molchanovskaya ul., 7
....(095) 291-60-18
Bulgaria, *Mon-Fri 9-13, 14-16:30*
Mosfilmovskaya ul., 66.........(095) 143-90-22
Canada, *Mon-Fri 8:30-13, 14-17*
Starokonyushennyy per., 23 .....(095) 241-58-82
China, *Mon-Fri 9-13; Bus 119*
Druzhby ul., 6.......................(095) 143-15-40
Czech Federal Republic, *Mon-Fri 8:30-12, 14-17*
Yuliusa Fuchika, 12/14...........(095) 251-05-40
Denmark, *Mon-Fri 9-13, 14-15*
Ostrovskogo N. A. per., 9 ....(095) 201-78-60
Fax ....(095) 230-20-72
Estonia, *Daily 0-24*
Sobinovskiy per., 5 ....(095) 290-50-13
Ethiopia, *Mon-Fri 9-13, 14-17*
Orlovo-Davydovskiy per., 6 .....(095) 280-16-16
Finland, *Mon-Fri 9-13, 14-17*
Kropotkinskiy per., 15/17.........(095) 246-40-27
France, *Mon-Fri 9-13, 15-18*
Bolshaya Yakimanka, 45 ....(095) 230-00-03
Germany, *Daily 0-24*
Mosfilmovskaya ul., 56 ....(095) 956-10-80
Great Britain, *Mon-Fri 9-12:30, 14-18*
Sofiyskaya nab., 14...............(095) 233-35-63
Greece, *Mon-Fri 10-16*
Stankevicha ul., 4 290-22-74
Hungary, *Mon-Fri 8:30-13, 14-17*
Mosfilmovskaya ul., 62...........(095) 143-86-11
Ireland, *Mon-Fri 9:30-13, 14:30-17:30*
Grokholskiy per., 5................(095) 975-20-66
Israel, *Mon-Fri 9-13*
Bolshaya Ordynka ul., 56 ......(095) 230-67-53
Italy, *Mon-Fri 9-13, 15-18*
Vesnina ul., 5........................(095) 253-92-89
Japan, *Mon-Fri 9:30-13, 14:30-18*
Kalashnyy per., 12 ....(095) 291-85-00
Korea, Peoples Republic of, *Mon-Fri 9-13, 14-17*
Mosfilmovskaya ul., 72.........(095) 143-62-44
Latvia, *Daily 0-24*
Chapygina ul., 3....................(095) 925-27-03
Lithuania, *Daily 0-24*
Pisemskogo per., 10..............(095) 291-26-43
Mexico, *Mon-Fri 9-15*
Shchukina ul., 4.....................(095) 230-20-42

Mongolia
Pisemskogo ul., 11 ....(095) 290-67-92
Netherlands, *Mon-Fri 9-13, 14:30-18*
Kalashnyy per., 6 ....(095) 291-29-99
New Zealand, *Daily 0-24*
Povarskaya ul., 44................(095) 290-46-66
Norway, *Mon-Fri 9-16*
Povarskaya ul., 7...................(095) 290-38-72
Poland, *Mon-Fri 9-14:30, 15-17*
Klimashkina ul., 4..................(095) 255-00-17
Romania, *Mon-Fri 9-13:30, 15-18*
Mosfilmovskaya ul., 64 ....(095) 143-04-24
Slovakia, *Daily 0-24*
Yuliusa Fuchika, 17/19 ....(095) 250-10-71
South Korea, *Mon-Fri 12:30-14*
Spiridonovka ul., 14 ....(095) 203-80-17
Spain, *Daily 0-24*
Gertsena ul., 50/8..................(095) 202-21-80
Sweden, *Mon-Fri 9-12*
Mosfilmovskaya ul., 60 ....(095) 147-90-09
USA, *Mon-Fri 9-18*
Novinskiy blvd., 19/23...........(095) 252-24-49
Fax.......................................(095) 230-21-01
Yugoslavia, *Daily 0-24*
Mosfilmovskaya ul., 46 ....(095) 147-41-06

☎ EMBROIDERY SHOPS
ВЫШИВКА
STICKEREIEN
BRODERIE, MAGASINS DE
HANDARBETSAFFÄRER
KORUOMPELULIIKKEET

Lace   **Tyul**
• Bolshoy pr., P.S., 69 233-04-53
Mon-Fri 10-19; Rbls
• Nevskiy pr., 124 277-30-21
Mon-Fri 10-14, 15-19; Rbls
T-bus 1; Metro Ploshchad Vosstaniya
Prestige
Reki Moyki nab., 3 312-77-18
Mon-Fri 10-18; Rbls, $

☎ EMERGENCY MEDICAL CARE
МЕДИЦИНСКАЯ НЕОТЛОЖНАЯ
ПОМОЩЬ
MEDIZINISCHE
NOTVERSORGUNG
SOINS D' URGENCE MEDICAUX
AKUTSJUKVÅRD
ÄKILLISET SAIRAUSTAPAUKSET

See also MEDICAL EMERGENCIES, MEDICAL CARE
AND CONSULTATIONS, *and* HOSPITALS

For Medical Emergencies
see pages 211-212

CITY AMBULANCE - 03
The best staffed and equipped ambulances
are the following:

POLICLINIC No. 2 AMBULANCE 110-11-02
Policlinic for foreigners

HOSPITAL NO. 20 AMBULANCE 108-48-08

GASTELLO HOSPITAL FOR FOREIGNERS.
Six Languages

☎ EMERGENCY SERVICES (24 Hours/Day)
СЛУЖБЫ НЕОТЛОЖНЫЕ, КРУГЛОСУТОЧНЫЕ
NOTDIENSTE
SERVICE D' URGENCE
AKUTMOTTAGNING DYGNET RUNT
HÄTÄNUMEROT 24h YÖTÄ PÄIVÄÄ

Round the clock, free of charge

FIRE	01
MILITSIYA (POLICE)	02
AMBULANCE	03
GAS LEAKS	04

EMERGENCY MEDICAL CARE
See MEDICAL EMERGENCIES
ACCIDENT INFORMATION 273-30-55
Information on people transported by ambulance
AUTOMOBILE ACCIDENTS
State Automobile Inspectorate ....(GAI)
Professora Popova ul., 42 234-26-46
....234-26-52
POLICE INFORMATION..............315-00-19
Information on people involved in accidents

EMERGENCY APARTMENT REPAIRS

Emergencies with electricity, locksmithing, sewer, heating, plumbing system, and water can be solved with the help of Municipal Residential Repair Departments ("PREO", ПРЭО *or* "REU", РЭУ). *The emergency numbers below should be able to refer you to the proper local REU.*

INFORMATION NUMBERS
SERVICES AVAILABLE DAILY 24 HRS
Dzerzhinskiy District
Chaykovskogo ul., 46/48................ 272-68-69
Kalininskiy District
Komsomola ul., 33........................524-25-51
Kirovskiy District
Stachek pr., 18 252-65-23
Kolpinskiy District
Karla Marksa ul., 8, Kolpino 484-80-20
Krasnogvardeyskiy District
Tarasova ul., 8................................227-48-98
Krasnoselskiy District
Veteranov pr., 131 130-65-32
Moskovskiy District
Moskovskiy pr., 146 298-13-60
Nevskiy District (Left bank of Neva)
Obukhovskoy oborony pr., 54 567-33-37
Nevskiy District (Right bank of Neva)
Podvoyskogo ul., 16, bldg. 1..........588-78-53
Oktyabrskiy District
Kazanskaya ul., 60 315-74-10
Petrogradskiy District
Bolshaya Monetnaya ul., 11 232-05-31
Primorskiy District
Sedova ul., 34................................301-40-77
Smolninskiy District
3-ya Sovetskaya ul., 42 274-25-54

Vasileostrovskiy District
Nakhimova ul., 5, bldg. 2 356-96-14
Vyborgskiy District
Parkhomenko pr., 24/9..................550-29-86

ELECTRICAL EMERGENCIES
Information.....................................311-15-00

GAS LEAKS
Lengaz Emergency Services
Avariynaya Sluzhba Lengaza
Sedova ul., 9/1 265-26-31

WATER PIPE BREAK & EMERGENCIES
Avariynaya Sluzhba Vodoprovodnoy Seti
Kavalergardskaya ul., 42 274-10-95
Cold water......................................232-18-80

☎ EMPLOYMENT AGENCIES
ПОДБОР ПЕРСОНАЛА
ARBEITSÄMTER
PLACEMENT, BUREAUX DE
ARBETSFÖRMEDLINGAR
TYÖNVÄLITYSTOIMISTOT

See also TEMPORARY HELP, SECRETARIAL SERVICES

ANCOR-PETERSBURG AGENCY
Gastello ul., 9
Tel 108-40-42
Fax..293-13-30
We Provide Qualified, Experienced Personnel for your Company

BCG, *Daily 10-18; Rbls, $; Eng*
Gertsena ul., 23...............................312-67-01
Fax...312-53-68
Business Link Company
13-ya Liniya, 20 218-69-00
Fax...218-79-40
Mon-Sat 9-18; Rbls, $; Eng, Ger
Employment Office for Youths
Smolnyy, entr. 9, rm. 332 271-30-12
Mon-Fri 10-18; Rbls
Inpredservice
Kutuzova nab., 34 272-15-00
Fax...279-50-24
Mon-Fri 9-13, 14-18; Rbls, $; CC
Bus 26; Metro Chernyshevskaya
Office of the Mayor Committee for Labor & Employment, *Mon-Fri 8-17; Rbls*
Galernaya ul., 7 312-92-36

 Personnel Corps

We find, screen and maintain a current data base of the finest professional & domestic employees.
• Temporary and Permanent Placement
• Personnel Training • Human Resource Consulting
• Employee Benefit Package Preparation
Nevskiy pr., 104 275-83-23
....275-45-86
Fax...275-83-23

Sovinform
Kamennoostrovskiy pr., 42 230-80-04
Daily 9-21; Rbls

☎ ENGINEERING CONSULTANTS
ТЕХНИЧЕСКИЕ КОНСУЛЬТАНТЫ
INGENIEURWESEN
INGENIEURS
INGENJÖRER
INSINÖÖRITOIMISTOT

See also BUSINESS CONSULTANTS

Budimeks
Robespera nab., 8/46, rm. 93 279-69-31
Fax 279-68-31
Mon-Fri 9-17; $, CC; Eng, Pol

Conbi
Lesnoy pr., 64 542-88-94
Mon-Fri 9-18; Rbls; Eng, Ger

Coop
Gorokhovaya ul., 48, apt. 45 311-16-75
Fax 311-70-94
Mon-Fri 9-13.30, 14:30-18; Rbls
T-bus 9; Metro Sennaya Ploshchad

Garantiya Center   **Warranty**
Bolshoy pr., V.O., 88, rm. 110,
Closed in July & August............... 217-26-70
Mon-Fri 9-19

Matra
Sirenevyy blvd., 18, floor 2 544-94-54
Mon-Fri 9-16; Rbls; Eng, Ger, Fr

Metra Representative
Bolshoy Sampsonievskiy pr., 31 542-06-59
Fax 542-68-42
Mon-Fri 9-17; Rbls; $; Eng, Finn

Permafrost Consultants, *See our ad under*
CONSTRUCTION & RENOVATION

Skaner
Doblesti ul., 18, bldg. 2 142-53-43
Mon-Fri 10-13, 13:30-17; Rbls
T-bus 45; Metro Leninskiy Prospekt

☎ ENTERTAINMENT ACTS
ВЫСТУПЛЕНИЯ АРТИСТОВ
VERANSTALTER, UNTERHALTUNG
MANIFESTATIONS ARTISTIQUES
UNDERHÅLLNINGSFÖRMEDLING
VAPAA-AJAN VIETE

St. Petersburg is full of musical talent. If you want to find a group to play for you try calling the Conservatory listed under UNIVERSITIES *or look up Music Schools in the St. Pb. Yellow Pages-93. Or listen to the many groups playing on the street or metros; they can be quite good.*

Art-Center Terem, *See our ad below*
Truda pl., 4, rm. 78 219-81-71
One of the best folk music groups; Daily 10-18; Rbls, $

Art-Sound Studio *Soundtrack production*
Pushkinskaya ul., 10, apt. 129 164-53-86
Fax 164-52-07

Center of Folk Arts
Galernaya ul., 33 311-43-11

Children School of Arts
Varshavskaya ul., 44 298-48-06

Dimitrin Yuriy, Librettist
Please call 164-79-51

Dyagilev Seasons Art Festival
Please call 351-03-54
Fax 315-17-01

Professional Movie Actors Guild
Reki Fontanki nab., 11, apt. 8 312-79-67
Mon-Fri 11-18; Rbls, $

St. Petersburg Incultcenter
Vyborgskaya nab., 5/2 542-90-56
Gorokhovaya ul., 1/8 315-96-63
Daily 10-20; Rbls

TEREM KVARTET
CLASSIC-MODERN-FOLK-ART
ST. PETERSBURG
"Unforgettable musical experience"
"Absolutely brilliant"
Exciting musical magic that's difficult to capture in words

Modern, classical and folk music woven into melodic Russian fantasy on ancient instruments: Domra, Domra-Alt, Bayan, and Balalaika-contrabas

The Saint Petersburg Conservatory
On Compact Disc **THE TEREM QUARTET**
Realworld/Virgin records CDRW23

Truda pl., 4, rm. 78 219-81-71

Torzhestvo
Lomonosova ul., 1 314-74-86
Fax 110-58-77
Mon, Wed-Sun 10-18; Rbls

☎ ETIQUETTE
ЭТИКЕТ
ETIKETTE
ETIQUETTE
ETIKETT
ETIKETTI

See also TIPPING and RAIL TRAVEL

When visiting Russia there are a few simple rules of etiquette that may be useful.

• Bring a gift to the family who invites you to their home for dinner. A bottle of wine, a cake, box of candy or a bouquet of flowers are traditional. A small gift for the child is always appropriate.

• If you bring flowers, make sure the number of flowers is uneven: 1, 3, 5, 7.

• Do not shake hands across the threshold of the door step, as this is traditionally bad luck.

• Take off your gloves when shaking hands.

• Be prepared to remove your shoes upon entering a home. You will be given a pair

of slippers (Тарки, Тапки) *to help keep the apartment clean.*

• *When entering or exiting a vehicle,* **men step out first** *so as to offer their hand to the woman whom they are accompanying.*

• *On public transportation,* **give your seat** *to mothers with children, the old or infirm.*

• **Check your coat,** *briefcase, or parcels at the front door of a restaurant, at theaters or any formal receptions.*

• **Do not cross your legs** *with the ankle on the knee or put your feet on the furniture. It's impolite to show people the soles of your feet. When in the metro or sitting on the bus, don't let your feet even come close to the seat.*

• *For business people traveling to Russia, make sure that you have plenty of* **business cards** *one side printed in English, the other in Russian. These can be printed quickly here. See* **BUSINESS CARDS.**

• *Offer to* **share your snacks and cigarettes** *with those around you, especially on the train or at the office. Be prepared to accept smoking.*

• *Be prepared to* **accept all food and drink** *offered when visiting friends, and it can be quite a lot, otherwise they might be offended.*

• *Be prepared to* **give toasts** *at dinners, etc. Be careful, the vodka can catch up with you.*

• **Dress up for the theater** *and check your coat and any large bags. Be on time. Absolutely no photographs.*

• **Women dress conservatively,** *and are not supposed to be assertive in public or pay for themselves in social situations.*

• **Dress.** *Business people dress conservatively with good shoes. Men should not take off their jackets without asking. Women wear a scarf or hat in Orthodox Churches. Dress casually for dinner in someone's home.*

• **Be careful in complimenting** *something in a home. Your host may offer it to you.*

• **Don't put your thumb** *between your first two fingers. It is a very rude gesture.*

• **Superstitions:**

Do not whistle inside or you will whistle away your money.

Never light a cigarette from a candle. It will bring you bad luck.

Never pour a wine back handed, it is impolite.

Black cats crossing your path is very bad luck.

Don't sit on the corner of a table or you will end up single.

If you leave something behind in Russia, it means you are coming back.

• **Admire the good & beautiful,** *don't make invidious comparisons or criticize.*

• **Warm smiles** *sympathy, patience, tolerance, and a good nature will get you through most difficulties.*

• *Learn some* **basic vocabulary** *and use whenever possible. It surprises and delights people.*

Please	Pozhalusta	Пожалуйста
Thank you	Spasibo	Спасибо
How are you	Kak Vy pozhivaete	Как Вы поживаете
Well	Khorosho	Хорошо
Good Morning	Dobroe utro	Доброе утро
Good day	Dobryy den	Добрый день
Good evening	Dobryy vecher	Добрый вечер
Good bye	Do svidaniya	До свидания

Many English words have no equivalents in Russian, such as "fun", and many Russian words no equivalents in English. Many difficulties arise from the differences in meanings given to similar words in English and Russian. Be careful to define your words carefully.

☎ EXCHANGES

See STOCK & COMMODITY EXCHANGES, *and* CURRENCY EXCHANGE

☎ EXCURSIONS

See TOURS-SAINT PETERSBURG *and* TRAVEL AGENTS

☎ EXHIBITION HALLS & GALLERIES, RENTAL
ВЫСТАВОЧНЫЕ ЗАЛЫ И ГАЛЕРЕИ
AUSSTELLUNGSRÄUME UND GALERIEN
EXPOSITIONS, SALLES D' ET GALLERIES A LOUER
UTSTÄLLNINGSLOKALER OCH GALLERIER
NÄYTTELYTILOJEN JA GALLERIOIDEN VUOKRAUS

Atus Gallery, *Mon-Sat 11-19; Rbls; Eng*
Ispolkomskaya ul., 9/11 275-32-15
Dom Arkhitektora   **Architect's House**
Gertsena ul., 52........................... 312-04-00
*Mon-Fri 11-20; Rbls, $; Eng, Ger, Fr, Finn;*F-5
Dom Ofitserov   **Officer's House**
Liteynyy pr., 20 278-86-40
Tue-Sun 8-20; Rbls, $; T-bus 3;
Metro Chernyshevskaya; H-7
Free Culture Humanities Foundation
Pushkinskaya ul., 10, apt. 1............ 164-53-71
Fax.. 164-52-07
Eng, Ger; Metro Ploshchad Vosstaniya; H-5
LDM Leningrad Youth Palace
Professora Popova ul., 47 234-32-78
Fax.. 234-98-18
Mon-Fri 11-18; Rbls, $; Eng; E-9
LenEXPO Exhibition
Bolshoy pr., V.O., 103 217-11-12
Fax.. 355-19-85
Daily 10-18; Rbls, $; Major European Languages; B-5

Manezh Central Exhibition Hall
Isaakievskaya pl., 1 314-82-53
Fax 314-82-54
Mon-Wed, Fri-Sun 11-19; Rbls; Eng, Ger, Fr
T-bus 5; Metro Nevskiy Prospekt; E-6

Sidlin School Art Gallery
Grafskiy per., 7 113-22-45
Mon-Sat 11-18; Rbls; Eng
Metro Mayakovskaya; Dostoevskaya; H-5

**Smolny Cathedral Concert &
Exhibition Complex**
Rastrelli pl., 3/1 311-35-60
Mon-Wed, Fri-Sun 11-16:30; Rbls;
Bus 14; Metro Chernyshevskaya; J-7

**St. Petersburg Art Union of Russia
Exhibition Center**
Gertsena ul., 38 314-30-60
Fax 314-64-12
Tue-Sun 13-19; Rbls, $; Eng; F-5

**St. Petersburg Art Union of Russia
Exhibition Hall**
Sverdlovskaya nab., 64 224-06-33
Tue-Sun 12-19; Rbls, $; K-7

Vakula
Tikhoretskiy pr., 9/9, apt. 8 534-26-92
Mon-Fri 9-17; Rbls, $; Eng, Ger

Zerkalo Gallery   **Mirror**
Nekrasova ul., 11 272-40-58
Fax 273-37-04
Mon-Sat 11-19; Rbls; Eng; Metro Chernyshevskaya; H-6

☎ **EXHIBITION SERVICES**
ВЫСТАВКИ, СЛУЖБЫ ПО
ОРГАНИЗАЦИИ
AUSSTELLUNGSGESELLSCHAFTEN
EXPOSITION, SERVICES
UTSTÄLLNINGSSERVICE
NÄYTTELYPALVELUT

*The following organizations help organize
exhibitions in various fields. Some offer
complete exhibition services from safe
transportation to St. Petersburg to setting
up modern displays, publicity and
translation services.*

Alinter
Nalichnaya ul., 6 356-37-21
Fax 356-24-14
Mon-Fri 9-18; Rbls, $; Eng

Ineks
Egorova ul., 18 292-50-46
Fax 292-77-29
Mon-Sat 9-18; Rbls, $; Eng, Fr, Finn, Swed

LenEXPO Exhibition
Bolshoy pr., V.O., 103 217-11-12
Fax 355-19-85
Daily 10-18; Rbls, $; Major European Languages

Leningrad-Impex
Gertsena ul., 35 310-94-41
Fax 319-97-09
Mon-Fri 9-13, 14-18; Rbls, $; Eng, Ger

**Leningrad Region Museums Board
Exhibition Hall**
Liteinyy pr., 57 273-16-23
Fax 273-57-92
Hrs 11-19, English, German

Russian Farmer
Gogolya ul., 8, of. 36 164-53-68
Fax 315-17-01
Mon-Fri 9:30-17:30; Rbls, $; Metro Ploshchad Vosstaniya

Samson International
Nevskiy pr., 30 219-92-66
Mon-Fri 9-18; Rbls

Sportservice
Millionnaya ul., 22 311-94-69
Fax 312-20-24
Daily 9-18; Rbls, $; Eng, Ger, Fr

Vakula
Tikhoretskiy pr., 9, bldg. 9, apt. 8 534-26-92
Mon-Fri 9-18

☎ **EXHIBITIONS**
ВЫСТАВКИ
AUSSTELLUNGEN
EXPOSITIONS
UTSTÄLLNINGAR
NÄYTTELYT

See also ART GALLERIES and MUSEUMS

COMMERCIAL EXHIBITIONS

*St. Petersburg is an exhibition center with
many exhibitions going on throughout the
year. Most large exhibitions are held on the
grounds of LenEXPO on the bank of the
Gulf of Finland.*

NON-COMMERCIAL EXHIBITIONS

*There are a large number of trade fairs
and commercial exhibitions. Below are
listed several permanent commercial and
non-commercial exhibitions*

ARTS EXHIBITIONS

*Art abounds in St. Petersburg and there
are always art exhibitions displaying the
works of today's artists going on somewhere
in the city. Many ART GALLERIES have
permanent displays as well as works of art
for sale. In addition, the major art MUSEUMS
The Hermitage and the Russian Museum,
have outstanding visiting exhibitions.*

Flower Exhibition Hall
Potemkinskaya ul., 2 272-54-48
Tue-Wed, Fri-Sun 11-19; Eng
Bus 6; Metro Chernyshevskaya

LenEXPO Exhibition
Bolshoy pr., V.O., 103 217-11-12
Fax 355-19-85
Daily 10-18; Rbls, $; Major European Languages; B-5

Palitra
Nevskiy pr., 166 277-12-16
Fax 274-09-11
Mon-Sat 11-18; Rbls; T-bus 10; Metro Pl. Vosstaniya; J-5

Perspective
*Commercial Information &
Exhibition Center*
Moskovskiy pr., 220a
Tel/Fax 293-54-97

Ritm-Tsenturion, *Daily 10-18*
Turbinnaya ul., 11, at Hotel Ritm 186-76-89

Russian Farmer
Gogolya ul., 8, off. 36 164-53-68
Fax 315-17-01
Mon-Fri 9:30-17:30; Rbls, $; Metro Ploshchad Vosstaniya

St. Petersburg Art Union of Russia Exhibition Center
Gertsena ul., 38 314-30-60
Fax 314-64-12
Tue-Sun 13-19; Rbls, $; Eng; F-5

☎ EXPORT-IMPORT FIRMS
ЭКСПОРТНО-ИМПОРТНЫЕ
ФИРМЫ
EXPORT/IMPORT FIRMEN
EXPORTES-IMPORTES, SOCIETES
EXPORT/IMPORT FIRMOR
TUONTI- JA VIENTILIIKKEET

This heading includes firms looking for export markets and partners to develop technology and to provide new equipment and management.

ABO Ltd.

Exclusive Retailer of Havana Cigars in CIS, Baltics & Scandinavia

Fine Tobacco

Distributors of European Consumer Goods

❖❖❖

Nevskiy pr., 176, P.B. 140
Tel 585-21-12
Tel/Fax 585-90-57

Alisa - Petersburg
ПЕТЕРБУРГ

Zanevskiy pr., 6 221-47-01
.... 528-77-38
Fax 528-62-11

AVEKS Association of Foreign Trade
3-ya Krasnoarmeyskaya ul., 12 292-48-37
Fax 292-14-53
Mon-Fri 10-17; Rbls, $

Balt Market-Trade House
Furshtadtskaya ul., 35 275-56-24
Fax 275-31-25
Mon-Fri 10-19; Rbls, $; Eng

Balt-Trade Company
Shpalernaya ul., 52 275-31-23
Fax 275-56-30
Mon-Fri 10-19; Rbls, $; Eng

Baltica, *Mon-Fri 9:30-17:30*
Dmitrovskiy per., 3/5 164-53-38

Baltica-1, *Daily 9:30-17; Rbls*
Konnogvardeyskiy blvd., 4, entr. 6 314-12-87

BONGRAIN SA

A EUROPEAN LEADER IN DAIRY PRODUCTS

Importer and distributor of a wide selection of cheeses, yogurts, fine chocolates and delicatessens in St. Petersburg

Konnogvardeyskiy blvd., 4/6
.... 311-24-13
Fax 312-72-92

Bosco Company
Nevskiy pr., 8 219-18-57
.... 311-65-60
Daily 11-18; Rbls, $; Eng

Center of Import & Export-Chemistry Products
Robespera nab., 8/46, apt. 66 273-41-64
Fax 273-00-78
Mon-Fri 9-17; $; Ger, Pol; Bus 14; Metro Chernyshevskaya

Center of Ultrasonic Technologies
Millionnaya ul., 5 110-62-30
Fax 311-60-16
Mon-Fri 10-18; Rbls; Eng, Ger, Fr T-bus 1; Metro Nevskiy Prospekt

Concern Goryachev
Vereyskaya ul., 39 112-75-96
Fax 315-24-21
Mon-Fri 9-13, 14-18; Rbls, $; Eng, Ital T-bus 3; Metro Tekhnologicheskiy Institut, Pushkinskaya

Fexima Trade House
Reki Fontanki nab., 34 275-75-10
Fax 275-50-96
Mon-Fri 9-18; Rbls, $; Eng, Fr

Gemma International Ltd.
Import-Export of Food & Consumer Goods
Sedova ul., 6 567-94-95
Fax 265-05-07

Ineks
Egorova ul., 18 292-50-46
Fax 292-77-29
Mon-Sat 9-18; Rbls, $; Eng, Fr, Finn, Swed

Karmal Trade
Lermontovskiy pr., 7/12 114-38-38
Fax 114-28-54
Mon-Fri 10-14, 15-18; Rbls

A/O KOMLIZ
Import-Export & Expediting Service
nab. reki Moyki, 20 311-88-54
Fax 312-67-05
Engl., Germ., Fr., Dutch, Fin., Estonian

Kompexim Petersburg
Kuznetsovskaya ul., 19 296-32-16
Mon-Sat 9-17

Kontrakt
Kronverkskiy pr., 63......................233-57-09
Fax 233-37-34
Daily 9-17; Rbls, $; Eng

anck

Export of Optics

Nab. reki Fontanki, 48 314-08-43
....314-12-73
Fax.......................................310-65-55

Leningrad-Impex
Gertsena ul., 35 310-94-41
Fax 319-97-09
Mon-Fri 9-13, 14-18; Rbls, $; Eng, Ger

Leningradintekh
Chkalovskiy pr., 52 235-58-74
Fax 230-13-07
Mon-Fri 9-13, 13:45-17:45; Rbls, $; Eng, Ger, Fr

Lenvneshtorg
Admiralteyskaya nab., 8.................312-42-54
Fax 312-40-12
Mon-Sat 9-21; Rbls; T-bus 1; Metro Gostinyy Dvor

MIR
Leninskiy pr., 161, bldg. 2 108-44-23
Tel/Fax...108-54-11

Oltes
Kovenskiy per., 17 275-51-82
Fax 275-89-07
Mon-Fri 10-18; Rbls, $; CC; Eng, Sp

Peter-West Brok
26-ya Liniya, 9 a 217-17-54
Fax 217-06-93
Mon-Fri 9-18; Rbls; Eng, Fr

Petrovskiy Trade House
Chaykovskogo ul., 60....................275-57-96
Fax 275-75-78
Mon-Fri 10-20; Rbls, $; Eng

Pilot
Ligovskiy pr., 58, apt. 20 164-12-69
Fax 164-13-69
Mon-Fri 10-18; Rbls, $; Eng, Ger; Metro Pl. Vosstaniya

PNN PTE LTD.
St Petersburg, 191186, P. O. Box 20
Fax 314-58-71
Telex...121722 Zarel
Import-Export Agent & Marketing Services

Polyus
Shpalernaya ul., 24 279-36-84
Fax 279-63-49
Mon-Fri 10-17; Rbls; Eng; Metro Chernyshevskaya

Potential
Pavlovskaya ul., 42, Kolpino 481-95-24
Fax 463-90-00
Mon-Fri 8:15-17:15; Rbls, $; Hun

RIK
Nab. Reki Monastyrki, 3 277-77-52
Fax 274-33-25
Wholesale Food Purchasing and Sales

Sankt Petersburg Baltic Co.
Dmitrovskiy per., 3/5......................164-53-38
Fax...311-48-64
Mon-Fri 9:30-18; Rbls

Scantrade Ltd.
Akademika Pavlova ul., 13 a............233-51-57
Daily 9-20; Rbls, $; Eng, Finn

Sfinks
Gertsena ul., 55.............................314-81-65
Fax...312-41-22
Mon-Fri 9-18; Rbls, $; Eng

SKM International
Export of Timber &
Finished Wood Products
Food Importing
Moskovskiy pr., 178, apt. 2
....294-62-29
Fax:...298-16-95
Telex................................621079 SKM

St. Petersburg Chamber of Commerce
Chaykovskogo ul., 46/48 273-48-96
Fax...272-64-06
Mon-Fri 9-13, 14-18; Rbls, $; Eng

Tellus
Egorova ul., 18...............................292-50-13
Fax...292-77-29
Daily 9-18; Rbls, $; Eng, Ger, Finn

Tradex Ltd.
Products from the Best Companies
in the World
Moskovskiy pr., 86.......................296-17-85

UniRem
Dekabristov pl., 3..........................311-78-95
Mon-Fri 9-18; Rbls, $; Eng, Fr

Valenius
Mozhayskaya ul., 1........................213-78-53
Daily 8:30-17; Rbls, $

Vneshenergomash
Reki Moyki nab., 67/69 311-99-96
Mon-Fri 9-17; Rbls; T-bus 5; Metro Gostinyy Dvor

Vneshlenstroyservice
Zakharevskaya ul., 31....................272-58-28
Fax...273-31-39
Mon-Fri 9-18; Rbls

YANTA LTD

Distributors of Footwear, Food,
Clothes, Cosmetics, etc. from
The Netherlands, Finland, USA, Italy
Network of Stores in St.Petersburg.

Liteynyy pr., 6/1
Tel 275-30-52
....275-70-45
Fax...279-50-66
English, German, French

☎ **EXPRESS MAIL & PARCEL SERVICE**
ЭКСПРЕСС-ПОЧТА
EILPOST/PAKETDIENST
EXPRESS, COURRIER
EXPRESS BREV/PAKET SERVICE
PIKA POSTI JA
PAKETTIPALVELUT

See also AIR CARGO

Aero-Balt Service Company, *Mon-Fri 9-17:30*
Shturmanskaya ul., 12 104-18-12

AES

Transportation & Distribution
Hand delivered letters and parcels
overnight between
⊠ Saint Petersburg and Moscow
Service to anywhere in the CIS.
Contact Moscow Office at:
.... (095) 256-45-02
Fax .... (095) 254-28-76

WORLDWIDE EXPRESS ®

DHL offers door-to-door express documents and
parcel service from Saint Petersburg to 215
countries worldwide!

♦ ♦ ♦

Overnight service to Western Europe and to major
U.S. business centers

DHL Express Center

Nevskij Palace Hotel
57, Nevskiy Prospekt
119-61-17
Mon-Fri 8:30-19, Sat 10-17

DHL Drop-of Points

Hotels: Grand Hotel Europe,
Astoria, Olympia,
Hotelship 'Peterhof'
Mon-Fri 8:30-19, Sat 9-18

DHL St. Petersburg

311-26-49, 210-76-54,
210-75-45, Fax: 314-64-73
≡ *WE KEEP YOUR PROMISES!* ≡

Express-Post
Nevskiy pr., 23, at Bure Salon .... No ☎
Federal Express
Mayakovskogo ul., 2 279-12-87
Fax.. 273-21-39
Mon-Fri 9-16; $; Eng

 FTE Official KLM agent
EXPRESS MAIL

Prof. Popova ul., 47, apt. 607...... 234-47-25
Tel./Fax: 234-51-92

Informkomset
Gagarina ul., 1, apt. 312 294-85-97
Mon-Fri 9-18; Rbls
Istok -K
Kantemirovskaya ul., 6 542-06-08
Mon-Fri 9-18; Rbls; Metro Lesnaya
ITEC
Manezhnyy per., 19 275-88-11
Fax... 275-57-73
Daily 12-18; $; Metro Chernyshevskaya
KLM Documents Delivery - See FTE ad
Document 2 Days to NY
LEK Telecom
Mytninskaya ul., 19 271-16-76
Mon-Fri 9-18; Rbls, $; Metro Ploshchad Vosstaniya
Sovmortrans
Dvinskaya ul., 8, bldg. 2 252-75-81
Fax.. 114-41-37
Mon-Fri 8:30-17; Rbls, $; Eng, Ger, Fr, Sp

TNT Express Worldwide

St. Petersburg
Liteynyy pr., 50

Express Parcels & Documents
Express Freight
Over 200 Countries Worldwide
Door to Door in 2-3 Days
Direct through Helsinki
Customs Clearance in St. Pb.

Immediate free pick-up
.... 273-60-07
.... 272-58-86
Fax............................ 104-36-84
Telex ....121741 ABS SU
Moscow Office: (095) 156-57-71

SHOULD YOUR AD BE HERE?

The most effective use of your
advertising dollar in St. Petersburg

Call TELINFO: (812) 315 -64-12

OUTSIDE OF RUSSIA
Call InfoServices International
USA + 516 549-0064

Express Mail
Door-to-Door in 1-3 Days Throughout Russia & CIS
Konnogvardeiskiy blvd., 4, 5th entrance, office 22

Tel/Fax 311-23-46

United Parcel Service

WORLDWIDE UPS SERVICE
CUSTOMS CLEARANCE & ELECTRONIC TRACKING
OVERNIGHT DOCUMENT DELIVERY TO MAJOR CITIES IN
EUROPE, UNITED STATES AND CANADA
THREE DAY PACKAGE DELIVERY, INCLUDING CUSTOMS,
FROM 100 G. TO 31.5 KG.
PICK-UP AT YOUR OFFICE OR HOME FROM 9-18
CORPORATE ACCOUNTS
& COLLECT BILLING AVAILABLE

Saltykova-Shchedrina ul., 31
☎ 312-29-15
☎ 314-78-37
Telephone will change to the following
numbers in Winter
☎ 275-44-05
Fax 275-88-78

☎ EXTERMINATORS
ДЕЗИНФЕКЦИЯ
DESINFEKTION
EXTERMINATEURS
OHYREBEKÄMPNING
DESINFIONNIT

Agroimpeks
Dobrolyubova pr., 25 232-05-03
Appointments 144-63-04
Mon-Fri 10-18; Rbls

Karavan
Kosygina pr., 23, bldg. 1 521-77-27
Mon-Fri 9-18; Rbls; T-bus 22; Metro Novocherkasskaya

Private Exterminator
Please call 314-86-07

Sanitarno-Dezinfektsionnye Stantsii
Exterminators
• Arsenalnaya ul., 1 542-57-80
Mon-Fri 8:30-16; Rbls
• Malookhtinskiy pr., 14/3 528-63-04
Mon-Fri 8:30-16; Rbls
• Marata ul., 25 112-02-11
Mon-Fri 8:30-16; Rbls
• Markina ul., 7................................233-81-88
Mon-Fri 9-15:30; Rbls; Tram 6; Metro Gorkovskaya
• Moskovskiy pr., 96 298-36-08
Mon-Fri 8:30-16; Rbls
• Professora Ivashentseva ul., 5 277-66-85
Mon-Fri 9-16; Rbls

☎ EYE GLASS REPAIR
See OPTICIANS *and* CONTACT LENSES

☎ FABRICS
ТКАНИ
STOFFE
TISSUS
TYGER
KANKAAT

*Russian fabrics and sewing notions are
bought in the numerous shops called
"cloth" (Tkani, Ткани).*

 BABYLON
shops

No. 5 The Fabric Shop
Imported Fabrics & Sewing Notions

A Complete Line of Fabrics
Imported Silks, Woolens,
Cottons, & Blends
Complete Sewing Notions Department
Pins and Needles, Scissors and Shears,
Buttons and Snaps, Zippers and Straps

Let our experienced staff help.

Nevskiy pr., 130 277-07-30
Daily 10-14,15-20; Rbls
Metro Ploshchad Vosstaniya

Dom Tkaney   **House of Fabrics**
Komsomola ul., 45 542-18-18
Mon-Fri 10-14, 15-19; Rbls

Tkani   **Fabrics**
• Moskovskiy pr., 42........................292-48-10
Mon-Sat 10-14, 15-19; Rbls
• Moskovskiy pr., 167......................298-09-62
Mon-Sat 10-19; Rbls
• Nevskiy pr., 32.............................311-06-90
Mon-Fri 10-19; Rbls
• Sadovaya ul., 95 114-60-81
Mon-Sat 10-14, 15-19; Rbls
• Sennaya pl., 9 315-90-45
Mon-Sat 10-19; Rbls
• Sredneokhtinskiy pr., 1 224-06-72
Mon-Sat 10-14, 15-19; Rbls
• Vladimirskiy pr., 4 113-13-36
Mon-Sat 10-19; Rbls
• Zagorodnyy pr., 21........................164-93-66
Mon-Fri 10-19; Rbls
• Zanevskiy pr., 8.............................528-16-89
Mon-Sat 10-19; Rbls

Favilla
Engelsa pr., 154 515-70-26
Fax...515-09-44
Mon-Fri 8:30-13, 13:30-17; Rbls, $; Eng, Ger

Knitted Fabrics   **Trikotazh**
Nevskiy pr., 136..............................277-08-96
Mon-Sat 10-19; Rbls

Shelen Petersburg
Vladimirskiy pr., 4...........................113-13-36
Mon-Sat 10-19; Rbls

☎ FAIRS (Trade)
See AUCTIONS, MARKETS, EXHIBITIONS
and FURS

☎ FARMERS' MARKETS

See MARKETS

☎ FASHION SALONS
САЛОН МОД
MODESALONS
MODE, SALONS DE
MODESALONGER
MUOTISALONGIT

See also DEPARTMENT STORES
and CLOTHING, WOMEN'S.

Fashion salons specialize in fashionable clothing for women, often imported.

Dom Mod, *Main Store*   **Fashion House**
Marshala Tukhachevskogo ul., 22
Director 226-86-20
Coats salon.................................... 225-19-19
Knitted wear salon 543-90-02
Men & Women clothing 225-18-18
Showroom....................................... 226-71-29
Mon-Sat 11-15, 16-20; Tram 14
Dom Mod   **Fashion House**
Kamennoostrovskiy pr., 37 234-90-40
Mon-Sat 10-19; Rbls
Gostinyy Dvor, *Various Departments*
Nevskiy pr., 35.............................. 110-54-08
Daily 9-21; Rbls
Kontinent   **Continent**
Sedova ul., 37 560-94-28
Fax 292-34-71
Mon-Fri 10-19

NEVSKIY PROSPECT FASHION HOUSE
Dom Modeley Nevskiy Prospect

Most fashionable clothes in St. Petersburg
Nevskiy pr., 21.............................. 311-44-48
.... 311-05-77
Mon-Fri 8-17; Rbls; Eng, Fr

Salon No. 1, *Mon-Sat 10-14, 15-19; $; Eng*
Suvorovskiy pr., 30....................... 271-20-92

☎ FAST FOOD
КАФЕ-ЭКСПРЕСС
IMBISS STUBEN
FAST FOOD
SNABBMAT
FAST FOOD

See also PIZZA, CAFES, *and* RESTAURANTS
The concept of "fast food" is catching on with "take out" and "stand up" restaurants. The following offer a quick stand-up snack. "Street food" can be rather good, especially the Russian Pizza. Try the cafes as well.

Diez Grill-Bar, *Whole Grilled Chickens*
Kamennoostrovskiy pr., 16 232-42-55
Daily 10-21; Rbls
Gino Ginelli, *Ice Cream*
Griboedova kan. nab., 14 312-46-31
Fax: 311-39-83
Daily 12-1; $, CC; Eng, Ger
Petrograd
Bolshoy pr., P.S., 17 232-34-93
Daily 9-14, 15-22; Rbls; T-bus 1; Metro Petrogradskaya

PIZZA-HOUSE

Formerly Pizza Express
Quick Home Delivery
From 10 am to 24 pm

13 Varieties of Pizza, Steak,
Wiener Schnitzel, Pastas & Salads
Lapin Kulta Beer & European Wines

Visit our restaurant
at Podolskaya ul., 23

7 minutes drive from center
Orders................................... 292-26-66
Fax....................................... 292-10-39
Daily 10-24; $, CC; Eng, Finn; D-3

Polyarnoe
Nevskiy pr., 79..............................311-85-89
Daily 10-18, 19-22; Rbls
Polar Wagons Fast Food
Hamburgers, Soft Drinks, Beer
LOCATIONS:
• Airport Pulkovo-1
• Corner of Gogolya ul. and St. Isaac's pl.
• Metro Elektrosila
• Moskovskiy pr., 220
• Ploshchad Iskusstv-Near the Russian Museum
Snack Bar at Palanga
Leninskiy pr., 127 254-56-49
Daily 0-24; Rbls, $; Eng

☎ FAX SERVICES
ФАКС-СЕРВИС
FAX-DIENSTE
FAX, SERVICE DE
FAX SERVICE
FAX-PALVELUT

Faxes are now common in St. Petersburg and can be sent and received at the following numbers as well as at BUSINESS CENTERS.

AsLANTIS

Fax Translation & Transmission

Desk: House of Books, Ground Floor

Nevskiy pr., 28; *Hrs: 16-20*

Dibunovskaya ul., 24, office 7

Tel./Fax 239-36-45

English, French; Metro Chernaya Rechka

Delta-Telecom - *See ad on next page*
Fax Service
Gertsena ul., 3, rm. 5 314-01-40
Fax... 315-17-01
Mon-Fri 8:30-17; Rbls
LTGS Fax Service - *See ad on next page*
Post Office
Nevskiy pr., 65.............................. 314-62-14
Fax... 311-45-62
Mon-Fri 9-12:30, 13-20; Rbls

Cellular Radio Telephone
In Saint Petersburg
Gateway to the World

Instant Access • Direct-Dial
Local and international phone & fax
From your home, office or car
Single calls & short-term rentals
Long-term subscriptions

Gertsena ul., 22	314-61-26
	315-71-31
Fax	314-88-37
Fax	275-01-30

LTGS Fax Service

Leningrad Telephone City Company
Fax Receiving Number 7-812-315-1701
Receive and send your faxes at the
LTGS Fax Center

Gertsena ul., 4 314-01-40
Faxes held for one month.
Mon-Fri 9-21

Sovam Teleport

Low-cost 1 hour express text fax/telex
Nevskiy pr., 30 311-84-12
Fax 311-71-29

Telegraph Office
Gertsena ul., 3/5 312-77-17
Fax 311-00-23
Daily 0-24; Rbls

☎ FERRIES & CRUISE SHIPS
ПАРОМЫ
SCHIFFSREISEN
FERRIES
FÄRJOR
LAUTAT

See also PASSENGER SHIP TERMINAL

Ferries (really cruise ships) sail back and
forth between St. Petersburg and
Stockholm, Helsinki, Riga and Kiel. Cars
can also go on some of the ferries. The
cruise ships-ferries leave from the SEA
PASSENGER SHIP TERMINAL *on Morskoy Slavy*
Ploshchad on Vasilevskiy Ostrov. Best
reached by taxi or trolleybuses 10 & 12.

TYP
LOOK FOR OUR ADVERTISERS BY
The Traveller's Yellow Pages
Decal 1993/94

Baltic Express Line Cruises
Treat yourself to a cruise on the Baltic.
Modern liners with restaurants,
entertainment, shops, business facilities
and car ferry deck.

M/S Ilich (year round) to Stockholm-Riga
Dep. St. Pb. .... Mon 18:00
Arr. Stockholm................. Tues 09:00
Arr. Riga........................... Wed 09:30
Dep. Riga .... Wed 18:00
Arr. St. Pb. ....Fri 17:30
M/S Anna Karenina (year round) to Kiel
Dep. St. Pb. .... Wed 18:00
Arr. Nyhnäshamn (Stockholm)Thur 17:00
Arr. Kiel.............................Fri 19:30
Dep. Kiel .... Sat 15:00
Arr. St. Pb. .... Mon 18:00
M/S Konstantin Simonov (April - Nov)
to Helsinki
Dep. St. Pb. .... Thurs & Sun 00:05
Arr. Helsinki.......... Thurs & Sun 14:00
Dep. Helsinki......... Mon & Thur 16:00
Arr. St. Pb. ....Tues & Fri 09:30
To Book Tickets
In Saint Petersburg
Morskoy Slavy Ploshchad ... 355-16-16
Fax 355-61-40
Mon-Fri 10:30-18:00, Eng
In Sweden .... 46 + (0)20-00-29
In Kiel .... 49-(0)431-98-20-000
In Helsinki............. 358-(9)-66-57-55
In Riga 7-013-883-00-40
In USA 1-305-529-30-00
.... 1-800-688-EURO

☎ FILM & FILM DEVELOPING

See PHOTOGRAPHY - FILM & DEVELOPING

☎ FIRE
ПОЖАРНЫЕ
FEUERWEHR
INCENDIE
BRAND KÅR
PALOKUNTA

In case of Fire Call 01
The Russian word for "fire" is
POZHAR (ПОЖАР)
pronounced
PA - JHAR

☎ FIRST AID STATIONS

See Page 211

☎ FISH STORES
РЫБНЫЕ МАГАЗИНЫ
FISCHGESCHÄFTE
POISSONNERIES
FISKHANDLARE
KALALIIKKEET

Fish are sold in two specialty stores,
"Fish" (Ryba, Рыба) and "Ocean" (Okean,
Океан)

Ryba   **Fish**
- Nevskiy pr., 21 *One of the best*......... 312-47-29
  Mon-Sat 10-20; Rbls
- Nevskiy pr., 43.............................. 319-98-51
  Daily 9-21, Metro Ploshchad Vosstaniya
- Nevskiy pr., 132............................. 277-29-27
  Daily 9-19
- Razezzhaya ul., 3 315-95-54
  Daily 8-20, Metro Dostoevskaya

Okean-1   **Ocean-1**
  Sadovaya ul., 39/41 310-75-52
  Mon-Sat 9-14, 15-20

Okean-3   **Ocean-3**
  Leninskiy pr., 121 254-56-15
  Mon-Sat 9-14, 15-20

☎ **FISHING & HUNTING**

See HUNTING & FISHING EXCURSIONS

☎ **FISHING & HUNTING EQUIPMENT**

See HUNTING & FISHING EQUIPMENT and
SPORTS EQUIPMENT

☎ **FLAT RENTALS**

See APARTMENT RENTALS

☎ **FLOWER SHOPS**
   ЦВЕТОЧНЫЕ МАГАЗИНЫ
   BLUMENGESCHÄFTE
   FLEURISTES
   BLOMSTERHANDLARE
   KUKKAKAUPAT

*The Russians love flowers and house
plants. Always bring an odd number of
flowers as a gift (1,3,5, etc.); even
numbers are only for funerals. The best
flowers are sold at Kuznechnyy Rynok
(Кузнечный Рынок) near Metro
Vladimirskaya. The following metro
stations have many flower sellers.*

Akademicheskaya	*Ploshchad Lenina*
Avtovo	*Pl. Vosstaniya*
Baltiyskaya	*Primorskaya*
Chernaya Rechka	*Pushkinskaya*
Lomonosovskaya	*Vasileostrovskaya*
Moskovskaya	*Vladimirskaya*
Park Pobedy	

See metro map on back cover

Some favorite flowers

Roses	*Rozy*	*Розы*
Carnations	*Gvozdika*	*Гвоздика*
Chrysanthemums	*Khrizantemy*	*Хризантемы*
Iris	*Iris*	*Ирис*
Lilies of valley	*Landysh*	*Ландыш*
Peonies	*Piony*	*Пионы*
Lilacs	*Siren*	*Сирень*
Violets	*Fialki*	*Фиалки*
Daffodils	*Nartsissy*	*Нарциссы*
Tulips	*Tyulpany*	*Тюльпаны*
Gladiolas	*Gladiolus*	*Гладиолус*

Alenkiy Tsvetochek
  Prosveshcheniya pr., 46, bldg. 1 597-26-94
  Mon-Sat 10-19
  Tram 57; Metro Prospekt Prosveshcheniya

Amela
  Vladimirskiy pr., 3 113-22-84
  Mon-Sat 10-20; Rbls; Eng
Azalea
  Bolshoy Sampsonievskiy pr., 70..... 245-46-19
  Mon-Fri 9-18; Bus 33; Metro Lesnaya
Babylon-7
  Bolshoy pr., P.S., 65 232-04-66
  Fax.. 279-63-49
  Daily 10-14, 15-20
Bakkara
  Bolshoy pr., P.S., 86 232-84-07
  Daily 9-19; T-bus 1; Metro Petrogradskaya
Buket   **Bouquet**
  Izmaylovskiy pr., 11 251-61-28
  Mon-Sat 10-14, 16-19
  Bus 60; Metro Tekhnologicheskiy Institut
Evrika
  Suvorovskiy pr., 3 277-50-41
  Daily 8-19; T-bus 5; Metro Ploshchad Vosstaniya

Exotica
Flowers, Seeds & Grill
Flower Bouquets &
Arrangements for Special
Occasions (order by phone)
Leninskiy pr., 119 254-75-91
Hrs: 10-23, closed 15-16

Fantaziya   **Fantasy**
  Zagorodnyy pr., 34......................... 315-95-27
  Daily 8-14, 15-20, Metro Pushkinskaya, Dostoevskaya
Fialka   **Violet**
  Stachek pr., 96............................... 183-22-87
  Tue-Sun 10-14, 15-19

FLORA ***
Home Delivery
Shpalernaya ul., 44 271-11-61
Daily 10-19; Rbls, $; Eng, Finn

Flora, *Daily 9-14, 15-20*
  Nevskiy pr., 110 275-71-24
Gera, *Daily 0-9, 10-24; Rbls*
  Bolshaya Konyushennaya ul., 1 315-74-90
Kameliya   **Camellia**
  Kosygina pr., 15.............................. 520-82-79
  Mon-Sat 10-13, 14-19; Bus 21; Metro Ladozhskaya
Karmen, *Daily 10-14, 15-19*
  Moskovskiy pr., 194........................ 298-42-42
Katya, *Mon-Fri 10-14, 15-19*
  Tipanova ul., 29 299-57-76
Kliviya, *Mon-Sat 10-14, 15-19*
  Leninskiy pr., 130 254-38-23
Lavanda   **Lavender**
  Kommuny ul., 23, Kolpino.............. 484-43-29
  Mon-Sat 10-14, 15-18:30
Liliya   **Lily**
  Sedova ul., 17................................ 265-04-89
  Mon-Sat 8-14, 15-20; Bus 31; Metro Elizarovskaya
Magiya, *Daily 10-14, 15-19*   **Magic**
  Narodnaya ul., 2............................ 263-40-13
Magnoliya   **Magnolia**
  Sadovaya ul., 46 310-08-63
  Daily 10-19

Mirta
Partizana Germana ul., 14/117 136-92-26
Mon-Sat 10-14, 15-19; T-bus 32; Metro Prospekt Veteranov

Nevskiy 5
Nevskiy pr., 5 312-64-37
Daily 8-14, 15-20; T-bus 1; Metro Nevskiy Prospekt

Nevskiy Buket   **Nevskiy Bouquet**
Nevskiy pr., 184 271-06-66
Mon-Sat 10-14, 15-19; Rbls

Nordiya
Zhukovskogo ul., 36 272-34-66
Fax 272-34-72
Mon-Sat 9-14, 15-20; Rbls

*** Oranzh, *Home Delivery*   **Orange**
Sezzhinskaya ul., 9/6 233-94-11
Daily 10-20

Polskiy Buket   **Polish Bouquet**
Morskaya nab., 15 352-20-75
Daily 10-14, 15-19; Bus 128; Metro Primorskaya

Rosinka   **Dew Drop**
Karpinskogo ul., 20 249-07-53
Mon-Sat 10-14, 15-19; Tram 9; Metro Akademicheskaya

Roza   **Rose**
Veteranov pr., 87 150-27-82
Mon-Sat 10-14, 15-19; Rbls; Eng, Ger

Strelitsya
Krylenko ul., 27 586-69-62
Mon-Sat 10-13, 14-19; Metro Prospekt Bolshevikov

Tsvety   **Flowers**
• Babushkina ul., 111 262-63-78
Mon-Sat 10-14, 15-19; Bus 11; Metro Proletarskaya
• Gorokhovaya ul., 8/13 312-16-26
Mon-Fri 8-14, 15-18
• Leninskiy pr., 119 254-75-91
Daily 10-15, 16-21
• Mayakovskogo ul., 19 272-83-58
Mon-Fri 10-13, 14-19
• Moskovskiy pr., 136 298-03-24
Daily 8-14, 15-20
• Potemkinskaya ul., 2 272-64-27
.... 271-44-19
Mon-Fri 10-13, 14-18:30; Bus 14; Metro Chernyshevskaya
• Staro-Petergofskiy pr., 52 252-41-50
Mon-Sat 10-14, 15-19
• Tipanova ul., 29 299-57-76
Mon-Sat 10-14, 15-19; T-bus 27; Metro Moskovskaya

Tsvety Bolgarii   **Bulgarian Flowers**
Kamennoostrovskiy pr., 5 232-46-85
Special bouquets can be made if ordered in advance
Daily 8-20

Tsvety Sankt-Peterburga
     Flowers of St. Petersburg
• Sredniy pr., 28 213-19-93
Daily 10-14, 15-19
• Liteynyy pr., 38 273-72-42
Daily 9:30-18:30

Zal Tsvetov   **Hall of Flowers**
Potemkinskaya ul., 2 272-54-48
Special bouquets can be made if ordered in advance
Daily 8-19; Rbls, $; Eng

☎ **FOOD DELIVERY**
ПРОДУКТЫ, ДОСТАВКА
LEBENSMITTELLIEFERUNG
NOURRITURE, LIVRAISON
MATLEVERERING
RUUAN KOTIINKULJETUS

Alfa Express
Please Call 234-39-68
Daily 19-5; Rbls

Exotica

Lunches & Dinners Delivered
to Your Home or Hotel Room
(order by phone)
Leninskiy pr., 119 254-75-91
Hrs: 10-23, closed 15-16

Inter-Latis Service
Daily 0-24 552-15-64
Daily 20-8 290-06-46

Orchid
Maklina pr., 60, apt. 11 113-65-46
Daily 0-24; Rbls, $, CC; Eng, Ital

PIZZA HOUSE

Formerly Pizza Express
Quick Home Delivery
From 10 am to 24 p.m.,
13 Varieties of Pizza, Steak,
Weiner Schnitzel, Pastas & Salads
Lapin Kulta Beer & European Wines
7 minutes drive from center
Podolskaya ul., 23
Orders 292-26-66
Fax 292-10-39
Daily 10-24; $, CC, Eng, Finn; Metro Frunzenskaya

Pizza-Rif, *Home delivery*
Please call 290-35-96
Reasonable Prices; Daily 19-8; Rbls, $

Royal Food, *Daily 0-24; Rbls, $*
Please call 542-79-35

☎ **FOOD MARKETS**

See MARKETS *and* FOOD STORES

☎ **FOOD RADIOACTIVITY
TESTING**
ПРОДУКТЫ, ПРОВЕРКА
НА РАДИОАКТИВНОСТЬ
LEBENSMITTELKONTROLLE,
RADIOAKTIVITÄT
NOURRITURE, ESSAI RADIOACTIF
RADIOAKTIVITETS TEST PÅ MAT
RUUAN RADIOAKTIIVISUUDEN
MITTAAMINEN

*Since Chernobyl, some Russians worry
and want to have their food tested.*

Radioactivity Tests for Food
4-ya Sovetskaya ul., 5 277-52-92
Mon-Fri 9-16

The Country Code for Russia
⇨ **7** ⇦
The City Code for Saint Petersburg
Dial 812 + Number

☎ FOOD STORES
ПРОДОВОЛЬСТВЕННЫЕ
МАГАЗИНЫ
LEBENSMITTELGESCHÄFTE
ALIMENTATION, MAGASINS D'
LIVSMEDELSAFFÄRER
RUOKAKAUPAT

See also SUPERMARKETS, FISH STORES, FOOD DELIVERY, DELICATESSENS, BAKERIES, BABY FOOD, MARKETS, and INTERNATIONAL SHOPS

For hints on how to shop for food see SHOPPING. *Food is bought in a variety of shops.*

• *A modest self-serve supermarket* (**Universam**, Универсам) *has canned and packaged goods, juices, pots, tableware, soap, paper products, dry goods, as well as meat, bread, fruits and vegetables.*

• *A* **Gastronom** (Гастроном) *usually has meat, fish, conserves, dairy products, and semi-prepared foods, but not dry goods or fruits and vegetables.*

• *A* **Diet** (Dieta, Диета) *grocery store is similar to a Gastronom but also has special foods for diabetics and others on special diets.*

• *A Farmer's* **Market** (Rynok, Рынок) *has fresh vegetables, fruit, sausage, meat, cheese, honey, flowers, etc. See* MARKETS. *In summer, fruits and vegetables are sold around metros.*

• *A variety of smaller shops, called* "**Products**" (Produkty, Продукты) *have a smaller selection of groceries, sugar, and coffee. Other types of food stores include:*

Dairy	Moloko	Молоко
Bakery	Bulochnaya	Булочная
Fruits	Frukty	Фрукты
Vegetables	Ovoshchi	Овощи
Fish	Ryba	Рыба
Meat	Myaso	Мясо

• **Supermarkets**: *Three large Western style supermarkets have opened in the past year: Kalinka-Stockmann ($), Spar ($), Super Babylon (rubles only). See* SUPERMARKETS.

• **Prices** *Many food stores have been privatized and set their own prices. Only a few products such as bread, milk, and eggs are subsidized and regulated. See also* CURRENCY EXCHANGE *and* MARKETS.

• **Hours** *See* HOURS. *Many smaller food shops and bakeries are open on Sunday; some commercial food shops are* OPEN 24 HOURS A DAY.

UNIVERSAMS   УНИВЕРСАМЫ
UNIVERSAL SELF-SERVICE FOOD STORES

Gavanskiy No. 14
Nalichnaya ul., 42 350-67-68
Mon-Sat 10-19; Rbls

Grazhdanskiy
Prosveshcheniya pr., 81 531-54-44
Mon-Sat 8-21

Izmaylovskiy
Novo-Izmaylovskiy pr., 3 296-51-45
Mon-Sat 9-13, 14-21; T-bus 17; Metro Elektrosila

Morskoy No. 29 near Hotel Pribaltiyskaya
Korablestroiteley ul., 21................ 356-86-59
Mon-Fri, Sun 8-21; Bus 128; Metro Primorskaya

Nevskiy
Bolshevikov pr., 6 588-30-13
Mon-Sat 8-21

Okhtinskiy No. 36 near Hotel Okhtinskaya
Sverdlovskaya nab., 62 227-08-47
Mon-Sat 9-21; Tram 7

Pulkovskiy No. 24
Pulkovskoe shosse, 3.................... 122-23-16
Mon-Sat 8-14, 15-21; Rbls

Severnyy
Prosveshcheniya pr., 74 558-52-01
Mon-Sat 8-21; Tram 22; Metro Grazhdanskiy Prospekt

Tallinnskiy
Veteranov pr., 89 150-78-71
Mon-Sat 8-14, 15-21; Bus 130, 68; Metro Prospekt Veteranov

Tulskiy
Tulskaya ul., 3......................... 275-68-50
Mon-Sat 8-14, 15-21

Vitebskiy
Dimitrova ul., 5 172-50-29
Daily 8-14, 15-21

Vostochnyy
Kollontay ul., 41, apt. 1 584-88-09
Mon-Sat 8-14, 15-20

Vyborgskiy
Nauki pr., 23 533-54-85
Mon-Sat 8-14, 15-21

Yuzhnyy
Yaroslava Gasheka ul., 6 176-18-29
Mon-Sat 8-14, 15-21; T-bus 39; Metro Kupchino

Zapadnyy, *Daily 9-14, 15-21*
Marshala Kazakova ul., 1 157-01-55

Zvezdnyy
Zvezdnaya ul., 16 126-93-37
Mon-Sat 8-14, 15-21; Bus 296; Metro Zvezdnaya

GASTRONOMS   ГАСТРОНОМЫ

Dieta   **Diet**
• Bolshoy pr., P.S., 5 232-11-92
Mon-Sat 11-13, 14-20; Rbls
• Bolshoy pr., P.S., 29 230-95-91
Mon-Sat 9-14, 15-21; Rbls
• Nevskiy pr., 30........................ 312-16-33
Mon-Sat 8-13, 14-19:30; Rbls
• Sadovaya ul., 38 315-94-48
Mon-Sat 9-14, 15-21; Rbls
• Suvorovskiy pr., 19 274-58-98
Mon-Sat 11-13, 14-20; Rbls

Eliseevskiy
Nevskiy pr., 56......................... 311-93-23
Built during Russia's brief period of capitalism in the early 1900's; Mon-Sat 9-21

Gastronomiya, Myaso, Ptitsa
                      Meat, Poultry
Nevskiy pr., 128........................ 277-14-31
Mon-Sat 8-13, 14-20

Liteynyy No. 13, *Mon-Sat 9-20*
Liteynyy pr., 12........................ 272-27-91

Produkty   **Food Store**
• Millionnaya ul., 23................... 315-86-73
Mon-Sat 10-14, 15-20; Rbls
• Nevskiy pr., 105 275-39-58
Daily 9-13, 14-21
• Nevskiy pr., 150 277-21-54
Daily 9-21; T-bus 1; Metro Ploshchad Vosstaniya

Strela, *Mon-Sat 9-13, 14-21*
Izmaylovskiy pr., 16/30 251-27-09
Vitebskiy, *Daily 9-13, 15-19*
Zagorodnyy pr., 45 113-52-01
Vladimirskiy
Zagorodnyy pr., 2 315-64-88
Daily 8-14, 15-20; Rbls; Metro Dostoevskaya

OPEN 24 HOUR FOOD STORES

Donon, *Nice selection of packaged meat, fruit, vegetables and cheese*
Gertsena, ul., 17 315-89-68
Daily 0-24; Rbls
Holiday, *Daily 0-13, 14-24; Rbls*
Bolshoy pr., P.S., 2 233-32-93
Nord Top, *Daily 0-8, 9-20, 21-24; Rbls; Eng*
Gorokhovaya ul., 11 314-64-54
Produkty   **Food Store (Delicatessen)**
Bolsheokhtinskiy pr., 25 227-16-33
Excellent Selection of Meats, Cheeses and Fruits
Daily 0-24; Rbls
Surprise, *Daily 0-24*
Nevskiy pr., 113 277-24-31
Tauras
Good deli, selection of Russian & imported foods
Kondratevskiy pr., 34 542-88-85
Daily 0-14, 15-24; Rbls

COMMERCIAL & PRIVATE FOOD STORES

Adamant, *Cold Beverages*
Reki Moyki nab., 72 312-10-55
Mon-Fri 10-14, 15-19; Rbls, $

Antanta Supermarket ***
Tuchkov per., 11/5 213-20-47
Fax 350-57-77
Amazing. Fresh fruits. The upscale grocery store.
Delicatessen with more than 2000 items
Daily 12-22; Rbls

BABYLON
shops

Mini-Market No. 3

Thirsty? Hungry? Forget Something?
Convenience Store on Nevskiy Prospect
Food, Snacks, Water, Cold & Refrigerated
Beer & Drinks, Martini & Rossi
and Other Imported Wine & Liquors

Nevskiy pr., 69 314-62-37
Mon-Sat: 10-14,15-20; Rbls
Metro Mayakovskaya

Balaton
Bolshoy Sampsonievskiy pr., 21 .... No ☎
Mon-Sat 10-14, 15-19; Rbls; Eng
Beriozka
Morskaya nab., 15 355-18-75
Daily 9-20; $
Best Department Store
Kupchinskaya ul., 15 261-64-53
Daily 9-20; Rbls
Bosco
• Ligovskiy pr., 130 166-00-11
Daily 11-15, 16-20; Rbls, $; Eng
• Nevskiy pr., 8 219-18-56
Daily 11-15, 16-20; Rbls, $; Eng
• Ulyany Gromovoy per., 3 275-57-11
Daily 11-15, 16-20; Rbls, $; Eng
• Zhukovskogo ul., 8 273-70-92
Mon-Sat 11-20; Rbls, $; Eng
Diodor Meat Store
Zagorodnyy pr., 43 112-42-78
Daily 9-20; Rbls
Dyuk
Kamennoostrovskiy pr., 69/71 234-57-33
Daily 8-13:30, 14-19; Rbls
Elf
Gertsena ul., 25/11 314-64-43
Mon-Sat 9-14, 15-20; Rbls
Europe-Shop
Gorokhovaya ul., 25 315-50-08
Fax 314-62-87
Daily 11-20; Rbls
Eurotrade
Lesnoy pr., 22 542-89-54
Mon-Sat 11-20; $, CC

Express Market   mini-market

Imported foods from Finland
The place to buy fresh fruit in St. Pb.

Fresh fruits, Meat, Cheese, Vegetables,
Coffees & Teas, Baked Goods, Beer,
Juices, Soft Drinks, Wines, Liquor,
Toiletries, Paper Goods, and much more.
AT VERY REASONABLE PRICES

Two Shops in St. Petersburg

Moskovskiy pr., 73 252-41-44
Nevskiy pr., 113 & Kharkovskaya ul., 1
(Entrance on Kharkovskaya ul)
.... 277-77-71
Daily 10-22, $, Finnish

Fart
Nevskiy pr., 160 277-48-38
Mon-Fri 10-13, 14-19; Rbls
Food Shop
Bolshoy pr., P.S., 5 .... No ☎
Mon-Sat 11-14, 15-20; $; Eng, Fr

Mon-Sat 10-21 Sun 12-20
Exchange office

ONE STOP SHOPPING AT SUPER BABYLON

Everything you need for an elegant last-minute dinner. Appetizers,
salad, prepared frozen foods, condiments, torte shells and
whipped cream for dessert. Great wines, delicious coffees and
teas and chocolate truffles to relish.

P.S., Malyy pr., 54 & 56 230-80-96
In the former Okean store off Bolshoy Prospekt

Gang, *Indian Spices*
Razezzhaya ul., 12, 2nd floor 164-85-46
Mon-Fri 10-14,15-20, Sat 11-15; Eng, Hindi, Urdu

Gushe
Vladimirskiy pr., 1 113-24-12
Daily 9-14, 15-21; Rbls, $; Metro Dostoevskaya

Intek
Ligovskiy pr., 137 112-21-11
Mon-Sat 10-20; Rbls

Ivakha
Bolshaya Konyushennaya ul., 5 315-79-52
Mon-Sat 10-14, 15-19; Rbls

Polar
Moskovskiy pr., 222 293-18-09
Fax 293-04-08
Daily 9-17; Rbls, $; Eng, Finn

Ropsha
Moskovskiy pr., 8 310-36-45
Mon-Fri 9-18; Rbls

Rozhdestvenskaya
Nevskiy pr., 120 277-59-05
Fax 277-31-03
Daily 8-14, 15-20; Rbls; Eng, Fr

Rus
Pestelya ul., 12 275-06-03
Daily 9-14, 15-19; Rbls, $

KALINKA

STOCKMANN
SUPERMARKET

Come and buy from the widest
selection in town
Fresh milk products, vegetables,
fruit, meat, fish, bread and
other food products.
We also have a good
selection of non-food products.

Finlandskiy pr., 1

542-22-97
542-36-76
Fax: 542-88-66

Open: Daily 10-21
$, DM, FIM,
Major Credit Cards
Metro: Ploshchad Lenina

Kuban
Bolshaya Zelenina ul., 2/42 230-58-58
Mon-Sat 9-20; Rbls

Lenkon
Podezdnoy per., 19 210-17-63
Mon-Fri 10-17; Rbls

Madlen, *Meat Store*
Sezdovskaya Liniya, 9 .... No ☎
Tues-Sat 10-14, 15-19

Minokhem Tradehouse
Zamshina ul., 29 543-39-20
Fax 543-49-10
Mon-Sat 8-14, 15-21; Bus 33

Nairi
Dekabristov ul., 6 314-80-93
Daily 10-20; Rbls

Nautilus
Gorokhovaya ul., 61 310-23-02
Fax 310-19-15
Mon-Sat 11-20

New Food Store
Grivtsova per., 7 315-86-63
Daily 9-21; Rbls, $; Eng

Podsolnukh   **Sunflower**
Liteynyy pr., 32 .... No ☎
Good selection of cheeses, vegetables, drinks, etc.
Mon-Sat 10-19, Rbls

✳ BABYLON

SUPER

THE SUPER SUPERMARKET
**Largest supermarket in Russia
for One-Stop Shopping in Rubles**

Everything from Soup to Nuts
Featuring Imported foodstuffs
from Holland and around the world

Hundreds and hundreds of items

in the five long aisles of our grocery
section, including a large frozen food
section, fresh produce, refrigerated dairy
and deli sections.

Choose your own fresh fruits & vegetables.
Dozens of deli items from French and Dutch
cheeses to sliced roast beef, smoked ham
and sausages, smoked fish, prepared foods,
and more.

Fresh French bread, rolls and croissants.

Large beverage section featuring fresh
juices, mixers, soft drinks and the finest
European wines and beers

Extensive selection of housewares, cleaning
supplies, paper products and
personal products

**OPEN MON-SAT 10-21
SUNDAY 12-20**

P.S., Maly pr., 54 & 56 230-80-96
.... 233-88-92
In the former Okean store right off Bolshoy Prospekt
Metro Petrogradskaya
Rubles only, Exchange office in store.

SPAR ⊕

MARKETS

featuring
Fine Foods from Finland
and the Rest of the World

Large Fresh Fruit and Vegetable Section
Fresh meat and fish, trimmed by our own
butcher, special marinated beef

In our dairy section dozens of cheeses,
sausages, smoke fish and meat, fresh
Finnish milk and butter

McCormick spices, condiments, peanuts by
the kilo, cereals, crackers, and more

Large frozen food section with many
varieties of ice cream, **Carolina turkeys**,
frozen fruits and vegetables.
Imported beer and soft drinks by the case.

Personal toiletries and paper products
Pampers your baby with **Pampers** and
imported formula and baby food

Our large Candy and Cookie Section
features **Fazer Sweets and Cookies**

At our corner cafe, treat yourself to a cup
of coffee, glass of wine and deli sandwich

SPAR MARKET SLAVA

Slavy pr., 30 260-41-21
....261-04-60
Fax.....................................261-29-70
*Daily 10-22; $, FIM, DM, Rbls; Eng, Finn, Ger
Metro Moskovskaya, then Bus 31, 114, or
T-bus 29, 27, 35*

SPAR MARKET KIROVSKIY

Stachek, 1 186-51-77
Fax.....................................186-94-11
*Daily 10-20; $, FIM, DM, Rbls; Eng, Finn, Ger
Right opposite Metro Narvskaya*

Tekhnolog,   *Daily 10-22; Rbls*
Dekabristov ul., 14 311-62-04
Tradehouse of Holland, *Large selection of
clothing, shoes and food from Holland*
Malookhtinskiy pr., 68 528-82-25
        Mon-Sat 11-19; Rbls, $
Tradehouse on Moyka, *Daily 10-14, 15-20; Rbls, $*
Reki Moyki nab., 59 315-08-84

UNIREM
FOOD STORE

- *Purified Water*
- *Food Items*
- *Grill*
- *Currency Exchange*

Marata ul., 3 311-30-45
Hrs: 9-21, 7 days a week

FRUIT & VEGETABLE STORES

Frukty, Konservy   **Canned Fruit**
Sadovaya ul., 56 315-59-20
     Mon-Sat 10-14, 15-19
Kooperator No. 48   **Cooperator No. 48**
Moskovskiy pr., 36-38 292-16-65
     Daily 8-14, 15-20
Dary Lesa   **Gifts from the Forest**
Poltavskaya ul., 4 279-42-30
     Mon-Sat 9-14, 15-20; Rbls
Frukty, Ovoshchi   **Fruits, Vegetables**
Malaya Posadskaya ul., 6 233-66-20
     Similar to a New York green grocer
   Mon-Sat 10-14, 15-20; Metro Gorkovskaya
Nevskiy pr., 132 277-21-63
     Daily 9-21
Gdansk Products from Poland
Leninskiy pr., 125 255-71-41
     Mon-Sat 9-14, 15-20
Gdynya
Zanevskiy pr., 20.............................528-27-08
     Mon-Sat 9-21
Ovoshchi-Frukty   **Vegetables-Fruits**
Nevskiy pr., 127 277-26-33
     Daily 8-13, 14-20; Metro Ploshchad Vosstaniya
Sopot Products from Poland
Sredniy pr., 25 218-49-75
     Daily 9-20
Sopot Vegetables-Fruits   **Ovoshchi-Frukty**
Sredniy pr., 34 213-10-43
     Daily 8-14, 15-20
Yablonka
Nevskiy pr., 65................................164-98-72
     Daily 9-21

☎ FOOD WHOLESALERS
**ПРОДУКТЫ, ОПТОВАЯ ПОСТАВКА
LEBENSMITTEL GROSSMARKT
ALIMENTATION,
LIVRAISON EN GROS
LIVSMEDELS GROSSISTER
TUKKULIIKE, RUOKA**

Barbara GmbH

Food Imports

St. Petersburg, 191011

Ostrovskogo pl., 9..........................310-26-24

Tel./Fax 310-26-86

Hrs: 10-19; Clsd. Sat, Sun; Rbls & $; Eng, Ger, Fr

The Bronze Lion Ltd.
Wholesale Distribution of Food and Beverages
Tel./Fax 314-72-92

Markit
Reki Moyki nab., 48 312-42-16
     Mon-Fri 9-18; Rbls, $

PROMETEY Ltd

Wholesale & Retail Distribution
of Imported Food Products &
Tobacco in St. Petersburg

Ochakovskaya ul., 7
St. Petersburg, 193015, Russia

Tel.: (812) 274-76-54
(812) 274-78-84
Fax. (812) 274-77-62

VISHNU

Priya International Co Ltd.
V.O. 19 Liniya, 12, 199026, St.Petersburg
"Especially for You"
Importers of the Best Quality Canned
Meat, Cheese, Confectionery
Fine Quality Tea & Coffee & All Types
of Preserved Foods
V.O., 19 Liniya,12 213-99-99
Fax....................................218-14-49

☎ FOREIGN CONSULATES

See CONSULATES

☎ FOREIGN FIRMS
ФИРМЫ, ИНОСТРАННЫЕ
FIRMEN, AUSLÄNDISCHE
COMMERCE EXTERIEUR,
SOCIETES DU
UTLÄNDSKA FIRMOR
ULKOMAALAISET YHTIÖT

*Foreign firms active in the following areas
are listed under:* ACCOUNTING, AIRLINES,
AUTOMOBILES, BANKS, COMMUNICATIONS,
COMPUTERS, LAW FIRMS, PHOTOCOPIERS,
PHOTOGRAPHY.

---

*This listing includes about 140 of the
better known Western foreign firms and
joint ventures out of more than 1200. For
a more complete listing, see* St. Pb. Yellow
Pages-93 *and* Ves St. Pb. 93 *or go to the
St. Petersburg Committee on Foreign
Economic Relations.*

A & A
Gertsena ul., 39, Hotel Astoria 312-76-88
A. J. EST S. U.
Konnogvardeyskiy blvd., 4, entr. 6, apt. 34
.... 110-64-96
Fax................................... 312-72-92
Mon-Fri 9-17; Rbls, $; Eng, Fr
Adra
Reki Pryazhki nab., 3/1 219-75-31
.... 219-79-25
Fax.................................... 219-56-45
Mon-Fri 10-18; Rbls, $; Eng; Tram 1; Metro Narvskaya
Amerex Intercontinental
Kamennoostrovskiy pr., 37 233-87-31
Mon-Fri 9-17; Rbls, $
American Express
at the Grand Hotel Europe
Mikhaylovskaya ul., 1/7 119-60-09
Fax.................................... 119-60-11
Mon-Fri 9-17; $, CC; Eng, Ger
Americar (Chrysler) - *See* Chrysler-Novak-
Motors under AUTOMOBILES SALES
Piskarevskiy pr., 39 544-05-90
Fax.................................... 544-58-24
Ameros Business Company
Ligovskiy pr., 87 164-21-28
Fax.................................... 112-18-44
Mon-Sat 10-18; Rbls, $
Antwerp
Kronverkskiy pr., 13/2 233-84-82
Mon-Fri 9-21; Rbls, $; Eng, Ger, Fr
Arnika
Lunacharskogo pr., 47 558-96-17
Mon-Fri 10-16; Rbls
Arthur Andersen
Bolshoy pr., V.O., 10 350-49-84
Fax.................................... 213-78-74
Daily 9-13, 14-18; Rbls, $; Eng, Ger
ASEA Brown Boveri
Bolshoy pr., V.O., 10 350-49-10
Fax.................................... 350-29-11
Mon-Fri 9-18; $; Eng, Ger
AT&T - St. Petersburg
Liflyandskaya ul., 4 186-75-37
Fax.................................... 252-12-52
Mon-Fri 8:30-17:30; Eng
Atlantic Investment
Nevskiy pr., 104 275-58-64
Fax.................................... 275-45-87
Autotur
Energetikov pr., 65, 2nd floor 226-95-39
Mon-Sat 10-18
Aytra
Sverdlovskaya nab., 52, bldg. 1 224-16-10
Badishe Anilin - und Sodafabrik BASF
Bolshoy pr., V.O., 10 350-72-56
Fax.................................... 218-53-81
Mon-Fri 9-18; Eng, Ger
Baker & McKenzie - *See* LAW FIRMS
Griboedova kan. nab., 36 310-54-46
Fax.................................... 310-59-44

Balkan Holidays-St. Petersburg
Artilleriyskaya ul., 1 279-61-38
Mon-Fri 9:30-18; Rbls, $; Eng, Ger, Fr
Balkancar - Ross
Ryleeva ul., 27, 1st floor 273-72-84
Fax 273-75-77
Baltic Bridge Ltd., *Mon-Fri 10-17; Rbls, $; Eng*
Kronverkskaya ul., 27 232-98-38
Fax 352-26-88
Baltic International Technopark
1-ya Krasnoarmeyskaya ul., 13 251-11-62
Fax 315-17-01
Mon-Sat 8:30-18; Rbls, $
Baltic Trading, *Mon-Fri 9-17; Eng, Ger*
Nevskiy pr., 176 230-88-32
Fax 277-09-35
Benson & Company
Rimskogo-Korsakova pr., 8, apt. 4
Tel/Fax 311-70-97
BIONT Corp.
Energetikov 2/60 226-44-56
Fax 226-91-00
Bronze Lion
Sadovaya ul., 51, rm. 10 314-72-92
Budimeks, *Mon-Fri 9-17; $, CC; Eng, Pol*
Robespera nab., 8/46, rm. 93 279-69-31
Fax 279-68-31

A/O **Bumar** Warinski

Construction Equipment, Sales & Repairs
Moscow office: Mira pr., 74, apt. 190
Tel./Fax .... (095) 284-45-55
In St. Petersburg: Yakornaya ul., 9
Tel./Fax .... (812) 528-84-90

Burrows Paper Corp.
Reki Fontanki nab., 23, rm.5, 5th floor
Tel/Fax 314-51-48
Business Link Company
13 Liniya, 14 218-69-00
Fax 218-79-40
Mon-Sat 9-18; Rbls, $; Eng, Ger
Business Management International (USA)
Please call 307-79-04
Mon-Fri 9-18; Rbls, $, CC; Eng

Carl Zeiss Jena GmbH   **ZEISS**
     Germany
V.O. Bolshoy pr., 10
199034 Sankt Petersburg

Tel: 350-48-35
Fax: 213-78-73
Telex: .... 121564 CZ LEN SU

Catalog Express
Sadovaya ul., 34 .... No ☎
Caterpillar
Millionnaya ul., 21/60 311-56-44
Fax 311-95-57
Central Europe Trust
Mayakovskogo ul., 46 275-58-20
Fax 279-28-69
Mon-Fri 10-18:30; Rbls, $; Eng; Metro Chernyshevskaya
Coca-Cola Saint Petersburg Bottlers
Shpalernaya ul., 55, 2nd floor 278-18-99
Fax 274-26-78
Mon-Fri 9-18; Rbls; Eng
Computerland - *See* COMPUTER STORES
Sverdlovskaya nab., 64 224-09-32
Fax 224-04-55
Coopers & Lybrand/Solutions for Business
See ACCOUNTING & AUDITING FIRMS
Gertsena ul., 39, Hotel Astoria, rm. 528
Tel/Fax 210-55-28
Mon-Fri 9-18; Rbls; Eng
Costa Inc.
Tavricheskaya ul., 39, rm. 353
Tel/Fax 271-41-10
DHL Express Courier
See EXPRESS MAIL & PARCEL SERVICE
Griboedova kan. nab., 5, rm. 325 ... 311-26-49
Fax 314-64-73
Mon-Fri 9-18; Rbls, $, CC
DTI SU
Bolshoy Sampsonievskiy pr., 23 541-81-46
Fax 541-05-05
Defis
Reki Fontanki nab., 117 278-50-88
Fax 110-60-97
Mon-Fri 10-17; Rbls, $; Eng
Delegation der Deutschen Wirtshaft
     Delegation of German Economics
Bolshoy pr., V.O., 10 213-79-93
Fax 350-56-22
Mon-Fri 9-18; Eng, Ger
Delta Airlines - *See* AIRLINES
Gertsena ul., 36 311-58-20
Mon-Fri 9-13, 14-17; $; Eng
Delta-Telecom - U.S. West
Chekhova ul., 18 275-41-49
Fax 275-01-30
Delta-Albion
Akademika Baykova ul., 9, bldg. 2 555-79-24
Daily 9-15, 16-20; Rbls, $
T-bus 13; Metro Politekhnicheskaya
Dialog Invest
Dostoevskogo ul., 19/21 164-89-56
Fax 164-93-92
Digital Equipment Corp.
Moskovskiy pr., 108 298-23-70
Fax 298-07-48

DELOVIE LYUDI

INDEPENDENT • OBJECTIVE • THOROUGH
Profsoyuznaya ul., 73; Tel.: (095) 333-33-40; Fax: (095) 330-15-68

Dresdner Bank
Isaakievskaya pl., 11 312-16-20
Fax 312-26-11
Mon-Fri 9-18; Rbls, $; Eng, Ger

ECO Stahl AG Eisenhuttenstadt
Bolshoy pr., V.O., 10 218-17-84
Fax 350-48-06
Mon-Fri 9-17; Rbls, $, CC; Eng, Ger

East Trade Polmot Holding
Nakhimova ul., 7, apt. 102 356-33-64
Mon-Fri 8-14; Rbls, $; Eng, Ger, Pol

Editions de L'espace European
Universitetskaya nab., 3 218-16-72
Fax 218-08-11
Daily 10:30-18; Rbls, $; Major European languages
T-bus 1; Metro Vasileostrovskaya

Elegant Logic, *Electronics*
Reki Fontanki nab., 46 312-38-86
Fax 311-04-52
Mon-Fri 10-18; Eng; Metro Mayakovskaya

Elektrim
Robespera nab., 8/46, apt. 66 273-41-64
Mon-Fri 9-17; $; Eng, Pol; Bus 14; Metro Chernyshevskaya

Eli Lilly & Elanco Pharmaceuticals Ltd.
Please call 550-30-26

Ernst and Young
See ACCOUNTING & AUDITING FIRMS
Gogolya ul., 11 312-99-11
Fax 312-53-20
Daily 9-18; $; Eng; Bus 22, 27; Metro Nevskiy Prospekt

Export Industries
Michurinskaya ul., 12 164-26-16
Mon-Fri 9-17; Rbls, $; Eng, Fr

Fexima Trade House
Reki Fontanki nab., 34 275-75-10
Fax 275-50-96
Mon-Fri 9-18; Rbls, $; Eng, Fr

Florman Information Russia, *Public Relations*
Kamennoostrovskiy pr., 14 b 233-76-82
Fax 232-80-17
Mon-Fri 9:30-18; Rbls, $; Eng, Ger, Finn, Swed

Gemma International
Sedova ul., 6 567-94-95
Fax 265-05-07
Mon-Fri 9-10-12, 13-18; Rbls, $; Eng

Gillette St. Petersburg Product Int'l
Sofiyskaya ul., 14 106-37-32
Fax 106-34-79

Goodwill Games, Inc.
Turner Broadcasting Systems
See GOODWILL GAMES
Bolshaya Monetnaya ul., 19
Tel/Fax 232-73-64

Harris Representative
Gertsena ul., 28 315-23-45
Fax 110-66-54
Mon-Fri 9-18; Rbls, $; Eng

Heerum, *Mon-Fri 10-17; Rbls, $; Eng, Ger*
Please call 542-69-70

Hill International
Gertsena ul., 23 312-67-01
Fax 312-53-68

Hollait
Baskov per., 6 279-09-03
Fax 272-23-69

Honeywell
Zakharievskaya ul., 31 275-35-04
Fax 275-28-04

International Business Services, Inc.
Rubinshteyna ul., 8 311-58-38

IBM, *Computer systems*
Admiralteyskiy pr., 6 312-60-17
Fax 312-38-87

Ibar, *Mon-Fri 9-18; $; Eng*
Energetikov pr., 24 227-47-98
Fax 227-47-14

Ilka, *Mon-Fri 9:30-17:30; Rbls; Eng, Bul*
Bolshoy pr., V.O., 70 218-29-68
Fax 217-22-42

IMID - International Market & Industry Development Inc.
Tel/Fax 264-66-14

In-Time Corporation
Gertsena ul., 42, 3rd floor, off. 149 311-65-10

Intermarco GmbH
Bolshoy pr., V.O., 10 350-46-56
Fax 350-56-22
Mon-Fri 9-18; Rbls, $; Ger
Bus 7; Metro Vasileostrovskaya

InterOccidental Inc.
Vosstaniya ul., 49 273-43-23
Fax 272-80-31

Interoptik, *Mon-Fri 9-21; Rbls, $; Eng, Ger*
Tuchkov per., 7 218-38-51
Fax 350-64-75

Interpicoat, *Mon-Fri 8:15-17*
Reki Moyki nab., 58 314-05-73

Intersigma
Tverskaya ul., 27/29, apt. 8 275-59-11
Fax 275-56-38

ITOCHU Corporation
Japanese Trading Firm

Phone: 311-86-78
Fax: 311-77-45
Telex: 121171 ITOCH SU

SC Johnson
Nevskiy pr., 1 311-89-90

Kamennyy Ostrov
Polevaya alleya, 6 234-10-11
Fax 234-12-66
Mon-Fri 9-18; Rbls; Eng, Ger

 KAUKOMARKKINAT
COMMERCIAL BUREAU

Import-Export & Barter Operations
Nakhimova ul., 7, office 39
.... 356-36-35
Fax 356-83-33
Telex .... 121309 LEDKA SU

Knoll AG, *Mon-Fri 10-18*
Bolshoy pr., V.O., 10.................. 218-53-81
Fax 119-60-40
Konwest
Reki Fontanki nab., 23 311-30-18
Mon-Fri 10-20; Rbls, $; Eng, Ger, Fr
Kushnareff Representative
12-ya Liniya, 17 355-89-25
Fax 218-00-32
Mon-Fri 10-18; Eng, Fr
LETI-Lovanium, *Mon-Fri 9-19; Rbls; Eng*
Professora Popova ul., 5 234-02-12
Lenkozhvest
Kozhevennaya Liniya, 1/3.............. 217-06-46
Fax 217-07-88
Mon-Fri 8:30-17; Rbls, $; Eng, Ger; Metro Primorskaya
Lentakeinvest, *Mon-Fri 9-18; Eng, Ital*
Obvodnogo kan. nab., 143 113-08-24
Fax 315-17-01
3M-Lentelefonstroy
Obukhovo, Grazhniy proezd, 1 110-15-34
.... 101-44-74

MS-AUDIOTRON

Professional audio, video and lighting
equipment for concert halls, theaters and studios.
Complete Installation • Musical Instrument Sales
P.O. Box 28, 00421 Helsinki, Finland
St. Petersburg:
Tel 310-55-13
Fax 310-48-01
Helsinki:
Fax .... +358-0-556-65-82

Madison Brands Inc.
Please call 543-54-62
Marine Computer Systems, *Mon-Fri 10-19*
Babushkina ul., 80 568-39-43
Fax 568-39-39
Matra, *Mon-Fri 9-16; Rbls; Eng, Ger, Fr*
Sirenevyy blvd., 18, floor 2 544-94-54
McKinsey & Co.
Hotel Olympia, Gavan................... 119-60-50
Fax 119-60-49

National / Panasonic / Technics

Matsushita Electric Industrial Co., Ltd

National

Nakhimova ul., 7, office 39
Tel.: 356-36-35, 355-63-05; Fax: 356-83-33
Telex: 121309 ledka su

METRA Engineering
  • Mechanical engineering
  • Building material technology
  • Porcelain bathroom fixtures
Bolshoy Sampsonievskiy pr., 31
Tel 542-06-59
Tel/Fax...................................... 542-68-42

Neyvo
Izmaylovskiy pr., 2 259-50-14
Fax 251-04-00
Mon-Fri 10-20; Rbls; Eng

Oil Data International Inc.
Geology, Geophysics,
Mathematical Analysis & Seismic Data
Moskovskiy pr., 1/2, apt. 21 310-32-92
Fax... 310-11-33

Otego International
Aptekarskiy pr., 6 234-54-44
Otis Saint Petersburg,
See our ad under CONSTRUCTION & RENOVATION
Khimicheskiy per., 12................... 252-36-94
Mon-Fri 8:30-17:30; Rbls; Eng, Ger
PPS in Saint Petersburg
Ryleeva ul., 27 273-24-18
Fax 272-57-18
Mon-Fri 9:30-18; Rbls, $; Eng, Bul

Personnel Corps
See EMPLOYMENT AGENCIES
Nevskiy pr., 104 275-45-86
Fax 275-83-23

Peterhouse
Chekhova ul., 14 272-30-07
Fax 272-63-57
Mon-Fri 10-19; Rbls, $; Eng, Ger
Metro Chernyshevskaya
Petroff Motors
Vyzovaya ul., 4............................ 235-23-86
Procter & Gamble, in the Grand Hotel Europe
4th floor.........................Ext. 456 113-80-66
Mon-Fri 9-18; Eng
Rank Xerox
Obvodnogo kan. nab, 93 a
Neptune Business Center 315-76-60
Fax... 315-77-73
RDW
Kuybysheva ul., 21 232-04-02
Fax... 232-44-16
Mon-Fri 10-18; Rbls, $
RJR Nabisco
Sredniy pr., V.O., 36/40................ 213-17-00
Fax... 213-19-55
Renlund
Bolshaya Zelenina ul., 14, Office..... 232-36-07
Mon-Fri 10-14, 15-19; Rbls, $; Finn
Rossa Trade
Khlopina ul., 11 534-10-86
Fax... 534-49-07
Moving in September 1993
Mon-Fri 9-19; Rbls, $
Russian-American Law Firm
Lermontovskiy pr., 7/12 114-56-60
Fax... 114-07-40

RusTex International - *See* LAW FIRMS
Belgradskaya ul., 6, apt. 46 273-44-40
Fax... 109-69-14

Ryland St. Petersburg
Gertsena ul., 31........................... 314-65-15
.... 314-75-36

SKL Motoren und System Technik AG
vorm Buckau-Wolf
Stavropolskaya ul., 10.................. 271-09-04
Fax 271-12-95
Mon-Fri 9-17; $; Ger

Saint Petersburg-Pure Water
Tavricheskaya ul., 10.................. 275-40-55
Fax 275-62-58
Mon-Fri 9-18

Santa Barbara Ltd.
Goncharnaya ul., 24/52.............. 552-13-30
Fax 312-41-28

Sampo
Bolshoy pr., V.O., 83, off. 336....... 217-58-20
Mon-Fri 9:30-17; Rbls, $, CC; Eng

Sara Lee
Lermontovskiy pr., 7/12.............. 114-56-60
Fax 114-07-40

Sevbek-Pererabotka
Narodnaya ul., 95....................... 263-80-79
Fax 263-15-60

Siemens AG
Gogolya ul., 18/20 315-31-97
.... 312-47-06
Fax 315-36-21
Mon-Fri 9-17; Rbls, $; Eng, Ger

Soft-Tronik GmbH Computers
Reki Fontanki nab., 88 311-23-14
Fax 311-23-25
Mon-Fri 9-18; Rbls, $; Eng, Ger
Metro Sennaya Ploshchad

Sogecred
Shpalernaya ul., 45 275-50-27
Fax 273-08-87
Mon-Fri 9-13, 14-18; Rbls, $; Eng

SovAm Teleport - *See* ELECTRONIC MAIL
Nevskiy pr., 30............................ 311-84-12
Fax 311-71-29

SPASSIS
Malyy pr., 1, apt. 3
Tel/Fax....................................... 218-63-13

Stern & Co - *See our ad under* LAW FIRMS
Nevskiy pr., 104.......................... 275-34-97
Fax 275-45-87

SULZER | SULZER LTD
| WINTERTHUR, SWITZERLAND

Representation in St. Petersburg:
Nab. Kan. Griboedova, 129, apt. 11
Tel 114-38-62
Tel/Fax....................................... 114-11-60
Telex................................. 621073 SUL SP
Chief Representative: Alexander Frygin
Administrative Assistant: Irina Otoka

Svelen
Serdobolskaya ul., 1 242-29-74
Fax 242-13-85

Tambrands St. Petersburg
Zhelezhnodorozhnyy pr., 20............. 560-13-19
Fax 560-97-14

Tatra Koprivnice
Tverskaya ul., 27/29, rm. 8 272-00-13
Mon-Fri 8:30-17; $; Ger, Czech

Taurus
Ispolkomskaya ul., 9/11 275-32-50
Fax 274-38-95
Mon-Fri 9-18; Rbls, $; Eng

TDV Ford - *See* AUTOMOBILE SALES
Kommuny ul., 16 521-37-20
Fax... 521-85-47

Telemecanique
Gastello ul., 12 291-81-15
Fax... 291-81-17
Mon-Fri 9-17; Rbls, $; Eng, Fr; T-bus 16; Metro Park Pobedy

Teleport St. Petersburg
Yuriya Gagarina pr., 1 567-37-31
Fax... 265-01-02

TELINFO

Telinfo is a wholly-owned subsidiary of
InfoServices International, Inc. NY, USA

TRAVELLER'S
YELLOW
PAGES

THE *TRAVELLER'S*
YELLOW PAGES
FOR
SAINT PETERSBURG
AND
THE CITY MAP OF
SAINT PETERSBURG

Moscow Edition Available October 1993
Baltics Edition Early 1994

✉190000, St. Petersburg, Russia:
Reki Moyki nab., 64 315-64-12
Fax... 312-73-41

Tetra Laval Stock Company
Russian Branch
Obvodnogo kan. nab., 93 a............. 315-22-87
Fax... 314-04-14
Mon-Fri 9-18; Rbls, $

Technoexan
Politekhnicheskaya ul., 26............ 247-93-78
Fax... 247-53-33
Mon-Fri 9:30-18; Rbls, $; Eng

Transnautik
Gapsalskaya ul., 10 251-85-37

Transworld Communications
Please call................................. 112--47-87

United Peleton
Lanskoe shosse, 14, bldg. 3........... 246-62-49
Fax... 242-10-97
Mon-Fri 9:30-18:30; Rbls, $, CC; Eng

UPS - *See* EXPRESS MAIL
Karavannaya ul., 12.................... 312-29-15
Fax... 314-70-37

VA Instruments
Rizhskiy pr., 26.......................... 252-67-59
Fax... 252-10-03
Mon-Fri 9-18; Rbls, $; Eng

Volkswagen
Toreza pr., 40............................. 552-46-64
Fax... 247-89-25
Mon-Sat 10-14, 15-18; Rbls, $; Eng, Ger

Wal-Rus Ltd.
Nekrasova ul., 40/47 273-67-46
Fax... 273-51-92

World Financial and
Trade Center Saint Petersburg
Griboedova kan. nab., 5 312-35-57
Mon-Fri 9-17; Rbls, $; Eng

PETERSBURG VNESHTRANS

International Sea-, Road-, River-, Rail-, Air-
    freight-forwarding
Terminal operations
Bonded warehouses
Custom clearance
Chartering
Luggage forwarding
Freight insurance

Russia, St. Petersburg,
198035 Mezhevoy kanal, 5
251-18-77
251-12-13
251-09-01
251-06-29
251-95-48
114-91-73
259-80-22
259-88-83
Fax: 186-28-83
Telex: 121511 SVT SU

VNESHTRANSAVIA Co. Ltd.

General air cargo forwarding to more than 200
destinations worldwide.
Agencies at all major airports of the CIS.
Fast delivery of transit cargo. Chartered flights.
Bonded warehousing, custom clearance of
distribution International & domestic courier service.

Russia, St. Petersburg,
196210 Pilotov ul., 8,
Pulkovo-2 Airport,
Cargo Terminal
104-34-97
104-37-25
104-37-79
Fax: 104-34-98
Telex: 121262 SVT AP

Forwarders for the Mariinskiy & other St. Petersburg theaters

VNESHTRANSAVTO Co. Ltd.
International & intercity trucking services
Road freight-forwarding
Local transfer & distribution
St. Petersburg-Helsinki weekly service
Bonded warehouse

Russia, St. Petersburg, 192236,
Sophiyskaya ul., 6
166-08-91
268-49-08
251-76-08
Fax: 166-08-91

ACTO-VNESHTRANS Co. Ltd
General Custom-brokers & freight-forwarders.
Specialized custom brokers for surface & air-traffic in
St. Petersburg area. Handling of traffic for "Turn-Key"
construction projects.

Russia, St.Petersburg,
Zaozernaya ul.,4
252-77-01, 294-86-75,
294-80-83
Fax: 252-77-01
Telex:121262 SVTAP

☎ FREIGHT FORWARDING AGENTS, EXPEDITERS
ДОСТАВКА, АГЕНСТВА
SPEDITION
COMMISSIONNAIRES
EXPEDITEURS
EXPEDITÖR
LAIVAKULJETUKSET

See SHIPPING AGENTS

Firms listed here arrange for the shipment of goods by air, truck, rail, and ship. They are often called EXPEDITERS.

AES

Transportation & Distribution

International and CIS Freight Forwarding
Customs Clearance for Air and Surface Cargo
Moscow-St. Petersburg Overnight Service

Contact Moscow Office at: .... (095) 256-45-02
Fax .... (095) 254-28-76

BALTLES

INTERNATIONAL EXPEDITER
GENERAL CUSTOMS
BROKER

Reki Fontanki nab., 118, bldg. 21
Tel 251-32-89
Tel./Fax 251-15-56
Telex .... 621161 BLTSP SU

EuroDonat FREIGHT FORWARDERS AND TRANSPORT

TRUCK, SHIP, RAIL
**Specializing in transport to/from
Russia, Baltic States, CIS,
USA, Canada & Europe
Customs Document Service
Modern Truck Fleet
St. Pb. Warehouse**

Yakornaya ul., 17
Tel .... (812) 224-11-44
Fax .... (812) 224-06-20
Telex .... 121118 DFS SU
Hrs: 9-18, $ & Rubles, English

INFLOT St. Petersburg Ltd.
*The most complete in-port service,
liner & tramp agency
Over 50 years experience
in the port of Saint Petersburg*

Gapsalskaya ul., 10 251-73-26
Director: 251-12-38
Fax: .... (812) 186-15-11
Telex: .... 121505 INF SU

Lenvneshtrans
Mezhevoy kan., 5 251-41-97
Fax 186-28-83
Mon-Fri 8:30-17:15; Rbls; Eng
Marin International Trade and Travel
Mayakovskogo ul., 30/32 273-90-66
Fax 158-40-44
*Mon-Fri 9-17; Rbls, $; Eng, Ger, Fr
Metro Chernyshevskaya*

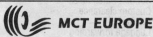 **MCT EUROPE**

FREIGHT FORWARDING & N.V.O.C.C.

Dvinskaya ul., 10, Korp. 3, 5th floor
.... 251-86-62
.... 251-36-51
.... 251-37-51
Fax 251-84-72
Telex .... 121691 MCT SU

Morservice, *Daily 0-24; Rbls, $; Eng*
8-ya Krasnoarmeyskaya ul., 23 251-06-46
Fax 251-86-47
PetersburgVneshTrans -
See ad on previous page
Petrotrans
Bolshoy Sampsonievskiy pr., 63 541-84-95
Shushary, *Mon-Fri 9-17*
Gastello ul., 17, Hotel Mir, rm. 601 108-47-60

SOVMORTRANS
St. Petersburg Branch
*Freight Forwarding & N.V.O.C.C.
Liner Agent for SEA-LAND SERVICE, Inc.
Port Agents
Container Trucking*

In Saint Petersburg
Dvinskaya ul., 8, bldg. 2 252-75-81
Fax 114-41-37
Telex .... 121115 SMTL SU
Mon-Fri 8:30-17; Rbls, $; Eng, Ger, Fr, Sp

St. Petersburg Freight Forwarding Agency
Kavalergardskaya ul., 6 275-89-46
Fax 274-29-66
Mon-Fri 9-12, 13-18; Rbls, $; Eng
Transnautik
Gapsalskaya ul., 10 251-85-37

☎ FUNERALS/UNDERTAKERS
ПОХОРОННЫЕ БЮРО
BESTATTUNGSINSTITUTE
POMPES FUNEBRES, BUREAUX
DES
BEGRAVNINGS BYRÅER
HAUTAUSTOIMISTOT

In case of death outside of a hospital, it is necessary to call a doctor to determine the cause of death. As a rule, the same ambulance which brought the doctor can take the body to the morgue of the "on-duty" hospital, where a pathologist examines the body and perhaps does an autopsy.

Births, deaths, weddings and divorces are registered at the ZAGS. See MARRIAGE BUREAU. *Consulates also usually offer help in the event of a death. See* CONSULATES.

Funeral Parlors & Undertakers
1-ya Sovetskaya ul., 8 279-40-67
Mon-Fri 9-13, 14-18
Funeral Store No. 1 *Caskets, silk flowers*
Dostoevskogo ul., 9/8 314-51-86
Mon-Sat 8-14:30, 15:30-19
Funeral Store No. 4 *Caskets, Silk Flowers*
Tipanova ul., 29 299-79-27
Daily 8-13, 14-19; T-bus 29; Metro Moskovskaya
Marshal, *Gravestones*
Furshtadskaya ul., 43 275-35-30
Mon-Fri 9-21; Rbls
Spetsservice
Voznesenskiy pr., 25, rm. 32 315-50-32
Mon-Fri 9-13, 14-18; Rbls, $; Eng

☎ FURNITURE STORES
МЕБЕЛЬНЫЕ МАГАЗИНЫ
MÖBELGESCHÄFTE
MEUBLES, MAGASINS DE
MÖBELHANDLARE,
MÖBELAFFÄRER
HUONEKALULIIKKEET

Furniture is sold in stores called "Furniture" (Mebel, Мебель). There are many atele called Atele po remontu i izgotovleniyu mebeli (Ателье по ремонту и изготовлению мебели) *that can custom make, repair and restore furniture.*

Alivekt
Lanskoe shosse, 27 246-15-15
Fax 234-90-96
Mon-Sat 10-14, 15-19; Rbls
AP & IT - *See ad below*
Bon Service, *Mon-Sat 10-18*
Bolshoy pr., V.O., 63 217-31-37
Capricorn - *See ad below*
Center-Mebel
Novocherkasskiy pr., 22/15 221-03-88
Mon-Fri 10-14, 15-19; Rbls
Concern Goryachev, *Antique reproduction*
Vereyskaya ul., 39 112-75-96
Fax 315-24-21
Mon-Fri 9-13, 14-18; Rbls, $; Eng, Ital
T-bus 3; Metro Tekhnologicheskiy Institut, Pushkinskaya
Arman
Bolshoy pr., V.O., 83, rm. 71 217-53-26
Mon-Fri 11-18; Rbls

Italian
Home & Office
Furniture

Kitchen • Bedroom • Living Room

Home Accessories

V.O., Kima pr., 28 350-55-48
Hrs: 10-13, 14-19; Clsd Sat, Sun; $, Rbls;
English, Italian

✳ BABYLON
shops

No. 8 The Furniture Store
Watch for Our Grand Opening
Complete Line of Quality Imported Furniture
for Your Home

P.S., Bolshoy pr., 38 232-52-43
Daily 10-14, 15-20; Rbls
Metro Petrogradskaya

capricorn
EXPORT   IMPORT

IMPORTED FURNITURE
WHOLESALE & RETAIL
Varshavskaya ul., 51 296-43-51
Fax 296-43-51
Telex ....121194 RUB SU

Creat
Kazanskaya ul., 49 311-13-01
Mon-Fri 10-18; Rbls, $
Delfin-Market
Yuriya Gagarina pr., 8 264-79-14
Mon-Sat 11-20; Rbls, $; Eng, Ger

DREZDEN
Home furnishings, Russian and imported
Toreza pr., 40 552-47-52
.... 552-28-08
Mon-Sat 10-14, 15-19; Rbls

Hallay
Prosveshcheniya pr., 80, bldg. 2 530-97-76
Mon-Fri 10-20, Sat-Sun 12-19; Rbls, $; Eng, Ger

Home □ Center
Furniture by Euromobil
Let Euromobil, Hilox and other fine
European Manufacturers furnish your home
Sofas, lamps, chairs, tables, coffee tables,
and other fine furnishings
Wet bars
Located in S.E. St. Pb., minutes from city center
Slavy pr., 30 261-15-50
....261-04-02
Fax...................................260-15-81
*Daily 10-20; $, FIM, DM, Rbls; Eng, Finn, Ger
Metro Moskovskaya, then Bus 31, 114, T-bus 29*

Interbalt
Pionerskaya ul., 63 235-66-50
Mon-Sat 10-19; Rbls

Interer   **Interior**
Nauki pr., 30........................... 550-72-73
Mon-Sat 10-18; Rbls

Inturist
Reki Karpovki nab., 27 234-96-49
Fax.................................... 234-09-02
Mon-Fri 8:30-17; Rbls, $

Jupiter-Holding
Tsiolkovskogo ul., 9.................... 251-27-16
Fax.................................... 251-34-00
Mon-Fri 8:15-17; Rbls, $

Kartas
Dibunovskaya ul., 37................... 239-47-28
Mon-Sat 10-19; Rbls

Klen   **Maple**
Nikolskaya pl., 6 114-37-71
Russian furniture; Mon-Sat 10-14, 15-19; Metro Sadovaya
Bolshevikov pr., 33 586-77-97
Fax 586-74-51
Ger, Finn, Czech; Mon-Sat 10-14, 15-19; Rbls, $

Kom-Invest
16-ya Liniya., 17 213-73-46
Fax 119-60-06
Mon-Fri 10-19; Rbls, $

Lenmebeltorg
Gogolya ul., 8 311-56-06
Mon-Fri 9-13:45, 14:30-18; Rbls, $

Lenraummebel
Dimitrova pr., 15....................... 101-43-36
Mon-Fri 11-14, 15-19; Rbls

Market Bridge Ltd.
Nevskiy pr, 82........................... 275-71-51
Fax 275-71-50
See our ad under OFFICE EQUIPMENT

Meandr Company Ltd.
Sofiyskaya ul., 56 106-09-15
Fax 106-09-04
Mon-Fri 9-18; Rbls

Mebel   **Furniture Stores**
• Bolshoy Sampsonievskiy pr., 21 542-49-01
Mon-Sat 10-14, 15-19; Rbls
• Bukharestskaya ul., 74 b 269-76-03
Mon-Fri 10-14, 15-19; Rbls
• Malyy pr., V.O., 35 213-70-89
Mon-Fri 10-14, 15-19
• Moskovskiy pr., 195 293-26-27
Mon-Fri 10-19:30; Rbls
• Olminskogo ul., 8..................... 567-14-38
Mon-Sat 10-19; Rbls

• Pogranichnika Garkavogo ul., 34 144-03-37
Mon-Fri 10-18; Rbls
• Prosveshcheniya pr., 75................. 530-77-69
Mon-Fri 10-19; Rbls
• Shevchenko ul., 17..................... 217-24-66
Mon-Fri 10-19; Rbls
• Sredneokhtinskiy pr., 10 224-29-00
Mon-Fri 10-19; Rbls
• Suvorovskiy pr., 1.................... 277-03-18
Mon-Sat 10-20; Rbls
• Zagorodnyy pr., 24.....................113-35-15
Mon-Sat 10-14, 15-19; Rbls

Mebel po Zakazam
Furniture to Order Showroom
Pestelya ul., 13/15 273-23-12
Mon-Sat 10-14, 15-19; Rbls

Nakhodka
Kustarnyy per., 3...................... 310-00-42
Mon-Fri 10-14, 15-18; Rbls, $; Eng

Nevka
Moskovskiy pr., 4/6,.....................113-53-75
Mon-Sat 9-18; Rbls

Nika, *Furniture shop*
Narodnaya ul., 10...................... 266-31-77
Mon-Fri 10-18; Rbls

Orion
Piskarevskiy pr., 20.................... 541-33-27
Mon-Sat 10-14, 15-19; Rbls

A/O Fund PENATES
High-Quality German Bathroom Fixtures
V.O., Bolshoy pr., 8 213-04-11

Petromebel
Tipanova ul., 18 291-11-59
Daily 10-20; Rbls

Plike
Blagodatnaya ul., 67.................... 298-37-38
Mon-Fri 10-16; Rbls; Ger

Prazdnik   **Holiday**
• Moskovskiy pr., 151 294-63-33
Fax.................................... 264-64-50
• Sveaborgskaya ul., 7.................. 294-05-03
Fax.................................... 264-64-50
Mon-Sat 10-19; Rbls

Russian Furniture
• Furniture Manufacturing & Design
• Office, Apartment & Store Interior Designers
• Interior Designers for Computerland St. Petersburg
• Professional Staff

Nevskiy pr., 82 272-47-82

Samshet
Slavy pr., 2, bldg. 1 260-18-33
Mon-Sat 10-19; Bus 114; Metro Moskovskaya

Soft Furniture Shop
Obvodnogo kan. nab., 121 292-01-66
Mon-Fri 9-18; Rbls

Spika
Mira ul., 25, rm. 19 ....No ☎
Mon-Fri 11-19; Rbls

Tradehouse on Moyka
Reki Moyki nab., 59, 2nd floor 315-86-63
Daily 10-14, 15-19; Rbls; $
Vetas, *Bamboo Furniture, may move*
Lva Tolstogo pl., 6/8 265-17-61
Mon-Sat 9-13, 14-19

☎ **FURS**
MEXA
PELZE
FOURRURES
PÄLSAR
TURKIKSET

See also DEPARTMENTS STORES, FASHION
SALONS and CLOTHING, WOMEN'S.
Fur auctions are held three times per year:
October, January, May or June.

Alisa
Reki Fontanki nab., 23 314-39-14
.... 312-96-10
Mon-Sat 10-18; Rbls
Atele po Poshivu Mekhovykh Izdelyy
Custom Fur Tailors
Rubinshteyna ul., 9 113-23-26
Mon-Fri 10-15, 16-19; Rbls
Commission Store No. 6, *Furs*
Liteynyy pr., 34 273-65-26
Mon-Sat 10-14, 15-19; Rbls
Dom Firmennoy Torgovli
Please Call 352-11-34
Mon-Sat 10-20
Gostinyy Dvor, *Sadovaya Line*
Nevskiy pr., 35, ... 312-41-74
.... 110-54-08
Mon-Sat 10-19; Metro Nevskiy Prospekt

♕ **ЛЕНА**
FINE FURS
ЛЕНА SAINT PETERSBURG

ЛЕНА **FUR SALON**
Vosstaniya ul., 23 273-75-42
1-ya Sovetskaya ul., 12 ... 277-55-79
Nevskiy pr., 50 (Main Store)
☎ 312-40-32
Suvorovskiy pr., 20 (Wholesale)
☎ 271-20-00
ЛЕНА **at HOUSE OF FASHION**
Kamennoostrovskiy pr., 37
☎ 233-85-17
Bolshoy pr., P.S., 29 233-85-17
ЛЕНА **for CHILDREN**
Nevskiy pr., 136 275-39-52

Custom Orders, Design, Exports
Myasnikova ul., 4-16
Tel: 310-23-22   Fax: 310-36-15

Hrs: 10-19, $ & Rubles, English

Mekha Rossii   **Furs of Russia**
Nevskiy pr., 57, next to Nevskij Palace
Mon-Sat 10-20; Rbls, $; Eng

Norka   **Mink**
Zagorodnyy pr., 26 113-32-38
Mon-Sat 11-14, 15-19; Rbls; Metro Dostoevskaya
Na Gorkovskoy
Kamennoostrovskiy pr., 2 233-51-53
Mon-Sat 11-14, 15-20
Olen   **Deer**
Liteynyy pr., 34 273-65-26
Mon-Fri 10-14, 15-19
Pushnoy Auktsion   **Fur Auction**
Moskovskiy pr., 98 298-45-43
Fax 293-34-59
Auctions held in January, June and October.
Mon-Fri 8:30-18:30; Rbls, $; Eng

Rot-Front Furs

Gertsena ul., 34 311-73-57
.... 114-81-05
Fax 114-05-73
Mon-Sat 10-19; Rbls, $

Russian Fur
Bolshoy pr., P.S., 82 232-02-83
Mon-Sat 10-14, 15-19; Rbls
Salon
Gertsena ul., 34 311-73-75
Mon-Sat 10-14, 15-19; Rbls, $; Eng
Salon No. 1
Suvorovskiy pr., 30 271-20-92
Mon-Sat 10-14, 15-19; $; Eng
Velona
Nevskiy pr., 139 277-56-33
Mon-Sat 11-15, 16-19; Rbls

☎ **GARDENS**
САДЫ
PARKS
JARDINS
TRÄDGÅRDAR
PUISTOT

Botanical Garden of
The Academy of Sciences
Botanicheskiy Sad
Professora Popova ul., 2 234-17-64
Five million plants from around the world
Mon-Thu, Sat-Sun 11-16; Rbls; Eng, Ger, Fr; G-9
* Summer Garden and Palace of Peter I
Letniy Sad i Dvorets Petra I
Letniy Sad 314-04-56
.... 314-03-74
The first summer estate laid out from 1704-1714 and
1710-1714, Architect: Trezzini, House: Schülter
Mon, Wed-Sun 11-18; Rbls; Bus 14; G-6,7
Garden of the Anichkov Palace
Sad Anichkova Dvortsa
Nevskiy pr., 39 314-72-81
This small garden is next to the famous Anichkov Palace
built in 1741-1750; Metro Nevskiy Prospect; G-5
Tavricheskiy Garden
Tavricheskiy Sad
Saltykova-Shchedrina ul., 50 272-60-44
Constructed in 1783-1789 next to the Tavricheskiy
Palace. Since the 19th century this has been a favorite
children's park. Metro Chernyshevskaya; I-7

GAS SERVICE
ГАЗ, СЛУЖБА
STADTGAS
GAZ, SERVICE
GAS SERVICE
KAASU

GAS EMERGENCY - CALL 04

For initiation and termination of service, billing information, installation and service of gas lines, call your district.

OPEN 24 HOURS

Dzerzhinskiy District
Liteynyy pr., 39 277-03-82
Kalininskiy District
Please call 592-74-62
Krasnoselskiy District
Veteranov pr., 154 130-36-51
Leninskiy District
5-ya Krasnoarmeyskaya ul., 12 292-25-39
Moskovskiy District
Sveaborgskaya ul., 8 294-84-36
Nevskiy District
Obukhovskoy Oborony pr., 137 265-12-24
Oktyabrskiy District
Soyuza Pechatnikov ul., 10 311-25-39
Petrogradskiy District
Bolshaya Pushkarskaya ul., 40 233-13-82
Primorskiy District
Shkolnaya ul., 68 239-28-60
Vyborgskiy District
Novorossiyskaya ul., 46, bldg. 2 550-08-65

 GAS STATIONS/PETROL
АВТОЗАПРАВОЧНЫЕ СТАНЦИИ
TANKSTELLEN
ESSENCE, POSTE A
BENSINSTATIONER
HUOLTOASEMAT

The petrol/gasoline situation improved dramatically with the opening of the 5 Neste Petro Service stations in St. Petersburg. Also, note those gas stations carrying Au-93, A-95 and A-98 (unleaded gas/petrol) and diesel fuel. Gas stations are self-service. Pay before you pump.

Gas Station No. 4, *A-95*
Teatralnaya pl. 312-21-35
Daily 9-22; E-5
Gas Station No. 6, *Au-93, A-95*
Aleksandrovskiy park, 6 232-45-23
Daily 8-15, 17-2; Rbls; F-8
Gas Station No. 9, *A-95*
Vitebskiy pr., 17, Bldg. 2 298-39-10
Daily 0-24; Rbls
Gas Station No. 10, *A-95*
Reki Fontanki nab., 156 251-38-71
Daily 7-22; Rbls; D-4
Gas Station No. 18, *Au-93,*
Tavricheskiy per., 18 273-49-62
Daily 7-23; Rbls; J-7
Gas Station No. 22, *Au-93*
Vyborgskoe shosse, 4 553-45-54
Daily 0-9, 10-24; Rbls

Gas Station No. 30, *Au-93, A-95*
Primorskiy pr., 56 239-09-45
Daily 0-13, 14-24, Rbls; B-11
Gas Station No. 32, *A-95*
Nepokorennykh pr., 15 534-17-16
Daily 0-24; Rbls
Gas Station No. 43
Sovetskiy per., 37 262-44-60
Daily 0-24; Rbls
Gas Station No. 52, *A-95*
Polyustrovskiy pr., 73 245-23-51
Daily 0-2, 6-24; Rbls; I-10
Gas Station No. 58, *Daily 8:30-20:30; Rbls*
Pilotov ul., 6 a 122-96-00
Gas Station No. 69, *A-95*
Narodnogo Opolcheniya pr., 16 254-37-48
Daily 0-24; Rbls
Gas Station No. 81, *A-95*
Suzdalskiy pr., 12 531-89-95
Daily 0-24; Rbls
Gas Station No. 85, *A-95*
Moskovskoe shosse, 35 293-24-19
Daily 0-9:30, 10:30-24; Rbls
Gas Station No. 87
Yuriya Gagarina pr., 32 293-72-10
Daily 0-24; Rbls
Gas Station No. 92
Pulkovskoe shosse, 27 293-47-80
Daily 0-24; Rbls
Gas Station No. 94, *Au-93*
Rustaveli ul., 40 249-42-57
Daily 0-24; Coupons only
Gas Station No. 103
Ekaterininskiy per., 11 225-70-60
Daily 0-24; Rbls

NESTE
Petro Service

GASOLINE and LUBRICANTS
ACCESSORIES • MINI-SHOP

24 HOURS A DAY
MAJOR CREDIT CARDS ACCEPTED
Gasoline: 76, 93, lead-free 95 E & 98E oct. for cars equipped with catalytic converters, automotive oils, fluids & accessories. Cigarettes, soft drinks, food & travel needs

5 LOCATIONS IN ST. PETERSBURG

STATION NESTE, on road to Pulkovo airport
Pulkovskoe shosse, 44a 123-34-23
Car Wash, GM-Service, Road Service, Tow-Truck, Diesel Fuel, First-Aid and Cafe
STATION No. 3, Near Moscow Gate
Moskovskiy pr., 100 298-45-34
Station No. 29, on Vasilevskiy Island; C-6
Malyy pr., V.O., 68a 355-08-79
STATION No. 45,
Avangardnaya ul., 36 135-58-67
STATION No. 66, B-11
Savushkina ul., 87 239-04-15
MAIN OFFICE: 295-54-49, FAX 295-81-72

Sovinteravto service

Selling Gas Coupons
to Foreigners

Visit Our Shop on Gogolya ul. 19,
near the Astoria Hotel

Gogolya ul., 19 315-97-58
Malodetskoselskiy pr., 26 ... 292-77-18
Moskovskiy pr., 73 296-57-90

Daily, 9 a.m. - 8 p.m.; Eng; $ & Rbls

IN SUBURBS

Gas Station No. 19, *Au-93, A-95*
Primorskoe shosse, 18 km., Olgino, Sestroretsk
.... 238-30-49
Daily 0-24; Rbls
Station No. 59, *Au-93, A-95*
Leningradskoe shosse, 45, Strelna
.... 420-11-04
Daily 0-24; Rbls
Gas Station No. 100, *Au-93, A-95*
Dachnaya ul., Gorelovo, Krasnoe Selo
.... 132-14-22
Daily 0-24; Rbls

☎ **GAS-PROPANE**

See PROPANE

☎ **GIFT SHOPS, SOUVENIRS**
ПОДАРКИ
GESCHENKARTIKEL
CADEAUX
SOUVENIRER, PRESENTAFFÄRER
MATKAMUISTOT

See also CRYSTAL AND PORCELAIN,
ART GALLERIES, ARTS & HANDICRAFTS,
FLOWERS, *and* ALCOHOL

It is customary to bring a small gift or flowers when you go visiting. Gifts are sold in special shops (Podarki, Подарки). Worth a visit, these stores carry everything from crystal and jewelry to toiletries. See ETIQUETTE.

In summer, there are many souvenir tables set up at the entrance to Peter and Paul Fortress and other tourist spots as well as along Nevskiy Prospekt opposite the Grand Hotel Europe.

Adonis
Dumskaya ul., 3 312-51-48
Mon-Sat 10-14, 15-19; Rbls; Eng
Babush
Lenina pl., 5, at the Finlyandskiy Station
.... 542-27-36
Mon-Fri 9:30-18:30; Rbls, $
Babylon - *See our ad on this page.*
P.S., Bolshoy pr., 65 232-04-66
Beriozka
Morskaya nab., 15 355-18-75
Daily 9-20; $

✳ BABYLON
shops

No. 7 The Gift Shop
Gifts that Last
Artificial Flowers, Jewelry and Perfumes
Watches for Men & Women
P.S., Bolshoy pr., 65 232-04-66
Daily 10-14, 15-20; Rbls
Metro Petrogradskaya

Connect
Zverinskaya ul., 12 232-56-22
Daily 10-18:30; Rbls; Eng
Decorative Arts Center
Toreza pr., 98, bldg. 1 553-98-50
Mon-Fri 9-17:30; Rbls; T-bus 10
Gera, *Porcelain, flowers, spirits. Open 24 hrs*
Bolshaya Konyushennaya ul., 1 315-74-90
Daily 0-15, 16-24; Rbls, $
Gildiya Masterov   **Master's Guild**
Nevskiy pr., 82 279-09-79
Daily 11-19; Rbls; Eng
Khudozhestvennyy Salon   **Artist's Salon**
Nevskiy pr., 45 311-21-96
Mon-Sat 10-14, 15-19; Rbls; Eng
Kollektsioner, *Will probably move*   **Collector**
Ligovskiy pr., 61 164-82-26
Mon-Sat 11-19; Rbls; Eng, Ger
Maska   **Mask**
Nevskiy pr., 13 311-03-12
Mon-Sat 10-14, 15-19; Rbls
Nasledie, *One of the best*   **Heritage**
Nevskiy pr., 116 279-50-67
Daily 10-14, 15-19; Rbls, $; Eng, Ger
Podarki   **Gifts**
• Bolshoy pr., P.S., 51 232-20-92
Mon-Sat 10-14, 15-19; Rbls; Eng
• Kosygina pr., 26 520-73-36
Mon-Sat 10-14, 15-19; Bus 174; Metro Ladozhskaya
• Nevskiy pr., 54 314-18-01
Daily 11-14, 15-19; Rbls
Polyarnaya Zvezda   **Pole Star**
Nevskiy pr., 158 277-09-80
Mon-Fri 10-14, 15-19; Rbls
Rozhdestvo   **Christmas**
Toreza pr., 43 247-09-45
Daily 10-14, 15-19; Rbls
Rossia   **Russia**
Bolshaya Konyushennaya ul., 5 315-29-70
Mon-Sat 10-19; Rbls
The Russian Arts
Saltykova-Shchedrina ul., 53 275-69-68
Mon-Sat 11-14, 15-20; Rbls
Russkiy Dom   **The Russian House**
Chaykovskogo ul., 65 275-15-65
Daily 9-19; Rbls, $; Eng, Ger, Fr
Serebryanye Ryady   **Silver Rows**
Dumskaya ul., 1 312-95-45
Fax 314-98-95
Mon-Sat 10-13, 14-20; Rbls, $; Eng
Suveniry   **Souvenirs**
Nevskiy pr., 92 279-42-79
Mon-Sat 10-14, 15-19; Rbls; Eng
Voski
Chaykovskogo ul., 36 275-71-47
Mon-Sat 10-14, 15-19; Rbls

Yubiley   Jubilee
Sverdlovskaya nab., 60 224-25-98
Mon-Sat 10-20; Rbls, $

☎ GOODWILL GAMES
ИГРЫ ДОБРОЙ ВОЛИ
SPIELE DES GUTEN WILLENS
LES JEUX DE BONNE VOLONTÉ
GODVILJANS SPEL
HYVÄN TAHDON KISAT

The St. Petersburg Organizing Committee of the 1994 Goodwill Games has selected The *Traveller's* Yellow Pages and Handbook for Saint Petersburg *to be the* Official Visitor's Directory for the 1994 Goodwill Games. The *Traveller's* Yellow Pages City Map, St. Petersburg *has been selected as the* Official Visitor's Map.

Uniting The World Best

1994 Goodwill Games
July 23 — August 7

For 16 days in the summer of 1994, St. Petersburg, Russia will host the 1994 Goodwill Games, featuring approximately 2,500 athletes from more than 50 countries competing in 24 sports. This international, multi-sport competition will take place in venues throughout historic St. Petersburg

For more information, contact the St. Petersburg Organizing Committee at
Tel 233-24-27
Bolshaya Monetnaya, 19
St. Petersburg, 197061
Russia

For further information about the 1994 Goodwill Games in St. Petersburg call:

In USA .... (404) 827-34-00
Fax .... (404) 827-13-94

☎ GOLF
ГОЛЬФ
GOLF
GOLF
GOLF
GOLF

Please send information to Telinfo if you have any additional information about golf in the St. Petersburg area.

St. Petersburg Golf Association
Millionnaya ul., 22 226-24-54
Fax 239-31-23

☎ GOVERNMENT, RUSSIAN
ПРАВИТЕЛЬСТВО РОССИИ
REGIERUNG, RUßLAND
GOUVERNEMENT
REGERING
KAUPUNGINNEUVOSTO

These ministries have offices in St. Petersburg. For a complete list of ministries, see The Traveller's Yellow Pages *for Moscow 1993/94.*

For government offices in St. Petersburg, see ST. PETERSBURG CITY COUNCIL, *and* ST. PETERSBURG MAYOR'S OFFICE.

Military Commandant's Office
Upravlenie Komendanta Sankt-Peterburga
Sadovaya ul., 3/5 311-81-04
Ministry of Culture and Tourism
Ministerstvo Kultury i Turizma
Griboedova kan. nab., 107 314-82-34
Ministry of External Economic Relations
Ministerstvo Vneshneekonomicheskikh Svyazey
Moskovskiy pr., 98 298-43-44
Fax 298-85-14
Ministry of Foreign Affairs
Ministerstvo Inostrannykh Del
Kutuzova nab., 34 272-00-76
Ministry of Internal Affairs
Ministerstvo Vnutrennikh Del
Liteynyy pr., 4 311-18-51
Ministry of Security
Ministerstvo Bezopasnosti
Liteynyy pr., 4 278-71-10
Procurator-General of the Russian Federation   *Generalnyy Prokuror RF*
Yakubovicha ul., 4 312-84-69
State Committee for Antimonopoly Policy and the Support of New Economic Structures
Gosudarstvennyy Komitet po Antimonopolnoy Politike i Podderzhke Novykh Ekonomicheskikh Struktur
Kazanskaya ul., 36 314-79-14
Fax 319-90-57
State Committee for Conversion Attached to the Presidium of the Russian Federation
Gosudarstvennyy Komitet po Konversii pri Prezidiume RF
Smolnyy 278-12-48
State Committee for Statistics
Gosudarstvennyy Komitet po Statistike
Professora Popova ul., 39 230-75-20

State Customs Committee
   Gosudarstvennyy Tamozhennyy Komitet
   Furmanova ul., 1 273-16-19
   Fax 275-31-54
State Tax Inspectorate
   Gosudarstvennaya Nalogovaya Inspektsiya
   Liteynyy pr., 53 272-01-88

☎ GRILL BARS

See RESTAURANTS

☎ GROCERY STORES

See FOOD STORES

☎ GYMS
   СПОРТИВНЫЕ ЗАЛЫ
   TURNHALLEN
   GYMS
   GYM, TRÄNINGS LOKAL
   LIIKUNTASALIT

See also SPORTS FACILITIES *and* HEALTH CLUBS
Dinamo
   Dinamo pr., 44 235-29-44
      Daily 6-24; Rbls
Elektrosila Sports Club
                  Sportivnyy Klub Elektrosila
   Moskovskiy pr., 156 297-17-44
      Daily 9-22; Rbls
Sport Center   *Sportivnyy Tsentr*
   Vyborgskoe shosse, 34 553-32-03
      Daily 8-23; Rbls
Yubileynyy Sports Palace
                  Dvorets Sporta Yubileynyy
   Dobrolyubova pr., 19 238-41-22
      Daily; Rbls; Trolleybus 1
Zenit Sport Palace   *Dvorets Sporta Zenit*
   Butlerova ul., 9 534-86-55
      Daily 8-23; Rbls
Winter Stadium   *Zimniy Stadion*
   Manezhnaya pl., 2 315-57-10
   Fax 312-40-46
      Mon-Fri 9-18; Rbls, $

☎ HABERDASHERY
   ГАЛАНТЕРЕЯ
   KURZWARENGESCHÄFTE
   MERCERIE
   ASSESSOARER, KLÄDER
   LYHYTTÄVARALIIKKEET

At the so-called HABERDASHERY *shops,*
(Galantereya, Галантерея), *you can buy
personal accessories, such as neckties and
belts, needles and thread, bags, and often
cosmetics, perfumes and toiletries. You
also can buy these personal accessories at*
DEPARTMENT STORES *and* COMMERCIAL SHOPS.
You can buy neckties at Necktie shops,
called (Galstuki, Галстуки). *See also*
COSMETICS.

Galantereya	Haberdashery Store
	Галантерея

• Babushkina ul., 9 265-00-40
      Mon-Sat 10-14, 15-19; Rbls
• Bolshoy pr., P.S. 28 232-30-49
      Mon-Sat 10-14, 15-19; Rbls

• Lanskoe shosse, 65 246-38-25
      Mon-Sat 10-14, 15-19; Rbls
• Moskovskiy pr., 134 298-94-28
      Mon-Sat 10-14, 15-19; Rbls
• Nevskiy pr., 141 277-15-89
      Mon-Sat 10-14, 15-19; Rbls
• Obukhovskoy Oborony pr., 227 262-40-17
      Mon-Sat 10-14, 15-19; Rbls
• Suvorovskiy pr., 56 274-82-32
      Mon-Sat 10-14, 15-19; Rbls
• Zagorodnyy pr., 6 315-88-37
      Daily 9-14, 15-19; Rbls
Piero Guidi in Russia
   Nevskiy pr., 54, Tel/Fax 314-25-38
      Mon-Sat 11-14, 15-20; $; Eng, Ital
Sphinx
   Nekrasova ul., 38 272-21-34
      Mon-Sat 11-14, 15-19; Rbls

☎ HAIRCUTTING SALONS
   ПАРИКМАХЕРСКИЕ
   FRISEURSALONS
   COUPE DE CHEVEUX
   HÅRKLIPPNING
   HIUSTENLEIKKAUS

*There are 100's of haircutting salons in
St. Petersburg called (Parikmakherskie,
Парикмахерские) for women (zhenshchin,
женщин) and men (muzhchin, мужчин).
Most large hotels, listed below, also have
haircutting salons where the staff may
speak English. There are a growing number
of private shops. Debut using Wella
products is one of the best for women and
Paris one of the best for men.*

IN HOTELS

Astoria
   Gertsena ul., 39 210-58-35
      Daily 8-20; $; Eng
Beauty Salon in the Hotel Pulkovskaya
   Pobedy pl., 1 264-51-15
      Daily 8-20; Rbls, $; Eng, Ger
Grand Hotel Europe
   Mikhaylovskaya ul., 1/7 113-80-75
      Daily 9-21; $; Eng, Ger
Hotel Oktyabrskaya Hair Salon No. 310
   Ligovskiy pr., 10 277-62-93
      Daily 8-21; Rbls

Hotelship Peterhof ★★★★
Nab. Makarova, near the Tuchkov Bridge
.... 213-63-21
Mon-Sat 10-20

Moskva
   Aleksandra Nevskogo pl., 2 274-20-97
      Daily 8-20; Rbls, $; Eng, Ger
Pribaltiyskaya
   Korablestroiteley ul., 14 356-28-02
   Fax 356-00-94
      Daily 8-21; Rbls, $; Eng-

HAIRDRESSERS/BEAUTY SALONS
FOR WOMEN

Aleksandra
   Bolshoy pr., P.S. 53 233-29-23
      Daily 8-21; Rbls

Barber Shop No. 108
Gertsena ul., 25 314-75-21
Daily 9-21; Rbls

Beauty Salon No. 35
Ligovskiy pr., 63 164-55-39
Daily 8-20; Rbls

Blondy
Kamennoostrovskiy pr., 64 234-04-38
Fax: 234-92-05
Mon-Sat 10-22; Rbls; Eng

Chao-Chao
Reki Fontanki nab., 5 314-00-80
Mon-Sat 10-19; Rbls, $; Eng; Tram 5

Debut, *using Wella products*
Nevskiy pr., 54 312-30-26
Mon-Sat 9-21; $, CC; Eng, Ger

Fotiniya
Professora Popova ul., 47 234-67-64
Mon-Sat 9-21; Rbls; Eng; Bus 25; Metro Petrogradskaya

Gloria
• Dekabristov ul., 32/2 312-38-07
Daily 10-20; Rbls
• Nevskiy pr., 168 277-41-09
Mon-Sat 8-20; Rbls

Parikmakherskaya   Hair Salon
• Babushkina ul., 131 267-33-40
Daily 7:30-21; Rbls
• Bolshoy Sampsonievskiy pr., 92 245-24-03
Mon-Sat 8-20; Rbls
• Nevskiy pr., 29 314-24-35
Mon-Sat 10-20; Rbls
• Nevskiy pr., 129 277-19-77
Mon-Sat 9-20; Rbls

Kalamis
Kamennoostrovskiy pr., 19 233-40-20
Mon-Fri 8-21; Rbls; Eng; Metro Petrogradskaya

Kameya Women's Salon
Zagorodnyy pr., 40 113-56-48
Daily 7:30-10; Rbls; Eng

Kliviya
Leninskiy pr., 130 254-38-23
Mon-Sat 10-14, 15-19

Kseniya
Bolshoy pr., P.S., 22/24 235-28-84
Mon-Sat 7:30-22; Rbls

Lucien in Dom Byta
Lermontovskiy pr., 1/44 114-29-81
Mon-Sat 8-21; Rbls

Lux-Service
Nevskiy pr., 22 311-40-34
Mon-Sat 8:30-21; Rbls; Eng; Bus 3; Metro Nevskiy Prospekt

Yuli-Anna
Malyy pr. V.O., 49 355-83-81
Mon-Sat 9-22; Rbls; Eng

MEN'S BARBERS

Alesha, Men's Barbers
Vosstaniya ul., 20 273-13-94
Mon-Sat 8-21; Rbls

Barber Shop No. 108
Gertsena ul., 25 314-75-21
Daily 9-21; Rbls

Debut, *using Wella products*
Nevskiy pr., 54 312-30-26
Mon-Sat 9-21, $; Eng, Ger

Men's Barbers, *Mon-Sat 7:30-21; Rbls*
Botkinskaya ul., 1 a 542-38-08

Paris
Kamennoostrovskiy pr., 9 232-41-46
Bus 1; Metro Gorkovskaya

CHILDREN'S HAIRDRESSERS/BARBERS

Men's and Children's Barbers
Ligovskiy pr., 91 164-15-11
Mon-Sat 7:30-20; Rbls

Monados
Myasnaya ul., 19 114-84-49
Mon-Sat 10-22; Rbls, $; Eng

Nadezhda
Liteynyy pr., 61 273-50-43
Mon-Sat 7:30-21; Rbls

Paris
Bolshoy pr., P.S., 10 232-18-88
Mon-Sat 7:30-21; Rbls

Saturn
Liteynyy pr., 43 273-29-71
Mon-Sat 7:30-22; Rbls

Sochi
Kazanskaya ul., 82 221-39-03
Mon-Sat 9-20; Rbls

Studio "M"
Toreza pr., 30 552-40-57
Mon-Fri 9-14, 15-21; Rbls

HAIRDRESSERS-UNISEX
MEN, WOMEN & CHILDREN

Smena, *Mon-Sat 8-20; Rbls*
Izmaylovskiy pr., 22 251-32-09

Yunona, *Daily 8-21; Rbls*
Chkalovskiy pr., 32 235-96-06

Yurtas, *Mon-Sat 8:30-20; Rbls*
Veteranov pr., 16 156-66-61

☎ **HARD CURRENCY SHOPS**

See INTERNATIONAL SHOPS

☎ **HARDWARE**
СКОБЯНЫЕ ТОВАРЫ
EISENWAREN
QUINCAILLERIES
JÄRNHANDLARE
RAUTATAVARAT

See also BUILDING SUPPLIES *and*
PAINT SUPPLIES

Building Supplies
Moskovskiy pr., 4 310-06-19
Mon-Sat 9-13, 14-18; Rbls

Hardware Store No. 158
Ligovskiy pr., 161 166-13-47
Mon-Sat 10-19; Rbls

✳ **BABYLON**
SUPER
Mon-Sat 10-21 Sun 12-20
Exchange office

Keep your house sparkling with supplies from our
housewares department. Brooms, detergents, sponges, paper
towels, wax and window cleaners, buckets, scrub brushes and
plastic bags. Proctor and Gamble cleaning products.

P.S., Maly pr., 54 & 56 230-80-96
In the former Okean store off Bolshoy Prospekt

Home □ Center
The Complete Hardware Source
Wide selection of tools including Ryobi electric hand tools, Stanley and Ironside tools including chisels, levels, pliers, cutters, planes, screwdrivers, hammers, axes, hex wrenches, socket wrenches, and more
Items For The Dacha,
Mc Culloch chain saws, pruning shears, rakes, shovels, and portable gas stoves and wood stoves, a bocci set and English darts to play.
Hardware For The Home
from door steps and heavy duty locks to nails, screws, nuts, and bolts.
Large Electrical Supply and Parts Dept

Plumbing Supplies and Fixtures
PFC pipe and fittings

Complete Paint Department
Custom-Mixed Paints
Located in S.E. St. Pb., minutes from city center
Slavy pr., 30 261-15-50
......................................261-04-02
Fax..................................260-15-81
Daily 10-20; $, FIM, DM, Rbls; Eng, Finn, Ger
Metro Moskovskaya, then Bus 31, 114, T-bus 29

Khozyaystvennye Tovary, *Mon-Sat 10-19*
• Yakornaya ul., 1 224-38-03
• Yakornaya ul., 2 224-34-86
Renlund - *See Building Supplies*

☎ HATS
ГОЛОВНЫЕ УБОРЫ
HÜTE
CHAPEAUX
HATTAR
HATUT

You can buy hats at DEPARTMENT STORES *and* FASHION SALONS *or specialized shops called* Atelier of Headgear (Atele golovnykh uborov, Ателье головных уборов), *where you can buy ready-made hats or have a hat made to order.*

Atele Golovnykh Uborov   Hatmakers
• Nevskiy pr., 98...............................279-33-30
Mon-Fri 11-15, 16-19; Rbls; Metro Ploshchad Vosstaniya
• Nevskiy pr., 107.............................275-39-68
Mon-Fri 11-20; Rbls
• Moskovskiy pr., 20 292-78-20
Mon-Fri 10-19; Rbls
Dom Mod   Fashion House
Marshala Tukhachevskogo ul., 22......225-18-18
Mon-Sat 11-15, 16-20; Tram 14

☎ HEALTH CARE
ЗДРАВООХРАНЕНИЕ
GESUNDHEITSWESEN
SOINS MEDICAUX
SJUKVÅRD
TERVEYDENHOITO

See EMERGENCY MEDICAL CARE, MEDICAL CARE AND CONSULTATIONS, HOSPITALS, OPTICIANS,

HEARING AIDS, DENTISTS, WATER, PHARMACIES, *and* WHAT-TO-BRING

SOME HEALTH INFORMATION
Body Temperature:
98.6 = 36.6° C   Normal
102   = 39° C   High

Normal Pulse Rate: **60 - 90 per minute**

WHAT TO BRING *lists important items you should be sure to have in your first aid kit. Be sure to have your diphtheria and other standard vaccinations up-to-date.*

☎ HEALTH CLUBS
ШЕЙПИНГ, ЗДОРОВЬЯ ЦЕНТРЫ
FITNESSCENTER
SPORT FITNESS, CLUB DE
HÄLSOKLUBBAR
LIIKUNTAKESKUKSET

Health Club at the Hotel Astoria
Gertsena ul., 39............................311-42-06
Sauna, Gym, Solarium, Massage
Opening September 1993
Intersport
Moiseenko ul., 22/17......................271-36-21
Daily 8-23; Rbls, $; Eng
Lawn Tennis Sports Center
Metallistov pr., 116........................540-18-86
Mon-Sat 9-21; Rbls; Tram 14; Metro Ploshchad Lenina
Olympia Shaping Center
6-ya Krasnoarmeyskaya ul., 14.......110-18-87
Fax..272-63-57
Mon-Sat 9-21; Rbls
Shaping Federation of Russia
Kazanskaya ul., 36 315-94-64
Sport Class Cooperative
Kamennoostrovskiy pr., 26/28........232-75-81
Daily 9-22
Sportservice Club at the Hotel Rossiya
Chernyshevskogo pl., 11 296-72-21
Mon-Sat 10-21; Rbls, $
The V. I. Alekseev Center
Raevskogo pr., 16..........................552-39-36
Fax..552-39-51
Daily 18-23; Rbls
Tonus, *Daily 9-24; Rbls*
Dinamo pr., 44, rm. 3.....................235-04-49
World Class, *Exercise and bodybuilding*
Kamennoostrovskiy pr., 26/28........232-75-81
Daily 9-22; Rbls, $; Eng, Swed; Metro Petrogradskaya; F-8
World Class at the Grand Hotel Europe
Mikhaylovskaya ul., 1/7 113-80-66
Fitness Center, Work-out Rooms, Sauna, Massage,
Solarium, Nike Sports Apparel, Mon-Fri 7-22,
Sat-Sun 9-22; $; Eng; Metro Nevskiy Prospekt; G-6

World Class ®
Fitness Center
At The Hotel Olympia

Sauna, Pool, Gym, Solarium, Massage
Morskoy Slavy pl. 119-68-00
Daily 14-22; $, CC; Eng, Swe
A Swedish-Russian Firm, F-5

☎ HEALTH RESORTS/SPA
КУРОРТЫ
KURORTE
STATIONS CLIMATIQUES
HÄLSOHEM
KYLPYLÄT

BELYE NOCHI
БЕЛЫЕ НОЧИ
HEALTH RESORT AND SPA
A most elegant health resort
nestled in a tranquil pine forest
on Gulf of Finland near Saint Petersburg.
For health therapy, exercise & recreation
Facilities include 75 ft. swimming pool, universal
exercise room, saunas, dry & water massage,
mineral water baths, mud therapy, tennis, bicycles,
row boats, hiking paths, volleyball & badminton,
solarium on beach.

Ideal for International Professional & Business
Conferences, 130 Rooms
Singles to 4 room luxury suites
38 km on St. Pb. - Vyborg road
PRIMORSKOE SHOSSE, 38 KM
Secretary............................ 237-31-93
24-Hour Phone: 237-21-38
Fax...................................... 237-36-32
Telex.................. 121104 SANAT SU
Open 24 hours/day, $ & Rubles, English, Finnish

Dyuny Health Spa
Primorskiy pr., 38 km, Sestroretsk 237-44-38

☎ HEARING AIDS
СЛУХОВЫЕ АППАРАТЫ
HÖRGERÄTE
APPAREILS, ACOUSTIQUES
HÖRSEL HJÄLP
KUULOLAITTEET

Medtekhnika
• 15-ya Liniya, 32............................ 213-06-09
   Mon-Tue, Thu-Fri 13-20; Rbls
• Svetlanovskaya pl., 35 552-21-92
   Mon-Fri 8:30-12:30, 13-17; Rbls
Slukh, *Mon-Fri 12-17; Rbls*
Galernaya ul., 55............................ 210-94-65

☎ HISTORY OF
ST. PETERSBURG
ИСТОРИЯ С.-ПЕТЕРБУРГА
GESCHICHTE SANKT PETERSBURG
HISTOIRE DE ST. PETERSBOURG
HISTORIA I ST. PETERSBURG
HISTORIA PIETARI

1703	Founding of St. Petersburg May 16- foundation stone laid for Peter & Paul Fortress
1712	St. Petersburg declared capital of Russian Empire
1725	Death of Peter the Great

1725-1727	Reign of Catherine I
1727-1730	Reign of Peter II
1730-1740	Reign of Anna Ioanovna
1740-1741	Reign of Ivan VI
1741-1761	Reign of Elizabeth I
1761-1762	Reign of Peter III
1762-1796	Reign of Catherine II
1764	Hermitage Museum established
1796-1801	Reign of Paul I
1801-1825	Reign of Alexander I
1825 December 14	Decembrist's Uprising
1825-1855	Reign of Nicholas I
1855-1881	Reign of Alexander II
1881-1894	Reign of Alexander III
1894-1917	Reign of Nicholas II
1898	Russian Museum opened
1914	St. Petersburg renamed Petrograd
1917	February Revolution, Nicholas abdicates
1917	October Bolsheviks seize power
1918	Moscow becomes the capital
1924 January 27	Petrograd renamed Leningrad
1941-1944	900 Day Siege of Leningrad
1991	Leningrad renamed St. Petersburg

☎ HOLIDAYS AND VACATIONS
ПРАЗДНИКИ
FEIERTAGE
FETES
HÖGTIDER
VAPAAPÄIVÄT

• **Holidays** *are in considerable flux. Note,
that if a holiday falls on Thursday, then
Friday and Saturday may also be holidays.
If a holiday falls on Saturday or Sunday,
then Monday will be a holiday.*

1 Jan	New Year's Day
7 Jan	Russian Orthodox Christmas
8 March	International Women's Day
March/April	Russian Orthodox Easter (Paskha)
1 & 2 May	Day of Spring and Labor
9 May	Victory (1945) Day
12 June	Independence Day for Russia
7 & 8 Nov	Holiday, no new name yet.

• **Other Special Days.** *There are some
other special days in Russia. January 18 is
the anniversary of Breaking the Blockade of
Leningrad in 1943. January 27 is the
anniversary of the complete liberation of
Leningrad in 1944. February 23 is Soviet
Army Day which is the day of men. Women
traditionally give men small gifts on this
day. The favor is returned on International
Women's Day which is an official holiday.
The last Sunday in May is St. Petersburg
Day.*

• **School & University Vacation.** *Schools
start September 1 and finish May 31 with a
week vacation in November, two weeks in
January at the New Year and one week in
March.*

Universities usually start the fall semester about September 1 and classes end the 20th of December, followed by examinations in January. Winter break is from the 25th of January to 8th of February. Spring semester starts on the second week of February. Classes the end of May followed by exams until about the 25th of June.

• **Vacation.** Most workers are entitled to 24 days of paid vacation and most people take their vacation in the summer at the dacha. While the 1st of May holiday is the traditional day for opening dachas, the November 7th holiday is already too cold to go to the dacha.

☎ HONEY
МЕД
HONIG
MIEL
HONUNG
HUNAJA

Honey from Altay region in Siberia is delicious. Look for Med Altay, (Мед Алтай).

Dary Lesa　　　　**Gifts of the Forest**
Poltavskaya ul., 4.......................... 279-42-30
Mon-Sat 9-13, 14-18; Rbls
Pchelovodstvo　　　　**The Beekeeper**
Liteynyy pr., 46............................. 273-70-74

☎ HORSEBACK RIDING
ЛОШАДИ, КАТАНИЕ
REITEN
EQUITATION
RIDNING
RATSASTUS

In summer, horseback and carriage rides are also available on Palace Square in front of the Hermitage.

Park Babushkina　　　**Babushkin Park**
Obukhovskoy Oborony pr., 149...... 560-01-57
Daily 10-20; Metro Lomonosovskaya
Campsite at the Olgino Motel
Primorskiy pr., 18 km 238-31-32
Tue-Sun 10-13, 15-19; Rbls, $
Kirov Stadium
Morskoy pr., 4 235-54-48
Mon, Wed-Sun 11-12:30, 16:30-20; Rbls, $; Eng
Konek
Marata ul., 86 164-07-22
Mon-Fri ; Rbls, $

PROSTOR-PARK

RIDING SCHOOL & STABLES

Horseback Riding & Carriages
Horseback Riding in Primorskiy Park
Instruction in Dressage & Jumping
Available for Film & TV Production

Horse Boarding & Sales • Carriages
Krestovskiy Ostrov, 20 230-78-73
Tues-Sat 16-20, Sun 10-15; Rbls, $, English

☎ HOSPITALS
БОЛЬНИЦЫ
KRANKENHÄUSER
HOPITAUX
SJUKHUS
SAIRAALAT

See also MEDICAL CARE

Listed below are some of the better hospitals in St. Petersburg.

HOSPITALS IN MEDICAL INSTITUTES

Bekhtereva Psychoneurological Institute
Psikhonevrologicheskiy Institut im. Bekhtereva
Bekhtereva ul., 3 265-24-30
Bus 8; Metro Ploshchad Aleksandra Nevskogo
Institute of Emergency Medical Care
　　　　　　Institut Skoroy Pomoshchi
Budapeshtskaya ul., 3 174-86-75
Fax.. 174-36-81
Open 24 Hours a Day

| **Kirov Academy of Military Medicine** |
| *Voenno-Meditsinskaya Akademiya im. S.M. Kirova* |
| Akademika Lebedeva ul., 6 .... 542-21-39 |
| Admitting .... 542-12-50 |
| Zagorodnyy pr., 47........................ 292-58-44 |
| *One of the best hospitals and universities in Russia* |

Neurological Institute
　　　　　　Institut Neyrokhirurgii
Mayakovskogo ul., 12 272-81-35
Petrov Institute of Oncology
　　　　Institut Onkologii im. Petrova
Poselok Pesochnyy-2,
Leningradskaya ul., 68 237-86-55
Trauma and Orthopedic Institute
Institut Travmatologii i Ortopedii im. Vredena
Akademika Boykova ul., 8.............. 556-08-31

CITY HOSPITALS

Emergency Hospital
　　　　Bolnitsa Skoroy Pomoshchi
Pionerskaya ul., 16........................ 235-71-13
General Hospital No. 15
　　　　Gorodskaya Bolnitsa No. 15
Avangardnaya ul., 4....................... 135-96-97
Bus 87; Metro Prospekt Veteranov
General Hospital No. 16
　　　　named after Kuybyshev
　　　　Gorodskaya Bolnitsa No. 16
Liteynyy pr., 56 278-89-24

| ***Hospital No. 20*** |
| Emergency & Inpatient Medical Care |
| Gastello ul., 21 |
| Reception desk .... 108-48-10 |
| Dept. for foreigners....... 108-40-81 |
| *English, German, French, 24 hours a day* |

Hospital No. 3 named after Grand Duchess Elizabeth
　　　　　　Bolnitsa No. 3
Vavilovykh ul., 14........................... 515-15-05
Fax.. 555-57-73

Mechnikov General Hospital Clinic
Klinicheskaya Bolnitsa im. Mechnikova
Piskarevskiy pr., 47 543-94-46
Pokrovskaya Hospital
Pokrovskaya Bolnitsa
Bolshoy pr., V.O., 85 217-26-31

St. George Hospital
120 Years of History

New technologies in surgery, cardiology,
gynecology, orthopedics, therapeutics,
physical therapy & other fields.

EKG, ultrasound, dental clinic, laboratory testing,
modern x-ray, radiology lab and endoscopy.

Severnyy pr., 1
Head Physician 511-96-00
Admitting office 511-97-94
Manager 511-95-00
Bus 33; Metro Ozerki

Volodarskiy General Hospital No. 14
Gorodskaya Bolnitsa No. 14
Kosinova ul., 19 186-76-76

CHILDREN'S HOSPITALS

Children's Hospital No. 1
Detskaya Bolnitsa No. 1
Highly recommended in an emergency
Avangardnaya ul., 14 135-12-07
T-bus 20; Metro Prospekt Veteranov
Children's Hospital No. 2 n. a. Krupskaya
Detskaya Bolnitsa No. 2 im. Krupskoy
1-ya Liniya, 58 213-29-37
Children's Hospital No. 6
Detskaya Bolnitsa No. 6
Chaykovskogo ul., 67 273-38-66
Children's Hospital No. 19 n. a. Raukhfus
Detskaya Bolnitsa No. 19 im. Raukhfusa
Ligovskiy pr., 8 279-40-20
Tram 13; Metro Ploshchad Vosstaniya

MATERNITY HOSPITALS

Itus Clinic & Maternity Hospital
Tambasova ul., 21 130-27-14
Fax 130-27-13
One of the best in the city. Mon-Sat 9-21; Rbls; Fr, Ital

Maternity Ward No. 1	**Rodilnyy Dom**
14-ya Liniya, 19	213-21-46
Maternity Ward No. 2	**Rodilnyy Dom**
Furshtadtskaya ul., 36	273-37-43
Maternity Ward No. 3	**Rodilnyy Dom**
Malyy pr., P.S., 13	235-11-51
Maternity Ward No. 4	**Rodilnyy Dom**
Sverdlovskaya nab., 36	225-06-86
Maternity Ward No. 6	**Rodilnyy Dom**
Mayakovskogo ul., 5	272-47-24
Maternity Ward No. 7	**Rodilnyy Dom**
Tambasova ul., 21	130-84-65

Maternity Ward No. 9	**Rodilnyy Dom**
Ordzhonikidze ul., 47	126-87-31
Maternity Ward No. 11	**Rodilnyy Dom**
Lesnozavodskaya ul., 10	262-42-12
Maternity Ward No. 12	**Rodilnyy Dom**
Kanonerskaya ul., 12	114-15-69
Maternity Ward No. 13	**Rodilnyy Dom**
Kostromskaya ul., 4	275-68-65

OPHTHALMOLOGY HOSPITALS

EYE MICROSURGERY CENTER
Tsentr Mikrokhirurgii Glaza
Branch of the famous Fedorov Clinic
Yaroslava Gasheka ul., 21 178-32-22
Fax.. 101-35-51
Mon-Fri 9-15

Ophthalmology General Hospital No. 7
Gorodskaya Oftalmologicheskaya Bolnitsa
Mokhovaya ul., 38 272-35-80

PSYCHIATRIC HOSPITAL

Psychiatric General Hospital No. 2
Gorodskaya Psikhiatricheskaya Bolnitsa
Reki Moyki nab., 126 114-10-83

SKIN & VENEREAL HOSPITAL

Skin & Venereal Hospital
Kozhno-Venerologicheskaya Bolnitsa
Vosstaniya ul., 45 272-79-34

TRAUMA HOSPITAL

Trauma Hospital No. 31
Gorodskaya Bolnitsa No. 31
Dinamo pr., 3 235-12-02

TUBERCULOSIS HOSPITAL

Tuberculosis Hospital No. 2
Tuberkuleznaya Bolnitsa No. 2
Toreza pr., 93 553-37-24

☎ **HOTELS**
   ГОСТИНИЦЫ
   HOTELS
   HOTELS
   HOTELL
   HOTELLIT

See also BED & BREAKFAST, MOTELS

For information and reservations, call the front desk, but if you have a problem, it is usually necessary to talk to the "Manager on duty", called the "Administrator".

Russian hotels vary greatly in quality and service. The Russian rating system for hotels is not the same as the Western system. A four star hotel rated in Russia is definitely a solid hotel but has a very different quality and ambiance than a four-star hotel in London or Paris. Most hotels listed here are rated first class by the Russia travel authorities. First class is acceptable to many guests, but quality is highly variable. Fourth class points toward students and low budget travelers. Joint-Ventures are rated on the Western scale.

★★★★★ means a great hotel;
★★★★ are really good;
★★★ good
Not all hotels are rated.

Astoria
Gertsena ul., 39
Reservations................................210-50-32
Director/Secretary........................311-42-06
Fax..315-96-68
Hairdresser's, bureau de change, clothing &, shoe repair, train & plane tickets, theater tickets, excursions, sauna, car rental, Osvas International shop, restaurants.
$, Eng, Ger; F-5

Belye Nochi Resort ★★★   White Nights
A most elegant health resort nestled in a tranquil pine forest on the Gulf of Finland near St. Petersburg.
See HEALTH RESORTS

Belye Nochi   White Nights
Narodnaya ul., 93, bldg. 1
Administrator.................................263-21-04
Director...266-25-57
Fourth Class Hotel for students

Long Term Living for Moderate Prices
Restaurant, Bar with Billiards,
Hard Currency Store, 24-Hour Parking,
Car Rental, with or without driver,
DHL Worldwide Express Service
Serebristyy blvd., 38
Reception.............................301-79-69
Office 301-56-63
Fax.......................................301-56-22
Telex ....121037 CHAI SU
Rubles, $, English
Metro Pionerskaya

Commodore Hotelship ★★★★
See ad below
1 Morskoy Slavy 119-66-66

Druzhba
Chapygina ul., 4
Administrator.................................234-18-44
Restaurant.....................................234-44-56
Restaurant 8:30-23, Bar: 12-23, Conference Hall Rbls, $; Metro Petrogradskaya; F-10

J.V. Fural
at the Hotel Rechnaya
Obukhovskoi Oborony pr., 195
Tel 262-84-00
Fax...279-65-16
Night bar 17-23, Rbls & $

GALAKT
Living Space Near Metro. Low Prices.
Krasnykh Zor blvd., 8
Administrator...................267-04-35
Metro Lomonosovskaya

★★★★

COMMODORE HOTEL St. Petersburg

Experience the best of an All-American Hotel
Join the party at the Commodore Hotel and
experience our theme restaurants, bars and
magical entertainment.

★ ★ ★ ★

High standard accommodation, 334 rooms
Meals in fabulously theme surroundings
Party the night away at our unique
entertainment center.

★ ★ ★ ★

The best of American entertainment
from Broadway.

★ ★ ★ ★

New York Restaurant, Los Angeles Bistro,
Las Vegas Show Lounge, Sky Bar, New
Orleans Night Club, Palm Beach Pool Bar,
Business Center, Conference Rooms,
Shop, Tours & Excursions,
24 Hour Room Service

★ ★ ★ ★

1 Morskoy Slavy
Tel...119-66-66
Fax..119-66-67

Grand Hotel Europe ★★★★★
See ad on next page

Hotel Helen
Lermontovskiy pr., 45/1
Administrator.................................251-61-01
Fax..113-08-59
Next to the Hotel Sovetskaya. Night bar, International shop, business center & communications
$; Finnish-Russian management; E-4

Hotel for Seamen
Gapsalskaya ul., 2
Administrator/Information 251-43-68
Fax..114-92-41
Cafe Daily 9-22; Rbls; C-3

Inpredservice
1-ya Berezovaya alleya, 20, E-10.....234-26-40
Kutuzova nab., 34, H-7 272-15-00
Fax..279-50-24
INPREDSERVICE is the municipal office for service to foreign representatives & their staff. Their Cottage No. 1 is ideal for visiting executives & negotiations, all meals cooked to order by your own chef, high security, chauffeured car or limousine. $; Metro Chernaya Rechka

Kareliya
Tukhachevskogo pr., 27, bldg. 2
Tel 226-35-15
Fax...226-35-11
Restaurant, Night Disco Bar & Casino, Pharmacy, Postal Service, Exchange Bureau

GRAND HOTEL EUROPE

★★★★★

ST. PETERSBURG
RUSSIA

The Restaurant Europe, The Brassiere
Chopsticks, Sadko's
Mezzanine Atrium Cafe, Lobby Bar
Night Club, Fitness Center, Business Center
Communication Center, 24 Hour Room Service

*Beautifully Restored to its Old World Elegance
On Nevskiy Prospect & Mikhaylovskaya
in the middle of Saint Petersburg*

*Within Walking Distance of the Hermitage
& the Russian Museum*

Mikhaylovskaya Street 1/7
Saint Petersburg, 191011

Information/Switchboard	119-60-00
Fax	119-60-01
Telex	64-121073 GHE SU

*English, Italian, France, Swedish
Spanish, German, Finnish;* G-6

$, All Major Credit Cards

"One of the Best". TYP editor

KIEVSKAYA

- Comfortable single & double
  rooms at low prices.
- Downtown location,
  less than five minutes drive
  from Nevskiy prospect.
- Convenient connections to
  airport & railway terminals.
- Restaurant, Bar, Post Office,
  Souvenir Shop.

Enjoy Our Hospitality

Dnepropertrovskaya ul., 49, H-3

Inquiries	166-04-56
Director	166-53-98

The LDM Complex
P.S., Professora Popova ul., 47, E-9
Reception 234-32-78
Business Center 234-97-93
Restaurant 234-14-02
Fax 234-98-18
See also BUSINESS CENTERS

Ladoga
Shaumyana pr., 26 528-56-28
Restaurant, hairdressers
Rbls, $; Metro Novocherkasskaya

Losevskaya
Pos. Losevo, Priozerskiy Region
.... (8-279) 6-72-29
.... (8-279) 6-72-16
*A small resort hotel on the beautiful Vuoksa River
in Losevo Natural Park Reserve on the Karelia Isthmus
Restaurant, bar, sauna, service bureau
Rbls, $; Eng, Finn "Beautiful," TYP editor*

Hotel Mercury

A small fashionable hotel

Located near Tavricheskiy Park
and Smolnyy Cathedral

Favorite of executives & professionals
for its cozy homelike atmosphere

Large, comfortable 1 to 3 room suites

Bar-Restaurant & Winter Garden
Two beautiful banquet rooms
All international communications
Audi cars & Ford mini-vans with drivers

Tavricheskaya ul., 39 278-19-77
Fax.................................... 278-19-77
IAC   Fax +7+502+222-1083
         Tel +7+502+222-1081+3388

$, English, I-7

Mir
Gastello ul., 17
Administrator 108-51-66
Director/Secretary 108-51-69
Restaurant 108-51-63
*Restaurant Daily 8-19, Cafe Daily 9-22, Hairdressers;
Rbls; Metro Moskovskaya "Good value," TYP editor*

Morskaya *(reopening fall 1994)*
Morskoy Slavy pl., 1
Head Engineer.............................. 355-13-87
Metro Primorskaya, B-5

Moskva
Aleksandra Nevskogo pl., 2 274-21-15
.... 274-21-00
Fax.. 274-21-30
*Restaurant & bar, sauna, currency exchange, duty-free
shop, clothing & shoe repairs, dry-cleaning, car rental, train & plane ticket desk, theater
ticket & excursion desk.
Metro Ploshchad Aleksandra Nevskogo; $;* J-5

Na Sadovoy
Sadovaya ul., 53
Director 310-65-37
Fourth Class Hotel; Rbls; F-4

Nauka   **Science**
Millionnaya ul., 27 315-86-96
Administrator.................................. 315-33-68
Hotel of the Russian Academy of Sciences; Rbls; F-6

Neptun, *See our ad on page 94*
Obvodnogo ka. nab., 93a 210-17-07
Fax 311-22-70

Neva
Chaykovskogo ul., 17..................... 278-05-04
Sauna, hairdressers, buffet; Rbls;
Metro Chernyshevskaya; H-7

★ ★ ★ ★ ★

NEVSKIJ PALACE
H O T E L
Nevskiy Prospect - St. Petersburg

Built in 1861 in the heart of St. Petersburg,
following careful restoration, the Nevskij Palace
Hotel opened in May 1993 as a brand new 5-star
hotel behind an antique facade.

287 rooms and suites • Cultural Center
Coffee Shop • Cafe-Bar • Beer Pub
Conference Facilities Shopping Arcade
Whirlpool Sauna and Massage • Choice of
restaurants with international
and "New Russian" cuisine.

WELCOME TO THE NEVSKIJ PALACE HOTEL
Nevskiy pr., 57............................... 311-63-66
Tel.. 112-52-38
Fax (via satellite)........................... 850-15-01
Telex...............................121279 HERMS SU

Reservations through finer travel agents or via UTELL
$ & CC, English, French, German, H-5
Managed by MARCO POLO HOTELS & RESORTS
Vienna, Austria

Oktivian (*under repair*) C-5
Sredniy pr., 88............................... 356-85-16

Oktyabrskaya
Ligovskiy pr., 10 277-60-12
Administrator.................................. 277-63-30
Secretary 277-61-48
Restaurant, bar, dry-cleaning, laundry, camera, clothing
& shoe repairs, International shop, telegraph.
Daily 9-20; Rbls; Metro Ploshchad Vosstaniya; I-5

HOTEL
OKHTINSKAYA

An International ★ ★ ★ Hotel

A comfortable, modern 1991 hotel
beautifully located on bank of the Neva
across from Smolnyy Cathedral.
Just 8 minutes to Palace Square

Double & deluxe suites, telephones
cable-satellite TV & air-conditioning.

This new mid-sized hotel is liked
by business people for its friendly staff.

Restaurant "Okhtinskaya" offers
excellent Russian-European cuisine.

Two Bars, Sauna, Conference Hall
Meeting Rooms, Business Center
International Communications
Kiosks & International Shops
Service desk and Mini-Bus

Bolsheokhtinskiy pr., 4

Tel....................................227-37-67
Tel....................................227-44-38
Fax....................................227-26-18
Telex ....121128 TUR SU

$ & CC, English, French and German; K-7

The Russian-French A/O "Victoria"

Olgino Motel Camping
Primorskoe shosse, 18 km, Sestroretsk
Director 238-34-89
Russian bath, hairdressers, air ticket desk ; Daily 0-24
Olympia - *See ad on next page*

Hotelship Peterhof ★★★★
A LITTLE BIT OF SWITZERLAND
IN THE CENTER OF ST. PETERSBURG

A la carte restaurant, open air cafe, Sky Bar
with live music, Panorama Bar, conference
facilities, business communications center,
fitness room, sauna, beauty center

Tel................................... 213-63-21
Fax 213-31-58
$, all major credit cards, English, German

DELOVIE LYUDI

INDEPENDENT • OBJECTIVE • THOROUGH
Profsoyuznaya ul., 73; Tel.: (095) 333-33-40; Fax: (095) 330-15-68

HOTEL OLYMPIA

★ ★ ★

ST. PETERSBURG

Welcome to the new Hotel Olympia!
Hotel Olympia now offers you generous value
for money in totally remodelled,
more spacious and comfortable rooms.

Exciting kitchen in a   Summertime rendezvous
friendly atmosphere.   under the midnight sun.

Hotel Olympia, Sea Glory Square,
199106 St. Petersburg, Russia.

Phone: .... 119 68 00.
Telex: .... 121 333.
Fax: .... 119 68 05.

🜨 Supranational Hotels

Pribaltiyskaya
Korablestroiteley ul., 14
Inquires 356-00-01
Fax 356-00-94
*Restaurants Neva, Leningrad, Daugava with
grill-bar, Panorama, Heineken & Stella Artois
beer bars, night club, casino, sauna,
swimming pool & bowling, The Baltic Star
International Shop, satellite TV, direct
international dialing, business center,
pharmacy, post, bank & photo service, 24
hour taxi, high-security parking
Rbls, $; A-6*

Pulkovskaya
Pobedy pl., 1
Bldg. 1 Administrator 264-51-22
Bldg. 2 Administrator 264-50-22
Fax 264-58-44
*Cafeteria, saunas, hairdressers, duty-free
shop, bureau de change, clothing & shoe
repairs, dry-cleaning, florist, fax facilities,
photocopying, car rental, air & rail ticket
desk, excursion desk, theater ticket desk
Rbls, $; Metro Moskovskaya*

Rechnaya
Obukhovskoy Oborony pr., 195
Director 262-89-00
Administrator 267-31-96
*Restaurant (under repair), grill-bar,
hairdressers, travel desk
Rbls; Eng, Ger; Metro Proletarskaya*

HOTEL REPINSKAYA
A Small Quiet Park Hotel in a beautiful pine
forest on the shore of the Gulf of Finland
Enjoy the beach, swim, bicycle in summer
X-Skiing & ice-fishing on Gulf in winter
Restaurant, Bar & Service Bureau
Less than an hour from St. Pb. by train

Repino, Primorskoe shosse, 428
Administrator 231-66-37
English, $ & Rubles

RETUR - Camping
Camping
On the beautiful Gulf of Finland
*Comfortable 2-rm cottages with bath
Breakfast, Bar & Restaurant
Sauna, Russian baths
Heated Swimming Pool & Tennis
Car Rental & Caravan Camping
with Hot Showers
Secure Parking Guaranteed*

*29 km from Saint Petersburg
on St. Pb. – Helsinki highway*

Primorskoe shosse, 29 km
Tel 237-75-33
Fax 273-97-83
Open 24 hrs, $, English, German, Finnish

Ritm
Turbinnaya ul., 11
Administrator 186-76-89
Director 186-76-88
*A small hotel with 8 comfortable rooms. Restaurant
Centurion with European and Chinese food
Rbls; Eng, Fr, Chinese; Metro Narvskaya*

Rossiya
Chernyshevskogo pl., 11
Administrator 296-73-49
Inquiries 296-76-49
*Restaurant, cafe, hairdressers, clothing & shoe
repairs, train & plane ticket desk, theater ticket &
excursion desk. Rbls; Metro Park Pobedy.*

In the Center of the City
Modern Comfortable Rooms
Bars • Cafe • Sauna • Hairdresser
Currency Exchange
Artilleriyskaya ul., 1
Secretary.......................... 272-03-21
Administrator 279-50-03
Rubles, $, English, H-6
*Metro: Chernyshevskaya, Mayakovskaya
Managed by the Russian-Italian Firm "Helios"*

Smolninskaya See ST. PETERSBURG: MAYOR'S OFFICE, SMOLNINSKAYA OFFICIAL GUEST RESIDENCE

St. Petersburg

★★★★

Just Across the Neva River
from the Summer Garden
Restaurants on floors A & B, Zerkalnyy
Three Night Clubs, Two Pools,
Fitness Center

Nab. Vyborgskaya, 5/2

Inquiries	542-91-23
Secretary	542-91-01
Administrator	542-94-11
Restaurant	542-91-55
	542-91-21
	542-90-12
Fax	248-80-02

Bars, Beriozka Shop, Sauna,
Chauffeur Driven Cars for Hire,
Exchange Bureau, "Viking" Food Store,
Duty-Free Shop, Travel Ticket Desk, Florist,
Clothing & Shoe Repair, Dry Cleaning,
Theater Ticket Desk, Concert Hall,
3 Conference Halls
Metro: Ploshchad Lenina; H-8

Sovetskaya Hotel

Single, Double & Deluxe Rooms
3 Restaurants, Grill, Bavaria Pub, Cafe, Hair
Salon, Sauna, Commercial Medical Center,
Conference Halls, Currency Exchange,
Business Center

Lermontovskiy pr., 43/1	259-25-52
Fax	251-88-90
Telex	121705 HOTS SU

Sportivnaya
Deputatskaya ul., 34
Administator	235-02-36
Director	235-13-17
Restaurant	230-42-23
Restaurant Daily 8-20; Rbls; D-10

Sputnik
Toreza pr., 34
Administrator	552-56-32
Director	552-81-00
Restaurant, bar, grill-bar, hairdressers; Rbls, $;
Metro Ploshchad Muzhestva

Turist Hotel
Sevastyanova ul., 3
Administrator	298-80-32
Director	298-58-81
Sauna, buffet; Tram 15; Metro Elektrosila

Vyborgskaya
Torzhkovskaya ul., 3
Administrator	246-91-41
Director	246-36-22
Restaurants, bar, clothing & shoe repairs, hairdressers,
bureau de change, train & plane ticket desk,
theater ticket desk, car rental.
Rbls; Metro Chernaya Rechka; F-11

ST. PETERSBURG'S
MODERN BUDGET
"WESTERN STYLE"
• CITY CENTER! •
RUSSIAN YOUTH HOSTEL
An American-Russian Joint Project
Tourist visas available!

3ʳᵈ Sovetskaya ulitsa, 28	277-05-69
Fax	277-51-02
International Reservation in USA	+1 (310) 379-4316
Fax	+1 (310) 379-8420

Yuzhnaya
Rasstannaya ul., 26
Administrator	166-10-88
Director	166-10-87
Cafe, sauna; Rbls; Tram 25, 49, Metro Ligovskiy Prospekt; G-3

☎ **HOURS, SHOPS, WORK**
ЧАСЫ РАБОТЫ
ÖFFNUNGSZEITEN
HEURES
ÖPPETTIDER, AFFÄRER
KAUPPOJEN AUKIOLOAJAT

See also HOLIDAYS and SCHOOLS

Hours of work. Organizations and institutes usually open between 9 and 10, take ½ - 1 hours off for lunch between 13 and 14 and end the work day about 18. Most are closed Saturdays and Sundays, although a few work Saturdays.

Most shops work Monday through Saturday, open around 10. Some close around 18, many stay open to 20 or 21. Food stores tend to be open from 8 to 20.

Lunch break. Most state shops and many organizations close for one hour in the middle of the day for a lunch break. You might see a sign Перерыв на обед (Pereryv na obed) on the door. Most new shops, Univermag, Universam and J.V. organization work without a lunch break

"Sanitary day". Many markets, museums, public institutions, and a few shops close one day per month in addition to their regular closing for "cleaning day" (sanitarnyy den, санитарный день). See MUSEUMS, MARKETS.

☎ **HOUSE CLEANING**
КВАРТИРЫ, УБОРКА
GEBÄUDEREINIGUNG
APPARTEMENTS, NETTOYAGE
STÄDNING, HUS
ASUNTOJENSIIVOUS

See APARTMENT CLEANING

☎ **HOUSEWARES**
ХОЗЯЙСТВЕННЫЕ ТОВАРЫ
HAUSHALTSWAREN
MENAGE, MARCHANDISES POUR
HUSHÅLLSARTIKLAR
TALOUSTAVARAT

See DEPARTMENT STORES and HARDWARE
Both housewares and hardware are sold in shops called Khozyaystvennyy Magazin (Хозяйственный Магазин).

BABYLON shops

No. 2 Everything for the Home

Make your home sparkle:

Paint, wallpaper, linoleum & throw rugs from Holland with tools & supplies to do it. Philips electrical appliances for the home. Procter & Gamble cleaning products.

Liteynyy pr., 63 279-01-48

Daily 10-14, 15-20; Rbls
Metro Mayakovskaya

Biomax

Hamburg — St. Petersburg

Production of environmentally safe detergents
Nab. reki Fontanki, 26 273-52-91
Tel 272-68-14

Ca Gi Ve
Nevskiy pr., 49/2...........................113-15-79
Fax 113-14-43
Mon-Sat 10:30-13, 14:30-19:30; Rbls, $; Ital

Dom   **Home**
Italian and Finnish bathroom fixtures, wall paper and locks
Grazhdanskiy pr., 13 535-03-63
Mon-Sat 10-14, 15-19; Rbls, $

Elma
Bolshoy Sampsonievskiy pr., 19 542-63-95
Mon-Fri 10-14, 15-19; Rbls

FAIRN & SWANSON

Electronics, Housewares, Toys
Nevskiy pr., 96...............................275-53-85
Fax 275-53-86
Mon-Sat 11-14, 15-19; Rubles; English

Hardware Store No. 158
Ligovskiy pr., 161 166-13-47
Mon-Sat 10-19; Rbls
Home Center - *See ad below*
Khozyaystvennye Tovary, *Table and Cookware*
Yakornaya ul., 1 224-38-03
Mon-Sat 10-19; Rbls
Konversiya-Service, *Mon-Fri 9-17; Rbls*
Chugunnaya ul., 14 248-03-52
Lama, *Daily 11-21; Rbls, $; Eng, Ger*
Nevskiy pr., 96/1...........................275-53-84
Fax 275-53-86

Home □ Center

Kitchen Appliances

Complete line of major kitchen appliances
Refrigerators, freezers, Seppel Fricke stoves, dishwashers, kitchen exhaust fans, Complete line of Philips microwaves, mixers, cookers, toasters, and small kitchen appliances,

Air conditioners, washing machines clothes dryers, vacuum cleaners, iron, fans Hot water heaters and more

In S.E. St. Pb., minutes from city center.
Slavy pr., 30.....................261-15-50
....261-04-02
Fax 260-15-81
Daily 10-20; $, FIM, DM, Rbls; Eng, Finn, Ger
Metro Moskovskaya, then Bus 31, 114, T-bus 29

Olesya, *Mon-Sat 10-14, 15-19; Rbls*
Nevskiy pr., 97...............................277-17-81
Podolsk-Sokol, *Sewing machines*
Bogatyrskiy pr., 10........................394-72-49
Mon-Sat 10-14, 15-19; Rbls
Prestige, *Mon-Fri 9-18; Rbls*
Reki Moyki nab., 3 312-77-18
Russkaya Bronza   **Russian Bronze**
Zhukovskogo ul., 36/1...................279-72-39
Mon-Sat 11-14, 15-19; Rbls
Shop No. 55
Maklina pr., 21 216-65-91
Mon-Sat 10-14, 15-19; Rbls
Terra
5-ya Liniya ,42 213-37-37

☎ **HUNTING & FISHING EQUIPMENT**
ОХОТА И РЫБОЛОВСТВО, ТОВАРЫ
JAGEN UND FISCHEN
CLUBS DE CHASSE
JAKT OCH FÖRENINGAR
METSÄSTYS-
JA KALASTUSTARVIKKEET

See also CAMPING EQUIPMENT *and* SPORTS EQUIPMENT
Altsec, *Mon-Fri 9-18; Rbls*
Kalinina ul., 39, Priozersk...... (8-279) 2-19-90
Commission Store No. 75
Apraksin Dvor, Section 13-15.........310-20-03
Sporting goods, hunting equipment
Mon-Sat 10-14, 15-19; Rbls
Dinamo Society
Dinamo pr., 44...............................235-47-17
Mon-Fri 9-17:30; Rbls

Keep your house sparkling with supplies from our housewares department. Brooms, detergents, sponges, paper towels, wax and window cleaners, buckets, scrub brushes and plastic bags. Proctor and Gamble cleaning products.

Mon-Sat 10-21 Sun 12-20
Exchange office

P.S., Maly pr., 54 & 56.................230-80-96
In the former Okean store off Bolshoy Prospekt

Hunting and Fishing Store No. 1
Liteynyy pr., 26 272-60-47
Mon-Fri 10-19; Rbls

Instant
Zheleznodorozhnyy pr., 40 560-66-85
Fax 560-43-85
Mon-Fri 10-19; Rbls, $; Eng
Bus 95; Metro Elizarovskaya

Neva-Broker
Bronnitskaya ul., 17 292-61-10
Fax 112-60-30
Mon-Fri 9-17; Rbls, $, CC; Eng, Fr

Okhota i Rybolovstvo
                    Hunting and Fishing No. 17
Nevskiy pr., 60 311-01-19
Mon-Sat 10-19; Rbls

Okhotnik   **Hunter**
Ligovskiy pr., 44 164-82-33
Mon-Sat 10:30-18:30; Rbls; Tram 25; Metro Ligovskiy Prospekt

Rybolov, *Excellent selection*   **Fishing**
Kamennoostrovskiy pr., 4 232-08-52

Voenokhot, *Backpacks, tents*
Kolpino, Trudyashchikhsya blvd., 16
☎ 481-45-44
Mon-Fri 9-18; Rbls

☎ **HUNTING & FISHING**
   EXCURSIONS
   ОХОТА И РЫБОЛОВСТВО,
   ЭКСКУРСИИ
   JAGD-UND ANGELVEREINE
   CHASSEURS ET DE PECHEURS,
   SOCIETES DE
   JAKT OCH FISKEFÖRENINGAR
   METSÄSTYS-
   JA KALASTUSRETKET

See also TRAVEL AGENCIES *for Hunting and Fishing Tours*

Evgeniya, *Mon-Fri 9-18; $; Eng, Ger*
Boytsova per., 4 114-26-60
Fauna, *Daily 9-18; Rbls, $; Eng, Ger, Swed*
Lenina ul., 120, Tosno 2-28-96

Hunting and Fishing Association of
Leningrad Voennyy Okrug
Reki Fontanki nab., 90, bldg. 4 219-23-74

Mon-Fri 9-13, 14-18; Rbls

INSTANT

SAFARI in Russia & Middle Asia
Zheleznodorozhnyy pr., 40 560-66-85
Fax 560-43-85

Obshchestvo Okhotnikov
                            Hunters' Society
Reki Fontanki nab., 90, bldg. 4 310-22-91
Mon-Fri 9-18; Rbls; Metro Pushkinskaya
Prostor-Sever
Nevskiy pr., 179 274-64-83
Fax 352-03-80
Mon-Fri 11-17; Rbls, $; Eng, Ger, Fr, Ital
Excursions in the Leningrad region and in Karelia
Vostr
Yablochkova ul. 5 232-95-41
Mon-Fri 9:30-18; Rbls, $; Eng

☎ **ICE CREAM**
   МОРОЖЕНОЕ
   EISCAFES
   GLACE
   GLASS
   JÄÄTELÖ

Ice cream is popular in St. Petersburg and is sold on the street as well as in numerous ice cream cafes (cafe-morozhenoe, Кафе-Мороженое). *Baskins and Robbins has come to St. Petersburg.*

BASKIN·ROBBINS

Thirty-one flavors of ice cream
American Ice Cream

Nevskiy pr., 79 164-64-56
Hrs: 10-22, Rubles

Cafe-Morozhenoe   **Ice Cream Cafe**
• 9-ya Liniya, 18 213-08-41
Daily 11-16, 17-21;
• Blagodatnaya ul., 35 294-33-67
Mon-Sat 10-19
• Kamennoostrovskiy pr., 41 232-53-89
10-16, 17-22
• Nevskiy pr., 154 277-07-25
Daily 10-15, 16-21
• Sadovaya ul., 33 310-82-31
Daily 11-16, 17-20
Gino Ginelli, *Italian ices*
Griboedova kan. nab., 14 312-46-31
Daily 12-20; $, CC; Eng, Ger
Ice Cream, *Daily 10-21; Rbls*
Moskovskiy pr., 45 292-13-83
Lyagushatnik   **Frogs Pool**
• Nevskiy pr., 24 311-00-71
Daily 11-15, 16-21
• Nevskiy pr., 3 312-65-45
Daily 10-15, 16-21
Morzh, *Daily 11-16, 18-23; Rbls, $*   **Walrus**
Sadovaya ul., 27 310-06-38
Na Pokrovke   **On Pokrovka**
Sadovaya ul., 97 114-39-37
10-16, 17-22; Rbls; Metro Sennaya Ploshchad
Pingvinchik   **Little Penguin**
Nevskiy pr., 54 312-24-60
Daily 10-15, 16-22; Rbls
Snezhinka   **Snow Flake**
Tipanova ul., 29 299-59-02
Daily 10-15, 16-21; Rbls
Store No. 42 Cafe, *Mon-Fri 10-14, 15-19; Rbls*
Potemkinskaya ul., 7 272-91-57
Tishutin and Co., *Mon-Sat 10-21*
Nevskiy pr., 100 279-33-11
Vorskla Ice Cream
Sredneokhtinskiy pr., 25 224-08-95
Daily 11-15, 16-24; Rbls
Zerkalnoe
Zagorodnyy pr., 8 315-89-48
Daily 10-15, 16-21; Rbls; Metro Dostoevskaya

☎ INFORMATION SERVICES
ИНФОРМАЦИОННЫЕ УСЛУГИ
INFORMATIONSDIENSTE
RENSEIGNEMENTS, BUREAU DE
INFORMATIONS SERVICE
INFORMAATIOPALVELUT

See also BUSINESS CONSULTANTS, BUSINESS PUBLICATIONS *and* TELEPHONE INFORMATION

Information services are provided by some ADVERTISING AGENCIES.

The following firms have databases including enterprises, banks, foreign firms and other organizations in St. Petersburg.

Asu-Impuls
Bogatyrskiy pr., 4, bldg. 1, 1st floor
☎ 394-02-44

Interbank Information Service
Nevskiy pr., 16 315-39-42
Currency Exchange Info 311-69-84
Information and Financial Services, Financial Management Consulting, Mon-Fri 10-18

Kontakt-Inform, *Information on foreign and Russian businesses, financial background checks, market specialization, etc.*
Please call 541-89-87
Fax 541-88-21
Mon-Fri 10-18; Rbls, $; Eng, Ger

Leninformatika
Pushkinskaya ul., 10, off. 13 164-85-00
Fax 164-53-60
Mon-Fri 10-19; Rbls

LIC, *Publisher of Directories of St. Petersburg*
Gertsena ul., 20 314-59-82
Fax 315-35-92
Mon-Fri 10-18:30; Rbls, $; Eng
Tram 31; Metro Nevskiy Prospekt

Petersburg Informational Channel
Rubinshteyna ul., 8 312-95-72
Fax 314-43-48
Pirs, *Mon-Fri 10-19; Rbls*
Ryleeva ul., 10 272-37-77
Fax 275-54-49
Polyform Ltd.
192242, P.O. Box 191 567-93-95

SEVERO-ZAPAD ®
BUSINESS NEWS INFORMATION

On your desk every morning, daily reports on business related news in St. Petersburg and throughout Russia.
Thorough reporting on issues in business and economics.
Transmitted by fax or E-mail in Russian and English.
The most available and useful source of information in St. Petersburg.

Reki Fontanki nab.,75/1 310-11-01
Fax 310-11-74

★ ★ *Recommended by TYP*

☎ INSTITUTES-RESEARCH
ИНСТИТУТЫ, НАУЧНО-
ИССЛЕДОВАТЕЛЬСКИЕ
FORSCHUNGSINSTITUTE
INSTITUTS
FORSKNINGSINSTITUT
TIETEELLISET
TUTKIMUSKESKUKSET

See also MEDICAL INSTITUTES *and* UNIVERSITIES

St. Petersburg is a research center of Russia with almost 100 research institutes. In this category we list only those attached to St. Petersburg State University. For information on other institutes, call the Russian Academy of Sciences.

Russian Academy of Sciences
Universitetskaya nab., 5 218-37-87
Fax 218-41-72
Mon-Fri 9-18

RESEARCH INSTITUTES OF THE
ST. PETERSBURG STATE UNIVERSITY
IN ST. PETERSBURG

Earth's Crust Research Institute
Universitetskaya nab., 7/9 218-97-75
Mon-Fri 10-17; Tram 31
Research Institute for Geography
Sredniy pr., 41 218-79-04
Mon-Fri 9-18
Research Institute for Social Studies
Galernaya ul., 60 311-84-45
Mon-Fri 9-17:30
Ukhtomskiy Physiology Research Institute
Universitetskaya nab., 7/9 218-37-21
Mon-Fri 9-17

RESEARCH INSTITUTES Of The
ST. PETERSBURG STATE UNIVERSITY
In PETERHOF (PETRODVORETZ)

Astronomy Observatory
Bibliotechnaya pl., 2 218-37-21
Mon-Fri 9-17:52
Radiophysics, Scientific Technological Bureau
Ulyanovskaya ul., 1, bldg. 1 428-72-89
Mon-Fri 10-16
Research Institute for Applied Mathematics & Process Control
Bibliotechnaya pl., 2 428-71-79
Mon-Fri 10-17
Research Institute for Biology
Oranienbaumskoe shosse, 2 427-54-51
Mon-Fri 9-17:20
Research Institute for Chemistry
Universitetskiy pr., 2 428-67-39
Fax 428-69-39
Mon-Fri 11-17
Research Institute for Mathematics and Applied Mechanics
Bibliotechnaya pl., 2 428-69-44
Mon-Fri 9:30-17:10
Research Institute for Physics
Ulyanovskaya ul., 1, bldg. 1 428-72-40
Mon-Fri 10-17

☎ INSURANCE
СТРАХОВАНИЕ
VERSICHERUNGEN
ASSURANCE
FÖRSÄKRINGAR
VAKUUTUKSET

See also MEDICAL INSURANCE

Alisa
Zanevskiy pr., 6 528-77-74
Fax 528-62-11

Asko-Peterburg, *Mon-Fri 10-18; Rbls, $*
Yuriya Gagarina pr., 1, 7th floor 294-88-81
Fax 294-65-36

Atalanta, *Mon-Fri 10-18; Rbls, $; Eng*
Shaumyana pr., 18........................ 528-96-03
Fax 528-97-07

Gosstrakh   State Insurance Company
Largest state insurance company in Russia
Zodchego Rossi ul., 1/3 311-24-02
Mon-Fri, Sun 9-13:30, 14:20-18; Rbls

Hi-Fi Trust
Vasi Alekseeva ul., 14 185-06-17
Mon-Fri 10-18; Rbls

Ingosstrakh
Largest state insurance company for foreign firms
Zakharevskaya ul., 17 275-77-10
Fax 275-77-12
Mon-Fri 9-13, 14-17; Rbls, $; Eng, Ger, Fr

Investstrakh
Professora Popova ul., 47, apt. 821
☎ 234-50-53

Kingdom Bosco, *Insurance*
Nevskiy pr., 8................................. 219-18-54
Tel./Fax.. 312-11-47
Daily 11-18; Rbls, $; Eng

Lefko
Lavrskiy proezd, 1......................... 277-11-14
Fax 277-52-00
Mon-Fri 11-17; Rbls, $

Medexpress Insurance
Pestelya ul., 4 275-65-05
Fax 275-88-95
Medical insurance
Mon-Fri 10-18

Prima-Polis, *Daily 10-17; Eng*
Lotsmanskaya ul., 20 114-79-62
Fax 106-19-43

Progress-Neva
Moskovskiy pr., 79 a...................... 298-13-39
Fax 298-01-09
Mon-Sat 9-20; Rbls, $; Eng, Fr

Rossia Insurance - *See ad below*

Rus
Kvarengi per., 4 278-16-94
Fax 278-15-54
Mon-Fri, Sun 9:30-13:30, 14:30-18; Rbls, $; Eng, Ger

Sabina
Podyacheskaya ul., 34 310-60-86
Fax 310-40-40
Mon-Fri 11-14, 15-18; Rbls

SKF-Express
Moskovskiy pr., 19 251-34-81
Fax 251-33-90
Mon-Fri 10-20; Rbls

ROSSIYA INSURANCE Co., Ltd.
Saint Petersburg Branch
Affiliate of Rossiya Insurance Company, Ltd., Moscow
All forms of insurance

Automobile, medical, property, liability,
exhibition, transport & cargo insurance
for residents and foreigners.
Coverage in rubles and hard currency
Reinsurance with Francona, München
Rückversicherung, Segewick & others

Gertsena ul., 33 314-46-21
Fax 153-91-10
Hrs: 11- 18, English and German
Colonia (Germany) and leading Russian banks
and companies are our shareholders.

Slaviya-Grumant, *Mon-Fri 9-17; Rbls*
Dachnyy pr., 21, bldg. 1 156-64-73
Fax.. 156-09-11

Virilis Insurance
Pestelya ul., 4 275-60-17
Daily 11-13, 14-17; Rbls

☎ INTERIOR DESIGNERS
ДИЗАЙНЕРЫ ПОМЕЩЕНИЯ
INNENAUSSTATTER
LOGEMENT AMENAGEMENT
HEMINREDNING
SISUSTUSSUUNNITTELIJAT

Concern Goryachev
Chandeliers and decorative wood panels
Vereyskaya ul., 39........................ 112-75-96
Fax.. 315-24-21
Mon-Fri 9-13, 14-18; Rbls, $; Eng, Ital
T-bus 3; Metro Tekhnologicheskiy Institut, Pushkinskaya

Decorative Arts Center
Morisa Toreza pr., 98, bldg. 1 553-98-50
Mon-Fri 9-17:30; Rbls; T-bus 10

Decorative Design Center
Rimskogo-Korsakova pr., 24/135 ... 114-37-66
Mon-Fri 9-17:30

Ecopolis
Zanevskiy pr., 32, bldg. 2 528-26-66
Mon-Fri 9:30-18; Rbls, $; Eng

Malakhit
Novo-Aleksandrovskaya ul., 22....... 227-29-20
Mon-Fri 9-17; Rbls, $; Eng, Ger

MARKET BRIDGE Ltd.
Nevskiy pr, 82............................... 275-71-51
Fax:.. 275-71-50
See OFFICE EQUIPMENT

Merkuriy   Mercury
Gorokhovaya ul., 19 312-75-14
Mon-Fri 8:30-18; Rbls

Mitrofanova T., *Personal Workshop*
Vitebskaya ul., 11.......................... 114-64-57
Mon-Fri 9-18; Rbls

Nancy
4-ya Sovetskaya ul., 13 277-60-58
Fax.. 527-80-78
Mon-Fri 9-17; Rbls; Eng

RosVuzdizayn
Solyanoy per., 13........................ 279-41-97
Fax 279-41-96
Mon-Fri 11-18; Rbls, $; Eng

Russian Furniture

- Furniture Manufacturing & Design
- Office, Apartment & Store Interior Designers
- Interior Designers for Computerland St. Petersburg
- Professional Staff

Nevskiy pr., 82 272-47-82

Sreda   **Wednesday**
Reki Fontanki nab., 118, floor 3, rm. 55
☎ 251-15-41
Mon-Fri 9-19; Rbls

Vselenie   **Housewarming**
Sizova pr., 24, bldg. 1 395-36-23
Fax 395-35-98
Mon-Fri 10-18; Rbls, $

☎ INTERNATIONAL ASSOCIATIONS & ORGANIZATIONS
МЕЖДУНАРОДНЫЕ
АССОЦИАЦИИ И ОРГАНИЗАЦИИ
INTARNATIONALE
GESELLSCHAFTEN UND VEREINE
ASSOCIATIONS ET
ORGANISATIONS
INTERNATIONALES
INTARNATIONELLA FÖRENIMGAR
OCH ORGANISATIONER
KANSAINVÄLISIÄ JÄRJESTÖJÄ

Alliance Francaise
Reki Moyki nab., 20 311-09-95
.... 312-02-39
Mon-Sat 10-19; Rbls; Fr

All-World Club of Petersburgers
Kuybysheva ul., 4 218-53-50
Fax 275-31-12
Mon-Sat 14-19; Tram 2; Metro Gorkovskaya

Center of German Culture
Grivtsova per., 10 315-83-35
.... 315-85-35
Mon-Fri 18-22

**Israeli Diaspora Cultural
and Educational Fund**
Shpalernaya ul., 52 275-56-20

Lions Club of St. Petersburg "Hermitage"
Marata ul., 17, rm. 305 315-51-27

**Provisional Rotary Club - St. Petersburg
Downtown**
Ploshchad Truda, 4 172-54-51
Meetings: Thurday 6:30; Eng; President: Vadim Panov

Red Cross Society of Russia
Italyanskaya ul., 25 311-36-96
Mon-Fri 9-17; T-bus 1; Metro Gostinyy Dvor

**Russian-Japanese Center of Science and
Culture Association**
Borovaya ul., 21 247-67-92
**St. Petersburg American Business
Association**
*Meets the 2nd Tuesday of each month
at various locations*
Executive Secretary 273-01-08
Fax 272-80-31
**St. Petersburg Association
for International Cooperation**
Reki Fontanki nab., 21 314-06-70
Fax 311-40-89
*Mon-Fri 9:30-18; Eng, Ger, Fr, Ital
Metro Mayakovskaya*
Swedish Club
Ploshchad Iskusstv, 5 315-57-23
UNESCO Center of St. Petersburg
Chaykovskogo ul., 28 272-52-22
Fax 273-27-12
Mon-Fri 10-18; Eng, Ger, Fr

☎ INTERNATIONAL SHOPS
ВАЛЮТНЫЕ МАГАЗИНЫ
VALUTALÄDEN
BOUTIQUES INTERNATIONALES
INTERNATIONELLA AFFÄRER,
VALUTAAFFÄRER
VALUUTTAKAUPAT

See also COMPUTERS, ELECTRONICS, FOOD
STORES, FOREIGN FIRMS, OFFICE EQUIPMENT,
PHARMACIES, PHOTOCOPIERS, RESTAURANTS,
STATIONERY, *and* SUPERMARKETS

International shops, often called Duty-free
shops or Hard currency shops (valyutnyy
magazin, валютный магазин) , *include
those shops that sell a selection of imported goods only for hard currency. Increasingly, shops sell imported goods for rubles
as well as dollars because of the increasing
legal convertibility of the ruble.*

*Here we give a full listing only to those
shops selling a rather limited selection of
everything from souvenirs, cigarettes and
liquors to imported foods, T-shirts and
electronics, all in one shop.*

*Other more specialized shops, which
have good selection of imported goods for
hard currency are cross-listed under their
own categories.* **Please look under that
category for the goods or service that you
seek.**

7 Ogney - *See* CLOTHING   **Seven Lights**
Adamant - *See* BUILDING SUPPLIES
& FOOD STORES
The Airport Shops - *See ad on next page*
Alina - *See* CLOTHING
Alivekt - *See* CLOTHING, COMMERCIAL STORES
& ELECTRONICS GOODS
Main Office
Professora Popova ul., 22 234-02-32
Fax 234-90-96
Mon-Sat 10-19

Astoria Duty-Free
Gertsena ul., 39, Hotel Astoria ....Closed
Closed: Moved to Pulkovo Airports

The Airport Shops
At St. Petersburg Airport

A LENRIANTA AEROFLOT Joint Venture

Largest selection of international brand goods, liquors, electronics and the best Russian souvenirs at real duty free prices.

The cafe bars at both terminals serve hot and cold drinks and snacks.

Pulkovo-1 Domestic Airport

Arrivals & Departures Shop and a Large Electronics Store
Open from 8-22

Pulkovo-2 International Airport

Two Arrivals & Departures Shops
Bar & Cafe

Great for Last Minute Gifts
Large Selection of Duty Free Spirits
Hours depend on airline schedules

Int'l Airport Pulkovo 2 (office) ...104-34-86
....104-34-91
....104-34-92
Fax......................................104-34-68

$, CC, English

Beriozka Shops - Main Office
Lebedeva ul., 10 a............... 542-07-42
Fax 542-98-53
Mon-Sat 10-14, 15-17; $; Eng, Ger

Beriozka Shops
• Gertsena ul., 26 315-46-47
Daily 9-20; $
• Malookhtinskiy pr., 6 528-63-98
Mon-Sat 10-20; $
• Morskaya nab., 9 356-55-98
Mon-Sat 10-20; $
• Morskaya nab., 15 355-18-75
Daily 10-20; $
• Nalichnaya ul., 35/1 351-74-57
Mon-Fri 10-13, 14-18; Metro Primorskaya, T-bus 10
• Nevskiy pr., 7/9 315-51-62
Daily 11-20; $

Beriozka at the Hotel Kareliya
Marshala Tukhachevskogo ul., 27, 7th floor
☎ 226-32-37
Mon-Sat 9-18; $

Beriozka at the Hotel Sovetskaya
Lermontovskiy pr., 43 251-76-40
Mon-Sat 10-14, 15-20; $

Bosco Stores
• Ligovskiy pr., 130 166-00-11
Daily 11-15, 16-20; Rbls, $; Eng
• Millionniaya ul., 8 311-88-51
Daily 11-19; Rbls, $; Eng
• Millionniaya ul., 10, *Jewelers* 314-66-56
Daily 11-19; Rbls, $; Eng
• Nevskiy pr., 8 219-18-56
Daily 11-15, 16-20; Rbls, $; Eng
• Ulyany Gromovoy per., 3 275-57-11
Daily 11-15, 16-20; Rbls, $; Eng
• Zhukovskogo ul., 8 273-70-92
Mon-Sat 11-20; Rbls, $; Eng

Castor Shop
Makarova nab., 30 213-71-61
Mon-Sat 11-14, 15-21; Rbls, $; Eng, Fr

Chao-Chao - *See* CLOTHING

City, *Clothing, shoes, audio/video, food*
Malaya Konyushennaya ul., 7 311-80-20
Rbls, $; Eng

Cristian - *See* CLOTHING

Diesel International, *Clothing, shoes*
Kamennoostrovskiy pr., 37............. 233-47-20
Mon-Sat 11-18; $; Eng, Ger

Electrolux - *See* AUDIO EQUIPMENT &
KITCHEN APPLIANCES

Eurotrade - *See* FOOD STORES

Express Market - *See* FOOD STORES

FAIRN & SWANSON

Electronics, Housewares, Toys
Nevskiy pr., 96............................... 275-53-85
Fax... 275-53-86
Daily 10-14, 15-20; Rubles; English

The Frontier Shop

At the Finnish-Russian Border. The shop offers a wide range of goods including liquor, perfumes, tobacco, soft drinks, delicatessen, leisure wear, fashion accessories, cameras and film, watches, jewelry, gifts and souvenirs
Town of "Torfyanovka"
on the Helsinki-St. Petersburg Road

Int'l Tel. 949-357-444
Telex .... 121015 SITOP SU

Aer Rianta-Vyborg Town JV
Open: 8-23 daily

Future Vision - *See* CLOTHING

Hard Currency Store, *Audio equipment, clothing*
Stachek pr., 14/2........................... 252-44-03
Fax... 252-49-96
Mon-Sat 9-13, 14-1:70; $; Eng

Kris Agro - *See* ELECTRONIC GOODS

Lenrianta, *Main Office*
Airport Pulkovo-2........................... 104-34-87
Fax... 104-34-86

Littlewoods
Wide selection of & imported goods
See our ad under DEPARTMENT STORES. *Fashions from abroad*
Nevskiy pr., 35, Gostinyy Dvor, Sadovaya Liniya
☎ 110-51-95
.... 110-54-47
Mon-Sat 10-20; Rbls, $; Eng; T-bus 1; Metro Gostinyy Dvor

Mitsar, *Audio, shoes, clothing*
Bolshoy pr., P.S., 15 232-04-82
Fax... 233-87-41
Mon-Sat 10-14, 15-19; Rbls, $; Eng

The Neva-Star Shop, The Baltic Star Shop
See ad on next page

Okhta, *Bathroom fixtures, clothing*
Bolshaya Pushkarskaya ul., 20 232-01-47
Fax... 277-23-12
Mon-Fri 10-19; Rbls, $

THE BEST SHOPS
IN ST. PETERSBURG!

Souvenirs	China
Food	Liquor
Tobacco	Electronics
Televisions	Audio/Video Equipment
Watches	Household Appliances
Perfume	Jewelry
Medicines	Goods for Children
Crystal	Household Goods
Magazines & Newspapers	Luggage
Automotive supplies	Gifts
Clothes	Cosmetics

INTERNATIONAL SHOPPING

The Neva Star Shop
Moskva Hotel, Alexander Nevsky Square
St. Petersburg, Tel: 274-0012/0024

The Baltic Star Shop
Pribaltiyskaya Hotel, Korablestroiteley 14
St. Petersburg, Tel: 356-2284/4185

Osvas

in the Astoria Hotel

Liquors • Perfumes • Soft Drinks

Snack Foods • Selected Clothing Items

Bolshaya Morskaya ul., 39, Block A

Tel 210-50-62

Hrs: 10.00-22.00, $, Engl., Ger., Fin.

Petr Velikiy   **Peter the Great**
See PHOTOGRAPHY, CAMERAS & SUPPLIES
Rospol - *See* CLOTHING
Rus
  Pestelya ul., 12 275-06-03
          Food Store
      Daily 9-14, 15-19; Rbls, $
**Skyshop Inflight Service Exclusively
on Aeroflot**
  Office at Airport Pulkovo-2 104-34-91
  104-34-92
  Fax 104-34-68
          Mon-Fri 9-18; $; Eng

Sovinteravto service

AUTO PARTS
*Parts, accessories & supplies
for foreign cars, trucks & buses
Visit Our Shop on Gogolya ul. 19,
near the Astoria Hotel*
Gogolya ul., 19 315-97-58
Telex .... 121412 LTOS SU
Fax 292-00-28
  Mon-Fri 10 a.m.- 6 p.m., Eng, $
Malodetskoselskiy pr., 26.. 292-77-18

TRAVEL SHOP
Imports from Germany and Holland
Sports clothing, leather jackets, shoes,
packaged foods, cosmetics, beer, liquor,
drinks, cigarettes, thermoses,
coffee makers, small refrigerators,
radios, etc.
Moskovskiy pr., 73 296-57-90
  *Metro: Frunzenskaya,
Hrs: 10-18 (Closed Sun & Mon), English, $*

The Art of Russia - See ARTS & HANDICRAFTS
The Electronic Store at the Airport Shop
  See ELECTRONIC GOODS
Tradehouse of Holland
See CLOTHING *and* FOOD STORES
Viking, *Food, soft drinks, perfume, audio/video*
  Vyborgskaya nab., 5/2.................. 542-80-32
        Daily 10-19; $, CC; Eng

☎ **INTERPRETERS**
    See TRANSLATION SERVICES

☎ **INTOURIST**
    ИНТУРИСТ
    INTOURIST
    INTOURIST
    INTOURIST
    INTOURIST

    See TRAVEL AGENCIES
*This once powerful monopoly has been
split into a number of semi-independent
firms including Intertrans, Interbureau and
many hotels.*

☎ **INTRODUCTION SERVICE**
    ЗНАКОМСТВ, СЛУЖБА
    BEKANNTSCHAFTEN
    RENCONTRES, SERVICE DE
    KONTAKTFÖRMEDLING
    KONTAKTIPALVELUT

*This category refers to Russian "dating
services" for singles to meet each other,
similar to those in Western countries.*
Fortune
  Furmanova ul., 30 279-76-49
        Tue-Sun 10-14, 15-20; Rbls

Noolis
Kamennoostrovskiy pr., 42 230-75-35
Daily 9-13, 14-21; Rbls

☎ **INVESTMENT COMPANIES**
ИНВЕСТИЦИОННЫЕ
КОМПАНИИ
ANGLAGEGESELLESCHAFTEN
INVESTISSEMENTS,
COMPAGNIES D'
INVESTERINGSBOLAG
SIJOITUSYHTIÖT

INVESTMENT COMPANY

ALEXANDER

Securities Market Operations
Consulting, Privatization,
Investment Analysis
Konnogvardeyskiy blvd., 4, apt. 11
Tel 311-64-61
Fax 311-78-22
Telex.............................621223 ALDR SU
E-mail .... rse@vsi.spb.su

**ARCA-American-Russian Commercial
Alliance**
Khlopina ul., 10.............................. 535-54-59
Fax 534-12-84
Mon-Fri 9-18; Rbls, $; Eng, Fr

Arean
Rastrelli pl., 2 110-73-19
Fax 274-18-94
Mon-Fri 9-18; Rbls, $; Eng

 Ciclon S.A.

St. Petersburg, Russia
Primorskiy pr., 6, office 7, 8, 25
Tel./Fax 239-53-74
....239-51-44
Tel./Fax 239-97-60
....239-63-67
Telex ....121497 NORD SU

General Investment Fund
Kapitanskaya ul., 3........................ 352-45-15
Fax 352-57-54
Mon-Fri 9-21; Rbls; Eng, Ger

Samson
Akademika Konstantinova ul., 8/2 .. 550-87-36
Fax 550-87-77
*Mon-Fri 9-18; Rbls; Eng, Ger, Fr
Tram 9; Metro Akademicheskaya*

Scorpion
Voznesenskiy pr., 4........................ 259-54-61
Fax 292-60-73
Mon-Fri 9-18; Rbls; Eng

St. Petersburg Finance Company
Kuznechnyy per., 14 a.................... 113-25-44
Fax 112-23-66
Mon-Fri 10-18; Rbls, $; Eng; Metro Dostoevskaya

Stern & Co.
Investment Banking and Venture Capital Operations
Commercial Consulting, Specialized Real Estate Brokerage
Nevskiy pr., 104 275-45-87
Fax.. 275-58-64

Vostok
Bumazhnaya ul., 6.......................... 186-66-22
Fax 275-54-38
Mon-Fri 9-17:30; Rbls, $; Eng

☎ **JAZZ**
ДЖАЗ
JAZZ
JAZZ
JAZZ
JAZZ

Art-Cafe

Jazz, Drama, Avant-garde, Poetry
Gertsena ul., 58, 1 flight up
510-46-52
Friday, Saturday, Sunday at 7 p.m.

Jazz
Philharmonic Hall

♪♪ **(Formerly Jazz Club)** ♪♪

*David Goloshchekin's jazz band
Nightly programs starting at 8 p.m.
Jam sessions past midnight
on Friday & Saturday
Sunday matinee " Jazz for the Children "*

Zagorodnyy pr., 27 164-85-65
.... 113-53-31

*TUE-SUN 14-20; RBLS; ENG
BUS 30, TRAMS 11,28,34, TROLLEYS 3,8,9,15, from
METRO: VLADIMIRSKAYA*

Kvadrat Jazz Club   **Concerts**
Pravdy ul., 10................................ 164-56-83
Concerts on Mon, Fri, Sun 19:00; Rbls; Eng, Ger

☎ **JEWELRY**
ЮВЕЛИРНЫЕ ИЗДЕЛИЯ
JUWELIERE
BIJOUTERIES
SMYCKEN
KULTASEPÄNLIIKKEET

---

7 Karat   **7 Carets**
Volynskiy per., 2 314-84-55
Mon-Sat 10-14, 15-19; Rbls

Akvamarin   **Aquamarine**
Novo-Smolenskaya nab., 1 352-07-66
Mon-Sat 10-19; Rbls

Almaz   **Diamond**
Veteranov pr., 87 150-82-38
Mon-Sat 10-14, 15-19; Rbls

Ametist   **Amethyst**
Bolshoy pr., P.S., 64 232-01-02
Mon-Sat 10-14, 15-19; Rbls

Russian Jewelry Art
Faberge by Ananov Collection

ANANOV

AT THE GRAND HOTEL EUROPE
Mikhaylovskaya ul. 1/7

Tel./Fax **119-60-08**

Hrs: 11-20, $, English, German,
French, Spanish, Italian

Biryuza	Turquoise
Nevskiy pr., 69	312-21-76

Daily 10-14, 15-19; Rbls; Metro Mayakovskaya

BOSCO
Trade Company

Large Selection of Fine Jewelry
Millionnaya ul., 8
Barmaleeva ul., 6
Malaya Konyushennaya ul., 8

Tel	311-88-51
	312-11-47
Fax	219-18-54

Granat	Garnet
Bukharestskaya ul., 72	268-22-75

Mon-Sat 10-14, 15-19; Rbls; Tram 25, 43

Handmade Jewelry and Repair
Barmaleeva ul., 8 232-17-67
Mon-Sat 9-19; Rbls

Iskorka	Sparkle
Ivanovskaya ul., 26	560-35-31

Mon-Sat 10-14, 15-19; Rbls

Izumrud, *Second Hand Store*	Emerald
Moskovskiy pr., 184	298-32-42

Tues-Sat 10-14, 15-19; Rbls; Metro Moskovskaya

Kristall	Crystal
Nevskiy pr., 32/34	311-30-95

Mon-Sat 10-14, 15-19; Rbls

Polyarnaya Zvezda	Pole Star
Nevskiy pr., 158	277-09-80

Mon-Fri 10-14, 15-19; Rbls

Rubin	Ruby
Stachek pr., 69	183-51-39

Mon-Sat 10-19; Rbls

Russkie Samotsvety
Russian Semi-precious Stones
Utkin pr., 8 528-10-91
Fax 528-23-78

Salon-Skupka, *Purchase and sale of jewelry*
Bolshoy Sampsonievskiy pr., 92 245-36-51
Mon-Sat 9-14, 15-19; Rbls; Metro Petrogradskaya

Samotsvety	Semi-precious Stones
Mikhaylovskaya ul., 4	110-49-15

Mon-Fri 10-14, 15-19; Rbls; Metro Nevskiy Prospekt

Sapfir	Sapphire
Engelsa pr., 15	550-00-80

Mon-Sat 10-19; Rbls

Yakhont	Ruby
Gertsena ul., 24	314-64-47

Mon-Sat 10-19; Rbls

Zhemchug	Pearl
Slavy pr., 5	261-37-20

Mon-Sat 10-19; Rbls

☎ KEROSENE
КЕРОСИН
KEROSIN/PETROLEUM
KEROSENE
GASOL
KEROSIINI

Kerosene is used in dachas and sold in the suburbs. Try the Russian version of a hardware-paint-dry goods store (Khozyaystvennye Tovary, Хозяйственные товары), otherwise try here.

Vega
Vokzalnaya ul., 2, Pargolovo 594-89-69
Mon-Sat 9-14, 15-18; Rbls

☎ KIOSKS
КИОСКИ
KIOSKE
KIOSQUES
KIOSKER
KIOSKIT

See NEWSPAPERS, MAGAZINES, BOOKS, *and*
MARKETS

Outdoor kiosks are shops in small booths on the sidewalks, squares, markets and around the metros of St. Petersburg. Most sell alcohol, drinks, and cigarettes, while others also specialize in newspapers, ticket sales, lotto, milk, souvenirs, fruits & vegetables, "bootleg" cassettes, or clothing.

Often they remain open late, some 24 hours a day, and they do most of their sales early and late. The largest collections of kiosks in St. Petersburg are found around metros and train stations, especially Ploshchad Mira (Sennaya Ploshchad), Gorkovskaya, Ploshchad Lenina, Moskovskaya and Ploshchad Vosstaniya.

In good weather, hundreds of tables appear on the sidewalks selling bananas, fruit, eggs, souvenirs, watches, books. Practically everything can be bought on the street and nearly everyone has something to sell, from the modern kiosks with Marlboro Cigarettes and Coca-Cola sponsors to the old man with four boxes of matches standing by the metro.

☎ **KITCHEN APPLIANCES**
БЫТОВЫЕ ПРИБОРЫ,
КУХОННЫЕ
KÜCHENGERÄTE
CUISINE, INSTRUMENTS DE
KÖKSAPPARATER
KOTITALOUSKONEET

Russian appliances are simple but effective and low-cost, especially toasters, coffee grinders, and electric tea kettles, refrigerators, space heaters and stoves. For fans, vacuum cleaners, and small appliances try ELECTRICAL GOODS, HARDWARE STORES and DEPARTMENT STORES. Large appliances (refrigerators, stoves, freezers) are sold in special stores called Kholodilniki (Холодильники). See REFRIGERATORS. Imported and Russian appliances are also available in COMMERCIAL STORES and some INTERNATIONAL SHOPS. Air conditioners are scarce but available.

For information on cost and availability of refrigerators in various appliance stores in St. Petersburg, call 184-98-14.

Electrolux, *Electrolux microwave ovens, mixers, food processors, etc.*
Robespera nab., 16 275-55-12
.... 275-00-52

Home □ Center
Custom Built Kitchens
Let us build your kitchen from bottom to top starting from tiles, counter top and kitchen cabinets, full range of kitchen appliances, counters exhaust fans, hot water heaters, sinks and dishwashers.

Located in S.E. St. Pb., minutes from city center
Slavy pr., 30 261-15-50
.... 261-04-02
Fax 260-15-81
Daily 10-20; $, FIM, DM, Rbls; Eng, Finn, Ger
Metro Moskovskaya, then Bus 31, 114, T-bus 29

Home □ Center
Kitchen Appliances
Complete line of major kitchen appliances
Refrigerators, freezers, Seppel Fricke stoves, dishwashers, kitchen exhaust fans, Complete line of Philips microwaves, mixers, cookers, toasters, and small kitchen appliances.

Air conditioners, washing machines, clothes dryers, vacuum cleaners, irons, fans, hot water heaters and more.

In S.E. St. Pb., minutes from city center.
Slavy pr., 30 261-15-50
....261-04-02
Fax.......................................260-15-81
Daily 10-20; $, FIM, DM, Rbls; Eng, Finn, Ger
Metro Moskovskaya, then Bus 31, 114, T-bus 29

INIS Stock Company
Nab. kan. Obvodnogo, 92 252-78-67
.... 108-44-23
Fax.. 293-56-03

Philips
Refrigerators, washing machines, coffee and juice makers, food processors, etc.
Suvorovskiy pr., 2 277-01-25
Fax.. 277-00-13
Tues-Sat 10-14, 15-19; Rbls, $

Rumit
Engelsa pr., 43 553-16-97
Daily 10-19; Rbls

Siemens
Refrigerators, microwaves, food processors
Robespera nab., 8/46 275-05-50
Mon-Sat 10-14, 15-19; Rbls, $

☎ **KITCHENWARE**
ПРЕДМЕТЫ ДЛЯ КУХНИ
GESCHIRR
CUISINE, ARTICLES POUR
KÖKSTILLBEHÖR
TALOUSTARVIKKEET

See also HARDWARE, HOUSEWARES, CRYSTAL & PORCELAIN, *and* DEPARTMENT STORES

This category includes tableware, pots & pans, dishes, teapots, etc. Most of these can be bought in the Russian equivalent of a HARDWARE store and in some COMMERCIAL STORES. These are specialized shops for tableware and small appliances.

HTH-Kukhni   **HTH-Kitchens**
Nevskiy pr., 3 311-82-79
.... 311-82-80
Mon-Fri 10-14, 15-18; Rbls, $; Eng

Khozyaystvennye Tovary
              Table and Cookware
Yakornaya ul., 1 224-38-03
Yakornaya ul., 2 224-34-86
Mon-Sat 10-14, 15-19; Rbls

Khrustal i Farfor   **Crystal and China**
Nice selection of glassware, china, vases and plastic housewares
Sadovaya ul., 38 310-07-34
Mon-Sat 10-19; Rbls

Kitchenware
Sezdovskaya Liniya, 25 213-21-17
Mon-Sat 10-14, 15-19; Rbls

Mapen
Toreza pr., 38................................ 552-77-22
Mon-Sat 10-14, 15-19; Rbls

Olesya
Nevskiy pr., 97 277-17-81
Mon-Sat 10-14, 15-19; Rbls

Tableware & Chemicals
Bolshoy pr., V.O., 40 355-81-96
Soap, cleaners
Mon-Sat 10-14, 15-19; Rbls

Tableware & Cookware
Bolshoy pr., P.S., 57 232-72-57
Mon-Sat 10-19; Rbls

Valeriya Tableware
Voznesenskiy pr., 18 314-81-48
Mon-Fri 10-19; Rbls

☎ LANGUAGE COURSES
КУРСЫ ИНОСТРАННЫХ ЯЗЫКОВ
SPRACHKURSE
LANGUES, COURS DE
SPRÅKKURSER
KIELIKURSSIT

There are many opportunities to learn languages in St. Petersburg. Private instructors are hesitant to give their names and addresses, but they have all been called. Try them for private tutoring. We know that at least one consulate offers language lessons; for French call the cultural section of the French consulate at 311-09-95. The large advertisers here are professional firms.

Advanced Humanities Courses
Voznesenskiy pr., 34 b 314-35-21
Fax 315-39-17
Mon-Fri 10-22; Rbls

A. J. EST S.U.
Russian Language Tours
St. Petersburg, Moscow, Odessa
Konnogvardeyskiy blvd., 4, Entry 6
Tel 312-72-92
Telex .... 121732 CGTT SU

All St. Petersburg
Gertsena ul., 8 312-67-72
Mon-Fri 11-19; Rbls; Eng
Alliance Francaise
Reki Moyki nab., 20 311-09-95
.... 312-02-39
Mon-Sat 10-19; Rbls; Fr

AsLANTIS
Russian as a Foreign Language
Major European Languages
Dibunovskaya ul., 24, office 7
Tel./Fax 239-36-45
English, French; Metro: Chernaya Rechka

Belye Nochi   **White Nights**
Utkin pr., 13, bldg. 1 528-56-46
Mon, Wed-Fri 17-20
Dialog *(including Russian)*   **Dialogue**
Avangardnaya ul., 20, bldg. 1, rm. 31
☎ 135-00-98
Daily 9-22
Ego Saint Petersburg Transit
Dumskaya ul., 3 242-97-05
Mon-Fri 9-21
Ego
Apraksin dvor, bldg. 1, rm. 69 310-12-88
Mon-Fri 9-19
Express-Linguistics
Shamsheva ul., 8 235-56-72
Mon-Sat 10-19; Rbls; Eng, Ger, Fr, Finn
Gallaks *(open from September 1993 till May 1994)*
Please call 310-37-34
Daily 9-20; Rbls; Eng, Fr, Finn

Humanities Center
Griboedova kan. nab., 92/1 310-20-90
Mon-Fri 9-17:30; Rbls
Kursy Inostrannykh Yazykov
    Language Courses *(including Russian)*
Bolshoy pr., P.S., 73 232-00-26
Mon-Wed, Fri-Sat; Rbls; Eng, Ger
LS-Language School
Moskovskiy pr., 1 310-58-28
Mon-Sat 9-20; Eng, Ger

Language Courses
Russian Language, Correspondence Classes
Narodnaya ul., 2, apt. 48 263-03-72

Language Courses
14-ya Liniya, 29 218-44-62
Mon-Sat 17-20; Rbls; Eng, Ger, Fr
Language Courses No. 4
Vitebskiy pr., 49, bldg. 2 299-63-21
Daily 17-23; Rbls; Eng, Fr
Lingva
7-ya Liniya, 36 218-73-39
Mon-Fri 9-22; Rbls; Eng
Marina International
Gorokhovaya ul., 26 310-54-65
Daily 9-23; Rbls; Eng
Mika
Kamennoostrovskiy pr., 34 232-08-23
Fax 312-41-28
Mon-Fri 10-20; Rbls, $; Eng
Obuchenie   **Education**
Zagorodnyy pr., 58 292-40-05
Daily 10-19; Rbls, $; Eng, Ger, Fr, Finn, Ital
Metro Tekhnologicheskiy Institut
Omis *(including Russian)*
Metallistov pr., 18/2, 4th floor 233-17-85
Daily 9-21; Rbls; Eng
Quazar - Center
Zhdanovskaya ul., 8 230-83-58
Mon-Fri 9-17

St. Petersburg State University
Russian Language Center
• Educational Programs
   from 2 weeks to 10 months, year-round
• 30 years experience teaching
   Russian to foreigners
Universitetskaya nab., 7/9 218-94-52
Fax 218-13-46

ST. PETERSBURG CHAMBER OF COMMERCE & INDUSTRY
LANGUAGE COURSES
Chaykovskogo ul., 46-48 ... 273-48-96

Tsentr Inostrannykh Yazykov
Center of Foreign Languages
Including Russian

Pobedy ul., 10, School No. 594 242-07-27
Daily 9-12; Rbls, $; Eng, Ger
Volodi Ermaka ul., 9 113-79-25
.... 110-68-82
Fax 219-73-29

VISIT IE Ltd.
Russian Language Courses
Reki Moyki nab., 24, apt. 18.......... 314-10-72
Tel./Fax................................. 314-06-44
Mon-Fri 10-17, Fr, Rbls, $; Metro Nevskiy Prospect

Vneshvuz Center
Morskaya nab., 9 355-60-56
Mon-Fri 10-18; Rbls, $; Eng, Ger, Finn

Yugoross
Moskovskiy pr., 33, rm. 13 292-46-34
Mon-Sat 14-20; Rbls, $, CC; Eng, Ger

☎ LAUNDROMATS
СТИРАЛЬНЫЕ АВТОМАТЫ
WASCHAUTOMATEN/
WASCHMASCHINEN
LAVOIRS
TVÄTTOMATER
ITSEPALVELUPESULAT

St. Petersburg has had Laundromats with self-service for years. Large antiquated commercial washers and dryers are, however, only for the brave and desperate. See below.

☎ LAUNDRY/DRY CLEANING
ПРАЧЕЧНЫЕ, ХИМЧИСТКА
WÄSCHEREIEN/CHEM. REIN.
BLANCHISSERIE
NETTOYAGE A SEC,
TVÄTT/KEMTVÄTT
PESULAT/KEMIALLISET PESUT

See also DRY CLEANING

Laundry can be a problem for travelers. Do it yourself like many Russians, ask at a hotel, find a Babushka to do it, or entrust it to the 210 "municipal laundries" listed in Ves St. Pb. 93. There are also three self-service Laundromats and dry cleaners in St. Petersburg. For an update on Laundromats, call the Central Administration of Laundries at 239-41-69.

Khimchistka, *Mon-Fri 8-17*   **Dry Cleaning**
Moiseenko ul., 24 271-29-06
Laundromat With Self-Service Machines & Dry Cleaning
• Metallistov pr., 73 540-19-35
Mon-Sat 8-20
• Tramvaynyy pr., 14 254-83-41
Mon-Sat 9-19
• Zanevskiy pr., 37 528-38-19
Mon-Fri 8-17
Laundromat & Service Center
Narvskiy pr., 18 252-00-58
Mon-Sat 10-14, 15-20; Rbls
Nezhnost Dry Cleaning
Kantemirovskaya ul., 19 245-20-64
Mon-Sat 8-20; Rbls, $
Private Dry Cleaner
Tikhoretskiy pr., 9, bldg. 4 555-08-57
Mon-Sat 10-14, 15-19; Rbls

Vista Laundry and Dry Cleaning
Chervonnogo Kazachestva ul., 36 a
☎ 183-07-42
Mon-Fri 9-12; Rbls, $; Ger; T-bus 127; Metro Kirovskiy zavod

☎ LAW COURTS
СУДЫ
GERICHTE
PALAIS DE JUSTICE
RÄTTSSAL
TUOMIOISTUIMET

City Court Presidium
Reki Fontanki nab., 16 273-32-36
.... 273-07-52
Mon-Fri 9:30-18
Gorodskoy Sud (City Court) of Saint Petersburg
Reki Fontanki nab., 16, floors 1,2,4
.... 273-07-52
.... 273-10-81
Leningrad Oblast Regional Court
Reki Fontanki nab., 16, floor 3, Secretary's Office
.... 273-14-52
Mon-Fri 9:30-18; Rbls

☎ LAW FIRMS & LAWYERS
ЮРИДИЧЕСКИЕ ФИРМЫ
И ЮРИСТЫ
RECHTSANWÄLTE UND NOTARE
NOTAIRES
ADVOKATBYRÅ, ADVOKAT
LAKIASIANTOIMISTOT
JA LAKIMIEHET

There are many types of lawyers in Russia. In particular, a jurist provides legal advice, registers firms and draws up contracts, while an advocat (similar to a barrister) is allowed to try cases before a court of law. There are many new private lawyers and law firms as well as the traditional "official legal consultation groups". We have listed Russian law firms and lawyers, legal consultation groups, and Western law firms.

WESTERN LAW FIRMS & LAWYERS
JOINT-VENTURE LAW FIRMS

BAKER & McKENZIE
St. Petersburg's International Law Firm

Resident Partner: Arthur L. George

Canal Griboedova 36	Telephones: +7 (812)
191023 St.Petersburg	310-5446; 310-5941;
Telex: 612151 BMSTP	310-5544
Fax: +7 (812) 310-59-44	for int'l dialing
	7-812-850-1425

Cheryl Ann Sigsbee, Attorney *(USA)*
Tel/Fax 109-69-14

Hans Eike von Oppeln-Bronikowski
Zagorodnyy pr., 28...................... 112-53-57
Fax....................................... 113-28-74
Mon-Fri 10-18; Rbls, $; Ger

MKD, *Russian-Italian*
Shpalernaya ul., 52 275-56-23
Fax....................................... 275-54-55
Mon-Sat 9-19; Rbls, $; Eng, Finn

Murray, Andronova & Associates
Privatization, Banking, Company Registration
An American-Russian Law Firm
Please call 110-66-33

NEVINPAT
St. Petersburg International Patent and Trade Mark Agency

Complete	Registration,
assistance	Searches
with patent,	Patent &
trademark,	Trademark
and design	Infringement

Nevskiy pr., 134, apt. 5, 4 floor
Tel.: 274-42-97, 274-43-20
Fax 274-36-06
English, German, Finnish
A Russian-Finnish Law Firm

RusTex International (USA)
Investment, Securities, & Privatization
Victor Konovalenko & Cheryl Ann Sigsbee
Tel/Fax.. 109-69-14

SHH INTERNATIONAL
(SALANS HERTZFELD & HEILBRONN)
L A W   O F F I C E S

TEMPORARY OFFICE
DOM ZHURNALISTOV, NEVSKIY PR., 70
TEL.:   (812) 272-45-72
TEL./FAX: (812) 273-68-44

SHH INTERNATIONAL
(Salans Hertzfeld & Heilbronn)
IN MOSCOW: Ogareva ul., 17/9
.... (501) or (095) 940-29-44
Fax............. (501) or (095) 940-28-06
Smart
Admiralteyskiy pr., 8/1 110-66-55
Fax 110-65-70
Mon-Fri 10-18; Rbls, $; Eng, Ger, Fr, Finn, Swed, Ital

Law Office of S.A. Stern
Russian & American Legal Expertise in
Contract, Property, Tax & Customs Law
Nevskiy pr., 104 275-34-97
Fax...................................275-45-87

ZVENITA   Consulting
Complete Registration of New Enterprises
Komsomola ul.,13 235-27-31

RUSSIAN LAW FIRMS & LAWYERS

ABC, *Daily 9-17*
Sadovaya ul., 55/57, rm. 505 310-84-36

The Law Firm "AZ St. Petersburg"
Alekseev and Zagaraev
Complete registration of new enterprises
Legal consultation and contracts
Representation in arbitrage and courts
Furshtadtskaya ul., 21 275-45-64
English Spoken

Alkor
Apraksin Dvor 33, floor 2 310-44-70
Fax... 255-76-56
Mon-Fri 10-18; Rbls, $; Eng, Fr
Ameroid
Kronverkskiy pr., 5........................ 312-86-06
Mon-Fri 9-18; Rbls
Argus
Stachek pr., 72, rm. 42 183-84-49
Mon-Fri 10-18; Rbls
Avil Law Firm
Bolshoy pr., P.S., 64 235-66-15
Mon-Fri 10-16

BALFORT, Inc. Law Firm
Bolshoy Smolenskiy, 36
....568-04-91
Fax...568-04-93

Noted lawyers from St. Petersburg University
LL.D. A.Ivanov, LL.D. Medvedev, I.Yeliseyev

English speaking staff; weekdays: 10-18; $, Rbl

BAZIS
Legal advice for start-up
companies, corporations and joint ventures.
Bolshoy pr., P.S., 4 213-48-89
Open: 10-17; English

Brotek, *Mon-Fri 9-17; Rbls*
Kurchatova ul., 6, bldg. 5 552-94-20
Concord
Antonenko per., 2, rm. 10 314-05-54
Mon-Fri 10-18; T-bus 5; Metro Sadovaya
Concord Agency
Rubinshteyna ul., 3 315-18-32
Fax... 315-06-59
Mon-Fri 10-18; Rbls, $; Eng
Foreign Law Representation
Pushkinskaya ul., 13 112-16-79
Mon-Tue, Thu, Sat-Sun 10-13, 14-17
Inaudit AKG, *Mon-Fri 10-18; Rbls, $*
Italyanskaya ul., 33 311-61-53
Fax... 310-53-33
Inkoslimited
Yakubovicha ul., 3, apt. 68............. 312-56-45
Fax... 110-67-09
Mon-Fri 10-18; Rbls, $; Eng
Inter-Consult, *Mon-Sat 10-18; Rbls, $; Eng*
Mirgorodskaya ul., 24/28 275-66-47

Interlaw
Ligovskiy pr., 31 275-34-01
Mon-Fri 10-18; Rbls, $; Eng, Ger, Fr
Kokuroshnikov Evgeniy
Ligovskiy pr., 108 b 164-60-60
Daily 10-18; Ger

Kopol Auditkonsult

Legal Services & Auditing

V.O., Bolshoy pr., 92G 355-32-19

Fax 355-09-84

Lant, *Mon-Fri 10-17; Rbls; Eng*
Voznesenskiy pr., 36, apt. 28 310-27-31
Lawyer
Please call 275-05-55
Lawyer Alexander Savochkin
Please call 225-00-71
Lawyer Mikhail Aksenov
Please call 427-78-09
Legis Law Firm
Chaykovskogo ul., 2, off. 594 279-07-30
Daily 10-18; Ger
Market Bridge Ltd.
Nevskiy pr, 82 275-71-51
Fax: 275-71-50
See OFFICE EQUIPMENT
Oferta
Nevskiy pr., 65, 7th floor 314-01-27
Mon-Fri 9:30-18:30; Rbls; Eng, Ger, Fr
Rosinteks International
Obvodnogo kan. nab., 93 a, rm. 54 210-13-96
Mon-Fri 9-18; Eng
Sherif
Obukhovskoy Oborony pr., 143 567-20-26
Mon-Fri 9-18; Rbls, $; Eng
Sodruzhestvo, *Mon-Fri 10-18*
Rubinshteyna ul., 3 315-18-34
Us
Please call 166-18-61
Yanols, *Mon, Wed-Thu 12-16*
Pravdy ul., 8, apt. 23 113-26-04
Yuriskon
Kazanskaya ul., 36, rm. 309 311-78-50

PUBLIC LEGAL CONSULTATION

Advocate Bar Central Legal
 Consulting No. 1
Nevskiy pr., 16 312-81-36
Municipal Legal Consultation Offices
Yuridicheskaya Konsultatsiya
• Apraksin per., 1 315-85-10
Mon-Sat 11-18
• Baltiyskaya ul., 3 252-60-08
Mon-Sat 10-19
• Bolshoy pr., P.S. 33 232-41-11
Mon-Sat 9:30-19
• Bolshoy pr., V.O., 61 213-50-00
Mon-Fri 9:30-19
• Bolshoy Sampsonievskiy pr., 88 245-89-82
Mon-Sat 10-19
• Gogolya ul., 9 312-24-95
Mon-Fri 9:30-19; Rbls
• Komsomola ul., 10 542-22-87
Mon-Sat 10-19
• Ligovskiy pr., 31 275-33-96
Mon-Fri 10-18; Rbls

• Liteynyy pr., 33 272-82-56
Mon-Sat 10-19
• Moiseenko ul., 2 275-28-12
Mon-Sat 9:30-19
• Moskovskiy pr., 127 298-70-55
Mon-Sat 9:30-19
• Nevskiy pr., 74 273-89-15
Mon-Sat 10-19
• Obukhovskoy Oborony pr., 90 567-54-82
Mon-Sat 10-19
• Sredneokhtinskiy pr., 12 224-05-90
Mon-Sat 10-19
• Toreza pr., 2/40 550-16-05
Daily 9-20
• Vokzalnaya ul., 21, Kolpino 484-50-90
Mon-Fri 10-19
• Voznesenskiy pr., 41 314-80-27
Mon-Sat 9:30-19
• Zagorodnyy pr., 22 164-96-26
Mon-Sat 9:30-19

☎ **LEATHER GOODS**
 КОЖАНЫЕ ИЗДЕЛИЯ
 LEDERWAREN
 CUIR, ARTICLES DE
 LÄDERVAROR
 NAHKAVALMISTEET

See also LUGGAGE

*These shops carry belts, wallets,
handbags, briefcases, etc. For suitcases,
see* LUGGAGE. *For leather clothing, see*
CLOTHING *and* FURS.

Elina, *Bags, Mon-Fri 10-14, 15-19; Rbls*
Nekrasova ul., 58 279-26-77
Favorit, *Leather bags, Mon-Sat 10-18*
Khudozhnikov pr., 15 511-61-09
InterArtBazaar, *Leather briefcases*
See ad on page 271
Luggage - Salon, *Tue-Sun 9:30-17:30; Rbls, $*
Ligovskiy pr., 123 164-05-56
Na Peskakh **On Sand**
Moiseenko ul., 22/17 271-30-00
Fax 271-41-88
*Mon-Sat 11-13, 14-18; Rbls; Eng
T-bus 10; Metro Ploshchad Vosstaniya*
Olya
Razezzhaya ul., 12 164-92-92
Mon-Sat 10-14, 15-19; Rbls; Metro Ligovskiy Prospekt
Piero Guidi in Russia
Nevskiy pr., 54
Fax 314-25-38
Mon-Sat 11-14, 15-20; $; Eng, Ital
Tovary v Dorogu **Travel Goods**
Nevskiy pr., 114 273-31-38
Mon-Sat 10-14, 15-19; Rbls

☎ **LIBRARIES**
 БИБЛИОТЕКИ
 BIBLIOTHEKEN
 BIBLIOTHEQUES
 BIBLIOTEK
 KIRJASTOT

See also UNIVERSITIES
Academy of Sciences Library
Biblioteka Rossiyskoy Akademii Nauk
Birzhevaya Liniya, 1 218-35-92
Fax 218-74-36
Daily 9-20; E-7

Agricultural Library
Tsentralnaya Nauchnaya
Selskokhozyaystvennaya Biblioteka
Gertsena ul., 44 314-49-14
Mon-Fri 9-18; F-5

Central Naval Library
Tsentralnaya Voenno-Morskaya Biblioteka
Sadovaya ul., 2 210-43-54
Mon-Sat 10-20; G-6

Geological Library
Vsesoyuznaya Geologicheskaya Biblioteka
Sredniy pr., 74 218-92-28
Mon-Fri 11-17; Rbls; C-6

Library of the Academy of Arts
Nauchnaya Biblioteka
Rossiyskoy Akademii Khudozhestv
Universitetskaya nab., 17 213-65-29
Mon-Sat 9:30-21; E-6

Library of the Blind
Gorodskaya Biblioteka dlya Slepykh
Shamsheva ul., 8 232-71-07
Daily 9-17; E-8

Lunacharskiy Theater Library
Teatralnaya Biblioteka im. Lunacharskogo
Zodchego Rossi ul., 2 311-08-45
Daily 11-18; G-5

Mayakovskiy Central City Library
Tsentralnaya Gorodskaya Biblioteka
im. Mayakovskogo
Main municipal public library, reading rooms, &
children's libraries in every district.
Reki Fontanki nab., 44 311-30-26
Daily 10-21; H-6

Medical Scientific Library
Nauchno-Meditsinskaya Biblioteka
Lunacharskogo pr., 45 592-71-58
Mon-Fri 11-18

Musical Library of the St. Petersburg Philharmonic
Muzykalnaya Biblioteka
Sankt-Peterburgskoy Filarmonii
Mikhaylovskaya ul., 2 110-40-95

Pushkin Central City Children's Library
Detskaya Gorodskaya Biblioteka
im. A.S. Pushkina
Gertsena ul., 33 312-33-80
Mon-Sat 10-20; F-5

Russian National Library
Rossiyskaya Natsionalnaya Biblioteka
One of the largest research libraries in Russia
Sadovaya ul., 18 310-28-56
Fax 310-61-48
Daily 9-21; Metro Gostinyy Dvor; G-5

St. Petersburg State University Library
Biblioteka Sankt-Peterburgskogo
Gosudarstvennogo Universiteta
Universitetskaya nab., 7/9 218-27-51
Mon-Fri 11-17; Rbls; Eng; G-6

☎ **LIGHTING FIXTURES/BULBS**
ОСВЕЩЕНИЕ/ЛАМПЫ
LAMPEN/BELEUCHTUNG
FIXATION D'ECLAIRAGE
LYSE/LAMPOR
VALAISTUSLAITTEET/
HEHKULAMPUT

See also ELECTRICAL GOODS

Remember that electricity is 220 volt, 50 Hz and is not compatible with US

standards. The following shops are centrally located and usually have a selection of lamps and lighting fixtures.

Keep a good supply of light bulbs on hand as they are often in "deficit". Try looking in a commercial shop. Halogen light bulbs are hard to find.

Coemar EST, *Professional lighting fixtures*
Nevskiy pr., 39 314-99-98
Fax 310-09-07
Mon-Fri 10-19; Rbls; Ital

Electrical Goods No. 164
Nevskiy pr., 65 311-04-45
Mon-Sat 10-14, 15-19

Gallikht, *Mon-Fri 10-18; Rbls*
Konnogvardeyskiy blvd., 4, ent. 5, rm. 26
☎ 315-95-02

Gepard, *Florescent fixtures & lamps*
Khlopina ul., 10 534-60-06
Mon-Fri 9-16; Ploshchad Muzhestva

Halogen Lamp Bulbs at Imperial
See Stationary

Renlund, *Finnish lighting fixtures and bulbs*
Bolshaya Zelenina ul., 14 232-36-07
Mon-Fri 10-14, 15-19; Rbls, $; Finn

☎ **LIMOUSINE SERVICE**
ЛИМУЗИНЫ
LUXUSWAGENVERMEITUNG
LIMOUSINES, SERVICE DE
LIMOUSIN SERVICE
LIMOUSIINIVÄLITYS

See also AUTOMOBILE RENTAL, TAXI *and* DRIVING

All levels of comfort and luxury in chauffeured automobiles are readily available in St. Pb. Service is offered by private individuals with a little old Moskvich to elegant stretch Volvos and Mercedes. Most car rentals in St. Petersburg come with driver.

Interavto, *Daily 0-24; Rbls, $; Eng, Ger*
Ispolkomskaya ul., 9/11 277-40-32
Fax 277-25-62

Svit
Korablestroiteley ul., 14 356-10-74
Fax 356-00-04
Daily 10-17; Rbls, $; Eng, Ger, Finn

☎ **LINENS**
БЕЛЬЕ, МАГАЗИНЫ
LEINENWÄSCHE
LINGES
LINNE
LIINAVAATTEET

See also DEPARTMENT STORES

If you need bed linens, try DEPARTMENT STORES. The feather comforters and pillows are exceptionally comfortable. Tailors can custom make beautiful covers for them. Good thick towels are hard to find. Bring your own.

You can find lovely hand embroidered or crocheted table clothes, place mats, dollies, etc. in some of the handicraft shops. See ARTS AND HANDICRAFTS.

Rigonda
  Makarova nab., 28 213-09-27
    Mon-Fri 10-19

☎ LINGERIE
БЕЛЬЕ ДЛЯ ЖЕНЩИН
DAMENUNTERWÄSCHE
LINGERIE
UNDERKLÄDER, DAM
ALUSVAATTEET,NAISTEN

See also DEPARTMENT STORES *and*
CLOTHING WOMEN'S

LiSS, *Imported lingerie from Italy and Germany*
  Engelsa pr., 111 510-41-10
    Mon-Fri 9-18; Rbls; Metro Ozerki
Lyudmila
  Torzhkovskaya ul., 7 246-48-09
    Mon-Sat 10-19
Silveross
  Makarova nab., 28 213-09-27
    Daily 10-19

☎ LIQUOR/SPIRITS

See ALCOHOL/OFF-LICENSE

☎ LOCKSMITHS
СЛЕСАРНЫЕ РАБОТЫ
SCHLOSSEREIEN
SERRURIER
LÅSSMEDER
LUKKOSEPÄT

See also APARTMENT REPAIR *and* ALARM
SYSTEMS & DEVICES

*Locksmith service is provided by munici-
pal organizations called PREO and REU
(ПРЕО и РЭУ) which provide a variety of
repair services such as plumbing, electrical,
redecorating and locksmithing to their
assigned region of the city. See APARTMENT
REPAIR on how to get service. There are a
number of other organizations and private
cooperatives providing such services as
well.*

*Many doors have two locks. Keys can be
cut in "metal repair shops" (Remont
metalloizdeliy, Ремонт металлоизделий).
Good solid doors installed by locksmiths are
highly recommended, especially on the first
floor along with metal window grills
(Reshetki, Решетки) .*

Korund, *Mon-Fri 18-20; Rbls*
  Gorokhovaya ul., 56 113-53-00
Peterburgskie Zori
  Nevskiy pr., 95, floor 5 277-45-47
    Mon-Fri 9-18; Rbls
Slesarnaya Masterskaya   Locksmith
  Bolshoy pr., P.S., 71 232-30-97
    Mon-Fri 9-14, 15-19; Rbls
Slesarnaya Masterskaya   Locksmith
  Nekrasova ul., 60 279-26-76
    Mon-Sat 10-14, 15-20
Sokol, *Mon-Fri 10-18; Rbls*
  Savushkina ul., 12 239-65-36
Usluga
  Lermontovskiy pr., 1 114-63-57
    Mon-Fri 9-17; Rbls

☎ LOST PROPERTY
СТОЛЫ НАХОДОК
FUNDBÜROS
OBJETS TROUVES, BUREAU DES
FÖRLORAD EGENDOM
LÖYTÖTAVARATOIMISTOT

*Per chance, if you left a bag behind on
the bus or metro, it might be turned over to
this agency.*
Lost Property
  Zakharevskaya ul., 19 278-36-90
    Mon-Fri 11-17:30

☎ LUGGAGE
БАГАЖ
REISEGEPÄCK
BAGAGE
RESVÄSKOR
MATKATAVARAT

See also DEPARTMENT STORES *and*
SPORTS EQUIPMENT *and* LEATHER GOODS

*Luggage, briefcases and leather goods
can be purchased in special TRAVEL SHOPS,
DEPARTMENT STORES, SPORTS EQUIPMENT SHOPS
and in DLT, Tsentr Firmennoy Torgovli and
Gostinnyy Dvor on the 1st floor on the
Sadovaya Line and Perinnaya Line.*

Elina, *bags, Mon-Fri 10-14, 15-19; Rbls*
  Nekrasova ul., 58 279-26-77
Favorit, *Leather bags, Mon-Sat 10-18*
  Khudozhnikov pr., 15 511-61-09
InterArtBazaar for Samsonite
    See ad on page 271
Luggage - Salon
  Ligovskiy pr., 123 164-05-56
    Tue-Sun 9:30-17:30; Rbls, $; Eng
Na Peskakh   On Sand
  Moiseenko ul., 22/17 271-30-00
  Fax 271-41-88
    *Mon-Sat 11-13, 14-18; Rbls; Eng
    T-bus 10; Metro Ploshchad Vosstaniya*

Rosin *handbags*
Fine canvas hand & sports bags
  Vosstaniya ul., 1 275-34-12
    Mon-Sat 10-14, 15-19; Rbls, $

Tovary v Dorogu   Travel Goods
  Nevskiy pr., 114 273-31-38
    Mon-Sat 10-14, 15-19; Rbls
Turist, *Mon-Sat 10-14, 15-19; Rbls*
  Nevskiy pr., 122 277-02-79

☎ MAGAZINES
ЖУРНАЛЫ
ZEITSCHRIFTEN
MAGAZINES
MAGASIN, VECKO-OCH
MÅNADSTIDNINGAR
AIKAKAUSLEHDET

See also NEWSPAPERS *and* BUSINESS
PUBLICATIONS

FOREIGN MAGAZINES

Many are available in St. Petersburg

including The Economist, Business Week, Match, Time, Newsweek, Der Spiegel, PC World. *There are Russian editions of* Business Week, Reader's Digest, PC World, ComputerWorld *and a bi-weekly edition of* The New York Times.

WHERE TO BUY: The widest selection of foreign magazines and newspapers are found in the shops and kiosks at the Grand Hotel Europe, Nevskiy Palace and other major hotels. Finnish magazines are available at Stockmanns Supermarket, German magazines at the Bahlsen-Le Café (see CAFE*). Also try some of the hard currency food stores. In general, foreign publications are sold for hard currency. To check on availability or to subscribe to a foreign magazine or newspaper, try calling:*

BUREAU "INPRESS"

Distributors of more than 60 foreign magazines and newspapers in St. Pb.

including *Economist, Business Week , Der Spiegel, Paris Match, Vogue, Burda Moden, & L'Europeo*

Available at Grand Hotel Europe, Pribaltiyskaya, Okhtinskaya, Astoria and other fine hotels.

Subscriptions (short-term and long-term)

Pochtamtskaya ul., 9 312-82-91

MARTINUS NIJHOFF

Book dealers
Subscription to foreign magazines
Marata ul., 86 315-25-86

Mon-Fri 10-18

A much smaller selection, mostly newspapers, is available at bookstores and street kiosks for rubles.

FOREIGN LANGUAGE MAGAZINES PUBLISHED IN RUSSIA BY
Russian And Western Firms

Business Contact *(bi-monthly)*, Commersant *(weekly)*, Delovye Lyudi *(monthly)*, Passport *(bi-monthly)*, Saint Petersburg News *(monthly)*, Saint Petersburg Premier *(quarterly)*, Russian Trade Express *(quarterly)*. *They are generally sold along with foreign magazines.*

BUSINESS CONTACT - *See ad below*

Commersant Publishing House
St.Petersburg Representation

Nevskiy pr., 3, office 25 315-04-20
Fax 315-79-67

Hrs: 10-20, English, German, French

Commersant, *Weekly news in English*
Best business, editorials, prices & policies
Nevskiy pr., 3 off. 25 315-04-20
Fax 315-79-67

BUSINESS CONTACT
ДЕЛОВЫЕ СВЯЗИ

- The business magazine bringing you news on the cutting edge of banking, privatization, industry trends and up-coming meetings in Russia.

- The most influential guide for industry leaders throughout the CIS and abroad

- Bi-monthly, published in English & Russian editions.

- Advertise today and reach a readership of 35,000!

- Subscribe for a yearly price of $54!

**113461, Moscow, Kakhovka ul., 31
☎ 331-89-00; Fax 310-70-05**

DELOVIE LYUDI

provides valuable and unique information on the CIS market enabling decision makers and entrepreneurs to follow the market economy transition in the former USSR.

DELOVIE LYUDI
also offers foreign business people an exceptional medium for communicating details concerning their companies, products and services.

DELOVIE LYUDI
is published in both English and Russian by a Moscow editorial team.

DELOVIE LYUDI
is independent, objective and thorough.

Moscow, Profsoyuznaya ul., 73

☎ .... (095) 333-33-40
Fax .... (095) 330-15-68

US Offices
1560 Broadway, 5th floor, N.Y., N.Y. 10036
2865 East Coast Hwy. Suite 308
Corona del Mar, CA. 92625

PASSPORT
to the
New World

Distributed in hotels throughout the former USSR and on Aeroflot international flights.

Passport not only gives you an inside look at life in the former USSR, it also gives you a helping hand in making business contacts as well.

"Passport to the New World" is your right choice.

Passport International Ltd.
15, New Arbat, Flat # 617, 619
Moscow, Russia 121019
Tel .... (095) 202-22-71
Fax .... (095) 202-69-17

ZigZag Venture Group
254, Fifth Avenue
New York, New York 10001, USA
Tel .... (212) 725-6700
Fax .... (212) 725-6915

Russian-American Centre

Publishers of:
Americans in St. Petersburg
St. Petersburg Theater Guide
The Russian Connection
The Christmas Catalogue

Alexandrovskiy Park 4, Office 131
Baltic House Theater
Tel./Fax 232-85-76

RTE Press
PUBLISHING HOUSE

Publisher of:

• InterBusiness Magazine
in Russian

• Russian Trade Express
in English

• Rules & Regulations in Russia
in English

Information about Russian Economy, Law & Business

Russia, 191014,
St. Petersburg, P.O. Box 151
Tel.: 164-41-78, 164-21-93
Fax: 164-40-78

Russian Trade Express, *English, quarterly*
Articles on business and trade in Russia
Pavlogradskiy per., 6 164-41-78
Fax 164-40-78
Mon-Sat 10-19; $

Pick Up Your Copy Today

Saint Petersburg PREMIER

Available FREE in all leading hotels

Saint Petersburg Premier, *Eng, quarterly.*
Interesting articles on culture, history and news.
For foreigners visiting and living in St. Petersburg.
Professora Popova ul., 47, off. 709
☎ 234-53-34
Fax 110-73-93

DELOVIE LYUDI

I N D E P E N D E N T • O B J E C T I V E • T H O R O U G H
Profsoyuznaya ul., 73; Tel.: (095) 333-33-40; Fax: (095) 330-15-68

Saint Petersburg News, *Eng, monthly; Timely articles on business & culture; publisher Florman Information Russia*
Kamennoostrovskiy pr., 14 b 233-76-82
Fax 232-80-17
Mon-Fri 9:30-18; Rbls, $; Eng, Ger, Finn, Swed

Saint Petersburg Today and Tonight
Eng & Ger; quarterly, information for tourists, Santa Ltd. Advertising Agency publisher
Makarova nab., 30 218-39-47
Fax 218-06-15
Daily 9-18; Rbls, $; Eng, Ger

RUSSIAN MAGAZINES IN RUSSIAN

WHERE TO BUY RUSSIAN MAGAZINES

Russian magazines and newspapers are sold largely in KIOSKS, *on the street near metros, and in hotels. Magazines are sold in Rospechat, (Роспечать) kiosks, now often denoted by a bright red Coca-Cola sign and by Novoe Vremya kiosks. Magazines are mainly distributed in the Rospechat stores listed below. To start a subscription, see* NEWSPAPERS.

You can receive information on any newspaper or magazine sold by Rospechat by calling:

Rospechat Commercial Department
☎ 315-44-78

Rospechat Stores
• Bolshoy pr., V.O., 72 217-25-22
Mon-Fri 1-14, 15-19; Rbls
• Bukharestskaya ul., 72, bldg. 1 268-08-57
Mon-Fri 10-14, 15-19; Rbls
• Dekabristov ul., 36 114-48-28
Mon-Sat 10-14, 15-19; Rbls
• Griboedova kan. nab., 27 311-70-58
Mon-Fri 11-14, 15-19; Rbls
• Ligovskiy pr., 34 164-66-24
Mon-Sat 9-14, 15-18; Rbls
• Ligovskiy pr., 171 166-11-51
Mon-Sat 10-14, 15-19; Rbls; Eng, Ger
• Mayakovskogo ul., 23 272-80-65
Mon-Fri 10-14, 15-19; Rbls; Ger
• Moskovskiy pr., 73 252-64-08
Mon-Sat 9:30-13, 15:30-19; Rbls
• Nauki pr., 42 249-09-00
Mon-Sat 10-14, 15-19; Rbls
• Razezzhaya ul., 16/18 312-95-00
Mon-Sat 11-14, 15-19; Rbls; Metro Dostoevskaya
• Rubinshteyna ul., 10 311-44-12
Mon-Fri 11-14; 15-18; Rbls
• Sennaya pl., 5 315-60-80
Mon-Sat 10-14, 15-19; Rbls
• Zhukovskogo ul., 4 273-65-18
Mon-Sat 10-14, 15-19; Rbls; Eng

MAJOR RUSSIAN MAGAZINES WITH OFFICES IN MOSCOW

Novyy Mir, *Monthly, serious fiction, politics, reviews*

Oktyabr, *Monthly, serious fiction, politics, reviews*

Moskva, *Monthly, serious fiction, politics, reviews*

Ogonek, *Weekly, politics, people, culture*

Nash Sovremennik, *Monthly, culture, history, politics*

Vokrug Sveta, *Geographical journal, travel, fiction*

MAGAZINES WITH OFFICES IN ST. PETERSBURG:

Avrora, *Rus, monthly, fiction, poetry & criticism*
Millionnaya ul., 4 312-13-23
Mon-Fri 10-18; Rbls, $

Gorodskaya Starina, *Rus, monthly*
                       City Antiques
Reki Moyki nab., 32 312-77-25
Mon-Sat 10-14, 15-19; Rbls; Eng

Neva, *Rus, monthly, fiction, poetry, reviews*
Nevskiy pr., 3 318-84-72
Fax 311-08-17
Mon-Fri 11-18; Rbls

Print and Publishing, *Rus, monthly, sub. only*
Pavlogradskiy per., 6/10 164-20-93
Fax 164-41-78
Mon-Sat 10-19; Rbls, $

Russkaya Literatura   **Russian Literature**
Makarova nab., 4, Pushkinskiy Dom ... 218-19-01
Mon-Fri 9-18; Rbls, $

Sankt-Peterburgskaya Panorama
Rus, monthly, culture & history of St. Petersburg
Nevskiy pr., 53 113-15-23
Mon-Fri 10-18; Rbls

Shop-Talk,Mon-*Sat 10-20; Rbls, $; Eng*
Pochtamtskaya ul., 5, apt. 30 311-63-19

Sudostroenie   **Shipbuilding**
Promyshlennaya ul., 14 a 186-16-09
Mon-Fri 8:30-11:30, 12:30-17:30; Rbls, $; Eng

Top-Shlep, *Rus, monthly, children's stories*
Pushkinskaya ul., 10, apt. 123 164-57-07
Mon-Fri 11-18; Rbls; Metro Ploshchad Vosstaniya

Zvezda *Rus, monthly, fiction, poetry, politics* **Star**
Mokhovaya ul., 20 272-89-48
Mon-Fri 10-18; Rbls, $

☎ MAPS & MAP SHOPS
КАРТЫ, МАГАЗИНЫ
LANDKARTEN
CARTES, MAGASINS DE
KARTOR
KARTTAKAUPAT

Finding good maps in English is difficult in St. Petersburg. There are special map shops and the selection of maps (especially published in the West and in English is small). Buy maps when you see them or bring them with you. Look for local maps in Russian, usually in KIOSKS *or* BOOKSTORES.

Our new Traveller's Yellow Pages City Map *for St. Petersburg in most hotels or by mail.*

MAPS OF ST. PETERSBURG AND RUSSIA

THE BEST MAPS OF ST. PETERSBURG IN ENGLISH & GERMAN

The *Traveller's* **Yellow Pages City Map for St. Petersburg *1:16,000,*

Free with The *Traveller's* Yellow Pages. *Additional copies available by mail ($4.95 plus s & h). Avaliable in Russia, in St. Petersburg and Moscow from our offices or from the many fine shops and hotels listed on page 349. Published as part of*

The *Traveller's* Yellow Pages *by InfoServices International, Inc., and PolyPlan St. Petersburg.*

In English, it features transport lines, names of almost all streets, both English-Russian and Russian-English street indexes and major points of interest, a list of new-old street names, map coordinates used by The Traveller's Yellow Pages, *maps of surrounding suburbs and metro maps, major streets in Russian too. Cartographically accurate.*

> ### Budget Edition of The Traveller's Yellow Pages City Map for St. Petersburg
> *1:16,000,* for students, staff and bulk use.
> Retail price $2.50 plus s&h.
> Discount for bulk purchases.
> Identical to above, *but considered "printers proofs" because poor "greens" We accepted delivery on this map to give you*
> A great map at a bargain price.

*St. Petersburg City Map Falk Plan

1:19,000 to 1:24,000, $12.95, *Falk-Verlag, Hamburg. Good map similar to the above, handy bilingual street index. Folding system hard to use, map rips easily. German transliteration difficult for English speakers. Variable distance scale. Available in St. Pb. at Bahlsen-Le Café.*

The New St. Petersburg City Map and Guide: 1:19,000, $7.00, Northern Cartographic, So. Burlington, VT., USA. *Basically good, no clear Russian or new/old street names, and no public transport lines. Available in St. Petersburg and by mail.*

THE FOLLOWING MAPS ARE AVAILABLE ONLY AT HOTEL NEWSSTANDS IN ST. PETERSBURG

Saint Petersburg City Plan 1:34000, $0 - 2.50, Karta , *General plan of city lacking detail and index.*

St. Petersburg Tourist Guide and Map. 1:27000, $2.50 - 5.00, TVP, Inc. St. Petersburg. *Russian transliteration difficult to understand. Lacks detail and index.*

One Day St. Petersburg, $0- 2.50, By One Day Advertising & Publishing Co. *Simple map with advertising, good for walking.*

For Tourists - About Sankt-Peterburg $0.25-2.00, *Clear little map, only major streets named. Availability?*

Leningrad City Plan, *$2.50 Len Art, Highlights only historic city center. Expensive for what is offered.*

MAPS AND PLANS OF ST. PETERSBURG IN RUSSIAN AVAILABLE IN ROSPECHAT KIOSKS

Маршруты городского транспорта *Municipal Transport Routes; Marshruty gorodskogo transporta; 1992, VTU GSH. and PolyPlan St. Petersburg. Most useful Russian map for English speakers - complete plan of metro, tram, bus, & trolleybus routes, to outskirts of city. Legend in English. About $0.25.*
*Санкт-Петербург 1992/93, карта, *Sankt-Peterburg 1992/93, karta, St. Petersburg, 1992/93 Map. Excellent for nearby suburbs and industrial & residential regions. No detail of center.* $1.50-2.50.
План С. Петербурга с ближайшими окресностями, *1914. Plan S. Peterburga s blizhayshimi okresnostyami, 1914, St. Petersburg and surrounding areas 1914, reproduction of 1914 map.*

1800 улиц, проспектов, набережных и.т.д. **Санкт-Петербурга;** (1800 ulits, prospektov, naberezhnykh, i.t.d. Sankt-Peterburga; Successful Drive Along St. Petersburg, 1800 streets, prospects, embankments, etc. in St. Petersburg). *Main routes to suburbs (Pushkin, Peterhof, Lomonosov), towns in English, streets in Russian. $0. 40.*

Шиномонтаж, авторемонт, запчасти карта-схема автолюбителя Санкт-Петербурга, Shinomontazh, avtoremont, zapchasti, karta-schema avtolyubitelya Sankt-Peterburga; Tire Repair, Auto Repair and Parts Map for Motorists in St. Petersburg. *Road scheme with detailed listing of where to get repairs, auto parts, etc 1993.*

*Карта-схема автодорог районов, прилегающих к Санкт-Петербургу, 1991, Karta-Schema avtodorog rayonov, prilegayushchikh k Sankt-Peterburgu; Map of Auto Roads and Areas Surrounding St. Petersburg, *1:200,000. Best map covering 200 km radius of St. Petersburg, good map for east of St. Petersburg, including Lake Ladoga.*

Автомобильные дороги юга Ленинградской Области; Automobile roads of the south Leningrad Oblast, 1:20,000. *And the similar* **Карельский перешеек,** The Karelian Isthmus, *north of St. Petersburg, 1:20,000. Excellent maps to find your way to the dacha with topographical markings.*

Vyborg City Map; 1992. *In Finnish, scale 1:10,000 city center, 1:20,000 city map, 1:500,000 Karelian Isthmus. Best map for Vyborg , limited English subheadings.*

From time to time, specialized maps such as this are published. Have fun looking in kiosks.

По грибы и ягоды в Карелию, 1991; Po griby i yagody v Kareliyu; Mushrooms and wild berries in Karelia. *Includes train schedules.*

MAPS OF WESTERN RUSSIA & EASTERN EUROPE

Western Soviet Union Road Map: *Cartographia, $7.00. Not available in St. Pb.*
Eastern Europe: *Freytag & Berndt, $10.00. Not available in St. Pb.*
Russia and Newly Independent Countries of the Former Soviet Union: *English, March 1993, National Geographic Society, $7.50. Not available in St. Pb. Shows principal communication lines and roads.*

STORES WHICH CARRY MAPS

Briz   **Breeze**
Bolshoy Sampsonievskiy pr., 92..... 245-19-48
Mon-Fri 7-18; Rbls, $; Eng

Dom Knigi   **House of Books**
Nevskiy pr., 28......................... 219-94-43
Mon-Sat 9-20; Rbls; Eng, Ger

Gidrogeologicheskaya Ekspeditsiya
7-ya Sovetskaya ul., 5 271-36-92
Mon-Fri 9-18; Rbls

Plakat   **Poster**
Lermontovskiy pr., 38 251-94-97
Mon-Fri 10-14, 15-19; Rbls; Eng; T-bus 3

PolyPlan ⊙ St. Petersburg
Shaumyana pr., 18....................... 542-19-47
Fax.. 528-97-02
Producer of The Traveller's Yellow Pages City Map for Saint Petersburg & The Traveller's Yellow Pages City Map for Moscow, 1993/1994 edition.
Mon-Fri 10-18; Eng, Finn, Estonian

☎ MARKETS
(Farmer's Markets, Kolkhoz Markets)
РЫНКИ
MÄRKTE
MARCHES
LIVSMEDELS MARKNAD
MARKKINAT

See also FOOD STORES *and* SHOPPING *for further information on food shopping.*

All St. Petersburg's Markets are open:
Daily 8:00 to 19:00, Sunday 8:00 to 16:00.
Note: all markets closed one day per month for cleaning. This "Sanitary Day" is given below. Rubles Only.

What: *The lively farmer's markets are the best place to buy fruit, vegetables, meat, sausage, cheese, milk, honey, eggs, jams, preserves, flowers, baked goods, usually at the best prices anywhere, if you know how to bargain. Some fruits and vegetables are imported; seasonal fruits and vegetables are from Russia or CIS.*

How: *Take along plenty of plastic shopping bags, egg cartons and jars for honey, etc., as none are provided. Prices are quoted per kilo (2.2 pounds), eggs are sold by tens. Don't be surprised by the "kilo" of bananas or bag of tomatoes used as a "counterweight", but do watch for thumbs on the scales.*

Haggle. *This is a bazaar. Smell, squeeze, select and taste before you buy. A "net" (no) can bring a price down.*

Caution. *Be very aware of pickpockets.*

***Kuznechnyy Rynok
Kuznechnyy Farmer's Market
In the center of city, the best market with widest selection and freshest produce. Worth a visit! An experience.
Kuznechnyy per., 3 312-41-61
Closed 2nd Tues; Metro Vladimirskaya; H-5

*Maltsevskiy Rynok, *formerly Nekrasovskiy,*
Maltsevskiy Farmer's Market
Nekrasova ul., 52........................... 273-17-34
Closed 4th Mon; Bus 22; Metro Ploshchad Vosstaniya; I-6

Moskovskiy Rynok
Moskovskiy Farmer's Market
Reshetnikova ul., 12 298-11-89
Closed 1st Tues; Metro Elektrosila

Narvskiy Rynok   Narvskiy Farmer's Market
Stachek pr., 54 184-84-01
*Daily 8-19, Sun 8-16; Closed 3d Mon
Metro Kirovskiy Zavod*

Nevskiy Rynok   Nevskiy Farmer's Market
Obukhovskoy oborony pr., 75 a 265-38-89
Closed 3rd Mon; Metro Elizarovskaya

Polyustrovskiy Rynok, *commonly called*
Kondratevskiy Rynok
Polyustrovskiy Farmer's Market
Kondratevskiy Farmer's Market
Famous for its large outdoors weekend pet market, called "The Bird Market" (Ptichiy Rynok, Птичий

рынок) *sells anything from purebred puppies to goats. Fur, clothing, & hat market in back, best selection on weekends.*
Polyustrovskiy pr., 45 540-30-39
Closed 3rd Tues, Metro Ploshchad Lenina, then T-Bus 3, 38, 43, Tram 6, 23, 51, Bus 138, J-9

Pravoberezhnyy Rynok
Pravoberezhnyy Farmer's Market
Dybenko ul., 16............................. 588-56-30
Fax...................................... 586-43-38
Closed 2nd Tues; Metro Dybenko

Sennoy Rynok   Sennoy Farmer's Market
Moskovskiy pr., 4/6................... 310-02-17
Closed 3rd Tues; Metro Sennaya Ploshchad; F-5

Sytnyy Rynok   Sytnyy Farmer's Market
Sytninskaya pl., 3/5.................. 233-22-93
Closed one day per month; Metro Gorkovskaya; F-8

Torzhkovskiy Rynok
Torzhkovskiy Farmer's Market
Torzhkovskaya ul., 20 246-83-75
Closed 1st Mon; Metro Chernaya Rechka; F-11

Vasileostrovskiy Rynok
Vasileostrovskiy Farmer's Market
Bolshoy pr., V.O., 18 213-66-87
Closed 1st Mon; Metro Vasileostrovskaya; D-6

SPECIAL MARKETS

Art Market, *see* Klenovaya Alleya *in* ART GALLERIES.
Auto Parts Market, *see* AUTO PARTS.
Bicycle Market, *see* BICYCLING
Bird and Pet Market
see above **Polyustrovskiy Rynok**
City Fair   Gorodskaya Yarmarka
*Daily at the SKK (Sportivno-Kontsertnyy Complex)
Imported goods market, sporting goods, clothes, electronics, shoes*
Yuriya Gagarina pr., 8 264-89-54
Daily 10-16, good on weekends, Rbls, $

Second-Hand Goods Market
Tovarno-Veshchevoy Rynok
Carries "used" (some new) goods. Electronic parts, housewares, clothing, etc. No food.
Marshala Zhukova ul., 21 157-86-44
Weekends

☎ MARRIAGE BUREAU (ZAGS)
ЗАГСЫ
STANDESÄMTER
MARIAGE,
   BUREAU DE L'ETAT CIVIL
ÄKTENSKAP, REGISTRERING
SIVIILIREKISTERITOIMISTOT

These "Marriage Bureaus" are really "Registration Offices of Vital Statistics; Marriages, Births, Deaths and Divorces". ZAGS *stands for Zapis aktov grazhdan-skogo sostoyaniya (Запись актов гражданского состояния). But the registration of marriages gives them their image as a marriage bureau. The marriage registration ceremony is often held in these beautiful buildings which are thus called "Wedding Palaces".*

See SHOPS, SPECIAL *for wedding dresses and tuxedos (both are often rented) wedding accessories, and items for newly-weds.*

Marriage Palace No. 1, *built 1890*
Palace of Grand Duke Andrei Vladimirovich
Krasnogo Flota nab., 28 314-98-48
.... 314-97-27
Daily 10-14, 15-20; Rbls
Marriage Palace No. 2, *built 1897*
Furshtadtskaya ul., 52 273-73-96
.... 273-36-15
Mon-Sat 9:30-14, 15-18; Rbls
Marriage Palace No. 3, *built 1910*
For marriages between foreigners and Russian citizens
Petrovskaya nab., 2 232-82-37
.... 233-07-43
Mon-Sat 10-14, 15-19; Rbls
Palace For Birth Registrations, *called Malyutka*
Furshtadtskaya ul., 58 272-83-78
Wed-Sun 9:30-14, 15-18:30; Rbls

☎ MASSAGE
МАССАЖ
MASSAGE
MASSAGE
MASSAGE
HIERONTA

See also MEDICAL CARE & CONSULTATIONS,
RUSSIAN BATHS, *and* HEALTH CLUBS

*Massages by highly qualified masseuse,
with advanced certification are given at
RUSSIAN BATHS, HEALTH CLUBS, and SPORTS
MEDICINE CLINICS. Newspapers often
advertise massage services. Some are
legitimate, others more exotic. Be careful.*

Danilov Mikhail
All types of massage
Please call 260-15-11

Hotel Kareliya, *Massage*
Marshala Tukhachevskogo ul., 27, bldg. 2
☎ 226-35-17
Daily 13-1; Rbls; Eng, Finn
Kositskaya Mariya, *Massage, Eng, Ger*
Please call 350-28-83
Medical Center DLT
Bolshoy pr., P.S., 29 a 233-25-42
Mon-Sat 9-21; Rbls; Eng; T-bus 1; Metro Petrogradskaya
Nevskie Baths, *Massage Center*
Marata ul., 5/7 311-14-00
Mon-Sat 12; Rbls
Pravoberezhnye Baths, *Massage Center*
Novoselov ul., 51 266-20-84
Mon-Sat 8-22; Rbls
Professor Medical Center
Liteynyy pr., 48........................... 272-16-58
Solarium No. 1
Soyuza Pechatnikov ul., 18/20 114-37-55
Daily 9-21; Rbls, $; Eng
Sports Medicine Clinic - *See* MEDICAL CARE
Vita
III-go Internatsionala ul., 16, bldg. 6
☎ 156-37-74
Mon-Sat 9:30-19; Rbls, $; Eng, Fr

☎ MAYOR'S OFFICE

See ST. PETERSBURG CITY GOVERNMENT,
THE MAYORS OFFICE

☎ MEASURES
РАЗМЕРЫ (Единицы измерения)
MASSEINHEITEN
MESURAGE
MÄTTENNETER
MITAT

For TABLES OF MEASURES, WEIGHTS *and* SIZES,
see pages 343-344

*Most scales are no longer inspected for
accuracy. It is also not uncommon to see a
bag of tomatoes or bunch of bananas used
as a counter weight in the markets.*

☎ MEDICAL ASSISTANCE
МЕДИЦИНСКАЯ СКОРАЯ
ПОМОЩЬ
ERSTE HILFE
MEDECINE, ASSISTANCE
MEDICALE
SJUKVÅRD
SAIRAANKULJETUS

See also MEDICAL CARE AND CONSULTATIONS,
HOSPITALS, DENTISTS *and* MEDICAL INSTITUTES

See MEDICAL EMERGENCIES
Page 211

☎ MEDICAL CARE & CONSULTATIONS
ЗДРАВООХРАНЕНИЕ И
МЕДИЦИНСКИЕ
КОНСУЛЬТАЦИИ
ARZTBESUCHE, MEDIZINISCHE
VERSORGUNG
SOINS MEDICAUX,
CONSULTATIONS MEDICALES
SJUKVÅRD, MEDICINSKA
KONSULTATIONER
LÄÄKÄRIT
JA LÄÄKÄRINKONSULTAATIOT

See also DENTISTS, EMERGENCY MEDICAL CARE,
HOSPITALS, *and* MEDICAL INSTITUTES

*Patients have free primary medical care in
the "Policlinics" in the district where they
live. Policlinics similar to an "official"
medical group for outpatient care.*

*The best known is Policlinic No. 2, which
used to be the clinic for foreign diplomats,
visitors and Russian officials and
executives. Also highly recommended is
Hospital No. 20 which has a special section
designated for foreigners with far better
service and treatment than most other
Russian hospitals offer. The American
Medical Center has opened a family
practice clinic; see below.*

*There are now a large number of
cooperative medical groups, and newly
independent hospitals and policlinics
offering similar services. Medical care is
changing rapidly as more and more*

physicians, dentists, medical professionals and even hospitals and policlinics open "fee for treatment" departments. In theory, however, all citizens can still receive free medical care. In fact, for many years, the level of your medical care could be improved by your rank, favors, and gifts. Many Russians are now buying medical insurance to ensure that they have the financial resources for "private paid" medical care.

For medical evacuations call your consulate and see MEDICAL EMERGENCIES. They will usually provide assistance in getting you home or to the nearest European hospitals for treatment.

MEDICAL GROUPS & CLINICS

There are dozens of Policlinics and private medical groups in St. Petersburg. See St. Pb. Yellow Pages 93 or Ves St. Pb. 93.

Aitis, *Internal diagnostics*
Serebristyy blvd., 14, bldg. 1 393-44-88
Mon-Fri 10-19; Rbls, $; Eng

American Medical Center **AMC** St. Petersburg	**American Medical Center**

Primary Outpatient, Emergency Care, Lab Tests, EKG & Medical Evacuations
Reki Fontanki nab., 77 119-61-01
Fax 119-61-20
24 Hour Service; $, Rbls; English

Avalanche, *Family care, amulance*
Vladimirskiy pr., 2........................... 311-85-49
Daily 0-24 210-84-04
Avicenna, *Mon-Fri 9-17; Rbls; Eng*
Professora Popova ul., 15/17 234-50-28

CENTER FOR MICROSURGERY

Hand surgery, plastic & reconstructive surgery, treatment of trauma and limb illnesses, fractures, battle injuries Highly experienced orthopedic and micro-surgeons
Stay in private & semi-private rooms in one of the best hospitals in St. Pb.
✉ Kultury pr., 4, St. Pb. 194291
Duty Doctor 558-88-71
Chief Surgeon.................... 558-85-17

Children's City Hospital
Gorodskaya Detskaya Bolnitsa
Chaykovskogo ul., 73.................... 273-38-66
Clinical Center of New Medical Technology
Severnyy pr., 1, 5th floor 511-09-61
Fax 511-81-02
Surgeons; Mon-Fri 9-16; Rbls; Eng, Ger

Cosmetics Salon, *Plastic Surgery*
Kronverkskiy pr., 23, apt. 39 232-59-07
Daily; Rbls, $
Cosmetics and Beauty Salon, *Plastic Surgery*
Karavannaya ul., 5........................ 315-52-37
Mon-Sat 9-21; Rbls, $
Cosmetologist, *Plastic Surgery, Mon-Fri 8-19*
Nevskiy pr., 111 277-00-44

SPORTS
MEDICINE CLINIC
PHYSICAL THERAPY SPECIALISTS

Personal programs of injury rehabilitation and therapy and physical fitness
Cardiac and physical fitness evaluation
Swedish and Eastern Massage, Hydrotherapy, ultrasound & electrotherapy
Neck and Back Therapy Program
Facilities include swimming pools, universal exercise & weight room
Large Experienced Staff of MD's, PT's & Chiropractors
Rentgena ul., 12............................232-25-49
Daily 9-15, $ & Rubles, English, German, Spanish

Elena-91, *Oxygen & music therapy*
Krasina ul., 4................................527-36-41
Mon-Sat 9-21; Rbls; Eng, Finn

EYE MICROSURGERY CENTER
Branch of the famous Fedorov clinic
Yaroslava Gasheka ul., 21 178-32-22
Fax...101-35-51
Mon-Fri 9-15

Gippocrat
Medical Cooperative

Treating Neurological Disorders for Adults & Children, Drug Abuse, Alcoholism
Marata ul., 57................................567-90-52
....315-18-68
Fax 567-71-27
Hrs: 11-20, English, Rbls & $

Gippokrat Pediatrician
Please call....................................107-37-92
Daily 9-21; Rbls
Harmony
Gastello ul., 9................................293-13-30
Psychiatric Care; Mon-Fri 10-20; Rbls; Eng

Hospital No. 20

Emergency & Inpatient Medical Care
Gastello ul., 21
Reception desk.................. 108-48-10
Dept. for foreigners 108-40-81
English, German, French, 24 hours a day

IMIS
Kultury pr., 4, ... 558-85-54
Daily Rbls; Metro Politekhnicheskaya

Dialysis Center
MEDELEN

*Kidney dialysis
for patients on vacation
in Saint Petersburg*

Lva Tolstogo ul., 17 234-50-01
Fax 234-54-78

Medical Association
Akademika Baykova ul., 8 550-95-84
.... 550-95-13
Fax 556-85-39
Mon-Fri 8:30-15

1st Medical Institute
Clinic of
Dermavenereal Diseases

Treatment of skin & venereal diseases
Lva Tolstogo ul., 6/8 234-92-31
Hrs: 9-16, Rbls & $, English

Medical Center at Policlinic No. 34
Drug and Alcohol Treatment
Zverinskaya ul., 15.......................... 233-11-08
Mon-Sat 9-20; Rbls, Metro Petrogradskaya

Medical Center DLT
Bolshoy pr., P.S., 29 a 233-25-42
*Physicians & Internal medicine; Mon-Sat 9-21; Rbls; Eng
T-bus 1; Metro Petrogradskaya*

Medical Center Deviz
Moskovskiy pr., 95, bldg. 3 299-72-55
*Physicians & Cosmetologists;
Mon-Fri 9-20, Sat 9-15; Rbls; Eng*

Medical Group Home Consultation
Please call 529-86-97
.... 520-60-20
Daily 8-23

Medical Rehabilitation Center
Zanevskiy pr., 12 221-76-20
.... 221-58-81
Fax 521-69-72
Mon-Fri 9-18; Rbls, $; Eng, Ger, Fr

Medikon
Borovaya ul., 55............................ 166-47-62
*Internal Medicine; Mon-Fri 9-19; Rbls;
Metro Ligovskiy Prospekt*

Nadezhda Medical Center for Women
Gynecologists and dentists
14-ya Liniya, 17 218-51-36
Mon-Fri 10-20; Rbls

Plastic Surgery Burn Specialists
Zagorodnyy pr., 47 292-38-88
.... 292-20-66
Daily 10-14

St. Petersburg Policlinic No. 2 - *See ad below*
Moskovskiy pr., 22 292-62-72

St. Petersburg Policlinic No. 2
An Independent Medical Group
World renown for over 25 years of service to
diplomats & visitors to St. Pb.
*Leading medical specialists in internal medicine,
cardiology, urology, surgery, pediatrics,
orthopedics, gynecology, & other fields.*
Complete Western Pharmacy
*Wide selection of Western drugs, antibiotics,
cortisone, vitamins, personal hygiene products.*
Modern X-Ray, EKG,
Ultrasound & Labs
Dental Clinic *with highly trained dentists,*
Italian & Finnish equipment
Highest Sanitary Standards *with all*
disposable syringes, etc.
Clinic Hours: M-F: 9:00 to 21:00
Sat.: 9:00 to 15:00
24-Hour Emergency Coverage
*House calls at your home or hotel
Well-equipped ambulance.
Call 24 Hours a Day*
Moskovskiy pr., 22............ 292-62-72
.... 110-11-02
Fax 292-59-39

CONSULTING MEDICAL CENTRE "PROFESSOR"
•••••••••••••••••••••••••••••••••••••
Highly Professional Staff
Diagnostics & Medical Treatment
Distributors of the Goldovskiy's
Biocorrector
*This Tiny Biocorrector Increases
Physical Fitness & Tone of your Body*
- Utilized for Years
- *An Effective Treatment for
Cardiovascular, Gastroenteric &
Kidney Diseases*
- *Over 500 Cases of Successful
Treatment of Oncological Diseases*
Head Office:
Kazanskaya ul., 49 311-39-02
Fax... 314-71-23
Reception:
Kirishskaya ul., 5, bldg. 3
Tel 532-18-18
.... 531-79-61

Professor Medical Center
Liteynyy pr., 48.............................. 272-16-58

Professor Sukhanov Clinic

Traditional Methods of Treating

Chronic Diseases

Beloostrovskaya ul., 26................. 245-63-32
.... 245-18-07
Hrs: 9-21, Closed Sunday; English, Italian

Prognoz,   *Mon-Sat 15-20; Rbls*
3-ey Pyatiletki ul., 30 100-83-15
Romashka
Chernyakhovskogo ul., 17, 3rd floor
☎ 164-98-79
Mon-Fri 9-21
Russian Gulf Company - *Urology*
Lva Tolstogo ul., 17 234-35-20
Mon-Fri 9-15; Rbls, $
Skin & Venereal Disease Clinics
Testing & Treatment
• Nalichnaya ul., 19 217-06-19
Daily 0-24
• Varshavskaya ul., 104 293-29-73
Mon-Sat 8-20
• Stremyannaya ul., 4 113-21-56
Daily 9-20

St. George Hospital
120 Years of History

New technologies in surgery, cardiology,
gynecology, orthopedics, therapeutics,
physical therapy & other fields.

EKG, ultrasound, dental clinic,
laboratory testing, modern x-ray,
radiology lab and endoscopy.

Severnyy pr., 1
Head Physician 511-96-00
Admitting office 511-97-94
Manager 511-95-00

St. Petersburg Regional Clinic
Lunacharskogo pr., 45 513-24-86
Tonus, *Chinese Breathing Method "Tsigun"*
Podvoyskogo ul., 14, bldg. 1, entr. 9
☎ 589-26-47
Mon-Wed, Fri 10-19; Rbls
Treatment Without Medicine
Lechenie Bez Lekarstv
Pionerskaya ul., 62/4 584-09-76
Daily 11-23
Vanga-Medika Women's Medical Center
Obstetrics, gynecology, ultrasound diagnosis
3-ya Sovetskaya ul., 6 271-08-20
Mon-Fri 10-20

Veronica - *Homeopathy, Dentists*
Vyborgskaya ul., 65....................... 246-90-93
Fax... 246-57-54
Mon-Sat 9-20
Victory - *Gynecologists, Physicians*
Kostyushko ul., 2 123-35-08
Mon-Fri 10-14, 16-19; Rbls

OBSTETRICS & GYNECOLOGY

Itus Clinic & Maternity Hospital
One of the outstanding maternity hospitals
Tambasova ul., 21.......................... 130-27-14
Fax... 130-27-13
Mon-Sat 9-21; Rbls; Fr, Ital

Lechmed
Mendeleevskaya liniya, 3 218-98-08
Mon-Fri 9-17; Rbls, $; Eng
Women's Health Center No. 2
Zhenskaya Konsultatsiya
Pestelya ul., 25 272-82-23
Mon-Fri 8-20
Women's Health Center No. 3
Zhenskaya Konsultatsiya
Reki Fontanki nab., 155.................. 114-29-58
Mon-Fri 8-20
Women's Health Center No. 30
Zhenskaya Konsultatsiya
Mayakovskogo ul., 5 272-00-69
Mon-Fri 8-20
Women's Health Center No. 35
Zhenskaya Konsultatsiya
2-ya Sovetskaya ul., 4 273-42-58
Mon-Fri 8-20

PHYSICIANS & DOCTORS

Bershtein L. M. - Endocrinologist
Please call...................................394-02-47
Daily 20-22

Sergey Victorovich Melnik, MD

Specialist in Internal and Family Medicine
Ultrasound & EKG

Asafeva ul., 2, Bldg. 2, Apt. 38

Tel 513-25-35
Hrs: 8-10, 17-24, German & English; Home Visits

N. D. Murtazaev, M.D., surgeon
*Painless immediate out-patient treatment of
ingrown nails & calluses*
Bolshaya Porokhovskaya ul., 45, apt. 169
☎ 227-20-71
Daily except Sun, 9-15, $, Eng, Ger, Fr
Professor - Neuropathologist V. N. Gurev
Institutskiy pr., 6, rm. 80................. 552-79-50
.... 247-25-39
Mon, Wed-Thu 11-18
Urologist
Please call................................... 157-13-32

TESTS

AIDS Testing
Mirgorodskaya ul., 3 277-56-71
Mon-Fri 9-14:30

American Medical Center, *See our ad on p. 206*
Blood Analysis and EKG
Reki Fontanki nab., 77 119-61-01
Fax 119-61-20
Metro Nevskiy Prospekt; $

Radioactivity Tests for Food
4-ya Sovetskaya ul., 5 277-52-92
Mon-Fri 9-16

Skin & Venereal Disease Clinics
Testing & Treatment
• Nalichnaya ul., 19 217-06-19
Daily 0-24
• Varshavskaya ul., 104 293-29-73
Mon-Sat 8-20
• Stremyannaya ul., 4 113-21-56
Daily 9-20

☎ MEDICAL EMERGENCIES
МЕДИЦИНСКАЯ СКОРАЯ
ПОМОЩЬ
ERSTE HILFE
MEDECINE, ASSISTANCE
MEDICALE
SJUKVÅRD
SAIRAANKULJETUS

See MEDICAL CARE AND CONSULTATIONS,
HOSPITALS, DENTISTS, *and* MEDICAL INSTITUTES

CITY AMBULANCE - 03
**The best staffed and equipped
ambulances are the following:**

POLICLINIC No. 2 AMBULANCE - 110-11-02
Policlinic for foreigners

HOSPITAL NO. 20 AMBULANCE - 108-48-08
Gastello Hospital for foreigners

CITY AMBULANCE SERVICE
EMERGENCY MEDICAL HELP SERVICE

*In St. Petersburg the city ambulance
service carries an attending physician and is
called:*

Emergency Medical Help Service
Skoraya Meditsinskaya Pomoshch
Скорая медицинская помощь
OPERATES 24 HOURS

Ambulance Service. *Use private
ambulance services, if possible. In general,
don't count on Western level of emergency
care from the extensive City EMS Service
of St. Petersburg. Equipment, medications
and standards have suffered greatly from
underfunding, but 150 new American
ambulances are coming this year.*

*For now, however, call one of the private
ambulances services, if possible.*

*To find out where a patient has been
transported with a City Ambulance, call.*

City Ambulance Information
☎ .... 278-00-25.

Central Ambulance Station office
Malaya Sadovaya ul., 1 .... 210-74-79.
Mon-Fri 9-17

*In general, **accident trauma victims** will
be moved to a* trauma center *(Travmotologi-*
cheskiy punkt, Травмотологический пункт)
*and then to a major hospital if necessary.
Other patients get transported to an appropriate medical facility (e.g. burn center,
emergency surgery, eye emergency).*

Eye injuries *are treated at:*
The Eye Trauma Center
Glaznoy Travmotologicheskiy Punkt
Глазной Травмотологический Пункт
Liteynyy pr., 25 272-59-55
24 hours a day.

Grave trauma and burn victims *from
accidents are often treated at:*
Institute for Emergency Medicine
Institut Skoroy Pomoshchi
Институт скорой помощи
Budapeshtskaya ul., 3 174-86-75
OPEN 24 HOURS

EMERGENCY MEDICAL CARE

EMERGENCY MEDICAL CARE. *Good
emergency medical care for diplomats, high
level officials and foreign visitors is offered
by several groups in St. Petersburg.*

*St. Petersburg Policlinic No. 2 is the lar-
gest organization with over 25 years of
experience in serving foreigners. This
independent medical group has imported
equipment, a modern pharmacy stocked
with many Western pharmaceuticals, and uses
disposable (syringes, catheters, etc.). They
have a well-staffed, well-stocked ambulance
and make emergency house calls around
the clock. For illnesses they use the Gastello Hospital No. 20; for emergency surgery they use Hospital No. 26, two of the
best hospitals in the city. Many doctors
speak English and translators are available
on short notice.*

*The American Medical Center can handle
basic medical emergencies at the family
practice level (lab tests, EKG, emergency
prescriptions). In case of more serious
emergencies, they will stabilize the patient
and arrange for medical evacuation to any
country (see below).*

American Medical Center
Reki Fontanki nab., 77 119-61-01
Fax 119-61-20
Metro Pushkinskaya; $, English

EMERGENCY MEDICAL EVACUATION

Emergency Medical Evacuation *to
Finland and to Europe and North America
is available. The cost is between $4,000
to $25,000. You may want to consider
purchasing insurance before you leave.*

For immediate evacuation *(within two hours) to a Finnish hospital, you have several choices:*

Jet Flite (Helsinki, Finland)
P.O. Box 86, 01531, Vanta, Finland
☎ .... (358)-(0)-822-766
Fax .... (358)-(0)-876-32-02
Answers 24 Hours a Day. Flight to Mehiläinen Hospital, Helsinki, Finland

EURO-FLITE
Box 187, 01531, Vantaa, Finland
☎ 358-0-870-2544
Fax 358-0-870-2507

The **American Medical Center** *can make all the arrangements for you. Cost is $8,000-10,000, payable by credit card or other financial guarantee.*

For less critical evacuation *on the next flight out basis to Europe and the USA, call the following airlines:*

SAS *offers a "stretcher service with accompanying doctor". Arrangements to complete forms and arrange payment must be made in advance. The cost is six seats plus one ticket for the patient and the doctor's fees.*

SAS
Nevskiy pr., 57 314-50-86
Fax 164-78-78

Lufthansa *offers a stretcher service with advanced booking. They provide a doctor and stretcher. A special plane can be ordered from Frankfurt, Germany. The cost of the stretcher service is 4 business class tickets plus one ticket for the patient and the doctor's fees. Prepayment required.*

Lufthansa
Voznesenskiy pr., 7 314-49-79
Fax 312-31-29
Pulkovo-2 104-34-32

Finnair *and* **Delta** *offer similar services.*

EMERGENCY MEDICAL EVACUATIONS FROM ANY POINT IN RUSSIA

Emergency Medical evacuations from anywhere in Russia can be arranged by **Delta Consulting.**

Delta Consulting
St. Petersburg: Tel/Fax 230-92-35
Moscow 24 hrs. .... (095) 229-65-36
24 hrs. .... (095) 229-78-92
Fax .... (095) 229-21-38
24 hour medical emergency assistance, worldwide and local evacuations, medical escorts and hospital access
Mon-Fri 9-18; $; Eng

Emergency evacuation from Russia can be arranged in the USA through the following services.

Aero Ambulance International
.... (800) 443-8042
Air Ambulance of America
.... (800) 843-8418
International SOS Assistance
.... (800) 523-8930

MEDICAL CARE WITH AMBULANCE SERVICES

St. Petersburg Policlinic No. 2
An Independent Medical Group
When you need medical care.
World renowned - over 25 years of service to diplomats and visitors to St. Petersburg
Leading medical specialists
Complete Western Pharmacy
Modern X-rays, EKG,
Ultrasound & Labs
Highest Sanitary Standards
Clinic hours: M-F: 9:00 to 21:00
Sat.: 9:00 to 15:00
24-Hour Emergency Coverage
House calls at your home or hotel
Well-staffed ambulance.
Moskovskiy pr., 22 292-62-72
24 Hours Around The Clock
Tel 110-11-02
Fax 292-59-39
Metro Tekhnologicheskiy Institut

City Diagnostic Center No. 1
Sikeyrosa ul., 10 554-19-00
Daily 9-17; Bus 33, 69, T-bus 13

Hospital No. 9
Krestovskiy pr., 18 235-20-58
Daily 0-24; Tram 21,33, T-bus 9

Hospital No. 20
Gastello ul., 21 108-48-08
.... 108-48-10
Specializing in the treatment of foreigners
Daily 0-24; Bus 61

Institute of Emergency Medical Care
Institut Skoroy Pomoshchi
Budapeshtskaya ul., 3 109-61-30
Daily 0-24; Bus 74, T-bus 39

Ophthalmology Clinic - Trauma Department
Liteynyy pr., 25 272-59-55
Daily 0-24

EMERGENCY ROOMS

Emergency Room	Travmpunkt
Травмпункт	
• Bolshoy pr., V.O., 85	217-02-82
• Engelsa pr., 37	554-17-21
• Gzhatskaya ul., 3	534-47-39
• Kavalergardskaya ul., 26	274-76-55
• Komsomola ul., 14	542-31-54
• Kosinova ul., 17	186-44-30
• Kryukova kan. nab., 25	114-52-98
• Lva Tolstogo ul., 6/8	234-57-72
• Malaya Konyushennaya ul., 2	311-43-96
• Moskovskiy pr., 87	298-45-96
• Obvodnogo kan. nab., 179	113-08-08
• Pravdy ul., 18	315-21-58
• Shaumyana pr., 51	221-23-32
Daily 0-24	

☎ MEDICAL EQUIPMENT
МЕДИЦИНСКОЕ
ОБОРУДОВАНИЕ
MEDIZINISCHE
AUSRÜSTUNGSGERÄTE
MEDECINE, ÉQUIPEMENT MEDICAL
SJUKVÅRDSMATERIAL
SAIRAALALAITTEET

See also PHARMACIES

Russian physicians buy their stethoscopes, blood pressure gauges, and other apparatus at Medtekhnika stores (Медтехника).

ALMED (Diamond - Instrument)
Koli Tomchaka ul., 24, bldg. 2........ 298-65-36
Fax 298-34-29
Mon-Sat 9-20

Annamed Ltd.
Voskova ul., 27/18 233-22-49
Fax 232-42-20
Mon-Fri 9:30-17:30; Rbls, $; Eng

A✛XIOM
Equipment for endoscopy, laparoscopy & gynecology

Suvorovskiy pr., 4 277-17-38

Fax 277-50-10

Dina, *Dental equipment, materials, instruments*
Moskovskiy pr., 186 294-12-98
Fax 294-16-52

Farmatekh
Mira ul., 14 232-10-36
Mon-Fri 9-17; Rbls, $; Eng, Ger

Lohman GmbH & Co. KG
Please Call 272-45-31
Sterile bandages, adhesives

DENTAL SUPPLY
EVERYTHING FOR DENTISTS

МЕДИ

Dental Equipment Sales.

Our sales representatives are experienced dental consultants.

All Equipment has been tested at the "MEDI" dental center.

St. Petersburg, Zanevskiy pr., 43
Tel./Fax: (812) 528-42-63
Tel: (812) 528-88-88

Medis
Instrumentalnaya ul., 6 234-13-11
Mon-Fri 9-17:30; Rbls, $

Medtekhnika   Equipment for Doctors
• Marata ul., 22/24 312-29-53
Fax 311-95-17
Mon-Fri 9-13, 14-17; Rbls; Metro Dostoevskaya
• Ruzovskaya ul., 18 292-19-77
Fax 112-60-70
Mon-Fri 8-12, 13-17; Rbls
• Svetlanovskaya pl., 35 552-21-92
Mon-Fri 8:30-12:30, 13-17; Rbls
• Voronezhskaya ul., 16 164-01-10
Fax 164-75-86
Mon-Fri 9-12:30, 13:15-17:45; Rbls, $

NORDMED

DENTAL EQUIPMENT

Representative for

FINNDENT

Latest Dental Technologies and
Equipment Used Worldwide

✉193124, Saint Petersburg, Russia
Tverskaya ul., 12/15

Tel 110-02-06
Fax 552-20-06
Hrs: 9-17:30, Thursday 9-20; English & German

Omilen, *Disposable medical supplies*
Sedova ul., 11 567-72-23
Fax 568-04-04
Mon-Fri 9-17; Rbls, $

**Pharmaceutical Products
                    Aptekarskie Tovary No. 10**
Nevskiy pr., 128 277-03-77

Siemens AG, *Medical equipment*
Gogolya ul., 18/20 315-31-97
Fax 315-36-21
Mon-Fri 9-17; Rbls, $; Eng, Ger

Yunimed, *Dental equipment & supplies from USA*
Svetlanovskiy pr., 60 559-43-50
Fax 557-70-75
*Mon-Fri 9-12:30, 13-17; Rbls, $; Eng
Tram 51; Metro Grazhdanskiy Prospekt*

☎ MEDICAL INSTITUTES
МЕДИЦИНСКИЕ ИНСТИТУТЫ
MEDIZINISCHE INSTITUTE
MEDECINE, INSTITUT DE
MEDICIN INSTITUT
LÄÄKETIETEELLISET
KORKEAKOULUT

The leading specialists practice at medical institutes, four of which are a combination of medical school and practicing clinic. The major medical institutes are listed below. The Institute of Radiology has newly acquired Western equipment to treat many internal diseases. The institute is famous, not only in Russia but also abroad, for its research and treatment of cancer. One of the few CAT scanners in St. Petersburg is found at the Petrov Institute of Oncology.

Bekhterev Psychoneurology Insitute
Psikhonevrologicheskiy Institut
im. Akademika Bekhtereva
Bekhtereva ul., 3 265-24-30
Fax 567-54-06

Institute of Cardiology *Institut Kardiologii*
Parkhomenko pr., 15 557-75-47
Mon-Sat 8-20

Institute of Children Infections
Institut Detskikh Infektsiy
Professora Popova ul., 9 234-60-04
Mon-Fri 9-16

Institute of Dental Cosmetics
Institut Protezirovaniya
Bestuzhevskaya ul., 50 544-21-89
Mon-Fri 11-14

Institute of Emergency Medicine
Institut Skoroy Pomoshchi
Burn and Trauma Center
Open 24 Hours
Budapeshtskaya ul., 3 174-86-75
Fax 174-36-81

Institute of Epidemiology & Microbiology
Institut Epidemiologii i Mikrobiologii
Bolshaya Monetnaya ul., 15 232-20-96

Institute of Hematology and
Blood Transfusion
Institut Gematologii i Perelivaniya Krovi
2-ya Sovetskaya ul., 16 274-57-21
Mon-Fri 9-17

Institute of Neurosurgery
Institut Neyrokhirurgii
Mayakovskogo ul., 12 272-81-35

Institute of Obstetrics and Gynecology
Institut Akusherstva i Ginekologii
Mendeleevskaya Liniya, 3 218-98-59

Institute of Orthopedics and Trauma
Institut Travmotologii i Ortopedii
Akademika Baykova ul., 8 550-95-50
Fax 556-06-47

Institute of Pediatrics
Pediatricheskiy Institut
Formerly 3rd Medical Institute
Medical school, Litovskaya ul., 2.... 542-93-57
Fax 542-80-14
Clinic 245-06-46

Institute of Radiology
Radiologicheskiy Institut
Leningradskaya ul., 70/4, Poselok Pesochnyy
☎ 237-85-43

Institute of Sports Medicine
Institut Sportivnoy Meditsiny
Rentgena ul., 12 232-25-49
Mon-Fri 9-16

Kirov Academy of Military Medicine
Voenno-Meditsinskaya Akademiya
im. S.M. Kirova
One of the best hospitals
and medical schools in Russia
Akademika Lebedeva ul., 6............. 542-21-39
Admitting 542-12-50
Zagorodnyy pr., 47 292-58-44

Pavlov Medical Institute
Sankt-Peterburgskiy Meditsinskiy Institut
im. Akademika Pavlova
One of the leading medical schools,
formerly The 1st Medical Institute
Lva Tolstogo ul., 6/8 ....
Medical school 234-08-21
Clinics 238-71-34
Mon-Fri 9-17

Petrov Institute of Oncology
Institut Onkologii im. Petrova
Leningradskaya ul., 68, Poselok Pesochnyy
☎ 237-86-55

Mechnikov Sanitary and Hygiene Institute
Sanitarno-Gigienicheskiy Institut im.
Former 2nd Medical Institute *Mechnikova*
Clinic Telephones
Piskarevskiy pr., 47,
Admissions to Clinic 543-03-01
Inquires 543-94-46
Head Doctor 543-93-29
School telephones
Secretary 543-96-09
Student Center 543-19-11

☎ **MEDICAL INSURANCE**
МЕДИЦИНСКОЕ СТРАХОВАНИЕ
KRANKENVERSICHERUNGEN
MEDECINE, ASSURANCE
MEDICAL
SJUKVÅRDSMATERIAL
SAIRASVAKUUTUS

Some reputable companies provide medical insurance to foreign tourists and businessmen that is comparable to Western standards. More and more Russian citizens are also buying medical insurance.

The American Consulate recommends that you carry medical evacuation insurance or have a credit card available with a minimum clear credit line of $5,000.

Delta Consulting Insurance -
See MEDICAL EMERGENCIES *for medical evacuation insurance*

Ingosstrakh
Zakharevskaya ul., 17 272-06-28
Daily 10-13, 14-18; $, CC; Eng, Ger, Fr

Medexpress Insurance
Pestelya ul., 4 275-65-05

Progress-Neva
Moskovskiy pr., 79 a 298-13-39
Fax 296-59-65

Rossiya Insurance Co. Ltd.
Leninskiy pr., 115 153-91-10
☎ 153-91-09
See our ad under INSURANCE

☎ **MEETING ROOMS**
See CONFERENCE ROOMS

☎ **MEN'S CLOTHING**
See CLOTHING - MEN'S

☎ METRO
МЕТРО
U-BAHN
METRO
TUNNELBANA
METRO

St. Petersburg Subway (Underground), called the Metro (Метро) for "Metropoliten", currently has 54 stations and operates from 5:30 in the morning to 00:30 (12:30 a.m.). Metro stations are identified by the blue and white (M) sign. Trains run at intervals of 4-6 minutes , 2-3 minutes during rush hours.

Tokens, (Zhetony, Жетоны) cost 15 rubles as of July 1993. Buy a good supply as they are also used in pay telephones. To enter the metro, place a token in the turnstiles, or use a monthly pass.

Monthly Pass. Monthly passes go on sale two weeks before the beginning of the next month at metro stations and kiosks. They are available for the Metro, for above ground transportation, and for any form of transportation, called an, "Unified City Transport Pass" (edinyy bilet, единый билет). Buy an edinyy bilet.

Transfer points (переходы, perekhody) close at 00:30 (12:30 a.m.). Watch the time so that you do not get stuck in the middle of the night.

St. Petersburg Metro

Moskovskiy pr., 28	259-71-11
	251-66-68

☎ MILITIA-POLICE
МИЛИЦИЯ
POLIZEI
POLICE
POLIS
POLIISI

POLICE - 02

Милиция	Militsiya	Militia
ГАИ	GAI	Traffic Police

The function of the police in Western countries are performed largely by both the militia (Militsiya, Милиция) and the related "traffic police" called "GAI" (ГАИ). The militia respond to emergencies, keep public order and do preliminary investigations of crimes. The GAI are traffic police and enforce traffic rules.

The militia and GAI both wear grey uniforms or dark blue with a beret and it takes a while to tell them apart. It is even more confusing as "special" militia units may wear camouflage. GAI vehicles are usually white with a blue stripe and flashing blue light. Militia vehicles also vary from yellow jeeps with a blue strip to an occasional brown jeep, brown military vehicle or bus.

There are dozens of militia stations throughout the city indicated by:

Отделение Милиции
Otdelenie Militsii

Ministry of Security of Russia, St. Petersburg Branch
Upravlenie ministerstva bezopasnosti Rossiyskoy Federatsii po gorodu Sankt-Peterburgu
(Formerly KGB)

Liteynyy pr., 4	278-71-10
Mon-Fri 9-18	

МИЛИЦИЯ

Militia   Open Daily 0 - 24   **Police**

Militia Headquarters (Main Office)
Liteynyy pr., 4 02

MILITIA HEADQUARTERS By DISTRICT

Dzerzhinskiy District
Chekhova ul., 15 272-02-02

Frunzenskiy District
Rasstannaya ul., 15 166-02-02
Bus 74; Metro Ligovskiy Prospekt

Kalininskiy District
Mineralnaya ul., 3 540-02-02

Kirovskiy District
Stachek pr., 18 252-02-02

Kolpinskiy District
Truda ul., 6, Kolpino 484-02-02

Krasnogvardeyskiy District
Krasnodonskaya ul., 14 224-02-02
Bus 174; Metro Novocherkasskaya

Krasnoselskiy District
Avangardnaya ul., 35 136-02-75
T-bus 32; Metro Prospekt Veteranov

Kronshtadt District
Lenina pr., 20, Kronshtadt 236-02-02

Kuybyshevskiy District
Krylova per., 3 310-02-02

Leninskiy District
Sovetskiy per., 9 292-02-02

Moskovskiy District
Moskovskiy pr., 95 298-02-02

Nevskiy District
Krupskoy ul., 30 560-02-02

Petrogradskiy District
Bolshaya Monetnaya ul., 20 233-02-02

Primorskiy District
Generala Khruleva ul., 15 394-02-02

Smolninskiy District
Mytninskaya ul., 3 271-02-02

Vasileostrovskiy District
19-ya Liniya, 10 213-02-02

Vyborgskiy District
Lesnoy pr., 20 542-02-02

☎ MONEY CHANGING
See CURRENCY EXCHANGE

☎ **MOTELS**
МОТЕЛИ
MOTELS
MOTELS
MOTELL
MOTELLIT

See also HOTELS, BED & BREAKFAST,
APARTMENTS

MOTEL "Natalino"

*20 km SW of Saint Petersburg
Motel, sauna & hot showers,
guarded parking
Hot breakfasts, lunch & dinner*
Krasnoe Selo,
Novozheleznodorozhnaya ul., 1

132-88-15

Daily 0-24; Rbls. Eng, Ger, Finn

Olgino Motel Camping
Primorskoe shosse, 18 km, Sestroretsk
.... 238-35-50
Fax 238-39-54
Daily 0-24; Rbls, $

RETUR - Camping

Camping
On the beautiful Gulf of Finland

*Comfortable 2-rm Cottages with Bath
Breakfast, Bar & Restaurant
Sauna, Russian Baths
Heated Swimming Pool & Tennis
Car Rental & Caravan Camping
with Hot Showers
Secure Parking Guaranteed
29 km from Saint Petersburg
on St. Pb.- Helsinki highway*

Primorskoe shosse, 29 km
Tel 237-75-33
Fax................................... 273-97-83
Open 24 hrs, $, English, German, Finnish

ST. PETERSBURG'S • *CITY CENTER!* •
MODERN BUDGET
"WESTERN STYLE" **ЯUSSIAN**
YOUTH HOSTEL
An American-Russian Joint Project

Tourist visas available

3ʳᵈ Sovetskaya ulitsa, 28.............................277-05-69
Fax...277-51-02
International Reservation in USA...+1 (310) 379-4316
Fax...+1 (310) 379-8420

☎ **MOTORCYCLES**
МОТОЦИКЛЫ
MOTORRÄDER
MOTOS
MOTORCYKLAR
MOOTTORIPYÖRÄT

For clubs and racetracks, see RACING.
Motorcycles can also be bought in SPORTS
EQUIPMENT *stores.*

BMW Sales Office
Bolshoy pr., V.O., 103, BMW Pavilon LenEXPO
☎ 355-51-18
Fax... 355-58-41
Mon-Fri 10-18; Rbls, $; Major European Languages
Motolyubitel **Motorcyclists**
Apraksin Dvor, sec 50-63
Sadovaya ul. 310-06-31
Mon-Fri 10-14, 15-19; Metro Gostinyy Dvor
Sport
Shaumyana pr., 2........................ 224-28-74
Mon-Sat 10-14, 15-19; Rbls

☎ **MOUNTAINEERING**
ГОРНЫЙ ТУРИЗМ
BERGSTEIGEN
ALPINISME
BERGSKLÄTTRING,
BERGSBESTIGNING
VUORISTOKIIPEILY

*Various sports clubs organize "treks",
"alpinist", and "rock climbing" outings.
"Big Rocks", near Lake Yastrebinoye, 180
km northwest of St. Petersburg is a favorite
spot for backpackers and rock climbers.
Ask a fellow climber or at a camping
equipment shop about how to get there.
See also* TRAVEL AGENCIES *for tours to the
Russian mountain ranges.*

Karat
Vosstaniya ul., 35/40..................... 275-15-31
Mon-Fri 9-18; Rbls
St. Petersburg Tourist Club
Bolshaya Konyushennaya ul., 27 311-45-17
Fax... 314-63-70
Mon-Fri 10-18; Rbls, $
Third Pole, *Travels and Adventures*
Professora Popova, 5 apt. 13 234-89-51
Fax... 234-27-58
Mon-Fri 10-18; Rbls, $; Eng

☎ **MOVIES**

See CINEMAS

☎ **MOVING COMPANIES**
ПЕРЕВОЗКИ ГРУЗОВЫЕ
MÖBELSPEDITIONEN
FRETS, COMPAGNIES DE
FLYTTBOLAG SE ÄVEN SHIPPING
KULJETUSLIIKKEET

See also FREIGHT FORWARDERS

*A number of Western moving companies
(removals) have offices in Moscow. See*
The *Traveller's* Yellow Pages for
Moscow, 1994.

There are dozens of companies with trucks for hire to help with moving furniture and things around the city. Eurodonat has a good reputation for international transport. See also TRUCKING.

Aspekt
3-ey Pyatiletki ul., 44 100-08-16
Mon-Fri 11-19; Rbls, $

EuroDonat FREIGHT FORWARDERS AND TRANSPORT

EXPERIENCED MOVERS
Modern Truck Fleet

Yakornaya ul., 17
Tel .... (812) 224-11-44
Dept. Manager .... (812) 222-55-95
Fax .... (812) 224-06-20
Telex .... 121118 DFS SU
Hrs: 9-18, $ & Rubles, English
Metro: Novocherkasskaya

Lakon
Vatutina ul., 19 540-90-05
Mon-Sat 8-20
Lenvneshtrans
Mezhevoy kan., 5 251-41-97
Fax 186-28-83
Mon-Fri 8:30-17:15; Rbls; Eng
Naydenov i Kompanony
Telezhnaya ul., 7/9 530-25-23
Daily 9-21; Metro Ploshchad Vosstaniya
San
Petropavlovskaya Krepost, 15, rm. 8
.... 238-42-41
Mon-Fri 9-17; Rbls
Shushary
Gastello ul., 17, Hotel Mir, rm. 601
.... 108-47-60
Mon-Fri 9-17

☎ **MUSEUMS**
МУЗЕЙ
MUSEEN
MUSEES
MUSEER
MUSEOT

See also CHURCHES *and* CEMETERIES
Most museums close one day each week. A few still close for a "sanitary day" the last Wednesday or Thursday or Friday of each month (indicated by "last"). These hours and days can change, especially in fall and winter, so check.

Palaces: *Many beautiful, old palaces, institutes, and grand houses of nobility and merchants are used as concert halls, "House of Culture" and government offices. Often special events are held there. Even though they are not operated as museums, we have listed them here.*

Anichkov Palace *Anichkov Dvorets*
Nevskiy pr., 39 .... Not open to the public
Built 1741-1754, Architects: Zemtsov, Dmitriev, Rastrelli. In the mid 1860's this palace was owned by Alexander III. It is now used by a children's organization. Metro Nevskiy Prospekt; H-5
Anna Akhmatova Museum at Fontannyy Dom
Reki Fontanki nab., 34,
Entrance from Liteynyy pr., 53 272-22-11
.... 272-58-95
Former home of Russian poet A. Akhmatova Tue-Sun 10:30-18:30, last Wed.; Eng, Ger, Fr; Metro Gostinyy Dvor; H-6
Applied Arts Museum
Muzey Prikladnykh Iskusstv
Solyanoy per., 15 273-32-58
Mon-Sat 11-17; Eng, Ger; Metro Chernyshevskaya; G-7
Beloselskikh-Belozerskikh Palace
Dvorets Beloselskikh-Belozerskikh
Nevskiy pr., 41 ....No ☎
Built in 1800, Architect: Demertsov, rebuilt in 1846, Architect: Stakenshneider, used for concerts & government functions;; H-5
Benua Family Museum - *See* PETERHOF
Blok House
Dekabristov ul., 57 113-86-16
Former home of Russian poet Alexander Blok Mon-Tue, Thu-Sun 11-18; Rbls, $; D-4
Bolshoy Petergofskiy Palace - *See* PETERHOF
Botanical Museum *Botanicheskiy Muzey*
Professora Popova ul., 2 234-84-70
.... 234-17-64
Five million plants from around the world "Orangery" in repair Mon-Fri 10-17; Rbls; Metro Petrogradskaya; G-9
Brodskiy House *Under repair until January 1994*
Iskusstv pl., 3 314-36-58
.... 213-64-96
Home of painter I. Brodskiy - paintings on display Mon-Sat 11-20; Metro Nevskiy Prospekt; G-9
Chinese Palace - *See* LOMONOSOV
Circus Art Museum
Muzey Tsirkovogo Iskusstva
Reki Fontanki nab., 3 210-44-13
More than 80,000 items chronicling the circus world Mon-Fri 12-18; Rbls; Metro Gostinyy Dvor; G-6
*Cruiser Aurora *Kreyser Avrora*
Petrogradskaya nab., 4 230-52-02
Fired the shot signaling the storming of the Winter Palace, the start of the October Revolution. Tue-Thu, Sat-Sun 10:30-16; Eng; Metro Ploshchad Lenina; Tram 6, 63; G-8
Dokuchaev Museum of Soil Science
Birzhevoy proezd, 6 218-56-02
.... 218-55-01
Displays of different soils & agricultural methods Mon-Fri 9-18; Rbls; Metro Vasileostrovskaya; F-7
Dostoevskiy Literary Memorial Museum
Kuznechnyy per., 5/2 164-69-50
.... 311-40-31
Home of great Russian writer Dostoevskiy Tue-Sun 10:30-17:30, last Wed; Eng, Fr; Metro Dostoevskaya; H-5
Exhibition of Musical Instruments
Vystavka Muzykalnykh Instrumentov
Isaakievskaya pl., 5 314-53-45
.... 314-53-94
Collection of musical instruments from 19th & 20th C. Wed-Mon 11-18; F-6

***THE HERMITAGE

ONE OF WORLD'S GREAT ART MUSEUMS
Dvortsovaya nab., 34 219-86-25
.... 311-37-25
One of the largest & most famous art museums with 2.7 million items on display. Housed in the Winter Palace, (1754-62), Small Hermitage (1764-67), Old Hermitage (1771-87), & New Hermitage (1839-52)
Tue-Sun 10:30-18, closed Mon; Rbls;
Eng, major European & Asian Languages
Metro Nevskiy Prospekt; T-bus 1, 7, 9, 10; F-6

**Kazan Cathedral   Kazanskiy Sobor
Also called **History of Religion Museum**
Kazanskaya pl., 2 311-04-95
See CHURCHES for description. Mon-Tue, Thu-Sat 11-17; Rbls, $; Eng; Metro Nevskiy Prospekt; G-6

Kirov Museum
Kamennoostrovskiy pr., 26/28 233-38-22
Former home of Leningrad Communist Party Boss Sergey Kirov, murdered by Stalin in 1934;
Mon-Tue, Thu-Sun 11-18; Metro Gorkovskaya; F-9

Krasin, *Icebreaker museum*
16-ya Liniya 356-29-69
Daily 9-18, D-5

Kshesinskaya Mansion
Osobnyak Kshesinskoy
Kuybysheva ul., 2/4 233-70-48
.... 233-73-22
Russian ballerina Kshesinskaya's home is a museum of Political History. Mon-Wed, Fri-Sun 10-17; Rbls; Eng; Metro Gorkovskaya; G-8

Leningrad Region Museums Board
Liteynyy pr., 57 279-71-35
Fax.................................... 273-57-92
Hrs: 9-18, English, German

Literary Plot of the Volkovskoe Cemetery
Rasstannaya ul., 30 166-23-83
See CEMETERIES for description.
Mon-Wed, Fri-Sun 11-19; Rbls; Metro Moskovskie Vorota H-2

Lomonosov Museum, *Tower of Kunstkamera*
Universitetskaya nab., 3 218-12-11
.... 218-14-12
Flat of Russian scientist Lomonosov; Mon-Thu, Sun 11-18; Rbls; Metro Nevskiy Prospekt; T-bus 1, 7, 9, 10; I-6

Manege Central Exhibition Hall
Isaakievskaya pl., 1 314-82-53
Fax 314-82-54
City's largest exhibition hall, built as a riding stables in 1804-1807 by architect Quarenghi.
Mon-Wed, Fri-Sun 11-19; Rbls; Eng, Ger, Fr
Metro Nevskiy Prospekt; T-bus 5; E-6

Marble Palace   Mramornyy Dvorets
Millionnaya ul., 5/1 312-91-96
Fax 314-41-53
Built by Catherine the Great for her favorite Grigoriy Orlov, 1768-1785, Architect: Rinaldi
Mon, Wed-Sun 10-18; Rbls, $; Eng
Metro Gorkovskaya; G-7

Mendeleev Museum
Universitetskaya nab., 7/9 218-29-82
Mendeleev developed the periodic table of the elements
Mon-Fri 10-17, T-bus 10; I-6

Menshikov Palace
Universitetskaya nab., 15 213-11-12
Palace of Alexander Menshikov, Peter the Great's favorite; 1710-1727; Architect: Fontana, Schädel
Tue-Sun 10:30-16; Eng, Ger, Fr;
Metro Nevskiy Prospekt; T-bus 10; I-6

Museum of the Academy of Art
Muzey Akademii Khudozhestv
Universitetskaya nab., 17 213-35-78
.... 213-64-96
Famous academy also displays paintings by alumni; 1764-1788, Architect: Kokorinov & Vallin de la Mothe
Wed-Sun 11-19; Rbls, $; Eng, Fr;
Metro Vasileostrovskaya; T-bus 1,7,9,10; E-6

Museum of the Arctic & Antarctic
Muzey Arktiki i Antarktiki
Marata ul., 24 a 311-25-49
The history of Arctic & Antarctic exploration; 1820-1826, Architect: Melnikov;
Wed-Sun 10-17; Rbls; Metro Mayakovskaya; H-5

*Museum of Artillery   Muzey Artillerii
Aleksandrovskiy Park, 7 232-02-96
Great display of arms from armor and swords to tanks and rockets. Favorite of military buffs & children.
Wed-Sun 11-18; Rbls; Metro Gorkovskaya, F-7,8

Museum of Ethnography   Muzey Etnografii
Inzhenernaya ul., 4, bldg. 1 219-11-74
Cultural life in former republics of USSR; 1900-1911
Tue-Sun 10-18, last Thu; Rbls; Eng, Ger, Fr;
Metro Gostinyy Dvor; G-6

*Museum of Ethnography & Anthropology
Also called **The Kunstkamera**
Universitetskaya nab., 3 218-14-12
Peter the Great's collection of curiosities; 1754 -1758, Architect: Chevakinskiy. Mon-Thu, Sun 11-18; Rbls; Eng; Metro Nevskiy Prospekt; T-bus 1, 7, 9, 10; E-6

Museum of Military Medicine
Voenno-Meditsinskiy Muzey
Lazaretnyy per., 2 315-53-58
.... 113-52-15
Military medicine exhibit
Mon-Fri 9-12, 13-16; Rbls; Metro Pushkinskaya; G-4

Museum of Urban Sculpture
Muzey Gorodskoy Skulptury
Located in the Church of the Annunciation at Alexander Nevskiy Monastery, See CHURCHES.
Aleksandra Nevskogo pl., 1 274-26-35
Models of the city's famous monuments.
Mon-Wed, Fri-Sun 11-15; Rbls
Metro Ploshchad Aleksandra Nevskogo; J-4

Nekrasov House
Liteynyy pr., 36 272-01-65
Home of 19th-century poet Nekrasov
Mon., Wed., Fri. 11-18, Thurs. 13-20, last Thur;
Metro Vladimirskaya; T-bus 3, 8 , 15, 38; H-6

Oreshek Fortress
Staroladozhskiy kanal, Shlisselburg
.... 238-47-20
Island fortress near the source of the Neva, famous for its prisoners. Daily 10-17; Rbls; Train from Finland RR; Metro Ploshchad Lenina

Palace of Catherine I - *See* PUSHKIN
Palace of Peter III - *See* LOMONOSOV
Pavlovsk Palace - *See* PAVLOVSK

***Peter and Paul Fortress
Petropavlovskaya Krepost
Petropavlovskaya Krepost, 3 238-45-40
.... 232-94-54
Built by Peter the Great to defend his new city of Saint Petersburg, founded in 1703. Site of St. Peter and Paul Cathedral with tombs of Peter the Great and Tsars.
Mon-Tue, Thu-Sun 11-17; Rbls, $; Metro Gorkovskaya F-7

Peter the Great's House   Domik Petra
Petrovskaya nab., 6 232-45-76
The city's oldest building, built in 1703
Mon, Wed-Sun 11-18; Rbls; Eng; Metro Gorkovskaya; G-7

Piskarevskoe Cemetery　　　See CEMETERIES
Nepokorennykh pr., 74.................... 247-57-16
*Contains the graves of more than 480,000 Leningraders
who died during the 1941-1944 Siege
Daily 10-18; Metro Ploshchad Muzhestva*

Popov's House
Professora Popova ul., 5.................. 234-59-00
*Home of the inventor of the first radio; Mon-Fri 11-17;
Rbls; Bus 10; Metro Petrogradskaya F-9,10*

Pushkin House
Nab. Reki Moyki, 12
Director 312-19-62
Tel/Fax... 311-38-01
Tour Reservations............................ 314-00-06
*Pushkin, Russia's greatest poet, lived here from
September 1836 till his death in January 1837
Guided & Self-Guided Tours; Hrs: 10:40-18, Closed Tues;
Eng, Ger; Metro Nevskiy Prospekt; F-6*

Pushkinskiy Dom
Makarova nab., 4 218-05-02
*Old Customs building houses displays of Russian
literature, manuscripts, first editions, 1829-32,
Architect: Lukini; Wed-Sun 11-17; Rbls; Eng E-7*

Railway Museum
　　　　　　　　　　Zheleznodorozhnyy Muzey
Sadovaya ul., 50 315-14-76
*Over 6000 exhibits illustrating the history of Russia's
railways, including operating models.
Mon-Thu, Sun 11-17:30; Metro Sadovaya; F-4*

Razliv Barn Museum
Sestroretsk, Emelyanova ul., 3
　　　　　*Barn & hay hut; Lenin hid here.
Trains from Finland RR; Metro Ploshchad Lenina*

Repin Museum (Penaty)
Primorskoe shosse, 411, Repino
*Location named after Russian painter Repin who lived
here from 1900 to 1930.　Mon, Wed-Sun 10-17; Rbls
Trains from Finland RR; Metro Ploshchad Lenina*

Rimskiy-Korsakov House
Zagorodnyy pr., 28, floor 3 113-32-08
*The former home of the 19th century Russian composer
Rimskiy-Korsakov.　Wed-Sun 11-18; Rbls;T-bus 3
Metro Vladimirskaya; G-4,5*

Rumyantsev Palace
　　　　　　　　　　Rumyantsevskiy Dvorets
Krasnogo Flota nab., 44 311-75-44
*Museum of the city's history from 1917, section on
1941-44 Siege;1826-1827; Architect: Glinka
Mon-Tue, Thu-Sun 11-16; Rbls, $; Eng; E-5*

**Russian Museum　　　　*Russkiy Muzey*
Inzhenernaya ul., 4......................... 219-16-15
Fax 314-41-53
*Over 315,000 paintings by Russian artists, in the former
Mikhaylovskiy Palace; Architect: Rossi 1819-1825
Mon, Wed-Sun 10-18; Rbls; Metro Gostinnyy Dvor; G-6*

Russian Political History Museum
　　　　　Muzey Russkoy Politicheskoy Istorii
Kuybysheva ul., 4 233-70-52
.... 233-70-50
*In the Kshesinskaya mansion
Mon-Wed, Fri-Sun 10-17:30; Metro Gorkovskaya; G-8*

Shalyapin House
Graftio ul., 26.................................. 234-26-98
*Home of Shalyapin, 1915-22, reformer of Russian opera
Wed-Sun; Metro Petrogradskaya; F-10*

***St. Isaac's Cathedral　*Isaakievskiy Sobor*
Isaakievskaya pl.............................. 315-97-32
.... 210-92-06
*One of the world's largest domed churches;
1818-1858, Architect: Monferrand
Mon-Tue, Thu-Sun 10-17; Rbls; T-bus 5; F-5, 6*

*Summer Garden & Summer Palace of Peter I
　　　　　Letniy Sad i Letniy Dvorets Petra I
Please call....................................... 314-03-74
*Summer estate laid out from 1704-1714 by Trezzini,
House built by Schülter ; Mon, Wed-Sun 11-18;
Rbls; Bus 14; G-6,7*

Tavricheskiy Palace　*Tavricheskiy Dvorets*
Shpalernaya ul., 47 .... Not open to public.
*Built, 1783-1789, for Prince Potemkin-Tavricheskiy,
now used by the government, architect: Starov
Metro Chernyshevskaya; I-7*

The Museum of the Defense of Leningrad
　　　　　　　Muzey Oborony Leningrada
Solyanoy per., 9.............................. 275-72-08
*Pictures and artifacts of the defense of Leningrad
during the 1941-1944 Siege
Mon-Tue, Thu-Sun 10-17; Rbls, $; Eng
Metro Chernyshevskaya; G-6,7*

Theater Museum　　　　*Teatralnyy Muzey*
Ostrovskogo pl., 6........................... 311-21-95
.... 312-36-23
*Evolution of Russian music and theater
Mon, Wed-Sun 11-18; Rbls; Metro Gostinnyy Dvor; G-5*

Modern Art Museum

Tsarskoe Selo Collection

Pushkin, Karla Marksa pr., 40

Director.. 466-55-81
Exhibition... 466-04-60

*Open Saturday, Sunday
Trains from Vitebskiy RR; Metro Pushkinskaya*

WOULD YOU VISIT
Usupov Palace
L i t e y n y y　p r . , 4 2

DiUP　　ZNANIE

KONTAKT　☎ 272-80-55
Tel.: 275-72-02, Ext. 6303; Fax: 275-70-01
● National Art of Russia.
■ Modern Art of St.Petersburg.
▲ Russian Bronze. Amber.
⚐ Composition "To New Civilization".

Wax Museum　　*Muzey Voskovykh Figur*
Kuybycheva ul., 2/4......................... 233-71-89
Daily 10-18; Metro Gorkovskaya; G-8

Winter Palace　　　　*Zimniy Dvorets*
*Built in 1754-1762 by the famous architect Rastrelli.
Now part of the Hermitage.　See HERMITAGE*

Yelagin Palace
Yelagin Ostrov, 1............................. 239-11-31
*Island summer residence of the tsars; 1818-1822,
Architect: Rossi; Wed-Sun 10-18; Rbls; Metro Chernaya
Rechka; Tram 2, 31, 37, 48; D-10*

Zoological Museum
Universitetskaya nab., 1 218-01-12
*Animal, fish & insect specimens from all over the world
Mon-Thu, Sat-Sun 11-17; Rbls; Eng
Metro Nevskiy Prospekt; T-bus 10; F-6*

📧 MUSIC AND ART SCHOOLS
МУЗЫКАЛЬНЫЕ ШКОЛЫ
MUSIKSCHULEN,
MUSIKUNTERRICHT
MUSIQUE, ECOLES DE ET COURS
MUSIKSKOLOR OCH
UNDERVISNING
MUSIIKKIOPISTOT

There are 30 or more special music schools which gifted children attend after their regular school program. Here are some of the best.

Art School   **Khudozhestvennaya Shkola**
- Nekrasova ul., 4/2 273-69-86
  Mon-Sat 10-22; Rbls
- Rizhskiy pr., 8 251-33-73
  Mon-Sat 10-22; Rbls; Tram 29; Metro Baltiyskaya

Children's Art School
       Detskaya Khudozhestvennaya Shkola
Marata ul., 68 112-00-09
  Mon-Sat 9-21; Rbls

Music School   **Muzykalnaya Shkola**
- Kamennoostrovskiy pr., 5 232-90-37
  Mon-Sat 10-20; Rbls
- Leytenanta Shmidta nab., 31 355-74-52
  Mon-Sat 10-22; Rbls
- Sadovaya ul., 32 310-04-62
  Mon-Sat 10-22; Rbls
- Sedova ul., 32 568-03-26
  Mon-Sat 10-22; Rbls; Bus 95; Metro Elizarovskaya

Rimskiy-Korsakov Conservatory
  Special School for Music
  The outstanding music school in St. Pb. Gifted students attend full-time.
Matveeva per., 1 a 114-11-61
  Mon-Sat 10-22; Rbls

📞 MUSIC SHOPS
МУЗЫКАЛЬНЫЕ МАГАЗИНЫ
MUSIKGESCHÄFTE
MUSIQUE, MAGASINS DE
MUSIKAFFÄRER
MUSIIKKILIIKKEET

See also RECORDS, COMPACT DISKS, and MUSICAL INSTRUMENTS

Alpina
  Zagorodnyy pr., 34 .... No 📞
  Daily 11-13, 14-20; Rbls

Diez
  Transportnyy per., 6 164-95-79
  Mon-Sat 11-19; Rbls

Dom Radio I Muzyki
           House of Radio & Music
  Large selection of CD's cassettes, records
  Grazhdanskiy pr., 15/1 534-42-18
  Mon-Sat 10-19; Rbls

Melodiya   **Melody**
- Bolshoy pr., P.S., 47 232-11-39
  Mon-Sat 10-14, 15-19; Rbls
- Nevskiy pr., 32-34 311-74-55
  Sheet music, records, cassettes, CDs, and books
  Mon-Sat 11-14, 15-19; Rbls; Eng

Muzyka No. 41   **Music No. 41**
  Sredniy pr., 48 213-41-88
  Mon-Sat 10-14, 15-19; Rbls

Rapsodiya
  Bolshaya Konyushennaya, 13 314-48-01
  312-35-05

Gramplastinki   **Records**
- Moskovskiy pr., 34/36 292-35-05
  Tue-Sun 10-14, 15-19; Rbls
- 7-ya Liniya, 40 213-35-88
  Mon-Sat 10-19; Rbls

Severnaya Lira   **Northern Lira**
  Classical compact disks, instruments, sheet music and literature on music
  Nevskiy pr., 26 312-07-96
  Mon-Sat 10-14, 15-19; Rbls; Metro Nevskiy Prospekt

📞 MUSICAL INSTRUMENTS
МУЗЫКАЛЬНЫЕ
ИНСТРУМЕНТЫ
MUSIKINSTRUMENTE
MUSIQUE, INSTRUMENTS DE
MUSIKINSTRUMENT
MUSIIKKI-INSTRUMENTIT

See also PIANOS

Apraksin Dvor
  Sadovaya ul., Apraksin Dvor, bldg.1, rm.13-15
  📞 310-20-03
  Mon-Sat 11-19; Rbls

Art-Sound Dvor
  Pushkinskaya ul., 10 164-52-96
  Fax 274-40-77
  Daily 11-19; Electronic and wind instruments

Barbara GmbH

Professional Sound Systems & Musical Instruments from Yamaha, Korg, Roland, Alesis, Kurzweil, Fostex, Tascam, C-LAB Atari, Vester, Tama, etc.
We Service What We Sell

Ostrovskogo pl., 9 310-26-24
Tel./Fax 310-26-86

PROFESSIONAL MICROPHONES

🅱 byetone

Designed for Professional Vocalists

Pervomaiskiy pr., 25 553-45-32
Fax 213-35-41

DLT (Leningrad Trading House)
  Bolshaya Konyushennaya ul., 21/23 ... 312-26-27
  219-95-02
  Fax 315-21-92
  Mon-Sat 10-20; Rbls, $; Eng

Factory of Musical Instruments
6-ya Krasnoarmeyskaya ul., 7 292-27-77
Fax 292-00-28
Mon-Fri 8:15-17; Rbls, $

Gostinyy Dvor
Nevskiy pr., 35, Perinnaya Liniya ... 310-53-66
Mon-Sat 10-21; Rbls, $

Dom Radio i Muzyki
                         House of Radio & Music
Grazhdanskiy pr., 15/1 534-42-18
Largest music store in St. Petersburg
Mon-Sat 10-19; Rbls

Muzyka No. 41   **Music No. 41**
Sredniy pr., 48............................... 213-41-88
Mon-Sat 10-14, 15-19; Rbls

⦿ POLYGON®

PROFESSIONAL MUSICAL EQUIPMENT

St. Petersburg, 195160, P.O. Box 160

Tel. 525-16-95

Tel/Fax... 525-62-48

REPAIR, MUSIC INSTRUMENTS

Remont Muzykalnykh Instrumentov
       Musical Instruments-Tuning & Repair
Apraksin Dvor, bldg. 3 314-24-51
Guitars, violins, pianos, accordions; Mon-Fri 9-17

Repair Workshop, *Brass Instruments*
Kharkovskaya ul.,.......................... 277-00-03
Mon-Fri 11-19

☎ MUSICIANS

See ENTERTAINMENT ACTS

☎ NEWS AGENCIES
АГЕНСТВА НОВОСТЕЙ
NACHRICHTENAGENTUREN
NOUVELLES, AGENCES DE
NYHETSBYRÅER
UUTISTOIMISTOT

See NEWSPAPERS *for local newspapers,* RADIO
STATIONS *and* TELEVISION STATIONS

RUSSIAN NEWS AGENCIES-ST. PETERSBURG

*Here are three St. Petersburg bureaus for
Russian news agencies.*

Interfax
Tavricheskaya ul., 39, rm. 347
☎ .... (812) 271-78-66
Fax .... (812) 271-76-02
Bus 46, 134; Metro Chernyshevskaya

ITAR-TASS
Sadovaya ul., 38 .... (812) 315-65-13
Metro Sennaya Ploshchad

RIA Novosti (News)
Kutuzova nab., 18 .... (812) 273-35-76

FOREIGN NEWS AGENCIES-MOSCOW

*In general foreign news agencies do not
have permanent representatives in St. Pb.*

These NEWS AGENCIES *are based in
Moscow. See* The *Traveller's* **Yellow Pages
for Moscow, 1994,** *and* Information
Moscow *for a complete list with names of
correspondents.*

Agence France Press (France)
Sadovaya-Samotechnaya ul., 13, apt. 34
☎ .... (095) 292-31-75

AP - Associated Press (USA)
Kutuzovskiy pr., 7/4, bldg. 5, apt. 33
☎ .... (095) 243-51-53
Fax...................................... (095) 230-28-45

BBC - British Broadcasting Corporation
Sadovaya-Samotechnaya ul., 12/24, apt. 9
☎ .... (095) 200-02-96

CBC - Canadian Broadcasting Corporation
Gruzinskiy per., 3 .... (095) 250-52-64
Fax...................................... (095) 230-28-75

CBS - Columbia Broadcasting System (USA)
Sadovaya-Samotechnaya ul., 12/24, apt. 38
☎ .... (095) 299-32-70

CNN - Cable News Network (USA)
Kutuzovskiy pr., 7/4, apt. 256-259
☎ .... (095) 243-70-95

DPA - Deutsche Press Agency (Germany)
Kutuzovskiy pr., 7/4, apt. 210
☎ .... (095) 230-25-63
Fax...................................... (095) 230-25-43

NBC - National Broadcasting Corporation (USA)
Berezhkovskaya nab., at the Hotel Slavyanskaya
☎ .... (095) 941-88-01

New York Times (USA)
Sadovaya-Samotechnaya ul., 12/24, apt. 65
☎ .... (095) 200-02-40

Newsweek (USA)
Kutuzovskiy per., 9, bldg. 2, apt. 78
☎ .... (095) 243-17-73

Radio - France & Télévision Française
       Internationale
Gruzinskiy per., 3, apt. 223
☎ .... (095) 253-92-94

RAI (Italy)
Mira pr., 74........................... (095) 280-76-89

Reuters (USA)
Sadovaya-Samotechnaya ul., 12/224, apt. 55-60
☎ .... (095) 200-39-48

Swenska Dagbladet (Sweden)
Kutuzovskiy pr., 9/2 .... (095) 243-67-47

Time (USA)
Kutuzovskiy per., 14............. (095) 243-17-93

Times (GBR)
Bolshaya Dorogomilovskaya ul., 14
☎ .... (095) 230-24-57

US News & World Report (USA)
Leninskiy pr., 36, apt. 53....... (095) 938-20-51

UPI - United Press International (USA)
Kutuzovskiy pr., 7/4, apt. 67
☎ .... (095) 243-70-11

Washington Post (USA)
Kutuzovskiy per., 7/4, apt. 2
☎ .... (095) 230-66-41

Welt (Germany)
Kutuzovskiy pr., 7/4, apt. 169
☎ .... (095) 243-52-86

Xinhua News Agency (China)
Druzhby ul., 6 .... (095) 938-20-07

Zuddeutsche Zeitung (Germany)
Kutuzovskiy pr., 7/4 .... (095) 243-11-66

☎ NEWSPAPERS
ГАЗЕТЫ, ЖУРНАЛЫ
ZEITUNGEN/ZEITSCHRIFTEN
JOURNAUX/MAGAZINES
TIDNINGAR/VECKOTIDNINGAR
SANOMA- JA AIKAKAUSLEHDET

See also MAGAZINES

WHERE TO BUY AND SUBSCRIBE TO MAJOR FOREIGN NEWSPAPERS

What is available: The International Herald Tribune, Wall Street Journal, Daily Express, Daily Mail, Die Welt, Financial Times, The Guardian, Le Monde, Sunday Times, The Times, The Economist, USA Today, Le Figaro *and more.*

Many of these foreign newspapers are available in news shops, at the Grand Hotel Europe, Nevskiy Palace, Pribaltiyskaya, Okhtinskaya, Astoria and other hotels. Some are available in newspaper kiosks on Nevskiy Prospect. To find out their availability and how to subscribe, call the following:

Bureau Inpress Co. Ltd.
Goncharnaya ul., 26 279-42-22
Mon-Fri 9-17:80; $, T-Bus 1; Metro Ploshchad Vosstaniya

MARTINUS NIJHOFF
Book dealers
Subscriptions to foreign magazines
Marata ul., 86 315-25-86
Mon-Fri 10-18

Where to subscribe to Russian Publications: *If the magazine or journal is sold by Rospechat (formerly Soyuzpechat) (see* MAGAZINES*), you can subscribe and pay for these magazines at any* POST OFFICE. *Or send the post card or form in the magazine to the publisher.*

ENGLISH AND FOREIGN LANGUAGE NEWSPAPERS PUBLISHED In ST. PETERSBURG And MOSCOW

Commersant
Best business news, editorials, prices & policies
Nevskiy pr., 3 off. 25 245-58-27
Fax 315-79-67

Monthly Publication
Kuznetsovskaya ul., 19 296-33-75
Fax 298-99-25

Golf Business
Millionnaya ul., 22 226-24-54
Fax 239-31-23

Moscow Business News, *Weekly, general news*
Moscow .... (095) 209-26-82
Fax....................................... (095) 209-17-28
Mon-Fri 10-18; Rbls, $

MOSCOW NEWS
W E E K L Y
Moscow News
The best way for you to know what's going on in Russia
- Politics
- Economics
- Editorials
- Culture
- Fashion
- Sports
Weekly editions in English and Russian

Tverskaya ul., 16/2, Moscow
Russian Edition......(095) 209-17-49
English Edition.......(095) 209-26-82
Fax ....(095) 209-17-28

Moscow Times, *Daily, general news*
Moscow .... (095) 257-32-01
Fax....................................... (095) 257-36-21
Mon-Fri 10-18; Rbls, $
Moscow Tribune, *Daily, general news*
Moscow .... (095) 135-11-14
Fax....................................... (095) 230-20-10
Mon-Fri 10-18; Rbls, $

WHAT'S HAPPENING IN ST. PETERSBURG
NEVA NEWS
An English language newspaper for foreign readers in Russia & abroad

Our prices for advertisements & classifieds are very competitive

Postal address: Pravdy ul., 10, St.Petersburg, 191126, Russia
Tel/Fax: 164-47-65

Neva Week, *City news*
Ligovskiy pr., 253, apt. 2, 3,4 166-37-96
Fax... 112-99-63
Mon-Fri 9:30-18; Rbls; Eng
Russian Business Review
Eng & Rus, reviews in Russian
Pochtamtskaya ul., 5, apt. 30 314-23-67
Fax... 315-47-74
Mon-Fri 10-18; Rbls, $

St. Petersburg For You, *Monthly, general news*
Kronverskiy pr., 29, apt. 1 232-00-39

☙ St. Petersburg Press ☙

Your English Language
News Source

119-60-80

Available in Consulates, Kiosks,
Hotels & Restaurants,
International Shops & Cafes

St. Petersburg Press
Eng, weekly on St. Pb., a must read
Professora Popova ul., 47, off. 624
☎ 119-60-80
St. Petersburglche Zeitung
Ger, monthly city-wide
Bolshoy pr., 83, rm. 76, V.O. 217-53-10
Mbl/WE *Monthly, Russian-American general events*
Moscow .... (095) 209-76-08

RUSSIAN NEWSPAPERS In RUSSIAN

24 Chasa   **24 Hours**
Daily reviews of Russian & foreign publications
Rimskogo-Korsakova pr., 9 310-63-75
Fax 312-80-74
Daily 10-18; Rbls, $
Aktsioner & Co., *Daily 10-17; Rbls*
Economic reports on small & medium sized businesses
Shpalernaya ul., 52, rm. 19 272-96-76
Fax 275-76-11
Baltic Courier, *Mon-Sat 10-19; Rbls*
Classifieds, book reviews & agriculture reports
Ligovskiy pr., 56 e 164-61-34
Fax 164-69-41
Birzha Truda   **Job Exchange**
Mainly job-related classifieds
Proletarskoy Diktatury, 6 278-52-01
Birzhevye Vedomosti   **Exchange News**
Weekly business paper
Moscow .... (095) 231-26-53
Fax .... (095) 233-38-63
Biznes-Shans   **Business-Chance**
Wholesale activities, stock & commodity exchanges
Reki Fontanki nab., 59 210-80-69
Mon-Sat 10-17; Rbls; Eng, Ger, Fr
Metro Sennaya Ploshchad
Business and Banks, *in Russian*
Reporting on the banking world
Moscow .... (095) 907-82-10
Chas Pik   **Rush Hour**
Weekly, politics, economics, culture
Nevskiy pr., 81 279-22-70
City *(moving fall, 1993) Mon-Sat 10-19*
Business news, industrial & technical advancements
Ligovskiy pr., 56 e 164-61-34

Commersant Publishing House
St. Petersburg Representation

Nevskiy pr., 3, office 25 315-04-29
Fax 315-79-67
Hrs: 10-20, English, German, French

Commersant, *Daily news in Russian*
Best business, editorials, prices & policies
Nevskiy pr., 3 off. 25 245-58-27
Commersant, *Weekly news in Russian*
Best business news, editorials, prices & policies
Nevskiy pr., 3 off. 25 245-58-27
Delovoy Peterburg
            Business Petersburg
Excellent financial and economic reviews
Malookhtinskiy pr., 68 528-00-56
Delovaya Zhizn   **Business Life**
News for the new class of Russian business owner
Nevskiy pr., 28 219-94-71
Domashniy Advokat   **Home Lawyer**
Free legal advice
Moscow .... (095) 209-36-34
Ekonomika i Zhizn   **Economics and Life**
Well respected weekly, reporting on economics
Moscow .... (095) 212-23-89
Fax .... (095) 200-22-97
Finansovaya Gazeta   **Financial News**
Weekly on international finance
Moscow .... (095) 208-43-26
Fax .... (095) 208-41-87
Finansovye Vesti   **Financial Times**
International Business Paper
Moscow .... (095) 927-10-01
Fax .... (095) 921-98-05

і ностранец

Member of the Commersant Publishing House
Newspaper Group
The perfect forum bringing together Russian
and foreign business contacts
Circulation: 100,000 Throughout the Former
USSR. 32 pages.

125080, Russia, Moscow, P.O. Box 21
Khoroshovskoe shosse, 17
Moscow .... (095) 941-09-00
Advertising & PR Dept .... (095) 940-02-33
Fax .... (095) 940-04-68

Izvestiya - *National paper*
Political, economic, cultural & scientific news
from Russia & abroad
Nevskiy pr., 19 311-87-33
Fax 311-85-06
Mon-Fri 10-18; Rbls
Kadr *Covering the cinema world*   **Frame**
Kamennoostrovskiy pr., 10 238-58-31
Located in the "Lenfilm" kinostudio
Kinonedelya Sankt Peterburga
    Film Week of St. Petersburg
Movie theater schedules
Reki Fontanki nab., 59 310-44-54
Mon-Fri 9-18; Rbls; Metro Sennaya Ploshchad
Komsomolskaya Pravda - *National Paper*
Outstanding: an old name with new views on politics,
economics, culture & science from Russia & abroad
(St. Petersburg correspondent)
Khersonskaya ul., 12 274-06-63
Mon-Fri 9-17; Rbls

Krasnaya Zvezda, *Military newspaper*   **Red Star**
Liteynyy pr., 20.............................. 272-58-25
Mon-Fri 10-18; Rbls

Labor   **Trud**
Politics, economics & culture from Russia & abroad
(St. Petersburg correspondent)
Truda pl., 4, rm. 57........................ 219-83-27
Fax 314-94-17
Mon-Fri 10-18; Rbls

Literaturnaya Gazeta   **Literary News**
(St. Petersburg correspondent)
Shpalernaya ul., 18 279-08-73
Mon, Fri 9-18; Rbls

Lvinyy Mostik, *Free Classifieds*
Ligovskiy pr., 253, apt. 2, 3,4......... 166-37-96
Fax 112-99-63
Mon-Fri 9:30-18; Rbls; Eng

Moscow News, *Weekly*
Politics, economics, editorials, culture, fashion, sports
Moscow................................(095) 209-17-07
Fax ....(095) 209-17-28

Natalie, *Russian women's news*
Sadovaya ul., 98/27 114-44-87

Nevskiy Vestnik   **Neva Bulletin**
Economic news of St. Petersburg
Reki Fontanki nab., 59 310-46-14
Fax 310-40-73
Mon-Fri 10-17; Rbls; Metro Sennaya Ploshchad

Nevskoe Vremya, *City News*   **Neva Times**
Gertsena ul., 47 312-40-40
Fax 312-20-78
Mon-Fri 10:30-18; Rbls, $

Omega, *Informational advertising newspaper*
Khersonskaya ul., 12...................... 312-78-31
Fax 274-08-52
Mon-Fri 10-18; Rbls

Pravda, *Old Communist Party paper*
Khersonskaya, ul., 12..................... 274-07-03
Fax 274-08-52
Mon-Sat 8:30-17:00

Pyat Uglov, *Children and teens*
Reki Fontanki nab., 59 311-88-74
Mon-Fri 10-18; Rbls; Metro Sennaya Ploshchad

Reklama-Shans, *Advertising newspaper*
Reki Fontanki nab., 59, rm. 116 210-84-57
Fax 315-62-83
Mon-Fri 10-18; Rbls; Metro Sennaya Ploshchad

Rock-Fuzz, *Chronicling the rock scene*
P.O. Box 127 528-76-87
Fax 227-29-83

Rynki Sankt-Peterburga i Oblasti
Markets in St. Petersburg & Region
Interesting, tells what is sold in stores & markets
Chkalovskiy pr., 15 235-98-26
Fax 235-51-17

Sankt Peterburgskie Vedomosti
Popular city news   **St. Petersburg News**
Reki Fontanki nab., 59 310-41-29
Fax 310-51-41
Mon-Fri 9:30-18; Rbls, $; Metro Sennaya Ploshchad

Sankt-Peterburgskoe Ekho
St. Petersburg Echo
Late-breaking city-wide news
Vosstaniya ul., 51 275-45-21
Fax 275-52-61

Segodnya *Daily political & business news* **Today**
Moscow...............................(095) 250-63-43

Sem Dney *Weekly TV & radio programs*   **7 Days**
Moscow...............................(095) 233-79-66

Slavic Bazaar

Weekly Publication in German

Kuznetsovskaya ul., 19...................296-33-75

Fax...298-99-25

Smena   *Politics & culture*   **New Generation**
Reki Fontanki nab., 59.................... 310-34-19
Mon-Fri 9:30-18; Rbls, $; Metro Sennaya Ploshchad

Soroka, *Free classifieds*
Proletarskoy Diktatury ul., 6 315-31-48
Mon-Fri 9-19; Rbls

Sovetskaya Rossiya   **Soviet Russia**
Political and economic news
Khersonskaya ul., 12.......................274-06-51
Mon-Sat 10-18; Rbls

Sovetskiy Sport, *Sports news*   **Soviet Sport**
Lomonosova ul., 22 314-24-17
Mon-Fri 10-18, Metro Dostoevskaya

SPORT, CHELOVEK, VREMYA
SPORT, MAN, TIME
Official publication of the Organizing Committee
of the 1994 St. Petersburg Goodwill Games
Reki Fontanki nab., 59.................... 310-43-70
Mon-Fri 10-17; Rbls

Segodnya S Utra Do Vechera, *City news*
This Day From Morning Till Night
Khersonskaya ul., 12.......................274-08-57
Mon-Fri, Sun 10-18; Rbls, $

Televidenie Radio   **Television, Radio**
Weekly television and radio programming
Reki Fontanki nab., 59.................... 310-57-75
Mon-Fri 10-18; Rbls; Metro Sennaya Ploshchad

Vecherniy Peterburg, *Popular evening newspaper*
Evening Petersburg
Reki Fontanki nab., 59.................... 311-88-75
Fax.. 314-31-05
Mon-Sat 9-17; Rbls; Metro Sennaya Ploshchad

Vesti   *St. Petersburg & Leningrad Region*   **News**
Millionnaya ul., 30...........................314-19-85
Mon, Wed, Fri 10-18; Rbls

Vse Dlya Vas   **Everything For You**
Free classifieds, wide circulation, regional editions
Pochtamtskaya ul., 5, off. 30.......... 315-52-25
Fax...315-47-74
Mon-Sat 10-18; Rbls; Eng

MbI/WE, *Monthly, Russian-American general events*
Moscow...............................(095) 209-76-08

☎ **NIGHTTIME**
ENTERTAINMENT
РАЗВЛЕЧЕНИЯ НОЧНЫЕ
UNTERHALTUNG/
VERANSTALTUNGEN, ABENDS
DIVERTISSEMENT NOCTURNE
NÖJESSTÄLLEN, NATTLIV
ILTAELÄMÄN HUVIT

See also THEATER/BALLET, RESTAURANTS, BARS,
CINEMAS, DISCOTHEQUE, ROCK CLUBS, CASINOS
& BOATS

Night time entertainment abounds in
St. Petersburg from concerts, cultural

evenings and THEATER *to elaborate variety shows at* RESTAURANTS *and intimate dancing at night bars. Information about shows can be found in newspapers, street billboards and signs, flyers and on TV.*

Bars, *see* BARS
Casinos, *see* CASINOS
Catherine the Great Erotic Variety Show
 Please call 248-82-64
Discotheques, *see* DISCOTHEQUES

NIGHT CLUB
ELDORADO
HOTEL KARELIA - ST. PETERSBURG
Tukhachevskogo ul., 27/2
226-3110
BAR, DISCO, DANCE SHOW, CASINO
OPEN DAILY 8 p.m. - 5 a.m., $

Europa Plus, Dance Hall, *Fri, Sat 23-6; Rbls, $*
 Kamennoostrovskiy pr., 68 .... No ☎
Galspe at Palanga
 Leninskiy pr., 127 254-55-82
 Variety Show; Daily 17-6; Rbls, $, CC

Hotelship Peterhof ★★★★
 Dine and Dance under the Sky
 Strictly no tennis shoes
 Nab. Makarova, near the Tuchkov Bridge
 213-63-21

Indie Club, *see* ROCK /POP MUSIC CLUBS
Jazz Philharmonic, *see* Jazz Clubs
Joy, *Discotheque, bar, casino*
 Lomonosova ul., 1/28 311-35-40
 Daily 22-5; Metro Nevskiy Prospekt; G-5
Landscrona in the Nevskij Palace
 Nevsky pr., 57............................... 113-15-18
 19-1; $, CC; Metro Mayakovskaya; H-5

NEVSKY
MELODY

European & Russian Cuisine,
Disco, Bars, Roulette, Blackjack.
Nab. Sverdlovskaya, 62 227-26-76
Tel./Fax 227-15-96
Hrs: 12-18 for Rubles, 18-1 $ & Rbls, $ for drinks.,
discotheque 21-1, CC, English, German, French

NIGHT RESTAURANT VOSTOK
"NIGHT RESTAURANT ORIENT"
Indian & European Cuisine
One of the best kitchens in the city
In beautiful Primorskiy Park Pobedy
New variety shows & orchestra
Primorskiy Park Pobedy 235-59-84
Hrs: 12-4:30; $ & Rubles, English

Night Theater
 Perekupnoy per., 12 274-94-67
Planetarium, *has a restaurant with a large, lively stage show and discotheque with laser lights and wild auctions. See* PLANETARIUM
Relax, *Discotheque*
 Prosveshcheniya pr., 80, bldg. 2 514-75-22
 Fri, Sat 22-6
Rock Around The Clock
 See SATURN SHOW *members only club, below*
Sadkos *on the weekend has live music or a Karaoke machine. See* RESTAURANTS

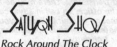

SATURN SHOW

Rock Around The Clock
Members Club
Sadovaya ul., 27 310-02-37

Schwabski Domik
 Krasnogvardeyskaya pl., 28/19.......528-22-11
 528-88-80
 Folk Music; Daily 11-2; Rbls, $; Eng, Ger
Star Dust Night Discotheque
 Aleksandrovskiy park, 4 233-27-12
 Live Music; Tue-Sun 10-16:30; Rbls; Metro Gorkovskaya
Tam Tam Club, *Rock & punk, soiled & seedy.*
 Malyy & 16-ya Liniya V.O. ....No ☎

A.O. TROIKA

• • • • •
The International-Russian Variety Show
Chorus Line, Song, Dance & Variety
"Moulin Rouge of Saint Petersburg"
A Great Show
• • • • •
Zagorodnyy pr., 27 113-53-43
Hrs: 19-24, $ & Rbls, English
A Russian-Swiss Company

Tunnel, *Located in a former bomb shelter, young crowd; techno music*
 Lyubanskiy per. (between Blokhina ul. and Zverinskaya ul.)...No ☎
Variety Shows *see* RESTAURANTS
 The following are just some of the restaurants which have variety shows: Assambleya, Nevsky Melody, St.- Petersburg, Schwabski Domik, Chayka, U Waltera, Vostok.

☎ NOTARY PUBLIC
НОТАРИАЛЬНЫЕ УСЛУГИ
NOTARIATE
NOTARIAT
NOTARIER
JULKISET NOTAARIT

Many forms must be notarized by an official NOTARY BUREAU (Notarialnaya Kontora, Нотариальная контора). Documents in a foreign language have to be translated or reviewed by an officially approved translator. There may be a long wait at the office, so call in advance or send someone to wait in line for you. Unfortunately, English is not spoken, so take your translator.

The Apostille. You may have to get your papers or forms notarized at your embassy or consulate as well. See CONSULATES. *Papers such as diplomas, transcripts, certificates, and incorporation papers needed for submission to authorities in Russia should be notarized before you leave for Russia using a form called an "Apostille" which states that the document is authentic. The process is lengthy and requires sending the documents to the state Secretary of State, who sends it to the Federal Secretary of States who sends it to the Russian Embassy for signature on the "stamped" form. In the USA, call the US Department of State, Authentication of Documents Division (202-647-5005). Once the papers get to Russia, they often will need to be translated into Russian by "official translators".*

Notary Bureau No. 1
Notarialnaya Kontora No.1
Nevskiy pr., 109.............................. 277-40-38
Mon-Fri 9-17; Rbls; Eng; Metro Ploshchad Vosstaniya
Notary Bureau No. 3
Nevskiy pr., 44................................. 110-50-44
Mon-Fri 9-13, 14-17:30; Rbls; Metro Nevskiy Prospekt
Notary Bureau No. 9
Zagorodnyy pr., 14 164-73-11
Mon-Fri 9-13, 14-18; Rbls; Metro Dostoevskaya
Notary Bureau No. 13
Serebristyy blvd., 22, bldg. 1 393-45-95
Mon-Fri 9-13, 14-17:30; Rbls; Metro Pionerskaya
Notary Bureau No. 14
Bolshoy Sampsonievskiy pr., 108..... 246-07-71
Mon-Fri 9-13, 14-17:30; Rbls; Tram 2; Metro Lesnaya
Notary Bureau No. 15
Manezhnyy per., 13 279-02-55
Mon-Sat 9-13, 14-17:30; Rbls; Metro Chernyshevskaya
Notary Bureau No. 18
Plovdivskaya ul., 9........................... 108-19-21
Mon-Sat 9-13, 14-17:30; Rbls; Tram 25; Metro Kupchino
Notary Bureau of Kronshtadt
Surgina ul., 15, Kronshtadt 236-27-53
Mon-Fri 9-13, 14-17:30; Rbls

☎ OBSTETRICIANS

See HOSPITALS, MEDICAL CARE & CONSULTATIONS

☎ OFFICE EQUIPMENT
ОФИСЫ, ОБОРУДОВАНИЕ
BÜROEINRICHTUNG
OFFICES, EQUIPEMENT
KONTORSUTRUSTNING
TOIMISTOKALUSTEET

See also PHOTOCOPIERS *and* COMPUTER STORES

ABC Electronics
Liteynyy pr., 22, apt. 30 272-96-58
Fax... 275-74-85
Fax machines, telephone equipment, calculators
Mon-Fri 10-13, 14-19; Rbls, $; Eng
Absolyut St. Petersburg
Kosmonavtov pr., 54...................... 264-65-15
In children's clinic, 3rd floor. Supplies for banks, telephones, beepers; Mon-Fri 10-18; Rbls, $; Eng
Aircom Russia - General Representative Minolta Austria
Komissara Smirnova ul., 15, off. 285
☎ 542-22-93
Photocopiers; Mon-Fri 10-18; Rbls, $; Eng, Ger
A. P. It, *Furniture for the Office*
Kima pr., 28..................................... 350-55-48
Mon-Fri 10-14, 15-19; Rbls; Eng, Ital
Arian, *Office furniture*
Revolyutsii shosse, 15 227-16-96
Mon-Fri 10-19; Rbls, $; Bus 22
Arman, *Office furniture, Mon-Fri 10:30-18; Rbls*
Bolshoy pr., V.O., 83, rm. 71 217-54-05
ASKoD, *Telephones, fax machines, calculators*
Reki Fontanki nab., 6...................... 275-58-15
Fax... 275-58-16
Mon-Fri 10-19; Rbls, $; Eng, Ger, Fr
Avista, *Office construction & design*
Radishcheva ul., 42......................... 273-31-06
Fax... 272-88-85
Mon-Fri 10-18

Baltex, *Computers, printers and computer supplies*
Blagodatnaya ul., 55....................... 294-10-23
Mon-Fri 10-18; Rbls, $; Eng, Ger, Fr
Ca Gi Ve, *Office furniture*
Nevskiy pr., 49/2, Tel/Fax 113-14-43
Mon-Sat 10:30-13, 14:30-17:30; Rbls, $; Ital
Canon Service Center, *Photocopiers*
Volkovskiy pr., 146, bldg. 3............ 269-05-04
Fax... 166-36-24
Mon-Fri 9-17; Rbls, $; Eng; Bus 36; Metro Elektrosila
Commark Ltd., *Photocopiers, laser printers*
Sablinskaya ul., 7............................ 233-30-08
Fax... 233-88-95
Mon-Fri 9-18; Rbls, $; Eng
Concom, *Mon-Fri 10-20; Rbls, $; Eng*
Reki Fontanki nab., 102................... 164-65-04
Fax... 164-56-77
Fax machines, calculators, modems, printers, streamers
Creat, *Professional audio & video equipment*
• Bakunina ul., 7/1 274-54-39
• Kazanskaya ul., 49 311-13-01
Mon-Fri 10-14, 15-18; Rbls, $; Eng
Etal Exhibition Hall, *Canon equipment*
Gertsena ul., 53............................... 312-33-82
Fax... 311-09-39
Mon-Fri 9-18; Rbls, $; Eng
Fotrelle, *Photocopiers*
Nevskiy pr., 58................................. 312-32-01
Mon-Fri 10-18; Rbls, $; Eng
Global USA - *See our color ad*
Moscow, Usacheva ul., 35
☎ ....(095) 245-56-57

High-Life Electronics
Karavannaya ul., 16 314-98-61
Mon-Sat 11-14, 15-19; Rbls, $; Eng, Ger

Impacto, *Safes from the USA*
Laboratornyy pr., 23, rm. 402 544-12-40
Mon-Fri 10-18; Rbls, $

Imperial, *Office supplies*
• Izmaylovskiy pr., 11 251-61-28
Office furniture, light fixtures, stationery
Mon-Sat 10-19; Rbls; Eng
• Nevskiy pr., 51 312-87-76
Fax machines, telephone systems, printers
Daily 10-14, 15-19; Rbls, $
• Vladimirskiy pr., 3 113-22-84
Lighting fixtures, stationery, fans
Mon-Sat 10-14, 15-20; Rbls; Eng; Metro Dostoevskaya

**INTER COMMERC
- FOR SHOPS**

Shop & Office Equipment from Leading World Companies

■ Computerized
  Cash Registers & Scales
■ Label Makers
■ Refrigerators & Freezers
■ Shelves & Counters
■ Outdoor Displays
■ Office Furniture
■ Equipment for Advertising &
  Printing Companies
■ Light Fixtures

Two Locations in St.Petersburg:

Professora Popova ul., 47
(in the Youth Palace) 234-37-82
Gagarina pr., 1 294-85-84
Tel./Fax 234-29-21

Mon-Sat 10-18, English, German

international printing systems
ipris

RANK XEROX

Authorized

Dealer

Apple Computer Inc. RESELLER
SALES & SERVICE

Primorskiy pr., 35a 239-57-96
Shvedskiy per., 2 311-18-10

Kopiya St. Petersburg   **Copy**
Partizana Germana ul., 37, apt. 4 ... 130-78-00
Photocopiers, fax machines
Mon-Fri 9-18; Rbls, $; Eng, Ger

LEK Tradehouse, *Mon-Fri 10-17; Rbls; Eng*
Mytninskaya ul., 19/48 274-38-85
Telephone equipment, fax machines, calculators

Linkomp, *Mon-Fri 10-18; Rbls, $; Eng*
Kuybysheva ul., 28 232-53-45
Telephone equipment, fax machines, briefcases

MacTech-St. Petersburg
Marata ul., 16 112-38-44
Mon-Fri 10-18; Rbls, $; Eng

Mega, *Office furniture, computers*
Nepokorennykh pr., 74 542-55-45
Mon-Fri 9:30-17;Rbls; Eng, Ger

MKS St. Petersburg
16-ya Liniya, 11 213-64-47
Fax machines, calculators, beepers
Mon-Fri 10-17; Rbls; Eng

**MARKET
BRIDGE LTD.**

EVERYTHING FOR YOUR OFFICE
Interior design
Office furniture • Lamps • Stationery
Computers- hardware & software
Nevskiy pr., 82 275-71-51
.... 275-79-83
Marshala Govorova ul., 16
Fax: 275-71-50
English, Rubles, $

POLRADIS
Network Design & Installation
Gagarina pr., 1 294-85-41

Quazar, *Fax machines, telephone equipment*
Kamennoostrovskiy pr., 3 233-45-87
Mon-Sat 10-19; Rbls, $; Eng
Raduga, *Telephones, fax machines*   **Rainbow**
Zaytseva ul., 41 183-30-96
Mon-Fri 10-17; $; Eng; Metro Avtovo

RANK XEROX

World leader in Photocopiers
For Sales, Service & Supplies
Regional Office
Obvodnogo kan. nab., 93a . 315-76-70
Fax 315-77-73

**Our Authorized Dealers in
Saint Petersburg**

Commark Ltd.
Sablinskaya ul., 7 233-30-08
IPRIS
Primorskiy pr., 35a 239-68-84
SKIF
Vosstaniya ul., 32 275-53-45
TEAM DEAX
Inzhenernaya ul., 9 314-02-15

Riso-Print, *Photocopiers; Riso copiers*
Antonenko per., 5 110-65-09
Fax 110-60-97
Mon-Fri 10-18; Rbls, $; Eng, Ger

Official Business Partner

РУБИКОН

Rubicon
Lesnoy pr., 19
542-00-65, 248-83-06
Fax.............542-09-89
Telex   121194 Rub SU

IBM MINOLTA Gold Star Hewlett Packard

Salam International, *Fax machines*
Politekhnicheskaya ul., 21, apt. 52/53 .. 247-52-48
Fax 247-42-18
Mon-Fri 11-18; Rbls, $; Eng

Sankt-Peterburg
Fax machines, telephone equipment, photocopiers
16-ya Liniya, 11 217-30-58
Mon-Fri 10-17; Rbls

Seldom, *Telephones, fax, beepers*
Kutuzova nab., 10 275-31-67
Mon-Fri 10-18; Rbls, $; Eng

Shchit, *Metal doors, window bars*   **Shield**
2-ya Liniya, 49 350-03-53
Daily 8-21; Rbls, $; Eng, Ger

Skif, *Photocopiers, typewriters*
Vosstaniya ul., 32 275-53-45
Fax 275-58-71
Mon-Fri 9-18; Rbls, $; Eng, Ger, Fr
Tram 5; Metro Chernyshevskaya

Svyatogor, *Typewriters*
Morisa Toreza pr., 34, bldg. 2,
Hotel "Sputnik", rm. 268 552-82-50
Mon-Fri 10-13, 14-18; Rbls, $

Tekhnopost, *Canon fax machine repair*
Grafskiy per., 4 292-25-62
Mon-Fri 9-17:30; Rbls, $; Eng, Ger
Metro Dostoevskaya

UMA LTD

Authorized **SAMSUNG ELECTRONICS** Distributor

Dealer for **NRG, Nashuatec, Aurora, Archiutti**

Malookhtinskiy pr., 68 528-95-66
....528-00-51
Fax 528-84-00

Venta, *Office alarm systems, beepers*
Kosygina pr., 28, bldg. 1 521-09-16
Mon-Fri 10-17; Rbls, $

Vita, *Office repair & design*
Shvedskiy per., 2 311-10-88
Mon-Fri 10-18; Rbls

Zodchiy, *Office building supplies*
Zagorodnyy pr., 1 311-60-98
Mon-Sat 11-14, 15-19; Rbls, $; Eng
Metro Dostoevskaya

☎ **OFFICE SPACE RENTALS**
ОФИСЫ, АРЕНДА
BÜROVERMIETUNG
OFFICES, BAIL
KONTORSLOKALER ATT HYRA
TOIMISTOTILOJEN VUOKRAUS

See also APARTMENTS *and*
REAL ESTATE AGENTS

Astoria-Service,   *Mon-Fri 9-17; Rbls, $; Eng*
Borovaya ul., 11/13, apt. 65 164-96-22

Crossroads,   *Mon-Fri 10-18; Rbls; Eng*
Poltavskaya ul., 10 277-41-97
Fax 273-43-04

А Г Е Н Т С Т В О
DOM PLUS Agency
Dvortsovaya nab., 16 312-88-73
Real estate agency

Ecopolis,   *Mon-Fri 9:30-18; Rbls, $; Eng*
Zanevskiy pr., 32, bldg. 2 528-26-66

Inform-Future
Tambovskaya ul., 12 315-17-01
Fax 312-30-78

Inpredservice
Kutuzova nab., 34 272-15-00
Mon-Fri 9-13, 14-18; Rbls, $, CC
Bus 26; Metro Chernyshevskaya

The LDM Complex, *See also* BUSINESS CENTERS
P.S., Professora Popova ul., 47 234-44-94
Fax 234-98-18
Long & short term office space

Petersburg Properties
Nevskiy pr.................................... 275-41-67

☎ **OFFICE SUPPLIES**

See STATIONERY

☎ **OPERA**

See THEATER/BALLET

☎ **OPHTHALMOLOGISTS**

See OPTICIANS, CONTACT LENSES, HOSPITALS
and MEDICAL CARE & CONSULTATIONS

☎ **OPTICIANS**
ОПТИКИ
OPTIKER
OPTICIENS
OPTIKER
OPTIKOT

See also CONTACT LENSES *and* MEDICAL
CARE & CONSULTATIONS

OPTICIANS/OPHTHALMOLOGISTS

Concor,   *Mon-Fri 11-19; Rbls, $; Eng*
Voznesenskiy pr., 9 311-50-93

Exclusive
Nevskiy pr., 13.............................. 311-45-88
Mon-Fri 10-14, 15-19; Rbls, $

Lincon, *Glasses and contact lenses*
• 14-ya Liniya, 97 355-83-88
• Furshtadtskaya ul., 36 272-28-52
• Liteynyy pr., 39 275-45-24
Mon-Fri 10-20; Rbls; Eng

Linkor-Kontakt
Galernaya ul., 46 312-10-92
Daily 9-19; Rbls

Ophthalmologist
Kultury pr., 4 558-89-14
Mon-Fri 9-16; Rbls; Eng

Optika-Atele
• Griboedova kan. nab., 18 314-31-63
Mon-Fri 10-19; Rbls
• Kamennoostrovskiy pr., 57 234-93-10
Mon-Sat 10-14, 15-19; Rbls
Bus 10; Metro Petrogradskaya
• Komsomola ul., 47 542-34-08
Mon-Sat 10-14, 15-19; Rbls
• Kuybysheva ul., 32 233-46-84
Mon-Sat 10-14, 15-19; Rbls;
Tram 2; Metro Gorkovskaya
• Lensoveta ul., 80 127-09-56
Mon-Fri 10-14, 15-19; Rbls

of St. Petersburg
Eyeglasses • Contact Lenses
Imported from Europe & USA
Eye Examinations • 1 Hour Service
Lomonosova ul., 5 310-15-95
Hrs: 10-19, English
A Russian-British firm

Visor, *Mon-Fri 11-19*
Liteynyy pr., 30 272-75-17

EYE GLASSES ONLY

Optika-Atele *Prescription glasses* **Opticians**
• 9-ya Liniya, 32 213-57-93
Mon-Sat 10-14, 15-19; Rbls
• 12-ya Krasnoarmeyskaya ul., 3 251-52-22
Mon-Fri 10-14, 15-19; Rbls
Tram 2; Metro Baltiyskaya
• 15-ya Liniya, 32 213-68-51
Mon-Fri 10-14, 15-19
Tram 5; Metro Vasileostrovskaya
• Chaykovskogo ul., 36 273-64-54
Mon-Fri 10-14, 15-19; Rbls; Eng
Bus 14; Metro Chernyshevskaya
• Chernoy Rechki nab., 51 246-36-91
Mon-Fri 10-14, 15-19; Rbls
• Maklina pr., 29 114-49-41
Mon-Fri 10-14, 15-19; Rbls
Tram 31; Metro Sennaya Ploshchad
• Moskovskiy pr., 54 292-47-71
Mon-Fri 10-14, 15-19; Rbls
Metro Frunzenskaya

• Nevskiy pr., 108 *(under repair)* 273-48-45
Mon-Sat 10-14, 15-19; Rbls; Metro Ploshchad Vosstaniya
• Sadovaya ul., 33 310-82-29
Mon-Fri, Sun 10-14, 15-19; Rbls
• Zhukovskogo ul., 6 272-57-66
Mon-Fri 11-14, 15-19; Rbls; T-bus 8; Metro Vladimirskaya

☎ ORCHESTRAS
ОРКЕСТРЫ
ORCHESTER
ORCHESTRES
ORKESTRAR
ORKESTERIT

Dmitriev's Academic Symphony Orchestra
Mikhaylovskaya ul., 2 110-42-26
Mon-Tue, Thu-Sun 10-18; Rbls, $
Symphony Orchestra, *Mon-Sat 10-15; Rbls*
Italyanskaya ul., 27 219-96-02
Temirkanov's Academic Symphony
Orchestra
Mikhaylovskaya ul., 2 110-42-26
Tue-Sun 10-18; Rbls, $

☎ PAINT SUPPLIES
КРАСКИ, ЛАКИ
FARBEN UND LACKE
PEINTURE, FOURNITURE
FÄRGHANDLARE
MAALAUSTARVIKKEET

Paints, lacquers, wallpaper, brushes, etc.
See also BUILDING SUPPLIES and HARDWARE

BABYLON
shops
No. 2 Everything for the Home
Make your home sparkle:
Paint, wallpaper, linoleum & throw rugs from
Holland with tools & supplies to do it.
Philips electrical appliances for the home.
Procter & Gamble cleaning products.
Liteynyy pr., 63 279-01-48
Daily 10-14, 15-20; Rbls
Metro Mayakovskaya

Home □ Center
PAINT AND WALLPAPER CENTER
Sadolin painting supplies
Custom color mixing
Latex, acrylic & spray paints
Brushes, rollers and cleaners
Wallpaper, Linoleum & Tile

Located in S.E. St. Pb., minutes from city center
Slavy ul., 30 261-15-50
.... 261-04-02
Fax 260-15-81
Daily 10-20; $, FIM, DM, Rbls; Eng, Finn, Ger
Metro Moskovskaya, then Bus 31, 114, T-bus 29

Khozyaystvennye Tovary
Yakornaya ul., 2 224-34-86
Mon-Sat 10-14, 15-19; Rbls
Lacquer, Paint, and Cleaning
Laki, Kraski, Skobyanye Tovary
Nevskiy pr., 146 274-02-84
Mon-Fri 10-19
Stroitelnye Tovary   Building Supplies
• Chernoy Rechki nab., 6 239-84-90
Mon-Sat 11-20
• Stachek pr., 34 186-77-22
Mon-Fri 10-14, 15-19; Rbls
Bus 2; T-bus 20, 8; Metro Narvskaya

☎ PARKING LOTS
АВТОСТОЯНКИ
PARKPLÄTZE
PARKINGS
PARKERINGSPLATSER
PARKKIPAIKAT

*These are "watched" lots for cars. For
trucks and buses, see* TRUCK PARKS. *The
Hotel Astoria and other hotels also have
attended parking lots.*

Automobile Parking No. 3
Vosstaniya ul., 7, Kronshtadt
☎/Fax 236-16-83
Daily 0-24
Automobile Parking No. 5, *Daily 6-24*
Piskarevskiy pr., 23 541-29-30
Automobile Parking No. 8 *(covered garage)*
Kronshtadtskaya ul., 19 183-51-67
Daily 6-24; Rbls
Automobile Parking No. 20
Kronshtadtskaya ul., 19 184-48-86
Daily 0-24
Automobile Parking No. 21
Rustaveli ul., 71 532-53-59
Daily 0-24; Rbls
Automobile Parking No. 35
Birzhevoy per., 2 218-21-01
*Daily 0-24; Bus 30, 44, 47, 7;
Metro Gostinyy Dvor, Nevskiy Prospekt*
Automobile Parking No. 42
Malaya Balkanskaya ul., 30/3 177-41-35
Daily 0-24
Automobile Parking No. 53
Zvezdnaya ul., 1 127-24-69
Daily 0-24; Rbls, $
Automobile Parking No. 69, *Daily 0-24*
Malaya Balkanskaya ul., 51 178-26-28
Avtodelo, *Mon-Fri 8-15; Rbls, $*
Zemledelcheskaya ul., 3 275-61-42
Nevskij Palace, *Daily 0-24*
Nevskiy pr., 57 (Hotel operator) 311-63-66

Sovinteravto service
High Security   AUTO PARK
Cars, Trucks & Buses
Varshavskaya ul., 42 296-58-20
Near the Russia Hotel
Daily 24 hrs; English; $ & Rbls

Startavto
Raevskogo pr., 16 247-74-12
Daily 0-24; Rbls, $; Bus 93; Metro Politekhnicheskaya
Supervised Car Parks for Foreign Vehicles
Varshavskaya ul., 42 296-58-20
Daily; Rbls, $; Eng, Ger

☎ PARKS
ПАРКИ
PARKANLAGEN
PARCS
PARKER
PUISTOT

See also GARDENS, CHILDREN IN ST.
PETERSBURG

*St. Petersburg has a variety of parks for a
Sunday afternoon excursion. They are
especially nice for children and some have
rides.*

Botanical Garden *See* GARDENS

Kirov Central Park (TsPKO)
Central Park of Culture and Rest
*A very large park NW of the center city
on Petrogradskaya Storona with walking
paths, lakes, boat rentals, tennis, badmin-
ton, summer theater for concerts, cafes, disco-
theques, and amusement rides for children.
Skating and X-country skiing in winter. A
favorite place in the summer to relax.*
Yelagin Ostrov., 4 239-09-11
Fax 239-12-61
*Daily 10-20; Rbls; Eng, Fr, Ital. Nearest Metro is
Chernaya Rechka, then Tram 2, 31, 37, C-10*

Moskovskiy Park Pobedy
Moscow Victory Park
*This 68 ha. park with beautiful lakes and
walking paths commemorates the victory
over Nazism. Boating, children's amusement park, skating and X-country skiing in
winter. The Sports and Concert Complex
(SKK) is located next to the park. Convenient to the Metro.*
Kuznetsovskaya ul., 25 298-08-81
Mon-Fri 9-18; Metro Park Pobedy

Park Babushkina   Babushkin Park
*Beautiful park in an industrial area with a
sports complex, lawn tennis, horseback
riding, photographers, cafe and a children's
amusement park.*
Obukhovskoy Oborony pr., 149 560-01-57
Daily 10-20; Metro Lomonosovskaya

Primorskiy Park Pobedy
Coastal Victory Park
*Beautiful commemorative park of 160 ha.
of English and French styles with alleys,
open meadows, ponds, boat rentals, cafe.
Its large Kirov Stadium on the Gulf of
Finland is the site of football matches.*
Krestovskiy pr., 21 230-04-55
Daily 9-17, No Metro. T-Bus 9, Tram 17, 21, 33, 34, C-9

Sosnovka   Pine Forest
*Large forest park north of St. Petersburg
with 310 ha. of pines and birches and*

oaks (and mushrooms), with walking paths, summer theater, tennis courts, X-country skiing. Peaceful. Open all the time.

Administrator's office at Manchesterskaya ul., 18
☎ 554-32-23
Metro Ploshchad Muzhestva, then Bus 9, 40, 123 or T-Bus 13

Summer Garden and Palace of Peter I
See GARDENS

Tavricheskiy Sad   **Tauride Garden**
See GARDENS

Tikhiy Otdykh   **Peaceful Rest**
This quiet 18th century park with broad alleys and walking paths is the site of Kamennoostrovskiy Palace and many beautiful dachas, now used as "recreation health spas".

Kamennoostrovskiy pr., 77 234-91-62
Mon-Fri 8-17, Tram 28 or Metro Petrogradskaya, then 15 minutes by foot along Kamennoostrovskiy or Metro Chernaya Rechka, E-10

Yuzhno-Primorskiy Park
South Coastal Park
50 ha. in French & English style with cafe, walking paths, fishing, children's amusements. Southwest St. Pb. on the Gulf of Finland.

Petergofskoe shosse, 27 151-52-85
Info Mon-Fri 8-17 151-52-87
Metro Leninskiy Prospekt, then Bus 83, 111, 142; T-Bus 35, 45

☎ **PASSPORT PHOTOS**
ФОТО ДЛЯ ДОКУМЕНТОВ
PASSFOTOS
PASSEPORT, PHOTOS POUR
PASSFOTO
PASSIKUVAT

See also PHOTOGRAPHERS

Many shops do "quick photos" quickly and inexpensively for your various passes and documents. Look under PHOTOGRAPHERS *for Express Photo (Срочное фото).*

AGFA *Agfa*
1 HOUR PHOTO
Polaroid Passport Photos in Color
Nevskiy pr., 20.......................... 311-99-74
Daily 10-20; Rbls, $

Passport Photos   **Foto dlya Dokumentov**
Фото для документов
Often better quality than "Fast photo"
• Bukharestskaya ul., 31/1 174-70-06
Mon-Sat 10-14, 15-18:30
• Moskovskiy pr., 34 292-38-47
Mon-Fri 9-14, 15-19; Rbls, $
• Nevskiy pr., 156....................... 277-14-61
Mon-Sat 11-20; Rbls, $; Metro Ploshchad Vosstaniya

Fast Photo   **Srochnoe Foto**
Срочное Фото
Quick photos for documents
• Chernyshevskogo pr., 17 279-52-33
Mon-Sat 11-19, Rbls, $
• Liteynyy pr., 23 273-21-53
Mon-Sat 10-14, 15-19; Rbls

• Malaya Konyushennaya ul., 7 311-80-20
One of the best. Daily 11-20; Rbls, $
• Novocherkasskiy pr., 22/15 221-22-87
Daily 10-14, 15-19; Rbls
• Sadovaya ul., 27 310-06-35
Mon-Sat 11-14, 15-19; Rbls, $
• Sredniy pr., 49 213-12-63
Mon-Sat 10-14, 15-19; Rbls
• Yuriya Gagarina pr., 24............... 264-60-34
Mon-Sat 10-14, 15-19; Rbls

Fotoavtomat *(Automatic), Mon-Sat 11-19; Rbls*
Nevskiy pr., 128 277-31-32

Photo Salon on Nevskiy
Nevskiy pr., 54......................... 314-33-01
Mon-Sat 10-15, 16-20; Rbls; Metro Nevskiy Prospekt

Photo Studios
Moskovskiy pr., 35...................... 292-48-88
Mon-Sat 9-18; Rbls
Moskovskiy pr., 130..................... 298-86-26
Mon-Fri 11-16; Rbls

Photography, *Mon-Sat 9-14, 15-20; Rbls*
Lermontovskiy pr., 1 114-09-57

☎ **PAWN SHOPS**
ЛОМБАРДЫ
PFANDHÄUSER
MONT-DE- PIETE
PANTBANKER
PANTTILAINAKONTTORIT

Into, *Antiques, Mon-Sat 11-19; Rbls, $*
Pochtamtskaya ul., 5 311-26-43
Lombard   *Main Office*   **Pawn Shop**
Bolshaya Pushkarskaya ul., 20 232-52-00
Mon-Fri 9-18; T-bus 1, 12; Tram 3; Metro Petrogradskaya
Lombard   **Pawn Shop**
• 8-ya Liniya, 25 213-10-46
Mon-Fri 9-17:45; Rbls
• Reki Moyki nab., 72 314-95-92
Mon-Fri 9-12, 13-18
• Vladimirskiy pr., 17 164-99-81
Mon-Sat 9-12, 13-17:45; Rbls

☎ **PAY PHONES**
ТЕЛЕФОНЫ-АВТОМАТЫ
TELEFONZELLEN
CABINES PUBLIQUES
TELEFONAUTOMATER
PUHELIN AUTOMAATIT

See TELEPHONES, INTERCITY
Pay phones on the street are often in disrepair and occasionally work. To place a call from a pay phone you now need a metro token instead of a 15 kopek coin. These tokens are available at metro stations and in July 1993 the price was 15 rubles.

Within the city. *To call within the city look for pay phones* Таксофоны *(Taksofony). 1) get your token ready by placing it in the slot, 2) dial number, 3) if phone answers, the token will drop. Officially you get three minutes, it is often longer.*

Between cities. *To call between cities look for an office or booth marked for* Intercity Telephone, Междугородный Телефон *(Mezhdugorodnyy Telefon). Have a good supply of tokens.*

Credit Card Phones. *Fifty new credit card phones are coming to St. Pb. courtesy BCL.*

☎ PETS
ЗООМАГАЗИНЫ,
ПРОДУКТЫ ДЛЯ ЖИВОТНЫХ
HAUSTIERE
ANIMAUX DOMESTIQUES
HUSDJUR
KOTIELÄIMET

See also DOGS *and* VETERINARIANS

You can buy birds, dogs, fish, cats, and other pets at the (Kondratevskiy) Pet Market in the Vyborgskiy region, see MARKETS. Imported pet food and other pet supplies can be purchased in many stores especially in Western-style SUPERMARKETS such as Babylon, Spar, or Stockmann. Also try KIOSKS in a pinch.

Aqua-hobby, *Cat and dog food*
Staro-Petergofskiy pr., 37 252-75-66
Daily 11-14, 15-19

Dom Prirody   **House of Nature**
Bolshaya Konyushennaya ul., 8 314-08-48
Daily 11-19

Kondratevskiy Pet Market, *see* MARKETS
Most active on weekends
Polyustrovskiy pr., 45 540-30-39
Mon-Sat

Vse Dlya Koshek i Sobak
                Everything for Cats and Dogs
Bukharestskaya ul., 23/13 174-87-46
Daily 12-14, 15-20; Rbls

Zoomagazin   **Pet Store**
• Akademika Lebedeva ul., 19 542-04-11
Mon-Sat 10-14, 15-19; Rbls
• Alexandrovskiy Park, 2 .... No ☎
Tue-Sun 11-18; Rbls
• Ligovskiy pr., 63 164-76-74
Mon-Fri 10-14, 15-19; Rbls
Bus 3, 30, 44, 74; Tram 10, 16, 25, 44, 49;
Metro Ploshchad Vosstaniya
• Ligovskiy per., 79 164-74-77
Mon-Sat 11-20; Rbls
• Moskovskiy pr., 6 310-79-51
Mon-Sat 9-14, 15-18; Rbls; Metro Sadovaya

☎ PHARMACIES
(DRUG STORES)
АПТЕКИ
APOTHEKEN
PHARMACIES
APOTEK
APTEEKIT

Until recently there was no equivalent to western pharmacies or drug stores, fully stocked with the latest medicine, and personal hygiene products. However, the situation is rapidly improving as can be seen from the ads in this section.

The standard Russian "Apteka" (Аптека) is an apothecary with a limited and uncertain supply of medicines and related products. Some pharmacies now have a "hard currency" section with well-known imported medicines and over the counter drugs (denoted by $ after hours). The control over prescription drugs is less strict. Equivalent Western prescription medicines, especially birth control pills, anti-depres-

sants and standard over-the-counter products such as antibiotic creams, antifungal, and good quality condoms are still hard to find. So bring along a good supply.

However, thanks to Proctor and Gamble and Tambrands, a wide variety of toothpaste, shampoos, etc. and personal hygiene products are now available in "APTEKA", DEPARTMENT STORES, SUPERMARKETS, *and* KIOSKS.

For availability of various medicines and drugs, call the following number:
Pharmacy info **164-44-10**

NIGHT PHARMACY

Apteka, *Daily 0-24, Rbls*
Nevskiy pr. 22 314-54-01
.... 311-20-04

АПТЕКА   АПТЕКА   PHARMACY

• 7-ya Liniya, 16 213-62-68
Mon-Sat 9-21; Rbls
• 10-ya Sovetskaya ul., 15/27 271-25-77
Mon-Sat 9-20; Rbls; Eng
• 17-ya Liniya, 8 213-71-40
Mon-Fri, Sun 8-20; Rbls
• Bolshoy pr., P.S., 43 232-46-79
Mon-Sat 8-20; $; Eng
• Gagarina pr., 42 127-05-29
Mon-Fri 9-20, Sun 11-18; Rbls; Children's pharmacy
• Korablestroiteley ul., 14,
Hotel Pribaltiyskaya, 2nd floor 356-25-38
Daily 9-14, 15-21; $; Eng, Ital
• Moskovskiy pr., 167 298-05-35
Mon-Fri, Sun 9-21; Rbls
• Nevskiy pr., 5 312-70-78
Mon-Sat 9-21; Rbls, $, CC; Eng, Ger
• Nevskiy pr., 50 311-44-98
Mon-Sat 9-20; Rbls; Eng
• Nevskiy pr., 66 314-56-54
Mon-Fri, Sun 9-21; Rbls; Eng
• Nevskiy pr., 111 277-29-31
Mon-Fri, Sun 9-21; Rbls; Eng
• Sadovaya ul., 36 310-88-68
Mon-Sat 8-20; Rbls
• Suvorovskiy pr., 48 271-98-09
Mon-Sat 9-21; Rbls
• Vosstaniya ul., 30 272-39-41
Mon-Sat 9-21; Rbls
• Vyborgskaya nab., 5/2,
Hotel Saint Petersburg, floor B .... No ☎
Tue-Sun 10-21; $; Eng, Ger

Aptekarskie Tovary No. 10
                    Pharmaceutical Products
Nevskiy pr., 128 277-03-77

THE PHARMACY DAMIAN
Of St. Petersburg Policlinic No. 2
*Wide selection of Western medicines,
antibiotics, cortisone, vitamins,
personal hygiene products,
baby needs and cosmetics.*
Pharmacy: M-F, 9:00 to 20:00

Moskovskiy pr., 22 110-17-44
Fax 292-59-39
English, Finnish, German

HS Petersburg AG

Wholesale Distribution of Pharmaceuticals
from Consignment Warehouses
V.O., Bolshoy pr., 9/6.....................218-55-37

KNOLL, AG
Producer of Pharmaceuticals
✉ 199034 Saint Petersburg, Russia
　　V.O., Bolshoy pr., 10
☎ 218-53-81
BASF:
☎ Fax 119-60-40
Subsidiary of BASF

Medhor, *Mon-Fri 9:30-17:30; Rbls*
Inzhenernaya ul., 13......................314-67-10

PetroFarm

Four Pharmacies in St. Pb.
Wide selection of imported medicines
and supplies from Western countries
Tel./Fax...315-45-67
In the Center of St. Petersburg
Nevskiy pr. 22................................314-54-01
　Open daily except Sat., 9-20, $ & Rbls, English
Nevskiy pr., 83...............................277-79-66
　Open daily except Sat., 9-20, $ & Rbls, English
On V.O. near the port & Metro Primorskaya
Zheleznovodskaya ul., 29..............350-59-79
　Open daily except Sat., 9-20, $ & Rbls
In Sestroretsk on the highway to Vyborg
Tokareva ul., 15..............................237-21-88
　Open daily except Sat., 9-17, $ & Rbls, English

Pharmadom

Medicines from World Leading
Pharmaceutical Companies
Zagorodnyy pr., 21...........315-96-36
Nevskiy pr., 5...................312-70-78
Hrs: 9:00 - 20:30

Pharmadom Pharmacies in St. Pb.
Zagorodnyy pr. 21 315-96-36
　Daily 9-20:30, Rbls & $, Eng. Metro Vladimirskaya
Nevskiy pr., 5................................312-70-78
　Daily 9-20:30, Rbls & $, Eng. Top of Nevskiy Pr.
Salute, *Imported medicine and supplies*
Kamennoostrovskiy pr., 38 234-96-00
　Daily 9-19; Rbls, $; Eng
Malookhtinskiy pr., 92 221-19-32
　Daily 9-19; $; Eng

☎ **PHONE**
See PAY PHONE

☎ **PHOTOCOPIERS SALES,**
　SERVICE & SUPPLIES
　ФОТОКОПИРОВАЛЬНАЯ
　　ТЕХНИКА
　FOTOKOPIERAUSRÜSTUNGEN
　PHOTOCOPIEURS, EQUIPEMENT
　FOTOKOPIERING UTRUSTNING
　KOPIOINTITARVIKKEET

Photocopier　Fotokopiya　Фотокопия
Xerox　　　 Kseroks　 Ксерокс

　Photocopiers, usually called "Kseroks",
supplies and services are readily available
here at fairly reasonable prices. Color
photocopiers are also available.
　Note that photocopiers from the US will
not work unless the 60 hertz timing chip is
replaced by a 50 hertz chip for about $15-
30. We can not guarantee that this will
work and the warranty will be voided, but
in a tight situation it is worth trying.

AUTHORIZED CANON DEALERS
Sales & Service
ABC Electronics
　Liteynyy pr., 22, apt. 30 272-95-58
　Fax...275-74-85
　　Mon-Fri 10-13, 14-19; Rbls, $; Eng
Azimut
　Malaya Posadskaya ul., 30 238-78-02
　Fax...232-25-81
　　Mon-Fri 9-18; Rbls
Bital
　Vitebskiy pr., 73, apt. 66
　Tel/Fax.......................................127-88-38
　　Mon-Fri 9-17; Rbls
Copy Service
　Reki Moyki nab., 48
　Tel/fax..312-42-08
　　Mon-Fri 9-17; Rbls, $; Eng
EastMarket
　Bolshaya Konyushennaya ul., 27 312-88-89
　Fax...314-22-73
Etal Exhibition Hall
　Gertsena ul., 53............................312-33-82
　Fax...311-09-39
　　Mon-Fri 9-18; Rbls, $; Eng
Inftel, *Moving fall 1993*
　Moldagulovoy ul., 7/6, 5th floor, apt. 51, 52
　...224-39-61
RiM
　Kosinova ul., 19 186-36-78
　Fax...186-20-09
　　Mon-Fri 10-18; Rbls, $
Venta
　Kosygina pr., 28, bldg. 1 521-09-16
　Fax...521-76-62
　　Mon-Fri 10-17; Rbls; Eng

Canon Service Center, *Authorized repair center*
　Volkovskiy pr., 146, bldg. 3............269-05-04
　Fax...166-36-24
　　Mon-Fri 9-17; Rbls, $; Bus 36; Metro Elektrosila

Commark Ltd., *Authorized Rank Xerox Dealer*
Sablinskaya ul., 7........................... 233-30-08
Fax 233-88-95
Mon-Fri 9-18; Rbls, $; Eng

Fotrelle
Morisa Toreza pr., 43.................... 552-01-75
Mon-Fri 10-18; Rbls, $

Fotrelle Service
• Volkovskiy pr., 146, bldg. 3............ 268-61-25
• Nevskiy pr., 58............................... 312-52-80
Fax 312-57-95
Mon-Fri 8-16; Rbls; Eng

Hitachi
Sinopskaya nab., 76....................... 271-50-51
Mon-Fri 10-18; Rbls; Eng, Pol

IPRIS, *Authorized Rank Xerox Dealer*
Primorskiy pr., 35a 239-68-84
See our ad under PHOTOCOPYING

Minolta-Representation *(moving fall 1993)*
Komissara Smirnova ul., 15 542-22-93
Mon-Fri 10-18

Nuklon, *Mon-Fri 10-17*
Bogatyrskiy pr., 7/2, apt. 10 394-28-61

RANK XEROX

World leader in Photocopiers
For Sales, Service & Supplies
Regional Office
Obvodnyy kan., 93a 315-76-70
Fax.....................................315-77-73

Our Authorized Dealers in
Saint Petersburg

Commark Ltd.
Sablinskaya st., 7 233-30-08
IPRIS
Primorskiy pr., 35a 239-68-84
SKIF
Vosstaniya ul., 32 275-53-45
TEAM DEAX
Inzhenernaya ul., 9 314-02-15
Tue-Thu, Sat-Sun 9-18

РУБИКОН

Official
Business
Partner
IBM
MINOLTA
Gold Star
Hewlett Packard

Rubicon
Lesnoy pr., 19
542-00-65, 248-83-06
Fax..............542-09-89
Telex 121194 Rub SU

Skif, *Authorized Xerox Dealer*
Vosstaniya ul., 32 275-53-45
Fax 275-58-71
Mon-Fri 9-18; Rbls, $, $; Eng, Ger, Fr
Tram 5; Metro Chernyshevskaya

TEAM DEAX
Inzhenernaya ul., 9........................ 314-02-15
Authorized Rank Xerox Dealer

☎ PHOTOCOPYING
ФОТОКОПИИ
FOTOKOPIEREN
PHOTOCOPIEURS
KOPIERING
KOPIOT

Sophisticated photocopying services including large-size A0 format and full-color photocopying are available in St. Petersburg. Regular copies cost $.05 to $.20 in rubles per page. IPRIS is the leading photo copy center in St. Petersburg.

Most BUSINESS CENTERS have photocopying services. Here are some others.

Commark Ltd.
Sablinskaya st., 7 233-30-08

Copy   **Kopiya**
Izmaylovskiy pr., 12 292-04-96
Mon-Fri 10-19

Copy Center, *Color copies*
Morisa Toreza pr., 30 552-54-20
Mon-Fri 10-13:30, 14:30-19; Rbls

INFORMATIKA
Photocopies
Prepared Business Cards
Company Letterhead
Reki Moyki nab., 64................ 314-68-96
.... 314-06-32
Fax 315-01-14
Mon-Fri 9-12, 13-18

Inmarkon
Bekhtereva ul., 3/2 265-38-50
Fax.. 567-02-52
Mon-Fri 9:30-18; Rbls, $

international
printing
systems
ipris

RANK XEROX
Authorized
Dealer

• *Photocopies*
• *Any size A0 - A4*
• *Business Cards*
• *Fax Services*
• *Full Color, Black & White Reduction and Enlargements*
• *Overhead Transparencies from 35 mm or other size film positive or negative*

Shvedskiy per., 2 311-18-10
.... 312-32-00
Near Malaya Konyushennaya

Kopirovalnyy Tsenter   **Copy Center**
Toreza pr., 30 552-54-20
Mon-Fri 10-19; Rbls, $; Bus 64; Metro Elektrosila
Lengiprotorg,   *Mon-Fri 9-12, 13-18; Rbls*
Avtovskaya ul., 16........................... 183-34-24
Optima Office,   *Mon-Fri 10-20; Rbls*
Chaykovskogo ul., 36.................... 273-29-64
Fax 273-78-82
Photo Service Center
Prazhskaya ul., 14......................... 268-61-43
Fax 113-27-30
Mon-Sat 11-18; Rbls; Eng; Metro Elektrosila
Poligrafiya,   *Mon-Sat 8:30-17:15*
Kuybysheva ul., 10........................ 230-81-13
Sever,   *Mon-Fri 9-18; Rbls; Eng, Sp*
Sadovaya ul., 54 310-37-80
Fax 567-16-08

☎ **PHOTOGRAPHERS, PHOTOS**
     ФОТОГРАФЫ, ФОТОАТЕЛЬЕ
     FOTOGRAFEN, FOTOSTUDIOS
     PHOTOGRAPHES
     FOTOGRAFER
     VALOKUVAAJIA
     JA VALOKUVAAMOITA

For quick photos for documents and visa see
PASSPORT PHOTOS

Alexander Alekseev – Photostudio
News & Commercial Photography,   Photodesign
Please Call 355-19-97
Fax 355-19-85
Telex................................. 121160 Lenex SU

Alenmaks
Liteynyy pr., 20, rm. 14.................. 278-86-81
Fax 394-02-10
Mon-Fri 10-18; Rbls, $; Eng, Finn
Amateur Photography Studio
Nevskiy pr., 54 311-08-38
Mon-Sat 10-14, 15-22; Rbls; Eng
Ametist
Bolshoy pr., P.S., 29 a 349-39-04
Fax 233-01-51
Mon-Fri 9:30-19; Rbls, $; Eng
Bogdanov Photography Studio
Griboedova kan. nab., 140, apt. 9
☎ 114-10-34
Fax 580-32-67
Express Photo,   *Daily 10-15, 16-19; Rbls*
Malaya Konyushennaya ul., 12....... 312-01-22

KITEZH

Professional photographers
Art, architecture and folk art
Illustration of art books & calendars
Custom work & museum slides
Write: Box 216, St. Pb., 199034
Telephone in St. Pb: 213-65-96

Photos,   *Mon-Sat 10-14, 15-19; Rbls*
Veteranov pr., 140 135-19-01
Photos,   *Mon-Fri 10-19; Rbls*
Krasnoputilovskaya ul., 9 184-64-76
Photos,   *Mon-Fri 10-14, 15-19; Rbls*
Bolshoy Sampsonievskiy pr., 75 245-00-94

Photos
Volodarskogo ul., 14, Sestroretsk
☎ 237-21-62
Mon-Sat 11-18; Rbls, $
Private Photographer, *Photos in your home*
Please call 235-65-49
Ralan Agency,   *Daily 11-19*
Reki Moyki nab., 61 312-15-78
Studio Photographer, *Art photos*
Nauki pr., 38 249-07-64
Mon-Sat 11-14, 15-20; Rbls

☎ **PHOTOGRAPHY CAMERAS
& SUPPLIES**
     ФОТОГРАФИЯ: АППАРАТУРА
     И ПРИНАДЛЕЖНОСТИ
     FOTOAPPARATE UND ZUBEHÖR
     PHOTO-CAMERAS
     ET FOURNITURES
     FOTO, KAMEROR OCH
     TILLBEHÖR
     VALOKUVAUSTARVIKKEET

See also shops listed under
PHOTOGRAPHY-FILM & DEVELOPING

AGFA,   *Daily 9-19; $, CC; Eng, Finn*
Nevskiy pr., 20 312-16-89
Firit
Tallinnskaya ul., 25, apt. 27............ No Phone
Mon-Sat 11-20; Rbls; T-bus 7; Metro Novocherkasskaya
LOMO,   *Mon-Fri 9-18; Rbls*
Malookhtinskiy pr., 94.................... 221-60-37
Petr Velikiy   **Peter the Great**
Gertsena ul., 32............................ 110-64-03
Malaya Konyushennaya ul., 7 110-64-97
Mon-Sat 9-21; Rbls, $; Eng
Photo Store No. 24
Veteranov pr., 110......................... 159-07-56
Mon-Sat 11-19; Rbls; T-bus 20; Metro Prospekt Veteranov
Photo Store No. 76
Bolshoy pr., P.S., 63 232-19-02
Mon-Sat 10-14, 15-19; Rbls

☎ **PHOTOGRAPHY FILM &
DEVELOPING**
     ФОТОГРАФИЯ:
     ПЛЕНКА И ЕЕ ПРОЯВЛЕНИЕ
     FOTO, FILME UND ENTWICKLUNG
     PHOTO-PELLICULE
     FOTO, FILM OCH FRAMKALLNING
     VALOKUVAUSLABORATORIOT

See also INTERNATIONAL SHOPS

*A wide selection of 110-size and 35 mm
print and slide (Ektachrome type) films are
available in most hotels,* INTERNATIONAL
SHOPS, *Petr Velikiy Photo Shops, and the
Agfa shop on Nevskiy which also has
Polaroid film.*

*Quick film processing using imported
chemicals is available for Kodak (Kodak
C41 process and Ektachrome E6 process),
Fuji and Agfa. Russian-made film is
supposedly compatible with Agfa process
only, but it is best processed in Russia.
Kodachrome slide processing still can not*

be done here and must be sent to Europe. According to our sources, Agfa will provide this service soon.

AGFA *Agfa*

1 HOUR PHOTO

THE BEST COLORPRINTS
In Saint Petersburg

PASSPORT PHOTO ON THE SPOT
WIDEST SELECTION OF FILMS AND
PHOTO SUPPLIES IN THE CITY

Open Every Day from 10 am to 8 pm
NEVSKIY PR., 20   (812) 311-99-74

Fuji Film and Processing

ANICHIKOV MOST'
PHOTOGRAPHY SHOP
1 HOUR FUJI PROCESSING
FUJI PHOTO SUPPLIES

Nab. reki Fontanki, 23 314-49-36

City, *Express developing of Fuji, Agfa, Kodak*
Malaya Konyushennaya ul., 7 311-80-20
.... 311-02-45
Daily 11-20; Rbls, $; Eng
Express-Photo, *Daily 10-20; Rbls; Eng*
Zagorodnyy pr., 9 314-19-14
Fotoeffekt, *Mon-Sat 11-15, 16-19; Rbls*
Prosveshcheniya pr., 87 530-09-04

Pyotr Velikiy, photography shop

KODAK *EXPRESS* SERVICE

All Kodak Paper, Chemicals, & Equipment
Enlargements to 28 by 36
Drop-off your film at night, back in the morning
at seven pick-up points.
Two shops in Saint Petersburg

KODAK *EXPRESS* SERVICE

Main Full Service Photo Stores
Malaya Konyushennaya ul., 7 110-64-97
Gertsena ul., 32 110-64-03

Pick-up Points and Film Sales
Barmaleeva ul., 6 in Dom Byta .... No ☎
Hotel Astoria, 1st floor .... No ☎
Hotel St. Petersburg, 1st floor .... No ☎
Slavy pr., 30 in Univermag .... No ☎
Nepokorennykh pr., 6 in Univermag ...... No ☎
Leninskiy pr., 138 in Univermag 255-39-54
Nevskiy pr., 103 275-39-57
Mon-Sat 9-21; Rbls, $; Eng

Pozifort
Koli Tomchaka ul., 28 294-01-25
Fax 294-04-11
Mon-Fri 9-17; Rbls; Eng

☎ PHOTOGRAPHY-REPAIRS
ФОТОАППАРАТЫ, РЕМОНТ
FOTO, REPARATUR
APPAREILS DE PHOTO,
REPARATION
KAMEROR, REPARATION
KAMERAKORJAAMOT

Camera Repairs, *Including movie cameras*
Nevskiy pr., 168 277-58-18
Daily 10-14, 15-19; Rbls
Electrical Repair Shops
Lenina ul., 16 232-06-48
Mon-Sat 10-14, 15-19; Rbls, Bus 10; Metro Gorkovskaya
12, 31, 49, 9, T-bus 1
Fotokinotovary No. 58 *(under repair)*
Nevskiy pr., 92 273-89-01
Mon-Sat 10-14, 15-19; Rbls
Kino-Foto Repair
Nevskiy pr., 92 273-89-01
Mon-Sat 10-14, 15-19; Rbls
LOMO Technical Center
Nevskiy pr., 20 315-49-88
.... 311-89-78
Mon-Sat 9-17; Rbls
Petrogradets
Bolshaya Pushkarskaya ul., 42/16 .. 232-06-48
Mon-Sat 10-14, 15-20; Rbls
Photography-Camera Repair
Zagorodnyy pr., 5 315-88-87
Mon-Sat 11-14, 15-20; Rbls
T-bus 3; Metro Vladimirskaya
Zvezdochka
Belinskogo ul., 1 272-70-70
Mon-Sat 10-14, 15-19; Rbls

☎ PIANOS
ПИАНИНО
KLAVIERE
PIANO
PIANO
PIANOT

Fortepyano   **Upright Piano**
A Commission Store selling used pianos
Rimskogo-Korsakova pr., 3 310-63-53
Mon-Sat 10-14, 15-19; Rbls
House of Radio & Music
Grazhdanskiy pr., 15/1 534-42-18
.... 534-54-95
Mon-Sat 10-19; Rbls

☎ PIZZERIAS
ПИЦЦЕРИИ
PIZZERIEN
PIZZERIAS
PIZZERIOR
PIZZERIAT

Bristol
Nevskiy pr., 22 311-74-90
Daily 10-20; Eng; Bus 22; Metro Nevskiy Prospekt
Daddy's Steak Room
Moskovskiy pr., 73 298-95-52
Daily 12-23; $

PIZZA-HOUSE

Formerly Pizza Express
Quick Home Delivery
From 10 am to 24 pm

13 Varieties of Pizza, Steak,
Wiener Schnitzel, Pastas & Salads
Lapin Kulta Beer & European Wines

Visit our restaurant
at Podolskaya ul., 23

7 minutes drive from center

Orders..292-26-66
Fax...292-10-39
Daily 10-24; $, CC; Eng, Finn; D-3

Pizza-Rif, *Home delivery*
Please call 290-35-96
Reasonable prices; Daily 19-8; Rbls, $
Pizzeria, *Daily 10-15, 16-21; Rbls*
• Rubinshteyna ul., 2.......................312-58-41
• Rubinshteyna ul., 30.....................314-57-18
Venetsiya, *Take-out pizzas* **Venice**
Korablestroiteley ul., 21 352-14-32
Daily 12-24; Rbls, $, CC; Eng, Ital; A-7

☎ **PLANETARIUM**
ПЛАНЕТАРИЙ
PLANETARIUM
PLANETARIUM
PLANETARIUM
PLANETAARIOT

Planetarium, *Mon-Thu, Sat-Sun 10-17*
Alexandrovskiy Park, 4..................233-31-53

☎ **PLUMBING**
САНТЕХНИКА
KLEMPNERARBEIT
KLEMPNER
RÖRMOSKARE
PUTKIMIES

See also BUILDING SUPLIES

Home □ Center
Bathroom & Plumbing Center

Everything you need for the bathroom
From bath tubs, washbasins, shower stalls, and
toilets by Arabia,
To tile, faucets, shower fixtures & curtains.
Extensive choice of PVC pipe and fittings

Located in S.E. St. Pb., minutes from city center
Slavy pr., 30 261-15-50
....261-04-02
Fax 260-15-81
Daily 10-21; $, FIM, DM, Rbls; Eng, Finn, Ger
Metro Moskovskaya, then Bus 31, 114, T-bus 29

A/O Fund PENATES
High-Quality German Bathroom Fixtures
V.O., Bolshoy pr., 8 213-04-11

Okhta, *Bathroom fixtures, Mon-Fri 10-19; Rbls, $*
Bolshaya Pushkarskaya ul., 20 232-01-47

☎ **POLICE**
See MILITIA
CALL 02

☎ **PORCELAIN**
See CRYSTAL & PORCELAIN

☎ **PORTS**
See SEA TERMINALS *and* RIVER TERMINALS

☎ **POST OFFICES**
ПОЧТА
POSTÄMTER
POSTE
POSTKONTOR
POSTIT

See also EXPRESS MAIL/PARCELS SERVICE,
POST RESTANTE, *and* POSTAL RATES

Mail Service: *The post office system in
Russia is responsible for "communications"
(svyaz, связь) which includes postal service, telegraph, intercity and international
telephone calls, and accepting subscriptions
to newspapers and magazines. Postal pick-
up boxes (pochta, почта) are blue and
white. Mail is delivered daily to your post
box in your building.*

*Outbound airmail to the UK & USA takes
about three weeks and is reliable. Inbound
mail is less reliable and can take three
weeks or more. American Express provides
a four day service for its card holders. See*
POST RESTANTE.

The **Main Post Office** *(Glavpochtamt
Главпочтамт) provides all services including
the mailing of international letters and
packages, domestic letters and packages,
subscriptions, and the sale of stamps for
collectors. Note, packages must be
wrapped at the post office.*

Glavpochtamt	Main Post Office
Главпочтамт	

*Stamps, express mail, packages, magazine &
newspaper subscriptions, telegraph, philately.*
Pochtamtskaya ul., 9.....................312-83-05
T-bus 5, 14, 22; Daily 9-21, Near St. Isaac's square

*All distances in Russia are measured from
the "Main Post Office", Glavpochtamt.*

Express mail *is part of the international
CMS express mail service and works rather
well. CMS operates out of a separate
building on Konnogvardeyskiy pr., 4. See*
EXPRESS MAIL/PARCELS. *Use better envelopes
than those provided.*

Branch Post Offices, *of which there are
about 700 are called odtelenie svyazi
(Отделение связи), sell stamps and take
subscriptions to newspapers and
magazines. They handle mailings only of
domestic and international letters and
books, but not international packages.*

There also are post office counters with limited services in the following hotels: Astoria, Kareliya, Moskva, Pribaltiyskaya, Pulkovskaya, and St. Petersburg.

The main regional post offices are:

DISTRICT POST OFFICES

Dzerzhinskiy Post Office
Furmanova ul., 17 272-75-13
Mon-Fri 8:30-17; Rbls
Frunzenskiy Post Office
Bukharestskaya ul., 23, bldg. 1 105-44-35
Mon-Fri 8:30-13, 13:30-17; Rbls
Kirovskiy Post Office
Stachek pr., 18 252-69-64
Daily 7-19; Rbls
Krasnogvardeyskiy Post Office
Energetikov pr., 42 225-60-82
Mon-Fri 8:30-12:30, 13-17
Bus 104, 106, 28, 37; T-bus 43
Krasnoselskiy Post Office
Tambasova ul., 32 130-49-07
Mon-Fri 9-12, 13-20; Rbls
Moskovskiy Post Office
Moskovskiy pr., 75 292-08-01
Mon-Fri 9-16; Rbls
Petrogradskiy Post Office
Vvedenskaya ul., 10 a 232-13-13
Mon-Fri 9-18; Rbls
Post Office No. 24
Nevskiy pr., 148 277-13-81
Mon-Fri 9-12, 12:30-20; Rbls
Sestroretskiy Post Office
Kommunarov ul., 2/4, Sestroretsk
☎ 237-37-73
Mon-Fri 9-13, 14-18; Rbls
Smolninskiy Post Office
Perekupnoy per., 11/15 274-06-27
Mon-Fri 8:30-12:30, 13:30-17; Rbls

☎ **POST RESTANTE**
ПОЧТА ДО ВОСТРЕБОВАНИЯ
POSTLAGERNDE SENDUNGEN
POSTE RESTANTE
POSTE RESTANTE
POSTE RESTERANTE

See also EXPRESS MAIL/PARCEL SERVICE

General Delivery. *Most post offices have a "general delivery" called "post restante" where you can pick up mail from the post office. Foreigners can use the following, but don't rely on it for highly critical items.*

Russia:
19044, St. Petersburg
Nevskiy Prospekt, 6
Poste Restante
Name of Addressee

You can address mail to any post office's "post office" by using the correct postal code, street address, including the words Pochta Do Vostrebovaniya (Почта до востребования) *and your name.*

American Express *card holders can have mail sent to their office, located in the Grand Hotel Europe. This service is via Finland, takes four days to arrive from the US, and mail will be held for two months.*

Name:
C/O American Express
P.O. Box 87
SF-53501, Lappeenranta
Finland

☎ **POSTAL ADDRESSES**
ПОЧТОВЫЕ АДРЕСА
POSTANSCHRIFT
REGLES POSTALES
POST ADRESS
POSTIOSOITTEET

Addresses on international mail into and out of Russia may be written in English and in standard Western format. The usual order of writing an address within Russia is the following:

Country
Six digit postal code, City or Town
Street Name
Name of Addressee
followed below by the return address.

☎ **POSTAL RATES**
ПОЧТОВЫЕ РАСЦЕНКИ
POSTGEBÜHREN
PRIX POSTAL
POST, AVGIFTER
POSTIMAKSUT

Postal rates are changing quickly. Consult the post office for current rates. Inland (domestic) postal rates are valid for the Commonwealth countries (CIS, СНГ) but not the Baltics and other totally independent republics.

DOMESTIC POSTAL RATES

All Postal Information is Current as of June 10, 1993

Russia:
Letters to 20 g. .... 7 Rbls.
Registered letters up to 20 g. .... 8 Rbls.
Insured Mail up to 20 g. .... 20 Rbls.

CIS:
Air Mail up to 20 g. .... 25 Rbls.
Postcards .... 15 Rbls.
Packages up to 500 g. .... 560 Rbls.

INTERNATIONAL POSTAL RATES

Letters (rubles)	Air	Surface
0 - 20 g	90	60
20 - 100 g	280	220
100 - 250 g	615	445
250 - 500 g	1225	850
Postcards (rubles)	60	45
Books (rubles)		
20 - 100 g	390	175
100 - 250 g	750	325
250 - 500 g	1680	580
500 g - 1 kg	2280	975
1 kg - 2 kg	3000	1365

PACKAGES BY SURFACE *(rubles)*

	Germany	GBR	Israel	USA
1 kg	13170	3495	3470	2480
10 kg	6060	7870	8085	8975

DOMESTIC EXPRESS MAIL

There is no domestic Express Mail service.
See EXPRESS MAIL or COURIER.

INTERNATIONAL EXPRESS MAIL RATES:

JV "EMC Garant Post"
Konnogvardeyskiy pr., 4 311-96-71

Ruble Zones:
    I USA, Europe (Excluding Countries listed
    in Dollar Zone I)
    II Japan, Tunisia, Israel, Iran, India
    III South America, Australia

Dollar Zones:
    I Canada, Germany, Netherlands, France,
    Sweden, II, III Africa

	Zone I	Zone II	Zone III

Documents to Ruble Zones
Dollars payable in rubles at Fx rate.

	Zone I	Zone II	Zone III
0 - 100 g	25	28	32
100 g - 1 kg	36	40	45
1 kg - 2 kg	42	50	59

Goods to Ruble Zones

	Zone I	Zone II	Zone III
0 - 250 g	45	50	55
250 - 500 g	50	55	60
500g - 1 kg	56	65	74
each add 1 kg	+6	+10	+14

Documents to Dollar Zones: (Dollars)

0 - 100 g	$25 For all Dollar Zones
100 g - 1 kg	$36 For all Dollar Zones
1 kg - 2 kg	$42 For all Dollar Zones

Goods to Dollar Zones: (Dollars)

0 - 250 g	$45 For all Dollar Zones
250 - 500 g	$50 For all Dollar Zones
500g - 1 kg	$56 For all Dollar Zones
1 kg - 2kg	$62 For all Dollar Zones

☎ PRINTING
ТИПОГРАФИИ
DRUCKEREIEN
IMPRIMERIE
TRYCKNING
PAINOTYÖPALVEWA

Many of these firms are really "desktop publishers".

Agency Igrek
Konnogvardeyskiy blvd., 19, floor 5, rm. 112 .
☎ 311-95-95
Fax 311-92-19

Aiyu, *Color printing, business cards, door plates*
Please Call 166-03-20

Alcor Technologes Incorporated
Stepana Razina ul., 8/50 310-26-87
Fax 310-44-70
Mon-Fri 10-19; Rbls, $; Eng, Ger, Fr

Autograph Avtograf
Printing & Design

In House Commercial Art & Design Studio
Offset Presses & Silk-screen Process
Quick Turn-Around Time on Rush Jobs
Lomonosova ul., 5 310-26-02
Hrs: 9-18, English, French, German, Japanese

Ales
Basseynaya ul., 20 294-18-66
Fax 294-04-44
Mon-Fri 9-17; Rbls

Baltica, *Mon-Fri 9-18; Rbls, $*
Bolshaya Monetnaya ul., 17 157-05-81

Color Printing, *Mon-Fri 8:30-17; Rbls*
Obukhovskoy Oborony pr., 110 262-20-77

ECS USA
Nevskiy pr., 147, apt. 49 277-68-70

EGO, *Mon-Fri 9-21; Rbls, $; Eng*
Gorokhovaya ul., 6 315-27-73
Fax 312-92-84

Ivan Fedorov Printing House
Zvenigorodskaya ul., 11 164-45-29
Fax 112-45-33
Mon-Fri 8:30-13, 13:30-17; Rbls, $

DESIGN & PRINTING

kella

Printers to the banks, businesses & government of Saint Petersburg.

Stationery, Cards, Announcements
Brochures, Presentation & Advertising Kits
Design of Logos & Trademarks
Color Separation and Silk-screen Process
Fine Quality Papers
  ✆ Kronverkskaya ul., 10

Tel/Fax 232-18-90
Hrs: 9-21, Closed Sundays

Printing House   **Tipografiya**
Chkalovskiy pr., 15 235-98-24
Mon-Fri 9-17; Rbls, $

Printing No. 4   **Tipografiya**
Sotsialisticheskaya ul., 14 164-87-06
Fax 315-32-53
Mon-Fri 8-12, 12:30-16:30; Rbls

Restavrator, *Mon-Fri 9-17; Rbls, $*
Staro-Petergofskiy pr., 3/5 251-63-03

Rikki-Tikki-Tavi, *Mon-Fri 9-18; Rbls, $; Eng*
Dekabristov ul., 62 219-76-92
Fax 114-19-20

Rotar, *Mon-Fri 9-17; Rbls, $; Eng, Fr, Finn*
Shpalernaya ul., 52, rm. 23 273-21-24
Fax 275-31-12

Silex, Mon-Fri 9-20; Rbls, $
Volodi Ermaka ul., 9 113-79-25
Fax 219-73-29
Smart, Color printing
Admiralteyskiy pr., 8/1 110-66-55
Fax 110-65-70
Mon-Fri 10-18; Rbls, $; Eng, Ger, Fr, Finn, Swed, Ital
Sova Owl
Liteynyy pr., 62, rm. 3 275-54-74
Mon-Fri 9-18; Rbls; Eng, Ger, Fr
Vals
Zagorodnyy pr., 10 164-49-39
Daily 9:30-17:30; Rbls; Eng, Ger, Fr
Vika Design Group
Obvodnogo kan. nab., 215 251-43-33
Mon-Fri 10-18; Rbls; Bus 2; Metro Narvskaya
Yuliya, Mon-Fri 10-17; Rbls, $, CC
Kamennoostrovskiy pr., 9/2, apt. 77
☎ 233-58-17

☎ PROPANE
ПРОПАН
PROPANGAS
PROPANE
PROPAN (GAS)
PROPAANIKAASU

For your dacha, hot water heater, or camper.

Lengaz, Daily 10-18; Rbls
Polyustrovskiy pr., 77 245-37-51
Lentekhgaz
Bolshoy Smolenskiy pr., 11 265-18-29
Fax 567-12-26
Mon-Thu 8:30-17, Fri 8:30-16; Rbls
Kalinina ul., 3 186-34-11
Mon-Fri 8-16:30; Rbls
Tere - Service, Mon-Fri 8-12, 12:30-16; Rbls
Saltykovskaya Doroga 15 226-18-33

☎ PSYCHIATRISTS

See MEDICAL CARE *and* CONSULTATIONS

☎ PUBLISHERS
ИЗДАТЕЛЬСТВА
VERLAGE
EDITEURS
FÖRLÄGGARE
KUSTANTAMOT

Amos
Pavlogradskiy per., 6/10 164-40-78

ART GRAPHIC™

Prints, Photography, Limited Editions

Please call 311-59-23

Art - Saint Petersburg
Nevskiy pr., 28 311-87-45
Mon-Fri 9-12, 12:45-17:45; Rbls
Art Literature, Mon-Fri 9-17:30; Rbls
Nevskiy pr., 28 219-90-10
Fax 311-75-68
Artists of Russia, Mon-Fri 9-17:30; Rbls
Bolsheokhtinskiy pr., 6, bldg. 2 224-06-37
August, Mon-Fri 10-17; Rbls
Kuznetsovskaya ul., 19 298-09-86

Aurora Art Publishers
Publishers of art and architecture books
Reproduction rights for all museums in Russia
Nevskiy pr., 7/9 312-37-53
Mon-Fri 9-13, 14-18; Rbls, $

Baltic Bridge Ltd., Mon-Fri 10-17; Rbls, $; Eng
Kronverkskaya ul., 27 232-98-38
Bureau-2, Mon-Fri 10-17; Rbls, $; Eng
Povarskoy per., 9, apt. 10 591-49-42
Children's Literature   Detskaya Literatura
Kutuzova nab., 6 273-78-46
Mon-Fri 9-12, 12:45-18; Closed Sat-Sun; Rbls

Commersant Publishing House
St.Petersburg Representation
Nevskiy pr., 3, office 25 315-04-29
Fax 315-79-67
Hrs: 10-20, English, German, French

Composer, music publishers
Gertsena ul., 45 314-50-54
Mon-Fri 10-18; Rbls; Eng, Ger, Fr, Finn, Swed, Ital
Contour-M
Chekhova ul., 8 272-55-45
Mon-Fri 9-18; Rbls, $; Major European languages
Cornfield, agricultural literature   **Niva**
Griboedova kan. nab., 15 311-02-03
Mon-Fri 9-17; Rbls
Defis, Mon-Fri 10-17; Rbls, $; Eng
Reki Fontanki nab., 117 278-50-88
Dom Natali, for women, Mon-Fri 10-18; Rbls
Dekabristov ul., 4 315-66-01
Foreign Trade Publisher
Kuybysheva ul., 34 233-52-63
Mon-Fri 8:30-12, 13-17:30
Graphic Arts, Mon-Fri 10-17; Rbls
Sadovaya ul., 89, apt. 7 114-69-62

InfoServices International Inc., USA
Represented in Russia by TELINFO

Publisher of

THE *TRAVELLER'S*
YELLOW PAGES
FOR
SAINT PETERSBURG
AND
THE CITY MAP OF
SAINT PETERSBURG

Moscow Edition Avaliable September 1993
Baltics Edition Early 1994
1 Saint Marks Place
Cold Spring Harbor, NY 11724, USA
Tel .... USA (516) 549-0064
Fax .... (516) 549-2032
Telex .... 221213 TTC UR
Telinfo is a wholly-owned subsidiary of
InfoServices International, Inc. NY, USA
Reki Moyki nab., 64 315-64-12
Fax 312-73-41

*i*ностранец

Information on Foreign Business Contacts
Member of the Commersant Publishing House
Newspaper Group
Circulation: 100,000 Throughout the Former USSR.
32 pages.

125080, Russia, Moscow, P.O. Box 21
Khoroshovskoe shosse, 17
Moscow....................................(095) 941-09-00
Advertising & PR Dept ....(095) 940-02-33
Fax ....(095) 940-04-68

Interpublish
Inzhenernaya ul., 6........................312-53-90
Fax 312-21-36
Mon-Fri 9-17

Kit, *Publisher of The Whole Saint*
Petersburg Business Directory
Marata ul., 86 112-50-51
Fax 112-42-11

Lenizdat
Reki Fontanki nab., 59 210-84-11
....311-14-51
Mon-Fri 10-17; Rbls. Metro Pushkinskaya

**LIC Information
& Publishing
Agency Ltd.**

**Gertsena ul., 20
191065, St. Petersburg, Russia
Tel.: 314-59-82
Fax: 315-35-92**

Ludmila Center for Revival of Russian Arts
Ligovskiy pr., 56 e, rm. 181 260-90-15
....164-61-34
Fax 164-69-41
Mon-Sat 10-19; Rbls

Moscow News - *See ad below*

Music
Ryleeva ul., 17 279-01-75
Mon-Fri 9-12:30, 13:30-18; Rbls

Mysl, *Philosophical works* **Thought**
Griboedova kan. nab., 26 314-33-45
Mon-Fri 10-19; Rbls

MOSCOW NEWS

WEEKLY

Moscow News

The best way for you to know what's going
on in Russia in the world of business.

♦ ♦ ♦

Weekly suppliments to keep you abreast of
local and worldwide economic events

♦ ♦ ♦

Tverskaya ul., 16/2, Moscow
Russian Edition .... (095) 209-17-49
English Edition............ (095) 209-26-82
Fax.............................. (095) 209-17-28

WHAT'S HAPPENING IN ST. PETERSBURG

NEVA NEWS

*An English language newspaper
for foreign readers
in Russia & abroad*

**Our prices for advertisements &
classifieds are very competitive**

Postal address: Pravdy ul., 10,
St. Petersburg, 191126, Russia

Tel/Fax: 164-47-65

New Times International
Pochtamtskaya ul., 5.....................314-23-67
Fax...315-47-74
Mon-Sat 10-20; Rbls, $

Palitra, *art magazine and books*
Perekupnoy per., 15/17 274-45-18
Fax...274-09-11
Mon-Fri 9-12:30, 13:30-18; Rbls

Petroart, *art books and graphics*
Novatorov blvd, 36 254-79-41
Mon-Fri 10-17; Rbls

PolyPlan St. Petersburg, *Mapmaker*
Shaumyana pr., 18.........................542-19-47
Fax...528-97-02
Mon-Fri 10-18

Restavrator, *art books*
Staro-Petergofskiy pr., 3/5 251-63-03
Mon-Fri 9-17; Rbls, $

Rotar
Shpalernaya ul., 52, rm. 23 273-21-24
Fax...275-31-12
Mon-Fri 9-17; Rbls, $; Eng, Fr, Finn

Pick Up Your Copy Today

Saint Petersburg PREMIER

Available FREE in all leading hotels

Saint Petersburg Premier, *Eng, quarterly.*
Interesting articles on culture, history and news.
For foreigners visiting and living in St. Petersburg.
Professora Popova ul., 47, off. 709
☎ 234-53-34
Fax 110-73-93

Science   **Nauka**
Mendeleevskaya Liniya, 1 218-39-12
Mon-Fri 9-11:30, 12:30-17:30; Rbls

Soviet Writer   **Sovetskiy Pisatel**
Liteynyy pr., 36 279-03-36
Mon-Fri 10-19; Rbls

ST. PETERSBURG CHAMBER OF
COMMERCE & INDUSTRY PUBLISHING
Chaykovskogo ul., 46-48 273-58-23

TEN-Inform, *Mon-Fri 10-20; Rbls; Eng*
Izmaylovskiy pr., 2 259-50-14
Fax 251-04-00

VlaS *(Publisher of the Izdatel-Kommersant)*
Nauki pr., 12, bldg. 7, rm. 24 555-08-39

☎ **QUALITY CONTROL**
КОНТРОЛЬ ЗА КАЧЕСТВОМ
ПРОДУКЦИИ
QUALITÄTSKONTROLLE
QUALITE DE LA PRODUCTION,
CONTROLE
KVALITETSKONTROLL, LAB
RUOKATUOTTEIDEN
LAATUKONTROLLIT

Product Quality Control Center
Admiralteyskaya nab., 8 210-88-30
Mon-Fri 9-18; Rbls; Tram 2; Metro Gorkovskaya

VA INSTRUMENTS

☑ Pure metals certification utilizing state-of-the-art technology (ICP-MS, GD-MS).

☑ Analytical Labs & Equipment Display

Rizhskiy pr., 26 252-67-59
Fax 252-10-03
Established 1989

Central Nutrition and Sanitation Laboratory
Baltiyskaya ul., 17, bldg. 2 252-57-32
Mon-Fri 10-18; Rbls; Tram 31; Metro Narvskaya

ST. PETERSBURG CHAMBER
OF COMMERCE & INDUSTRY
QUALITY CONTROL
Chaykovskogo ul., 46-48 275-09-89
Quality & Quantity Control
of Import-Export Goods

Water Tests
Laboratoriya Issledovaniya Vody
Bolshoy pr., V.O., 13 213-76-59
Mon-Fri 9-17

☎ **RACING**
БЕГА, ГОНКИ
WETTRENNEN, RENNEN
COURSES
RACING, (HÄST, KAPPLÖPNING,
BILRACING)
KILPAILUT(RATSASTUS-JA RALLI)

There is no official horse racing in St. Petersburg but a racetrack is being built in Kupchino. For automobile racing, try the following for information on competitions or to participate in them.

The track in Yukki is used for training for automobile and motorcycle racing. The Mototrek track at Zhaka Duklo is used for international competitions.

Avtomotosport in St. Petersburg, *Office*
Perekupnoy per., 9 274-66-53
Mon-Fri 9-17

Mototrek Stadium, *Daily 9-18; Rbls*
Zhaka Dyuklo ul., 67 553-84-83

Skachki
Chekistov ul., 20 136-73-83
Daily 9-22; Bus 87; Metro Prospekt Veteranov

☎ **RADIO STATIONS**
РАДИОСТАНЦИИ
RADIOSENDER
RADIO, STATIONS DE
RADIOSTATIONER
RADIOASEMAT

A small good quality multi-band radio with FM, MW (AM), short-wave and long wave bands is a great companion on any trip to listen to local stations and to tune into BBC,& Voice of America. The Russians and Europeans sometimes use wavelength *in meters rather than our* kilohertz & megahertz.

Note, the Russian and European FM band goes from 66 to 107 MHz, the American from 87 to 107 MHz. Try to buy a radio that tunes from the lower 66 MHz to 107 MHz. Voice of America and BBC broadcast in English on short wave (See chart below).

What to listen to in St. Petersburg. *There are three official stations and a growing number of commercial stations in St. Pb. The BBC World Service broadcoast in St. Pb. in English and in Russian on AM 1260, The Deutsche Welle in German on AM 1200. The best stations for popular music* *are Magic Radio, Europa Plus and Radio Baltica. Most radio stations can be contacted through Petersburg 5th Channel.*

Many old Russian radios have three selection buttons, because historically many apartments were wired for three-channel inexpensive radios. New and important radios can tune in a variety of programs on FM, short-wave, middle wave and long wave.

AM Radio Stations

KHz	Mtrs	Station, Type, Hours
198	1515	**MAYAK** *Music and News, 3:00-2:00*
234	1282	**RADIO-1** *Music and News, 5:00-3:00*
549	550	**MAYAK** *Music and News, 4:00-3:00*
684	439	**RADIO BALTICA** *Music, News, Local Ads,* *7:00-24:00*
801	374	**PETERSBURG-5th CHANNEL** *Music, News, Local Ads,* *5:00-1:00*
873	345	**RADIO ROSSII** *Music and News, 5:00-3:00*
1053	285	**POLIS** *City News, Music, 0:00-24:00*
1125	267	**ORFEY** *Classical Music, 6:00-24:00*
1200	251	**DIE DEUTSCHE WELLE** *Broadcasting in German*
1260	238	**BBC WORLD SERVICE** *In English & in Russian*

FM Radio Stations

MHz	Mtrs	Station, Type, Hours
66.3	4.52	**RADIO ROSSII** *Music and News, 5:00-3:00*
67.45	4.45	**MAYAK** (stereo) *Music and News, 5:00-4:00*
68.22	4.39	**MAGIC RADIO** (stereo) *Music, News, Ads, 6:00-2:00*
69.47	4.32	**RADIO KLASSIKA** (stereo) *5:00-1:00 - Music* *1:00-5:00 - News*
71.24	4.21	**RADIO BALTICA** (stereo) *Music, News, Ads, 7:00-24:00*
71.66	4.19	**RADIO-1** (stereo) *World News and Music,* *7:00-24:00*
72.68	4.13	**EUROPA PLUS** (stereo) *Music, News, Ads, 6:00-4:00*
100.5	2.99	**EUROPA PLUS** (stereo) *Music, News, Ads, 6:00-4:00*
102.0	2.94	**RADIO ROX** (stereo) *Music, News, 6:00-2:00*

Short Wave Radio Stations

St. Pb time is 3 hours later than Greenwich Mean Time (GMT) in winter, 4 hours during summer time
VOA=Voice of America, BBC=BBC World Service

Short wave Radio Broadcasts in English

Mhz	Greenwich Mean Time
	0 2 3 4 5 6 7 8 9 10 11 12 13
5.995, 6.040	VOA
6.140, 7.170	VOA
6.180, 7.325	BBC
6.195	BBC
9.410	BBC
12.095	BBC
13.070	BBC
15.205	VOA
17.640	BBC

Mhz	13 14 15 16 17 18 19 20 21 22 23 24
5.930	BBC
6.040	VOA
6.180, 7.325	BBC
9.410	BBC
9.700	VOA
9.760	VOA
12.095	BBC
13.070	BBC
15.205	VOA
17.640	BBC

Europa Plus, *Mon-Fri 10-18; Rbls, $*
  Professora Popova ul., 47 234-98-78
  Fax.. 234-98-60
Magic Radio, *Mon-Fri 9-18*
  Reki Karpovki nab., 43 234-90-85
Petersburg 5th Channel
  Telephones will be changed in Summer 1993.
  Italyanskaya ul., 27
  Advertising.................................... 219-96-94
                      Mon-Fri 10-18
Polis, *Mon-Fri 10-18*
  Ligovskiy pr., 253, apt. 8 166-37-96
Radio Baltica, *Mon-Fri 10-18*
  Kamennoostrovskiy pr., 67 235-58-50
Radio Klassika, *Mon-Fri 10-18*
  Italyanskaya ul., 27 315-36-37
Radio Rossii
  Italyanskaya ul., 27, rm. 308-310
  ☎ 219-96-08

☎ RAIL INFORMATION
ЖЕЛЕЗНОДОРОЖНАЯ ИНФОРМАЦИЯ
ZUGAUSKUNFT
INFORMATION FERROVIAIRE
TÄGINFORMATION
JUNIEN AIKATAULUTIEDOITUS

TRAIN SCHEDULES

Printed "long distance" train schedules are available at all stations, suburban electric commuter schedules are only available at the station serving those lines. One central number provides information for all stations.

Railway Information for All Stations
  Please call.................................... 168-01-11
  162-33-44
                 Daily 0-24
Moscow Departures ..... (095) 266-90-00/09
  .... (095) 921-45-13

TICKETS

Same day tickets. *Tickets for same day departure can be purchased only at the station of departure at the "same-day window"* (sutochnaya, суточная), *for rubles, (or at hotels or Intourist kassas for $) if available. Last minute tickets can sometimes be obtained from speculators-scalpers with an inside track, but at a stiff premium.*

Tickets in advance: *Tickets for the next day up to 45 days in advance can be purchased only at the:*

Central Railway Agency Office
Tsentralnye Zheleznodorozhnye Kassy
Griboedova kan. nab., 24 162-33-44
Right off Nevskiy marked by a locomotive sign.
Open 9-19, Metro Nevskiy Prospekt, G-5

Tickets by telephone: *You can order tickets in advance by telephone and they will be delivered in two or three days to your home or office. You pay when they are delivered. Call 162-33-44.*

Tickets for foreigners: *In theory, foreigners are supposed to buy tickets at special Intourist windows at the station, Intourist ticket offices or special windows in the Central Railway Office. Basically, foreigners are supposed to pay more for their tickets. Foreigners on tourist visas are supposed to pay in dollars, foreigners on commercial visas pay for tickets in rubles and a $4 per ticket commission. Such tickets are accompanied by a receipt showing that you paid properly.*

In practice, many foreigners ask a Russian to buy tickets for them. A name must be put on the tickets to prevent scalping and in theory, the purchaser must show passports for the tickets they buy. Often, the ticket agent just asks your name. Try to have your name put on the ticket.

International train tickets *are sold only for hard currency to all travelers.*

TRAIN TRAVEL IN RUSSIA

Train travel is the least expensive and the most efficient way in most cases to travel to Moscow, the Baltic's, and North-west Russia.

Comfort and classes: *There are three basic classes for long distance train travel:* **luxury-soft** (lyuks, люкс *or* SV, CB) *with two soft beds which pull out for more space,* **coupé-soft** (kupe, купе) *with four soft beds, and* **platskart** (плацкарт) *with six beds per compartment, a choice to be avoided at all costs.*

Electric commuter trains, *called* elektropoezda, (электропоезда) *usually have hard wooden benches, no amenities and can be very crowded on weekends in summer when people go off to the dacha.*

For really good service between St. Pb. and Moscow, take the new "commercial trains" (kommercheskiy poezd, коммерческий поезд). *The improved service*

usually includes clean bathrooms, hot tea and snacks, restaurant cars, new equipment, polite conductors and overall less hassle. Tickets are sold at a separate window. The price includes the linen supplement.

For real comfort, *always buy all the tickets for the compartment, even if just one or two people are traveling. You have privacy and on overnight trips, you can make yourself a king-size bed by putting your luggage & extra blankets between the two beds. It is not advisable for women to travel alone. If they must, it's mandatory to have a compartment to themselves.*

Getting to your train: *Your ticket will indicate the train* (poezd, поезд) *number, wagon* (vagon, вагон) *and compartment* (kupe, купе). *People meeting you will often ask for your compartment and wagon number. Russian trains are long, so it is handy to have someone there where you step off the train.*

On the train: *When you board the train, the conductor* (provodnik, проводник) *will put your ticket into his/her black pouch (and should return it to you the next morning). He/she may or may not check your passport; few conductors bother. On night trains the conductor will usually collect a small sum of money for the bed linen, and towel ($0.25-0.50 in rubles). They should also offer you tea at night and in the morning. Some will have a selection of alcohol, cold beer, soda and snacks for sale. For good service, a small tip ($0.50 in rubles) at the end of the trip is appropriate.*

If you have purchased your tickets at the window for Russians, the conductor will occasionally try to collect the "Intourist" commission for himself. Good humor and a sum of between $1-$4 per person will solve the problem. Resist those persons who may try to collect more for unused tickets or for linen service.

Porters (nosilshchik, носильщик) *expect no less than $1.00 in rubles from foreigners for one or two bags and about $0.30 for each additional bag. Indulge yourself, because "Wagon Number 3" is a long way down the platform. They share their tips with their "foreman" who "assigns" work.*

Toilets *on most trains are in disrepair and without supplies. Bring your own toilet paper and soap tucked in a bag.*

What to bring: *To make your trip more enjoyable bring food, water and nonalcoholic drinks, beer and spirits, a pocket knife (to prepare food). On overnight trips bring slippers, light bed clothes, toilet paper, and a 2 ft piece of 1/8 inch nylon cord.*

Safety at the station and the train: *Be alert around railway stations, especially the Moscow, Warsaw and Baltic stations. At night, be accompanied by someone.*

As on most European trains, each compartment door has a door lock and a second security lock for ventilation. The door lock can be opened with an easily-available special key; the ventilation lock can also be quietly defeated from outside. Voila! We carry a short nylon cord to loop over the top of the door handle to prevent the door from being opened. Most conductors approve of this method and often warn travelers to store valuables in a special compartment under the bed. Women should always travel with a companion. Now, you have peace of mind.

NUMBER OF HOURS FOR SELECTED TRIPS

ABROAD And To The REPUBLICS:

Berlin: 36 , Brest: 21.5, Budapest: 59, Bucharest: 48.5, Helsinki: 6.5, Kharkov: 27.5, Kiev: 27 Minsk: 17.5, Odessa: 36.5, Riga: 2, Sofia: 59, Tallinn: 9, Vilnius: 15, Warsaw : 26 , Alma-Ata: 90 hours.

DOMESTIC:

Arkhangelsk: 28.5, Kaliningrad: 24, Moscow: 6-8.5 (15 times daily), Novgorod 4-5.5, Petrozavodck: 8-9, Samara: 41, Pskov: 6.5, Smolensk: 16.5, Volgograd: 38, Gorkiy (renamed Nizhniy Novgorod): 18, Kazan: 29, Murmansk: 31, Vyborg: 1.75 hours.

When crossing the Russian border, the train will stop for about three hours to change the trucks (wheels) from the wider Russian track width to the narrower European width.

☎ RAILWAY STATIONS
ЖЕЛЕЗНОДОРОЖНЫЕ ВОКЗАЛЫ
BAHNHÖFE
GARES FERROVIAIRES
TÅGSTATIONER
RAUTATIEASEMAT

Commuter electric trains leave from all stations.

🚂 Baltic Station

Baltiyskiy Vokzal   Балтийский вокзал
Trains to Western suburbs such as Gatchina, Lomonosov & Peterhof
Obvodnogo kan. nab., 120 168-01-11
Rbls, Eng, Ger; Metro Baltiyskaya
Buses: 10, 49, 60, 67,109; T-bus: 3, 24
Trams: 1, 2, 19, 29, 34, 36, 43; E-3

🚂 Finland Station

Finlyandskiy Vokzal   Финляндский вокзал
Trains to Helsinki, local trains to northern suburbs Vyborg, Zelenogorsk, Sestroretsk, Repino and to Lake Ladoga, etc.
Passenger Station, Lenina pl., 6
  ☎ Passenger Information............... 168-01-11
Container Freight Service, Mineralnaya ul., 25
  ☎ 168-72-72
Metro: Ploshchad Lenina;
Buses: 2, 28, 37, 47, 49, 78, 104, 106, 107, 136; 137
T-bus: 3, 8, 12, 19, 23, 38, 43;
Trams: 6, 17, 19, 20, 23, 26, 30, 32, 38, 51; H-8

🚂 Moscow Station

Moskovskiy Vokzal   Московский вокзал
Trains to Moscow, Northern Russia, Caucasus, Crimea, Georgia, Central Asia
Nevskiy pr., 85 .... 168-45-97, 277-16-21
Metro: Ploshchad Vosstaniya, Mayakovskaya; Buses: 3, 7, 22, 26, 27, 44, 74, 174; T-bus: 1, 6, 7, 10, 14, 16; I-5

🚂 Vitebsk Station

Vitebskiy Vokzal   Витебский вокзал
Trains to Smolensk, Novgorod, Kiev, Odessa, Moldova, & locals to suburbs of Pavlovsk, Pushkin
Zagorodnyy pr., 52......................... 168-57-05
Freight office.................................... 314-02-35
Metro: Pushkinskaya; T-bus: 3, 8, 9, 15; G-4

🚂 Warsaw Station

Varshavskiy Vokzal   Варшавский вокзал
Trains to Baltics, Pskov, Lvov, Poland and Eastern Europe and local trains to Gatchina.
Obvodnogo kan. nab., 118 168-26-55
Metro: Baltiyskaya; Buses: 10, T-bus: 15, 17; F-3

☎ REAL ESTATE AGENTS
АГЕНТЫ ПО КУПЛЕ-ПРОДАЖЕ НЕДВИЖИМОСТИ
MAKLER, IMMOBILIEN
ACHAT ET VENTE, AGENTS D' FASTIGHETSMÄKLARE
KIINTEISTÖVÄLITYS

Real estate is the hottest growth sector in Russia as privatization gives people the opportunity to own property. There are dozens of real estate agents and even newspapers devoted to the sale of apartments and offices. Ownership is not always clear and neither are the laws.

Agency XXI Century

Office Space & Apartments Available in St.Petersburg.

PURCHASE & SALES

Real Estate in South East USA

Vladimirskiy pr., 9
Tel.: 113-1676, 113-1370
Fax: 113-1673

Alivekt
Reki Moyki nab., 40 315-73-02
Antaks Tur
Metallistov pr., 119, rm. 206 540-51-42
Mon-Fri 10-18:30; Rbls, $; Eng
Autocomp
Razezzhaya ul., 9 166-53-18
Fax 166-12-52
Mon-Fri 9-18; Rbls, $; Eng, Ger, Fr
Avers
Bolshoy Sampsonievskiy pr., 75 245-52-69
Fax 245-07-38
Mon-Fri 9-17; Rbls
Deon
Kolpinskaya ul., 10, rm. 10 230-94-25
Mon-Fri 10-20; Rbls, $

DOM PLUS Agency

We buy, sell and rent commercial,
industrial and residential properties.
Full service agency providing assistance
with negotiations and documents.

Griboedova kan. nab., 3 312-11-32

Fax 312-83-51

InterOccidental
Vosstaniya ul., 49 273-43-23
Fax 272-80-31
Daily 9-21; Rbls, $; Eng

 K-Keskus
We Buy & Sell Apartments
Business Space & Land
232-07-23, 233-48-33

Lek-Estate
Please call 272-10-97
Mon-Fri 10-17; Rbls; Eng

 **LENALP**

We Sell Apartments
Office Space & Stores
Vladimirskiy pr., 10 310-09-61
Fax 567-28-71
Telex .... 121619 VYSOT SU

Luch, *Mon-Sat 9-18; Rbls, $*
Please call 292-78-35
Nadezhda
Griboedova kan. nab., 15 314-43-34
Fax 314-67-87
Mon-Fri 9-18; Rbls

OVEN
Real Estate Agency

❖❖❖

Sales of Premium Office Space &
Apartments in the Center of
St. Petersburg
All Legal Documents Prepared

❖❖❖

Mokhovaya ul., 27/29, apt. 21

Tel.: 275-40-69
Fax: .... (812) 275-36-59

Hrs: 10-20, Sat. 10-18, Clsd. Sun.
Metro Chernyshevskaya

A/O **PETER-HAKA** Real Estate Development Services
Admiralteyskiy pr., 6, 191065, St.Petersburg
Tel .... +7-812-312-31-18
Fax .... +7-812-315-93-58
Peterburgskiy Auktsion
Grivtsova per., 5, rm. 409, 414, 417 311-07-74
Fax 311-06-01
Mon-Fri 9:30-18:30; Rbls; Eng, Ger

Petersburg Properties
Extraordinary Flats for Long Term Rent or Purchase
Buildings and Commercial Space
Property Management Services
"Everything But the Hermitage"

Nevskiy pr. 275-41-67

 SAVVA
REAL ESTATE S.Pb

Excellent Apartments &
Office Space

SAVVA 234-36-01

S. FitzLyon F.R.I.C.S.

Reki Moyki nab., 11, apt. 32
London, England .... (0181) 994-5678
Services in English & French
Opening in September 1993

Sovex
Leninskiy pr., 117/1 153-91-96
Fax 252-26-32
Taurus, *Mon-Fri 9-18; Rbls, $; Eng*
Ispolkomskaya ul., 9/11 275-32-50

VMB
Energetikov pr., 37........................ 114-76-04
Fax 114-75-89
YUS
Prilukskaya ul., 12, apt. 1 166-58-12
Fax 166-18-61
Mon-Fri 9-18; Rbls, $, CC; Eng
Zolotoy Medved
Nekrasova ul., 2 279-23-61
Fax 279-26-09

☎ **RECORDS**
ПЛАСТИНКИ
SCHALLPLATTEN
DISQUES
SKIVOR
LEVYT

See also MUSIC SHOPS

Records, tapes, and CD's can be bought in many DEPARTMENT STORES *and in* KIOSKS.

Diez
Transportnyy per., 6 164-95-79
Mon-Sat 11-19; Rbls
Dom Radio i Muzyki
House of Radio & Music
Grazhdanskiy pr., 15/1 534-42-18
.... 534-54-95
Mon-Sat 10-19; Rbls
Gramplastinki **Records**
• 7-ya Liniya, 40 213-35-88
Mon-Sat 10-19; Rbls
• Nevskiy pr., 32/34 311-74-55
Mon-Sat 11-14, 15-19; Rbls
• Moskovskiy pr., 34/36 292-35-05
Tue-Sun 10-14, 15-19; Rbls
• Obukhovskoy Oborony pr., 81 265-13-01
Mon-Sat 10-14, 15-19; Rbls
Tram 7; Metro Elizarovskaya
• Veteranov pr., 110 159-07-56
Mon-Sat 11-19; Rbls
T-bus 20; Metro Prospekt Veteranov
Izabel
Tsvetochnaya ul., 7 298-73-64
Fax 296-12-54
Mon-Thu, Sat-Sun 8:30-17; Rbls
Melodiya **Melody**
• Bolshoy pr., P.S., 47 232-11-39
Mon-Sat 10-14, 15-19; Rbls
• Nevskiy pr., 32-34 311-74-55
Mon-Sat 11-14, 15-19; Rbls; Eng
Sonata
Novocherkasskiy pr., 41/14 528-16-90
Mon-Sat 10-14, 15-19; Rbls

☎ **REFRIGERATORS**
ХОЛОДИЛЬНИКИ
KÜHLSCHRÄNKE
REFRIGERATEURS
KYLSKÅP
JÄÄKAAPIT

See KITCHEN APPLIANCES & DEPARTMENT STORES

Russian freezers and refrigerators are basic solid appliances without many features. Consider buying one from a specialty store called "Refrigerators" (Kholodilniki, Холодильники) *or a department store or rent one. See* RENTALS.

Energiya
9-ya Sovetskaya ul., 11 271-21-61
Mon-Sat 10-19; Rbls
Kholodilniki **Refrigerators**
• Bolshoy pr., P.S., 31 232-92-06
Mon-Sat 10-14, 15-19; Rbls; Eng
• Bolshoy Sampsonievskiy pr., 80 245-27-68
Mon-Sat 10-19; Rbls
T-bus 46; Metro Petrogradskaya
• Dostoevskogo ul., 22 164-94-07
Mon-Sat 10-19; Rbls
• Moskovskiy pr., 208 293-14-00
Mon-Sat 10-19; Rbls
Siemens
Refrigerators, microwaves, food processors
Robespera nab., 8/46 275-05-50
Mon-Sat 10-14, 15-19; Rbls, $
Tradehouse on Moyka
Reki Moyki nab., 59, 2nd floor........ 315-86-63
Daily 10-14, 15-19; Rbls, $

☎ **REMOVALS**

See MOVING COMPANIES

☎ **RENTALS**
(Furniture,Bicycles, TV's)
ПРОКАТ ОБОРУДОВАНИЯ,
ТЕЛЕВИЗОРОВ
VERLEIH
LOUAGE DE T.V., D' EQUIPMENT
UTHYRNING, MÖBLER, CYKLAR,
TV-APPARATER ETC.
VUOKRAUS (TV, POLKUPYÖRÄ,
HUONEKALU)

A person can rent a number of items, such as refrigerators, baby carriages, TVs, coffee pots, furniture, and bicycles and much more. Try the official rental stores in the nearest "rental point" (punkt prokata, пункт проката). *Selection will vary from store to store. Note that a Russian passport must be presented for identification when renting from state owned bureaus. Ask a friend. There are dozens of rental points, here are only a few.*

Dzerzhinskiy District
Mokhovaya ul., 31 272-40-46
Mon-Sat 13-19; Rbls; Eng
Frunzenskiy District
• Dimitrova ul., 20 172-53-46
Mon-Fri 10-14, 15-19; Rbls
• Kupchinskaya ul., 32 176-77-45
Mon-Fri 10-14, 15-19; Rbls
Kalininskiy District
• Akademika Lebedeva ul., 15 542-11-34
Mon-Fri 11-18; Rbls
• Grazhdanskiy pr., 92, bldg. 1 555-11-12
Mon-Sat 11-14, 15-20; Rbls
• Timurovskaya ul., 8 557-66-83
Mon-Fri 10-14, 15-19; Rbls
Kirovskiy District
• Avtovskaya ul., 32 184-20-38
Mon-Fri 11-14, 15-19; Rbls
• Leninskiy pr., 117 157-76-18
Mon-Fri 11-19; Rbls
Krasnogvardeyskiy District
Novocherkasskiy pr., 12 528-94-83
Mon-Fri 10-14, 15-19; Rbls

Krasnoselskiy District
Veteranov pr., 141 144-33-75
Mon-Sat 10-14, 15-18; Rbls

Kuybyshevskiy District
• Kolokolnaya ul., 2 113-38-82
Mon-Sat 10-14, 15-19; Rbls
• Gorokhovaya ul., 36 310-88-53
Mon-Sat 11-14, 15-19; Rbls

Leninskiy District
Uglovoy per., 5 292-79-38
Mon-Fri 11-18; Rbls; Metro Frunzenskaya

Moskovskiy District
• Novo-Izmaylovskiy pr., 28 295-43-06
Mon-Sat 10-14, 15-19; Rbls
• Leninskiy pr., 147 295-63-67
Mon-Sat 10-14, 15-19; Rbls

Nevskiy District
• Dybenko ul., 25, bldg. 1 585-42-80
Mon-Fri 10-14, 15-19; Rbls
• Narodnaya ul., 1 263-60-23
Mon-Fri 11-14, 15-19; Rbls
• Narodnaya ul., 2 263-74-00
Mon-Fri 10-14, 15-19; Rbls

Oktyabrskiy District
Sadovaya ul., 49 314-82-47
Mon-Sat 11-14, 15-20; Rbls

Petrogradskiy District
• Bolshoy pr., P.S., 19 232-48-58
Mon-Fri 10-18; Rbls
• Kamennoostrovskiy pr., 52 234-54-76
Mon-Sat 11-14, 15-19; Rbls

Primorskiy District
• Torzhkovskaya ul., 1 246-17-21
Mon-Fri 10-18; Rbls
• Shkolnaya ul., 56 239-01-20
Mon-Sat 10-14, 15-19; Rbls

Sestroretsk Rental Bureau
Vokzalnaya ul., 17, Sestroretsk 237-64-02
Mon-Fri 9-17; Rbls

Smolninskiy District
Tverskaya ul., 7 271-97-12
Mon-Fri 11-14, 15-19; Rbls

Vasileostrovskiy District
• Nalichnaya ul., 11 356-54-15
Mon-Fri 11-19; Rbls
• Morskaya nab., 17 356-98-83
Mon-Fri 11-18; Rbls

Vyborgskiy District
• Gavrskaya ul., 4 553-88-48
Mon-Sat 11-15, 16-21; Rbls
• Neyshlotskiy per., 23 542-30-03
Mon-Fri 9-13, 14-18; Rbls

Zolushka, *Wedding & Evening wear rental*
Bogatyrskiy pr., 11, 5th floor 393-42-77
Tues-Sat 12-14, 15-19

☎ **REPAIR SERVICES**
РЕМОНТ, СЛУЖБЫ
RENOVIERUNG
REPARATION, SERVICE DE
REPARATIONER
KORJAUSTYÖT

See also AUTOMOBILE REPAIR, SHOE REPAIR,
TAILORS, LOCKSMITHS, PLUMBERS,
CARPENTERS, CONSTRUCTION AND RENOVATION,
BOOKBINDERS, PHOTOCOPIERS, WATCH REPAIRS

*Almost anything can be repaired and
renovated here from umbrellas in a "Remont
Metalloizdeliy" to computers.*

APARTMENT REPAIR

See APARTMENT REPAIR

BICYCLE REPAIR

Reved
Bryantseva ul., 7 531-76-95
Mon-Sat 10-14, 15-19; Rbls

COMPUTERS

See COMPUTER REPAIR

ELECTRICAL APPLIANCES

Minsk - Snige, *refrigerators*
Baltiyskaya ul., 3 186-12-06
.... 186-65-42
Mon-Fri 9-16; Rbls, $; Lit, Belorus

Petrogradets, *Film, Photo, Radio*
Bolshaya Pushkarskaya ul., 42/16
☎ 232-06-48
Mon-Sat 10-14, 15-20; Rbls

Ravenstvo
Repair of precision equipment, optical & mechanical
Promyshlennaya ul., 19 252-92-89
.... 186-18-60
Mon-Fri 9-17; Rbls, $

Vera - Service, *Repair all types of refrigerators*
Nevskiy pr., 104 535-04-88
Mon-Fri 9-17; Rbls
Grazhdanskiy pr., 33, bldg. 2 535-78-97
Fax 273-84-71
Mon-Sat 9-17:45; Rbls

ELECTRONICS

Electrical Repair, *Daily 9-21; Rbls*
Budapeshtskaya ul., 15, bldg. 2, rm. 64
☎ 174-33-34

Progress Service
Reki Moyki nab., 59, 2nd floor 315-86-63
Fax 213-53-56
Daily 11-19; Rbls; Tram 2, 28, 3; Metro Sadovaya

Rus, *TV, Audio and Video Repair*
• 9-ya Liniya, 54 213-25-88
Mon-Sat 10-14, 15-20; Rbls
• Lanskoe shosse, 2 246-49-68
Mon-Sat 10-20; Rbls
• Kamennoostrovskiy pr., 17 232-28-94
Mon-Sat 10-14, 15-20; Rbls
• Shkolnaya ul., 7 239-84-41
Fax 239-62-07
Mon-Sat 10-14, 15-20; Rbls

Toshiba Authorized Service Centre
Grivtsova per., 1/64 210-69-84
Audio and Video Repair

OFFICE SUPPLIES, CALCULATORS

Bureau-2, *Mon-Fri 10-17; Rbls, $; Eng*
Povarskoy per., 9, apt. 10 312-23-49
Fax 312-33-11

PHOTOCOPIERS

See PHOTOCOPIERS, SALES, SERVICE, SUPPLIES

TYPEWRITERS

Service Center, *Mon-Sat 9-14, 15-19; Rbls*
Lermontovskiy pr., 1/44 114-49-01

SEWING MACHINES

Mekhanik, *Mon-Sat 9-21; Rbls*
Barochnaya ul., 8 235-19-04
Podolsk-Sokol
Razezzhaya ul., 12 315-23-84
Fax 394-72-53
Mon-Fri 9-20; Rbls; Metro Dostoevskaya, Vladimirskaya
Reved, *Mon-Sat 10-14, 15-19; Rbls*
Bryantseva ul., 7 531-76-95
Sewing Machine Repair
　　　　　　　Remont Shveynykh Mashin
• Finskiy per., 4 542-03-29
　　Mon-Sat 9-14, 15-20; Rbls
• Vosstaniya ul., 44 275-61-00
　　　　　Mon-Fri 9-19; Rbls

VIDEO AND TELEVISION REPAIR

See VIDEO/TELEVISION REPAIR

☎ RESTAURANTS & CAFES
РЕСТОРАНЫ И КАФЕ
RESTAURANTS
RESTAURANTS
RESTAURANGER
RAVINTOLAT JA KAHVIOT

See also CAFES, FAST FOOD, PIZZA, FOOD DELIVERY, DELICATESSENS & ICE CREAM

Saint Petersburg has over 1000 eating establishments from the numerous very basic, inexpensive cafeterias to the most elegant restaurants in old palaces and hotels.

In addition to restaurants and cafes, there are many other types of places to eat in Saint Petersburg and the food, while simple, can be quite good. Try some of the ones listed below.

TYPES OF EATING ESTABLISHMENTS:

Restaurant　　Restoran　　Ресторан
The Russians make a very clear distinction between the Russian word for "restaurant" and all other places to eat. The "classic Russian restaurant" means high-class, good-quality, expensive with a special cuisine and champagne, wine and vodka and often an orchestra, variety show or music. This type of restaurant is frequently found in large hotels .

Cafe　　　　Kafe　　　　Кафе
The word "Cafe" (кафе) is loosely used in Russian and could refer to anything from an elegant little restaurant serving steak and lobster to a basic coffee shop serving tea, juice, pastries, and ice cream but no coffee. In general cafes are smaller and less formal. In this book those cafes that serve something hot and substantial to eat, from sandwiches, soup, pizzas and good pancakes to steaks and fish are included under RESTAURANTS AND CAFES. Those cafes that serve only drinks, pastries and ice cream are listed under CAFES.

Grill Bar　　Gril Bar　　Гриль Бар
Serve drinks, grilled meats, often chicken & sometimes "shashlyk" (shish kabobs).

Beer Bar　　Pivnoy Bar　　Пивной Бар
Serve beer and appetizers; a beer restaurant has a more extensive menu.

"Blinnaya"　　Blinnaya　　Блинная
Serve Russian blinys, thin pancakes filled with jam or meat and baked pastries.

Pizzeria　　Pitstseriya　　Пиццерия
The imported pizza from Finland is tasty, so is the Russian pizza. Try some. Neither is like American pizza.

Bistro　　　Bistro　　　Бистро
Means "fast" in Russian and is a stand-up place for a quick cup of coffee, open-faced sandwich, salad and soup.

Ice Cream　　Kafe-　　　　Кафе-
Cafe　　　　morozhenoe　　мороженое
Serve ice cream, coffee, chocolates, sweets, champagne and cognac.

"Donuts"　　Pyshechnaya　　Пышечная
Serve coffee & Russian-style donut-puffs

Cafeteria　　Kafeteriy　　Кафетерий
Stolovaya　　Stolovaya　　Столовая
"Buffet"　　Bufet　　　　Буфет
These are basically "cafeteria", very cheap and very basic. Only eat here if recommended by a Russian. The better ones are often operated by an organization, factory, or firm.

IN THE RESTAURANT

Reservations are highly recommended, especially for larger and popular restaurants. For reservations, call and ask for the "Administrator" or "Maitre D'Hotel.".

*When asking for a table, ask for a **"clear table without zakuski"** (chistyy stol bez zakuski, чистый стол без закуски) which means that it has not been preset with expensive hors d'oeuvres (zakuski, закуски). If you are given a table laden with zakuski, make it clear that you want to make your own selection.*

TERMINOLOGY IN THIS BOOK:

"Rubles" *means only rubles,* **"$"** *means hard currency only, and* **"$ & rubles"** *can mean several things: a ruble menu with a more limited selection (or even in a different hall, "Зал") than for $, or drinks are paid in $ and meals in rubles, or an entrance fee is paid in $ and the rest in rubles.*

"Light snacks" *usually means "open-faced sandwiches" (buterbrod, бутерброд) with cheese, meat, caviar, some baked goods, juices, cognac and champagne.*

"Music" *usually means recorded music. Look for "Orchestra", "Chamber Music" or "Band" for live music. Some restaurants have dance floors. "Variety show" usually means singing of contemporary music, dance line and comedy. Those "shows" that feature striptease will be obvious from their advertising. A "cultural evening" may include classical music, poetry and Russian romantic ballads.*

"Folklore" and "gypsy" *are usually in national costumes and feature folk and national songs.*

Related Topics: TIPPING, FOOD STORES, BREAD, FISH, *and* ETIQUETTE.

Afrodita   **Aphrodite**
Nevskiy pr., 86...........................275-76-20
Seventeen different cuisines; Italian, Spanish, etc. Fresh seafood, wine list. Daily 12-24; $; Eng, Fr, Ger; Metro Mayakovskaya, H-5

Ambassador

Elegant Dining in the Classic Tradition of St. Petersburg Outstanding Russian & European cuisine, accompanied by soft piano music Warm, distinctive atmosphere with fireplace and candlelight

Fontanka emb., 14

Reservations

273-74-40

Hrs: 12-24; Rbls & $; English

Ambassador - G-6

Angleterre, *European Cuisine*
Gertsena ul., 39 at the Hotel Astoria ... 210-59-06
Daily 12-23:30; Rbls, $, CC; F-5

Antwerpen, *European Cuisine*
Kronverkskiy pr., 13/2....................233-97-46
Daily 12-24; Rbls, $; Eng, Ger; F-8

Aragvi, *Georgian Cuisine*
Marshala Tukhachevskogo ul., 41 ... 225-00-82
Variety show, casino, striptease, billiards; Daily 12-24; Rbls

Assambleya, *Russian Cuisine, Open 24 hrs*
Bolshaya Konyushennaya ul., 13 314-15-37
Daily 0-24; Rbls, $; Eng; Metro Nevskiy Prospect; G-6

Assol, *Cafe - Russian Cuisine*
Ivanovskiy ul., 13 560-88-22
Daily 12-16, 17-23; Rbls

Astoria, *European Cuisine*
Gertsena ul., 39 210-59-06
Daily 12-23:30; Rbls, $, CC; F-5

Austeria NB, *18th C. and modern Russian cuisine*
Petropavlovskaya Krepost
Ioannovskiy Ravelin 238-42-62
Daily 12-24; Rbls; Eng, Ger; Metro Gorkovskaya; F-7

Bagdad, *Uzbek (Central Asian) Cuisine*
Furshtadtskaya ul., 35 272-35-33
Daily 12-23; Rbls; Eng; Metro Chernyshevskaya; H-7

Balkany, *Russian Cuisine*
Nevskiy pr., 27.............................315-47-48
Daily 11-22; Rbls; Metro Nevskiy Prospect; F-6

Baltica, *Russian Cuisine*
Sennaya pl., 4/1 310-71-21
Daily 12-23; Rbls; Metro Sennaya Ploshchad; F-5

Baltiyskiy Vokzal Restaurant, *Russian Cuisine*
Obvodnogo kan. nab., 120 168-23-30
Daily 12-22; Rbls, $; Metro Baltiyskaya; E-3

Baskin-Robbins, *American Ice Cream*
See our ad below.
Nevskiy pr., 79.............................164-64-56
Hrs 10-21; Rbls; Metro Mayakovskaya; H-5

Bavariya at the Hotel Sovetskaya, *Warsteiner*
Lermontovskiy pr., 43 259-22-25
German Cuisine; Daily 12-3; E-3

Beer Garden
Nevskiy pr., 86.............................273-31-89
Summer open-air bar; $

Bella Liona, *European Cuisine*
Vladimirskiy pr., 9 113-16-70
Daily 13-24; Rbls; Metro Vladimirskaya; H-5

Belye Nochi, *Russian Cuisine*   **White Nights**
Voznesenskiy pr., 43 314-84-32
Daily 12-18, 19-23; Rbls; F-4

Bingo, *Spanish Cuisine, Opening Fall 1993*
Leninskiy pr., 127 254-55-82

THE BRASSERIE

Relaxed but Elegant Dining Featuring an International Menu & Winelist

At the GRAND HOTEL EUROPE
Nevskiy pr. / Mikhaylovskaya ul., 1/7

119-60-00

Ext. 6340
Daily 11-23, Sunday 15-23, $, English

The Brasserie - G-6

Brigantina, *Russian Cuisine*
Dvinskaya ul., 3............................259-08-15
Daily 12-23; Rbls, $; Eng, Ger

Bristol, *Cafe - Pizza, Snacks*
Nevskiy pr., 22.............................311-74-90
Daily 11-22; Eng, Bus 22; Metro Nevskiy Prospect; F-6

Cancan, *Cabaret Hall*
Izmailovskiy pr., 7 251-70-27
Restaurant, Musical Performances, Daily 20-24; $; F-3

Cafe-Automat, *Daily 10-15, 16-20; G-6*
Nevskiy pr., 45.............................319-97-36

Chayka, *Northern German Cuisine*
Griboedova kan. nab., 14................312-46-31
Fax...311-39-83
Daily 11-3; $, CC; Eng, Ger; Metro Nevskiy Prospect; G-6

CHOPSTICKS

WHERE EAST MEETS WEST EXCITING CANTONESE FOOD FROM CHINA

At The GRAND HOTEL EUROPE
Mikhaylovskaya ul., 1/7

119-60-00

Ext. 6391
Daily 12-15, 18-23, $, English

Chopsticks - G-6

DADDY'S STEAK ROOM

The Best Steaks in Saint Petersburg

Moskovskiy pr., 73 298-77-44

Fax.......................................298-95-52

Hrs: 12-23, $, CC, English & German & Finnish

Pizza Express , A Russian-Finnish Firm; F-2

Daugava at the Hotel Pribaltiyskaya, *Grill*
Korablestroiteley ul., 14 356-44-09
Daily 8-23:30; Rbls, $, CC; Eng, Ger; A-6

Demyanova Ukha

Russian Seafood Dishes

Kronverkskiy pr., 53.......................232-80-90

Demyanova Ukha   Demyan's Fish Chowder
Kronverkskiy pr., 53.......................232-80-90
Daily 12-22; Metro Gorkovskaya; F-8

Diamond Jack
Bubnovyy Valet

Outstanding Russian Cuisine

P.S., Lenina ul., 32

230-88-30

Diamond Jack
P.S., Lenina ul., 32 230-88-30
Metro Petrogradskaya; E-9
Diana
Sadovaya ul., 56 310-33-22
Daily 12-23; Rbls; Metro Sennaya Ploshchad; F-5
Diez Grill, *Whole Grilled Chicken - Take-out*
Kamennoostrovskiy pr., 16 232-42-55
Daily 10-21; Rbls; Metro Gorkovskaya; F-8

Dom Arkhitektora

The Place for Classic Russian Cuisine
In the beautiful turn-of-the century hall
A favorite of St. Petersburg
RESERVATIONS REQUIRED

Gertsena ul., 52......................311-45-57

Hrs: 12 - 23

DR. OETKER NEVSKIY 40

A Bar - Pub in the German Style

Essen, Trinken, Geniessen
Eating, Drinking and Enjoyment
Imported German Beers & Good Food

Nevskiy pr., 40 312-24-57

Fax 311-90-66

Hrs: 12 - 24; Rbls, $, English and German; G-6

Druzhba, *Russian Cuisine*
Nevskiy pr., 15..............................315-95-36
Daily 11-23; Rbls; Eng; F-5

DUKE KONSTANTIN

Outstanding Italian cuisine in the beautiful
Marble Palace.
Music and Folklore Ensemble
Call for reservations

Millionnaya ul., 5/1........................312-18-59
Hrs: 11-until the last customer leaves
Rubles, $, English, F-6

E THE RESTAURANT EUROPE

A Beautiful,
Old Restaurant with Interior
Design from the Beginning
of the Century
At The GRAND HOTEL EUROPE
Russian Specialties
Classic European Cuisine
Sunday Brunch

Mikhaylovskaya ul., 1/7

119-60-00
Ext. 6330
Daily for
Breakfast 7-10 & Dinner 18-23,
Sunday Brunch 12-15,
Closed Sunday Dinner

Reservations Required
Tie & Jacket Required

Galspe at Palanga, *Spanish Cuisine*
Leninskiy pr., 127 254-55-82
Daily 17-2; Rbls, $
Gino Ginelli, *Ice Cream*
Griboedova kan. nab., 14...............312-46-31
Daily 12-20; $, CC; Eng, Ger; Metro Nevskiy Prospect; G-6
Goluboy Delfin, *Russian Cuisine*   **Blue Delfin**
Sredneokhtinskiy pr., 44 227-21-35
Daily 12-16, 17-23; Rbls; K-8
Gridnitsa, *Russian and European Cuisine*
Griboedova kan. nab., 20................310-34-20
Daily 11-22; Rbls; Metro Nevskiy Prospect; G-6
Grill Bar, *Russian and European Cuisine*
Nalichnaya ul., 5 356-55-24
Daily 12-16, 17-23; Rbls; Metro Primorskaya; B-5
Grot, *Coffee*
Aleksandrovskiy Park 238-46-90
Daily 11-21; Rbls Metro Gorkovskaya; F-8
Hebei - *See ad on next page* F-9
Imereti, *Georgian cuisine, Daily 11-22; Rbls*
Bolshoy Sampsonievskiy pr., 104 245-50-03

Imperial in the Nevskij Palace,
Fine European Cuisine
Nevskiy pr., 57, ...113-15-18
Daily 7-11, 12-15, 19-23; $, CC; Metro Mayakovskaya; H-5

HEBEI CHINESE RESTAURANT
EXOTIC HEBEI PROVINCE CHINESE CUISINE
PREPARED BY EXPERIENCED CHINESE CHEFS
CHINESE MUSIC
P.S., BOLSHOY PR., 61
233-2046
METRO: PETROGRADSKAYA
Hrs: 12-23, Rbls, Eng.

Imperial Restaurant, *Russian Cuisine*
 Kamennoostrovskiy pr., 53 234-17-42
 Fax 234-32-96
 Daily 12-16, 17-24; Rbls; Eng; Metro Petrogradskaya; F-9
Iveriya
 Marata ul., 35 164-74-78
 Daily 11-22; Rbls; Metro Vladimirskaya; H-5
Izmaylov, *Russian Cuisine*
 6-ya Krasnoarmeyskaya ul., 22 292-68-38
 Package price meal & variety show; Daily 13-16, 20-23; Rbls; $; Eng, Ger, Fr; F-3
John Bull Pub   John Bull and Skol on Draught
 ****See our ad below****
 Nevskiy pr., 79 164-98-77
 Hrs 12-5, Rbls, $; Eng; Metro Ploshchad Vosstaniya; H-5
Kareliya, *A Variety of Cuisines*
 Marshala Tukhachevskogo ul., 27/2..... 226-35-49
 Daily 8-23:30; Rbls, $; Eng
Kingswood Trust
 Chapygina ul., 4 234-44-56
 Daily 11-22; Rbls, $, CC; Eng; F-10
Koelga, *A Variety of Cuisines*
 Narodnaya ul., 15......................... 263-18-93
 Daily 21-4; Rbls, $; Eng
Kolomna
 Griboedova kan. nab., 162 ....No ☎
 Daily 11-22; Rbls, $; Eng; E-4
Korean House, *Great Korean Food*
 Reki Fontanki nab., 20 275-72-03
 Daily 13-21; Rbls; Eng; H-6
Kurazh Grill Bar, *German Cuisine*
 Mokhovaya ul., 41 273-53-79
 Daily 0-24; Rbls; H-6

Landscrona in the Nevskij Palace
 Nevskiy pr., 57............................. 113-15-18
 European Cuisine; Daily 19-1; $, CC; Metro Mayakovskaya; H-5

Le Café - *See ad below*
 Nevskiy pr., 142............................ 271-28-11
 Fax 271-30-60
 Bakery Daily 9-20, Restaurant Daily 12-24, Rubles Cafe Daily 12-21; Metro Ploshchad Vosstaniya; I-5
Leningrad at the Hotel Pribaltiyskaya
 Korablestroiteley ul., 14   *European Cuisine*
 Reservations 356-44-09
 Daily 8-24; Rbls, $, CC; Eng, Ger; A-6
Lera, *Cafe - Russian Cuisine*
 Masterskaya ul., 4........................ 114-03-08
 Daily 10-21; Rbls, $, CC; E-4

Bahlsen
Gepfelegte Gastlichkeit
Hospitality at its best
Nevskiy Prospekt 142,
Tel. 271-28-11, 271-30-37
Fax 271-30-60
Le Café

THE LITERARY CAFE
Elegant Cafe-Restaurant
in the Old Tradition
Fine Russian Cuisine
Classical Music, Literary Readings
Poetry & Good Conversations
Nevskiy Prospekt, 18 312-60-57
.... 312-85-43
Daily 12-16:30, 19-23, Rubles
Metro Nevskiy Prospekt; F-6

Lukomore, *Russian Cuisine*
 Leytenanta Shmidta nab., 19 218-59-00
 Daily 12-23; Rbls; D-6
Metropol, *European Cuisine, Orchestra*
 Sadovaya ul., 22 310-18-45
 311-02-33
 Daily 12-24; Rbls, $; Eng, Ger; Metro Gostinyy Dvor; G-5

The Mezzanine Café
Meet at the Atrium Cafe
for a cup of coffee with fine pastry
or glass of wine
with a gourmet sandwich
At The GRAND HOTEL EUROPE
Nevskiy pr. / Mikhaylovskaya ul., 1/7
119-60-00
Daily 9-22   Ext. 6340 $, English

Moskovskiy Station Restaurant
 Nevskiy pr., 85 277-30-31
 Daily 12-23; Rbls; Metro Ploshchad Vosstaniya; I-5
Moskva, *Russian Cuisine*
 Aleksandra Nevskogo pl., 2 274-95-03
 274-00-28
 Daily 8-11, 12-23:30;
 Metro Ploshchad Alexandra Nevskogo; J-5
Na Fontanke, *Russian and European Cuisine*
 Reki Fontanki nab., 77 310-25-47
 Orchestra; Daily 13-17, 19:-23; Rbls, $; Eng; G-5

Nataly, *Russian Cuisine*
Kollontay ul., 30.............................. 580-81-39
Daily 19-2; Metro Prospekt Bolshevikov

Neptun, *Russian Cuisine*
Stachek pr., 25 a.............................. 186-61-10
Fax 223-64-51
Daily 12-24; Rbls, $, CC; Eng; Metro Narvskaya; D-1

Neva, *Russian and European Cuisine*
Nevskiy pr., 46.............................. 110-59-80
Mon-Sat 12-24; Rbls, $; Eng, Fr, Finn
Metro Nevskiy Prospect; G-6

Neva at the Hotel Pribaltiyskaya
Korablestroiteley ul., 14   *European Cuisine*
Reservations.................................. 356-44-09
Tue-Sun 8-24; Rbls, $, CC; Eng, Ger; A-6

Nevskie Zvezdy   **Cabaret Neva Stars**
Babushkina ul., 91 262-54-90
.... 262-25-37
Russian, European and Central Asian Cuisine
Daily; Eng, Ger, Fr

Nevskie Berega
Sverdlovskaya nab., 62 229-65-71
Daily 12-24; Rbls, $; Eng; K-7

J̶o̶h̶n̶ ̶B̶u̶l̶l̶®

The English Pub

Nevskiy pr., 79............164-98-77
Hrs: 12-5, Rbls & $; English
Metro: Ploshchad Vosstaniya

restaurant
NEVSKIY

Classic Russian Dining Experience
With first-class service

The Winter Garden for
Russian-European Cuisine

The St. Petersburg Gallery for
A Great Variety Show

The Nevskiy Room for
A Pleasant Lunch and Supper

Great for small intimate parties or
the largest banquets with orchestra

Nevskiy pr., 71 311-30-93

At Metro Mayakovskaya, H-5
Hrs: 12-23; Rubles; English

BASKIN-ROBBINS

Thirty-one flavors of ice cream
American Ice Cream

Nevskiy pr., 79 164-64-56
Hrs: 10-22; Rubles

 NEVSKY
MELODY

European & Russian Cuisine,
Disco, Bars, Roulette, Blackjack.
Sverdlovskaya nab., 62...... 222-51-80
Tel.................................... 227-15-96
Hrs: 12-18 for Rubles, 18-1 $ & Rbls, $ for drinks.,
Discotheque 21-1, CC, English, German, French

Nevskii 40 *See* DR. OETKER NEVSKIY 40

Nevsky Melody
Sverdlovskaya nab., 62 227-26-76
Tel./Fax 227-15-96
Daily 12-18 Rbls, 18-1 $, CC; Eng, Ger, Fr, Swed; K-7

NIGHT RESTAURANT VOSTOK
"NIGHT RESTAURANT ORIENT"
Indian & European Cuisine
One of the best kitchens in the city
In beautiful Primorskiy Park Pobedy
New variety shows & orchestra
Primorskiy Park Pobedy........... 235-59-84
Hrs: 12-4:30 am, $ & Rubles, English; B-9

OCEAN

Floating Restaurant
Traditional Russian Seafood Dishes
Russian Folk Music

Primorskiy pr., 31b 239-63-05
.... 239-28-77
Hrs: 12-24; Rbls & $; English, Finnish; D-11

Okhotnichiy Club   **The Hunter's Club**
Gorokhovaya ul., 45 315-36-94
Daily 12-24; Metro Sennaya Ploshchad; G-5

Okolitsa, *Russian Cuisine*
Primorskiy pr., 15 239-69-84
Daily 11-23; Rbls; E-11

Oktyabrskiy at Hotel Oktyabrskaya
Nevskiy pr., 118 277-67-38
European Cuisine; Daily 12-23:30; Rbls; Eng;
Metro Ploshchad Vosstaniya; I-5

Oreshek, *Russian Cuisine*
Tovarishcheskiy pr., 20/27 583-01-38
Daily 12-24; Rbls

Panorama at the Hotel Pribaltiyskaya
Korablestroiteley ul., 14 356-00-01
Russian and European Cuisine with a great view
Daily 8-23:30; Rbls, $, CC; Eng, Ger; A-6

Hotelship Peterhof ★★★★

Fine European Cuisine
Makarov Embankment near
the Tuchkov Bridge
Reservations.................................. 213-63-21
Hrs: 12-14 & 18-22, $ & CC, English, German; D-7

Petro Star, *A Variety of Cuisines*
Bolshaya Pushkarskaya ul., 30 232-40-47
Fax 232-10-80
Daily 13-24; Rbls; Metro Petrogradskaya; F-8
Petrogradskoe, *European & Russian Cuisine*
Bolshoy pr., P.S., 88 232-34-55
Daily 12-24; Metro Petrogradskaya; F-9
Petrovskiy, *Russian Cuisine*
Mytninskaya nab., 3, on the ship "Petrovskiy"
Daily 12-24; Rbls; $; Eng; F-7

PICCOLO
R E S T A U R A N T

Exciting kitchen in a friendly atmosphere.
Breakfast, lunch and dinner daily.

Hotel Olympia, Sea Glory Square,
199106 St.Petersburg, Russia.

Phone: .... 119 68 00.

Pietari
bar & restaurant

Great European Cuisine
with First Class Service
Live Pop Music & Dance, Moderately Priced

Moskovskiy pr., 222 293-18-09
Fax 293-04-08
Metro: Moskovskaya, Opposite Pulkovskaya Hotel
Hrs: 12-2; $; English

Pirosmani, *Georgian Cuisine*
Bolshoy pr., P.S. 14 235-64-56
Decorated with art by Georgian artist Pirosmani
Daily 12-23; Metro Petrogradskaya; F-9
Pizza-Express *(but no pizza) Daily 11-23; Rbls; E-3*
Rizhskiy pr., 48.............................. 251-17-24

PIZZA-HOUSE

Formerly Pizza Express
Quick Home Delivery
From 10 am to 12 p.m.

13 Varieties of Pizza, Steak,
Wiener Schnitzel, Pastas & Salads
Lapin Kulta Beer & European Wines

Visit our restaurant
at Podolskaya ul., 23

7 minutes drive from center city
Orders 292-26-66
Fax 292-10-39
Daily 10-24; $, CC; Eng, Finn; D-3

Pogrebok, *Russian Cuisine* **The Cellar**
Gogolya ul., 7................................ 315-53-71
Relax with pizza, grilled dishes & wine
Daily 11-22; Rbls; F-6
Polese, *Belorussian Cuisine*
Sredneokhtinskiy pr., 4 224-29-17
Daily 12:30-23:30; Rbls; Eng; K-7
Polyarnoe, *European Cuisine*
Nevskiy pr., 79.............................. 311-85-89
Daily 10-18, 19-22; Rbls; H-5
Prazdnik **Holiday**
Yuriya Gagarina pr., 14.................. 298-61-81
Fax 264-64-50
Daily 9-19; Rbls
Prestol Beer Hall, *Russian Cuisine*
Mayakovskogo ul., 2/94 272-27-90
Daily 10-21; Rbls; H-5
Primorskiy, *Russian and European Cuisine*
Bolshoy pr., P.S., 32 233-27-83
Fax... 230-99-13
Daily 12-24; Rbls; Eng; E-8
Restaurant at the River Terminal
(Opening Fall 1993) European Cuisine
Obukhovskoy Oborony pr., 195 262-02-39
Daily 12-23:30; Rbls
Restoranchik, *Russian Cuisine*
Bolsheokhtinskiy pr., 31 222-90-36
A quiet, intimate restaurant; Daily 12-24; Rbls; Eng; K-8
Rossiya, *Russian Cuisine*
Chernyshevskogo pl., 11 296-75-49
Daily 12-24; Rbls, $
Rus, *Russian and Chinese Cuisine*
Veteranov pr., 53 152-19-45
Daily 12-23:30; Rbls; F-5
Russkie Samovary, *Desserts, Good Bliny*
Sadovaya ul., 49 314-82-38
Daily 8-15:30, 16:30-20; Rbls; F-4
Ryabinushka, *A Variety of Cuisines*
Oskalenko ul., 11 239-40-80
Tue-Sun 11-18; Rbls, $; Eng
Sadko's - *See ad on next page*
Saigon-Neva, *Vietnamese*
Kazanskaya ul., 33 315-87-72
Mon, Wed-Sun 12:30-23; Rbls, $; Eng; F-5
Saint Petersburg Restaurant, *Russian Cuisine*
Griboedova kan. nab., 5 314-49-47
Fax... 314-35-86
Daily 12-1:30; $; Eng, Ger; G-6
Saint Petersburg, *European Cuisine*
at the Hotel St. Petersburg
Vyborgskaya nab., 5/2................... 542-91-21
Daily 7-11, 12-23; Rbls, $, CC; Eng; G-8

Russian & International Cuisine
Live Musical Entertainment
Reservations Recommended

Mikhaylovskaya ul. 1/7.
At The
Grand Hotel
Europe

SADKO'S *Bar & Restaurant*

119-60-00   Ext. 6390

S. English, Swedish

STARAYA DEREVNYA CAFE

A restaurant in the tradition of
the "Russian family salon"
of the 1900's.
Dine on classic Russian cuisine
surrounded by beautiful antiques
and art by contemporary painters
Gypsy & Russian songs on Fri & Sat
15 minutes from central St. Pb.
Well worth the trip

Ul. Savushkina, 72

Tel./Fax: 239-00-00
Daily 12 noon to evening. Eng. Ger. Sp: D-11

SCHWABSKI DOMIK

Come join us for
Schnitzel, Wurst and German Beer
The German Gaststätte-Pub in St. Pb
International & German Cooking
Great selection of European Wines
Music and Folklore Ensemble

Just ten minutes drive from center city

Krasnogvardeyskiy pr., 28/19......... 528-22-11
.... 528-88-80
Take the Metro to Metro Novocherkasskaya.
Daily 11-2; Rbls, $; Eng, Ger; K-5

Semenovskiy Traktir   Semenov's Pub
Vereyskaya ul., 4................................No Phone
Mon-Sat 11-20; Rbls
Sever, *A Variety of Cuisines*   **North**
Nevskiy pr., 46.............................. 110-55-03
Daily 12-24; Rbls; Eng, Ger, Fr; G-6
Shanghai, *Chinese Cuisine*
Sadovaya ul., 12/23 311-27-51
Fax 312-12-74
Daily 12-24; Rbls, $; Eng; G-6

SHLOTBURG

Fine dining in a cozy, intimate atmosphere
Old style "Merchant's Kitchen"
Reservations Required
Bolsheokhtinskiy pr., 41 227-29-24
Daily 12-24; Rbls & $, English; K-8

Solnyshko, *A Variety of Cuisines*   **Little Sun**
Dekabristov per., 8.......................... 350-29-38
Mon-Fri 16-20; Rbls
Sovetskiy, *Slavic Cuisine*
Lermontovskiy pr., 43/1 259-24-54
Daily 9-24; Rbls; E-3
Staraya Derevnya - *See ad below*
Stroganov - *See ad below*
Sudarynya, *Russian Cuisine*
Rubinshteyna ul., 28 312-63-80
Daily 12-23; Rbls; Eng, Ger, Fr; Metro Dostoevskaya; H-5

STROGANOV

Russian specialties & delicious Italian cooking
Traditional Russian music
Elegant Old Decor
Reservations Suggested

Nevskiy pr., 17............................... 312-18-59
Hrs: 11-until the last customer leaves
Rubles, $, English; F-6

Swedish Connections
                    In the Nevskij Palace Hotel
Nevskiy pr., 57 113-15-18
Swedish Cuisine
Daily 11-23; $, CC; H-5

TBILISI, *Classic Georgian Cuisine*
Sytninskaya ul., 10............ 232-93-91
Daily 12-23; F-8

Tête-à-Tête
A favorite of St. Pb., *European Cuisine*
Bolshoy pr., P.S., 65 232-75-48
Daily 13-17, 19-24; Rbls; Eng; F-9

A Thousand and One Nights -
See ad on next page
Troika - *See ad on next page*
Turku, *European Cuisine*
Pobedy pl., 1.................................. 264-57-16
Daily 7-16, 17-23:30; Rbls, $, CC; Eng, Ger
U Kazanskogo, *Russian Cuisine*
Nevskiy pr., 26.............................. 314-27-45
Daily 11-22; Rbls; G-6
U Moskovskikh Vorot, *Russian Cuisine*
Moskovskiy pr., 126....................... 298-55-58
Daily 11:30-23; Rbls; F-1
Universal
Nevskiy pr., 106............................. 279-33-50
Daily 12-23:30; Metro Ploshchad Vosstaniya; I-5

☪ A Thousand and One Nights

A night restaurant in the heart of St. Petersburg near the Hermitage.

Elegant Central Asian Decor

Private seating available for up to 14 people.

Uzbek & European Cuisine

Variety Show and Late Night Striptease

Millionnaya ul., 21/6

Reservations 312-22-65

Hrs: 19-5, English; F-6

A.O. TROIKA

A LUXURIOUS RUSSIAN STYLE RESTAURANT

TROIKA

From Salmon & Chicken a la Kiev to Troika Roulade, Champagne & Caviar

• • • • •

The International-Russian Variety Show
Chorus Line Song, Dance & Variety
" Moulin Rouge of Saint Petersburg"
A Great Show

• • • • •

Great Vodkas & European Wine Cellar

Zagorodnyy pr., 27 113-53-43

Hrs: 19-24, $ & Rbls, English; G-5
A Russian-Swiss Company

• • • • •

"Restaurant on Fontanka"
Nab. Reki Fontanki, 77 310-25-47

U Petrovicha - *See ad below*
U Prichala, *Central Asian Cuisine, Daily 12-24; B-5*
  Bolshoy pr., V.O., 91 217-44-28
Urartu, *Caucasian cuisine, Daily 12-23; Rbls*
  Rudneva ul., 25............................... 558-69-19
U Waltera, *European Cuisine*
  Nalichnaya ul., 51 350-91-13
  Daily 13-24; Rbls; Metro Primorskaya; B-7

U Petrovicha

An Intimate 18th Century
Merchant-Style Restaurant
Authentic Russian Cuisine
Specially Prepared Game, Smoked Eel & Ham
Light dinner music and dancing
Sredneokhtinskiy pr., 44 227-21-35
Hrs: 12-17, 18-24; Rbls, English, K-8

Vardziya, *Central Asian Cuisine, Shish Kabobs*
  Bolshaya Podyacheskaya ul., 33.....310-11-41
  Daily 11-22; Rbls; F-4
Varshavskiy Vokzal Restaurant
  Obvodnogo kan. nab., 118 259-45-33
  (To be closed for repair) *Daily 10-23; Rbls;* F-3
Venetsiya, *Italian Cuisine*   **Venice**
  Korablestroiteley ul., 21.................. 352-14-32
  Pizza to-go; Daily 12-24; Rbls, $, CC; Eng, Ital; A-7
Veronika, *Russian Cuisine, Daily 12-24; Rbls;* I-5
  Nevskiy pr., 87 279-67-33
Viktoriya, *Russian Cuisine*   **Victoria**
  Kamennoostrovskiy pr., 24............. 232-51-30
  Daily 12-16, 18-23; Rbls; Eng; F-8
Vyborgskiy, *Russian Cuisine, Daily 7-24; Rbls;* F-11
  Torzhkovskaya ul., 3 246-91-19
  246-91-36

RESTAURANT
"Warsteiner Forum"

Newski 120
277-29-14

Warsteiner Forum, *German Bierstube*
  Nevskiy pr., 120 277-29-14
  Daily 12-2; Metro Ploshchad Vosstaniya; I-5

The Winter Garden

in The LDM Complex

*A Beautiful Winter Garden
in a Tropical Setting
Overlooking Malaya Nevka*

P.S., Professora Popova ul., 47

.... 234-44-94

.... 234-97-93

Fax 234-98-18

Hrs: 8-24, Rbls., English; E-9

Zastole, *Russian Cuisine*
  Nevskiy pr., 74 272-90-17
  Daily 12-24; Rbls; Eng, Ger; H-5
Zerkalny Restaurant   Mirror Restaurant
  See ad on next page
  Daily 12-23; Rbls, $, CC; Eng; G-8
Zhemchuzhina   Pearl Oyster
  Shkiperskiy protok, 2 355-20-63
  Azerbaijani and European Cuisine
  Daily 11-23; Rbls, $

Zerkalny Restaurant
HOTEL
Sankt Petersburg
Come Enjoy Authentic Russian Cuisine
Together with Russian Romance Folksong
Nab. Vyborgskaya, 5
542-91-55
Hrs: 12-23, $, Ruhles, CC, English

Zimniy Sad, *European Cuisine* **Winter Garden**
in the Astoria Hotel
Gertsena ul., 39 210-59-06
Daily 12-23; Rbls, $; Eng; F-5
Zurbagan, *A Variety of Cuisines*
Ordinarnaya ul., 21 235-09-49
Daily 12-22; Rbls; Tram 17; Metro Petrogradskaya; F-9

IN PETERHOF *(PETRODVORETS)*

RESTAURANT PETERHOF
A Fine Restaurant in Petrodvorets
For Lunch and Dinner
In a small congenial restaurant
International and Russian cuisine from steak &
french fries to bliny & caviar
German beers & fine European wines

At the entrance to the lower Park
in the Peterhof - Petrodvorets

427-90-96 & 314-49-47

Daily 12-2, $ & Rbls, German & English

IN PUSHKIN *(TSARSKOE SELO)*

Admiralteystvo Restaurant
Ekaterinenskiy park 465-35-49
Daily 12-20; Rbls, $; Eng
Hermitage Restaurant
Kominterna ul., 27 476-62-55
Daily 11-22; Rbls, $; Eng

VITYAZ

A classic Russian dining experience
with first class service
Russian folk music

Tsarskoe Selo, Moskovskaya ul., 20

466-43-18

Hrs: 11-until the last customer leaves
Rubles, $, English

IN SESTRORETSK

Cafe U Ozera, *Russian and Korean Cuisine*
Cafe by the Lake
Primorskoe shosse, 352, Sestroretsk
☎ 237-48-17
.... 237-38-38
Daily 12-23; Rbls

OLGINO

Olgino at the Motel Olgino, *A Variety of Cuisines*
Primorskoe shosse , Olgino, 18 km
☎ 238-36-74
Daily 8-23, 24-4; Rbls, $; Eng, Ger, Finn

☎ RESTROOMS
ТУАЛЕТЫ
TOILETTEN
TOILETTES
TOALETTER
VESSAT

*Restrooms in Russia often have no toilet
paper or use recycled newspaper. This is
especially true on trains & in public places.
Carry a couple of small packs of tissues
(Kleenex) in your purse or bag.*

*These restrooms are "pay" toilets which
should be cleaner with amenities. As of
June, 1993, they cost about 10 rubles.*

*Restrooms can be identified by the
following signs: WC, or "Туалет" (Tualet).
Men by "M" and women by "Ж".*

- ◆ Dinamo pr. & Petrogradskaya ul. (corner) D-9
- ◆ Dobrolyubova ul., in the garden E-7
- ◆ Dumskaya ul., 13 G-5
- ◆ Gogolya ul., 9 F-6
- ◆ Kirovskiy pr., 37b F-9
- ◆◆ Malaya Konyushennaya ul., 12 G-6
- ◆ Marata ul., 4 H-5
- ◆ Moskovskiy pr., 205
- ◆ Muchnoy per., 9 G-5
- ◆◆◆ Nab. Reki Moyki, 37 G-6
- ◆◆◆ Nab. Petrogradskaya, 10 G-8
- ◆ Nekrasova ul., 21 H-6
- ◆◆ Nevskiy pr., 20, 39, 50/13 F-6, G-6, H-5
- ◆ Plekhanova ul., 6 G-5
- ◆◆ Rubinshteyna ul., 3 H-5
- ◆ Sadovaya ul., 69 E-4
- ◆ Saltykova-Shchedrina ul., 2 H-7
- ◆ Stachek pr., 9 D-2
- ◆◆ Vosstaniya ul., 1 I-5

☎ RIVER BOAT EXCURSIONS
See BOAT EXCURSIONS

☎ RIVER TERMINALS
ВОКЗАЛЫ, РЕЧНЫЕ
FLUSSHÄFEN
GARE FLUVIALE
FLODTERMINALER
JOKITERMINAALIT

See also SHIP TERMINAL *and* BOAT EXCURSIONS

RIVER PASSENGER TERMINAL
Rechnoy passazhirskiy vokzal
Речной пассажирский вокзал
*Departure for trips to Moscow and on to
the Black Sea leave from this terminal.*
Obukhovskoy Oborony pr., 195 262-02-39
Information 262-13-18
*In Southeast St. Pb. on left bank of Neva River at
Metro Proletarskaya, Bus 11; Daily 9-21; Rbls; Eng*

RIVER CARGO PORTS

Vasileostrovskiy Cargo River Port
Vasileostrovskiy Gruzovoy Port
Василеостровский грузовой порт
Kima pr., 19 350-00-20
*For inland river transport on barges; located near to
Metro Primorskaya;* B-8

Nevskiy Cargo River Port
Nevskiy Gruzovoy Port
Невский грузовой порт
Oktyabrskaya nab., 40 588-86-96
*This port is for inland river shipping on barges and is
located in Southeast St. Pb. on the right bank of the
Neva not far from the Volodarskiy Most.
Metro Ulitsa Dybenko, then Bus.*

Pristan Ermitazh   **Hermitage**
Dvortsovaya nab. 311-95-06
Hydrofoil to Peterhof and tours on Neva Rbls, $; F-6

Pristan U Tuchkova Mosta
Tuchkov Most Dock 236-33-17
Hydrofoil to Kronshtadt, Near the Hotelship Peterhof

Pristan Kronshtadt
At Kronshtadt.................................236-33-17
....236-19-56
Daily 0-24; Rbls; D-7

☎ ROCK/POP MUSIC CLUBS
РОК-/ПОП-КЛУБЫ
ROCK-/POPMUSIK-CLUBS
ROCK/POP MUSIC CLUBS
ROCK/POPMUSIKKLUBBAR
ROCK/POPMUSIIKKI KLUBIT

See also JAZZ CLUBS *and* CONCERT HALLS
*Rock music is very popular and is played
in large stadiums and little clubs alike.
Large rock concerts are advertised in street
posters, in newspapers & on radio and are
held in the following* CONCERT HALLS: *Sports
and Concert Complex (SKK), Yubileynyy
Sport Palace , LDM Palace of Youth,
October Concert Hall.*

Rock-Club
Rubinshteyna ul., 13 312-34-83
Fax 314-96-29
Mon-Sat 12-20; Eng

Rock Around The Clock
*At the Saturn movie theater. Live bands & festive
crowds in a small club atmosphere.*
Sadovaya ul., 27 310-02-37
Metro Sennaya Ploshchad

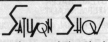

*Rock Around The Clock
Members Club*

Sadovaya ul., 27 310-02-37

Tam Tam Club, *Rock & punk, soiled & seedy.*
Malyy pr. & 16-ya Liniya, V.O.................No ☎

Indie Club, *Bar & occasional live music*
Obukhovskoy Oborony pr., 223.............No ☎

☎ ROWING CLUBS
ГРЕБНЫЕ КЛУБЫ
RUDERVEREINE
CANOTAGE, CLUBS DE
RODDKLUBBAR
MELONTASEURAT

Energiya Rowing Club, *Mon-Fri 10-21*
Deputatskaya ul., 15......................235-15-44
Rowing School, *Daily 9-20; Rbls*
Reki Bolshoy Nevki nab., 24 234-04-66
Spartak Rowing Club, *Mon-Fri 9-18; Rbls*
Reki Bolshoy Nevki nab., 24 234-36-22

☎ RUGS & CARPETS
КОВРЫ И ДОРОЖКИ
TEPPICHE UND LÄUFER
TAPIS
MATTOR
MATOT

Rugs are also found in DEPARTMENT STORES
Crazy Bert, *Imported American, Finnish and Dutch
carpets and floor coverings*
Kultury pr., 26, bldg. 1 559-30-44
Daily 11-20; Rbls
Kovry
Pogranichnika Garkavogo ul., 4 144-82-83
*Mon-Sat 10-14, 15-19; Rbls; Eng
Bus 130; Metro Prospekt Veteranov*
Prado, *Mon-Sat 10-14, 15-19; Rbls, $; Eng*
Suvorovskiy pr., 2 277-43-19
Fax...277-00-13
Skif, *Daily 10-14, 15-19; Rbls*
Sadovaya ul., 42 310-13-15

☎ RUSSIAN LANGUAGE COURSES

See LANGUAGE COURSES

☎ SAFETY
БЕЗОПАСНОСТЬ
SICHERHEIT TIPS FÜR
PERSÖNLICHE
SECURITE PERSONNELLE
SÄKERHET
TURVALLISUUS

*As any large city, there are crime and
safety problems here. St. Petersburg is
safe and most people are honest, helpful,
and eager to be friends. Russians take a
number of precautions against crime, and
you should too. All foreigners are thought
to be rich. Thus, they are sometimes sin-
gled out. Be on guard, act defensively.
Here are some reminders and recommendations for St. Petersburg.*

CRIME PREVENTION HERE AND EVERYWHERE

**Money and documents must be put
away, best inside** of your clothing *and your
bag zipped and over your shoulder. Be
aware.*

Carry a pocket flashlight. *Many entrance
halls and stairways have no lights. And in
the winter the nights are long and dark.*

Carry a small can of "Mace", "Pepper Shield", or similar product and know how to use it. If you feel threatened, take it out and let it be seen. This is an effective deterrent. And don't hesitate to use it.

Never get into a taxi carrying anyone other than the driver. Look at the driver and condition of the car. When in doubt, wave the taxi on. Taxis ordered by phone or through organized services at hotels will be more expensive but more reliable. Many "official state taxis", once the benchmark of safety have been privatized & are no longer subject to official supervision on rates or safety. See TAXIS.

Never give your home address to a stranger. The Russians never do; they often don't even let the taxi driver know exacty where they live. Foreigners are even better targets for thieves. Exchange phone numbers & business addresses.

Don't show large amounts of money, especially hard currency. For small purchases, carry some rubles in one pocket and some dollars in another. Carry your documents and large sums of money separately inside your clothing in a money belt or pouch hung around your neck.

Changing Money. Safest at currency exchange offices. Stay away from Gostinyy Dvor and Apraksin Dvor. On the street, never change money alone. See CURRENCY EXCHANGE.

Fraud. Most fraud occurs when changing money and buying "bargains" on the street.

Beware. Be specially alert around railroad, metro, and bus stations, markets, and Apraksin Dvor. On overnight trains take a few simple precautions. See RAIL TRAVEL.

CRIME PROBLEMS

Thieves, pickpockets and muggers. They come in all sizes and ages. Be especially careful of thieves and pickpockets from elderly well dressed gentlemen and pretty prostitutes to scruffy drunks, pushy money changers, and swarms of young children.

Street urchins. Like in many European cities, roving gangs of children are perhaps the most visible and the most aggressive thieves. Much to the dismay of the gypsy community, many are gypsy children. So, beware of gangs of dirty, ill dressed, poor-looking children (under 14 because they can not be arrested). Don't be sympathetic about their condition. You may actually be in imminent danger of being robbed.

These gangs work by swarming around you like bees, begging, even grabbing your legs or arms and distracting you. Then, in a flash they cut your purse from around your neck, grab your parcels, unzip your backpack, rip off headphones, and knock you to the ground to take what they want.

What to do. Stay with or go over to other people, go into a shop. Don't look at them, move away quickly. Don't be distracted, by begging. If you have a mace or pepper shield canister, take it out and let them see it. Use it if necessary. If they come near you, threaten to hit them and loudly shout "von" or "militia". And if a child (or even woman beggar) actually comes close to you, act aggressively at once. From our experience we know that they will not hesitate to rob you in broad daylight.

PERSONAL SAFETY AND HEALTH

Unmarked and unprotected street hazards. Be careful when walking on sidewalks and streets for open stairwells, deep holes, iron bars sticking out from walls and other hazards. Safety laws are not enforced.

Don't jaywalk. Cross busy streets only at the light or use the underpass (perekhod, переход) denoted by a blue and white sign with a picture of a person walking down a stairway. Russians observe these rules and with good cause.

Poor enforcement of sanitary standards. Food handling and sanitation standards are not enforced. While refrigeration, food handling and food preservation is improving, it is still primitive in many shops and eating establishments which may or may not have hot water. Water is a particular problem in St. Petersburg. Russians don't drink the water, you shouldn't either. See WATER.

Medical problems. Traveler's requiring periodic injections should bring there own syringes needles and prescriptions. Check that your immunizations are current especially DPT. Go to medical care facilities using disposable products.

☎ **SAILING**

See YACHT CLUBS

☎ **SAINT PETERSBURG**

See ST. PETERSBURG

☎ **SAUNAS**
САУНЫ
SAUNA UND FITNESSCENTER
SAUNAS
BASTU/BAD
SAUNAT, SUOMALAINEN

See also HEALTH CLUBS, BATHS, *and* SWIMMING

Home ☐ Center

Sauna in Your Home

Install a sauna in your own home or dacha
Complete from Finland

Located in S.E. St. Pb., minutes from city center
Slavy pr., 30.................................261-15-50
....261-04-02
Fax...260-15-81

Daily 10-20; $, FIM, DM, Rbls; Eng, Finn, Ger
Metro Moskovskaya, then Bus 31, 114, T-bus 29

SAUNAS IN HOTELS

Hotel Kareliya
  Marshala Tukhachevskogo ul., 27, bldg. 2
  ☎ 226-35-17
Daily 13-1; Rbls; Eng, Finn
Hotel Pribaltiyskaya
  Korablestroiteley ul., 14 356-17-92
Tue-Sun 9-13, 14:30-22; $; Eng, Finn
Hotel Pulkovskaya
  Pobedy pl., 1 264-51-16
  Fax 264-63-96
Tue-Sun 9-22:30; Rbls, $, CC; Eng, Ger, Fr, Finn, Ital
Hotel Saint Petersburg
  Vyborgskaya nab., 5/2 542-37-98
Daily 12-21:30; Rbls, $
Sportserviceclub at the Hotel Rossiya
  Chernyshevskogo pl., 11, 2nd floor...... 296-31-44
Daily 22-5; Rbls, $; Eng
World Class at the Grand Hotel Europe
  Mikhaylovskaya ul., 1/7 113-80-66
Daily 7-22; $; Eng
World Class at the Hotel Astoria
  Gertsena ul., 39 311-42-06
  Sauna 210-58-69

OTHER SAUNAS

Bast Sports Center
  Raevskogo pr., 16........................... 552-39-36
Tennis Courts, Sports Halls, Sauna. Daily 8-23; Rbls;
Eng, Ger; Bus 93, Metro Politekhnicheskaya
Bathhouse No. 41
  Fonarnyy per., 1............................. 312-31-51
Tue-Sun 8-21; Rbls; Eng
Intursport
  Moiseenko ul., 22/17 271-36-21
  Fax 271-41-88
Daily 8-23; Rbls; Eng
Sauna-Lux
  Karbysheva ul., 29 a 550-09-85
Mon-Wed, Fri-Sun 9-21; Rbls, $

☎ SCHOOLS/PUBLIC, PRIVATE
ШКОЛЫ, ГОСУДАРСТВЕННЫЕ
И ЧАСТНЫЕ
SCHULEN, STAATLICHE UND
PRIVATE
ECOLES D'ETAT ET PRIVEES
SKOLOR, ALLMÄNNA OCH
PRIVATA
KOULUT, YKSITYISET JA
JULKISET

See also MUSIC *and* ART SCHOOLS

There are about 730 primary schools
(grades 1-3), lower middle schools (grades
4-9) and middle schools (equal to secondary
school or high school grades 10-11) in St.
Petersburg. Some children go to private or
state kindergartens (Detskiy sad, Детский
сад) and enter primary school when they
are six or seven years old. Education
usually lasts 9 to 11 years.

Specialized schools Some schools
specialize in certain areas such as mathematics, physics, foreign languages and
humanities. These elite schools require a
special exam and interview and are being
renamed as "gymnasiums", "colleges" or

"lyceums". There are also specialized
music and art schools which selected
children attend after their regular school
day. See MUSIC AND ART SCHOOLS.

The School Year There are four quarters
in the school year: the first from September
1st to November 1st followed by one week
vacation; the second from November 10th
to the end of December followed by a two-
week New Year vacation; the third term
from mid January to mid March is followed
by a one week vacation. The spring term
starts in late March and ends May 31
followed by a three month summer
vacation.

The following committee is responsible
for the school system in St. Petersburg:

Committee on People's Education
Komitet po Narodnomu Obrazovaniyu
  Antonenko per., 8.......................... 319-91-79
  319-91-40

While schools are listed in Ves Sankt
Peterburg-93, a good description of state
and private, primary and secondary schools
is found in (in Russian) "St. Petersburg for
Children, Teenagers and Parents" 1992
(Санкт-Петербург для детей подростков и
родителей) published by IMA-press, 1992.

STATE SCHOOLS

German National School "Peterschule"
  Zanevskiy pr., 53, bldg. 2 221-79-76
Gymnasia No. 30
  Shevchenko ul., 23, bldg. 2 217-21-57
Mathematics, Physics, English, French
Gymnasia No. 209, *Humanities Lyceum*
  Vosstaniya pl., 8 279-04-73
English, Arts, Journalism. Mon-Fri 9-15; Eng, Ger, Fr
Gymnasia No. 610
  Krasnogo Kursanta ul., 6/9 235-13-02
Latin, Ancient Greek, English, German, World Literature
Jewish Gymnasia "Migdalyor"
  Reki Fontanki nab., 112.................. 292-76-01
Hebrew, Jewish History and Culture
Physics and Mathematics Lyceum
  Saltykova-Shchedrina ul., 8 a 272-96-68
Mon-Sat 9-18; Eng, Ger, Fr
Russian Museum Gymnasia
Gimnaziya pri Russkom Muzee
  Mikhaylovskaya pl., 3..................... 311-46-44
Mythology, Art History, Latin

PRIVATE SCHOOLS

**Anglo-American School of Moscow
St. Petersburg**
*St. Petersburg branch for English-speaking foreigners.
Curriculum compatible with British and American schools*
  Furshtatskaya ul., 15...................... 275-17-01
Aquilon
  Konnogvardeyskiy blvd., 4, entr. 7
  ☎ 311-29-09
  Fax... 315-20-03
Mon-Fri 9-18; Rbls
Kilchichakov Governesses' School
Shkola Guvernerov Kilchichakova
  Bolshevikov pr., 2, entr. 7 589-17-29
*Training for governesses and nannies
Foreign languages, Arts, Etiquette*

Krasnoselskiy Business Lyceum
Marshala Zhukova ul., 43/2 143-87-79
Business management, Foreign languages
Mon-Fri 9-18; Rbls; Eng, Ger, Fr
Vzmakh Business School
Dmitrovskiy per., 18 311-80-19
Foreign languages, Business management
Mon-Sat 10-18; Rbls; Eng, Fr; Metro Dostoevskaya

☎ SEA TERMINALS

See SHIP TERMINALS, FERRIES *and* RIVER
TERMINALS

☎ SEATING PLANS
ПЛАН МЕСТ В ТЕАТРЕ
THEATERPLATZANORDNUNG
PLAN DE THEATRE
KARTA ÖVER SITTPLATSER,
TEATER
TEATTEREIDEN
ISTUMAPAIKKAJÄRJESTYKSET

See THEATER SEATING PLANS *on pages* 336-341

☎ SECOND HAND SHOPS

See ANTIQUES, ANTIQUITARIAN SHOPS,
COMMISSION STORES,
and COMMERCIAL STORES

☎ SECRETARIAL SERVICES
СЕКРЕТАРСКИЕ РАБОТЫ
BÜRODIENSTLEISTUNGEN
SECRETARIAT, SERVICE
SEKRETERARSERVICE
SIHTEERIPALVELUT

See also TEMPORARY HELP

Ekos
13-ya Liniya, 12, apt. 1 355-91-51
Mon-Fri 11-17; Rbls, $; Eng, Ger, Fr

Optimum
Nekrasova ul., 15 299-68-34
Mon-Fri 10-15, 16-18; Rbls; Eng, Ger, Fr

Personnel Corps
Nevskiy pr., 104 275-83-23
.... 275-45-86
Fax 275-83-23

Stenography and Typewriting
Ligovskiy pr., 63/65 164-77-74
Mon-Fri 9:30-17:30; Rbls; Metro Ploshchad Vosstaniya
Typewriting Works, *Daily 9-20; Rbls; T-bus 3*
Liteynyy pr., 28 272-40-63

☎ SECURITY
СИСТЕМЫ БЕЗОПАСНОСТИ
SICHERHEIT(SYSTEME)
SECURITE
SÄKERHET
TURVALLISUUS

See also LOCKSMITHS, ALARM SYSTEMS, *and*
SECURITY DEVICES

These firms provide a variety of security
services from armed bodyguards and

armored transport to installation of fire
alarm systems, metal doors, and secure
warehouses.
Adamas Service
Shvetsova ul., 36 252-14-40
Mon-Fri 8-19; Rbls, $; Eng; Metro Narvskaya

Alex Security Ltd.

Fully Licensed Security Service
Offices, Industries, Banks & Hotels
Transport & Technical Systems Security
Licensed Training School
Branches and Subsidiaries
Throughout Russia

Security Doesn't Cost...It Pays

St. Petersburg .... (812) 352-59-42
Moscow .... (095) 318-03-11
Fax .... (095) 318-50-01

Bikar
Mytninskaya ul., 1 274-42-91
Mon-Fri 9-18; Rbls; Eng
T-bus 1; Metro Ploshchad Vosstaniya
Business Security
Shkapina ul., 4 252-45-22
Confident, *Information Security*
Smolnyy , entr. 4, rm. 410 278-13-39
Fax 278-10-92
Mon-Fri 9-18; Rbls

Contact
Moskovskiy pr., 182 294-04-75
Fax 298-86-35
Mon-Fri 9-17; Rbls; Eng; Tram 15; Metro Elektrosila

CREDO
LOKTIONOV
DETECTIVE AGENCY

Private Investigations
Protection of Individuals and Property

196070, St. Petersburg, P.O. Box 231
Tel./Fax: 293-68-80

EVS, *Security systems*
Krasnogvardeyskiy pr., 60 223-58-38
Fax 221-14-58
Mon-Fri 9-18; Rbls, $; Eng
Express-Service
Lenina ul., 11 232-93-55
Mon-Fri 10-18; Rbls, $; Eng
Institute of Modern Technology
Moskovskiy pr., 75 294-33-71
Fax 294-33-62
Security Systems; Mon-Sat 10-18; Rbl, $; Eng, Finn

Leader
Professora Popova ul., 21 232-56-63
Mon-Fri 11-15; Rbls; Eng
Metra Engineering, *ABLOY locks*
Bolshoy Sampsonievskiy pr., 31 542-06-59
Fax 542-68-42
Mon-Fri 9-17; Rbls; Eng
Neva, *Mon-Fri 9-18; Rbls*
Svechnoy per., 9............................ 112-30-19
Fax 164-94-94
RDW
Kuybysheva ul., 21........................ 232-04-02
Rbls, $; Eng, Ger, Fr
SBS-Neva
Svechnoy per., 9............................ 112-30-19
Fax 164-94-94
Mon-Fri 10-17; Rbls, $; Eng
Sredstva Bezopasnosti
Security Items Store
Rubinshteyna ul., 9........................ 315-47-74
Fax 311-12-89
Metro Vladimirskaya
Strazha   **Guard**
5-ya Sovetskaya ul., 28 274-38-48
Mon-Fri 10-18; Rbls
Zashchita   **Defense**
Dobrolyubova pr., 13 233-82-62
Mon-Fri 9-18; Rbls, $

☎ SHIP TERMINALS & PORTS
МОРСКИЕ ВОКЗАЛЫ
SCHIFFDOCKS
GARES MARITIMES
HAMNTERMINALER, FARTYG
LAIVATERMINAALIT

See also FERRIES AND CRUISES
and RIVER TERMINALS

Association of Maritime Trade Ports
Gapsalskaya ul., 4.......................... 186-68-21
.... 114-92-06
Fax 251-14-92
Mon-Fri 8:30-17; Rbls, $; Eng, Fr

Passenger Ocean Ship Terminal
Morskoy Passazhirskiy Vokzal
Морской пассажирский вокзал
See FERRIES AND CRUISE SHIPS for *schedule.*

The Passenger Ocean Ship Terminal is on the Gulf of Finland near the end of Bolshoy prospect on Vasilevskiy Island. The port is the home of the Baltic Line, and has The Hotel Morskaya with a restaurant and bar (temporarily closed for renovation), kiosks, and the cruise ship and ferry terminal. There are no nearby metros, so take a taxi or Bus Э-30 from Metro Vasileostrovskaya.

Morskoy Slavy pl. 1
Information about terminal............. 355-13-10
.... 355-13-88
Mon-Fri 9-21, Rbls, $, Eng, Swed, Ger, Fin

Ocean Timber Trade Port
Morskoy Lesotorgovyy Port
Морской лесоторговый порт
Gladkiy ostrov, 1 252-14-89
Located on Gladkiy Island southwest of the city center. Handles all timber trade. No close transport, B-1

Ocean Cargo Port   **Morskoy Torgovyy Port**
Морской торговый порт
Mezhevoy kanal, 5 251-02-38
.... 259-81-70
Located southwest of city center. General cargo port. Metro Baltiyskaya, then take Bus 22; C-3

Association of Russian Commercial Sea Ports
Gapsalskaya ul., 4 186-68-22

☎ SHIPPING
МОРСКАЯ ДОСТАВКА
SEETRANSPORTE
TRANSPORT MARITIME
BÅTSPEDITION
MERIKULJETUKSET

See also TRUCKING, AIR CARGO, SHIPPING
AGENTS, EXPRESS MAIL/PARCELS SERVICE

This listing only includes companies with ships or that handle cargo to and from ships. To book passenger tickets, see FERRIES AND CRUISE SHIPS.

For land transportation see FREIGHT
FORWARDERS AND EXPEDITERS, TRUCKING, *and*
MOVING.

Alers-Line
Goncharnaya ul., 24, rm. 46.......... 277-53-16
Fax.. 277-30-00
Mon-Fri 9:30-18; $; Eng, Ger, Fr
Baltic Shipping Company
Mezhevoy kan. nab., 5.................... 251-07-42
Fax.. 186-85-44
Mon-Fri 8:30-17; $; Eng

INFLOT St. Petersburg Ltd.
The most complete in-port service,
liner, tramp agency
Over 50 years experience
in the port of Saint Petersburg

Gapsalskaya ul., 10 251-73-26
Director: 251-12-38
Fax: .... (812) 186-15-11
Telex: .... 121505 INF SU

Kron-Flot
Lomonosov, Volodarskogo ul., 1......422-46-04
MAERSK Private Limited
Tambovskaya ul., 12 a 112-82-68

(((⫸ MCT EUROPE

HANDLING & DELIVERY OF CARGOES
VIA PORT OF ST. PETERSBURG
CONTAINER STORAGE IN ST. PB.

MEZHEVOY KANAL, 5....... 251-86-62
FAX .... (812) 251-84-72
TELEX..................... 121691 MCT SU
Mon-Sat 9-18; $; Eng, Ger, Fr

North-Western River Shipping Company
Gertsena ul., 37 312-01-45
Fax 312-03-59
Representative for cargo shipping on inland rivers
Daily 8:30-17:30; Rbls, $; Eng

ROMAR INTERNATIONAL INC.
SHIPPING & TRADING COMPANY
Baltic, North, Black &
Mediterranean Sea Operations
Import & Export to Europe, Israel and China
197042 St. Petersburg, Elagin Ostrov, 10
....239-18-41
....239-18-51
Fax...239-14-71

Russian Dream Company
Reki Fontanki nab., 92, bldg. 2 312-34-23
Fax 113-25-55
Mon-Sat 10-18; Rbls, $; Eng
Shipping Agency
Please call 520-07-89
Daily 0-24; Rbls, $; Eng
The Sea Shipping Company
Kazanskaya ul., 17 314-06-59
Fax 312-33-59
The first private shipping company in Russia
Mon-Fri 9-17; Rbls; Eng

Sovavto - St. Petersburg
Shipping Company
Vitebskiy pr., 3 298-55-56
....298-46-50
Fax 298-77-60
Mon-Fri 8:30-17; Rbls; Eng, Ger

Sovmortrans, *Sealand Representative*
See ad in Freight Forwarders
Dvinskaya ul., 8, bldg. 2 252-75-81
....259-89-94
Fax 114-41-37
Mon-Fri 8:30-17; Rbls, $; Eng, Ger, Fr, Sp

UNIREM SHIPPING

Cargo Shipping
to Finland, Baltic States & Iran

Konnogvardeyskiy blvd, 1
Tel.: 311-79-93 Fax: 312-79-58

☎ **SHIPPING AGENTS,**
FREIGHT FORWARDERS
МОРСКИЕ АГЕНТСТВА,
ДОСТАВКА
SEESPEDITIONEN
AGENTS MARITIMES,
EXPEDITEURS
HAMN SPEDITÖRER, EXPEDITÖR
LAIVAMEKLARIT JA KULJETUKSET

See FREIGHT FORWARDERS AND EXPEDITERS

All firms that arrange for the shipping of
packages and freight by a variety of

transportation methods such as by truck,
air, rail, and ship are listed under the
category FREIGHT FORWARDERS & EXPEDITERS.

All firms that provide their own trucking
services are listed under TRUCKING, *all firms*
that specialize in shipping freight by ship
are listed under SHIPPING, *and all firms that*
specialize in transporting freight by air are
listed under AIR CARGO.

☎ **SHIPS**
КОРАБЛИ
SCHIFFE
NAVIRES
FARTYG
LAIVAT

St. Petersburg is the center of ship-
building for Russia and has many ship
building design institutes.
Okeanotekhnika, *Small ships and yachts*
Please Call 114-14-84
MTU Deutsche Aerospace - *Marine Propulsion*
Systems. See our ad under TECHNOLOGY TRANSFERS

Poul Christensen (Russia) Ltd.
A Danish Company
Shipbuilding, Purchase & Sale of Ships
in the Russian Market
Leninskiy pr., 161/2 108-49-32
Fax 293-52-49
Telex .... 121665 PCRUS SU

Sredne-Nevskiy Sudostroitelnyy Zavod
Pontonnaya stantsiya 265-55-10
Yachts and small ships; Mon-Sat 8-17; Rbls, &

☎ **SHOE REPAIRS**
РЕМОНТ ОБУВИ
SCHUHMACHER
CHAUSSURES, REPARATION DES
SKOMAKARE
SUUTARIT

Shoemakers, called Atele po poshivu
obuvi (Ателье по пошиву обуви) *can*
custom make shoes and boots as well as
do repairs. See Ves St. Pb. 93 and St. Pb.
Yellow Pages 93 for a complete list. There
are also many shoe repair shops called
Remont Obuvi (Ремонт обуви), *which are*
very skilled at restoring shoes, or instant
shoe repair in small kiosks.

Nitro, *Mon-Fri 10-19*
Lva Tolstogo ul., 1/3 233-56-53
Salon-Service
Nevskiy pr., 153 277-30-27
Mon-Fri 11-14, 15-19; Rbls; Eng
Bus 30; Metro Ploshchad Aleksandra Nevskogo
Remont Obuvi   **Shoe Repair**
Ремонт Обуви
• Gorokhovaya ul., 33 310-62-71
Mon-Sat 10-19
• Kamennoostrovskiy pr., 54............. 234-57-80
Mon-Sat 11-20
• Reki Moyki nab., 42 311-08-39
Mon-Fri 11-19

- Rubinshteyna ul., 16 113-23-94
  Mon-Fri 11-19
- Sadovaya ul., 51 310-66-70
  Mon-Sat 9-19
- Sadovaya ul., 85 114-58-21
  Mon-Fri 10-19
- Vosstaniya ul., 23 272-77-23
  Mon-Fri 11-15, 16-19; Rbls; Eng
- Vosstaniya ul., 40 272-29-27
  Mon-Sat 11-20

Zolushka
  Bolshaya Monetnaya ul., 9 232-41-34
  Mon-Fri 11-20

☎ **SHOE STORES**
   ОБУВНЫЕ МАГАЗИНЫ
   SCHUHGESCHÄFTE
   CHAUSSURES, MAGASINS DES
   SKOAFFÄRER
   KENKÄKAUPAT

*State shoe stores (obuv, обувь) mostly
carry domestic shoes.*

*Try DEPARTMENT STORES and the shops
listed below for stylish women's shoes and
good winter boots. Imported sneakers,
sport shoes (often copies) and dress shoes
are sold everywhere including COMMERCIAL
STORES, in KIOSKS, & even outdoor MARKETS.*

*See our TABLE OF SIZES on page 343 to
translate Russian sizes into American,
British and European sizes.*

Babylon-4, *See our ad under CLOTHING*
  Sadovaya ul., 26 310-18-15
  Daily 10-14, 15-20; Rbls; Eng
  Metro Gostinyy Dvor

Boutique-Joy
  Zagorodnyy pr., 9 315-53-13
  Mon-Sat 11-14, 15-20; Rbls; Eng, Ital
  Metro Dostoevskaya

**IMPORTED
MEN'S & WOMEN'S SHOES**
  Varshavskaya ul., 51 296-27-09
  Fax 296-43-51
  Telex .... 121194 RUB SU

Cinti
  Zagorodnyy pr., 33 315-96-78
  Fax 351-12-04
  Mon-Sat 11-14, 15-19; Rbls, $; Eng, Ger
  Tram 3, 5, 8, 15, 17; Metro Pushkinskaya

Diesel International, *Clothing, shoes*
  Kamennoostrovskiy pr., 37 233-47-20
  Mon-Sat 11-18; $; Eng, Ger
  Metro Petrogradskaya

Dom Obuvi   **Shoe House**
  Krasnogvardeyskaya pl., 6 224-02-24
  Mon-Sat 10-14, 15-19; Rbls

Gorizont   **Horizon**
  Shelgunova ul., 4 262-02-67
  Mon-Sat 10-19; Rbls; Eng
  Metro Lomonosovskaya

Lenwest Shoes

For the latest models and best selection

The Lenwest Shoe Salons

Dress shoes for men, women & children
Wet weather and winter footwear
Stylish boots for women

Outstanding footwear produced with the best
materials and German technology
designed by world-renown Salamander

  Aviagorodok, Vzletnaya ul., 7B 104-35-91
  Daily 10-14, 15-19
  Industrialnyy pr., 15 524-08-48
  Tues-Sat 10-14, 15-19
  Nevskiy pr., 11 314-72-43
  Mon-Fri 10-14, 15-19, Sat 10-14, 15-18
  Nevskiy pr., 119 277-30-22
  Mon-Sat 10-14, 15-19
  Rimskogo-Korsakova pr., 55/9 113-62-20
  Savushkina ul., 17 239-63-44
  Mon-Fri 10-14, 15-19
  Sofiyskaya ul., 57 108-62-04
  Suvorovskiy pr., 36 275-22-28
  Mon-Sat 10-14, 15-19
  Varshavskaya ul., 120 123-11-75
  Mon-Fri 10-14, 15-19
  Rubles, English

Marcopizzi
  Kamennoostrovskiy pr., 37 233-86-64
  Fax 233-85-54
  Tue-Sat 10-20; Rbls; $; Eng, Ital

Mitsar
  Bolshoy pr., P.S., 15 232-04-82
  Fax 233-87-41
  Mon-Sat 10-14, 15-19; Rbls, $; Eng

Na Vosstaniya 24 Shoe Store
  Vosstaniya ul., 24 273-36-48
  Mon-Sat 10-14, 15-19; Rbls; Eng

Nika, *Mon-Sat 11-14, 15-19; Rbls*
  Vladimirskiy pr., 2 314-00-48

Novyy Rim   **New Rome**
  Nevskiy pr., 48, at the Passage, 2nd floor
  219-17-83

Obuv   **Shoes**
- Bolshoy pr., P.S., 33 232-42-44
- Nevskiy pr., 116 279-57-64
- Suvorovskiy pr., 17 271-44-92
  Mon-Sat 10-14, 15-19; Rbls

Orthopedic Shoes
  Soyuza Pechatnikov ul., 14 114-08-08
  Mon-Fri 12-18 ; Rbls

Pell Kuir St. Petersburg, *Italian Shoes*
  Bolshaya Konyushennaya, 21/23
  In DLT 219-95-26
  Mon-Sat 10-20; Rbls, $

Shoes for Men & Women
  Moskovskiy pr., 153 298-27-73
  Mon-Sat 10-14, 15-19; Rbls; Eng
  Metro Elektrosila, Park Pobedy

Troika-RO
  Zagorodnyy pr., 28 112-47-46
  Daily 10-19; Rbls, $; Eng

Vityaz   **Knight**
  Narodnaya ul., 6 266-35-62
  Mon-Sat 10-14, 15-19; Rbls

☎ SHOOTING RANGES
ТИРЫ
SCHIESSSTÄNDE
TIR, CLUB DE
SKJUTBANOR
AMPUMARADAT

Shooting ranges are really shooting galleries (Tir, Тир) *include both air guns (pnevmaticheskoe oruzhie,* пневматическое оружие*) and live ammunition.*

St. Petersburg Shooting Center
Aptekarskiy pr., 14 234-35-62
Mon-Fri 9:30-13:30, 14:30-17
Tir No. 83, *Daily 12-21; Rbls; Eng*
Nevskiy pr., 20 311-68-29

☎ SHOPPING
МАГАЗИНЫ
GESCHÄFTE
MAGASINS
AFFÄRER
OSTOKSET VINKKEJÄ JA NEUVOJA

The *Traveller's* Yellow Pages *is designed to help travelers shop. With perseverance, most products and services can be found.*

SOME BASIC TIPS FOR SHOPPING IN RUSSIA

Plastic bags. *Always take plastic bags with you which the Russians call a "paket". Most products are sold without packaging and many stores don't have plastic bags. So always take along a good supply of plastic bags, an egg container, and jars for honey, cream, etc. Most Russians keep a couple of bags in their handbag or briefcase.*

"Buy it when you see it". *If you see something you like, or might need in the future, buy it now. Most likely you will not be able to find it when you want it.*

"Small bills and coins". *Have small bills and coins with you, whether paying in rubles or dollars.*

"Three times in line". *In many stores, the collection of cash is centralized with separate cashiers called "kassa" (касса) rather than in the individual departments. This "three times in line" system is still used in many stores, especially food stores.*

First, stand in line to select and weigh the goods (e.g. butter, meat, cheese) you want to buy; the clerk often adds up your selections on an abacus and hands you a piece of paper with the total amount. In some stores, like bread stores, you simply have to remember the price of each item you want to buy. Better write it down.

Second, stand in line at the cashier (kassa, касса) to pay. Give the slip with the amount or tell her the price of each item and the department (otdel, отдел) it comes from. You will get a cash-register receipt.

Three, you go back to the line at the sales counter, hand over the receipts, and pick up your purchases. Hint. Two people

shopping together is faster; one stands in the cashier's line and the other selects the goods.

Prices *are given in cost per **100 grams** (about a quarter pound) or **kilograms** (2.2 pounds). A half kilogram is called a polkilo. See WEIGHTS AND MEASURES.*

Prices in dollars, payable in rubles. *Dollars circulate almost as a second currency and some establishments have the legal right to sell (imported) goods for dollars. On the street, vendors often ask foreigners for outrageous sums in dollars compared to what they are willing to sell to Russians in rubles. Haggle!*

Recently, a new pricing practice has emerged. Because of inflation (and, until recently, the continual decline in the ruble) some prices may be stated in dollars, but payable only in rubles at the current rate of exchange. This is especially true in shops selling imported goods.

When to shop. *State stores are most crowded in early mornings, lunch hour and late evenings when people are shopping before or after work. Many older establishments close for a one hour lunch break (pereryv na obed,* перерыв на обед*): stores from 1-2 or 2-3, restaurants in late afternoon. One day per month, food shops close for a "sanitary day". Many modern shops and large department stores work without a break. See HOURS.*

How to find the shops. *Many nice small shops, cafes, and restaurants are located in strange places, in courtyards of apartment buildings, behind plain strong wooden doors, or up or down a flight of dark stairs and with minimal advertising. If you are given directions to a shop or restaurant on the second floor of a factory and it seems to be in an unlikely place, you are probably at the right place. Hotel restaurants and bars are often on the upper floors.*

WHERE TO SHOP

- *Department store* (Univermag - Универмаг)
- *Supermarket* (Universam - Универсам)
- *Market* (Rynok - Рынок)
- *Shop* (Magazin - Магазин)

Department stores (Univermag, Универмаг) *have a number of departments which sell a variety of manufactured goods such as clothing, linens, toys, housewares, shoes. Often they have separate boutiques selling selections of imported goods, sometimes for hard currency.*

Supermarkets (Universam, Универсам) *sell food and some housewares. They are Western-style, self-service (samoobsluzhivanie) and use the regular Western checkout system. The old Russian supermarkets listed under FOOD SHOPS, however, carry a much more limited selection than the Western-type supermarkets listed in* SUPERMARKETS.

Markets (Rynok, Рынок) *are true farmers' markets with fresh meats, vegetables, nuts,* cheeses, etc. from all over Russia, Central Asia and the world. See MARKETS.

Shops of any kind are called **Magazin** (Магазин) and come in many different varieties and in the past they were simply given the name of the product sold and a number, like Meat No. 28 or Fabrics No. 12. These Russian names are usually given in the essays or heading. Shops are now adopting more sophisticated names.

Shops called **"Magazin-Salon"** (Магазин-Салон) were at one time supposed to be shops with higher quality, more fashionable goods, especially clothing and furs. The term is now overused. A store of any type called a **"DOM"** (which means "House") tends to be one of the best in the city with wider selection and better quality, such as the Dom Mod (Дом Мод), the House of Fashion.

SHOPS, SPECIAL
МАГАЗИНЫ,
СПЕЦИАЛИЗИРОВАННЫЕ
GESCHÄFTE, ANDERE
MAGASINS, AUTRES
AFFÄRER
MUUT LIIKKEET

Here are a few unique shops in St. Petersburg including Coins, Military Uniforms, Theater Costumes, Wedding Dresses, Stamps, Garden Plants and Seeds.

Agroservice, Wide selection of seeds
Grivtsova per., 5 315-64-20
Mon-Fri 10-14, 15-19, Sat 11-14, 15-18

Maska, Theater and ballet accessories   **Mask**
Nevskiy pr., 13................................ 311-03-12
Mon-Sat 10-14, 15-19; Rbls

MS·AUDIOTRON
Professional audio, video and lighting
equipment for concert halls, theaters and studios.
Complete Installation • Musical Instrument Sales
P.O. Box 28, 00421 Helsinki, Finland
St. Petersburg:
Tel 310-55-13
Fax 310-48-01
Helsinki:
Fax .... +358-0-556-65-82

Numizmat   Coins   **Numismatic**
Astrahanskaya ul., 23.................... 541-84-10
Old coins, metals, pins; Mon-Sat 11-18; Rbls

PETROPOL
G A L L E R Y
MAMMOTH-IVORY
and
Peter the Great's Turnery
27 Millionnaya St. 315-34-14
Hrs: 10-18, Rbl, English

Rospechat, Philately
• Industrialnyy pr., 26/24 520-30-45
• Sennaya pl., 5 315-60-80
Mon-Sat, 10-14, 15-18
Voennyy Univermag
                          Military Supply Store
• Nepokorennykh pr., 6.................... 247-19-14
Mon-Sat 10-14, 15-19; Rbls
• Nevskiy pr., 67 311-77-33
Military Uniforms. Mon-Sat 11-14, 15-20; Rbls
Yubiley, Wedding and evening gowns
Sverdlovskaya nab., 60 224-25-98
Accessories for the newly engaged and newlywed;
Marital aides in department "Intim"
Mon-Sat 10-14, 15-20; Rbls, $
Zolushka, Wedding & Evening wear rental
Bogatyrskiy pr., 11, 5th floor.......... 393-42-77
Tues-Sat 12-14, 15-19

☎ SIGHTSEEING

See TOURS-SAINT PETERSBURG
and TRAVEL AGENTS

☎ SIGNS
ВЫВЕСКИ
AUSHÄNGESCHILDER
ENSEIGNES
SKYLTAR, TILLVERKNING
KYLTIT

See also ADVERTISING AGENCIES
for other sign makers.

Composit, Neon Signs
Narodnaya ul., 8............................. 312-07-34
Fax 110-76-60
Mon-Fri 8-21; Rbls; Eng, Ger
Gazosvet, Mon-Fri 9-18; Rbls
Yakornaya ul., 11 224-35-61
Interplast
Sedova ul., 37, 2nd floor 560-21-43
Rostorgreklama, Mon-Fri 9-18; Rbls
Sedova ul., 13................................. 567-47-02
SignArt, Posters, signs, Mon-Fri 10-21
Leninskiy pr., 168 290-20-02

☎ SIZES
РАЗМЕРЫ
GRÖßEN
TAILLE, POINTURE
STORLEKAR
KOOT

See TABLES OF MEASURES, WEIGHTS AND SIZES

☎ SKATING
КАТАНИЕ НА КОНЬКАХ
SCHLITTSCHUHLAUFEN
PATINAGE
SKRIDSKOÅKNING
LUISTELU

Little neighborhood outdoor rinks dot the city and are flooded in winter. For skating we recommend the Yubileynyy Palace of Sports. Skates can be rented at RENTALS.

Ice Rink Moskovskogo Parka Pobedy
Kuznetsovskaya ul., 25................... 298-08-01
Mon-Fri, Sun 9-18, Metro Park Pobedy

Ice Rink Tavricheskogo Sada
Saltykova-Shchedrina ul., 50......... 272-60-44
Daily 9-20 in Winter; Metro Chernyshevskaya; I-7

Summer Ice Skating   Letniy Katok LVO
Skating all year round
Reki Fontanki nab., 112............... 292-21-28
Daily 7-23; Metro Tekhnologicheskiy Institut; F-4

Yubileynyy Palace of Sports
Large well-maintained indoor rink for year round skating. Skates can be rented.
Dobrolyubova ul., 18.................... 238-40-61
11:00 a.m.-6:00 p.m. Skates can be rented. Metro Vasileostrovskaya, then Tram 18, 37, 40

☎ **SKIING**
КАТАНИЕ НА ЛЫЖАХ
SKIFAHREN
SKI
SKIDÅKNING
HIIHTOURHEILU

The best places to cross-country ski in St. Petersburg during the winter season are in nearby Kavgolovo and Komarovo, which can be reached by the electric commuter trains that leave from Finlyandskiy railway station. Another beautiful place for skiing is Pavlov-skiy Park in PAVLOVSK.

In the city center you can ski at Park Po-bedy on Moskovskiy prospect near Metro Park Pobedy. Other popular spots are Pri-morskiy Park Pobedy on Krestovskiy Island (B-9) and TsPKO Central Park of Culture & Rest on Yelagin Island (C-10). Take a taxi, since buses are not frequent. In past years, you could rent skis on site at the sports complexes at the parks and it may still be possible.

☎ **SKIN & VENEREAL DISEASES**

See MEDICAL CARE & CONSULTATIONS, HOSPITALS *and* MEDICAL ASSISTANCE

☎ **SOUVENIRS/GIFTS**

See ART GALLERIES, ARTS & HANDICRAFTS, CRYSTAL & PORCELAIN, FURS, GIFTS SHOPS, INTERNATIONAL SHOPS, *and* JEWELRY

☎ **SPORTS CLUBS**
СПОРТИВНЫЕ КЛУБЫ
SPORTVEREINE
SPORT, CLUBS
SPORTKLUBBAR
URHEILUSEURAT

See also BICYCLING, HORSEBACK RIDING, ROW-ING CLUBS, SAILING, TENNIS, MOUNTAINEERING, HUNTING, VOLLEYBALL, *and* SWIMMING

Azimut, *Sports Orienteering*
Mayakovskogo ul., 27.................. 279-76-35
Mon, Fri, Sun 15-20; Rbls; Eng, Finn
Metro Chernyshevskaya

Baltic Blades *Fencing Club* **Baltiyskie Klinki**
Chaykovskogo ul., 63.................... 273-61-68
Mon-Fri 10-18; Rbls

Motoclub, *Professional motorcycle racing*
Perekopskaya ul., 6/8 186-90-14
Daily 0-24

Russian Curling Association
Dekabristov ul., 35, rm. 46............ 219-51-18
Information in English 291-83-76
Daily 11-15; Rbls, $; Eng

Russian Federation of Shaping
Kazanskaya ul., 36 315-94-64
Fax... 312-85-65
Mon-Sat 9-21

Russian Federation of Bodybuilding
Yuria Gagarina pr., 8 264-79-11
Mon-Sat 10-22, Sunday 10-15, Winter 10-23;
Metro Park Pobedy; in the Sports & Concert Complex

Shaping Club
10-ya Liniya, 47 218-80-15
Mon 9-23, Tues 16-20:30, Thurs 16-20:30
Tram 40, Metro Vasileostrovskaya

Shooting Club
Aptekarskiy pr., 14 234-16-16
Mon-Fri 9-20; Metro Pertogradskaya

Sportservice, *Sports Group Coordinators*
Millionnaya ul., 22....................... 311-94-69
Fax... 312-20-24
Daily 9-18; Rbls, $; Eng, Ger, Fr

St. Petersburg City Air Club, *Mon-Fri 10-17*
Gorodskoy Aeroklub
Karavannaya ul., 4....................... 210-46-32

St. Petersburg Federation of Baseball & Softball
Pirogova ul.,13............................ 312-75-02
Fax... 314-62-18
Mon-Sat 10-18

The V. I. Alekseev Center, *Olympic Training*
Raevskogo pr., 16........................ 552-39-36
Fax... 552-39-51
Daily 18-23; Rbls

Zenit Football Club, *Soccer Club*
Konnogvardeyskiy blvd., 4, rm. 23 314-61-45
Fax... 311-77-98
Mon-Fri 10-12, 13-18

☎ **SPORTS EQUIPMENT**
СПОРТИВНОЕ ОБОРУДОВАНИЕ
SPORTAUSRÜSTUNGEN
SPORT, EQUIPEMENT
SPORTUTRUSTNING
URHEILUVÄLINEET

Sports equipment can be purchased in "Sports Equipment" stores (Sporttovary, Спорттовары) and also DEPARTMENT STORES, TRAVEL SHOPS, HUNTING AND FISHING EQUIPMENT stores and CAMPING SUPPLIES.

Sports equipment stores carry a wide variety of sports wear (tennis clothes, parkas swim wear, , and warm-up suits) and equipment (some imported) including ice skates, hockey helmets, tennis rackets and free weights. You may also find stores with a camping department selling tents, packs, camp ware, and pocket knives.

Apraksin Dvor, *Mon-Sat 11-19; Rbls*
Sadovaya ul., Apraksin Dvor, bldg.1, rm.13-15
☎ 310-20-03

Kompas   Compass
Malaya Posadskaya ul., 30 238-78-57
Special Order Sporting Equipment
Mon-Fri 9-17; Rbls, $; Eng, Ger

Olimpiets **Olympian**
Bolshoy pr., P.S., 76 232-96-28
Sports Wear, Cycling, Fishing, Outdoor Supplies
Mon-Sat 10-14, 15-19; Rbls
Store No. 9, *Mon-Sat 10-14, 15-19; Rbls*
Moskovskiy pr., 171 298-27-68
Store No. 10, *Mon-Fri 10-14, 15-19; Rbls*
Moskovskiy pr., 6 310-16-37
Sportlyuks
Liteynyy pr., 57 272-67-51
Sports Wear, Cycling, Fishing, Outdoor Supplies
Mon-Sat 10-14, 15-19; Rbls; Eng
Sport
Shaumyana pr., 2 224-28-74
Mon-Sat 10-14, 15-19; Rbls
Sporttovary **Sporting Goods**
Moskovskiy pr., 37 292-58-33
Mon-Sat 10-14, 15-19; Rbls
Tourist, *Mon-Sat 10-14, 15-19; Rbls*
Nevskiy pr., 122 277-02-79
Sports Wear, Cycling, Fishing, Outdoor Supplies
Yukon, *Exercise Equipment*
Sinyavinskaya ul., 4 227-47-47
Fax 227-60-80

☎ SPORTS FACILITIES
СПОРТИВНЫЕ СООРУЖЕНИЯ
SPORTANLAGEN
SPORT, ACTIVITES
SPORTHALLAR
URHEILUHALLIT

See also STADIUMS, TENNIS, SPORTS CLUBS,
HEALTH CLUBS, SAILING, BICYCLING, HEALTH
CLUBS, HUNTING & FISHING, *and* RACING

Army Sport Club
Inzhenernaya ul., 13 219-29-67
Swimming Pool, Volleyball, Basketball
Metro Gostinyy Dvor; G-6
Dinamo Sports Center
Dinamo pr., 44 235-01-70
Volleyball, Football, Track and Field, Horseback Riding
and Swimming Pool; Tram 21; D-9
Mototrek Club, *mototrack*
Zhaka Dyuklo ul., 67 553-84-83
Daily 9-18; Rbls; Motorcycle track
Metro Politekhnicheskaya, T-bus 25; F-8
Zenit Sport Palace, *Sports Complex*
Butlerova ul., 9 534-86-55
Daily 8-23; Rbls; Metro Akademicheskaya

☎ ST. PETERSBURG
CITY COUNCIL
ГОРОДСКОЙ СОВЕТ
STADTRAT, ST. PETERBURG
COMITE EXECUTIF
DE ST.PETERSBOURG
STATSFULLMÄKTIGE
PIETARIN KAUPUNGINNEUVOSTO

See also RUSSIAN GOVERNMENT *and*
ST. PETERSBURG MAYOR'S OFFICE

St. Petersburg is governed by an elected
City Council (Gorsovet, Горсовет) *of 400*
members, which meets 3 or 4 times a year
and a mayor (Meriya, Мэрия). *The Small*
Council works throughout the year and
consists of 36 members including the
chairman, and many of the chairmen of the

Standing Commissions. For a quick
overview of City Government, see St. Pb.
Business Guide 1993, *pp. 32-35.*

All Commissions of the City Council are
in the City Council Building (Mariinskiy
Palace) on St. Isaac's Square *unless*
otherwise noted.

City Council	**Gorodskoy Sovet**
Isaakievskaya pl., 6 319-94-85	
Fax 310-47-76	

Head of the City Council
Belyaev, Alexander Nikolaevich
☎ 310-00-00

DEPARTMENTS & COMMISSIONS

Commission on Communications and
Informational Technologies
Komissiya po Svyazi i Informatike
Isaakievskaya pl., 6, rm. 316 319-95-19
Commission on Culture and Historical
Heritage *Komissiya po Kulture i Kulturno-*
Istoricheskomu Naslediyu
Isaakievskaya pl., 6, rm. 337 319-94-79
Secretary 315-42-73
Commission on Ecology
Komissiya po Ekologii
Isaakievskaya pl., 6, rm. 336 319-95-04
Commission on Economic Reform
Komissiya po Ekonomicheskoy Reforme
Kazanskaya ul., 36, rm. 516, 517 310-12-84
Moving in September to Isaakievskaya pl., 6
Commission on Education and Adult
Education *Komissiya po Vospitaniyu i*
Narodnomu Obrazovaniyu
Isaakievskaya pl., 6, rm. 250 319-90-96
Commission on Glasnost and Mass Media
Komissiya po Glasnosti i Sredstvam
Massovoy Informatsii
Isaakievskaya pl., 6, rm. 227 310-42-34
Commission on Housing Policy
Komissiya po Zhilishchnoy Politike
Isaakievskaya pl., 6, rm. 327 319-90-27
Rm. 325 319-94-33
Commission on Human Rights
Komissiya po Pravam Cheloveka
Isaakievskaya pl., 6, rm. 357 319-92-06
Commission on Industry
Komissiya po Promyshlennosti
Isaakievskaya pl., 6, rm. 334, 381 319-95-24
Commission on International and Foreign
Trade Links
Komissiya po Mezhdunarodnym i
Vneshneekonomicheskim Svyazyam
Isaakievskaya pl., 6, rm. 243, 244 319-97-06
Commission on Law and Public Order
Komissiya po Zakonnosti i Pravoporyadku
Isaakievskaya pl., 6, rm. 303 319-98-19
Commission on Legislative Matters
Komissiya po Voprosam Zakonodatelstva
Isaakievskaya pl., 6, rm. 319 319-98-12
Commission on Medical Supplies
Komissiya po Meditsinskomy Obespecheniyu
Isaakievskaya pl., 6, rm. 365 319-94-17

Commission on the Military-Industrial Complex, Conversion of Defense Enterprises & Armed Forces Relations
Komissiya po Voenno-Promyshlennomu Kompleksu, Konversii Predpriyatiy i Organizatsiy Oboronnogo Kompleksa i Vzaimodeystviyu s Territorialnymi Strukturami Vooruzhennykh Sil
Isaakievskaya pl., 6, rm. 360.......... 319-95-81

Commission on Planning, Budget and Finance
Planovo i Byudzhetno-Finansovaya Komissiya
Isaakievskaya pl., 6, rm. 243.......... 314-41-56

Commission on Property Matters
Komissiya po Voprosam Sobstvennosti
Isaakievskaya pl., 6, rm. 247.......... 310-07-07

Commission on Science and Higher Education
Komissiya po Nauke i Vyssherny Obrazovaniyu
Isaakievskaya pl., 6, rm. 364.......... 319-97-07

Commission on Social Policy
Komissiya po Sotsialnoy Politike
Isaakievskaya pl., 6, rm. 246.......... 319-94-19

Commission on Trade and Communal Services *Komissiya po Torgovle i Sfere Bytovykh Uslug*
Isaakievskaya pl., 6, rm. 123.......... 319-95-73

Commission on Transportation
Komissiya po Transportu
Isaakievskaya pl., 6, rm. 383, 384...... 319-94-48

Commission on Urban Planning and Land Use
Komissiya po Gradostroitelnoy Politike i Zemlepolzovaniyu
Isaakievskaya pl., 6, rm. 227.......... 319-97-07

Commission on Youth Affairs, Physical Culture and Sports
Komissiya po Delam Molodezhi, Fizicheskoy Kulture i Sportu
Isaakievskaya pl., 6, rm. 367.......... 319-93-66

Property Management Fund
Fond Imushchestva
Grivtsova per., 5 311-04-74
Fax 319-94-26

☎ ST. PETERSBURG THE MAYOR'S OFFICE
МЭРИЯ
ST. PETERBURG,
BÜRGERMEISTER
MAIRE DE PETERSBURG
BORGMÄSTARE
PIETARIN KAUPUNGINJOHTAJA

See also RUSSIAN GOVERNMENT *and* ST. PETERSBURG CITY COUNCIL

The Mayor is the highest elected official. The Mayor's Offices (Meriya, Мэрия) are now located in the Smolnyy Institute at Proletarskoy Diktatury pl., 1. Anatoliy Alexandrovich Sobchak, Prof. of Law at the St. Petersburg State University is the current mayor. He has a number of deputy mayors and advisory staff.

The major committees in the Mayor's office are:

Mayor's Office at Smolnyy Institute
Smolnyy 315-98-83
Information 278-19-68

Committee on Culture and International Tourism
Komitet po Kulture i Mezhdunarodnomu Turizmu
Nevskiy pr., 40 312-24-71

Committee on Trade, Public Catering, Communal Services and Supply of Foodstuffs to the City
Komitet po Torgovle, Obshchestvennomu Pitaniyu, Bytovomy Obsluzhivaniyu i Snabzheniyu Goroda
Admiralteyskaya nab., 8 315-46-01

Department of Religious Societies Relations *Otdel po Svyazyam s Religioznymi Obedineniyami*
Saltykova-Shchedrina ul., 17 273-08-76
Mon-Fri 9-16

Development of International Humanitarian Relations Department
Komitet po Mezhdunarodnym Gumanitarnym Svyazyam
Smolnyy, rm. 123 278-14-82

Economic Development Committee
Komitet po Ekonomicheskomy Razvitiyu
Smolnyy, rm. 382 278-11-68

Education Committee
Komitet po Obrazovaniyu
Antonenko per., 8 319-91-79

Finance Committee *Finansovyy Komitet*
Voznesenskiy pr., 16 315-51-52

Foreign Economic Relations Administration
Upravlenie Vneshneekonomicheskikh svyazey
Antonenko per., 6, rm. 22 314-73-69

Foreign Relations Committee
Komitet Vneshnikh Svyazey
Smolnyy, rm. 112 278-11-13
Fax... 278-16-33

Free Trade Zone Committee
Komitet po Upravleniyu Zonoy Svobodnogo Predprinimatelstva
Smolnyy, rm. 286 278-17-24
.... 278-16-78

Health Committee
Komitet po Zdravookhraneniyu
Malaya Sadovaya, 1 210-85-14

Housing Committee *Zhilishchnyy Komitet*
Antonenko per., 4 319-99-01

Housing and Energy Committee
Komitet po Zhilishchnomu Khozyaystvu i Energetike
Gogolya ul., 12............................... 312-58-11

Inpredservice, Foreign Company Representation in St. Petersburg Commmittee
Kutuzova nab., 34 272-15-00
Fax... 279-50-24

Investment Committee
Investitsionnyy Komitet
Reki Moyki nab., 76 319-94-40

Labor and Employment Committee
Komitet po Trudu i Zanyatosti
Galernaya ul., 7/8 312-92-36

Land Reform and Land Resources Committee
Komitet po Zemelnoy Reforme i Zemelnym Resursam
Smolnyy 278-12-31

Legislation Committee
Yuridicheskiy Komitet
Smolnyy, rm. 341 278-16-51

Municipal Property Appropriations Committee
Komitet po Upravleniyu Gorodskim imushestvom
Smolnyy, rm 260 278-15-57

Municipal Utilities Committee
Komitet Gorodskogo Khozyaystva
Gogolya ul., 12 312-58-11

Physical Culture and Sports Committee
Komitet po Fizicheskoy Kulture i Sportu
Millionaya ul., 12 312-15-41

Press and Mass Media Committee
Komitet po Pechati i Sredstvam Massovoy Informatsii
Smolnyy, rm. 272 278-12-61

Public Improvements & Roads Committee
Komitet po Blagoustroystvu i Dorozhnomu Khozyaystvu
Smolnyy, rm. 231, 233 278-18-42
Fax 278-15-67

Requests and Appeals Committee
Komitet po Obrashcheniyam i Zhalobam
Smolnyy, rm. 343, 345 278-12-57

Smolninskaya Official Guest Residence
To contact guests, call 278-10-99
.... 278-15-99

Social Affairs Committee
Komitet po Sotsialnym Voprosam
Smolnyy 273-60-90

Social Welfare Committee
Komitet po Obshchestvennomu Blagosostoyaniyu
Smolnyy, rm. 333 278-17-20

Transport and Communication Committee
Komitet po Transportu i Svyazi
Smolnyy, rm. 252 278-12-06

Urban Planning and Architecture Committee
Komitet po Gradostroitelstvu i Arkhitecture
Lomonosova pl., 2 315-52-16

🕿 STADIUMS
СТАДИОНЫ
STADIEN
STADES
ARENOR/STADIOS
STADIONIT

Unless otherwise noted, these are open air stadiums.

Baltica, *Seats 1300*   **Baltika**
Petrovskiy pr., 16 235-51-64
Daily 8-23; T-bus 7; C-8

Kirov Stadium   Stadion im. Kirova
Seats 74,000, Football
Morskoy pr., 1 235-00-78
Mon-Fri 9-20; Rbls, $; A-10

Petrovskiy Stadium   Petrovskiy Stadion
Formerly "Lenin Stadium", football, seats 30,000
Petrovskiy Ostrov (Island), 2 g 238-41-29
Metro Vasileostrovskaya, Tram 37, 40; E-7

Sports and Concert Complex
Sportivno Kontsertnyy Kompleks (SKK)
Hockey & concerts, seats 20,000, indoor facility
Yuriya Gagarina pr., 8 298-21-64
Fax 298-01-07
Mon-Fri 9:30-17; Rbls, $; Eng, Ger
Bus 12; Metro Park Pobedy

Yubileynyy Sports Palace
Dvorets Sporta Yubileynyy
Hockey arena & concerts; seats 6000, indoor facility
Dobrolyubova pr., 19 238-41-22
Daily 9-20; Rbls; T-bus 1; Metro Petrogradskaya; E-7

Zimniy Stadium   Zimniy Stadion
Seats 2000, indoor
Manezhnaya pl., 2 315-57-10
Fax 312-40-46
Mon-Fri 9-18; Rbls, $; Metro Gostinyy Dvor, Tram 14; G-6

🕿 STAMPS/SEAL
ШТАМПЫ И ПЕЧАТИ
STEMPEL UND SIEGEL
EMPREINTES ET CACHETS
FRIMÄRKEN, SIGILL
POSTIMERKIT JA SINETIT

Business in Russia is highly dependent on the "official stamp" (pechat, печать) on documents rather than relying just on a signature. Only one stamp is allowed per company registration and this stamp can only be obtained after registration of a company and submission of papers to the local authorities. Buy a good quality self-inking stamp. Company stamps are usually locked up at night.

Western companies coming to Russia to sign contracts or to open a branch here, may want to bring their corporate seal and stamp along. Note, only companies registered in Russia have any legal right in ARBITRAGE COURT.

Comtrade
Nevskiy pr., 44 311-54-23
.... 110-50-92
Fax 314-90-76
Mon-Fri 10-17; Rbls; Eng, Ger

Dilar, *Mon-Fri 9-17; Rbls*
Komsomola ul., 33 541-83-30
Kontrade, *Mon-Fri 10-17; Rbls*
Gogolya ul., 14, rm. 114 311-64-57

LT SHTAMP
Seal Manufacturing in 3 Hours
Rimskogo-Korsakova pr., 71
Lermontovskiy pr., 24
.... 114-58-31
Fax 114-22-87

Photo Service Center
Prazhskaya ul., 14 268-61-43
Fax 113-27-30
Mon-Sat 11-18; Rbls; Eng; Metro Elektrosila

Roderic Ltd.
Professora Kachalova ul., 9 314-69-05
Fax 312-53-35
Mon-Fri 9-13, 14-17; Rbls, $; Eng
T-bus 16; Metro Ploshchad Aleksandra Nevskogo

Standard-Collection
Reki Moyki nab., 51 312-66-21
Fax 311-75-35
Mon-Sat 10-14, 15-19; Rbls;Eng
Technolog
Galernaya ul., 22 219-82-69
Mon-Fri 9:30-12:30, 13-16:30; Rbls
UNO
Maklina pr., 17/19 114-29-25
Daily 10-18; Rbls; Eng

☎ STATIONERY
КАНЦЕЛЯРСКИЕ ТОВАРЫ
SCHREIBWAREN
BUREAUX, FOURNITURES
PAPPERSHANDLARE
PAPERIKAUPAT

See also COMPUTER SUPPLIES,
PHOTOCOPIERS *and* ART SUPPLIES

*Private stores stocking Western station-
ery goods are quickly opening in St. Petersburg. Existing state shops, usually called
Kantselyarskie Tovary (Канцелярские
товары) are opening "commercial" departments with a good selection of imported supplies. Good quality photocopy paper,
both imported and domestic is also available. See* PHOTOCOPIERS. *Note that it is
impossible to buy American standard
stationery supplies, especially 8 1/2 X 11
letterhead, but it can be cut to size.*

Agency Igrek
Stachek pr., 72 183-61-74
IMPERIAL Shops
• Izmaylovskiy pr., 11 251-61-28
• Nevskiy pr., 51 312-87-76
• Vladimirskiy pr., 3 113-22-84
*Imported stationery and office supplies
Mon-Sat 10-14, 15-19; Rbls; Eng*
InterArtBazaar - *See ad below*
Kantselyarskie Tovary   Stationery
• Bolshoy pr., P.S., 69 232-79-06
Mon-Fri 10-14, 15-19; Rbls
• Bolshoy pr., P.S., 72 232-01-26
• Suvorovskiy pr., 24 279-37-16
• Novo-Izmaylovskiy pr., 40 295-39-26
Mon-Sat 10-14, 15-19; Rbls
Koyan
Chernyshevskogo pr., 9 273-34-91
Daily 9:30-14, 15-18:30; Rbls, $; Eng
Kulttovary
Robespera nab., 8 279-20-66
Mon-Sat 10-14, 15-19
Lenkulttorg Shops
• Kamennostrovskiy pr., 2 233-50-53
• Moskovskiy pr., 34 (in record shop)
.... 292-35-05
• Sadovaya ul., 31 310-82-49
*Fine imported stationery and office supplies
Mon-Sat 10-14, 15-19; Rbls*
Lotor No. 1
Prosveshcheniya pr., 78 557-87-09
Mon-Sat 10-19; Rbls
Natali
Lermontovskiy pr., 1/44 114-30-50
Mon-Sat 10-14, 15-17; Rbls
Polako
Kolokolnaya ul., 9 .... No ☎
Mon-Sat 10-18; Rbls

InterArtBazaar

*Everything for Businessmen
Wholesale and Retail*

♦ Stationery and office equipment by
  *PENTAL, KING JIM, MAX, KAMENSTEIN,
  ELDON RUBBERMAID, AVERY MYERS*
♦ Business organizers by *FILOFAX*
♦ Exclusive writing instruments by
  MONT BLANC AND SHEAFFER
♦ Luggage and briefcases by *SAMSONITE*
♦ Genuine leather attache and briefcases
♦ Quality paper, envelopes and notebooks

At these fine shops in Saint-Petersburg:
LENCULTTORG shops:

Kamennostrovskiy pr., 2

Sadovaya ul., 31

Moskovskiy pr., 34

IMPERIAL shops: .... (812) 113-22-85

Vladimirskiy pr., 3

Nevskiy pr., 51

Izmaylovskiy pr., 11

Moscow office:
Serpukhovskiy val., 24/2 954-30-09
.... 952-30-08
Fax 954-23-00

S & A Stationery Co.

Established by Statfall Inter'l, Ltd.
Supplier of imported office products
and stationery to businesses
& visitors in St. Petersburg

Full line of 3M, Stabilo, Staedtler, Pelican,
High-quality Finnish paper
Wholesale & retail, delivery, ask for price list.
Located in central St. Petersburg.
Bolshaya Konyushennaya ul., 27, rm. 3
(Formerly Zhelyabova ul.)
Tel 311-87-20
Mon-Fri 9-18; Eng, Ger; $, Rbls

Sovremennik
Ligovskiy pr., 51 277-79-82
*Mon-Fri 10-18; Rbls
Metro Ligovskiy Prospekt*
Store No. 24
Veteranov pr., 110 159-07-56
*Mon-Sat 11-19; Rbls
T-Bus 20; Metro Prospekt Veteranov*
Trud, *All types of paper, wholesale*
Saltykova-Shchedrina ul., 30 279-77-31
*Mon-Fri 10-17; Rbls, &
Metro Chernyshevskaya*

Vial Stationers

High Quality Stationery & Office Supplies
Large Selection of Products from Finland,
Germany, Italy and Switzerland
School Supplies
While-u-wait European standard
bookbinding

Belinskogo ul., 11 278-86-80

☎ **STOCK & COMMODITY
EXCHANGES**
БИРЖИ, ТОВАРНЫЕ И
ФОНДОВЫЕ
WARENBÖRSE WERTPAPIERBÖRSE
BOURSE DES VALEURS
ET DES MARCHANDISES
AKTIEMARKNAD
TAVARA-JA ARVOPAPERIPÖRSSIT

*There are more than 20 so-called
"Exchanges" in St. Petersburg now, some
with very similar names. Two examples
are, the older, larger regular Stock and
Commodity Exchange for St. Petersburg
and the smaller St. Petersburg Stock and
Commodity Exchange. Here are few of the
more active exchanges.*

Alisa-Petersburg
Zanevskiy pr., 6 528-71-45
....528-05-29
Fax 528-62-11
Mon-Fri 9-19; Rbls, $; Eng
International Wood Exchange
                                Interlesbirzha
Mikhaylova ul., 17........................541-87-27
Fax 541-87-50
Mon-Sat 9-17; Rbls, $; Eng

Ladoga
Ochakovskaya ul., 7 274-76-54
Fax 274-77-62
Mon-Fri 11-18; Rbls, $; Eng, Ger, Fr

North-West Agricultural Product Exchange
Rustaveli ul., 31...........................538-24-07
Fax 184-63-36
Mon-Fri 9-18; Rbls, $; Eng

Planet   **Planeta**
Khlopina ul., 5 232-09-42
Fax 233-99-45
Mon-Fri 10-13, 14-17; Rbls

Resource   **Resurs**
Kamennoostrovskiy pr., 5...............233-87-48
Fax...233-80-45
Mon-Fri 9-18; Rbls, $; Eng
Russian Paper in St. Petersburg
Griboedova kan. nab., 126, rm. 216
☎...114-38-25
Mon-Fri 9-18; Rbls, $; Eng
St. Petersburg Currency Exchange
Zagorodnyy pr., 68.......................292-56-60
Mon-Sat 10-19
St. Petersburg Stock Exchange, *oldest*
Bolshoy pr., V.O., 103 355-51-48
Fax...355-59-55
Mon-Sat 9:30-20; Rbls, $; Eng
T-bus 10 ; Metro Primorskaya
**Stock & Commodity Exchange
St. Petersburg**
26-ya Liniya, 15 217-44-92
Fax...355-68-59
Mon-Fri 9-13, 14-19; Rbls, $; Eng, Ger, Fr

☎ **STORAGE**
СКЛАДСКИЕ ПОМЕЩЕНИЯ
LAGERHÄUSER
ENTREPOTS
LAGER
VARASTOINTI

See also WAREHOUSES

AB
Reki Fontanki nab., 95...................310-76-84
Mon-Fri 9-18; rbls

EuroDonat   *FREIGHT
FORWARDERS
AND TRANSPORT*

**Custom Heated & Refrigerated
Warehouse Space
Armed Security
Direct Railway Connections
to / from Warehouse
Customs Document Service
Modern Truck Fleet**

Yakornaya ul., 17
Tel......................... (812) 224-11-44
Fax .... (812) 224-06-20
Telex .... 121118 DFS SU
Hrs: 9-18, $ & Rubles, English

DELOVIE LYUDI

INDEPENDENT • OBJECTIVE • THOROUGH
Profsoyuznaya ul., 73; Tel.: (095) 333-33-40; Fax: (095) 330-15-68

Interservice, *Mon-Fri 10-18*
  Liteynyy pr., 35 275-35-61
  Fax 275-28-03
Kirovspek, *Mon-Fri 8:30-17*
  Stachek pr., 47 183-67-38
Poliservice
  Tsimlyanskaya ul., 6 224-14-47
    Mon-Fri 8-16; T-bus 14; Metro Lomonosovskaya

☎ **STREETCARS, TRAMS**

See TRAMS

☎ **SUBWAY (Underground)**

See METRO

☎ **SUPERMARKETS**
    УНИВЕРСАМЫ
    SUPERMÄRKTE
    SUPERMARCHES
    STORMARKNAD
    SUPERMARKETIT

See FOOD STORES, MARKETS & DELICATESSENS

These are large true Western style supermarkets with a variety of foodstuffs, housewares, deli sections and shopping carts. For Russian "supermarkets" (Universamy), see FOOD STORES.

KALINKA STOCKMANN

SUPERMARKET

Come and buy from the widest
selection in town
Fresh milk products, vegetables,
fruit, meat, fish, bread and
other food products.
We also have a good
selection of non-food products.

Finlandskiy pr., 1

542-22-97
542-36-76
Fax: 542-88-66

Open: Daily 10-22
$, DM, FIM,
Major Credit Cards
Metro: Ploshchad Lenina

✳ BABYLON SUPER

THE SUPER SUPERMARKET

**Largest supermarket in Russia
for One-Stop Shopping in Rubles**

Everything from Soup to Nuts

Featuring Imported foodstuffs
from Holland and around the world

Hundreds and hundreds of items
in the five long aisles of our grocery
section, including a large frozen food
section, fresh produce, refrigerated dairy
and deli sections.

Choose your own fresh fruits & vegetables.
Dozens of deli items from French and Dutch
cheeses to sliced roast beef, smoked ham
and sausages, smoked fish, prepared foods,
and more.

Fresh French bread, rolls and croissants.

Large beverage section featuring fresh
juices, mixers, soft drinks and the finest
European wines and beers

Extensive selection of housewares, cleaning
supplies, paper products and
personal products

**OPEN MON-SAT 10-21
SUNDAY 12-20**

P.S., Maly pr., 54 & 56 230-80-96
In the former Okean store right off Bolshoy Prospekt
Metro Petrogradskaya

Rubles only, Exchange office in store.

Spar Markets

Now two markets in Saint Petersburg!
Just turn the page for information

✳ BABYLON SUPER

Mon-Sat 10-21 Sun 12-20
Exchange office

ONE STOP SHOPPING AT SUPER BABYLON

Everything you need for an elegant last-minute dinner. Appetizers,
salad, prepared frozen foods, condiments, torte shells and whipped
cream for dessert. Great wines, delicious coffees and teas and
chocolate truffles to relish.

P.S., Maly pr., 54 & 56 230-80-96
In the former Okean store off Bolshoy Prospekt

SPAR Ⓐ

MARKETS
featuring
Fine Foods from Finland
and the rest of the world

Large Fresh Fruit and Vegetable Section

Fresh meat and fish, trimmed by our own
butcher, special marinated beef

In our dairy section dozens of cheeses,
sausages, smoked fish and meat, fresh
Finnish milk and butter

McCormick spices, condiments, peanuts by
the kilo, cereals, crackers, and more

Large frozen food section with many
varieties of ice cream, **Carolina turkeys**,
frozen fruits and vegetables.

Imported beer and soft drinks by the case.

Personal toiletries and paper products
Pamper your baby with **Pampers** and
imported formula and baby food

Our large Candy and Cookie Section
features **Fazer Sweets and Cookies**

At our corner cafe, treat yourself to a cup
of coffee, glass of wine and deli sandwich

SPAR MARKET SLAVA
- Slavy Prospekt, 30 260-41-21
 261-04-60
Fax....................................261-29-70
*Daily 10-22; $, FIM, DM, Rbls; Eng, Finn, Ger
Metro Moskovskaya then Bus 31, 114, or
T-bus 29, 27, 35*

SPAR MARKET KIROVSKIY
- Stachek Prospekt, 1 186-51-77
 186-94-11
*Daily 10-20; $, FIM, DM, Rbls; Eng, Finn, Ger
Right opposite Metro Narvskaya*

☎ SWIMMING
ПЛАВАНИЕ
SCHWIMMBÄDER
NATATION
BAD/SIM HALLAR/PLATSER
UINTI

*Also try some of the pools listed under
HEALTH CLUBS. If you are going to visit a
swimming pool in St. Petersburg, generally,
it's a good idea to phone ahead. It may
also be necessary to have documentation
from a physician certifying your health.
Bring a bathing cap, soap, rubber sandals,
towels, a swimming suit and a plastic bag.
Shoes are often left in the cloak room.*

Delfin, *Daily 6-24; Rbls*
Dekabristov ul., 38........................ 114-20-54

Dinamo, *Daily 6-24; Rbls*
Dinamo pr., 44................................ 235-29-44

Lokomotiv Swimming Pool, *Opens October '93*
Konstantina Zaslonova ul., 23......... 164-46-10
*Daily 6:15-22:30; T-bus 1; Metro Ploshchad Vosstaniya
Bus 10, 47; T-bus 1, 9; Metro Petrogradskaya*

Naval Sports Club Swimming Pool
Novocherkasskiy pr., 5 a 528-73-28

Popular Education Committee
Bolshaya Raznochinnaya ul., 20 235-38-77
Daily 6:30-23

SKA　　　　　　　　　**Army Sports Clubs**
- Inzhenernaya ul., 12 219-29-67
  Daily 6-24
- Litovskaya ul., 3 542-01-62
  Opens January '94; Daily 6-24;

Spartak Swimming Pool
Konstantinovskiy pr., 19................. 235-05-83
Daily 6:30-22:30

Yunost
Pravdy ul., 11.................................. 315-01-17
Daily 7-22:30; Rbls; T-bus 15, 8; Metro Dostoevskaya

☎ SYNAGOGUES
СИНАГОГИ
SYNAGOGEN
SYNAGOGUES
SYNAGOGER
SYNAGOOGAT

*If you find kosher food stores or
restaurants, please, call us.*

Choral Synagogue
Lermontovskiy pr., 2 114-11-53
Mon-Fri, Sun 10-20; Tram 29

Synagogue, *at the cemetery*
Aleksandrovskoy Fermy pr., 2 264-39-81
Metro Lomonosovskaya, Bus 53

☎ TAILORS/SEAMSTRESSES
ПОРТНЫЕ
SCHNEIDER
TAILLEUR/COUTURIER
SKRÄDDARE/SÖMMERSKOR
RÄÄTÄLIT

*There are many skilled tailors and seam-
stresses in St. Petersburg working in "Atel-
iers" (Atele, Ательe). There are three levels
of quality: 2nd, 1st and deluxe "Lyuks". In
addition there are many private tailors and
seamstresses who can custom tailor your
dress with your pattern and material. Get a
recommendation from Dom Mody (House of
Fashion) or your friends.*

ANDY'S 🏠 FASHION - *See on Next page*

Atele, *Mon-Fri 11-20*
Nevskiy pr., 134............................. 277-11-72

Atele Mod, *Mon-Sat 11-19; Rbls*
Liteynyy pr., 27 272-65-51

Atele No. 3
Nevskiy pr., 95............................... 277-19-22
Mon-Sat 10-19; Rbls; Metro Ploshchad Vosstaniya

Lux, *Mon-Fri 10-19; Rbls*
Moskovskiy pr., 125....................... 298-30-92

Soyuz, *Theatrical clothes*　　　　　　**Union**
Piskarevskiy pr., 16........................ 540-21-65
Mon-Fri 9-14, 15-19; Rbls, &

Velona, *Mon-Sat 11-15, 16-19; Rbls*
Nevskiy pr., 139............................. 277-56-33

ANDY'S 🛡 FASHION

—— HONG KONG ——

Made to Measure Clothing

World-Wide Custom Tailoring
for Diplomats, Travellers & Business
Persons, Ladies & Gentlemen

We Stock Fabrics from
World Renowned Manufacturers
of Silks & Cashmeres, British Wools,
Egyptian Cottons, etc.

Wide Selection of Fashion & Classic Styles
Handmade Suits, Jackets, Trousers
Skirts, Jodhpurs, Shirts & Blouses

Every Style, Any Fabric, Every Season
Any Time, All Year

**Impeccable Made to Measure Clothes by
Hong Kong's Most Distinguished Tailors**

*To arrange your personal appointment
in* St. Petersburg, *please call us at* 556-08-09

In Moscow, *contact our representative*
Jimmy K. *at* ☎ (O95) 302-34-95,
302-81-55 *or* Fax 131-04-20

FAIR PRICES & FAST DELIVERY GUARANTEED

YOUR SATISFACTION IS OUR AIM

☎ TAX CONSULTING

See ACCOUNTING & AUDITING FIRMS
and BUSINESS CONSULTANTS

☎ TAXIS/LIMOUSINES

ТАКСИ
TAXIS
TAXI/LIMOUSINE
TAXI
TAKSIT/LIMOUSIINIT

See also AUTOMOBILE RENTAL,
LIMOUSINE, AIRPORT TRANSPORTATION

Types of Taxis: *There are official taxis,
private taxis, and private cars. All are
called taxis. Furthermore, there is little real
difference between renting a car by the
hour or day with a driver and taking a taxi,
except that taxis are for specific destinations and car rentals are for time. Even
taxis can be hired by the hour.*

*Official (and private) taxis can be iden-
tified by a small green light on the windshield. Official taxis have the distinctive T
and checkered emblems on the doors and
may have yellow lights on the roofs.*

*Many private cars also stop to pick up
passengers, often by drivers going to work
or on business. Taking private cars for*

*taxis, however, can be risky and is only for
the adventuresome who know some
Russian. Evaluate all drivers carefully.
Travel in twos and never get into cars
already occupied by two people.*

Hailing and Negotiating: *To hail a taxi
that looks OK, hold out your arm, palm
down. Tell or show the driver the address
(written in Russian) where you are going
and ask the price. It will often be higher
than normal if you are not Russian. You
can often bring the price down if you say
that it is too much and begin to walk away.
There will usually be another taxi. Unless,
of course, it is 2 a.m. and pouring rain. The
market works here.*

You Can't Get There from Here. *If the
driver seems to be taking a circuitous route
to your destination, it may be because of
road closings, one-way streets and "no-left-
turns". See* DRIVING.

Prices: *The rates for all types of taxis are
basically the same. Late at night expect to
pay at least double the rate you would pay
in the daytime. The official rate for a taxi
ride is 1000 times what is shown on the
meter, if the driver still uses it (August 1,
1993). Note, however, that many taxi
drivers now have the legal right to negotiate
a price for each ride rather than to charge
the official price. For a short ride Russians
pay the ruble equivalent of $0.50-$0.60 as
of August 1, 1993 or about $0.25 per kilo-
meter. By the hour, Russians pay the
equivalent of $3.00-$4.00.*

*For a lower price, negotiate in Russian.
For foreigners the standard rate in the front
of hotels is around $5 to most places, and
for longer trips, such as to or from the airport
it may cost as much as $15-25. Ruble taxis
can be found if you walk a block or two from a
hotel. Getting a reasonably priced taxi at the
airport is nearly impossible due to price fixing
by local drivers. Arrange for a ride or call
for an official cab to pick you up.*

Tipping: *If a meter is used, "round up,"
no other tip is expected . A good driver and
a low "negotiated" price warrants a small
tip.*

Ordering an official taxi: *Even though
most taxis are being "privatized", ordering
an official taxi usually works quite effi-
ciently - in the center city during the day.
Officially two hours notice is required, they
often come sooner.*

OFFICIAL TAXI (FOR RUBLES)	
Orders:............................	312-00-22
Inquiries:	315-11-17

Private taxi services: *The most reliable
and comfortable taxis are, of course, the
private taxi services listed below. Often
the drivers speak some English.*

Astoria-Service
Borovaya ul., 11/13, apt. 65 164-96-22
Mon-Fri 9-17; Rbls, $; Eng

INTERAUTO

Hertz Int. Lic.

Large selection of cars & minibuses with or without drivers. Reservations at the Grand Europe & Moscow Hotels
Ispolkomskaya ul., 9/11 277-40-32
Complete 24 Hrs service, Rbls, $, English

Lingva
Pochtamtskiy per., 7 312-18-24
Mon-Sat 9:15-19:45

Matralen
Lyubotinskiy pr., 5 298-12-94
.... 298-36-48
Mon-Sat 8-20; Rbls, $; Eng, Ger

STV
Konnogvardeyskiy blvd., 4 315-29-55
Mon-Fri 9-17; Rbls

 TAXI

At Pribaltiyskaya Hotel
Taxi and Limousine Service
24 Hours/Day,
Featuring Fords

Korablestroiteley ul., 14
Dispatcher.......................... 356-93-29
Director .... 356-00-01 *Ext. 10-74*
Fax..................................... 356-00-94
Fax..................................... 356-38-45
$, English, German, Finnish

Taxi (on call)
Konyushennaya pl., 2..................... 312-00-22
Daily 0-24; Rbls; Eng, Ger

Taxi transportation to and from
Airport ● Railway Station ● Seaport
Lermontovskiy pr., 37.................... 113-72-53
Fax 114-38-03

☎ **TECHNICAL INSTITUTES**
ИНСТИТУТЫ ТЕХНИЧЕСКИЕ
TECHNISCHE INSTITUTE
INSTITUTS TECHNIQUES
TEKNISKA INSTITUT
TEKNISET OPPILAITOKSET

See UNIVERSITIES AND INSTITUTES for educational institutions and conservatories, INSTITUTES, RESEARCH for research institutes and MEDICAL INSTITUTES for medical institutes and medical schools. Education and research are major industries in St. Petersburg and it has one of the best educated populations in the world.

☎ **TECHNOLOGY TRANSFERS**
ТЕХНОЛОГИИ, ОБМЕН
TECHOLOGIETRANSFER
TECHNOLOGIES, TRANSFERT DES
TEKNISK ÖVERFÖRING
TEKNINEN VAIHTO

See EXPORT-IMPORT FIRMS and BUSINESS CONSULTANTS

Many Russian firms and research institutions are offering "technology" and are looking for foreign partners.
Alba, *Mon-Fri 8:30-17:10; Rbls, $; Eng, Ital*
3-ya Liniya, 52 213-31-17
Fax.. 218-39-35

Alcor Technologies, Inc.
Stepana Razina ul., 8/50
.... 235-69-24
Fax 235-54-35
*Optical, Spectral & Laser Instruments
Optical Crystals & Elements*

Alinter
Nalichnaya ul., 6 356-37-21
Fax.. 356-24-14
Mon-Fri 9-18; Rbls, $; Eng
Alyuma System Monolitstroy
Ryleeva ul., 29 273-26-46
Fax.. 272-79-30
Mon-Fri 9-18; Rbls, $; Eng
Association for Foreign Economic Cooperation
Millionnaya ul., 27, apt. 49 315-86-27
Fax.. 311-77-58
Mon-Fri 9-18; Rbls, $; Eng, Ger, Finn
Baltic Technologies
Torzhkovskaya ul., 3, Hotel Vyborgskaya
☎ 246-98-35
Mon-Fri 9-20; Rbls
Center of New Technologies
Dinamo pr., 3................................. 235-00-27
Fax.. 235-03-34
Mon-Fri 10-19; Rbls, $, CC; Eng, Ger

Institute of Energy Electronics

*Uninterrupted Power Supply 0.4-6-10 kV
for Industrial Enterprises*

V.O., 26-ya Liniya, 9 a, P.O. Box 962
.... 164-07-03
Fax 217-06-93

Intekhcenter
Chkalovskiy pr., 52........................ 234-92-23
Fax.. 230-13-07
*Mon-Fri 8:30-17:45; Rbls, $; Eng, Ger
Tram 31; Metro Petrogradskaya*
Konsofin
Rizhskiy pr., 58 259-91-06
Fax.. 251-76-11
Mon-Fri 8:35-17:30; Rbls, $; Eng
LST-Metall, *Mon-Fri 7:45-16:30; Rbls, $; Ger*
Petroslavyanka Doroga, 5.............. 267-08-24
Fax.. 100-32-63

Laser Center St. Petersburg ITMO
Grivtsova per., 14 210-69-36
Fax 315-71-33
Daily 10-19; Rbls, $; Eng

Laser Technology Center
Politekhnicheskaya ul., 29 535-52-47
Fax 552-01-00
Mon-Fri 9-18; Rbls, $; Eng

Lentep
Zaozernaya ul., 1 259-67-17
Fax 252-60-00
Mon-Fri 8:30-17:15; Rbls, $; Fr

Maksud
Angliyskaya nab., 38 311-34-83
Mon-Fri 9-17; Rbls, $; Eng

Marine Computer Systems
Babushkina ul., 80 568-39-43
Fax 568-39-39
Mon-Fri 10-19

Mineral Processing Engineers
21-ya Liniya, 8 a 213-99-86
Fax 350-20-24
Mon-Fri 9-12, 13-18; Rbls, $; Eng

mtu
Deutsche Aerospace

Manufacture, sales and service of diesel engines, gas turbines, gearboxes and electronic control and monitoring systems for marine, railroad, current generating, vehicular and industrial applications.

COMPACT and RELIABLE
Marine Propulsion Systems

Diesel, gas turbine or combined systems with: fixed-pitch, controllable pitch, surface-piercing propellers or water-jets

In Germany:
P.O. Box 2040
7990 Friedrichshafen 1, Germany
Tel.: + 7541-900, Telex: 734280-0 MT D

In Turkey:
Istanbul
Tel.: +1 - 288 27 59, Fax: + 1 - 266 47 63
Telex: 26706 MOBN TR

MTU - THE MARINE POWER SYSTEMS EXPERTS

New Informational Technologies
Leninskiy pr., 101, Shipbuilding Inst., rm. 210
Fax 157-25-33
Mon-Fri 9-18

Otis *(See our ad in CONSTRUCTION)*
Khimicheskiy per., 12 252-37-58
.... 252-36-94
Fax 252-53-15

Saint Petersburg-Pure Water
Tavricheskaya ul., 10 275-40-55
Fax 275-62-58
Mon-Fri 9-18

Sigmatek, *Mon-Fri 9-20; Rbls, $; Eng, Ger*
Krasnogo Flota nab., 8 315-27-98
Fax 312-28-73

Texnoexan, *Mon-Fri 9:30-18; Rbls, $; Eng*
Politekhnicheskaya ul., 26 247-93-78
Fax 247-53-33

Vetas Ltd

- *Know-How in Thermoelectricity*
- *Bamboo Furniture*
- *Automobile Radiators*
- *Custom Manufacturers of Slot-Machine Tokens*
- *Assembly Line Set-Up*

Gertsena ul., 61 312-10-39
.... 315-56-37

☎ **TELEGRAM**
ТЕЛЕГРАММЫ
TELEGRAMME
TELEGRAMME
TELEGRAM
SÄHKEET

See COMMUNICATIONS, TELEPHONE and BUSINESS CENTERS
You can send internal telegrams from most post offices and telegram posts (Telegraf, Телеграф). You can send international telegrams from several post offices in each district including the main post office in each region. See POST OFFICE.

Express-Post, *Mon-Fri 10-18*
Konnogvardeyskiy blvd., 4, off. 22
☎ 311-23-46

Telegraph, *Daily 0-24; Rbls*
Sinopskaya nab., 14 277-31-92

Telegraph Office, *Daily 9-20; Rbls*
Pochtamtskaya ul., 15 314-57-54

☎ **TELEPHONE BOOKS**
ТЕЛЕФОННЫЕ КНИГИ
TELEFONBÜCHER
DIRECTOIRES TELEPHONIQUES
TELEFONKATALOGER
PUHELINLUETTELOT

See also BUSINESS PUBLICATIONS
Finding Phone Numbers. *Phone numbers change very frequently and many numbers are not available in official phone books or from Phone Information which only has the Official Subscribers list. In particular organizations and people that rent offices and apartments will not be listed with the phone company.*

All the phone numbers in The *Traveller's* Yellow Pages *have been checked twice, the last time in July 1993. We continually check phone numbers through the year and plan to provide a supplement to our registered readers. Send in your card.*

Note, the first three digits of the phone number indicates the specific area and even the street in St. Petersburg. Satellite telephones have special codes and can be difficult to reach inside the city.

Phone books. *Contrary to common belief, there are telephone books for St. Petersburg. The Leningrad Telephone Company published two telephone books in the last 5 years:* Telephone Book of Leningrad 1988 (Telefonnyy Spravochnik Leningrada 1988, Телефонный Справочник Ленинграда 1988) *and an updated and better organized* Short Telephone Book of Leningrad 1991 (Kratkiy Telefonnyy Spravochnik 1991, Краткий Телефонный Справочник Ленинграда 1991). *They are a combination of non-residential white pages and yellow pages without any informational advertising.*

For Western readers, the principal problems are that the books are in Russian, are hard to find, very incomplete, out-of-date and are poorly organized for those accustomed to the Western-style Yellow Pages. The books are basically organized by type of organization and institution rather than by category of goods and services.

Our Traveller's *Yellow Pages for Saint Petersburg is the first yellow pages in the city and earned the reputation of being the most accurate, up-to-date, and easy to use. Information is collected by a staff of 24 researchers and all numbers are verified twice. Readers who send in their address card will get a* free *"up-date" in Feb. 1994.*

There are now two other Yellow Pages *in St. Petersburg. We* recommend *both of them for business use along with* The *Traveller's* Yellow Pages (TYP). *They are useful for finding chemical factories, a complete list of bakeries, public schools, etc. in the state economy. Unfortunately, both have an error and omission rate of 20-30% because they are based on official telephone company listings so that many private firms and numbers are not yet listed and many listed firms are no longer active. They have little other information and very few ads.*

Желтые Страницы Санкт-Петербург-93, Saint Petersburg Yellow Pages-93 *(St. Pb. Yellow Pages-93) is bilingual with Russian headings and English index. It is difficult to use, heavy, with little information and few ads. Its 20,000 listings are mostly from the state sector and phone company listings. Cost was $15.00. Available from the address listed below.*

Ves Sankt Peterburg, 1993 The Whole St. Petersburg Directory *(in Russian with Russian and English indexes), cited as* **Ves St. Pb-93.** *Large A-4 size with listings first in a white pages format followed by a yellow page section, with listings in Russian for $12.00. There are many other directories about St. Petersburg. See* BUSINESS PUBLICATIONS *and* DIRECTORIES.

St. Petersburg Yellow Pages 1993
Antonenko per., 6b, 5th floor, rm. 507, 510
Fax...315-66-95

The *Traveller's* **Yellow Pages and Handbook for Saint Petersburg 1993-1994**
Reki Moyki nab., 64 315-64-12
Fax...312-73-41

Mon-Fri 9-18
Ves Sankt-Petersburg 1993
The Whole Saint Petersburg-93
Business Directory
Marata ul., 86...............................112-50-51
Fax...112-42-11

☎ **TELEPHONE EQUIPMENT**
ТЕЛЕФОННОЕ ОБОРУДОВАНИЕ
TELEFON-ZUSATZGERÄTE
TELEPHONE, EQUIPEMENT
TELEFONUTRUSTNING
PUHELINLAITTEET

Western telephones can be bought at most ELECTRONIC SHOPS. *They should work on "*Pulse*" as well as "*Tone*" and have "*Redial*" and "*Pause*"; speed-dial memory is especially useful in Russia. To use your "*Redial*" button when accessing numbers through "8", dial "8" first, the "*Pause*" button twice and then the number. To redial, you simply push "*Redial*", the "*Pause*" waits again for the tone after "8".*

Don't buy the cheapest phone, they burn out from voltage fluctuations. Western phones can be installed by rewiring the plug. Easier yet, bring or buy an adapter outlet to rewire into the Russian outlet and just plug in the phone. They work.

Alen, *Mon-Fri 0-24; Rbls; Eng*
Kronverkskaya ul., 47.....................233-48-22

THE WORLD LEADER IN TELECOMMUNICATIONS

Offers for your Russian Office Telephone Systems
from 8 up to 4000 Extensions

▼ *supply on a turn-key basis*

▼ *all equipment adapted
to the Russian telephone network*

▼ *full guarantee and technical support*

Bolshaya Morskaya ul., 16 315-89-38
....315-82-10
Fax...315-94-74
Telex................................121246 ALCSP SU

We'll help you to see the difference
▼

ALCATEL

Belam

*Sales, Installation & Service
of Office Telephone Systems &
Telecommunications Equipment*
192007 Russia, St. Petersburg, P.O. Box 140
Tel 315-23-45
Fax 110-66-54

Contract
Chekhova ul., 17 272-97-21
Mon-Fri 10-17; Rbls

Delta Telecom
(See our ad under TELEPHONE SERVICE)
Gertsena ul., 22 314-61-26
Fax 314-88-37
Mon-Fri 9-18; Rbls, $

Kopiya   **Copy**
Partizana Germana ul., 37, apt. 4
☎ 130-78-00
Fax 130-80-98
Mon-Fri 9-18; Rbls, $; Eng, Ger

Lyceum of Radio Electronics
Kamennoostrovskiy pr., 21/14 232-97-44
Fax 233-04-75
Mon-Fri 8:30-17:30; Rbls; Eng; Metro Petrogradskaya

NOKIA

SWITCHING SYSTEMS

Bolshoy Sampsonievskiy pr., 60
Tel 542-56-63
Fax.....................................542-88-60

*Complete telephone systems
Manufacture & installation*

Peterstar
(*See our ad under* TELEPHONE SERVICE)
Bldg. 31, Line 16, V.O., 199178, St. Petersburg
Tel 119-60-60
Fax 119-90-02

Petrocont, *Mon-Fri 9-18; Rbls, $; Eng*
Tyushina ul., 4 164-00-11

☎ TELEPHONE INFORMATION
СПРАВКИ ПО ТЕЛЕФОНУ
TELEFONAUSWEISE
INFORMATIONS TELEPHONIQUES
TELEFONINFORMATION
PUHELINNUMEROT

*The phone company has a list of "free
information numbers" and "paid information
numbers". Look in the Ves St. Pb.-93 for a
more extensive listing.*

FREE INFORMATION IN RUSSIAN

- FIRE 01
- MILITIA (POLICE)......................... 02
- EMERGENCY MEDICAL 03
- GAS EMERGENCY 04
- TELEGRAPH.............................. 066
- INTERCITY CALLS 07

- EXACT TIME 08
- DIRECTORY ASSISTANCE........... 09
- "REKLAMA DUBL" BUSINESS
  DIRECTORY listing businesses 050
- MEDICAL CENTER INFORMATION 002
- BUSINESS DIRECTORY 008

☎ 050 Information Service Reklama Dubl

Selected Information about:

- *Businesses*
- *Services*
- *Goods*

Hrs: Mon.-Fri.: 9-21

*Reklama Dubl is a free information service
to callers.*

PAID INFORMATION IN RUSSIAN

*Costs between 20-50 Rbls.
DIAL 8, WAIT FOR DIAL TONE
Then DIAL the NUMBER*

- *Residential/commercial numbers 009*
- *Telephone number
  or address of St. Pb. residents 061*
- *Addresses of courts 062*
- *Public transportation info and
  commercial telephone info............ 063*
- *Legal advice 065*
- *Children's stories 068*
- *Information on Moscow telephone
  numbers........................... 314-73-52*

☎ TELEPHONE INTERCITY CALLING
ТЕЛЕФОНЫ МЕЖДУГОРОДНИЕ
TELEFON, FERNGESPRÄCHE
TELEPHONE INTERURBAIN
TELEFON RIKSSAMTAL
PUHELUT, KAUPUNKIEN VÄLISET

*You can dial most cities in Russia directly
from St. Petersburg using either your home
or office phone or from special telephone
booths/offices, called "Mezhdugorodniy",
(Междугородний).*

**HOW TO CALL OTHER CITIES
DIAL 8
WAIT FOR DIAL TONE
DIAL CITY CODE + NUMBER**

*Special service for calling people without
telephones. It is called the "07" service.
You order a call for a specific date and time
and length of call; the person called is not-
ified and comes to the "Telephone Post" to*

talk with you. This is a good way to get in touch with people at their dachas.

If you don't know the telephone code or telephone number in the distant city, call Information "07". For a more complete listing of codes, see "Ves St. Pb. 93".

INTERCITY CODE - LENINGRAD REGION

Boksitogorsk	266
Gatchina	271
Kingisepp	275
Kirishi	268
Kirovsk	262
Lodeynoe Pole	264
Luga	272
Podporozhie	265
Priozersk	279
Slantsy	274
Sosnovyy Bor	269
Tikhvin	267
Tosno	261
Volkhov	263
Volosovo	273
Vsevolozhsk	270
Vyborg	278

INTERCITY CODE - NORTHWEST RUSSIA

Arkhangelsk	818
Murmansk	815
Novgorod	816
Petrozavodsk	814
Pskov	81122
Syktyvkar	82122
Vologda	81722

INTERCITY CODES OTHER MAJOR CITIES IN RUSSIA

Moscow	**095**
Bryansk	0832**, 08322
Cheboksary	8352
Chelyabinsk	3512
Cherepovets	820
Chita	30222
Irkutsk	3952
Ivanovo	0932**, 09322
Kaliningrad	0112
Kazan	8432
Khabarovsk	81732
Kirov	833
Krasnodar	8612
Krasnoyarsk	3912
Kursk	071
Lipetsk	0742
Mineralnye Vody	86531
Nizhniy Novgorod	8312
Novosibirsk	3832
Omsk	3812
Penza	8412
Perm	3422
Pyatigorsk	86533
Rostov-na-Donu	8632
Ryazan	0912
Samara	8462
Saratov	8452
Smolensk	081
Sochi	8622
Suzdal	09231

Sverdlovsk	3432
Tomsk	3822
Tula	0872
Tver	08222
Ufa	3472
Ulyanovsk	8422
Vladikavkaz	86722
Vladimir	09222
Volgograd	8442
Vorkuta	82151
Voronezh	0732
Yaroslavl	0852

**First code is used with telephone with 6 numbers; the second code is used with telephones with 5 numbers.*

Delta Telecom

Gertsena ul., 22	314-61-26
Fax	314-88-37

Mon-Fri 9-18; Rbls, $

Peterstar, *Daily 0-24*

16-ya Liniya, 31	119-90-00
Fax	119-90-02

☎ TELEPHONE INTERNATIONAL CALLS
МЕЖДУНАРОДНЫЙ ТЕЛЕФОН
AUSLANDSGESPRÄCHE
TELEPHONE INTERNATIONAL
UTRIKES SAMTAL
PUHELUT, KANSAINVÄLISET

INTERNATIONAL CALLING

International calling is much easier now than a few years ago because the St. Petersburg telephone company installed facilities to direct dial most of Western Europe, the United Kingdom and North America. For more information on international calling, dial 315-00-12 and ask for an English speaking operator. For information in Russian about international or Russian calls, dial 274-93-83 or 274-93-83.

Direct dialing. You can direct dial to the United States, Western and Eastern Europe from many homes and offices. Dial "8", wait for second dial tone and then dial "10", the country code and telephone number. Here are some international codes from St. Petersburg:

Belgium	32
Bulgaria	359
Canada	1
Denmark	45
Finland	358
France	33
Germany	49
Great Britain	44
Hungary	36
Israel	972
Italy	39
Japan	Operator Assisted Only
Norway	47
Netherlands	31
Poland	48
Spain	Operator Assisted Only
Sweden	46
USA	1

CODES TO FORMER REPUBLICS OF THE USSR

To dial former republics of the USSR, dial 8, then wait for a dial tone and dial the appropriate code and number.

Armenia
Erevan 8852

Azerbaijan
Baku 8922

Belorus
Minsk 0172
Brest 01622
Gomel.......................... 0232**, 02322
Mogilev... 0222
Vitebsk 0212**, 02122

Estonia
Tallinn 0142
Narva 01435

Georgia
Tbilisi 8832
Sukhumi 88122

Kazakhstan
Alma-Ata 3272
Dzhambul................... 3262**, 32622
Karaganda 3212

Kyrgyzstan
Bishkek 3312

Latvia
Riga.. 0132

Lithuania
Vilnius 0122
Kaunas 0127
Klaypeda 01261
Palanga 01236
Panevezhis 01254

Moldova
Kishinev 0422

Tajikistan
Dushanbe 3772

Turkmenistan
Ashkhabad 3632

Ukraine
Kiev 044
Chernovtsy...................................03722
Dnepropetrovsk 0562
Donetsk 0622
Kharkov 0572
Kherson 055
Lvov 0322
Odessa 0482
Sevastopol.................................... 069
Simferopol.................................... 0652
Vinnitsa 04322
Zaporozhe 0612**, 06122
Zhitomir 0412

Uzbekistan
Tashkent....................................... 3712
Fergana...37322
Bukhara...36522
Samarkand 3662
Termez 37622
Urgench 36222

Cities in bold type are capitals of the former republics of the USSR.

** First code is used with telephone with 6 numbers; the second code is used with telephones with 5 numbers.

For a complete listing of international codes, see the Ves St. Pb. 93.

DIRECT ACCESS DIALING

Direct access dialing is supposed to be arriving in St. Petersburg in late 1993. In the meantime, call through Moscow.
ATT USA Direct *Call ATT-Direct in Moscow at (095) 155-50-42. To call anywhere in the USA, it costs $6.75 for 1st min. plus $2.50 each add. minute. Collect calls have a $3.75 surcharge per call.*

Sprint Express *Call Sprint Express in Moscow number at (095) 155-61-33. The cost to access Sprint Express is $3.75 for the 1st min. plus $2.50 each add. min. plus a $2.00 charge.*

Note that you can not access the toll-free MCI and Sprint Express numbers in Helsinki from Saint Petersburg.

OTHER WAYS OF CALLING THE REST OF THE WORLD

Direct dialing is still somewhat of an ordeal with "no rings", busy signals, and lost connections. Try these other methods.

1. Order a Call in Advance. *The traditional way to place an international call is to order a call in advance. You can order an international call for a specific time and date up to two days in advance. You must give them the number you will be at the time but you can change it before the call is placed.*

To call home from a private phone or business, you can place a reservation with the overseas operator after 9 am, up to two days in advance. Dial 315-00-12 and ask for an English speaking operator. Explain that you want to place an international call, and when you want to call . They will tell you dates and times available. Give the number you are calling and the number you will be at the time of the call. (Note you are reserving a time slot and can change both numbers before the call is placed). You will be called back when the call goes through.

In a hotel, the operator or service bureau will assist you in ordering a call, but you may still have to wait. Book in advance for calls in rubles. In other hotels, they have direct dial via satellite. This is expensive.

2. Place a Direct Call at the Telephone Station. *Try going to the "long-distance and international point" at Gertsena ul., 3/5, daily from 9-17 to place a call directly. Expect to wait in line & pay rubles. Or go to the DELTA TELECOM office.*

3. Place an Immediate Direct Call by Satellite and by Leased Lines. *For immediate calls via satellite, go to one of* the "BUSINESS CENTERS", DELTA TELECOM, a COMMUNICATION company or a hotel that lists "phone or satellite phone". It costs between $3-10 per minute, but it is quick and clear.

4. Subscribe to your own International Access Service. Several firms listed under COMMUNICATIONS and CELLULAR PHONE provide the instant access to international lines from your office, home phone, or even car. These are ideal for business & industries that want their own instant access to international lines. Prices are reasonable and competitive, especially to the USA.

Telephone Company Tariffs: The costs of regular calls has run up rapidly, but it remains remarkably low to many countries, but not to the United States. Ordinary telephone company tariffs are lowest from homes and state financed organizations. Ordered calls and offices are charged about twice the home rate, so direct dial from your home if your can. The latest price rates are available from 315-00-12.

Some sample Telephone Company rates as of July 10, 1993:

Country	Direct Dial		Operator Assisted
	Evening 18-8	Daytime 8-18	
USA, Canada & Israel	756	1512	2268
Europe	378	756	1134
Australia	756	1512	2268
Indonesia, Turkey	567	1512	1701

For information about international calls: Dial 315-00-12 and ask for an English-speaking operator.

Alcatel
Gertsena ul., 16 315-89-38
.... 315-82-10
Fax 315-94-74
Mon-Fri 9-18; Rbls, $; Eng, Fr, Finn, Ital

BCL
Konnogvardeyskiy blvd., 4 311-14-88
Fax 314-86-60
Mon-Fri 8-17; $; Eng

Delta Telecom
See ad under CELLULAR PHONES
Gertsena ul., 22 314-61-26
Fax 314-88-37
Mon-Fri 9-18; Rbls, $

Lenfincom
Gertsena ul., 3/5 110-69-17
.... 314-75-84
Fax 312-32-73
Mon-Fri 8:30-17; $; Eng; T-bus 5; Metro Nevskiy Prospekt

Peterstar
Bldg. 31, Line 16, V.O., 199178, St. Petersburg
Tel 119-60-60
Fax 119-90-02
Daily 0-24

☎ **TELEPHONE REPAIRS INSTALLATION**
ТЕЛЕФОНЫ, УСТАНОВКА, РЕМОНТ
TELEFONINSTALLATION, REPARATUR
TELEPHONE, INSTALLATION, REPARATION
TELEFONINSTALLATIONER, REPARATIONER
PUHELIMIEN ASENNUKSET JA KORJAUKSET

To get your phone repaired or to check on service, call the service number for your telephone district. There are too many to list here. Ves St. Pb. 93 has a complete listing at the back of the book. Or try these numbers (in Russian) to find out the number to call for your telephone:

Vyborgskiy Telefonnyy Uzel.......... 054
Moskovskiy Telefonnyy Uzel......... 055
Nekrasovskiy Telefonnyy Uzel....... 053
Petrogradskiy Telefonnyy Uzel 052
Tsentralnyy Telefonnyy Uzel......... 051

Alen,   *Mon-Fri 0-24; Rbls; Eng*
Kronverkskaya ul., 47 233-48-22

Alfa,   *Daily 9-12:30, 13:30-17; Rbls*
Ryabchikova ul., 11/3, Krasnoe Selo
☎ 132-62-26

Contract,   *Mon-Fri 10-17; Rbls*
Chekhova ul., 17 272-97-21

NOKIA
SWITCHING SYSTEMS
Bolshoy Sampsonievskiy pr., 60
Tel 542-56-63
Fax 542-88-60
Complete telephone systems
Manufacture & installation

PETERSTAR
Bldg. 31, Line 16, V.O., 199178, St. Petersburg
Tel 119-60-60
Fax 119-90-02
Daily 0-24

Petrocont
Tyushina ul., 4 164-00-11
Mon-Fri 9-18; Rbls, $; Eng

☎ **TELEPHONE SERVICE**
ТЕЛЕФОННОЕ ОБСЛУЖИВАНИЕ
FERNSPRECHDIENSTE
TELEPHONE
TELEFON
PUHELINPALVELUT

See also TELEPHONE-INTERNATIONAL; TELEPHONE-INTERCITY; TELEPHONE REPAIR & INSTALLATION, TELEPHONE EQUIPMENT *and* CELLULAR TELEPHONES

The telephone situation is rapidly improving in St. Petersburg as the St. Pb.

Telephone Company works with Western telephone companies to improve service and as more firms enter the market to supply telephones and telephone services. In addition to the official St. Petersburg Telephone Company, there are a number of new foreign telephone companies. Prices tend to vary among them. Count on $400-$500 for installation charges and $2-$8 for long-distance calls to Europe or America. Given the price discrimination against calls to North America, these private services are not that expensive. Try: Peterstar 119-90-00, B.C.L. 311-86-87, LenFinCom 314-00-60 and Delta Telecom 314-61-26 (mo-bile phones) for immediate installation in offices and enterprises.

Alcatel

Gertsena ul., 16	315-89-38
	315-82-10
Fax	315-94-74

Mon-Fri 9-18; Rbls, $; Eng, Fr, Finn, Ital

International phone, fax and data communications

Just call St. Petersburg 311-1488 To get connected!

BCL Head Office/Shop
Konnogvardeyskiy Blvd, 4,
190000 St.Petersburg, Russia

Phone	311-14-88
Fax	314-86-60

Delta Telecom - *See ad below*

Harris Representative

Gertsena ul., 28	315-23-45
Fax	110-66-54

Mon-Fri 9-18; Rbls, $; Eng

Cellular Radio Telephone In Saint Petersburg and the World

For businesses and individuals.
See our ad under cellular phones.

Gertsena ul., 22	314-61-26
Fax	314-88-37
Fax	275-01-30

Lenbell, *Telephone systems*

Malookhtinskiy pr., 68	528-02-35
Fax	528-74-14

Mon-Fri 10-18

LENFINCOM

Complete communication services for
business at down-to-Earth prices
Direct access to all major electronic
computer networks worldwide
Prepaid international cardphone services
International connections
for your office phones

**CALLING THE WORLD SHOULD NOT
COST YOU THE EARTH**

Call us	110-69-17
Fax	312-32-73

LENINGRAD INTERCITY TELEPHONE STATION

Intercity and International Calls for
Residents and Visitors of St.Petersburg
Long Distance Service from Any Number
in St.Petersburg

Bolshaya Morskaya ul., 3-5
Fax: (812) 315-17-10

Tel	07

"Mezhdugorogniy"
(intercity calls)

Tel	274-93-83

"Mezhdunarodnyy"
(international calls ordered from hotel)

Tel	314-47-47

"Mezhdunarodnyy"
*(international calls ordered from
home or business)*

Tel	315-00-12

Rubles, English, French, German, Spanish

ПЕТЕРСТАР ✦ PETERSTAR

ТЕЛЕКОММУНИКАЦИИ • TELECOMMUNICATIONS

- The *only* telecommunications company in St. Petersburg offering instant local, national and international connections from *one* phone and from any country in the world and any city in the former USSR
- Voice and Data Services
- 24 hour technical and operator support by English speaking personnel
- Design and installation of office and hotel communications systems
- Star services available
  - Call Waiting
  - Call Diversion
  - Roll Out Number Groups

CALL: 119-60-60

Address: Bldg. 31, Line 16, V.O.,
               199178, St. Petersburg
               Fax: (812) 119-90-02

☎ **TELEVISION-CABLE**
ТЕЛЕВИДЕНИЕ КАБЕЛЬНОЕ
KABELFERNSEHEN
TELEVISION DE CABLE
TV, KABEL
KAAPELITELEVISIO

See also TELEVISION SATELLITE

Cable TV first appeared in St. Petersburg about three years ago. One of the best centers, "Petr Velikiy", has 5 channels. Many buildings and small regions of the city have their own cable TV system which improves reception and broadcast films, etc. A small monthly fee must be paid. Ask the residents of your apartment building how to arrange cable TV.

Baltic-Sputnik (Satellite TV) *30-40 programs*
 Litovskaya ul., 10........................... 245-21-60
Mon-Thu 8-17; Rbls

Cable TV
 Vereyskaya ul., 34/36.................... 273-51-29
 Fax... 110-68-83
Mon-Fri 9-17; Rbls; Tram 28; Metro Vladimirskaya

Central Cable Television Studio
 Sadovaya ul., 55/57, apt. 416......... 113-49-89
Mon-Fri 11-17; Rbls, $

Lenceltel, *Mon-Fri 9:30-17; Rbls; Eng*
 Kostromskaya ul., 1 274-46-41

Navigator, *Satellite systems*
 Promyshlennaya ul., 19................. 186-56-06
Mon-Fri 9-18; Rbls, $

 Peter the Great A/O
ПЕТР
ВЕЛИКИЙ
CABLE-SATELLITE
TELEVISION St. Pb.

Excellent opportunity to advertise to the residents of Saint Petersburg
Sredneokhtinskiy pr., 52.....526-66-31
Fax....................................526-66-24
Telex .... 121637 DISK SU
Daily 11-20; Rbls, $; Bus 77; Metro Ladozhskaya

Sprut TV
 Prosveshcheniya pr., 87................ 594-72-94
Mon-Fri 10-18; Rbls

☎ **TELEVISION REPAIR**
ТЕЛЕВИЗОРЫ, РЕМОНТ
FERNSEHGERÄTE, REPARATUR
TELEVISION, REPARATION
TV, REPARATION
TELEVISIOIDEN KORJAUKSET

See also ELECTRICAL REPAIRS *and* REPAIRS

Graviton, *Mon-Sat 11-15, 16-20; Rbls*
 Krasnoputilovskaya ul., 12 183-14-74
Interservice. *Mon-Fri 9-18; Rbls*
 Bolsheokhtinskiy pr., 1/1 224-15-74
 Fax... 224-12-58
Orbita-Service, *Mon-Sat 10-19; Rbls*
 Kosmonavtov pr., 25...................... 293-65-01
Petro TV, *Mon-Sat 9-14, 15-19; Rbls*
 Zverinskaya ul., 38........................ 233-05-33
Pole-Service   **Polyus-Servis**
 Kuznetsovskaya ul., 44.................. 298-97-88
 Fax... 298-24-08
Daily 10-13, 14-20; Rbls, $; T-bus 24; Metro Elektrosila
Rekord, *Mon-Fri 10-19; Rbls*
 Prosveshcheniya pr., 62................. 598-89-09
Repair Agency, *Mon-Sat 10-14, 15-18; Rbls*
 III-go Internatsionala ul., 18 156-46-93
Rubin TV, *Mon-Sat 11-19; Rbls*
 Reki Fontanki nab., 28................... 273-45-81
Rus, *TV, Audio and Video Repair*
- 9-ya Liniya, 24 213-25-88
- Lanskoe shosse, 2 246-49-68
- Kamennoostrovskiy pr., 17.......... 232-28-94
- Shkolnaya ul., 7 239-84-41
 Fax... 239-62-07
Mon-Sat 10-14, 15-20; Rbls
Sonex, *Mon-Fri 11-18; Rbls, $*
 Professora Popova ul., 7/8 234-58-00
Technical Center No. 4
 Krasnoputilovskaya ul., 12 184-63-61
Mon-Sat 10-14, 15-19; Rbls; Metro Kirovskiy Zavod
Teleservice, *Mon-Sat 10-19; Rbls*
 Veteranov pr., 43 152-03-52
Veta
 Gavanskaya ul., 13 217-21-16
Mon-Sat 9-14, 15-18; Rbls; Tram 11, 63; Metro Primorskaya
Vid
 Gertsena ul., 14............................. 315-61-65
Mon-Sat 10-19; Rbls; T-bus 1; Metro Gostinyy Dvor

☎ TELEVISION SALES
ТЕЛЕВИЗОРЫ, ПРОДАЖА
FERNSEHGERÄTE, VERKAUF
TELEVISION, VENTE
TV, FÖRSÄLJNING
TELEVISIOIDENMYYNTI

See also ELECTRONICS

Imported and Russian televisions can be bought at a variety of shops including domestic electrical goods shops as well as some of the INTERNATIONAL SHOPS *and* COMMERCIAL SHOPS. *You can even get your own satellite TV system installed and receive dozens of international programs.*

Electron
Grivtsova per., 1/64 312-41-93
Electronica Gallery and Shop
Yuriya Gagarina pr., 12 299-38-49
Mon-Sat 10-14, 15-19; Rbls, $
Elektrolux, *Bang & Olufsen Distributor*
Robespera nab., 16....................... 275-55-12
Daily 10-20; Rbls, $; Eng, Fr
Elektronika-Video, *Mon-Fri 10-19; Rbls*
Lesnoy pr., 22 542-62-17
Eridan
Zagorodnyy pr., 11 314-23-18
Mon-Sat 10-14, 15-19; Rbls, T-bus 3, 8; Metro Dostoevskaya
Everest, *Mon-Sat 10-14, 15-19; Rbls*
Sredniy pr., 19 213-02-81
Goldstar, *Mon-Sat 10-19; Rbls, $; Eng*
Lesnoy pr., 20 542-19-59
Fax 542-09-89
Gorizont, *Daily 10-14, 15-19; Rbls*
Shvernika pr., 14 550-44-84
Fax 552-35-21
LEMI'S, *Mon-Sat 10-14, 15-19; Rbls, $*
Moskovskiy pr., 20 110-12-95
Lans, *Mon-Fri 10-17; Rbls, $*
Kostyushko ul., 3, bldg. 2, floor 10 290-73-05
Philips Electronics, *Daily 10-14, 15-20; Rbls, $; Eng*
Suvorovskiy pr., 2.......................... 277-43-19
.... 277-22-25
Record-Service
Rubinshteyna ul., 20 310-59-71
Mon-Sat 10-14, 15-19; Rbls; Metro Dostoevskaya
Rigonda, *Mon-Sat 11-14, 15-20; Rbls*
Moskovskiy pr., 171 298-08-40
Rumit, *Daily 10-19; Rbls*
Engelsa pr., 43.............................. 553-16-97
Sadko
• Petra Alekseeva ul., 11 315-63-09
Daily 11-19; Rbls, $
• Mozhayskaya ul., 40 292-41-36
Mon-Fri 10-19; Rbls
Signal
Nekrasova ul., 4............................ 272-02-59
Mon-Sat 10-14, 15-19; Rbls; Metro Chernyshevskaya
Skif
Vosstaniya ul., 32 275-53-45
Fax 275-58-71
Mon-Fri 9-18; Rbls, $; Eng, Ger, Fr
Tram 5; Metro Chernyshevskaya
Vesta-Tauras, *Mon-Sat 10-19; Rbls*
Primorskiy pr., 27 239-97-61
Fax 239-98-21
Zolotoy Klyuchik, *Mon-Sat 10-14, 15-19; Rbls*
Marshala Govorova ul., 10 184-83-18

☎ TELEVISION SATELLITE
ТЕЛЕВИДЕНИЕ СПУТНИКОВОЕ
FERNSEHAN
TELEVISION
TELEVISION SATELLIT
TELEVISION

About 40 satellite TV channels can be received with the proper TV and satellite dish. See TELEVISION SALES, TELEVISON CABLE. *The Moscow Tribune and Moscow Times publish schedules for satellite TV and for BBC, Super Channel, Eurosport, MTV, RTL (Ger), Pro7 (Ger), TV5 (Fr).*

A & A
Tikhoretskiy pr., 4 247-72-81
Fax 247-34-06
Mon-Sat 10-14, 15-19; Rbls, $; Eng, Ger, Fr
Baltic-Sputnik, *30-40 programs*
Litovskaya ul., 10 245-21-60
Mon-Thu 8-17; Rbls
Delisat, *Satellite systems*
Truda pl., 2 311-89-22
Fax 311-75-43

Peter the Great A/O
ПЕТР ВЕЛИКИЙ
CABLE-SATELLITE
TELEVISION St. Pb.

See our ad in Television-Cable

☎ TELEVISION STATIONS
ТЕЛЕВИЗИОННЫЕ СТАНЦИИ
FERNSEHANSTALTEN
TELEVISION, STATIONS DE
TV, STATIONER
TELEVISIOKANAVAT

See also ADVERTISING AGENCIES, TELEVISION-CABLE *and* TELEVISION, SATELLITE

St. Petersburg is served by four TV stations and by several cable TV systems in different areas of the city and by satellite television. The TV schedules for the week are published in several places including Televidenie & Radio and Baltiyskiy Kurier.

Traditional Russian TV had four channels plus two more for local cable systems inside of building complexes.

The four TV stations are:

Channel 1: "Ostankino" National channel
Concerts, culture, news, films

Channel 2 "TV Petersburg"
St. Petersburg's independent TV with films, interviews, round tables, local news, concerts and advertising

Channel 3: "Rossiya" National channel
Sports, news, films, features

Channel 4 "Educational"
Foreign language lessons, physics, economics, and educational films

Availability of cable TV depends on location.

Petersburg 5th Channel
Coordinates the broadcasting of Russian TV from its TV tower. Telephones may change.

Chapygina ul., 6	232-02-21
Fax	234-77-66
Advertising	234-78-70
Mon-Fri 9:30-18:30; Rbls, $

TV Broadcasting
Movie & Video Production, Advertising
International Art Exhibitions & Auctions

Malaya Nevka, 4	234-54-92
Fax	234-00-88

TV-Neva Show Business
Pushkinskaya ul., 10, apt. 9	112-32-73
Fax	112-36-29
Mon-Fri 10-18; Rbls, $; Eng, Fr

☎ TELEX
ТЕЛЕКС
TELEX
TELEX
TELEX
TELEX

Telex, a form of telegraph, operates independently of phone lines and in some circumstance can be the only way to send information quickly. It is still popular in Russia and Europe where the fax is less common. Most BUSINESS CENTERS offer "telex" services.

☎ TEMPORARY HELP
ВРЕМЕННАЯ РАБОТА
ZEITARBEIT
TRAVAIL TEMPORAIRE
VIKARIER, EXTRAHJÄLP
VÄLIAIKAINEN APU

Since the publication of the first edition of our book, temporary employment agencies have appeared in St. Petersburg. This is a great move from a year ago when they did not exist at all.

EKOS
Specializing in temporary help
Trained secretaries & translators
English, German and other languages
13-ya Liniya, 12 355-91-51
Mon-Fri 10-18; Rbls; Eng, Ger

Personnel Corps
Nevskiy pr., 104	275-83-23
	275-45-86
Fax	275-83-23

Professional Technical College No. 2
Varshavskaya ul., 7 296-37-13
Mon-Fri 8:30-18; Rbls

☎ TENNIS
ТЕННИС
TENNIS

Dinamo Sports Center, *Indoor*
Dinamo pr., 44 235-01-70
Daily 8-21; Tram 21; D-9

Kirov Stadium, *Outdoor*
Morskoy pr., 1 235-48-77
Mon-Fri 9-17; Rbls; Bus 71; Metro Petrogradskaya

Lawn Tennis Sports Center, *Outdoor*
Metallistov pr., 116 540-18-86
Shaping, Sauna, Swimming Pool, Summer Outdoor Courts
Mon-Sat 9-21; Rbls; Tram 14; Metro Ploshchad Lenina

Mars, *Outdoor*
Aptekarskiy per., 16 ....No ☎

Park Babushkina   **Babushkin Park**
Obukhovskoy Oborony pr., 149 560-01-57
Daily 10-20; Metro Lomonosovskaya

Tennis Court, *Indoor*
Primorskiy Park Pobedy 235-20-77
Daily 8-24; Rbls, $

Tennis Court, *Indoor*
Kazanskaya ul., 37 315-62-20
Daily 8-23; Rbls

THE TENNIS CLUB

*Located on the banks
of the beautiful Nevka River
Training, court & racquet rental, racquet
repairs, pro-shop, cafe, shower & sauna*

Konstantinovskiy proezd, 23............235-04-07
Mon-Fri 8-23, Rbl, $

☎ THEATERS/BALLET
ТЕАТР, БАЛЕТ
THEATER/BALLETT
THEATRE/BALLET
TEATER/BALETT
TEATTERIT/BALETIT

*For tickets, see THEATRICAL TICKET OFFICE
For seating plans of Mariinskiy Theater, Malyy Theater of Opera and Ballet, Russian Academic Bolshoy Dramatic Theater, Theater of Opera and Ballet, Bolshoy Philharmonic Hall, Glinka Chamber Philharmonic Hall and the Bolshoy Concert Hall "Oktyabrskiy", see pages 336-341 of this book. There is a Russian book of seating plans for theaters, palaces of culture, and sports arenas, called Teatry, konsertnye zaly, dvortsy kultury, dvortsy sporta Leningrada (1984).*

The theater and ballet begin between 7 - 7:30 p.m. Be on time, as the ushers are strict about curtain time. When you arrive check your coat, "rent" opera glasses, and buy a program. At each intermission, drinks and light snacks are sold in the lobbies, but pay attention to the bells signaling the end of intermission. The ushers may not let you in.

Rock concerts and "spectaculars" are often held in stadiums.

Academic Bolshoy Dramatic Theater
Reki Fontanki nab., 65 310-92-42
Fax 110-47-10
Tue-Sun 11-17; Rbls; Metro Gostinyy Dvor; G-5

Academic Comedy Theater
Nevskiy pr., 56................................ 314-26-10
Fax 314-25-01
*Tue-Sun 11-13:30, 14:30-20; Rbls
Bus 22; Metro Gostinyy Dvor; G-5, 6*

Baltic House   *Baltiyskiy Dom*
Aleksandrovskiy Park, 4 232-62-44
Fax 233-99-36
Tue-Sun 12-15, 16-20; Rbls, $; Metro Gorkovskaya; F-8

Benefis Theater
Reki Moyki nab., 24
Fax 314-07-36
Daily 12; Rbls, $; Eng, Ger, Fr; Metro Nevskiy Prospekt; F-6

Bolshoy Philharmonic Hall
Mikhaylovskaya ul., 2..................... 311-73-33
Fax 311-21-26
Daily 11-15, 16-19:30; Rbls; Metro Nevskiy Prospekt; G-6

Bolshoy Puppet Theater
Nekrasova ul., 10 273-66-72
Wed-Sun 10:30-15, 16-19; Rbls; Metro Chernyshevskaya; H-6

Boris Eyfman's Contemporary Ballet
Lizy Chaykinoy ul., 2 232-02-35
Fax 232-18-62
Mon-Sat 10-18; Rbls, $; Metro Gorkovskaya; F-8

Bosse Mansion Chamber Concert Hall
4-ya Liniya, 15 213-34-88
Rbls; Metro Vasileostrovskaya; E-6

Bryantsev Theater for Young Audiences
Pionerskaya pl., 1 112-41-02
Tue-Sun 11-14, 15-19; Rbls, Tram 34; Metro Pushkinskaya; G-4

Buff Theater
Narodnaya ul., 1 263-67-67
Fax 263-83-00
Tue-Sun 12-20; Rbls; Metro Ulitsa Dybenko

Comedian's Refuge   *Priyut Komedianta*
Gogolya ul., 16 312-53-52
Daily; Rbls; Metro Nevskiy Prospekt; F-6

Da-Net
Pushkinskaya ul., 10, apt. 124 164-53-86
Metro Ploshchad Vosstaniya; H-5

Da-Theater, *Metro Vasileostrovskaya;* C-6
Malyy pr., V.O., 124 ....No ☎

Dimitrin Yuriy, Librettist
Please call 164-79-51

Drama Theater, *Metro Chernyshevskaya;* H-7
Liteynyy pr., 19.............................. 275-41-92

Efim Shkolnik Opera
St. Petersburg
Millionnaya ul., 23, apt. 13
Tel 315-46-19
Metro Nevskiy Prospekt; G-6

Etno
Mokhovaya ul., 3 275-42-26
Fax 275-10-86
Metro Chernyshevskaya; H-6

Experiment State Theater
Bolshoy pr., P.S., 35/75 233-94-28
*Tue-Sun 12-15, 16:30-19:30; Rbls, $
Bus 128; Metro Petrogradskaya; E-8*

Glinka Chamber Hall
St. Petersburg City Philharmonic
Nevskiy pr., 30............................... 312-45-85
Daily 11-20; Rbls, $; Metro Nevskiy Prospekt; G-6

Hermitage Theater
Dvortsovaya nab., 34 311-90-25
Tue-Sun ; Rbls, $; Bus 7; Metro Nevskiy Prospekt; F-6

Improvisational -Children's Theater on Ice
Improvizatsiya -Detskiy Ledovyy Teatr
Ligovskiy pr., 148 112-86-25
Mon-Fri 11-15; Eng, Fr

Interernyy Theater
Nevskiy pr., 104 275-53-72
Tue-Sun; Rbls; Metro Ploshchad Vosstaniya; I-5

Komissarzhevkaya Theater (Drama)
Italyanskaya ul., 19 311-31-02
Mon, Wed-Sun 11-15, 16-19:30; Metro Gostinyy Dvor; G-6

MALY
OPERA & BALLET THEATER
(Musorgskiy)
Iskusstv pl., 1
Artistic Director - Stanislav Gaudasinskiy

Tel	219-19-88
Fax....................................	312-27-74

Executive Director:

Tel	314-71-54
Fax....................................	314-36-53

Chief Administrator:

Tel	314-37-58

Box Office:

Tel	219-19-78
Fax....................................	314-36-53
Telex......................	121080 OPERA SU

Metro Nevskiy Prospekt; G-6

Malyy Drama Theater
Rubinshteyna ul., 18 113-20-28
Fax... 113-33-66
*Mon, Wed-Sun 12-15, 16-19:30; Rbls;
Metro Vadimirskaya; H-5*

Mariinskiy Theater of Opera & Ballet
*Former Kirov Theater, for opera & ballet
major theater*
Teatralnaya pl., 1/2........................ 114-12-11
.... 114-45-40
Fax... 314-17-44
Daily 11-17; Rbls; E-5

Miniature Theater   *Teatr Miniatyur*
Mokhovaya ul., 15 .... (Fax) 272-00-15
Metro Chernyshevskaya; H-6

Musical Comedy Theater
Italyanskaya ul., 13 542-14-60
Mon, Wed-Sun 11-19; Rbls; Metro Gostinyy Dvor

Neva Fairytales   *Skazki na Neve*
Sovetskiy per., 5............................ 251-01-13
Metro Moskovskie Vorota

Neva-Kontsert
Lenina pl., 1 542-09-44
Daily 9-21; Rbls; Metro Ploshchad Lenina; I-6

New Theater   *Novyy Teatr*
Oboronnaya ul., 7............................ No Phone
Ger; Metro Narvskaya; D-1

On Mokhovaya
Mokhovaya ul., 35........................... 273-07-30
Fax... 273-07-32
Tue-Sun 9-18; Rbls; Metro Chernyshevskaya; H-6

Open Theater   *Otkrytyy Teatr*
Vladimirskiy pr., 12...................... 113-22-07
Tue-Sun 11-15, 16-18; Rbls; Metro Vladimirskaya; H-5

Osobnyak
Kamennoostrovskiy pr., 55 .... No ☎
Metro Petrogradskaya; F-9

Perelom
Stachek pl., 88/2........................... 255-17-19
Metro Navskaya; D-2

Puppet and Marionettes Theater
Nevskiy pr., 52............................. 311-19-00
Tue-Sun 10:30-15, 16-17; Rbls, $; Eng
T-bus 5; Metro Nevskiy Prospekt; G-5

Puppet Theater (Children's)
Moskovskiy pr., 121 298-00-31
Tue-Sun 10:30-14, 14:30-16; Rbls
Tram 29; Metro Moskovskie Vorota

Pushkin Academic Drama Theater
Ostrovskogo pl., 2 312-15-45
.... 311-61-39
Tue-Sun 11-15, 16-19; Rbls, Bus 22; Metro Gostinyy Dvor; G-5

Rain Theater   *Teatr Dozhdey*
Reki Fontanki nab., 130................. 251-19-50
Metro Technologicheskiy Institut; F-4

Russian-American Theatre

Theatre of the North,
Where East Meets West
Baltic House Theater

Alexandrovskiy Park, 4

Tel./Fax... 232-85-76

Metro Gorkovskaya; F-8

Saint Petersburg
Chaykovskogo ul., 63..................... 273-60-93
Metro Chernyshevskaya; H-7

Satire Theater   *Teatr Satiry*
Sredniy pr., 48............................... 213-00-12
Metro Vasileostrovskaya; D-6

Saturday   *Subbota*
Pravdy ul., 10 315-01-54
Metro Pushkinskaya; G-4

Shapito Big Top Summer Circus
Avtovskaya ul., 1 a........................ 183-15-01
.... 183-14-98
Rbls; Metro Avtovo

Sharmanka
Moskovskiy pr., 151 a.................. 294-63-11
Metro Moskovskie Vorota

Small Petersburg Theater
Malenkiy Peterburgskiy Teatr
Perekupnoy per., 12....................... 274-94-67
Metro Ploshchad Aleksandra Nevskogo; I-5

St. Petersburg Music Hall

Best musical shows in the city

Alexandrovskiy Park, 4.................. 233-02-43

Box Office.................................... 232-92-01

Metro Gorkovskaya; F-8

THE CHAMBER MUSIC THEATER
COMPANY

ST. PETERSBURG OPERA

LISTEN TO CHAMBER OPERAS
IN PETERSBURG'S MOST BEAUTIFUL
PALACES
RUSSIA'S BEST YOUNG VOICES
THEATRE AT ITS BEST
ARTISTIC DIRECTOR
YURI ALEXANDROV

TEL...315-67-69
FAX...271-40-22

St. Petersburg State Academic Ballet Theater
Mayakovskogo ul., 15 273-19-97
Fax... 273-05-89
Daily 10-18; Rbls, $; Metro Mayakovskaya; H-6

St. Petersburg State Conservatory Theater of Opera and Ballet
Teatralnaya pl., 3........................... 312-25-07
Fax... 311-50-34
Mon, Wed-Sun 12-18; Rbls
Tram 1; Metro Sennaya Ploshchad; E-5

State Youth Theater
Reki Fontanki nab., 114................. 292-68-70
Tue-Sun 15-19; Rbls; T-bus 3;
Metro Tekhnologicheskiy Institut; F-4

Teatr Estrady
Bolshaya Konyushennaya ul., 27 314-70-60
Tue-Sun 11-15, 16-19; Rbls; Metro Nevskiy Prospekt; G-6

Theater of Folk Art
Teatr Narodnogo Tvorchestva
Rubinshteyna ul., 13 311-04-06
Metro Vladimirskaya; H-5

Theater OF
Pushkinskaya ul., 10, apt. 109........ 249-59-48
Metro Ploshchad Vosstaniya; H-5

Theater of Realistic Art
Teatr Realnogo Iskusstva
Chernyshevskogo pr., 3.................. 273-98-01
Metro Chernyshevskaya; H-7

Theater on Liteynyy
Liteynyy pr., 51 273-53-35
Tue-Sun 11-14, 15-22; Rbls; Metro Mayakovskaya; H-6

Theater under the Open Sky
Teatr Pod Otkrytym Nebom
Ligovskiy pr., 65 164-94-38
Metro Ligovskiy Prospekt; H-4

The Curved Mirror   *Krivoe Zerkalo*
Bolshaya Konyushennaya ul., 27 314-70-60
Bus 100; Metro Nevskiy Prospekt; G-6

The Parrot Flaubert   *Popugay Flober*
Bolshaya Pushkarskaya ul., 44 238-59-77
Fax... 314-86-62
Metro Gorkovskaya; F-8

The Peacock's Feather   *Pavline Pero*
Ligovskiy pr., 65 164-76-77
Daily 14-18; Metro Ligovskiy Prospekt; H-4

The People's Theater
Rubinshteyna ul., 13 312-34-84
Daily; Rbls; Metro Vladimirskaya; H-5

The Puppet Opera   *Opera Kukol*
Tavricheskaya ul., 4 275-60-90
Fax... 311-58-60
Metro Chernyshevskaya; I-6

The State Circus, *Former Cinizelli Circus*
Reki Fontanki nab., 3 314-84-78
Mon-Wed, Fri-Sun; Rbls; Metro Gostinyy Dvor; G-6

Through the Looking Glass
Children's Theater   *Zazerkale*
Shamsheva ul., 8 238-12-05
Tue-Sun 12-17; Rbls; Metro Petrogradskaya; E-8

*Organization of Performances of
Leading Musical Troupes
in St.Petersburg*
Nevskiy pr., 70
Tel/Fax **273-47-33**

VISIT IE Ltd.
Leading Tours of Ballet Troupes
Performances on the Stages
of St. Petersburg Theaters
Reki Moyki nab., 24, apt. 18.......... 314-10-72
Tel./Fax............................. 314-06-44
*Mon-Fri 10-17, Fr, Rbls, $
Metro Nevskiy Prospekt*

Yusupov Palace, *Daily 11-22; E-5*
Reki Moyki nab., 94 314-98-83

☎ **THEATRICAL TICKET OFFICE**
ТЕАТРАЛЬНЫЕ КАССЫ
THEATERKASSE
THEATRE, VENTE DE TICKETS
TEATER, BILJETTKONTOR
TEATTERILIPPUJENMYYNTI

Tickets for rubles. *You can buy tickets
to most ballets, theaters and concerts in
advance at the theater or at kiosks called
Theater Box Offices* (Teatralnaya kassa,
Театральная касса).

Theater Box offices *are most often
located at the entrances of metros and on
the sidewalks of St. Petersburg. You can
also purchase tickets at the* **Central Box
Office** *on Nevskiy Prospect, 42. To be sure
of the best seats, however, try a tourist
service or service bureau at the major
hotels (in hard currency at much higher
prices). You can also try buying tickets
from "scalpers" at the door of the theater
on the night of the performance. Negotiate.
See our* SEATING PLANS *on page 336.*

Central Box Office No. 1
Nevskiy pr., 42............................. 311-31-83
*11-19; Rbls
T-bus 1, 10, 14, 22, 7; Metro Nevskiy Prospekt*

Kassa   **Box Office**
• Bolsheokhtinskiy pr., 10................ 224-23-92
• Bolshoy pr., P.S., 40 273-07-30
• Bolshoy Sampsonievskiy pr., 80..... 245-30-16
  Mon-Sat 11-15, 16-19; Rbls
• Dvortsovaya nab., 46, Hermitage...... 311-19-20
  Tue-Sun 11-15, 16-18; Rbls
• Griboedova kan. nab., 2 b
  in Russian Museum 219-16-10
  Mon, Wed-Sun 11-15, 16-18; Rbls
• Metro Gostinyy Dvor 251-99-88
  Mon-Sat 11-15, 16-19; Rbls
• Metro Leninskiy Prospekt.............. 254-91-31
  Mon-Sat 11-15, 16-19; Rbls
• Metro Narvskaya 259-77-84
  Mon-Sat 11-15, 16-19; Rbls
• Metro Pushkinskaya 251-90-19
  Mon-Sat 11-15, 16-19; Rbls
• Metro Vladimirskaya 311-11-89
  Mon-Sat 11-15, 16-19; Rbls
• Moskovskiy pr., 130...................... 298-33-20
  Mon-Sat 11-15, 16-19; Rbls
• Nevskiy pr., 22/24 311-15-39
  Mon-Sat 11-15, 16-19; Rbls
• Nevskiy pr., 39............................. 310-42-40
  Mon-Sat 11-15, 16-19; Rbls
• Nevskiy pr., 107 272-65-12
  Mon-Sat 11-18; Rbls; Metro Ploshchad Vosstaniya
• Nevskiy pr., 185........................... 271-51-40
  Mon-Sat 11-19; Rbls
• Sadovaya ul., 24/26...................... 310-46-77
  Mon-Sat 11-19; Rbls
• Sredniy pr., 27 213-18-85
  Mon-Sat 11-15, 16-19; Rbls

☎ **TICKET BUREAUS**
ПРОДАЖА БИЛЕТОВ
KARTENVORVERKAUF
VENTE DE TICKETS
BILJETTFÖRSÄLJNING
LIPPUPALVELUT

See also AIRLINES, BUSES *and* RAIL TRAVEL

Airline Tickets - Aeroflot
Gogolya ul., 7/9............................. 311-80-72
Railroad Tickets
Griboedova kan. nab., 24................ 162-33-44
River Boat Tickets (*only tours*)
Obukhovskoy Oborony pr., 195...... 262-89-94

☎ **TIME & TIME ZONES**
ВРЕМЯ И ВРЕМЕННЫЕ ЗОНЫ
ZEIT & ZEITZONEN
HEURE, TEMPS
KORREKT TID (FROKEN UR)
AIKAVYÖHYKKEET

For the exact time (in Russian), call 08

Daylight Savings. *St. Petersburg goes on
Daylight Savings (Summer) Time on the last
Saturday of March and goes off Daylight
Savings Time on the last Saturday of
September.*

World Time. *St. Petersburg is 3 hours
ahead of Greenwich Mean Time and is in
the same time zone as Moscow. Call 315-
00-12 (in Russian) for the time difference
with a particular city, ask for an English
speaking operator (if needed).*

If the time is 11:00 in the morning
in St. Petersburg, Russia, then the time:

To the West of St. Petersburg is:
10:00	Baltics, Kiev, Helsinki, Tel Aviv
9:00	Warsaw, Paris, Berlin, Rome
8:00	Lisbon, Dublin, London
3:00	New York
2:00	Chicago
1:00	Denver

To the East of St. Petersburg is:
13:00	Tashkent
14:00	Omsk
15:00	Novosibirsk
16:00	Irkutsk (Russia), China
18:00	Vladivostok
19:00	Japan

☎ TIPPING
ЧАЕВЫЕ
TRINKGELD
POURBOIRE
ATT GE DRICKS
JUOMARAHAT

See TRAIN TRAVEL, RESTAURANTS *and* TAXIS
There is no standard for tipping in Russia. As elsewhere, the citizen on the street would be offended if offered a tip for helping you. Service people, however, expect tips for helping with luggage, for service in restaurants or any other substantial help. Hotels and restaurants occasionally add a 5-15% service charge to your bill as well as a 20% value added tax.

☎ TIRES
АВТОПОКРЫШКИ
REIFEN
PNEUS
DÄCK
AUTONRENKAAT

See also AUTOMOBILE PARTS *and*
AUTOMOBILE SERVICE
Avto Technica, *Tire and wheel repair*
  Nekrasova ul., 14a 273-24-26
5th Wheel   **Pyatoe Koleso**
  Sinopskaya nab., 30 274-00-51
       Mon-Sat 10-14, 15-19; Rbls

Sovinteravto service

AUTO PARTS

*Parts, Accessories & Supplies
for Foreign Cars, Trucks & Buses*
Visit Our Shop on Gogolya ul., 19,
near the Astoria Hotel

Gogolya ul., 19 315-97-58
Malodetskoselskiy pr., 26 ... 292-77-18
Fax 292-00-28
Telex .... 121412 LTOS SU
       Mon-Fri 10-18; Eng; $

Sovinteravtoservice (towing service)
  5-yy Predportovyy proezd 290-15-10

☎ TOBACCO
ТАБАК
TABAK
TABAC
TOBAK
TUPAKKA

Many Western cigarettes can be bought in INTERNATIONAL SHOPS, *many* COMMERCIAL SHOPS *and* KIOSKS. *R.J.R. Reynolds products are most popular.*

Commercial Store
  Kamennoostrovskiy pr., 2 233-52-53
       Mon-Fri 10-14, 15-19; Rbls
Store No. 1
  Nevskiy pr., 64 314-42-58
       Mon-Sat 9-14, 15-21; Rbls; Metro Nevskiy Prospekt
Tobacco No. 38
  Ligovskiy pr., 65 164-48-47
       Mon-Sat 9-14, 15-21; Rbls
Tobacco No. 57
  Sadovaya ul., 29 315-94-96
       Mon-Fri 10-14, 15-18; Rbls; Metro Sennaya Ploshchad
Tobacco No. 70
  Rimskogo-Korsakova pr., 13 314-84-14
       Mon-Sat 9-13, 14-17; Rbls

☎ TOILETS

See RESTROOMS

☎ TOURS-RUSSIA
ЭКСКУРСИИ ПО РОССИИ
REISEN DURCH RUßLAND
TOURISME ET EXCURSIONS
EN RUSSIE
UTFLYKTER - RYSSLAND
EKSKURSIOT ,VENÄJÄLLÄ

See TRAVEL AGENCIES,
TOURS - SAINT PETERSBURG
For the most exciting tours of Russia see the ads in TRAVEL AGENCIES, *for local tours see* TOURS-SAINT PETERSBURG *below.*

☎ TOURS SAINT PETERSBURG
ЭКСКУРСИИ ПО
САНКТ-ПЕТЕРБУРГУ
EXKURSIONEN IN
ST.PETERSBURG
TOUR DE VILLE,
SAINT-PETERSBOURG
TURISTBYRÅ
EKSKURSIOT, PIETARISSA

See also TRAVEL AGENCIES, BOAT EXCURSIONS,
and AIR CHARTER

Here are a few firms and individuals specializing in tours of St. Petersburg and the surrounding areas. They often offer tours to the rest of Russia also. In several places of the city (on Nevskiy Prospect at the corner of Dumskaya Street and at Dvortsovaya Square) people are available for immediate excursions of the city.

Aslantis - *See ad under* TRAVEL AGENCIES

Avista-Tur
Millionnaya ul., 7 275-66-35
Mon-Fri 10-18; Rbls, $; Eng, Ger, Chin, Kor

City Excursion Bureau
Krasnogo Flota nab., 56 311-24-45
Mon-Fri 10-18; Rbls; Eng, Ger, Fr, Ital, Pol

Eksta
4-ya Liniya, 45 213-00-71
Mon-Fri 10-18; Rbls, $; Bus 128; Metro Vasileostrovskaya

Epol - *See ad under* TRAVEL AGENCIES

GRIFFON

Furshtadtskaya ul., 9 275-72-15
.... 275-71-21
Fax 275-81-51

Tours of St. Petersburg in any language.

Mon-Fri 10-13, 14-18; Rbls; $; Eng

Helen
Lermontovskiy pr., 43/1 113-08-60
Fax 113-08-59
Mon-Fri 9-18; $, CC; Eng

Itus
Gorokhovaya ul., 47 310-87-43
Fax 310-93-94
Mon-Fri 9:30-18; Rbls

Lasan
Dmitrovskiy per., 6, apt.4 164-27-05
Daily 10-22; Rbls, $; Metro Ploshchad Vosstaniya

LenArt
Nevskiy pr., 40 312-48-37
Fax 110-66-14
Mon-Fri 9-18; Rbls, $, CC; Metro Nevskiy Prospekt

Monuments of Culture   *Pamyatniki Kultury*
Shpalernaya ul., 35 a 273-30-50
Fax 275-79-95
Mon-Fri 9-17; Rbls; Eng, Fr, Pol
Bus 14; Metro Chernyshevskaya

Nevskie Zori
Nevskiy pr., 95 274-00-90
Daily 10-19; Rbls

Panorama
Nevskiy pr., 95, floor 3 277-31-26
Fax 314-16-85
Daily 9:30-19; Rbls; Tram 34; Metro Nevskiy Prospekt

PETER THE GREAT
PERSON TO PERSON TOURS

Let us show you the shops, markets, factories,
museums, the best restaurants, art galleries,
concerts, theater, and night life.
Visit villages, farms & forests.
The parks & palaces of
Pushkin, Pavslosk, & Peterhof.
From early morning to late at night.
English, German & other languages.
Dmitrovskiy per., 16 311-80-19
Fax 526-66-24
Mon-Sat 10-20; Rbls, $; Eng, Ger, Fr

Profi Travel Agency
Yakovlevskiy per., 2 298-13-00
Fax 298-07-00
Daily 9-17; Rbls; Tram 43; Metro Elektrosila

Saint Petersburg
Isaakievskaya pl., 11 315-51-29
Daily 9-21; Rbls; Metro Sennaya Ploshchad

Sphinx
Gatchinskaya ul., 1/56, apt. 68 232-44-02
Mon-Fri 10-18; Rbls, $

Sputnik
Chapygina ul., 4, rm.10, 27 234-02-49
Mon-Fri 9:30-12, 13-18; Rbls, $; Eng, Ger, Fr

STARAYA DEREVNYA
Savushkina ul., 72
239-00-00
Custom Tours of
St. Petersburg

St. Petersburg City Excursion Bureau
Krasnogo Flota nab., 56 311-40-19
Fax 311-86-66
Mon-Fri 10-18; Rbls; Eng, Ger, Fr, Ital, Pol

TEMP-Service, Ltd
Individual Tours for Businessmen
Nevskiy pr., 176 271-04-86
.... 218-55-46

Troika Tours
The Nights of St. Petersburg Tour
Four exciting days and nights
Complete tours include Hermitage, Peter
and Paul Fortress, sightseeing, Pushkin or
Pavlovsk, great restaurants & gala dinner
including the Famous Troika Show.
From $270 depending on hotel.
Zagorodnyy pr., 27 113-53-76
Fax 310-42-79
Telex .... 121299 TROJK SU
Tue-Sun 19-24; Eng; Metro Dostoevskaya

Vet
Reki Fontanki nab., 90, bldg. 1, apt. 17
☎ 314-42-26
Daily 10-17; Rbls; Eng, Ger, Fr; T-bus 17, Metro Pushkinskaya

Vi Tur
Sredniy pr., 5 350-93-54
Fax 213-60-36

☎ **TOY STORES**
ИГРУШКИ, МАГАЗИНЫ
SPIELWARENGESCHÄFTE
MAGASINS DE JOUETS
LEKSAKSAFFÄRER
LELUKAUPAT

Toys can be bought in department stores
and toy stores called Igrushki (игрушки).
Barbie dolls and Legos are the most popular
toys in Russia at the moment.

Detskiy Mir   **Children's World**
Moskovskiy pr., 191 293-50-82
Mon-Sat 10-14, 15-19; Rbls

DLT (Leningrad Trading House)
• Bolshaya Konyushennaya ul., 21/23
☎ 312-26-27
Fax 315-21-92
Toys are on the 1st floor. Mon-Sat 10-20; Rbls, $; Eng
• Sedova ul., 69 560-61-92
Mon-Sat 10-14, 15-19

FAIRN & SWANSON
Electronics, Housewares, Toys
Nevskiy pr., 96.............................. 275-53-85
Fax 275-53-86
Daily 9-14, 15-21; Rubles; English

Foros, *Daily 11-14, 15-19; Rbls, $*
7-ya Liniya, 28 213-46-63
From Clay to Porcelain Art
Please Call 232-35-83
Daily 9-18; Eng

Home □ Center
The Children's Room
Toys, children's furniture,
cribs, strollers and car seats

Located in S.E. St. Pb., minutes from city center
Slavy pr., 30 261-15-50
.... 261-04-02
Fax 260-15-81
Daily 10-20; $, FIM, DM, Rbls; Eng, Finn
Metro Moskovskaya then Bus 31, 114, T-bus 29

Igrushki   **Toy Store**
• Detskaya ul., 26 217-07-20
        Mon-Sat 10-19; Rbls
• Nevskiy pr., 95 279-20-12
        Daily 10-14, 15-20
• Sofiyskaya ul., 29 268-64-93
        Mon-Sat 10-19; Rbls
• Suvorovskiy pr., 15...................... 271-59-67
        Mon-Sat 10-19; Rbls
• Tipanova ul., 18 293-01-24
Lego & Mattel
Nevskiy pr., 48, at the Passage, 3rd floor
☎ 219-17-62
Lotor No. 1, *Mon-Sat 10-19; Rbls*
Prosveshcheniya pr., 78................. 557-87-09
Lyudmila, *Mon-Sat 10-19; Rbls*   **Ludmila**
Prosveshcheniya pr., 46-1 597-33-16
Zolotoy Klyuchik   **Golden Key**
• Marshala Govorova ul., 10 184-83-18
        Mon-Sat 10-14, 15-19; Rbls
• Liteynyy pr., 36............................ 273-66-02

☎ TRADEMARKS
ФАБРИЧНЫЕ МАРКИ,
ТОВАРНЫЕ ЗНАКИ
WARENZEICHEN
MARQUES DE FABRIQUES
FÖRETAGSREGISTRERING
TAVARAMERKIT

Copyrights and trademarks are becoming
important in Russia. Be sure to register any
trademarks.
Informpatent-   **Office & Trademark Agency**
Ligovskiy pr., 87 164-07-38
Fax 164-74-04
     Mon-Fri 9-18; Rbls; Eng, Ger, Fr
     Metro Ploshchad Vosstaniya
Nevinpat - *See ad below*
Petruz Patent Office
Prazhskaya ul., 19, rm. 100, in Dental Clinic
☎ 268-13-89
   Mon,Wed-Fri 10-14, 15-19; Rbls; Eng
   Bus 116; Metro Elizarovskaya

NEVINPAT
St. Petersburg International Patent and Trade Mark Agency

Complete   Registration,
Assistance   Searches
with Patent,   Patent &
Trademark,   Trademark
and Design   Infringement

Nevskiy pr., 134, apt. 5, **4th floor**
Tel.: 274-42-97, 274-43-20
Fax 274-36-06
English, German, Finnish
A Russian-Finnish Law Firm

☎ TRAIN INFORMATION
See RAILWAY STATIONS

☎ TRAIN TRAVEL
See RAIL INFORMATION

☎ TRAMS (TROLLEYS)
ТРАМВАЙ, ИНФОРМАЦИЯ
STRAßENBAHNAUSKUNFT
TRAM, INFORMATION
SPÅRVAGN TROLLEY
RAITIOVAUNUT

See also BUSES, METRO

Trams. *Trams are what Americans call*
"trolleys" and run on rails. "Trolley buses"
*(**T-BUSES**) are really buses powered by elec-*
tricity from overhead wires. The signs for
tram stops hang on wires over the street
and tell you which trams stop there. It is
not unusual to find trams, trolley buses,
and buses all operating along the same
street.

These are the signs for various forms of
street transportation.

SIGNS FOR PUBLIC TRANSPORT		
A	**Ⓜ**	12 33 44 55
BUS STOPS	TROLLEYBUS STOPS	TRAM STOPS
on street	on street	hanging on wire

As with the METRO they run from 5:30
a.m. to 12:30 a.m.

Trams can be the best way to get around,
especially when there are no taxis in sight.
They are often very crowded at rush hour,
but join the crowd.

Fares: *You need "transport coupons"*
called "talony" (талоны) or a "monthly
transport card" (for information about the
"transport cards", see METRO). Buy talony
coupons at special kiosks selling

transport coupons and cards, at Rospechat kiosks, on the bus, trolley bus or tram, and in shops. When you get on, you are supposed to punch the "talony" yourself with a simple punch attached to the wall. If you can't reach it, pass your "talony" along, someone will help you punch it. The cost is minimal but fares are changing quickly. The "honor" system is checked at random and you should be prepared to show your "talony" or pass.

TRANSPORT MAPS

On The Traveller's Yellow Page's City Map of St. Petersburg, the TRAM lines are indicated by SOLID RED lines, boxes and numbers, the BUS lines by SOLID BLUE lines, boxes and numbers, the TROLLEYBUS (T-Bus) lines by DOTTED RED lines, boxes and numbers.

Buy a metro map and also a transport map of St. Petersburg called Skhema Passazhirskogo Transporta (Схема Пассажирского Транспорта) at kiosks, Rospechat and book stores. They are in Russian with some English and the route numbers are clear. These are designed and published by Poly-Plan, St. Petersburg.

☎ TRANSLATION SERVICES
ПЕРЕВОДЫ, СЛУЖБА
ÜBERSETZER/DOLMETSCHER
TRADUCTION, SERVICE DE
ÖVERSÄTTNINGSBYRÅER
KÄÄNNÖSTOIMISTOT

St. Petersburg is well supplied with translators and interpreters of all languages, many are graduates of the Philological Faculty of St. Petersburg State University. Most BUSINESS CENTERS offer translating (writing) and interpreting (spoken) services.

AsLANTIS

All Types of Translation & Interpreting

Guided Tours & Fax Services

Desk: House of Books, Ground Floor

Nevskiy pr., 28; *Hrs: 16-20*

Dibunovskaya ul., 24, office 7

Tel./Fax... 239-36-45

English, French, Metro: Chernaya Rechka

Assco, *Daily 11-19; Rbls; Eng, Ger, Fr*
Ligovskiy pr., 197, Messages......... 166-55-48
Asta, *Eng, Ger, Fr, Finn, Swed, Ital*
Bolshoy pr., P.S., 82, rm. 17.......... 230-88-29
Fax 232-75-35
Mon-Fri 10-12, 13-17; Rbls, $
Belye Nochi **White Nights**
Sredneokhtinskiy pr., 18/12 224-30-97
Mon-Sat 10-21; Rbls
City Center Translation
Bronnitskaya ul., 15 292-50-96
Fax 259-62-52
Mon-Fri 10-13, 14-18; Rbls

Congress-Service
Kazanskaya ul., 36, rm. 705 319-93-70
Fax... 312-85-56
Mon-Fri 9-17
Contact Tourism for Students
Professora Popova ul., 5 234-69-59
Mon-Fri 10-18; Rbls

BUSINESS CENTER 🕮 GRAND HOTEL EUROPE

★★★★★

ST. PETERSBURG RUSSIA

Fax, telex, telephones, computers, photocopies
Audio-visual support and projectors
Secretaries and interpreters
Six meeting rooms

Mikhaylovskaya Street 1/7
Saint Petersburg, 191011

Info/Switchboard .... 119-60-00, Ext. 6234
Fax:.. 119-60-01

Iakinf, *Eng, Chinese*
Grecheskiy per., 15, apt. 28...............274-72-18
Mon-Fri 10-18; $
Inkont
Kazanskaya ul., 36, rm. 215 314-78-48
Mon-Fri 10-16
Inter
Bronnitskaya ul., 15 259-62-52
Mon-Fri 10-18; Rbls
Interpreter, *Swed, Dan, Nor*
Please call....................................... 232-13-42
Interpreter, *English*
Please call....................................... 219-51-48
Introkon, *Eng, Ger, Fr, Finn, Swed, Ital*
Marshala Govorova ul., 52.............. 252-10-08
Fax... 252-10-03
Mon-Fri 9-18; Rbls, $
Intourist, *Eng, Ger*
Isaakievskaya pl., 11, rm. 127 210-09-32
Fax... 315-55-54
Mon-Fri 10-18; Rbls, $
Kontakt, *Eng, Dutch, Swed* **Contact**
Professora Popopa ul., 5, rm. 60....... 234-69-59
Mon-Fri 10-18; Rbls
Konwest, *Eng, Ger, Fr*
Reki Fontanki nab., 23...................... 311-30-18
Mon-Fri 10-20; Rbls, $
LenArt
Nevskiy pr., 40................................. 312-48-37
Fax... 110-66-14
Mon-Fri 9-18; Rbls, $, CC; Metro Nevskiy Prospekt

Anna V. Letoutchaia
Official interpreter
Please call 277-33-88
Fax............................541-81-46

Lingvakhim
Zheleznodorozhnyy pr., 40 560-43-34
Fax... 568-14-98
Mon-Fri 9-17; Rbls, $
Optima-Office
Chaykovskogo ul., 36..................... 273-29-64
Fax... 273-78-82
Mon-Fri 10-20; Rbls

Personnel Corps
Nevskiy pr., 104............................ 275-83-23
.... 275-45-86
Fax 275-83-23

RAmbus Ltd.

Interpreting & Translation Services
Personal Computer Programs
Kosmonavtov pr., 18/2, apt. 6
Tel 299-46-24

Retur Business Center, *Eng, Fr*
Gertsena ul., 39, 2nd floor, Hotel Astoria
☎ 311-73-62
Fax 311-42-12
Daily 9-23; $, CC
Sezam, *Eng, Ger, Fr, Ital, Sp*
Zheleznovodskaya ul., 66, apt.116
☎ 350-45-42
Daily 9-17; Rbls, $
Sphinx, *Eng, Ger*
Bronnitskaya ul., 15 259-62-52
Fax 112-65-15
Mon-Fri 9:30-13, 14-18; Rbls, $

St. Petersburg Chamber of
Commerce & Industry
Translation Services
Chaikovskogo ul., 46-48.....279-05-90

Transelectro OY
Moskovskiy pr., 171 294-06-35
Fax 294-04-43
Mon-Fri 9-18; Rbls, $
Translation Services, *Eng*
Please call 525-88-83
Daily 11-23; Rbls
Translation Services, *Eng, Sp*
Please call 542-76-46
Varyag Tours
Kamennoostrovskiy pr., 27 232-03-60
Mon-Fri 10-14, 15-19; Rbls, $
Ves St. Petersburg
Gertsena ul., 8 312-67-72
Mon-Fri 11-19; Rbls; Eng
Yuniks, *Mon-Fri 12-18; Rbls, $, CC*
Italyanskaya ul., 23 315-17-01
Znanie   **Knowledge**
Kavalergardskaya ul., 10, rm. 19 278-50-35
Znanie Society, *Eng, Ger*
Liteynyy pr., 42.............................. 279-52-85
Fax 279-53-90
Mon-Fri 10-17:30; Rbls, $

☎ **TRAVEL AGENCIES**
ТУРИСТИЧЕСКИЕ АГЕНТСТВА
REISEBÜROS
VOYAGES, AGENCES
DE/AGENCES
RESEBYRÅER
MATKATOIMISTOT

The tourist industry and travel agency
situation has changed dramatically in the
past year. The once powerful Intourist
Agency has been split into many indepen-
dent hotels, travel agencies and travel
services and the competition between
travel agencies and tour-excursion services
is growing. Quality in many hotels is
rapidly improving.

A B C EducATion CenTer
Custom tours for business,
education and pleasure.
Attractive rates.

Moscow, Ger. Panfilovtsev, ul., 9/1, suite 38
Tel.. (095) 494-14-92
Fax .... (095) 494-65-75
Mon-Sat 9:30-19:30; Rubles, $; English

AMERICAN EXPRESS
TRAVEL SERVICE
In the Grand Hotel Europe

Air Tickets ● Business Travel
Card Member Services ● Foreign Exchange
Mikhaylovskaya ul., 1/7............ 119-60-09
Fax 119-60-11
Telex .... 621198 AMEX SU

ARS, *Mon-Fri 10-18; Rbls, $*
Sezzhinskaya ul., 21 235-68-50
Artell Ltd.
Nevskiy pr., 48.............................. 311-96-10
Fax.. 110-55-10
Mon-Fri 10-18; Rbls, $; Eng, Ger; Metro Nevskiy Prospekt

ATLAS 🖋 АТЛАС
Cultural, Business & Specialized
Tours Throughout CIS
Bolshaya Morskaya ul., 35....... 312-20-60
Fax.. 319-97-09

DELOVIE LYUDI

I N D E P E N D E N T ● O B J E C T I V E ● T H O R O U G H
Profsoyuznaya ul., 73; Tel.: (095) 333-33-40; Fax: (095) 330-15-68

Avista-Tur
Millionnaya ul., 7 275-66-35
Mon-Fri 10-18; Rbls, $; Eng, Ger, Chin, Kor

BALTIC BRIDGE LTD.

Tourist Services. Russian Language Courses.
Kronverkskaya ul., 27 232-98-38
Fax...................................352-26-88

Baltic Travel Company
Fax 251-50-27
Telex................................121331 BALTR SU

All-Inclusive & Specialized Tours
Throughout Russia Including
Cultural Tours
Wide Choice of Cruise Lines
Trekking, Rafting, Mountaineering
Skiing, Hunting & Fishing Trips
Specialized Tours for
Businessmen and Professionals
Visa Support & Hotel Reservations
Russian Language and
Business Courses
Ballet School Led by
Kirov Ballet Dancers

P.O. Box 375, St. Petersburg 197198, Russia
Tel 168-88-04
Fax 312-41-28
Telex.............................. 21345 BOUZINENKO
E-mail............................tour@fabcb.spb.su

CGTT Lepertours
Konnogvardeyskiy blvd., 4, entr. 6 apt. 34
.... 312-72-92
Mon-Fri 9-17; $; Eng, Fr; T-bus 14, 22
Metro Nevskiy Prospekt
Central Travel Bureau
Bolshaya Konyushennaya ul., 27 315-45-55
Mon-Fri 9-18; Rbls
Contact Tourism for Students
Professora Popova ul., 5 234-69-59
Mon-Fri 10-18; Rbls; Most European languages
Da Tur
Reki Karpovki nab., 25 234-49-98
Fax 232-68-63
Mon-Fri 9:30-13, 14-18; Rbls, $, CC; Eng, Fr
Duncan, *Name to change*
Mayakovskogo ul., 8 272-99-86
Fax 275-13-36
Mon-Fri 10-18; Rbls, $; Eng, Ger, Fr
Edelveys   **Edelweis**
4-ya Liniya, 29 218-21-24
Fax 213-26-57
Mon-Fri 14-17
Eksta
4-ya Liniya, 45 213-00-71
Mon-Fri 10-18; Rbls, $; Bus 128
Metro Vasileostrovskaya

EPOL
Travel
Agency

A Full Service Travel Agency

All-Inclusive Tours of Saint Petersburg, Moscow,
Kiev and the Baltics

SPECIALIZING IN CUSTOM TOURS IN RUSSIA
Art, Ballet, Music & Theatrical, Church Pilgrimages,
Architecture, Photography, Sports,
Mountaineering, Hunting & More.

Business Travel Arrangements & Transit

Liteynyy pr., 6/1 279-50-60
.... 278-09-52
Fax 279-50-66
Hrs: 9:30-18:00, English, German, French

ESCAPE TRAVEL LTD.

Hotel & Travel Arrangements
Meeting & Seminar Planning
Corporate Incentive Programs
Special Events & Theme Parties
Krasnoselskoe shosse, 46/4 134-16-11
.... 135-55-92
Fax 312-41-28

Etno, *Mon-Fri 10-18*
Kurskaya ul., 40 166-84-97
Fax 230-18-06
Galatur
Reshetnikova ul., 15 298-83-09
Fax 298-85-33

USA TRAVEL AGENCY IN RUSSIA

GRIPHON
TRAVEL

- **Any Destination • Any Airline**
- **Lowest Airfares on the Market**

Moskva Hotel, Service Bureau 274-00-22
Hrs: 10-18, $, English
Subsidiary of Griphon Travel, USA
Representation in St. Petersburg

Helen, *Mon-Fri 9-18; $, CC; Eng*
Lermontovskiy pr., 43/1 259-20-48
Fax 113-08-60
Imac Inc., *Mon-Fri 11-18; Rbls, $; Eng*
Tuchkov per., 24, off. 1 213-64-04
Intant-Tour - *See ad on next page*
InterAries
Konnogvardeyskiy blvd., 4, apt. 26..... 314-92-37
Fax 311-81-39
Mon-Fri 10-18; Rbls, $; Eng; T-bus 5; Metro Sennaya Ploshchad

INTANT-TOUR travel agency

*A Full Service Travel Agency
Deluxe Tours to Belgium,
The Netherlands, Luxembourg*

Blokhina ul., 15	230-98-40
Tel/Fax	230-47-06
Fax	311-77-58
Telex	121320 NAUKA SU

International Tourist Center
Professora Popova ul., 47, rm. 710 234-52-34
Mon-Fri 12-18
Intertrans in the Hotel Moskva
Aleksandra Nevskogo pl., 2, entr. 5....274-20-92
Fax 274-21-21
Daily 9-19; Rbls, $; Eng, Ger, Fr
Intourservice
Gorokhovaya ul., 69 113-18-51
Fax 113-59-83
Mon-Fri 9-17:30; Rbls

INTURBUREAU
Travel Agency

Accommodations in 3 and 4 Star Hotels
Rail and Aeroflot Ticket Service
Guided Tours by Professional Staff in
Comfortable Mini & Full Sized Buses

| Galernaya ul., 22 | 315-78-76 |
| Fax | 315-76-12 |

Lats
6-ya Sovetskaya ul., 25/20 271-28-18
Mon-Fri 10-18; Rbls; Eng, Ger, Finn
Laval
Stachek pr., 12, P.O. Box 349 255-37-60

AGENCY **LENALPTOURS**

*Trekking, Mountaineering & Exotic Tours
in Altai, Pamirs, Tian Shian, Kamchatka
Kyzylkumy Desert, Russian Arctic &
North Pole. City Tours in the CIS.*

193029, Bolshoy Smolenskiy pr., 2

Tel	567-95-51
Fax	567-98-34
Telex	121619 VYSOT SU

LenArt
Nevskiy pr., 40.............................. 312-48-37
Fax 110-66-14
Mon-Fri 9-18; Rbls, $, CC; Metro Nevskiy Prospekt

Litota
Reki Moyki nab., 42, apt. 25........... 314-53-40
Mon-Sat 9-18; Rbls, $; Eng, Ger, Fr, Ital, Sp
Lotto, *Mon-Fri 10-18; Rbls, $; Eng*
Nevskiy pr., 170, apt. 2 277-41-45
Margeu-Tour
Liteynyy pr., 62 279-47-07
Fax 275-88-36
Mon-Sat 9:30-19; Rbls, $; Eng, Ger, Fr
Mila
Mokhovaya ul., 27/29, off. 21 275-44-42
Fax 275-36-59
Mon-Fri 11-18; Rbls; Eng, Ger, Fr, Ital
Monuments of Culture *Pamyatniki Kultury*
Shpalernaya ul., 35 a..................... 273-30-50
Fax 275-79-95
*Mon-Fri 9-17; Rbls; Eng, Fr, Pol
Bus 14; Metro Chernyshevskaya*
Neva, *Mon-Fri 9:30-18; Rbls; Eng*
Sablinskaya ul., 7 230-45-62
Fax 230-80-65
Neva, *Water Tourism Club, River Tours in Russia*
Martynova nab., 94 235-27-22

NORD-SOYUZ

River & Canal Tours of St. Petersburg

Cruises to Kizhi & Valaam

Various Tours through Russia

| Bolshaya Posadskaya ul., 9A | 238-82-61 |
| Fax | 232-59-13 |

Orbita, *Mon-Fri 10-17; Rbls, $*
Saltykova-Shchedrina ul., 30, rm. 54
☎ 273-42-95
Panorama, *Mon-Sat 10-19; Rbls*
Nevskiy pr., 95, 3rd floor................ 277-31-26
Fax 277-30-64

PETRO NTEX

Serving Tourist Groups & Visitors
to St. Petersburg in 5,4,3 Star Hotels
Tours Throughout Russia & Bulgaria
Ligovskiy pr., 10, rm. 404
(In Hotel Oktyabrskaya)

Tel	277-64-00
Tel/Fax	277-64-04
Telex	121667 LEC SU

Pomoshchnik
Reki Moyki nab., 72 310-00-52
Fax 164-37-26
Mon-Fri 9-18; Rbls; Bus 22; Metro Gostinyy Dvor
Profi Travel Agency
Yakovlevskiy per., 2 298-13-00
Fax 298-07-00
Daily 9-17; Rbls; Tram 43; Metro Elektrosila
Retur, *Mon-Fri 10-18; $, CC; Eng, Ger, Fr*
Shpalernaya ul., 16 273-93-32
Fax 273-97-97

Romos-Tur, *Mon-Fri 10-19; Rbls, $; Eng*
Goncharnaya ul., 11 275-38-48
Russian Dimensions, Ltd.
Millionnaya ul., 27 315-45-05
Satellite phone 850-15-50

R U S S I A N   F A I R
Accommodations, Tours & River Cruises in
St. Petersburg, Moscow, Novgorod, Pskov,
Petrozavodsk, Siberia, Sochi, Tallinn
Pobedy pl., 1 (Pulkovskaya Hotel, Bldg. 2)
Tel. 264-58-70
Tel/Fax 592-02-45

Russian Travel
Liteynyy pr., 64, 2nd floor 273-41-33
Fax 275-61-42
Saint Petersburg Tourist Company
Formerly part of Intourist
Isaakievskaya pl., 11 315-51-29
Fax 315-55-54
Daily 9:30-18; Rbls, $

SANKT-PETERSBURG
CULTURE-SCIENCE-TECHNOLOGY-BUSINESS

Specialized tours in St. Petersburg for
groups & individuals
Accommodations in any hotel or
individual apartment with
personal cook.
Transportation around the clock
Guides, Interpreters, Business Center
We Bring Business People Together

Reki Fontanki nab., 21

☎ 210-45-13
☎ 117-21-77
Fax 117-21-76
Fax 314-70-53

Severnaya Palmira, *Mon-Fri 10-18; Rbls*
Reki Fontanki nab., 109 310-15-47
Fax 310-13-45

---

siti Since 1989
Co., Ltd.

*A Name You Can Trust
in Travel*
**Your Full Service
Travel Agency**

Smolnyy, "Porch" 9,
Tel./Fax 273-08-71
Telex: 121350 VEPS SU, Attn. SITI

Skate-Tour, *Mon-Fri 11-17; Rbls*
Blokhina ul., 33 233-16-16
Slita, *Mon-Fri 10-18; Rbls, $; Eng, Ger, Fr*
Kazanskaya ul., 5 312-41-88
Soyuz
Shaumyana pr., 22 221-39-42
Fax 528-01-67
Mon-Fri 9-17
Sputnik, *International Youth Travel Bureau*
Chapygina ul., 4, rm.10, 27 234-02-49
Mon-Fri 9:30-12, 13-18; Rbls, $; Eng, Ger, Fr

⌘⌘ *SPCT* ⌘⌘
St. Petersburg Council for Tourism
Leader in travel and tour services
in the St. Petersburg Region

Head Office: Italyanskaya ul., 3
St. Petersburg 191011, Russia
Tel 314-87-86, 110-67-39
Fax 110-68-24, 311-93-81
Telex .... 321893 TURIST
12 Hotels
Okhtinskaya**** 227-44-38
Oktivian*** (Closed for repair) 356-11-62
Russ** 272-03-21
Mir** 108-51-66
Fedorovskiy Gorodok[1] 476-36-00
Repinskiy**[2] 231-65-09
Repinskiy Camping[2] 231-68-84
Terioki[3] 231-44-20
Losevskaya**[4] .... (279) 6-72-29
Nakhimovskaya (camp)[5] (278) 6-51-22
Poddubskaya (camp)[6] .. (272) 7-74-83
Tolmachevskaya*[7] ...... (272) 7-43-73
[1] Pushkin, [2] Repino, [3] Zelenogorsk,
[4] Losevo, [5] near Priozersk,
[6] near Luga, [7] near Tolmachevo

Travel & Tour Service Bureaus
Central Travel Bureau of SPCT
Bolshaya Konyushennaya ul.,27 315-30-74
Regional
Volkhov .... (263) 2-26-11
Vyborg .... (278) 2-06-46
Gatchina .... (271) 3-87-40
Kirishy .... (268) 2-31-89
Kolpino 484-12-50
Lodeynoe Pole .... (264) 2-00-81
Luga .... (272) 2-28-02
Peterhof 422-12-08
Priozersk .... (279) 2-19-31
Sestroretsk 231-66-09
Tikhvin .... (267) 2-33-49
Tosno .... (261) 2-18-88
Other Travel Services
Intourbureau 315-78-76
Coaches (TOURIST) 225-06-55
Tourist Club 311-14-19
Tourist Sports Union 311-42-75

St. Petersburg City Excursion Bureau
See our beautiful city with us
Krasnogo Flota nab., 56 311-40-19
Fax 311-86-66
Mon-Fri 10-18; Rbls; Eng, Ger, Fr, Ital, Pol

◢◣ SVELEN

Full service travel agency

Please call.....................242-27-31
Fax................................242-13-85
Telex.................121340 MEDIN SU

Temp-Service, *Moving Fall 1993*
Nevskiy pr., 176.............................271-04-86
Fax 278-12-10
Mon-Fri 10-13:30, 14:30-18; Rbls

Tourist Firm 33
Muchnoy per., 3, rm. 27 310-53-64
Fax 315-17-01
Mon-Fri 9:30-17; Rbls, $ Tram 54; Metro Sennaya Ploshchad

Travel Agency, *Mon-Fri 9-17; Rbls*
Storozhevoy Bashni ul., 11........(278) 2-06-46

Tur-Rossa
Khlopina ul., 11..............................534-48-44
Fax 534-49-07
Mon-Fri 9:30-18; Rbls, $; Ger

Turbus
Sapernyy per., 16........................273-00-67
Mon-Fri 10-19; Rbls, $; Tram 5; Metro Chernyshevskaya

Turist
Reki Moyki nab., 58 311-25-20
Fax 311-59-49
Mon-Fri 10-17:30; Rbls, $; Eng, Ger, Finn

◢ UNiREM TRAVEL AGENCY

Full Service Travel Agency
Group & Individual Tours in
Russia, CIS & Europe
International Bus Routes
Restaurant & Hotel Reservations
Bus & Automobile Rentals
Excursion & Theater Tickets
Translators

Konnogvardeyskiy blvd., 1
Tel: **311-78-95**; Fax: **314-92-48**
Telex: 121054 UREM SU

Valaam-Tur
Turbinnaya ul., 7, apt. 13 186-72-55
Mon-Fri 10-18; Rbls, $; Eng

Valentina-Reisen International
Podezdnoy per., 3 a 311-78-23
Daily 9-18; Rbls, $

Varyag Tours
Kamennoostrovskiy pr., 27 232-03-60
Mon-Fri 10-14, 15-19; Rbls, $; T-bus 6; Metro Petrogradskaya

Vet
Reki Fontanki nab., 90, bldg. 1, apt. 17
☎ 314-42-26
Daily 10-17; Rbls; Eng, Ger, Fr; T-bus 17; Metro Pushkinskaya

Violetta
Rizhskiy pr., 29..............................259-92-16
11-19; Bus 22, 27; Metro Ploshchad Vosstaniya

VISIT IE Ltd.

Full Service Educational Tours Including
Ballet & Master Musician Classes and
Russian Language Courses
Reki Moyki nab., 24, apt. 18..........314-10-72
Tel./Fax...................................314-06-44
Mon-Fri 10-17, Fr, Rbls, $; Metro Nevskiy Prospekt

Voyage

Please call 110-62-56
....312-10-01
Guided tours

Yana-Print, *Mon-Fri 9:30-18; Rbls, $; Eng*
Konnogvardeyskiy blvd., 4, entry 6, apt. 33
☎ 311-97-15
Fax..312-72-92

☎ TRAVEL BOOKS/GUIDES to ST. PETERSBURG
ПУТЕВОДИТЕЛИ ПО САНКТ-ПЕТЕРБУРГУ
REISEFÜHRER FÜR ST. PETERSBURG
GUIDES DE VOYAGES POUR ST. PETERSBOURG
RESEGUIDER, ST. PETERSBURG
MATKAOPPAAT

See also BUSINESS PUBLICATIONS
Most English language guides are still available only outside of Russia, except for our Traveller's Yellow Pages for Saint Petersburg 1993-1994. Because changes occur so rapidly, most directories quickly become out dated and incomplete with many wrong names and numbers. Here are some of the best.

☒ *Not Available in St. Petersburg*
☑ *Available in St. Petersburg*

***Baedeker's Leningrad, *1991,(NY: Prentice Hall), 295 pp., $15.95. "Best general guide to St. Petersburg. Look for new edition soon, the German edition is already out." Editors of TYP.* The Traveller's Yellow Pages *is designed to complement Baedeker's Guides in size and content.* ☒

Baltic States & Russia Through the Back Door *1993, 77 pp. $3.00* ☑

***Blue Guide to Moscow and Leningrad, *1989, (Black, Landon, Norton: England), 392 pp., $16.95 . A classic "must-bring". "Absolute best on history, architecture, art, music, culture with great walking tours." TYP editors.* ☒

City Breaks in Moscow & Leningrad. *1990, 80 pp., $6.95. Another short guide, outdated.* ☒

Essential Moscow and Leningrad. *1991,128 pp. $7.95. A good start for the tourist. Outdated.* ☒

Fodor's Russia and the Baltic Countries *1993, $18,00. One of the best general guides to the former Soviet Republics. "A good read."* ☒

Guide to Budget Accommodations (International Youth Hostel Federation) 1993, $8.00 ⊠

Harper's Independent Traveler, Soviet Union. 1990, (NY, Harper & Row) 352 pp., $10.95. "Good tours, well written with historical, cultural, and practical information." Outdated ⊠

Hippocrene Insider's Guide to Moscow, Leningrad & Kiev. 1990, 175 pp. $11.95.

Insight City Guides. St. Petersburg (Leningrad), 1992 (APA Publications) 297 pp. $19.95. Excellent guide to St. Petersburg, with photos and cultural & historical commentary. ⊠

Leningrad Atlas Turista. 1990, 95 pp. Available in kiosks in Russian. Excellent street maps. ☑

Leningrad Guide 1990. 134 pp. Available in Kiosks in English, very useful with good information on buses, trains, and metro. ☑

Leningrad Success Guide. Available in kiosks in English, useful but incomplete with good maps. ☑

Moscow-Leningrad Handbook including the Golden Ring by Masha Nordbye, 1991, (CA: Moon) 205 pp., $12.95. ⊠

Motorist Guide To The Soviet Union, 1980, by Leonid Zadvorny (Moscow, Progress Publisher, out-of-print, available in several book shops). Very biased, very interesting itinerary descriptions; distances & driving conditions, facilities. Not much has changed. ☑

*Russia Business Survival Guide. March 1993. $24.50. An excellent informative guide with good references to business publications for those coming to Russia. Interesting read. ☑

Russiawalks, Seven intimate walking tours of Moscow and Leningrad, with maps, photos, and select list of restaurants, cafes and shops, by David & Valeria Matlock, Henry Holts; NY 1991, $12.95.

Sankt-Peterburg, Petrograd, Leningrad Entsiklopedicheskiy Spravochnik 1992 (Saint-Petersburg, Petrograd, Leningrad, An Encyclopedic Handbook), 1992, 687 pp., (St. Petersburg: Nauchnoe Izdatelsvo Bolshaya Russiyskaya Entsiklopediya). A fantastic guidebook about everything in St. Pb., for the Russian reader.

St. Petersburg Visitor's Guide 1992, 171 pp. $5.00.

The Economist Guide USSR, 1990. About $20.00.(Hutchinson, London). Outdated, but a must read for a quick overview of the resources and of the old Soviet economy, business and cultural awareness. ⊠

The Fresh Guide to Saint Petersburg 1993, (San Francisco: Fresh Air), $7.00. Useful information especially for young travelers. Good companion to The Traveller's Yellow Pages for St. Petersburg. ☑

The St. Petersburg Rough Guides. Rob Humphreys and Don Richardson 1993. The Rough Guides, England, 1993.

A great eclectic travel guide. Fun and practical. But times move quickly.

***The Traveller's Yellow Pages For Saint Petersburg, 1993-1994 with City Map. June 1993, 348 pp., map, $8.95, plus s&h. The first Yellow Pages for St. Petersburg, the most up-to-date, with useful information and over 4000 telephone numbers and addresses listed in over 440 categories from Accounting Firms and Art Galleries to Yachts and Zoos. Ideal for the tourist, student, business traveler and resident. InfoServices International, Inc. NY, USA and Telinfo, St. Petersburg, Russia. Updates will be available to registered readers. ☑

In Russia: **TELINFO**

⊠ 190000, St. Petersburg, Russia, Nab. Reki Moyki, 64,
☎ .... (812) 315-64-12
Fax: .... (812) 312-73-41
⊠ 103001, Moscow, Russia, Granatnyy per., 3
☎ .... (095) 290-22-12
Fax: .... (095) 290-43-79

For the rest of the world:

InfoServices International, Inc.,
⊠ 1 Saint Marks Place,
Cold Spring Harbor, NY 11724, USA
☎ .... (516) 549-0064,
Fax: .... (516) 549-2032,
Telex: .... 221213 TTC UR
*USSR, 1991,(Berkeley CA: Lonely Planet), 810 pp. $21.45. Interesting with good, practical information and maps, but outdated. Still very useful for all-Russia travel.

Where in St. Petersburg. $13.50 about 130 pp. New edition in September ?1993. (Vermont: Russian Information Service). Useful "white pages" directory, but incomplete "yellow pages". Street & metro maps.

ST.PETERSBURG
TOURIST GUIDE

Russian & English Edition

Contains the Most Complete & Reliable Information about the City's History, Businesses, Cultural & Religious Life, Entertainment, Transportation, Communications, etc.

Gertsena ul., 20
191065, St.Petersburg, Russia

Tel.: 314-59-82 Fax.: 315-35-92
LIC Information & Publishing Agency Ltd.

☎ TRAVELER'S CHEQUES
ДОРОЖНЫЕ ЧЕКИ
REISESCHECKS
CHEQUES DE VOYAGE
RESECHECKAR
MATKASHEKIT

See BANKS *and* CURRENCY EXCHANGE

Some banks in St. Petersburg will cash traveler's cheques for dollars, however, be sure to purchase better known cheques such as American Express, VISA or Bank of America. Also, be sure to take your passport along. These banks include: Bank Saint Petersburg, I&C (Promstroybank), Vneshtorgbank, Credo-Bank, or at the American Express office in the Grand Hotel Europe. Many other banks refuse them. Less than $100 can be cashed into dollars when purchasing at the better hard currency shops.

While credit cards are increasingly accepted by shops, restaurants and hotels, traveler's cheques often are not accepted in place of dollars. Your passport is needed when paying by traveler's cheque or credit card.

☎ TROLLEYS (TRAMS)
ТРАМВАЙ, ИНФОРМАЦИЯ
STRAßENBAHNAUSKUNFT
TRAM, EXCURSIONS EN
SPÅRVAGN TROLLEY
TROLLEYBUSSIT

See TRAMS

What Americans call "TROLLEYS" running on tracks are called TRAMS. We are using TRAM, as the Europeans do here in this book.

☎ TRUCK PARK
ГРУЗОВИКИ, СТОЯНКИ
PARKPLÄTZE, LASTKRAFTWAGEN
PARKINGS, CAMIONS
PARKERINGSPLATSER LASTBIL
KUORMA-AUTOJEN
PAIKOITUS

Guarded truck parks are mandatory.
Motel Olgino, *Daily 0-24, $*
Primorskoe shosse, 18 km............. 238-37-18
Motel Retur, *Daily 0-24, $*
Primorskoe shosse, 29 km............. 237-75-33

High Security AUTO PARK
Cars, Trucks, Buses
Varshavskaya ul., 42..........296-58-20
Near the Russia Hotel
Daily 24 Hrs; English, $ & Rbls

☎ TRUCK RENTALS
ГРУЗОВИКИ, АРЕНДА
PARKPLÄTZE LASTKRAFTWAGEN
CAMIONS, LOCATION DE
LASTBILSLUTHYRNING
KUORMA-AUTOJEN VUOKRAUS

See also MOVING COMPANIES *and* TRUCKING

Naydenov i Kompanony
Telezhnaya ul., 7/9 530-25-23
Daily 9-21; Metro Ploshchad Vosstaniya

☎ TRUCK SALES
ГРУЗОВИКИ, ПРОДАЖА
LASTKRAFTWAGEN, VERKAUF
CAMION, VENTE
LASTBIL, FÖRSÄLJNING
KUORMA-AUTOJEN MYYNTI

East Trade Polmot Holding
Nakhimova ul., 7, apt. 102.............. 356-33-64
Mon-Fri 8-14; Rbls, $; Eng, Ger, Pol

RENAULT ◆ TRUCKS

Sales & Leasing

Lyubotinskiy proezd., 5 298-36-48
.... 298-12-94
Fax 298-00-73
Telex .... 121028 MATRA SU
24 Hours Daily; $; English, German

Morilen GAZ Trucks, *Mon-Sat 10-18; Rbls*
Narodnogo Opolcheniya pr., 207 136-68-86

SOVAVTO ST. PETERSBURG
VOLVO Truck Sales
Volvo Authorized Truck Dealer
Sales, Service, Repairs & Parts
Used Volvo & Maz Trucks
Large Stock of Used Trailers
Distributor of Volvo truck parts for Russia
Full Warranty in Russia and Abroad
Vitebskiy pr., 3............................298-46-50
Fax 298-77-60
Telex ....121535 AVTO
Hrs. 8:30-17:30; English, German

TRUCKCENTRUM SLIEDRECHT

First Class Used Trucks And
Trailers From Holland
From Our Stock Of More Than
300 Units We Can Offer:
MAN, VOLVO, MERCEDES, DAF, SCANIA,
RENAULT, IVESCO, TANK, FRIGO and
Open & Closed Trailers
For More Information Please Contact Us

Tel	31-0-1840-10811
Fax	31-0-1840-11865
Telex	23155 TRUCK NL

☎ TRUCK SERVICE & REPAIRS
ГРУЗОВИКИ, ОБСЛУЖИВАНИЕ
И РЕМОНТ
LASTKRAFTWAGEN, SERVICE
UND REPARATUR
CAMION, REPARATION
LASTBIL, SERVICE OCH
REPARATION
KUORMA-AUTOJEN KORJAUS
JA HUOLTO

MATRALEN
Lyubotinskiy proezd., 5.......298-36-48
Fax....................................298-00-73
Telex .... 121028 MATRA SU

SOVAVTO ST. PETERSBURG
TRUCK SERVICE
TRUCK AND TRAILER
REPAIRS and PARTS
Volvo, DAF & Maz trucks
All Russian & European trailers
Large inventory of tires, brake parts, axles
Warranty work
Factory tested mechanics, modern paint and
test facilities

Sovtransavto

Vitebskiy pr., 3	298-55-56
Shushary Railroad Station	293-73-71
Fax	298-77-60
Telex	121535 AVTO

Mon-Sat, 7-22, $ & Rbls., German,
Translators available

Swed Car, *Volvo truck repair and service*
Energetikov pr., 59/3 225-40-51
Mon-Fri 10-19, Sat 10-15; Rbls, $

☎ TRUCKING
ПЕРЕВОЗКИ ГРУЗОВЫЕ
LASTTRANSPORT
CAMION, TRANSPORTS EN
LÄNGTRADAR TRANSPORT
RAHDINKULJETUS

*The advertisers in this section are profes-
sionals in the industry with modern fleets
and extensive experience in international
transport. For trucking and moving of
goods within the city, see also* MOVING
COMPANIES.

Acto-VneshTrans Co. Ltd
Zaozernaya ul., 4 294-80-83
See our ad on page 167
Aspekt, *Mon-Fri 11-19; Rbls, $*
3-ey Pyatiletki ul., 44..................... 100-08-16
Avtotrans, *Mon-Fri 8:30-19:30; Rbls, $*
Griboedova kan. nab., 5 314-66-73
Fax... 314-66-76

EuroDonat   *FREIGHT
FORWARDERS
AND TRANSPORT*

TRUCK, SHIP, AIR, RAIL
Specializing in transport to / from
Russia, the Baltic States, CIS,
USA, Canada & Europe
Customs Document Service
Modern Truck Fleet
St. Pb. Warehouse

Yakornaya ul., 17

Tel	(812) 224-11-44
Fax	(812) 224-06-20
Telex	121118 DFS SU

Hrs: 9-18, $ & Rubles, English

Faster
Kanala Griboedova nab., 5.............. 210-76-60
Fax... 314-32-78
Mon-Fri 8:30-17:15

Joint Venture INGER

International Trucking
Bolshaya Morskaya ul., 53/8, apt. 12
Tel..................................314-83-02
Telex......................121027 ETS SU

Iskra-Balt
Pobedy ul., 11 293-44-62
Fax 291-97-95
Mon-Fri 9-18; Rbls, $; Eng, Ger

KAMKO freight-carriers

Truck freight routes to and from Russia with
France, Germany, Scandinavia & rest of Europe
Seaport service to all Russia.
Specializing in transport of mfg. goods,
containers, equipment, bulk commodities.
Fleet of 125 trucks incl. many refrigerated
trailers. Express freight service
Outstanding security record.
European Expediters: Whilhelm Rotermund,
S.T.E., M.C.T, & others In Rybatskoe

Yunnatov tupik, 1 107-35-90
....262-30-34
Fax....................................267-60-38
Mon-Fri 8-16:45; $; Rbls, Eng, Ger
A Russian-Austrian Company

Lenvneshtrans
Mezhevoy kan., 5...........................251-41-97
....251-76-08
Fax 166-08-91
Mon-Fri 8:30-17:15; Rbls, $; Eng
Logis
Manezhnyy per., 19, apt. 37...........273-14-29
....275-79-16
Mon-Fri 9-18; Rbls

International & Domestic Shipping
Within CIS & Baltics
Fast, Complete Door to Door Service
Large Trucking Fleet
Including Refrigerated Trailers
Expediting Services
All Documents Prepared

Lyubotinskiy proezd, 5........298-36-48
....298-12-94
Fax...................................298-00-73
Telex ....121028 MATRA SU
24 Hours Daily, $, English, German

(((MCT EUROPE

FREIGHT FORWARDING & N.V.O.C.C.
Dvinskaya ul., 10, Korp. 3, 5th floor
................................251-86-62
................................251-36-51
................................251-37-51
Fax 251-84-72
Telex ....121691 MCT SU

Mobile-Service, *Trucking, local and throughout CIS*
Borovaya ul., 11/3, bldg. 2 164-60-66
Mon-Fri 9-18; Rbls, $
Motorcade
Khrustalnaya ul., 27 567-98-65
Fax...567-90-54
Mon-Fri 7-18; Rbls, $
Naydenov i Kompanony
Telezhnaya ul., 7/9 530-25-23
Daily 9-21; Metro Ploshchad Vosstaniya
RMS-Peterburg, *Local delivery*
Moskovskoe shosse, 13A...............291-11-38
Mon-Fri 10-17:30; Rbls, $

Rubicon
TRUCKING

Lesnoy pr., 19
542-00-65, 248-83-06
Fax.............542-09-89
Telex 121194 Rub SU   РУБИКОН

SCANSPED

- A member of the Bilspedition Group -

• *Transportation*
• *Freight Forwarding
  Operations*
• *Custom Clearance*
• *Terminal Services*

**We can ship your cargo to and
from any European country
through our Scansped Network
Daily service to Finland**

Vitebskiy pr., 3...............................298-0055
Fax..294-8233
Telex...121535

24 hours; $ & Rbls; English

Scantrade Ltd., *Daily 9-20; Rbls, $; Eng, Finn*
Akademika Pavlova ul., 13 a........... 233-51-57
Soppol
2-ya Krasnoarmeyskaya ul., 7 110-14-32
Fax 110-12-09
Mon-Fri 10-18; Rbls, $; Eng, Ger
Bus 10; Metro Tekhnologicheskiy Institut

SOVAVTO ST. PETERSBURG

FREIGHT & SHIPPING

General and consolidated cargoes
Heavy cargo transport

All countries in Europe, Scandinavia and ME.
Representatives in 29 countries

SOVTRANSAVTO's modern fleet
580 tractors, & 700 trailers with 150 refrigerated

SovAvto Cargo Express
Twice daily service through Finland,
Daily departures to Western Europe &
Scandinavia
Insurance, crating, secure truck park
Bonded warehouse & customs clearance

Vitebskiy pr., 3 298-46-50
Fax.. 298-77-60
Telex...................................... 121535 AVTO
Hrs. 8:30-17:30, English, German

Sovmortrans
Dvinskaya ul., 8, bldg. 2................. 252-75-81
Fax 114-41-37
Mon-Fri 8:30-17; Rbls, $; Eng, Ger, Fr, Sp
Transcontinentalservice
Mayakovskogo ul., 5...................... 272-14-24
Mon-Fri 9-18; Rbls, $; Eng, Ger

Truck Routes to Finland,
Baltic States & Europe

Konnogvardeyskiy blvd., 1
Tel.: 210-95-98 Fax: 312-79-58

Volan, *Mon-Fri 9-17; Rbls*
Gastello ul., 17, Hotel Mir, rm. 603 108-47-64
VneshTransAvto Co. Ltd
Sofiyskaya ul., 6 166-08-91
See our ad on page 167

Welz-Saint Petersburg Ltd., *Mon-Fri 9-18*
Isaakievskaya pl., 9 312-85-49

☎ **TV DOCUMENTARY**
See VIDEO/FILM PRODUCTION

☎ **TYPEWRITER REPAIR**
ПИШУЩИЕ МАШИНКИ, РЕМОНТ
SCHREIBMASCHINENREPARATUR
MACHINES A ECRIRE, REPARATION
SKRIVMASKINER, REPARATIONER
KIRJOITUSKONEHUOLTO

Souvenir, *Mon-Fri 11-18* **Suvenir**
Baskov per., 4 272-41-67

☎ **TYPING SERVICES**
МАШИНОПИСНЫЕ РАБОТЫ
SCHREIBDIENSTE
DACTYLOGRAPHIE, SERVICE DE
SKRIVMASKIN, SERVICE
KONEKIRJOITUSTOIMISTOT

See also BUSINESS CENTERS *and*
SECRETARIAL SERVICES
Optima-Office, *Mon-Fri 10-20; Rbls*
Chaykovskogo ul., 36.................... 273-29-64
Fax.. 273-78-82
Referent, *Mon-Fri 9:30-20; Rbls*
Please call..................................... 272-56-37
Typist, *Daily 3-22; Rbls; Eng*
Poeticheskiy blvd., 1, apt. 77.......... 516-37-70

☎ **UMBRELLAS**
ЗОНТИКИ
SCHIRME
PARAPLUIES
PARAPLYER
SATEENVARJOT

Buy umbrellas (zontik, зонтик) *at* Haberdashery *shops called* Galantereya (Галантерея) *and raincoats at department or*
clothing stores. It is very useful to have an
umbrella that opens automatically.

☎ **UNIVERSITIES & INSTITUTES**
УНИВЕРСИТЕТЫ И ИНСТИТУТЫ
UNIVERSITÄTEN UND INSTITUTE
UNIVERSITES ET INSTITUTS
UNIVERSITET OCH INSTITUT
YLIOPISTOT JA INSTITUUTIT

St. Petersburg is a leading educational
and research center with major universities,
technical educational institutes, major re-
search institutions and leading medical re-
search centers. Here we list major educa-
tional institutions including technical insti-
tutes. The research institutes associated
with the university are listed under INSTI-
TUTES-RESEARCH.
The leading educational institution is St.
Petersburg State University, formerly Lenin-
grad State University. Its faculty and facil-
ities are situated on Vasilevskiy Ostrov as
well as throughout St. Petersburg and
Peterhof (Petrodvorets).

There are about 20 technical institutes for post-graduate studies and continuing education for managers and specialists in different branches of an industry, for example, the Institute for Managers of Building industry. Here are three for doctors and teachers.

UNIVERSITY INSTITUTES AND FACILITIES

See INSTITUTES, RESEARCH

Academy of Civil Pilots
Akademiya Grazhdanskoy Aviatsii
Pilotov ul., 38 104-15-19
Fax 104-18-32
Mon-Fri 9-17:30

Admiral Makarov State Maritime Academy
Gosudarstvennaya Morskaya Akademiya im. adm. Makarova
Kosaya Liniya., 15A 217-50-02
Fax 217-06-82
Mon-Sat 9-18

Advanced Humanitarian Courses
Vysshye Gumanitarnye Kursy
Voznesenskiy pr., 34 b 314-35-21
Fax 315-39-17
Mon-Fri 10-22; Rbls

Aviation Instrumentation Institute
Institut Aviatsionnogo Priborostroeniya
Gertsena ul., 67 312-21-07
Fax 110-66-43
Mon-Fri 8:30-17

Baltic State Mechanical Engineering University
Baltiyskiy Gosudarstvennyy Mekhanicheskiy Universitet
1-ya Krasnoarmeyskaya ul., 1/21 ... 292-23-94
Mon-Fri 9-17

Center for International Education
Tsentr Mezhdunarodnogo Obucheniya
Smolnogo ul., 1/3, Smolnyy, entr 9, rm. 304
☎ 110-00-29
Fax 143-85-21
Mon-Fri 10-19

Construction Engineering Institute
Inzhenerno-Stroitelnyy Institut
2-ya Krasnoarmeyskaya ul., 4 292-56-92
Mon-Fri 9-18

Electrotechnical Institute of Communication
Elektrotekhnicheskiy Institut Svyazi
Reki Moyki nab., 61 315-89-10
Mon-Fri 9-17

Engineering Economics Institute
Inzhenerno-Ekonomicheskiy Institut
Marata ul., 27 164-30-87
Mon-Fri 9-18

Frunze Naval College
Voenno-Morskoe Vysshee Uchilishche im. Frunze
Leytenanta Shmidta nab., 17 213-71-47
Mon-Sat 9-17

Humanities Center   *Gumanitarnyy Tsentr*
Griboedova kan. nab., 92/1 310-20-90
Mon-Fri 9-17:30; Rbls

Hydro-Meteorological Institute
Gidrometeorologicheskiy Institut
Maloookhtinskiy pr., 98 221-25-96
Mon-Sat 9-16; Metro Ploshchad Aleksandra Nevskogo

Institute of Film and Television
Institut Kino i Televideniya
Pravdy ul., 13 315-72-85
Fax 315-01-72
Mon-Fri 9-17:30

International Humanities University
Mezhdunarodnyy Gumanitarnyy Universitet
Gastello ul., 12 293-23-30
Mon-Fri 9-21

Institute of Culture   *Institut Kultury*
Dvortsovaya nab., 2/4 314-11-21
Mon-Sat 8:30-21

Institute of Trade & Economics
Torgovo-Ekonomicheskiy Institut
Novorossiyskaya ul., 50 247-78-06
Fax 247-43-42
Mon-Fri 9-17

Kirov Academy of Military Medicine
Voenno-Meditsinskaya Akademiya im. S.M Kirova
Akademika Lebedeva ul., 6 542-21-39
Admitting 542-12-50
Zagorodniy pr., 47 292-58-44
One of the best hospitals and medical schools in Russia

Machine Tools Building Institute
Mashinostroitelnyy Institut
Polyustrovskiy pr., 14 540-01-54
Mon-Fri 9-17:40

Marine University   *Morskoy Universitet*
Lotsmanskaya ul., 3 114-07-61
Fax 113-81-09
Mon-Sat 9-17

Mining University   *Gornyy Universitet*
21-ya Liniya, 2 218-82-38
Mon-Fri 9-18

Mukhina Advanced Commercial Arts College
Khudozhestvenno-Promyshlennoe Uchilishche im. V. I. Mukhinoy
Solyanoy per., 13 273-38-04
College Branch at Chaykovskogo ul., 3
Mon-Sat 10-17:30, Metro Chernyshevskaya; Bus 14, 46, 134

Musorgskiy Music College
Muzykalnoe Uchilishche im. M. P. Musorgskogo
Mokhovaya ul., 36 273-03-39
Mon-Fri 10-17, Sat 10-16; Metro Gostinyy Dvor

North-West Correspondence Politechnical Institute
Severo-Zapadnyy Zaochnyy Politekhnicheskiy Institut
Millionnaya ul., 5 312-28-22
Fax 311-60-16
Mon-Fri 9-19

Painting, Sculpture & Architecture Institute
Institut Zhivopisi, Skulptury i Arkhitektury im. Repina
The leading art school in Saint Petersburg located in the Academy of Art
Universitetskaya nab., 17 213-61-89
Mon-Sat 9:30-17

Pedagogical University
Pedagogicheskiy Universitet
Reki Moyki nab., 48 312-44-92
Fax 312-11-95
Mon-Fri 9-17

Pharmaceutical Institute
Khimiko-Farmatsevticheskiy Institut
Professora Popova ul., 14 234-57-29
Fax 234-60-44
Mon-Fri 9-18

Physical Culture Institute n.a. Lesgaft
Institut Fizicheskoy Kultury im. Lesgafta
Dekabristov ul., 35 219-51-39
Fax 114-10-84
Mon-Sat 10-18

Polygraphical Institute of Moscow,
St. Petersburg Branch
Sankt-Peterburgskoe Otdelenie
Moskovskogo Poligraficheskogo Instituta
Dzhambula per., 13 315-06-37
Fax 164-65-56
Mon-Fri 10-18; T-bus 3; Metro Pushkinskaya

Precise Mechanics & Optics Institute
Institut Tochnoy Mekhaniki i Optiki
Sablinskaya ul., 14 238-87-94
Fax 315-71-33
Mon-Fri 10-17

Railway Engineering Institute
Institut Inzhenerov Zheleznodorozhnogo
Transporta
Moskovskiy pr., 9 310-25-21
Mon-Sat 8:30-21; Metro Sadovaya

Refrigeration Industry Institute
Tekhnologicheckiy Institut Kholodilnoy
Promyshlennosti
Lomonosova ul., 9 315-36-17
Fax 315-05-35
Mon-Sat 9-18; T-bus 15, 8; Metro Dostoevskaya

Religious Academy
Dukhovnaya Akademiya i Seminariya
Obvodnogo kan. nab., 17 277-33-50
Mon-Sat 9-17

Rimskiy-Korsakov State Conservatory
Gosudarstvennaya Konservatoriya
im. Rimskogo-Korsakova
The leading music conservatory in St. Pb.
Teatralnaya pl., 3 312-21-29
Fax 311-62-78
Tram 5, 15

Russian-American University
Russko-Amerikanskiy Universitet
Millionnaya ul., 6 219-19-32
.... 314-00-01
Educational programs, English lessons; Mon-Fri 13-18

Sea & River Transport Institute
Institut Vodnogo Transporta
Dvinskaya ul., 5/7 259-03-25
Mon-Fri 9-17; Bus 66; Metro Narvskaya

Serov Art College (for gifted 14-16 year olds)
Khudozhestvennoe Uchilishche im. V. A. Serova
Grazhdanskiy pr., 88, bldg. 2 555-84-44
Man-Sat 9:30-16, Metro Akademicheskaya

St. Petersburg University
of Finance & Economics
Sankt-Peterburgskiy Universitet
Ekonomiki i Finansov
Sadovaya ul., 21, entr. from nab. kan.Griboedova 30
.... 310-50-24
Fax 110-56-74
Mon-Fri 10-19; Rbls; Eng

SAINT PETERSBURG STATE UNIVERSITY

Founded 1819
former Leningrad State University
MAIN OFFICE

Universitetskaya nab. 7/9 218-20-00
.... **218-97-88**
.... **213-11-68**
Fax.. 218-13-46
Mon-Fri 9-17

DEPARTMENTS

Faculty of Applied Mathematics &
Process Control
Peterhof, Bibliotechnaya pl. 2 428-71-59

Faculty of Biology & Soil Sciences
Universitetskaya nab., 7/9 218-08-52

Faculty of Chemistry, *Mon-Sat 9:30-20*
Peterhof, Universitetskaya ul. 2.......... 428-67-33

Faculty of Economics, *Mon-Fri 9-22*
Chaykovskogo ul., 62 273-40-50

Faculty of Geography, *Mon-Sat 9-22*
10-ya Liniya, 33/35 213-06-27

Faculty of Geology, *Mon-Sat 9-16:20*
Universitetskaya nab., 7/9 218-94-68

Faculty of History, *Mon-Sat 9-22:30*
Mendeleevskaya Liniya 5................. 218-94-47

Faculty of Journalism, *Mon-Sat 9-18*
1-ya Liniya, 26 218-59-37

Faculty of Law, *Mon-Sat 9-15, 19-23*
22-ya Liniya, 7 213-49-49

Faculty of Oriental Languages & Studies
Universitetskaya nab., 11 218-95-17

Faculty of Philology, *Mon-Sat 9-21:20*
Universitetskaya nab., 11 218-95-18

Faculty of Philosophy, *Mon-Sat 9:30-22:30*
Mendeleevskaya Liniya, 5............... 218-94-39

Faculty of Physics, *Mon-Sat 9:10-16:35*
Peterhof, Ulyanovskaya ul. 1............428-72-00

Faculty of Psychology, *Mon-Sat 9:30-22:20*
Universitetskaya nab., 7/9 218-00-01

Faculty of Russian Languages Studies
Makarova nab., 6 218-96-53

Faculty of Sociology, *Mon-Fri 9:00-21:40*
Smolnogo ul., 1/3, Smolnyy, etr. 9..... 271-91-65

St. Petersburg Electrical Engineering
University
Gosudarstvennyy
Elektro-Tekhnicheskiy Universitet
Professora Popova ul., 5 234-89-47
Mon-Fri 9-17

State Technical University
Gosudarstvennyy Tekhnicheskiy Universitet
Formerly the Politechical Institute, one of the leading
institutes in science & engineering
Politekhnicheskaya ul., 29 247-20-95
Mon-Fri 9-17

Technological Institute
Tekhnologicheskiy Institut
Zagorodnyy pr., 49.......................... 259-48-39
Mon-Fri 9-18

Technological Institute of Pulp & Paper
 Industry *Tekhnologicheskiy Institut*
 Tsellyulozo-Bumazhnoy Promyshlennosti
 Ivana Chernykh ul., 4 186-57-44
 Fax 186-86-00
 Mon-Fri 9-17

Textile and Light Industry Institute
 Institut Tekstilnoy i Legkoy Promyshlennosti
 Gertsena ul., 18 315-75-25
 Mon-Fri 9:30-17; Metro Nevskiy Prospekt

Theater, Music & Cinema Institute
 Institut Teatra, Muzyki i Kinematografii
 Mokhovaya ul., 34 273-15-81
 Mon-Fri 9:30-17:30

A. Ya. Vaganova Academy of Russian
 Ballet *Akademiya Russkogo Baleta*
 im. A. Ya. Vaganovoy
 Zodchego Rossi ul., 2 312-17-02

Veterinarian Institute *Veterinarnyy Institut*
 Moskovskiy pr., 112 298-36-31
 Mon-Fri 9-17

INSTITUTES FOR CONTINUING EDUCATION & POST GRADUATE STUDY

There are about 20 technical institutes for post-graduate studies and continuing education for managers and specialists in different branches of an industry for example, the Institute for Managers of Building industry. Here are three for doctors and teachers.

Institute for Post Graduate
 Education and Training (regional)
 Institut Usovershenstvovaniya
 Uchiteley (oblastnoy)
 Chkalovskiy pr., 25 a 235-49-77
 Mon-Fri 9-18

Institute for Post-Graduate Studies
 for Physicians
 Institut Usovershenstvovaniya Vrachey
 Saltykova-Shchedrina ul., 41 272-63-43
 Mon-Fri 9:30-17

University for Post Graduate
 Education and Training
 Universitet Pedagogicheskogo Masterstva
 Lomonosova ul., 11 315-35-53
 Mon-Fri 9-18

☎ **VETERINARIAN**
 ВЕТЕРИНАРЫ
 TIERÄRZTE
 VETERINAIRES
 VETERINÄRER
 ELÄINLÄÄKÄRIT

There are numerous municipal and private veterinarians in St. Petersburg. Here are several.

Noev Kovcheg **Noah's Ark**
 Rescue of animals
 Please call 222-14-65
 394-39-84
 Daily 0-24; Rbls

Veterinarnoe Delo **Veterinarian**
 Obukhovskoy Oborony pr., 68 567-91-95
 Daily 10-13, 15-22; Rbls, $, T-bus 44; Metro Elizarovskaya

Veterinarian
 • Please call, *Daily 9-21* 210-44-04
 • Please call 217-03-36
 • Please call 254-66-52

Veterinary Station - Moscow District
 Ligovskiy pr., 291 298-46-94
 Daily 10-13, 14-18; Rbls

☎ **VIDEO EQUIPMENT AND**
 REPAIR
 ВИДЕО АППАРАТУРА И РЕМОНТ
 VIDEOAUSRÜSTUNG/ZUBEHÖR
 EQUIPMENT VIDEO
 VIDEO, UTRUSTNING
 VIDEOLAITTEET JA HUOLTO

See also REPAIRS

US standard video recorders and players can be converted to SECAM/PAL by a simple operation. If buying new equipment consider dual US/European equipment.

Baltica
 Morisa Toreza pr., 2/40 247-23-79
 Mon-Sat 11-14, 15-20; Rbls

A/O CREAT
 Please call 274-54-39
 Computer Design, Video Advertisements

Intep
 Ryleeva ul., 10 275-55-36
 Fax 275-53-60
 Mon-Fri 10-18; Rbls, $; Eng

Magius
 Politekhnicheskaya ul., 22 556-92-81
 Mon-Fri 10-17; Rbls; Eng

Peterhouse
 Chekhova ul., 14 272-30-07
 Fax 272-63-57
 Mon-Fri 10-19; Rbls, $; Eng, Ger; Metro Chernyshevskaya

Polyus-Service
 Kuznetsovskaya ul., 44 298-97-88
 Fax 298-24-08
 Daily 10-13, 14-20; Rbls, $, T-bus 24; Metro Elektrosila

Progress Service
 Reki Moyki nab., 59, 2nd floor 315-86-63
 Fax 213-53-56
 Daily 11-19; Rbls

Romos - Alpha
 Rubinshteyna ul., 38 314-07-77
 Fax 315-82-89
 Mon-Sat 12-19

РУБИКОН
Rubicon
Lesnoy pr., 19
542-00-65, 248-83-06
Fax............542-09-89
Telex 121194 Rub SU

Official Business Partner

IBM
MINOLTA
Gold Star
Hewlett Packard

Sadko
 Petra Alekseeva ul., 11 315-63-09
 Daily 11-19; Rbls, $

Toshiba Authorized Service Centre
Grivtsova per., 1/64 210-69-84
Audio and Video Repair

LTD

Authorized **SAMSUNG ELECTRONICS** Distributor

Supra Dealer

Malookhtinskiy pr., 68 528-95-66
....528-00-51
Fax 528-84-00

☎ **VIDEO/FILM PRODUCTION**
ВИДЕОФИЛЬМЫ,
ПРОИЗВОДСТВО
VIDEOFILMPRODUKTION
FILMS -VIDEO, CREATION ET
REALISATION DE
VIDEO, FILM PRODUKTION
VIDEO/FILMITUOTANTO

Aprel-Video, *Mon-Fri 10-17*
Obukhovskoy Oborony pr., 163...... 267-33-45

BLAZE PRODUCTIONS
TV commercials and corporate video
training, informational and sales tapes

Join Our Clients: ABC, CBS, NBC,
Apple Computer, American Express,
Russian Privatization Commercials

Griboedova kan. nab., 97 311-04-09

Wholly owned subsidiary of Blaze Productions, USA.

In USA, call .... (612) 925-8357

A/O CREAT

Please call 274-54-39
Computer Design, Video Advertisements

Film Consulting Leningrad
Kamennoostrovskiy pr., 10 233-97-47
Fax 233-21-74
Mon-Fri 10-17

Intep, *Mon-Fri 10-18; Rbls, $; Eng*
Ryleeva ul., 10............................... 275-55-36
Fax 275-53-60

Kronverk St. Petersburg Productive
Creative Firm A.O.
TV documentaries and feature film
Gertsena ul., 56 311-70-27
Fax 311-84-49
Mon-Fri 10-19; Rbls, $; Eng, Ger, Fr, Finn, Swed, Ital

Ladoga
Kamennoostrovskiy pr., 10 238-52-28
Fax 238-52-96
Mon-Fri 10-17; Rbls, $; Eng

Lenfilm, *Mon-Fri 9-17*
Kamennoostrovskiy pr., 10 232-83-74
Fax 232-88-81

Lennauchfilm
Melnichnaya ul., 4 265-01-51
Fax 567-70-24
Mon-Fri 9-17

Lentelefilm
Chapygina ul., 6 234-77-75
Fax 234-39-95
Mon-Fri 10-20; Eng

Luch, *Daily 11-20; Rbls, $; Eng*
Leninskiy pr., 134 254-80-16

Mars-Video
Robespera nab., 10 278-82-34
Mon-Fri 9-17; Rbls, $, CC; Eng

Peterburgskiy Predprinimatelskiy Dom
Please call 177-74-59

Rumb, *Daily 8:30-12, 13-18:30; Rbls*
Zaytseva ul., 41 183-46-39
Fax 185-08-69

Russkoe Video
Reki Maloy Nevki nab., 4 234-54-92
Fax 234-00-88
Mon-Fri 9-18; Rbls, $; Eng

TRIONIKS, film-video production

Documentary & Advertising Videos
Scripts, Takes, Editing, Dubbing

Povarskoy per., 8 112-38-44
Fax 112-53-59
Telex ....121222 SPRES SU

T V I D STUDIOS
Video Productions
Shooting, Editing, Sound Effects
Dubbing in Russian, English & Japanese

Kamennoostrovskiy pr., 42, rm. 430
Tel 230-85-55

Znanie Society
Liteynyy pr., 42 279-52-85
Fax 279-53-90
Mon-Fri 10-17:30; Rbls, $; Eng

☎ **VIDEO RENTAL/TAPE,**
RENTAL/SALES
ВИДЕОКАССЕТЫ, ПРОКАТ
И ПРОДАЖА
VIDEOKASSETTENVERLEIH
CASSETTES VIDEO LOCATION
VIDEO, UT HYRNING
VIDEOKASETTIEN VUOKRAUS

Remember that there are two video tape standards: the European standard "PAL" for European TV's and VCRs, and the American standard NTSC for American TV's & VCRs.

The Russians use the European "PAL" so that an American VCR will not play Russian or European videocassettes. And vice versa. Many VCR's on sale here are dual standard and can play both cassette formats. If you have US video cassettes be sure that you can play them.

Video rental stores (video prokat, видео прокат), *are found all over in St. Petersburg.*

Electronica Gallery and Shop
Yuriya Gagarina pr., 12 299-38-49
Mon-Sat 10-14, 15-19; Rbls, $

Foton
Nekrasova ul., 25 272-63-98
Daily 14-20; Rbls; Eng
Bus 22; T-bus 12, 5; Metro Chernyshevskaya

Lida
Liteynyy pr., 62, apt. 15 a 272-52-41
Daily 14-20; Metro Mayakovskaya

Romos - Alpha, *Mon-Sat 12-19*
Rubinshteyna ul., 38 314-07-77
Fax 315-82-89

Viza
Rubinshteyna ul., 9 315-47-54
Fax 311-12-89
Daily 11-14, 15-21; Rbls; Eng; Metro Dostoevskaya

☎ **VISA REGISTRATION (OVIR)**
ОВИР
VISA-AMT
VISAS, BUREAU DE
VISUM, KONTOR
VIISUMIKONTTORI,(OVIIRI)

At present, you must still register your passport with the (OVIR, ОВИР) which means the Department of Visas and Registration, (Otdel Viz i Registratsiy, Отдел Виз и Регистраций) *within three workings days of your arrival. If you are staying at a hotel, they will do this for you. If you are living with a friend or in a rented apartment, you should also register with the OVIR in the district where the apartment is located, especially if you need to extend your visa.*

See OVIR offices for each district.

Visa extensions. *To extend your visa, you must comply with certain regulations from the very beginning of your stay including registration of your passport and visa. For any extension, you usually need to have an official statement requesting an extension, and if you are staying in a rented apartment or private home, permission to stay a longer time from your host. You then take these papers along with your visa to the OVIR in your district (listed below) and apply for an extension. They are pretty efficient there.*

Multiple entry visas. *Businesses may be interested in a* Commercial multi entry visa *which allows unlimited entries for 6 month period. Employees of Russian companies and joint ventures apply to OVIR and pay in rubles. Employees of 100% foreign-owned companies, apply to the consulate department of MID (Ministerstvo Inostrannykh Del) Ministry of Foreign Affairs. There must be a good reason for having a multiple entry visa and the company must be registered with MID . The process takes about two weeks.*

Central office OVIR is for difficult cases and your local OVIR may send you there.

OVIR Visa Registration - Central Office
Main registration office for foreigners
• *Open for extensions of visas and similar visa problems:*
Mon, 10-12, 15-17,
Wed 15-17, Fri 15-17
• *Multi visa application accepted on Tues 10-12 and are issued Fridays 15-17.*
Saltykova-Shchedrina ul., 4 278-24-81
.... 273-90-38
Mon-Fri 9:30-17:30; Rbls, $; Eng, Ger

Dzerzhinskiy District
Chekhova ul., 15 272-55-56
Frunzenskiy District
Obvodnogo kan. nab., 48 166-14-68
Kalininskiy District
Mineralnaya ul., 3 540-39-87
Kirovskiy District
Stachek pr., 18 252-77-14
Krasnogvardeyskiy District
Krasnodonskaya ul., 14 224-01-96
Krasnoselskiy District
Avangardnaya ul., 35 136-89-06
Kuybyshevskiy District
Krylova per., 3 310-41-17
Leninskiy District
Sovetskiy per., 9 292-43-56
Moskovskiy District
Moskovskiy pr., 95 294-81-55
Oktyabrskiy District
Sadovaya ul., 58 315-49-01
Petrogradskiy District
Bolshaya Monetnaya ul., 20 232-11-19
Primorskiy District
Generala Khruleva ul., 15 394-72-13
Smolninskiy District
Mytninskaya ul., 3 274-57-10
Vasileostrovskiy District
19-ya Liniya, 10 355-75-24
Vyborgskiy Dstrict
Lesnoy pr., 20 542-21-72

☎ **VISA SERVICES**
ВИЗОВЫЙ СЕРВИС
VISA-DIENST,
VISAANGELEGENHEITEN
VISAS, SERVICES DE
VISUM, SERVICE
VIISUMIPALVELUT

You need a visa to travel to Russia. If you are traveling with a travel agency or a tour, they will take care of this problem.

Now, however, there are many other ways to get a visa. Basically you need an "invitation" either from your host or some sort of host organization, institute, or official agency, stating that they will take all responsibility for your needs. You then send the invitation to the Russian Embassy along with three photos, a visa application, photocopy of your passport, the processing fee, and a stamped return envelope. Some organizations, for example the new Bed &

Breakfast Associations, will get a visa for you. There are also visa services that will help you get the "invitation" that is necessary for a visa if you are not traveling with a tour.

The Russian Embassy in Washington and the Consulates in New York and San Francisco now have accelerated processing: five business day service is $20, four days $40, and overnight (if you submit your application by 11:30 a.m.) is $120. A multiple entry visa for business purposes can be obtained under special circumstances and costs $120 for a six-month visa. Prices may change.

Alyuri, *Mon-Fri 11-18; Rbls*
Reshetnikova ul., 15 298-85-29
Ministry of Foreign Affairs of Russia
Kutuzova nab., 34 272-00-76
Mon-Fri 10-17; Rbls; Eng

☎ **VOLLEYBALL CLUBS**
    ВОЛЛЕЙБОЛЬНЫЕ КЛУБЫ
    VOLLEYBALLVEREINE
    VOLLEYBALL CLUB DE
    VOLLEYBOLL
    LENTOPALLOKERHOT

Automobilist St. Pb. Volleyball Center
2-ya Liniya, 5, 2nd floor 218-69-51
World class volleyball team; Mon-Fri 10-17; Rbls, $; Eng

☎ **WAREHOUSES**
    СКЛАД
    LAGERHÄUSER
    ENTREPOT
    LAGER
    VARASTOT

See also STORAGE

Logis, *Mon-Fri 9-18; Rbls*
Manezhnyy per., 19, apt. 37 273-14-29

MATRALEN (See our ad under Trucking)
Lyubotinskiy proezd., 5 298-36-48
                          298-12-94
Fax 298-00-73
Telex .... 121028 MATRA SU

Poliservice, *Mon-Fri 8-16; Metro Lomonosovskaya*
Tsimlyanskaya ul., 6 224-14-47
PetersburgVneshTrans - *See ad on p. 167*
Rosvneshterminal
Belinskogo ul., 11 279-75-86
Fax 279-75-62
Mon-Fri 9:30-13, 14-18:30; Rbls, $; Eng
VneshTransAvia Co. Ltd - *See ad on p. 167*
VneshTransAvto Co. Ltd - *See ad on p. 167*

☎ **WATCHES**
    ЧАСЫ
    UHREN
    MONTRES
    ARMBANDSUR/KLOCKOR
    KELLOT

See also WATCH REPAIR
You can buy watches in specialized departments of DEPARTMENT STORES, in specialized

shops called "Watches", (Chasy, Часы) and in many small commercial shops. Souvenir peddlers will try to sell you "Soviet army watches" at outrageous prices.

Antique Watch
Sales & Repair of Antique Watches
Bolshaya Konyushennaya ul., 19
314-15-59
Hrs: 10-14, 15-19; Rbls; Eng, Metro Nevskiy Prospekt

Bure Salon, *For watches*
Nevskiy pr., 23 312-27-59
Mon-Sat 10-19:30; Rbls

Chasy   **Watches**
• Bolshoy pr., P.S., 30 230-70-78
Mon-Sat 10-14, 15-19
• Nevskiy pr., 93 277-13-62
Mon-Fri 10-19, Sat 10-18; Rbls
• Sredniy pr., 27 213-18-56
Mon-Fri 10-14, 15-19; Rbls
Gostinyy Dvor, Sadovaya Liniya
Nevskiy pr., 35, 1st floor 110-52-49
Kristall   **Crystal**
Nevskiy pr., 32/34 311-30-95
Mon-Sat 10-14, 15-19; Rbls
Vikont, *Mon-Sat 10-14, 15-19*
Moskovskiy pr., 130 298-58-01
Vse dlya Vas   **Everything for You**
Obukhovskoy Oborony pr., 81 265-13-01
Mon-Sat 10-14, 15-19; Rbls; Tram 7; Metro Elizarovskaya

☎ **WATCH REPAIRS**
    ЧАСЫ, РЕМОНТ
    UHRREPARATUR
    HORLOGERIE
    KLOCKREPARATIONER
    KELLOJENKORJAUKSET

Buy watch batteries in specialized departments of big DEPARTMENT STORES (Univermag Универмаг), WATCH SHOPS, and in some repair shops. An extra watch battery could save a lot of time.

Anker-Z, *Mon-Sat 10-14, 15-19; Rbls, $; Eng, Ger*
Ligovskiy pr., 173 166-56-33
Antique Watch, *Mon-Sat 10-19; Rbls; Eng*
Bolshaya Konyushennaya ul., 19 314-15-59
Bure, *Mon-Sat 10-19:30; Rbls*
Nevskiy pr., 23 312-27-59
Interface
Sadovaya ul., 29 310-00-47
Mon-Sat 10-14, 15-19; Rbls; Metro Sadovaya
Vikont, *Mon-Fri 10-14, 15-19*
Moskovskiy pr., 130 298-58-01
Watch Repairs
• 12-ya Krasnoarmeyskaya ul., 14 251-42-15
Mon-Sat 11-14, 15-18; Rbls
• Liteynyy pr., 45 273-64-05
Mon-Fri 10-14, 15-19; Rbls
• Mira pl., 3 ....No ☎
Mon-Sat 11-14, 15-19; Rbls
Watch Repair and Exchange
Moskovskiy pr., 190 298-33-42
Mon-Sat 10-14, 15-19; Rbls

WATER
ВОДА
WASSER
EAU
VATTEN
VESI

Don't drink the water. *Many Russians don't drink tap water in St. Petersburg and you should probably not drink the water either. You can drink all the water you want at the five star hotels which have their own water purifying systems. Enjoy the ice too. In other places avoid cold tap water and ice, and items rinsed in cold tap water, both in winter and especially in summer, even though the water is frequently tested. For short-term visits and peace of mind, you can buy water in plastic bottles.*

Water Treatment:
1. Boil for 10 minutes, or
2. Iodine treatment (Tablets of Potable Aqua, Globulin or 2 drops of iodine per liter of water, 1/2 hour)

Possible health problems. *Water is almost always a problem for world travelers and St. Petersburg is no exception. In addition to the usual problems, St. Petersburg is thought by some to have two additional problems. The first is with heavy metal, not really a problem for short-term visitors. The second problem is with "Giardia Lamblia," a parasite found throughout the world (especially in mountain streams with mountain sheep grazing nearby). The symptoms may appear after days, weeks or months and include stomach cramps, nausea, bloated stomach, diarrhea and frequent foul gas. The current state of these problems is unresolved. Treat under care of a doctor (some use Metronidazole, 200 mg 3x per day for fourteen days, available in Russia as Trikapol). See* MEDICAL CARE & CONSULTATIONS *and* WHAT TO BRING.

Getting fluids. *When traveling getting enough fluids can be a problem. Drink lots of weak tea, soft drinks and beer. Mineral water can be salty. Juices are usually OK.*

Here boil all your water and to put extra hot water from morning coffee and afternoon tea in pitchers and bottles to cool. You can use a little one cup water heater (bring with you). Some long term residents use water filters. But pure water from Finland and even as far away as Ireland can be very refreshing (try Stockmann's or other INTERNATIONAL SHOPS*). In an emergency, use water purification tablets (bring) and brush your teeth and fill your water bottles with the hottest tap water available.*

Hot Water Supply Interruption in Summer. *The hot water to apartments and offices is often supplied by central power stations. In summer, the hot water is usually turned off for "planned repairs" for two to four weeks. Boil some water & take a sponge bath. Even better, find an apartment with a gas or electric water heater.*

CLEAR WATER

Hot and cold water dispensers
for home or office

Imported Finnish spring water completely
free of any harmful bacteria,
metals or minerals.

Free Home and Office Delivery

6-ya Liniya, V.O., 37 213-57-33

Lensey, *Water purification and wholesale, large bottles and/or fill your own.*
Sadovaya ul., 93 114-25-89
Mon-Fri 10-19; Rbls, $; Eng, Ger
Nayada, *Water purifiers for home and office*
Rizhskiy pr., 26 251-67-33
Mon-Fri 9-18; Rbls, $; Eng
Saint Petersburg-Pure Water, *Mon-Fri 9-18*
Tavricheskaya ul., 10 275-40-55
Water Tests, *Mon-Fri 9-17*
Laboratoriya Issledovaniya Vody
Bolshoy pr., V.O., 13 213-76-59

🕿 **WEATHER**
ПОГОДА
WETTER
TEMPS, MÉTÉO
VÄDER
ILMA

See CLIMATE *for Hi/Lo Temperature, Sunny Days, Rainfall, etc.*

For a four day weather forecast in Russian, dial 001. For monthly weather forecast for the entire country, dial 062. Even better, watch the weather report on the morning TV news.

Weather Bureau
Professora Popova ul., 78 234-13-92

🕿 **WEIGHTS & MEASURES**

See TABLES OF WEIGHTS & MEASURES p. 330

🕿 **WHAT TO BRING**
ЧТО ВЗЯТЬ С СОБОЙ
REISECHECKLISTE
CE QU'IL FAUT AMENER
VAD TAR JAG MED/
RESECHECKLISTA
MITÄ OTTAA MUKAAN

See CLIMATE *for a discussion of clothes.*

The supply of most goods is rapidly increasing in St. Petersburg. Some things can take incredible amounts of time to find. So, save time and money, and be sure to have essential things, consider bringing the following items (listed in order of priority) not only to Russia, but on most trips.

Usefulness.

*** *Essential for traveling in Russia*
** *Very useful*
* *Nice to have*

Availability in St. Petersburg

> ⊠   *Almost impossible to find*
> **?**   *Limited selection & variable supply*
> ☑   *Readily available*

* * * *All prescription medicines and prescription RX* ⊠ *&* **?**

* * * *Medicine for Giardia Lamblia* ⊠ *(Consult with your doctor before you leave),& an antibiotic for bacterial dysentery* **?**.

* * * *Small packages of Kleenex* ☑ *and pre moistened witch hazel packets.*

* * * *Extra pair of glasses / contact lenses***?***, hearing aids* ⊠, *and your prescriptions.*

* * * *Special batteries for cameras, hearing aid and watches* ⊠.

* * * *Contraceptives/condoms* ⊠, *sanitary napkins* ☑.

* * * *Photo copies of passport, visa, air tickets, etc. (keep in two places)* ☑.

* * * *Business cards (lots), See* ETIQUETTE

* * * *Swiss army knife with scissors and can opener* **?**

* * * *Small flashlight* **?**

* * * *Toilet paper* ☑

* * * *Umbrella that opens automatically* **?**

* * * *Standard first aid items: antibiotic cream* ⊠, *cortisone cream* ⊠, *fungal cream or powder* ⊠, *band aids* ⊠ *moleskin for blisters , pseudo- ephedrine , antihistamine , aspirin* ☑, *Dramamine* ⊠, *thermometer* ☑, *small needle, tweezers, Pepto- Bismol* ⊠, *alcohol wipes* ⊠.

* * *Small transformer (if needed)* **?**

* * *Small multi-voltage hair dryer* ☑

* * *Decaffeinated Coffee***?***, Tea* ⊠

* * *1/2 liter plastic water bottle* **?**

* * *Small water heater* ☑, *2% iodine water tablets (Potable Aqua, Globulin)* ⊠

* * *Flat water stopper & bar of soap* ☑

* * *Batteries* **?***(AA, C & D cells* ☑*).*

* * *Sunscreen, lip salve, sunglasses* **?**

* * *Mosquito repellent in summer* ⊠

* * *Foldable nylon string shopping bags* **?**

* * *Dictionary***?***, *phrase book* **?**

* *All special film in x-ray proof bag* ⊠ *(Regular film is now widely available)*

* *Little thin calculator (for exchange rates)* ☑

* *Thermos, insulated mug, spoon & knife* **?**

* *Walkman radio/ tape with tapes and batteries, blank cassette tapes* ☑, *small short wave radio* **?**

* *Small binoculars* **?**

* *Travel guides in English* ⊠

* *Address-phone book, extra pens & pencils, pen refills* **?**, *lead, erasers, scotch tape, plastic folders, paper clips and rubber bands* **?**.

* *Laundry soap* ☑, *15 ft of light nylon line & clothes pins* **?**, *lightweight hangers for pants and clothes* **?**,*shoe polish* ☑, *small plastic bags* ⊠, *needle & thread*☑

**The good small yellow* Pocket Langenscheit Russian/English, English- /Russian *dictionary is everywhere. The* excellent two volume Oxford Dictionary *is not available here.*

☎ WOMEN'S CLOTHING

See CLOTHING-WOMEN'S

☎ YACHT CLUBS
ЯХТ-КЛУБ
JACHTKLUBS
YACHT-CLUBS
SEGELKLUBBAR
PURJEHDUSSEURAT

Baltic Shipping Company Yacht Club
Martynova nab., 92 235-19-45
Fax.. 230-75-85
Daily 0-24;Rbls;$; T-bus 9; Bus 71, C-10

Malakhit Yacht Rentals
Frunze ul., 18 264-65-10
Fax.. 298-17-19
Mon-Fri 8:30-12, 14:30-16:30; Rbls, $; Eng,

Neva
Martynova nab., 94 235-27-22
Daily 0-24;Rbls;$; T-bus 9; Bus 71, C-10

Rowing School
Reki Bolshoy Nevki nab., 24 234-04-66
Daily 9-20; Rbls, D-10

St. Petersburg River Yacht Club
Petrovskaya Kosa, 7 235-72-17
Fax.. 235-70-67
Mon-Sat 10-18; Rbls; Eng, B-9

Yacht Club No. 55, *Military Naval Base*
Shkiperskiy protok 12 217-09-03
Tue-Sun 9-18; Rbls, $, B-5

☎ YOUTH HOSTELS
ХОСТЕЛИ, МОЛОДЕЖНЫЕ
JUGENDHERBERGE
AUBERGE DEJEUNESSE
UNGDOMSHOTEL
RETKEILYMAJAT

Tourist visas available!

ST. PETERSBURG'S MODERN BUDGET "WESTERN STYLE"   *CITY CENTER!*   **ЯUSSIAN YOUTH HOSTEL**   An American-Russian Joint Project

3rd Sovetskaya Ulitsa, 28...........................277-05-69
Fax...277-51-02
International Reservation in USA..+1 (310) 379-4316
Fax...+1 (310) 379-8420

Metro Ploshchad Vostaniya; I-5

☎ ZOO
ЗООПАРК
ZOO
ZOO
ZOO
ELÄINTARHAT

The Zoo
Alexandrovskiy Park, 1 232-28-39
Daily 10-20; Rbls; Metro Gorkovskaya; F-7

The Suburbs of Saint Petersburg
LOMONOSOV • PAVLOVSK • PETERHOF • PUSHKIN

We include telephone numbers and addresses of basic services, banks, hotels, museums and restaurants in four suburbs of St. Petersburg. Most of this information was collected personally by our staff. Our readers are invited to add to this list. Peterhof is now the official name for Petrodvorets and Tsarskoe Selo will probably be the new "old" name for Pushkin.

LOMONOSOV
ЛОМОНОСОВ

Lomonosov is 40 km west of St. Petersburg. The commuter train to Lomonosov leaves from the Baltic Station and takes one hour. Get off at Oranienbaum-1 Station. From May to September hydrofoils come to Lomonosov from Morskaya Pristan on Vasilevskiy Island (V.O.) near Tuchkov Bridge every 30 minutes.

BANKS

Sberbank No. 1886
Yunogo Lenintsa ul., 43/6 423-03-40
Fax: 423-08-47
Mon-Sat 9-19; Rbls

CHURCHES RUSSIAN ORTHODOX

Archangel Michael Cathedral
           Sobor Arkhangela Mikhaila
Yunogo Lenintsa ul., 63 422-39-62
Daily 6:30-12, 15-19

CITY GOVERNMENT

City Council   Gorodskoy Sovet
Krasnykh Partizan ul., 11 422-46-08
Mon-Fri 10-18

CONSTRUCTION & RENOVATION

Akater, *Daily 8:30-20; Rbls, $; Eng*
Fedyuninskogo ul., 3 423-17-11

DENTISTS

Dental Clinic
Sverdlova ul., 2 423-03-49
Fax: 423-07-56
Mon-Fri 9-15; Rbls

HOSPITALS

Hospital, *Daily 0-24; Rbls*   **Bolnitsa**
Leninskaya ul., 13 423-07-69

JEWELRY

Akvamarin
Yunogo Lenintsa ul., 53 422-31-19
Mon-Sat 10-14, 15-19; Rbls

LAW FIRMS & LAWYERS

Law Consulting, *Mon-Sat 9-18; Rbls*
Yunogo Lenintsa ul., 43/6 422-47-56

MARKETS
(Farmer's Markets, Kolkhoz Markets)

Lomonosovskiy Rynok   Market
Rubakina ul., 16 422-98-70
Daily 7:30-19; Rbls

MILITIA-POLICE

Militia/Internal Affairs Department   UVD
Kronshtadtskaya ul., 5 423-07-02
Daily 0-24; Rbls
Traffic Police, *Daily 0-24; Rbls*   **GAI**
Kronshtadtskaya ul., 5 423-02-32

MOVIES

Zarya
Filatovykh ul., 14 .... No ☎

MUSEUMS

** Grand Palace   Bolshoy Dvorets
Yunogo Lenintsa ul., 48 422-88-06
Built 1710-1727; Architects Fontana, Schädel
Wed-Sun 11-17; Rbls
Chinese Kitchen
Yunogo Lenintsa ul., 48 422-88-06
Small pavilion with Chinese motifs, Wed-Sun 11-17; Rbls
Chinese Palace
Yunogo Lenintsa ul., 48 422-37-53
Built 1762-1768; Architect: Rinaldi; Beautiful small palace; interiors in Chinese style, Wed-Sun 11-17; Rbls
Pavilion Katalnoy Gorki
Yunogo Lenintsa ul., 48 422-37-53
Built 1762-1774; Architect: Rinaldi. Previously this was a hill used for sledding. Today only the French styled pavilion survives. Wed-Sun 11-17; Rbls
Palace of Peter III   Dvorets Petra III
Yunogo Lenintsa ul., 48 422-37-53
Built 1758-1762; Architect: Rinaldi. Wed-Sun 11-17; Rbls

NOTARY PUBLIC

Notary Bureau
Yunogo Lenintsa ul., 43/6 423-08-89
Mon-Tue, Thu-Sat 10-13, 14-18; Rbls

PARKING LOTS

Automobile Parking (24 hours)
Yunogo Lenintsa ul., 67 .... No ☎

Automobile Parking No.9
Oranienbaumskiy pr. 422-47-50
Daily 10-19; Rbls

PHARMACIES (DRUG STORES)

Apteka   **Pharmacy**
• Pobedy ul., 2.............................. 422-77-60
Daily 8-20; Rbls
• Yunogo Lenintsa ul., 55, bldg. 8.. 422-60-13
Mon-Sat 9-20; Rbls

POST OFFICES

Pochta   **Post Office**
Krasnykh Partizan ul., 27 422-97-87
Mon-Fri 9-14, 15-20; Rbls

RENTALS (Furniture, Bicycles, TV's)

Petrodvotsovyy District
Botanicheskaya ul., 18 428-72-53
Mon-Fri 10-18; Rbls

SHIPPING

Kron-Flot, *Mon-Fri 8:30-18; Rbls, $*
Volodarskogo ul., 1 423-18-86

TRUCKING

Transagenstvo, *Daily 8-19; Rbls*
Yunogo Lenintsa ul., 63 423-07-14

PAVLOVSK
ПАВЛОВСК

Pavlovsk is about 30 km south of St. Petersburg and is known for its Palace of Paul I and large beautiful park in the French style. The electric commuter train from Vitebsk Station leaves every 20-30 minutes and takes about 30 minutes. Bus No. 479 from Metro Zvezdnaya will also take you to Pavlovsk.

BAKERIES

Bulochnaya, *Daily 8-20*   **Bakery**
Krasnykh Zor ul., 2 470-60-14

BANKS

Sberbank, *Mon-Fri 10-20*   **Savings Bank**
Krasnykh Zor ul., 16/13................. 470-61-03

BATHS, RUSSIAN

Banya, *Thu-Sun 8-20; Rbls*
Lunacharskogo ul., 12 470-60-53

BOOKS

Kniga, *Mon-Sat 11-14, 15-19*   **Book**
Krasnykh Zor ul., 25...................... 470-23-92

CAFES

Otdykh, *Daily 11-19; Rbls*
Krasnykh Zor ul., 1 470-23-62

CHURCHES RUSSIAN ORTHODOX

St. Nicholas Cathedral
Sobor Svyatogo Nikolaya
Artilleriyskaya ul., 2, *Sat-Sun* 465-19-99

CINEMAS, MOVIES

Rodina, *Daily; Rbls*
Krasnykh Zor ul., 7 470-61-94

CITY GOVERNMENT

City Council   *Gorodskoy Sovet*
Rozy Lyuksemburg ul., 11/16......... 470-20-27

CONFERENCE ROOMS

Pavlovsk Palace, *Mon-Thu, Sat-Sun 9-17:30*
Revolyutsii ul., 20 470-22-16

ENTERTAINMENT ACTS

Pavlovsk Palace, *Mon-Thu, Sat-Sun 9-17:30; Rbls*
Revolyutsii ul., 20 470-22-16

HAIR CUTTING

Ruslan Men's Barbers, *Mon-Sat 8-20*
Krasnykh Zor ul., 12 470-60-64

LAUNDRY/DRY CLEANING

Laundry, *Mon-Sat 10-18; Rbls*
Krasnykh Zor ul., 2 465-13-27

MEDICAL CARE & CONSULTATIONS

Policlinic No. 67, *Mon-Sat 8-20; Rbls*
Marata ul., 1................................... 470-21-71

MILITIA-POLICE

Militia/Internal Affairs Department   **UVD**
Marata ul., 17................................. 470-20-23

MUSEUMS

Pavlovsk Palace
Revolyutsii ul., 20 470-21-55
Built 1782-1786, Architect Cameron a lassic style. Official Summer residence of Paul I in 1796-1801. Mon-Thu, Sat-Sun 10-17:30; Rbls

PARKS

Pavlovsk Park
Revolyutsii ul., 20 470-69-65
The largest park in Russia is known for its beautiful landscape. Built at the end of the18th century. Architects: Cameron, Gonzago, Brenna

PHARMACIES (DRUG STORES)

Apteka No.100   **Pharmacy**
Krasnykh Zor ul., 14/12................. 470-60-73
Mon-Sat 8-20

PHOTOGRAPHERS, PHOTOS

Photographers, *Mon-Thu, Sun 11-13, 14-20*
1-go Maya ul., 30/42...................... 470-76-41

POST OFFICES

Pochta　　　　　　　　　**Post-Office**
　Karla Libknekhta ul., 8/14.............. 470-28-77
　　　　　Mon-Fri 11-19

RENTALS (Furniture, Bicycles, TV's)

Byuro Prokata, *TVs, Furniture, etc.*
　Detskoselskaya ul., 6 470-61-06
　　　　Mon-Sat 10-19; Rbls

RESTAURANTS & CAFES

Leto　　　　　　　　　　　**Summer**
　Krasnykh Zor ul., 35..................... 470-62-16
　　　　Daily 12-22; Rbls, $

SHOE REPAIRS

Remont Obuvi　　　　　**Shoe Repair**
　Vasenko ul., 28............................. 470-24-14
　　　　Mon-Sat 10-19; Rbls

SHOPS

Detskiy Mir, *Clothing, toys*　**Children's Shop**
　Kommunarov ul., 12/15 470-25-71
　　　　Mon-Sat 10-19; Rbls
Tovary dlya Doma　　　**Goods for Home**
　Kommunarov ul., 24 470-61-44
　　　　Mon-Sat 10-19; Rbls
Raduga Department Store
　Detskoselskaya ul., 5 470-61-16
　　　　Mon-Sat 10-19; Rbls

TAILOR/SEAMSTRESS

Atele, *Mon-Sat 10-19; Rbls*
　Detskoselskaya ul., 17 470-62-13

PETERHOF
(PETRODVORETS)
ПЕТЕРГОФ
(ПЕТРОДВОРЕЦ)

Peterhof, known as Petrodvorets from 1919 to 1992, is about 30 km west of St. Pb. on the Gulf of Finland. It is known for beautiful palaces, parks and especially for its fountains. The electric commuter train leaves from Baltic Station to Novyy Petergof Station every 30 minutes and takes about 40 minutes. From Novyy Petergof Station, take bus No. 350, 351, 352, 356. It is about 10 minutes to the Park. From May to September you may go to Petrodvorets by hydrofoil from The Hermitage (Dvortsovaya Naberezhnaya). It leaves every 30-40 minutes and takes about half an hour.

BAKERIES

Bulochnaya　　　　　　**Bakery No. 9**
　Sankt-Peterburgskaya ul., 41 427-97-30
　　　　Daily 7:30-13, 14-19:30; Rbls

BANKS

Saint Petersburg Bank
　Mezhdunarodnaya ul., 10 427-54-88
　　　Mon-Sat 10-14, 15-20; Rbls, $; Eng, Ger
　Sankt-Peterburgskaya ul., 12.......... 427-53-64
　　　Mon-Fri 9:30-13; Rbls, $; Eng; Bus 351

BATHS, RUSSIAN

Banya, *Wed-Sun 9-20; Rbls*
　Lenina blvd., 10 427-35-88

BOOKS

Knigi　　　　　　　　　　**Book Store**
　Sankt-Peterburgskaya ul., 10.......... 427-76-74
　　　　Mon-Sat 10-15, 16-19; Rbls

CAFES

Kafe　　　　　　　　　　　　**Cafe**
　Kominterna ul., 4 427-96-01
　　　　Daily 12-20; Rbls; Bus 351

CHURCHES RUSSIAN ORTHODOX

St. Peter & Paul Cathedral
　　　　Sobor Svyatogo Petra i Pavla
　Sankt-Peterburgskaya ul., 32.......... 427-92-68
　　　　Daily 9-19

CITY GOVERNMENT

City Council　　　　　**Gorodskoy Sovet**
　Dvortsovaya ul., 7 427-74-12
　　　Mon-Sat 9-12:30, 14:30-18; Rbls; Eng, Ger
　　　　Bus 351; Metro Avtovo

DENTISTS

Dental Clinic
　Proletarskaya ul., 1 427-92-41
　　　　Daily 8-20; Rbls; Eng, Ger, Finn

EMERGENCY SERVICES　(24 Hours/Day)
Apartment Repair

Emergency Station of Petrodvorets
　Tolmacheva ul., 3.......................... 427-99-39
Petrodvortsovyy District, *Daily 0-24*
　Lunacharskogo ul., 11.................... 427-98-16

FLOWER SHOPS

Yukka, *Mon-Sat 10-14, 15-19*
　Sovetskaya ul., 12......................... 427-92-17

GAS STATIONS/PETROL

Gas Station No. 17, *A-93*
　Sankt-Peterburgskaya ul., 67.......... 427-92-19
　　　　Daily 0-24; Rbls;
Gas Station No. 99, *A-93, A-95*
　Universitetskiy pr., 2 427-79-62
　　　　Daily 0-24; Rbls, $; Eng, Finn;

HOSPITALS

Hospital No. 37
　Sankt-Peterburgskaya ul., 20.......... 427-92-22
　　Daily 0-24; Rbls, $; Eng, Ger; Bus 352; Metro Avtovo

HOTELS

Chayka, *Daily 0-24; Rbls*
Shakhmatova, 16 428-68-92
Hotel of Watch Making Factory
Checherinskaya ul., 11, bldg. 3 428-70-02
Daily 0-24; Rbls; Bus 359; Metro Avtovo

LAUNDRY/DRY CLEANING

Laundry
Lenina blvd., 2 427-36-10
Mon-Sat 8-22; Rbls; Bus 355; Metro Avtovo

MARKETS (Farmer's and Kolkhoz Markets)

Rynok, *Daily 8-19; Rbls* **Market**
Torgovaya pl., 8 427-90-57

MILITIA-POLICE

Internal Affairs Department, Militia **UVD**
Morskogo Desanta ul., 1 427-74-02
Daily 0-24; Rbls; Bus 351; Metro Avtovo

MOVIES

Avrora, *Daily 10-22; Rbls*
Sankt-Peterburgskaya ul., 17 427-54-54

MUSEUMS

Benua Family Museum
Sovetskaya pl., 8 427-99-32
Built 1853-1858; Architect Benua, opened 1988. Displays over 700 works of art by the Benua family.
Mon-Fri 10:30-17; Rbls; Eng, Fr
Bolshoy Petergofskiy Dvorets
Grand Peterhof Palace
Kominterna ul., 2 427-95-27
A gem of Russia built 1714-25; by Braunshteyn, Zemtsov; then rebuilt 1745-1755, by Rastrelli
The main country residence of the Russian tsars.
Tue-Sun 10:30-18; Rbls, $; Eng, Fr ; Bus 351
Dvorets "Cottage"
Aleksandriya park, 7 427-99-53
Built 1829, by Menelaws. This beautiful small classic pavilion overlooking the Gulf of Finland;
Sat-Sun 10:30-18; Rbls; Eng, Fr; Bus 351
Dvorets Marli **Marli Palace**
Kominterna ul., 2 427-77-29
Built 1721-1723, A small palace located in the lower park by the pond. Mon-Fri 10:30-18; Rbls; Eng, Fr
Ekaterininskiy Korpus
Kominterna ul., 2 427-91-29
Built 1747-1754, Architect: Rastrelli. Displays interiors dating back to the 18th & 19th centuries.
Mon-Fri 10:30-18; Rbls; Eng, Fr
Monplaisir
Kominterna ul., 2 427-91-29
Built 1714-1725, Architects: Braunstein, Le Blond, supervised by Peter the Great. The favorite palace of Peter the Great. Open May-October. Closed Wednesdays

NOTARY PUBLIC

Notary Bureau, *Mon-Fri 9-13, 14-18; Rbls; Eng*
Sankt-Peterburgskaya ul., 28 427-98-40

PARKING LOTS

Automobile Parking No. 5, *Daily; Rbls*
Konoplyannikovoy ul., 1 427-78-42

PARKS

***Parks and Fountains of Petrodvorets
Kominterna ul., 2 427-74-25
Upper Park and famous 102 hectare Lower Park, world's finest system of French fountains ; Rbls, $; Eng, Fr

PHARMACIES (DRUG STORES)

Pharmacy No. 3 **Apteka**
Kalininskaya ul., 6 427-95-78
Mon-Fri, Sun 8-20; Rbls, $; Eng, Ger

POST OFFICES

Pochta **Post Office**
Sankt-Peterburgskaya ul., 15 427-53-91
Mon-Sat 10-12, 13-19; Rbls

PUBLISHERS

Avrora, *Daily 10-22; Rbls*
Sankt-Peterburgskaya ul., 17 427-54-54

REPAIR SERVICES

Audio Repair, *Mon-Sat 10-13, 14-17*
Ozerkovaya ul., 45 427-23-11

RESTAURANTS & CAFES

Parkovyy *(under repair)*
Sankt-Peterburgskaya ul., 14 427-90-96
Daily 20-1; Rbls; Eng, Ger

RESTAURANT
PETERHOF
A Fine Restaurant
in Peterhof
For Lunch and Dinner
In a small congenial restaurant
International and Russian cuisine from
steak & french fries to bliny & caviar
German beers & fine European wines

At the entrance to the lower Park
in the Peterhof - Petrodvorets

427-90-96 & 314-49-47
Daily 12-2; Rbls, $; Eng, Ger

RIVER TERMINALS

Pristan Petrodvorets (in Peterhof)
Hydrofoil to St. Petersburg
Petrodvortsovaya nab. 427-72-12

ROWING CLUBS

Rowing Club Volna, *Daily 8-18; Eng*
Krylova ul., 17 421-44-65

TAILOR/SEAMSTRESS

Making & Mending of Clothes
Sankt-Peterburgskaya ul., 29 427-92-49

TRUCKING

Lentransagentstvo
Sankt-Peterburgskaya ul., 8/9 427-74-27
Daily 9-14, 15-18; Rbls

UNIVERSITIES & INSTITUTES

See UNIVERSITIES for departments of the St. Petersburg State University located in Peterhof.

VISA REGISTRATION (OVIR)

Department of Visa and Registration OVIR
Morskogo Desanta ul., 1 427-77-12
Mon-Wed, Fri 16-18; Rbls

WATCHES

Raketa, *Mon-Sat 8-17; Rbls*
Sankt-Peterburgskaya ul., 60 420-29-66
Fax: 420-28-04

PUSHKIN
(TSARSKOE SELO)
ПУШКИН
(ЦАРСКОЕ СЕЛО)

Pushkin is 24 km south from the city and known for its Catherine Palace in baroque style, parks and also for the Lyceum where Pushkin, Russia's favorite poet, studied in 1811-1817.

Its name seems to be in the process of being changed back to its original name Tsarkoe Selo.

The electric commuter trains leave from Vitebsk Station every 20 minutes and the trip takes about half an hour. You get off the train at Detskoe Selo (Детское село) Station.

From Ploshchad Pobedy you can also reach Pushkin by bus no. 287 and fixed route buses 20 and 28, "marshrutnoe" taxi (really mini-buses).

ADVERTISING AGENCIES

Art Designer
Alekseya Tolstogo blvd., 38, apt. 3..... 465-85-48
Rbls

AIR CARGO

Kustanay Air
Leningradskoe shosse, 11 466-61-61
Fax: 465-88-10
Daily 8:30-23; Rbls, $; Eng

AIRLINES

Aeroflot Tickets
Leningradskaya ul., 1 470-13-06
.... 466-48-65
Mon-Sat 9-14, 15-19; Rbls

ART GALLERIES

Modern Art Museum
Tsarskoe Selo Collection

Pushkin, Karla Marksa pr., 40
Director 466-55-81
Exhibition 466-04-60
Open Saturday, Sunday

AUTOMOBILE PARTS

Glass, *Mon-Fri 9-17; Rbls, $*   **Steklo**
Moskovskoe shosse, 55 a 466-03-41

AUTOMOBILE SERVICE AND REPAIRS

GAZ (Warranty Service), *Mon-Fri 8:30-20*
Kolpinskoe sh., , proezd 2 470-40-83

BANKS

Bank Saint-Petersburg, *Mon-Fri 9:30-13*
Oktyabrskiy blvd., 16...................... 470-02-06

CAFES

Hermitage, *Daily 12-23*
Kominterna ul., 29........................... 476-62-55

CEMETERIES

Kazanskoe Cemetery, *Daily 10-16*
Lermontovskiy pr., 1 465-28-53

CHURCHES OTHER

Lutheran Church
Proletkulta ul., 4............................. 470-77-63

CHURCHES RUSSIAN ORTHODOX

Cathedral of Sofiya, *Daily 9-18*
Sofiyskaya ul., 1............................. 465-47-47

CITY GOVERNMENT

City Council   **Gorodskoy Sovet**
Oktyabrskiy blvd., 24...................... 466-62-81
Mon-Fri 10-19

COSMETICS

Gortenziya, *Mon-Sat 10-14, 15-19*
1-go Maya ul., 30/42...................... 470-76-70

DENTISTS

Dentists No. 19, *Daily 10-14, 15-21*
Ivana Pushchina ul., 33 470-10-17

DEPARTMENT STORES

Gostinyy Dvor
Moskovskaya ul., 25 476-87-52
Daily 10-14, 15-20; Rbls

EMERGENCY MEDICAL CARE

Emergency Medical Care, *Daily 0-24*
Moskovskaya ul., 15 470-75-52

FLOWER SHOPS

Liana, *Mon-Sat 10-14, 15-19*
Privokzalnaya ul., 4 470-48-01

GAS STATIONS/PETROL

Gas Station No. 2, *Daily 8-2, 4:30-8*
Vasenko ul., 1 476-57-31
Gas Station No. 97, *Daily 8-2, 4:30-8*
Zheleznodorozhnaya ul. 470-16-77

GIFT SHOPS, SOUVENIRS

Gortenziya, *Mon-Sat 10-14, 15-19*
1-go Maya ul., 30/42 470-76-70

HOSPITALS

Hospital, *Daily 0-24; Rbls*
Proletkulta ul., 5, bldg. 7 466-61-88

HOTELS

Chayka, *Daily 0-24; Rbls, $*
Shishkova ul., 32/15 465-88-37

MARKETS (Farmer's and Kolkhoz Markets)

Tsarskoselskiy Rynok., *Daily 8-19*   **Market**
Moskovskaya ul., 19/25 476-80-19

MEDICAL INSTITUTES

Institute of Children Orthopedics
Parkovaya ul., 64/68 465-34-31
Daily 9-18

MILITIA-POLICE

Militia, Dept. Internal Affairs, *Daily 0-24*
Pushkinskaya ul., 34 470-02-02
Traffic Police   **GAI**
Novaya ul., 1, Pushkinskiy Dis., Pos. Tyarlevo
☎ 466-48-66

MOVIES

Ruslan, *Daily 10-20; Rbls*
Karla Marksa ul., 42 476-26-77

MUSEUMS

Dom Pushkina   *Pushkin House-Museum*
Pushkinskaya ul., 2 476-69-90
Wed-Sun 11-18; Rbls
***Palace of Catherine I**   *Dvorets Ekateriny I*
Komsomolskaya ul., 7 465-34-29
Built 1751-1756, Architect: Rastrelli. Magnificent baroque palace built by Empress Elizabeth as summer residence of the Imperial family. Daily 10-17; Rbls
Pushkin History Museum
Truda ul., 28 466-55-10
Established 1967. Illustrates the various stages of Pushkin's life. Mon-Wed, Sat-Sun 10-17; Rbls

Pushkin Lyceum
Komsomolskaya ul., 2 470-77-92
Built 1789-1791. Poet A. Pushkin studied in this elite school from 1811-1817. Mon, Wed-Sun 10:30-16:30
Pushkin's Country House
Pushkinskaya ul., 2 476-69-90
Built 1827, home of poet A. Pushkin from May-October 1831. Displays of pictures, documents and other materials related to the great Russian poet. Wed-Sun 11-17

Modern Art Museum

Tsarskoe Selo Collection

Pushkin, Karla Marksa pr., 40
Director 466-55-81
Exhibition 466-04-60
Open Saturday, Sunday

PHOTOGRAPHY-REPAIRS

Photography Cameras Repair
Kominterna ul., 60 a 470-10-39
Mon-Fri 10-13, 14-19; Rbls

POST OFFICES

Post Office, *Mon-Sat 11-20; Rbls*
Revolyutsii ul., 11/29 476-34-11

RENTALS (Furniture, Bicycles, TV's)

Rental Bureau, *Mon-Sat 10-19; Rbls*
Leningradskaya ul., 45 470-11-33

REPAIR SERVICES

Radio Equipment Repair, *Mon-Fri 10-19; Rbls*
Ivana Pushchina ul., 23 466-64-08

RESTAURANTS & CAFES

Admiralteistvo
Ekaterinenskiy park 465-35-49
Daily 12-20; Rbls, $; Eng
Hermitage, *Daily 11-22; Rbls, $*
Kominterna ul., 27 476-62-55
Kolobok Cafe-Konditorei, *Daily 9-21; Rbls*
Kominterna ul., 29 476-62-55
Shampur, *Daily 11-16, 17-22; Rbls*
1-go Maya ul., 39 470-74-23
Tsarskaya Myza, *Daily 12-23; Rbls, $*
Kominterna ul., 23 476-62-55

⚓ **VITYAZ**

A classic Russian dining experience
with first class service
Russian folk music

Tsarskoe Selo, Moskovskaya ul., 20

466-43-18

Hrs: 11-until the last customer leaves
Rubles, $, English

SHOE REPAIRS

Remont Obuvi   **Shoe Repair**
  Kominterna ul., 60 a...................... 470-10-33
  Mon-Sat 10-14, 15-19; Rbls

SHOPS

Gloria, *Clothing, shoes, cosmetics*
  1-go Maya ul., 39........................... 470-33-76
  Mon-Sat 10-14, 15-19; Rbls

TELEGRAM

Telegraph Office, *Daily 0-24; Rbls*
  Revolyutsii ul., 52 470-49-01

THEATRICAL TICKET OFFICE

Theatre Ticket Box Office
  1-go Maya ul., 29 470-98-25

UNIVERSITIES & INSTITUTES

Agricultural Institute
  Leningradskoe shosse, 2 470-05-39
  Mon-Fri 9-17

WATCHES

Gortenziya
  1-go Maya ul., 30/42 470-76-70
  Mon-Sat 10-14, 15-19

VYBORG

Information on Vyborg is difficult to find in Russian as well as in English so we sent our staff there to collect information and addresses of the most important services, shops, banks, museums, etc. Our readers are invited to add to this list.

The dialing code is 278.

Vyborg is located in the Karelian peninsula and shares a Finnish and Russian heritage. It is the border town on the Saint Petersburg-Helsinki highway 160 km northwest of St. Petersburg. Vyborg is one of the oldest cities in Europe. The two fast trains to Helsinki, which also stop at Vyborg leave daily at 6:20 a.m. and 3:55 p.m. from Finland Station and take 1½ hours. Electric commuter trains leave from Finland Station every hour or two. The trip takes about 2½ hours by train or by car and there are scheduled sailings to/from Finnish ports.

On the highway to Helsinki, there are two border crossings to Finland: at Torfyanovka (to Vaalimaa) and at Brusnichnoe (to Nuijamaa).

ART GALLERIES

Sinyaya Loshad Salon   **Marine Horse**
  Vyborgskaya Krepost 3-09-44
  Tue-Sun 11-18

• TRIADA • 🐈

Vyborg, Suvorova pr., 4 (in Aalto Library)
Tel .... (278) 2-20-90
  Mon-Sat 12-19; English, Finnish

AUTOMOBILE SERVICE

VAZ Avtoservice
  Leningradskoe shosse, 60 2-53-82

BANKS

Stolichnyy, *Mon-Fri 9-18*
  Nikolaeva ul., 3 2-55-84
Vneshtorgbank
  Leningradskiy pr., 14 2-53-02
  Mon-Fri 9:30-12:30; Rbls, $
Vyborg Bank, *Mon-Fri 9-18*
  Pionerskaya ul., 2 2-18-45

BARS

Flamingo, *Daily 15-2*
  Vokzalnaya ul., 2 2-78-38

Night Star
  Primorskoe Shosse, 14 ....(278) 2-50-10
  Excellent Food & Service

Pub/Beer Bar, *Daily 9-4; Rbls, $; Eng, Finn*
  Zheleznodorozhnaya ul., 7 2-59-42

U Olega
  Vyborg, 188900, Lenina pr.
  (in the Palace of Culture "50 Let Oktyabrya")
  Tel .... (278) 210-42
  Tues-Sun 14-4, English, Finnish

BUSINESS CENTERS

Business Center, *Mon-Fri 9-18*
  Nikolaeva pr., 3 2-06-83

CHURCHES RUSSIAN ORTHODOX

Cathedral of the Transfiguration
                              Preobrazhenskiy Sobor
  Teatralnaya pl., 1 2-58-37

CINEMAS, MOVIES

Rodina
  Mira ul., 7 2-02-04
Vyborg
  Krepostnaya ul., 25 2-13-70

CITY GOVERNMENT

City Council of Vyborg   *Gorodskoy Sovet*
  Krepostnaya ul., 35 2-47-14
Economic Chamber, *Mon-Fri 9-18; Rbls*
  Sovetskaya ul., 12 2-47-92

CLUBS & SOCIETIES

Staryy Vyborg   **Old Vyborg**
  Oktyabrskaya ul., 31 2-19-61
  Tue-Sun 11-17; Eng, Finn

CURRENCY EXCHANGE

AVTOVAZBANK
Currency exchange
Progonnaya ul., 1, office 2
(278)257-06, (278)338-80
Daily 9-21

CUSTOMS

Customs
- Brusnichnoe 7-05-04
- Luzhayka 9-61-21
- Port 2-88-59
- Torfyanovka 2-84-70
- Vysotsk 5-25-78
- Zheleznodorozhnaya ul., 9/15 2-66-97

DENTISTS

Dental Clinic, *Mon-Fri 9-19, Sat 9-14*
Lenina pr., 12 2-57-03

DEPARTMENT STORES

Univermag   **Department Store**
Lenina pr., 11 2-04-52
Daily 10-15, 16-19; Rbls

EMERGENCY MEDICAL CARE

Emergency Medical Care, *Daily 0-24*
Mayakovskogo ul., 2 2-40-12

FURNITURE

Mebel, *Mon-Sat 10-19; Rbls*   **Furniture**
Pobedy pr., 9 2-10-76

GAS STATIONS/PETROL

Gas Station No. 1, *A-92, 95, 98, Diesel*
Vokzalnaya ul., 1 2-35-53
Daily 0-24; Rbls
Gas Station No. 2, *A-93, Diesel*
Leningradskoe shosse 9-67-59

NESTE
Petro Service
GASOLINE and LUBRICANTS
DIESEL • CAFE
24 HOURS A DAY
MAJOR CREDIT CARDS ACCEPTED
*Gasoline: 76, 93, lead-free 95 E &
98E oct. for cars equipped with
catalytic converters, automotive oils,
fluids & accessories. Cigarettes, soft
drinks, food & travel needs*
NESTE-VYBORG
Leningradskiy pr.,16 3-18-70

GAS STATION
H a n s a   O i l

Gasoline A-96, Diesel Fuel
Bar, Currency Exchange
On the Finnish Border

Vyborg, pos. Gvardeyskiy
Tel.: (278) 319-01
Tel./Fax: (278) 288-16
Hrs: 9-24, Rbls & $

GIFT SHOPS, SOUVENIRS

Suveniri, *Mon-Sat 10-15, 16-19*   **Souvenirs**
Severnaya ul., 12 2-19-21

INTERNATIONAL (Hard Currency) SHOPS

Beriozka
Zheleznodorozhnaya ul., 9/15 2-17-98
Daily 10-14, 15-19; Rbls, $; Eng, Finn
Helen, *Daily 9-24; $; Eng, Finn*
Railway Station 2-84-29
Ross, *Mon-Sat 11-13, 14-19; $; Eng, Finn*
Dimitrova ul., 1 2-09-55

HOSPITALS

Central Hospital, *Daily 0-24*
Oktyabrskaya ul., 2 2-45-52
Rodilnyy Dom   **Maternity Hospital**
Leningradskoe shosse, 24/26 2-39-92
Zheleznodorozhnaya Bolnitsa, *Daily 0-24*
Leningradskoe shosse, 23 9-65-15

HOTELS

Druzhba Hotel ***
Zheleznodorozhnaya ul., 5 2-49-42
Daily 0-24; Rbls, $; Eng, Ger, Finn
Hotelship Korolenko *(near Hotel Druzhba)*
Please call 9-44-78
Vyborg Hotel
Leningradskiy pr., 19 2-23-83

INSURANCE

Ingosstrakh, *Daily 9-18; Rbls*
Leningradskiy pr., 31 2-57-04

INTERNATIONAL SHOPS

The Frontier Shop
At the Finnish-Russian Border.
Liquor, perfumes, tobacco, soft drinks,
delicatessen, leisure wear, fashion
accessories, cameras and film, watches,
jewelry, gifts and souvenirs
Town of "Torfyanovka"
on the Helsinki-St. Petersburg Road

Int'l Tel. 949-357-444
Aer Rianta-Vyborg Town JV; Open: 8-23 daily

JEWELRY

Almaz, *Mon-Sat 10-15, 16-19; Rbls*   **Diamond**
Krepostnaya ul., 43 2-03-73

LAW FIRMS & LAWYERS

Law Consulting, *Mon-Sat 9-13, 14-18; Rbls*
Krepostnaya ul., 41 2-31-70

MAPS - VYBORG

*Viipuri Map and Guidebook published by
Modus OY, Vega SPb. OY and PolyPlan St.
Petersburg, 1992. The guide is published
mostly in Finnish with categories in English.*

MARKETS (Farmer's and Kolkhoz Markets)

Rynok, *Daily 8-18; Rbls*   **Market**
Severnyy Val ul., 1 2-53-13

MEDICAL CARE & CONSULTATIONS

City Policlinic, *Mon-Sat 8-22*
Onezhskaya ul., 8 2-53-09
Rodilnyy Dom   **Maternity Hospital**
Leningradskoe shosse, 24/26 2-39-92

MILITIA-POLICE

GAI Traffic Police, *Daily 0-24*
Leningradskiy pr., 13 2-55-90
Militia/Internal Affairs Department   **UVD**
Leningradskiy pr., 13 2-47-26

MUSEUMS

Regional Museum, *Tue-Sun 10-19; Rbls*
Vyborgskaya krepost. 2-39-40

NOTARY PUBLIC

Notary Bureau, *Mon-Sat 9-17; Rbls*
Mira ul., 10 2-25-15

PHARMACIES (DRUG STORES)

Apteka   **Pharmacy**
• Lenina pr., 22, *Daily 8-20* 2-79-13
• Rubezhnaya ul., 18, *Mon-Fri 9-19* 2-52-16
• Severnyy Val, 19, *Mon-Sat 9-19* 2-01-09
• Vokzalnaya ul., 4, *Mon-Fri 9-20* 9-68-07

PORTS

Sea Terminal, *Daily 0-24*   **Morskoy Port**
Severnyy Val, 1 9-32-20

POST OFFICES

Post Office
• Leningradskoe shosse, 27 2-33-45
• Sportivnaya ul., 4 2-51-24
                    Mon-Sat 9-19
• Tsentralnaya ul., 12 2-30-03

RESTAURANTS & CAFES

Brigantina   **Brigantine**
Yuzhnyy Val, 16 2-37-19
                Russian Cuisine; Daily 12-24
Krepost Cafe, *Daily 10-19*   **Castle**
Vyborgskiy Zamok (Castle) .... No ☎

Nochnaya Zvezda   **Night Star**
Primorskoe shosse, 14 2-50-10
                Russian Cuisine; Daily 12-24
Ogonek, *Russian Cuisine; Daily 9-20*
Vokzalnaya ul., 11 2-39-42
Pantserlaks Cafe
Luzhskaya ul., 1 2-63-01
                Western Ukrainian Cuisine; Daily 9-21
Railway Station Restaurant
Zheleznodorozhnaya ul., 7 2-11-74
                Russian Cuisine; Daily 12:30-23:30
Sever, *Russian Cuisine; Daily 13-24*   **North**
Lenina pr., 11 2-18-37

SHOPS

Gera *Tableware, linen, gifts, porcelain*
Poselok Roshchino 6-40-47
                Mon-Sat 10-19; Rbls

SPORTS EQUIPMENT

Spartak, *Mon-Fri 10-19, Sat 10-17; Rbls*
Moskovskiy pr., 11 2-59-57

TELEGRAM

Telegraph Station, *Daily 0-24*   **Telegraf**
Moskovskiy pr., 24 2-50-49

TELEVISION STATIONS

TV–Vyborg, *Mon-Fri 9-18*
Vodnoy Zastavy ul., 3 2-41-31

TRAVEL AGENCIES

Sputnik, *Mon-Fri 10-18; Rbls, $*
Leningradskoe shosse, 31 2-50-47
Travel Agency, *Mon-Fri 9-17; Rbls*
Storozhevoy Bashni ul., 11 2-06-46

TRUCKING

Sovtransavto

SOVAVTO ST. PETERSBURG

VYBORG TRUCK PARK

FUEL, SERVICE and REPAIRS
WAREHOUSE and SECURE PARKING

On the Helsinki - St. Petersburg
Road at Vyborg

Tel .... (278) 2-14-63

VISA REGISTRATION (OVIR)

Visa Registration   **OVIR**
Leningradskiy pr., 13 2-58-61
                Mon-Fri 9-13, 14-18; Rbls, $

Russian Jewellery Art

FABERGE
by Ananov collection

Grand Hotel Europe
Mikhaylovskaya ul., 1/7
daily from 11 a.m. to 8 p.m.
Collection/Store, $
tel./fax 119-6008

ANANOV

English·German·French·Spanish·Italian

GLOBAL

SUPER SHOP

COMPUTERS
ELECTRONICS
&
HOME
APPLIANCES

LOWEST PRICES IN RUSSIA

Our Own Global Computers
MADE IN THE USA
ONE YEAR GUARANTEE

Matrix & Laser Printers, Plotters & Scanners,
Network Hardware & Software, Modems, Software
& Peripherals PLUS: Photocopiers, Telephones,
Audio-Video & HIFI and Household Appliances
Products from: Sony, Panasonic, Sharp, Canon,
Konica, Funai, Casio, Citizen, Brother, Olivetti,
Hitachi, Orion, National, Pioneer, Kenwood, Aiwa,
Sencor, Braun, Black & Decker, Phillips and
Goldstar

Visit Our Showroom in Moscow

GLOBAL-USA AUTOLAND

Jeep Cherokee
Lincoln Towncar
Cadillac SE Deville
Dodge Caravan
Ford Taurus

Extensive Selection of
Quality American Cars

USA

Usacheva ul., 35
Moscow, 119018
Metro: Sportivnaya
Fax: (095) 246-89-17

TELEPHONE: (095) 245-56-57/245-50-39/245-48-66/245-52-24/245-58-79/245-44-72/244-16-46

Industry & Construction Bank

The widest network of branches in St. Petersburg

Branches throughout Russia with a representative office in Berlin

Close ties with both foreign and Russian banks and companies

Investment, leasing, stock and insurance options

Worldwide service with payments, Letters of Credit, and Documentary Collection through our correspondent banks

Secured Loans

Buying and selling of non-cash currency through Inter-bank Currency Exchanges in St. Petersburg, Moscow and directly through Industry and Chemical Bank

Traveler's Cheque cashing

Exchange Offices:
Head-office
Mikhailovskaya ul., 4
Admiralty Branch
Galernaya ul., 24
Hotel "Oktyabrskaya"
Ligovskiy pr., 10
Motel "Olgino"
Hotel "Sovetskaya"
Lermontovskiy pr., 43
Beriozka shop
Shop "Luma"
Nevskiy pr., 164
Shop "Imperial"
Vladimiriskiy pr.,3

Nevskly ps., 38, 191011,
St. Petersburg, Russia
Tel.: +7 (812) 110-4958
Fax: +7 (812) 310-6173
Telex: 121612 ICB SU

**Industry & Construction Bank
Saint Petersburg, A/O**

Est. Volzhsko-Kamskiy Bank, 1863

CORRESPONDENT WITH: Bank of New York · Bankers Trust Company · Deutsche Bank · Midland Bank · Credit Suisse · ABN AMRO Bank · Societe Generale · Kreditanstalt Bankverein · Bank of Tokyo · Kansallis-Osake-Pankki · Unibank · Svenska Handelsbanken

THE JOINT STOCK COMPANY
SOVAVTO - SAINT PETERSBURG

is the largest carrier of cargo and passengers in Northern Europe. Sovavto has great experience in rendering a diverse range of shipping, transportation and travel services both within Russia and abroad.

SOVAVTO FREIGHT & SHIPPING: General, consolidated and heavy cargo shipping to and from all countries in Europe, Scandinavia, and the Middle East. Representatives in over 29 countries.

SOVAVTO CARGO EXPRESS: Daily Departures to Western Europe and Scandinavia, twice daily through Finland.

SOVAVTO VYBORG TRUCK PARK: A range of maintenance and storage services, including fuel, repairs, warehousing and secured parking.

SOVAVTO TRUCK SALES: An authorized Volvo truck dealer. Sovavto stocks used Volvo & Maz truck as well as a large stock of used trailers. Full Warrenty services in Russia and abroad.

SOVAVTO SERVICE CENTER: Repair and parts (including warrenty services) for Volvo, SAF, MAZ trucks and all Russian and European trailers. Factory tested mechanics, modern paint and test facilities and a large parts inventory.

SOVAVTO AUTOMOBILES: A wide selection of used foreign cars such as Volvo, Opel and Ford Scorpio from stock or by order.

SOVAVTO EXPRESS BUS TO FINLAND: The quick and most comfortable way to Finland in modern coaches at a reasonable price.

MAIN OFFICE

Russia, 196199, Saint Petersburg, Vitebskiy pr., 3
Tel.: (812) 298-5556, Fax: (812) 298-7760, Telex: 121535 avto

MAGAZINE
PASSPORT
TO THE
NEW WORLD

THE QUALITY CHOICE

"Passport to the New World" published by "Passport International Ltd" (Russian-American Joint Advertising and Publishing Company). "Passport to the New World" is a high quality bimonthly English language magazine with a circulation of 100,000 copies distributed on Aeroflot International flights, in hotels in Moscow, Saint Petersburg, Kiev, Sochi, Alma-Ata, Minsk, Odessa as well as in diplomatic and foreign trade missions in Moscow.

In addition, our magazine is distributed through Aeroflot's 150 representatives in 93 countries of the world.

"Passport to the New World" will help you not only know better the life in the former USSR but it will also give you a helping hand in making business contacts with leading companies and enterprises in the CIS. It will also become your reliable guide in this beautiful country. "Passport to the New World" is your right choice.

The Magazine is presented by its founders

"Passport International Ltd"
15, New Arbat, flat # 617, 619,
Moscow, 121019, Russia
Tel: (095) 202-22-71
Fax: (095) 202-69-17

"ZigZag Venture Group"
254, Fifth Avenue,
New York, 10001, USA
Tel: (212) 725-67-00
Fax: (212) 725-69-15

DELOVIE LYUDI

THE MAGAZINE FOR BUSINESS LEADERS

**DELOVIE LYUDI
(Business in the ex-USSR)**
provides valuable and unique information on the CIS market. This enables decision-makers and entrepreneurs to follow the transition to a market economy in the former USSR. DELOVIE LYUDI also offers foreign business-people an exceptional medium for communicating details concerning their companies, products and services. DELOVIE LYUDI is available in two editions with identical contents: 100,000 copies in Russian and 30,000 copies in English for the international edition. Written by a Moscow editorial team, well-connected in top economic and social circles, DELOVIE LYUDI is independent, objective and thorough.

Editorial Office:
Ul. Profsoyusnaya, 73, Moscow, 117342, Russia
tel.: (7-095) 333-33-40; fax (7-095) 330-15-68
telex 414741
International Edition Subscription Service
Postal enquiries and subscription fees:
4, rue Brunel, 75017 Paris (France)
Telephone and fax enquiries:
Yuri ALeonidov, Vera Kuznetsova
tel. (7-095) 193-42-81; fax (7-095) 943-00-05
US Offices:
New York: DELOVIE LYUDI,
1560 Broadway, 5th FL, New York, NY 10036
Orange County: DELOVIE LYUDI
2865 East Coast Highway, Ste 308.
Corona del Mar, CA 92625, USA

THE INDEPENDENT ECONOMIC MONTHLY

TRAVELLER'S YELLOW PAGES

Seven Basic Reasons To Advertise in

The *Traveller's* Yellow Pages and Handbook Series

Michael R. Dohan, Ph.D., Editor

Written and designed for English-speaking
foreign residents, businessmen and tourists
in Russia and Eastern Europe.

1. **Efficient and cost-effective**
   in promoting your business to the
   upscale market of English-speaking foreign residents, tourists and
   business travellers in Russia and
   Eastern Europe.

2. **Year round advertising.**
   • 24 hours/day, 365 days/year.

3. **Excellent demographics.**
   • Most foreign residents & businesses.
   • Majority of foreign business
   executives and official visitors.
   • Many individual tourists & visitors.
   • Used for referral by most hotels and
   travel agencies and tour guides.

4. **Extensive free distribution.**
   1000's of copies to foreign businesses, hotels, consulates, and travel
   agencies in Moscow and Saint
   Petersburg and in the United States.

5. **Large local & overseas sales
   network for book sales.**
   • More than 100 booksellers in Russia.
   • More than 60 in US, UK, Germany,
   France, Norway and Finland.
   • Worldwide mail order.

6. **Acclaimed by its readers, who write:**
   Recommend it to all my colleagues.
   Most useful book ever written!
   Most up-to-date and accurate.
   Absolutely the easiest to use.
   Essential, indispensable!
   We use it every day!

7. **Internationally acclaimed design!**
   More than just a telephone book.
   • 1000's of selected listings and more
   than 100 essays and tables, yet
   compact and convenient to carry.
   • Index and headings in 5 languages.
   • Extensive use of local language.
   • Outstanding maps and graphics.
   • Professionally written ads & text.
   • Nominated as Official Directory
   1994 Goodwill Games Saint Petersburg.

*Join 100's of international and
local firms when you*

ADVERTISE IN

The *Traveller's* Yellow Pages

1994-1995 EDITIONS

NORTHWEST RUSSIA, 1994/95
15,000 copies, Publication July 1994

ESTONIA 1994-95
15,000 copies, Publication July 1994

LATVIA 1994-95
15,000 copies, Publication August 1994

LITHUANIA 1995-late 1994
15,000 copies, Publication October 1994

SAINT PETERSBURG 1994-95
Special 3d Edition for the 1994 Goodwill games
in Saint Petersburg in July-August 1994. 20,000
copies , 8,000 copies distributed free.
Publication June 1994

MOSCOW 1995 (2d ed.)
30,000 copies, Publication, December 1994

FUTURE EDITIONS IN 1995
*KIEV-1995, RUSSIAN FAR EAST-1995,
WARSAW-1995, PRAGUE-1995,
BUDAPEST-1995, BUCHAREST-1995*

*Advertising rates from $50 to $2600.
Ask about the Russian language editions.
Discounts for Multiple Editions.
Write /Call/Fax for Advertising Kits
and Closing Dates*

EDITORIAL OFFICES
THE *TRAVELLER'S*
YELLOW PAGES™

InfoServices International, Inc.

⊠ 1 Saint Marks Place
Cold Spring Harbor, NY 11724, USA

Tel	USA (516) 549-0064
Fax	(516) 549-2032
Telex	221213 TTC UR
Internet	71147.2275@compuserve.com

*Editorial offices also in
Saint Petersburg and Moscow.*

Information for the World Traveller™

Examples of Advertising
in editions of
The *Traveller's* Yellow Pages

A typical free listing always includes ↗ name, street address and telephone number. Other information may be included.

Even the smallest one centimeter ad ↗ attracts attention, gets a box and allows **four lines. Economical!**

This ad is about two centimeters → and allows for a good solid presentation of the firm with a few graphics. Very cost-effective advertising.

Your Advertising and Rate Kit
for The *Traveller's* Yellow Pages
is available from
InfoServices International, Inc.
1 Saint Marks Place,
Cold Spring Harbor, New York, 11724 USA
☎ 1 (516) 549-0064 ❖ Fax 1 (516) 549-2032

This 3.5 cm size is very effective → when using the **firm's logotype.** Our designer **scanned the trademark** and **created a fancy border** to make this ad even more effective. **This size is the best advertising buy in the book.**

This **larger 5.5 cm ad** was chosen to **convey the atmosphere and status of** → **the firm.** This ad conveys the "turn-of-the-century Russian family salon atmosphere" of this little restaurant. The **largest column ad is 8 centimeters** so that our smaller advertisers can be seen also.

Some **large firms** choose a **full page four-color ad** to present more visual information and to convey an appropriate image of their company. These firms also receive additional advertising free of charge in the appropriate categories of the yellow pages.

Other advertisers place their advertising message throughout the book by using **running footers** in various categories. Look at the Babylon ads (all different with the same logo) and the Delovie Lyudi ads (all similar) in this edition. ↓

John Bull Pub John Bull and Skol on Draught
Nevskiy pr., 79 164-98-77
Hrs 12-5, Rbls, $; Eng; Metro Ploshchad Vosstaniya; H-5
Staraya Derevnya,
Savushkina, ul., 72 239-00-00
Russian Cuisine Daily 12-11, Rbls, Eng, Ger, Span, D-11

☙ STARAYA DEREVNYA ☙
In the tradition of the Russian family salon
Savushkina, ul., 72 239-00-00
Russian Cuisine, Daily 12-11, Rbls, Eng, Ger, Span, D-11

JOHN BULL PUB 🍺
A PUB IN THE ENGLISH TRADITION
WITH GREAT PUB SNACKS
John Bull and Skol on Draught
Nevskiy pr., 79 164-98-77
Hrs 12-5, Rbls, $; Eng; Metro Ploshchad Vosstaniya; H-5

The English Pub
Nevskiy pr., 79 164-98-77
Hrs: 12-5, Rbls & $; English
Metro: Ploshchad Vosstaniya

A restaurant in the tradition of
the "Russian family salon"
of the 1900's.
Dine on classic Russian cuisine
surrounded by beautiful antiques
and art by contemporary painters
Gypsy & Russian songs on Fri & Sat
15 minutes from central St. Pb.
Well worth the trip
Ul. Savushkina, 72
Tel./Fax: 239-00-00
Daily 12 noon to evening, Eng, Ger, Sp; D-11

DELOVIE LYUDI
I N D E P E N D E N T   •   O B J E C T I V E   •   T H O R O U G H
Profsoyuznaya ul., 73; Tel.: (095) 333-33-40; Fax: (095) 330-15-68

329

The Ideal Advertising Media In Russia & The Baltics
The *Traveller's* Yellow Pages and Handbook Series
For English-Speaking Residents & Travellers to Russia & the Baltics

THE *TRAVELLER'S*
YELLOW PAGES
and HANDBOOK for
ESTONIA
1994 - 1995

ESTONIA 1994-95 including Tallinn, Tartu and other towns. More than 4,000 addresses. New maps of Estonia, Tallinn & major towns. In English with headings in Estonian, Russian, German, Swedish & Finnish. pp. 256, Pub. mid-1994.

THE *TRAVELLER'S*
YELLOW PAGES
and HANDBOOK for
NORTHWEST RUSSIA
From MURMANSK to NOVGOROD
1994 - 1995

NORTHWEST RUSSIA 1994-95 From Murmansk to Novgorod with 3,400 addresses. With maps of towns and Northwest Russia. pp. 304. Pub. June 1994.

THE *TRAVELLER'S*
YELLOW PAGES
and HANDBOOK for
MOSCOW
1994

MOSCOW 1994, with more than 6,000 addresses of shops, offices, services, restaurants, etc. New large Moscow City Map. pp. 448, Pub. December 1993.

THE *TRAVELLER'S*
YELLOW PAGES
and HANDBOOK for
SAINT PETERSBURG
VYBORG AND SUBURBS OF LOMONOSOV, PAVLOVSK, PETERHOF AND PUSHKIN
1994

Жёлтые Страницы
с алфавитным указателем
для иностранных гостей
Санкт-Петербурга
Gelbe Seiten
für Reisende mit
deutschem Suchwortregister
Pages Jaunes
pour le voyageur
avec index en français
Guía Sidorna
för resande med
invining på svenska
Keltaiset Sivut
suomenkielinen
aakkosellinen hakemisto

ST. PETERSBURG 1994 including suburbs and Vyborg with more than 4,500 addresses. Large new City Map. pp. 356, October 1993.

Special 1994-95 Edition for the 1994 Goodwill Games in Saint Petersburg with the most up-to-date information and special maps. Late June 1994.

Michael R. Dohan, Ph.D., Editor

Essential for travellers on business and pleasure: Contains more than 4000 phone and fax numbers and addresses of selected shops, art galleries, hotels, restaurants, tour guides, translators, tailors, museums, churches, medical care, pharmacies, food markets, department stores, offices and apartment rentals, business services and supplies, lawyers, shipping and trucking, auto service and 411 more categories. Practical information includes postal rates, telephones and communications, transportation, climate, size, what-to-bring, theater seating plans, hours, signs, Cyrillic alphabet, holidays, customs, visas and Metro map.

INFOSERVICES INTERNATIONAL, INC.,
New York, USA

Official Visiter's Directory

"Absolutely indispensable for the businessman and visitor to Saint Petersburg."
Marshall Goldman
Harvard University

Each Copy of The *Traveller's* Yellow Pages Includes:

Thousands of addresses of selected shops, restaurants, auto rentals, food stores, hotels, medical, legal and business services, office and apartment rentals, and 402 more categories, all organized like the traditional Yellow Pages. More than 150 essays, charts, tables, plans and maps on topics from shopping, taxis and telephones to seating charts and radio stations. Each includes a full-size fold-out map in English and bilingual indexes.

TRAVELLER'S
YELLOW
PAGES

Advertise to the Upscale Russian Market
The "Лучшее В - Best in" Editions in Russian
Written and designed for Russian residents in Saint Petersburg and in Moscow

ANNOUNCING
The New Лучшее в *Series*
Edited by Michael R. Dohan, Ph.D. & Associates
In Russian

Лучшее в Санкт-Петербурге
1994/95
The Best in Saint Petersburg 1994/95
20,000 copies

Лучшее в Москве 1994/95
The Best in Moscow 1994/95
30,000 copies

Created at the request of our Russian readers and our current advertisers in The *Traveller's* Yellow Pages.

More than just a telephone book!

FEATURES:
1. Organized like its cousin, The *Traveller's* Yellow Pages.

2. Completely rewritten to meet the needs of the upscale Russian resident and businesses looking to buy the best domestic and imported goods, to dine out, to travel, to get the best medical care, to find professional craftsmen & other services.

3. Many categories expanded and 100's of new shops & services added, such as medical care, tailors, theaters, education, travel, craftsmen, etc.

4. Contains 1000's of selected listings of the best shops, restaurants and services in each city, evaluated by local staff, and organized into 440 categories like The *Traveller's* Yellow Pages.

5. More than 100 essays, tables and charts, providing hard-to-find data and information such as seating plans of theaters and concert halls, shopping maps, tables of sizes and multilingual glossaries for main categories of consumer goods, etc.

Don't Miss This Opportunity!
This exciting, new directory promises to be a best seller and one of the most important advertising media to the new Russian consumer in the 1990's.

Six Reasons to Advertise
to Russian businesses & households in the new **Best In** *editions for* **Moscow and Saint Petersburg.**

1. Profitable and cost-effective in promoting your business to the upscale market of Russian residents.

2. Get a competitive edge in the new market economy.

3. Year round advertising *24 hours/day, 365 days/year at home and in the office.*

4. Excellent demographics focused on the well-to-do and educated Russian household, professionals, business staff and visitors in each city.

5. Extensive free distribution of 1000's of copies to major Russian and foreign businesses, consulates and government offices, hotels and travel agencies in Moscow & St. Petersburg.

6. Large local book sales network.

For Advertising Information Kits
The New Лучшее в *Series*
EDITORIAL OFFICES
THE *TRAVELLER'S* YELLOW PAGES™

InfoServices International, Inc.
Information for the World Traveller™
✉ 1 Saint Marks Place
Cold Spring Harbor, NY 11724, USA

Tel .... USA (516) 549-0064
Fax ....(516) 549-2032
Telex .... 221213 TTC UR
Internet. 71147.2275@compuserve.com
Editorial offices also in
Saint Petersburg and Moscow.
Plan also for the Future Best In *Editions*
NORTHWEST RUSSIA, 1994/95
KIEV-1995

Лучшее в Санкт-Петербурге
Лучшее в Москве

The New "Best In" Series in Russian
For the Russian-Speaking Market in Saint Petersburg and Moscow

An outstanding opportunity to advertise to Russian consumers
and businesses. In Russian for Russians.

Advertise in these prestigious publications, designed and written especially for well-to-do Russian consumers and businesses wishing to buy "The Best" in domestic and imported goods and services. *"The Best in Saint Petersburg"* and *"The Best in Moscow"* are similar in concept, design, size and quality to **The *Traveller's* Yellow Pages,** but have been completely rewritten with many special features for the Russian market.

NEVSKIY PROSPEKT
From Neva to Kanal Griboedova

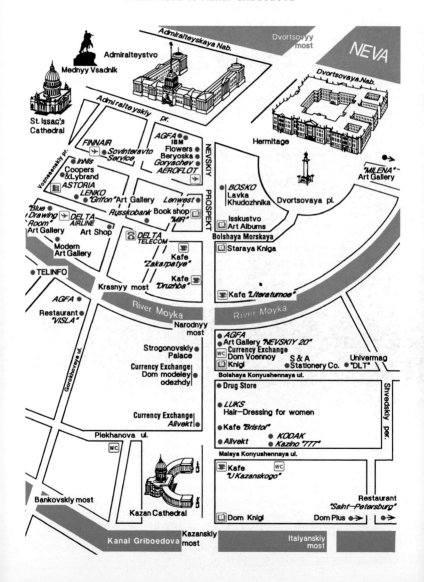

Admiralteyskaya Nab.

Dvortsovyy most

NEVA

Admiralteystvo

Mednyy Vsadnik

Dvortsovaya Nab.

St. Issac's Cathedral

Admiralteyskiy pr.

Hermitage

Voznesenskiy pr.

FINNAIR

Sovinteravto Service

InNis

Coopers &Lybrand

ASTORIA

LENKO

"Grifon" Art Gallery

"Blue Drawing Room" Art Gallery

DELTA-AIRLINE

Art Shop

Modern Art Gallery

TELINFO

AGFA

IBM

Flowers

Beryoska

Goryachev

AEROFLOT

NEVSKIY PROSPEKT

Lenwest

Russkobank Book shop

"MIR"

DELTA TELECOM

Kafe "Zakarpatye"

Kafe "Druzhba"

Krasnyy most

"MILENA" Art Gallery

BOSKO

Lavka Khudozhnika

Dvortsovaya pl.

Isskustvo Art Albums

Bolshaya Morskaya

Staraya Kniga

Kafe "Literaturnoe"

AGFA

Restaurant "VISLA"

Gorokhovaya ul.

River Moyka

River Moyka

Narodnyy most

Strogonovskiy Palace

Currency Exchange Dom modeley odezhdy

Currency Exchange Alivekt

Plekhanova ul.

WC

AGFA

Art Gallery "NEVSKIY 20"

Currency Exchange

Dom Voennoy

Knigi

S & A Stationery Co.

Univermag "DLT"

Bolshaya Konyushennaya ul.

Drug Store

LUKS Hair—Dressing for women

Kafe "Bristol"

Alivekt

KODAK

Kazino "777"

Shvedskiy per.

Malaya Konyushennaya ul.

Kafe "U Kazanskogo"

WC

Bankovskiy most

Kazan Cathedral

Restaurant "Saint—Petersburg"

Dom Knigi

Dom Plus

Kazanskiy most

Kanal Griboedova

Italyanskiy most

NEVSKIY PROSPEKT
From Kanal Griboedova to Liteynyy prospekt

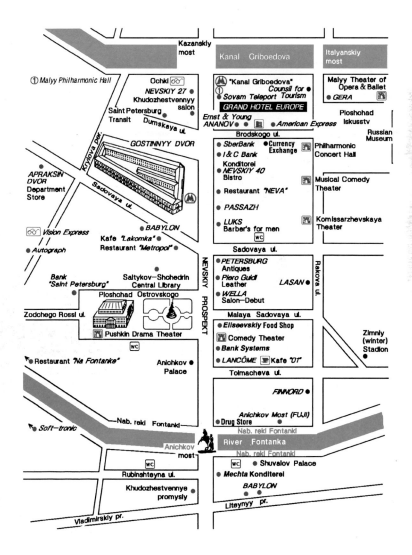

Kazanskiy most

Kanal Griboedova

Italyanskiy most

① Malyy Philharmonic Hall

Ochki 👓

NEVSKIY 27 ●
Khudozhestvennyy salon

Saint Petersburg ●
Transit

Dumskaya ul.

"Kanal Griboedova"
Sovam Teleport

Counsil for
Tourism

GRAND HOTEL EUROPE

Ernst & Young
ANANOV ● ● ● 🏛 ● American Express

Malyy Theater of
Opera & Ballet
● GERA 🏛

Ploshohad
Iskusstv

GOSTINNYY DVOR

Brodskogo ul.

Russian
Museum

Krylova per.

● SberBank   ● Currency
● I & C Bank   Exchange 🏛

Philharmonic
Concert Hall

APRAKSIN
DVOR
Department
Store

Sadovaya ul.

Konditorei
● NEVSKIY 40
Bistro

● Restaurant "NEVA"

● PASSAZH

Musical Comedy
Theater 🏛

● BABYLON

👓 Vision Express

Kafe "Lakomka" ●
Restaurant "Metropol" ●

● LUKS
Barber's for men
WC

Komissarzhevskaya
Theater 🏛

● Autograph

Sadovaya ul.

Bank
"Saint Petersburg"

Saltykov–Shchedrin
Central Library

● PETERSBURG
Antiques
● Piero Guidi
Leather   LASAN ●
● WELLA
Salon–Debut

Rakova ul.

Ploshohad Ostrovskogo

Zodchego Rossi ul.

Pushkin Drama Theater 🏛
WC

Malaya Sadovaya ul.

● Eliseevskiy Food Shop

🏛 Comedy Theater

● Bank Systems

● LANCÔME 🏛 Kafe "01"

Zimnly
(winter)
Stadion
●

NEVSKIY PROSPEKT

⚘ Restaurant "Na Fontanke"

Anichkov ●
Palace

Tolmacheva ul.

FINNORD ●

⚘ Soft–tronic

Nab. reki Fontanki

Anichkov Most (FUJI)
● Drug Store   ●

Nab. reki Fontanki

Anichkov
most

WC

River Fontanka

Nab. reki Fontanki

WC ● Shuvalov Palace

Rubinshteyna ul.

● Mechta Konditerei

BABYLON

Khudozhestvennye
promysly

Liteynyy pr.

Vladimirskiy pr.

NEVSKIY PROSPEKT
From Liteynyy prospekt to Ploshchad Vosstaniya

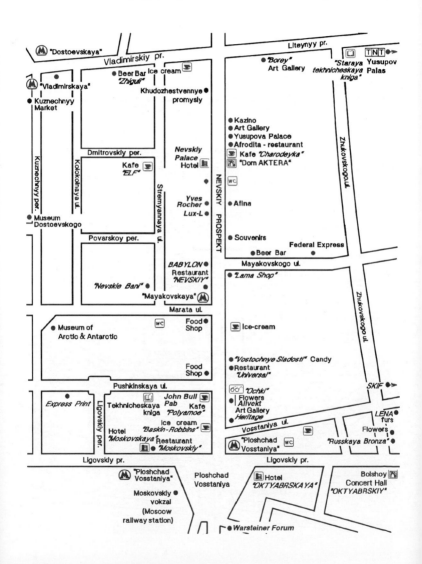

NEVSKIY PROSPEKT

From Ploshchad Vostaniya to Aleksandro-Nevskaya Lavra

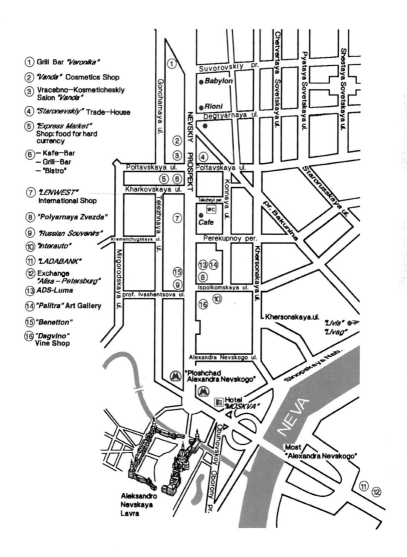

1. Grill Bar *"Veronika"*
2. *"Vanda"* Cosmetics Shop
3. Vracebno—Kosmeticheskiy Salon *"Vanda"*
4. *"Staronevskiy"* Trade—House
5. *"Express Market"* Shop: food for hard currency
6. — Kafe—Bar
   — Grill—Bar
   — "Bistro"
7. *"LENWEST"* International Shop
8. "Polyarnaya Zvezda"
9. *"Russian Souvenirs"*
10. *"Interauto"*
11. *"LADABANK"*
12. Exchange *"Alisa – Petersburg"*
13. ADS-Luma
14. "Palitra" Art Gallery
15. "Benetton"
16. "Dagvino" Vine Shop

SEATING PLAN OF

Malyy Theater of Opera and Ballet

Academic Malyy Theater of Opera and Ballet n.a. Musorgsky
(1239 Seats)

Iskusstv pl., 1
Bus: 14, 22, 25, 27
Tram: 2, 3, 5, 12, 13, 14, 34
Trolleybus 1, 5, 7, 10, 14, 22
Metro: Nevskiy prospekt, Gostinyy Dvor

Tickets: 219-19-78
Administration & Information: 219-19-80
Map: J-8

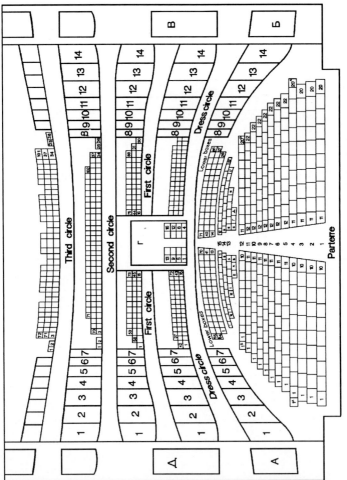

SEATING PLAN OF
Russian Academic Bolshoy Dramatic Theater by Tovstonogov
(Formerly Gogkiy Theater, 1402 Seats)

Nab. reki Fontanki, 65   Tickets: 310-92-42
Tram: 2, 5, 13, 15, 14, 28   Administration & Information: 310-04-01
Trolley: 1, 3, 5, 7, 8, 9, 10, 15, 17, 14, 22   Map: J-7
Metro: Nevskiy prospekt, Gostinyy Dvor

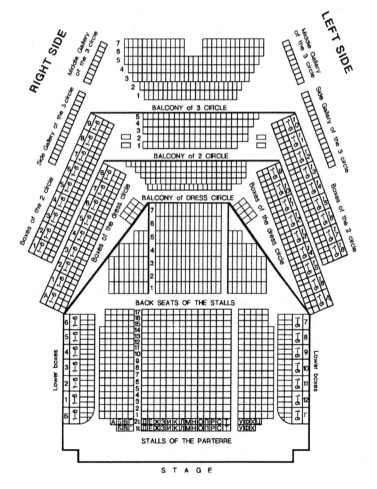

RIGHT SIDE   LEFT SIDE

Middle Gallery of the 3 circle

Side Gallery of the 3 circle

BALCONY of 3 CIRCLE

BALCONY of 2 CIRCLE

Boxes of the 2 circle

Side Gallery of the dress circle

BALCONY of DRESS CIRCLE

Boxes of the dress circle

BACK SEATS OF THE STALLS

Lower boxes

STALLS OF THE PARTERRE

STAGE

SEATING PLAN OF

Bolshoy Philharmonic Hall

Philharmonic n. a. Shostakovich, Bolshoy Hall

(1318 Seats)

Mikhaylovskaya (formerly Brodskogo) ul., 2   Tickets: 110-42-90
Bus: 14, 22, 25   110-42-57
Tram: 2, 3, 5, 13, 14, 34   Administration & Information: 311-73-33
Trolley: 1, 5, 7, 10, 14, 22   Map: J-8
Metro: Nevskiy prospekt, Gostinyy Dvor

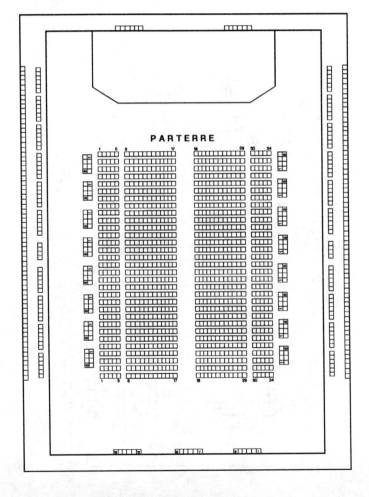

SEATING PLAN OF
Glinka Cappella (Choral Hall)
Academic Cappella n.a. Glinka

Nab. reki Moyki, 20   Tickets: 314-10-58
Bus: 14, 22   Administration: 314-10-34, 312-76-00
Trolleybus: 1, 5, 7, 10, 14, 22   Information: 314-11-59
Metro: Nevskiy prospekt, Gostinyy Dvor   Map: H-8

SEATING PLAN OF

Oktyabrskiy Concert Hall

Bolshoy Concert Hall "Oktyabrskiy"

(3738 Seats)

Ligovskiy pr., 6   Information: 275-12-73 (answering machine)
Bus: 22,   Administration: 275-13-00
Tram: 13, 16, 19, 44, 49   Tickets: 275-12-73
Trolleybus: 1, 5, 7, 10, 14, 22   Map: L-8
Metro: Ploshchad Vosstaniya, Mayakovskaya

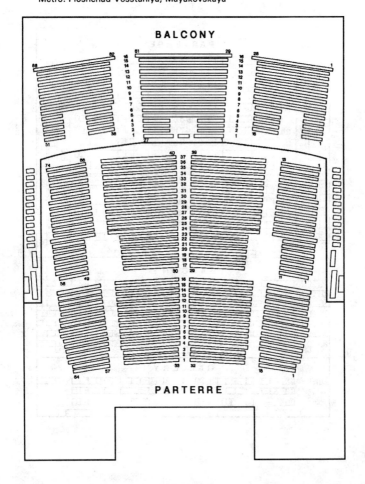

SEATING PLAN OF
Mariinskiy Theater of Opera and Ballet
(Formerly Kirov Theater, 1625 Seats)

Teatralnaya pl., 1
Bus: 22, 27
Tram: 1, 5, 15, 21, 33, 42

Tickets: 114-43-44, 114-52-64
Administration & Information: 114-12-11
Map: F-6

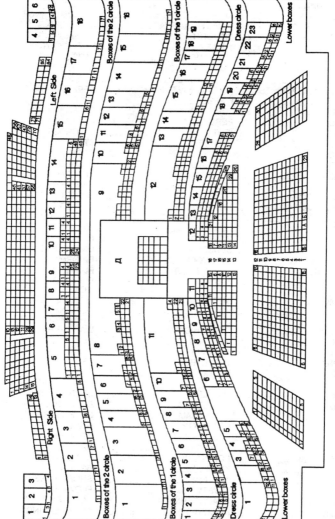

Marinskiy Theater of Opera and Ballet

SIGNS YOU MAY SEE

ВЫВЕСКИ • AUSHÄNGESCHILDE • ENSEIGNES • SKYLTAR • KILVET

RUSSIAN	TRANSLITERATION	ENGLISH
ВЫХОД	VYKHOD	EXIT
ВХОД	VKHOD	ENTRANCE
ВХОДА НЕТ	VKHODA NET	NO ENTRANCE
ВХОД ВОСПРЕЩЕН	VKHOD VOSPRESHCHEN	NO ADMITTANCE
ПОСТОРОННИМ ВХОД ВОСПРЕЩЕН	POSTORONNIM VKHOD VOSPRESHCHEN	NO ADMITTANCE
ХОДА НЕТ	KHODA NET	NO ADMITTANCE
У НАС НЕ КУРЯТ	U NAS NE KURYAT	NO SMOKING
НЕ КУРИТЬ	NE KURIT	NO SMOKING
ТУАЛЕТ	TUALET	LAVATORY/TOILET
Ж	ZH (ZHENSKIY)	LADIES
М	M (MUZHSKOY)	GENTLEMEN
ОКРАШЕНО	OKRASHENO	WET PAINT
ПО ГАЗОНАМ НЕ ХОДИТЬ	PO GAZONAM NE KHODIT	KEEP OFF THE GRASS
К СЕБЕ	K SEBE	PULL
ОТ СЕБЯ	OT SEBYA	PUSH
ПЕРЕХОД	PEREKHOD	CROSSING
ИДИТЕ	IDITE	GO/CROSS
СТОЙТЕ	STOYTE	STOP
ОТКРЫТО	OTKRYTO	OPEN
ЗАКРЫТО	ZAKRYTO	CLOSED
ПЕРЕРЫВ НА ОБЕД	PERERYV NA OBED	CLOSED FOR LUNCH
ОБЕД	OBED	LUNCH (CLOSED)
РУКАМИ НЕ ТРОГАТЬ	RUKAMI NE TROGAT	DO NOT TOUCH
НЕ ФОТОГРАФИРОВАТЬ	NE FOTOGRAFIROVAT	DO NOT PHOTOGRAPH
ЗАПРЕЩАЕТСЯ	ZAPRESHCHAETSYA	PROHIBITED
ОПАСНО	OPASNO	DANGER
ЗАНЯТО	ZANYATO	OCCUPIED
СВОБОДНО	SVOBODNO	UNOCCUPIED
СПРАВОЧНОЕ БЮРО	SPRAVOCHNOE BYURO	INFORMATION
ЧАСЫ РАБОТЫ	CHASY RABOTY	BUSINESS HOURS
КАССА	KASSA	BOOKING OFFICE / CASHIER
МЕДПУНКТ	MEDPUNKT	MEDICAL SERVICES
ВОКЗАЛ	VOKZAL	TERMINAL / RAILWAY STATION
ЗАЛ ОЖИДАНИЯ	ZAL OZHIDANIYA	WAITING HALL
АВТОБУС	AVTOBUS	BUS
ТРАМВАЙ	TRAMVAY	TRAM
ТРОЛЕЙБУС	TROLEYBUS	TROLLEYBUS
МЕТРО	METRO	SUBWAY / UNDERGROUND
МАГАЗИН	MAGAZIN	STORE/SHOP
УНИВЕРМАГ	UNIVERMAG	DEPARTMENT STORE
УНИВЕРСАМ	UNIVERSAM	SUPERMARKET
ПРОДУКТЫ	PRODUKTY	GROCERY
ГАСТРОНОМ	GASTRONOM	GROCERY
БУЛОЧНАЯ	BULOCHNAYA	BAKERY
КОНДИТЕРСКАЯ	KONDITERSKAYA	KONDITOREI
КНИГИ	KNIGI	BOOKS
ОБУВЬ	OBUV	SHOE STORE
ЦВЕТЫ	TSVETY	FLOWERS
ПРАЧЕЧНАЯ	PRACHECHNAYA	LAUNDRY
ХИМЧИСТКА	KHIMCHISTKA	DRY CLEANING

CLOTHING AND SHOE SIZES (APPROXIMATE)

MEN'S CLOTHES

Suits & Coats

American		36	38	40	42	44	46	48
		S	← M →		L	← XL →		
European		46	48	50	52	54	56	58
Russian		46	48	50	52	54	56	

Shirts

American	14	14½	15	15½	16	16½	17	18
	← S →		← M →		← L →		← XL →	
English	34	36	38	40	42	44	46	48
European	36	37	38	39	41	42	43	45
Russian	36	37	38	39	41	42	43	45-46

Shoes (All size comparisons are approximate.)

American		6½	7	7½	8½	9½	10	10½	11½
English &	Ger.	6	6½	7	8	9	10	10½	11
European	French			39	41	43	44½	45½	
European	Italian	38	39	40	42	44	45	46	47
Russian		37	38	39	41	43	44	45	46

Socks

American	9½	10	10½	11	11½	12
English	9½	10	10½	11	11½	12
Russian	39	40	41	42	43	44

WOMEN'S CLOTHES

Dress & Coats

American	6	8	10	12	14	16
	S	← M →		← L →		XL
English	8	10	12	14	16	18
European		40	42	44	46	48
Russian	44	46	48	50	52	54

Shoe (All shoe sizes are approximate and should be checked.)

American	4½	5½	6½	7	7½	8	8½	9	9½
English	3	4	4½	5	5½	6	6½	7	7½
Italian		36	36	37		38	39	40	41
French	35½	36½	37	38	38½	39	40	41	41½
Russian	33½	35	35	36	36½	37	38	39	40

CHILDREN'S CLOTHES

American	4	6	8	10	12	14
English (in.)	43	48	55	58	60	62
European (cm.)	125	135	150	155	160	165

Editor's note: This information is only approximate and there were considerable differences in the data for shoe sizes. Readers are invited to contribute more precise information to this table.

THE METRIC SYSTEM OF MEASUREMENT
Linear Measures

1 kilometer (km)	=	1000	meters
1 hectometer (hm)	=	100	meters
1 decameters (dm)	=	10	meters
1 meter (m)	=	1000	millimeters
	=	100	centimeters
1 decimeter (dm)	=	10	centimeters
1 centimeter (cm)	=	10	millimeters
1 millimeter (mm)	=	0.1	centimeter
	=	0.001	centimeter

Square (sq.) Measures

1 sq. kilometer (km^2)	= 100 hectares
1 hectare (ha)	= 10,000 m^2
1 sq. meter (m^2)	= 10,000 cm^2
1 sq. meter (m^2)	= 10^6 mm^2
1 sq. centimeter (cm^2)	= 100 mm^2
1 sq. meter (mm^2)	= 0.01 cm^2

Cubic Measures

1 cubic meter (m^3)	=	1000 dm^3
	=	1,000,000 cm^3
1 cubic centimeter (cm^3)	=	1000 mm^3
1 cubic millimeter (mm^3)	=	0.001 cm^3

Liquid Measures

1 kiloliter (kl)	=	1000	liters
1 hectoliter (hl)	=	100	liters
1 decaliter (dl)	=	10	liters
1 liter (l)	=	10	deciliters
	=	100	centiliters
	=	1000	milliliters
	=	1000	cm^3
1 deciliter (dl)	=	10	centiliters
1 centiliter (cl)	=	10	milliliters
1 milliliter (ml)	=	0.001	liter
	=	0.01	cm^3

Weight Measures

1 metric ton (mt)	=	1000	kg.
1 kilogram (kg)	=	1000	grams.
1 gram (g)	=	1000	mg.
1 milligram (mg)	=	0.001	gram.

US & British Cooking Measures
Volume Measures

1 teaspoon	=	04.9	milliliters
1 tablespoon	=	14.8	milliliters
1 cup	=	236	milliliters
1 pint	=	472	milliliters

BRITISH-AMERICAN UNITS OF MEASUREMENT AND METRIC EQUIVALENTS
Linear Measures

British/American		Metric	
1 inch (in.)	=	25.40	millimeters
	=	2.540	centimeters
1 foot (ft)	=	12	inches
	=	30.48	centimeters
	=	0.3048	meters
1 yard (yd)	=	3 feet = 36 inches	
	=	0.9144	meters
1 mile (ml)	=	5280	feet
	=	1760	yards
	=	8	furlongs
	=	1.6093	kilometers
1 naut. mile	=	6080	feet
	=	1.832	kilometers
1 inch	=	12	lines
	=	2.54	centimeters
1 line	=	6	point
	=	2.1	millimeters
1 point	=	1/72	inch
	=	0.3528	millimeter

Metric		British/American	
1 millimeter	=	0.03937	inches
1 centimeter	=	0.3937	inches
1 meter	=	39.37	inches
	=	3.2808	feet
	=	1.0936	yards
1 kilometer	=	3280.8	feet
	=	1093.6	yards
	=	0.62139	miles

Square (sq.) Measures

English		Metric	
1 square inch	=	645.16	mm^2
	=	6.4516	cm^2
1 square foot	=	929.03	cm^2
	=	9.2903	dm^2
	=	0.092903	m^2
1 square yard	=	0.83613	m^2
1 acre	=	43,560	ft^2
	=	0.4047	hectare
1 square mile	=	2.5900	km^2

Metric		English	
1 $millimeter^2$	=	0.001550	sq. inches
1 $centimeter^2$	=	0.15500	sq. inches
1 $decimeter^2$	=	0.10764	sq. feet
1 $meter^2$	=	10.764	sq. feet
	=	1.1960	sq. yards
1 hectare	=	2.47	acres
1 km^2	=	0.38608	sq. miles

Cubic Measures

English		Metric	
1 cubic inch	=	16.387	cm^3
1 cubic foot	=	1728	$inches^3$
	=	0.028317	m^3
1 cubic yard	=	27	ft^3
	=	0.76455	m^3
1 cubic mile	=	4.16818	km^3
Metric		**English**	
1 cm^3	=	0.061023	$inches^3$
1 m^3	=	35.315	$feet^3$
	=	1.3079	$yards^3$
1 km^3	=	0.23990	$miles^3$

Liquid Measures

British/US		Metric	
1 US fluid ounce	=	29.57	milliliters
1 Br. fluid ounce	=	28.4	milliliters
1 US pint	=	16 fluid	ounces
	=	0.4732	liter
1 British pint	=	20 fluid	ounces
	=	0.570	liter
1 quart	=	2	pints
1 US quart	=	0.94635	liter
1 British quart	=	1.140	liter
1 gallon	=	4	quarts
1 US gallon	=	3.7854	liters
1 British gallon	=	4.546	liters
1 US barrel	=	119.24	liters
1 British barrel	=	160.42	liters
1 Barrel of oil	=	158.98	liters
Metric		**British/US**	
1 milliliter	=	0.033814	US oz.
1 liter	=	33.814	US ounce
	=	1.0567	US quarts
	=	0.26417	US gallons

Weight Measures

Troy (apothecary & precious metals)

1 carat	=	200.	mg
1 grain	=	64.799	mg
	=	0.002285	ounces
1 ounce	=	31.103	grams
1 pound (lb)	=	373.24	grams

Avoirdupois (common)

1 ounce (oz)	=	28.35	grams
1 pound	=	453.59	grams
1 stone	=	14	lbs.
	=	6.35	kg
1 centner (British)	=	50.6	kg
1 centner (US)	=	45.3	kg
1 centner (Russian)	=	100	kg
1 ton (short)	=	907.18	kg
1 ton (long)	=	1016	kg
Metric		**Avoirdupois**	
1 gram	=	15.432	grains
	=	0.035274	oz avoir
100 grams	=	3.5274	oz avoir
1 kilogram	=	2.2046	pounds
1 ton metric	=	0.98421	ton long
	=	1.1023	ton short

Dry Measures

English		Metric	
1 quart	=	1.1012	liters
1 peck (pk)	=	8.8098	liters
1 bushel (bu)	=	35.239	liters
1 liter	=	0.90808	quarts
	=	1.11375	pecks
	=	0.028378	bushel

Temperatures

Fahrenheit		Celsius	Comparisons
212	—	100°	Boiling
176	—	80°	
140	—	60°	
122	—	50°	
104	—	40°	Very high fever
102	—	38.9°	High fever
100	—	37.8°	Mild fever
98.6	—	36.6°	Normal temperature
90	—	32.2°	Roasting hot day
86	—	30°	Very hot day
80	—	26.6°	Warm day
70	—	21.1°	Pleasant
68	—	20°	Pleasant
60	—	15.5°	Cool & Refreshing
50	—	10°	Warm winter day
40	—	4.4°	
32	—	0°	Water Freeze
30	—	-1.1°	
20	—	-6.7	Vermont winter day
14	—	-10°	
10	—	-12.2	
0	—	-17.8°	Really cold
-4	—	-20°	
-10	—	-23.3°	
-31	—	-35°	Winter in Siberia
-459.67	—	-273.15°	Absolute zero

$$Celsius = (Fahrenheit - 32) / 1.80$$
$$Fahrenheit = (Celsius \times 1.8) + 32$$

Old Russian Measures

1 versta (верста)	=
	= 500 sazhen (сажень)
	= 1066.78 meters
1 sazhen	= 3 arshin (аршин)
	= 2.13356 meters
1 arshin	= 16 vershok (вершок)
	= 0.71 meters
1 vershok	= 0.0444 meters
1 pood (пуд)	= 16.38 kg
1 desyatina (десятина)	
	= 2400 $sazhen^2$ (кв. сажень)
	= 109.254 arcres

NOTES, NUMBERS & ADDRESSES

NOTES, NUMBERS & ADDRESSES

NOTES, NUMBERS & ADDRESSES

Where To Buy The *Traveller's* Yellow Pages Books & Maps
Available in Russia:
In Saint Petersburg *at the following places:*

Hotels and Restaurants

Ambassador	Kievskaya	Oktyabrskaya	Rus
Astoria	Moskva	Olgino Motel	St. Petersburg
Grand Hotel Europe	Mercury	Olympia	Smolninskaya
Helen	Nevskiy 40	Peterhof	Sovetskaya
Jazz Club	Nevskiy Palace	Pribaltiiskaya	Staraya Derevnya
Kvartet	Okhtinskaya	Pulkovskaya	

Shops

Agfa photography	Dom Knigi	Petroservice, gas station
Airport Shop	Eurotrade	Silver Lines, Art Shop
Anichkov Most photography	Inmar bookstore	S&A Stationery
Baltic Star	Neva Star	Stockmann Supermarket
Beryozka	Petr Velikiy photography	VT-Service Travel Agency
Computerland	Petropharm Pharmacy	

Art Galleries, Museums, Universities, and Offices

Adreevskiy Dom	Lenart	Russian Language Centre
DK "Mayak"	St. Peter & Paul Cathedral	Bank Exhange Bureau
Heritage	Finansovo-	at Nevskiy 38
Hermitage	Economicheskiy Universitet	

In Moscow *at the following fine hotels, shops, and offices*

Aerostar Hotel	Pullman Hotel	Stockmann shops
Marco Polo Hotel	Radisson-	American Embassy
Metropol Hotel	Slavjanskaya Hotel	Americom Business Center
Palace Hotel	Ukraine Hotel	SovIncenter Business Center

In the United States *at the following book stores*

Phileas Fogg's, Palo Alto, CA	Travel Books Unlimited,	Traveller's Bookstore,
Distant Lands, Old Pasadena, CA	Bethesda, MD	New York, NY
Tattered Cover, Denver, CO	Latitudes Bookstore Minn., MN	Rand McNally Map & Travel
Great Explorations,	Airport Bookstores, JFK, NY	Stores
New Canaan, CT	B. Dalton, New York, NY	#002 New York, NY
Map Store, Washington, D.C.	Book Revue, Huntington, NY	#003 San Francisco, CA
Travel Merchandise, Wash., D.C.	Univ. of Pittsburgh, Pitt, PA	#008 Boston, MA
Travel Genie, Ames, IA	The Map Shop, Greenville, SC	#009 Washington, DC
Globe Corner, Cambridge, MA	Davis-Kidd, Memphis, TN	#015 Bethesda, MD
Passenger Stop, Towson, MD	Wide World, Seattle, WA	#018 Houston, TX

Available in Europe for direct purchase and mail order:

England: Collets, Denington Road, Northamptionshire NN8 2QT, England,
☎ 44 (0933) 224-351 Fax 44 (0933) 276-402

Germany: Kuban and Sagen, Post Fach 340108/ Hess Str. 39-41, D-8 Munich
☎ 49 (89) 543-180 Fax 49 (89) 542-18218

Finland: Akademiska Bokhanden, P.O. Box 218, Helsinki, SF-00381
☎ 358 (0) 121-41 Fax: 358 (0) 121-44-41

France: IGET International, 127 Avenue de la Republic, Montrouge, 92120
☎ 33 (89) 542-180, Fax 33 (89) 542-18 218

Norway: Unisales A/S
☎ 47 (02) 550-366 Fax: 47 (02) 444-777

Available from anyplace in the world by mail/fax/phone order
↦ *Next day express delivery available in the US, 2-3 days for Europe from* ↦

USA, InfoService International, Inc.
1 Saint Marks Place, Cold Spring Harbor, NY 11724,
☎ (516) 549-0064, Fax (516) 549-2032

Library & University Subscriptions to The *Traveller's* Yellow Pages Series:
Faxon Fulfillment Center, 345 Metty Drive, P.O. Box 964, Ann Arbor, MI 48106, USA.
For information on **wholesale purchases**, availability, purchases on account in Moscow
and St. Petersburg, or to become a distributor for our books and maps, contact one of our
offices in New York, St. Petersburg, or Moscow.

Become a Contributing Reader
to The *Traveller's* Yellow Pages

The TYP is designed for and by you, the "traveller-reader". Help make the next edition of the *Traveller's* Yellow Pages better and more available. Fill out the form on the last page and send it in. Or just send a letter. The source of all information is kept confidential.

1. **Evaluate a firm, a restaurant, or a service, good or bad!**
   Send us your *critical* evaluation of an establishment, especially restaurants, special shops, hotels, professional services (such as lawyers, translators, etc.) in Saint Petersburg, Russia. We will use this information to award the TYP ☆'s, write descriptive lines, or even to drop an establishment from our listings.

2. **Find a good new shop, restaurant, scenic spot, cafe, etc.**
   which is *not already in our* Traveller's *Yellow Pages* or our latest supplement. We are particularly interested in new shops and restaurants, air conditioners, snow blowers, luggage shops, camping, lingerie, dacha rental, hardware stores, child care, skilled craftsmen, moving companies, translators and guides, and map shops. We are particularly interested in shops selling top-quality Russian goods as well as imported.

   Be sure to include the following information: 1) Category (type of shop or service, cafe or restaurant, etc.), 2) Name of establishment, 3) Address, 4) Telephone/Fax . Your description and/or comments/evaluation cover the following points. What was especially good or bad about the establishment: service, cleanliness, professionalism, quality of product, interesting, size, interesting, convenience, selection, honesty, friendliness, price versus value, atmosphere.

3. **Find a new book shop or map distributor.**
   Put us in contact with a distributor or local bookstore in a new city or country which is interested in caring our books or maps, especially travel book stores and in your home country. Send us the name of the Bookstore and manager/owner, address, telephone and fax

Receive As a Contributing Reader,

1. A free *Traveller's* Yellow Pages **City Map of your choice**
2. **50 % off a Traveller's Yellow Pages of your choice**
3. Announcements of future Traveller's Yellow Pages.
4. A permanent discount of 25% off the list price of future Traveller's Yellow Pages publications
5. An acknowledgment on our Contributing Readers Page
6. A free address update, when published.

Be sure to include:Your Name, Address,Country and Telephone.

Send or fax to:

InfoServices International, Inc., 1 Saint Marks Place,
Cold Spring Harbor, NY 11724, USA, Fax 1 (516) 549-2032.

Suggestions and Reader's Contributions:

1. **Your evaluation of one firm, a restaurant, or a service, good or bad.**
2. **The name and address of one good new shop, restaurant, scenic spot, cafe, doctor or service**
3. **The name of one new book shop or map store, not already on our list.**

Description of establishment _____

Name of establishment _____

Name of owner/manager _____

Address:_____

Telephone and Fax _____

What is especially good or bad about the establishment	
Quality of products, food, knowledgeable, professional & craftsmanship.	
Service: friendly, quick, professional, knowledgeable, helpful, or cold & inattentive	
Cleanliness and safety Was it clean, did you feel safe, did everything work?	
Location & decor. beautiful, convenient, interesting, safe, dangerous	
Size of store, & selection of goods (or menu) relative to other firms.	
Clientele: young, old, tourist, businessman, expat, foreigner, etc.	
Atmosphere: Friendly, formal, stuffy, arrogant, lively, loud, businesslike.	
Price versus value: Bargain, costly for what you get, expensive & good	
Other Comments and overall rating	Please use additional paper for more comments
Your name, address, telephone.	

All "Contributions" acknowledged and the sources kept confidential.
Mail or fax form to: InfoServices International, Inc.
1 Saint Marks Place, Cold Spring Harbor, NY 11724, USA.
☎ (516) 549-0064 Fax: (516) 549 - 2032

MAIL/FAX/TELEPHONE ORDER FORM
FOR *TRAVELLER'S* YELLOW PAGES® PUBLICATIONS
Information for the World Traveller

For fastest service, call us at 1 (516) 549-0064 or fax your order to 1 (516) 549-2032
Inquire about discounts for large orders. Prices in US dollars.

Please send me the following publications:

COPIES

____ *Traveller's* Yellow Pages and Handbook for Saint Petersburg . @ 8.95 _____
1993/94 (2nd ed.) Include the new City Map of Saint Petersburg

____ *New Traveller's* Yellow Pages City Map of Saint Petersburg 1993 @ 3.50 _____

____ *Traveller's* Yellow Pages and Handbook for Moscow .... @ 9.95 _____
1994 Including City Map of Moscow

____ *Traveller's* Yellow Pages City Map of Moscow (1993 ed.) ..... @ 3.50 _____

(New York residents, add 8.5% sales tax.) _____

Please ship by the following method and add shipping and handling:
Within the United States
TYP Handbooks are usually sent Priority Mail, *same day shipping.*
Add $4.00 for first copy, plus $1.00 for each additional copy.
Maps ordered with TYP Handbook shipped free
Maps ordered separately: Shipping and handling
$1.50 for first copy, $.50 for each additional copy. _____
Overnight Express Delivery: please inquire about cost. _____

TOTAL COST .... _____

Rest of world except Russia and CIS: In your home country, order from our
distributors listed on page 349. Elsewhere and for bulk orders, order
from our US office for fastest shipment and large-volume discounts.
In Russia: Same-day delivery to your office or home in Moscow and Saint
Petersburg. Courier shipping to other points. Call for details.

SHIPPING ADDRESS

Name _____

Company (optional) _____

Street Address _____

Town _____

State _____ Zip/Post code _____ Country _____

Phone _____ Fax: _____

METHOD OF PAYMENT

____**Personal check** enclosed for the full amount, payable to *InfoServices
International, Inc* in US$, payable on a US bank. *We prefer this method
of payment.*
____**Company purchase order** for the full amount of the order.
Please send an invoice to the address above.
____**Please charge my credit card** for the total cost above.

Credit Card (circle one)   VISA   Master Card   AMEX

Credit Card Number _____ Expires _____

Name On Card _____

Total Amount of Purchase Above (including shipping & handling) $ _____

Authorized Signature:_____

Complete form and mail or fax to:
InfoServices International, Inc.
1 Saint Marks Place, Cold Spring Harbor, NY 11724, USA.
☎ (516) 549-0064 Fax: (516) 549 - 2032